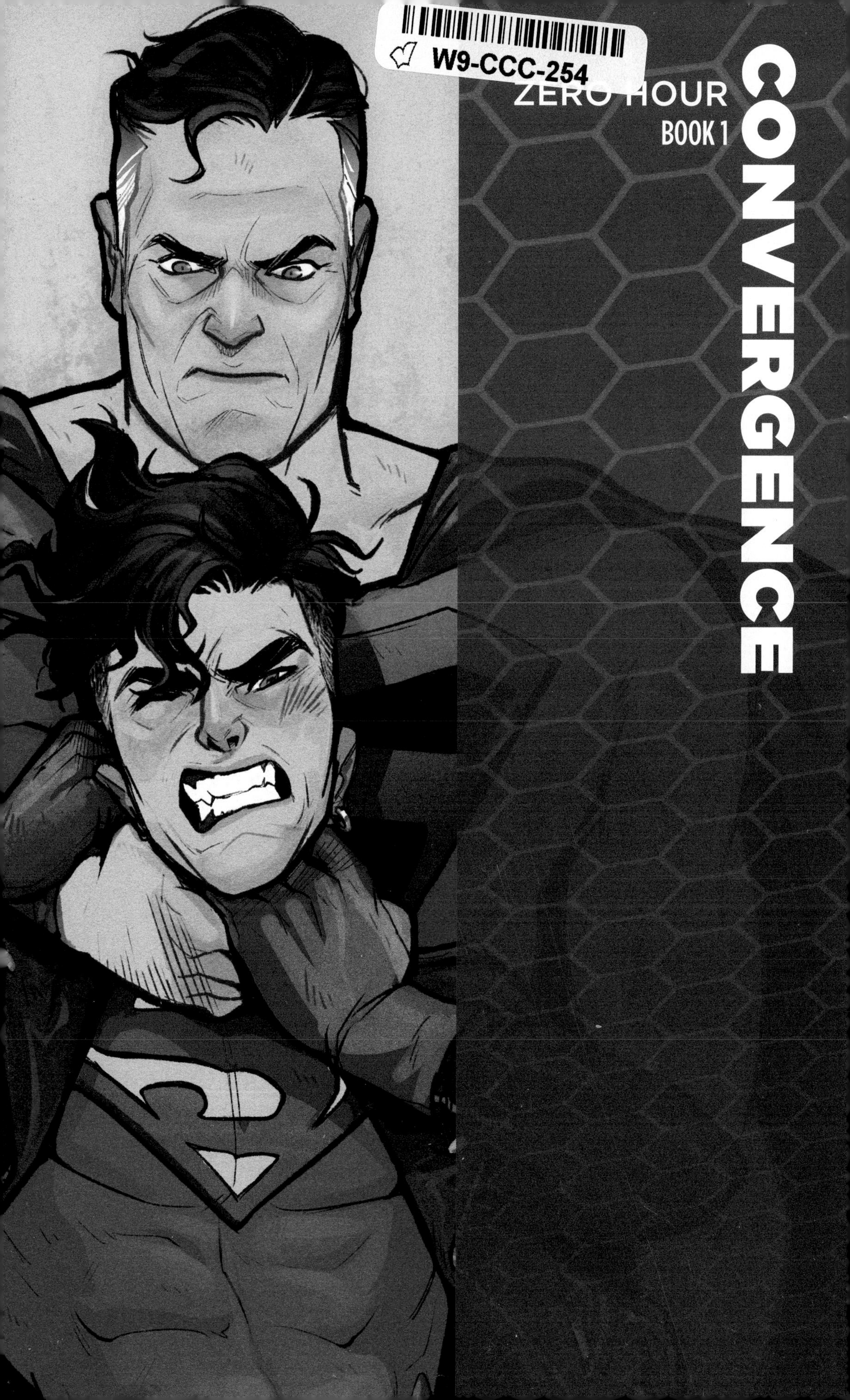
CONVERGENCE
ZERO HOUR
BOOK 1

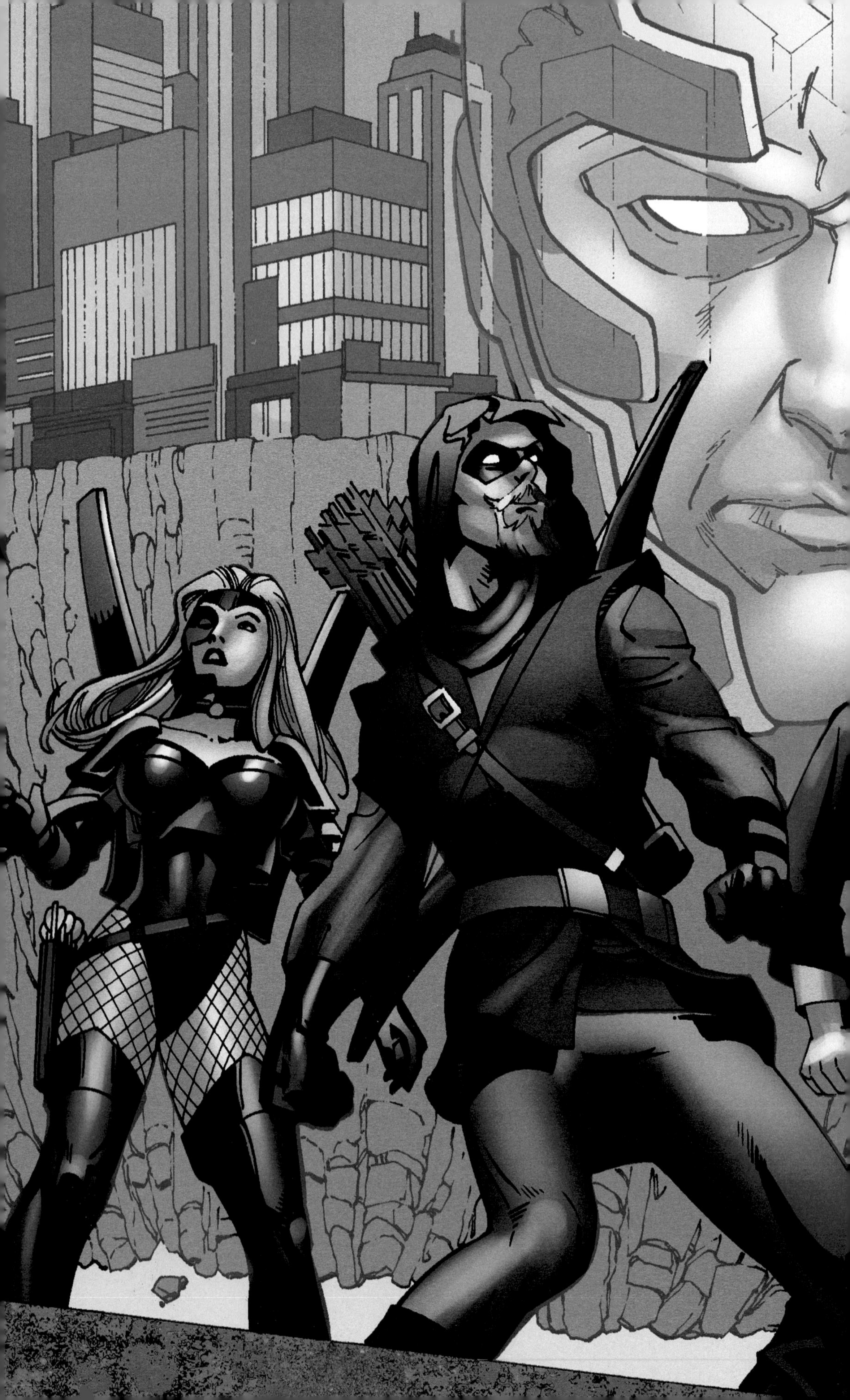

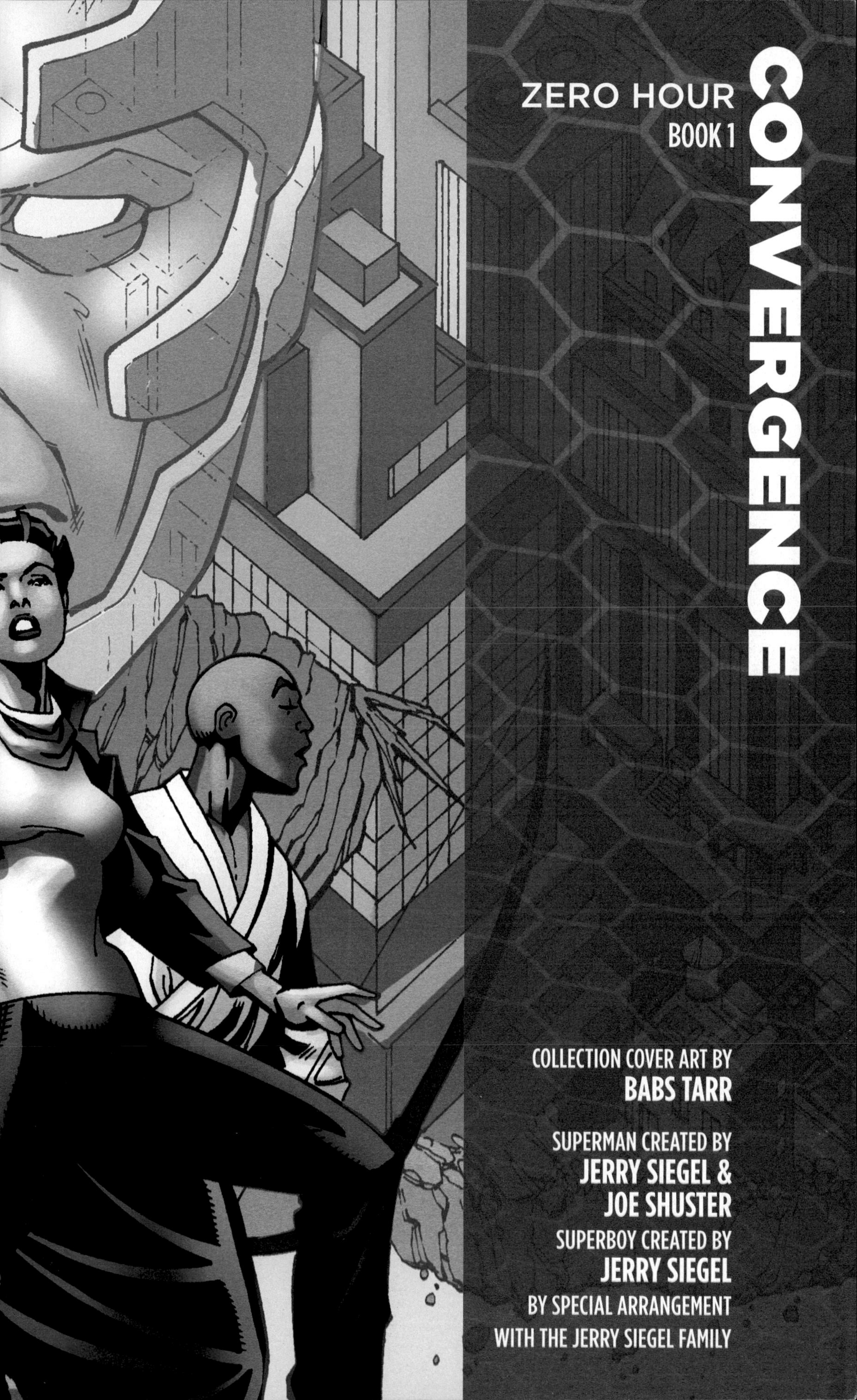

CONVERGENCE

ZERO HOUR
BOOK 1

COLLECTION COVER ART BY
BABS TARR

SUPERMAN CREATED BY
JERRY SIEGEL & JOE SHUSTER
SUPERBOY CREATED BY
JERRY SIEGEL
BY SPECIAL ARRANGEMENT
WITH THE JERRY SIEGEL FAMILY

MARIE JAVINS Editor – Original Series
BRITTANY HOLZHERR MICHAEL KRAIGER Assistant Editors – Original Series
ROBIN WILDMAN Editor
JEB WOODARD Group Editor – Collected Editions
DAMIAN RYLAND Publication Design

BOB HARRAS Senior VP – Editor-in-Chief, DC Comics

DIANE NELSON President
DAN DIDIO and JIM LEE Co-Publishers
GEOFF JOHNS Chief Creative Officer
AMIT DESAI Senior VP – Marketing & Global Franchise Management
NAIRI GARDINER Senior VP – Finance
SAM ADES VP – Digital Marketing
BOBBIE CHASE VP – Talent Development
MARK CHIARELLO Senior VP – Art, Design & Collected Editions
JOHN CUNNINGHAM VP – Content Strategy
ANNE DePIES VP – Strategy Planning & Reporting
DON FALLETTI VP – Manufacturing Operations
LAWRENCE GANEM VP – Editorial Administration & Talent Relations
ALISON GILL Senior VP – Manufacturing & Operations
HANK KANALZ Senior VP – Editorial Strategy & Administration
JAY KOGAN VP – Legal Affairs
DEREK MADDALENA Senior VP – Sales & Business Development
DAN MIRON VP – Sales Planning & Trade Development
NICK NAPOLITANO VP – Manufacturing Administration
CAROL ROEDER VP – Marketing
EDDIE SCANNELL VP – Mass Account & Digital Sales
SUSAN SHEPPARD VP – Business Affairs
COURTNEY SIMMONS Senior VP – Publicity & Communications
JIM (SKI) SOKOLOWSKI VP – Comic Book Specialty & Newsstand Sales

CONVERGENCE: ZERO HOUR BOOK 1

Published by DC Comics. Compilation Copyright © 2015 DC Comics. All Rights Reserved.
Originally published in single magazine form as CONVERGENCE: CATWOMAN 1-2, CONVERGENCE: GREEN ARROW 1-2, CONVERGENCE:
JUSTICE LEAGUE INTERNATIONAL 1-2, CONVERGENCE: SUICIDE SQUAD 1-2, CONVERGENCE: SUPERBOY 1-2 © 2015 DC Comics.
All Rights Reserved. All characters, their distinctive likenesses and related elements featured in this publication are trademarks of
DC Comics. The stories, characters and incidents featured in this publication are entirely fictional.
DC Comics does not read or accept unsolicited ideas, stories or artwork.

DC Comics, 4000 Warner Blvd., Burbank, CA 91522
A Warner Bros. Entertainment Company
Printed by RR Donnelley, Salem, VA, USA. 9/4/15.
ISBN: 978-1-4012-5839-9
First Printing.

Library of Congress Cataloging-in-Publication Data

Marz, Ron.
Convergence : zero hour book one / Ron Marz, Rags Morales, Christy Marx.
pages cm
ISBN 978-1-4012-5839-9
1. Graphic novels. I. Morales, Rags. II. Marx, Christy. III. Title.
PN6728.C676M37 2015
741.5'973—dc23
2015011793

PEFC Certified

Printed on paper from
sustainably managed
forests and controlled
sources

PEFC/29-31-75

www.pefc.org

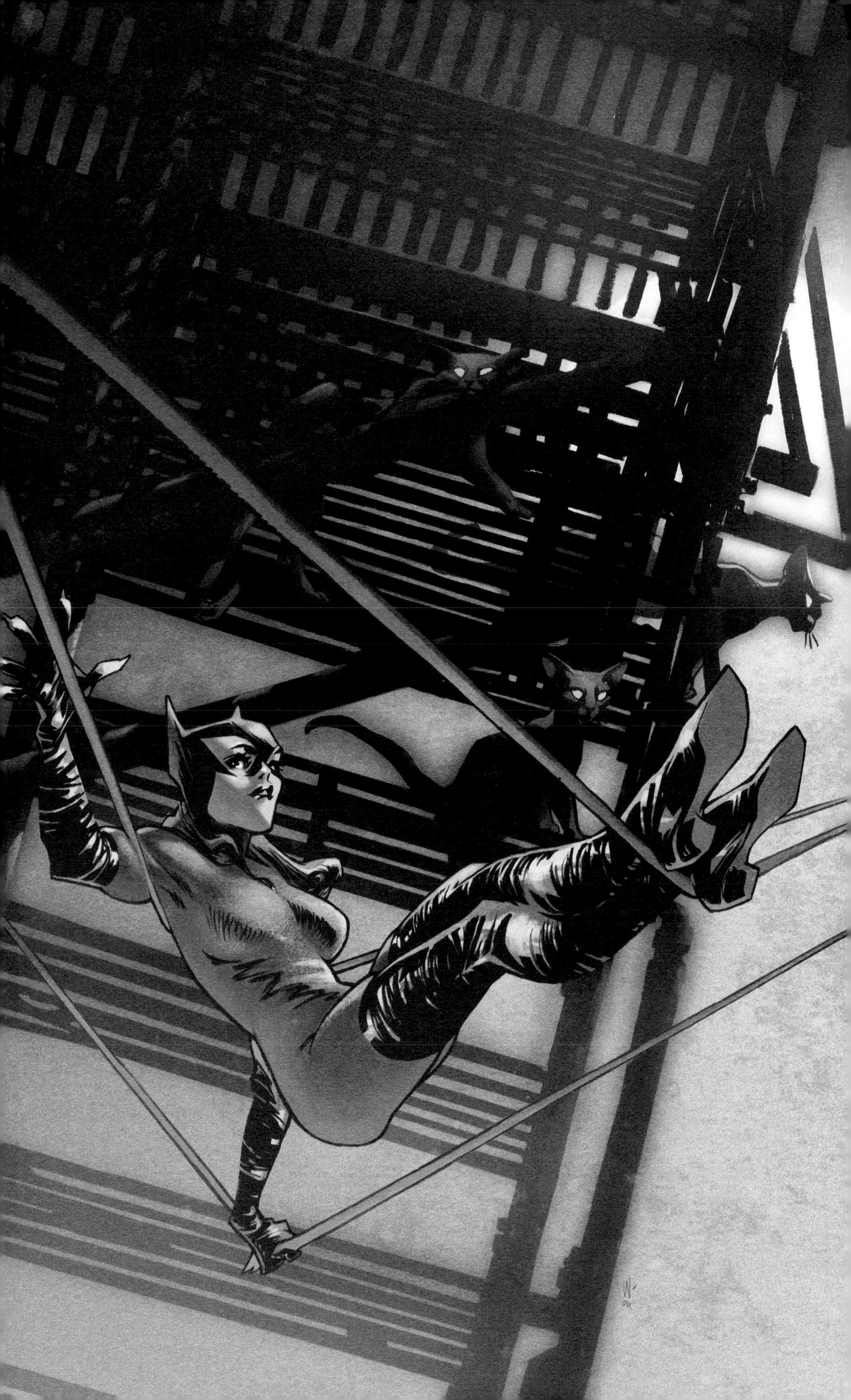

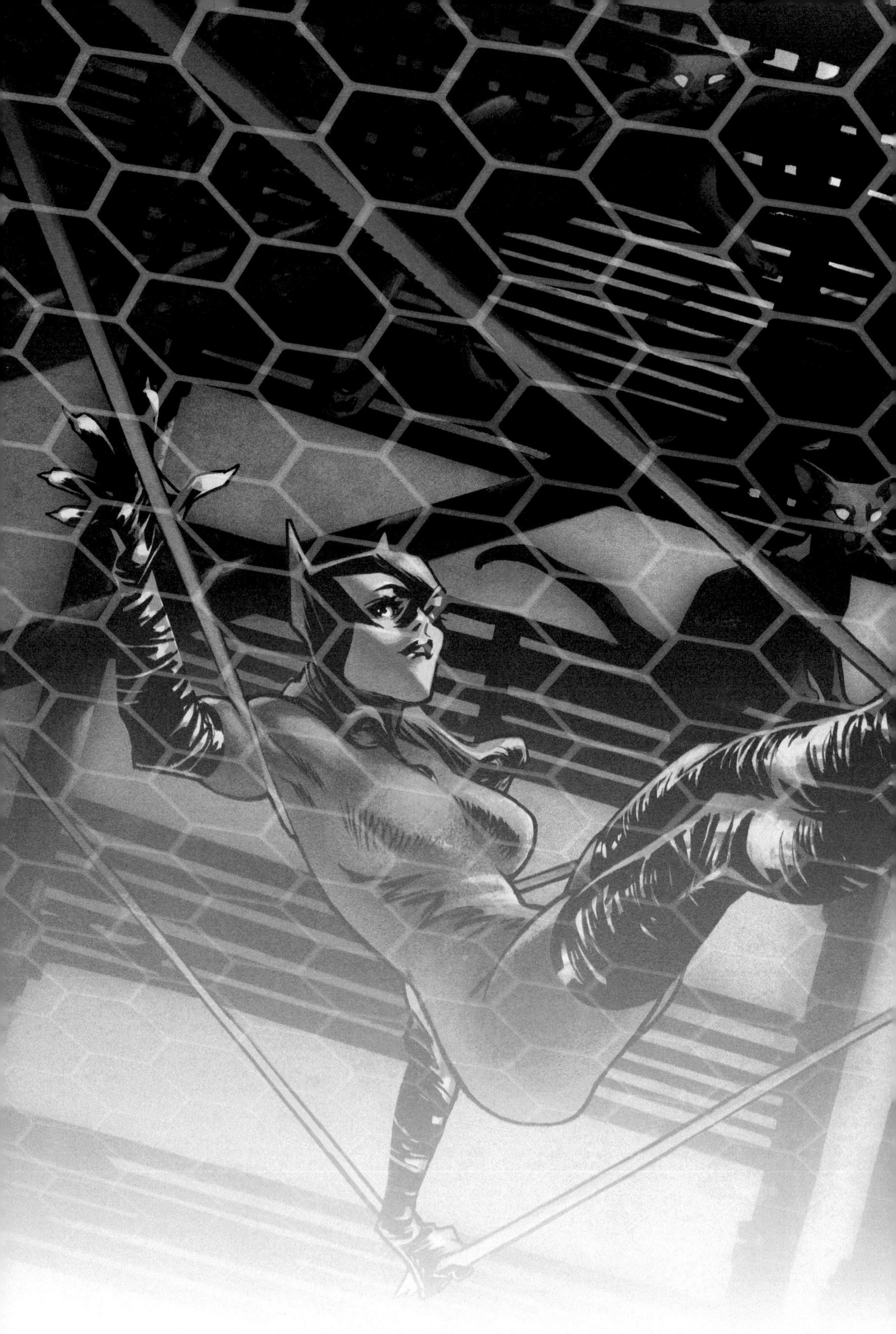

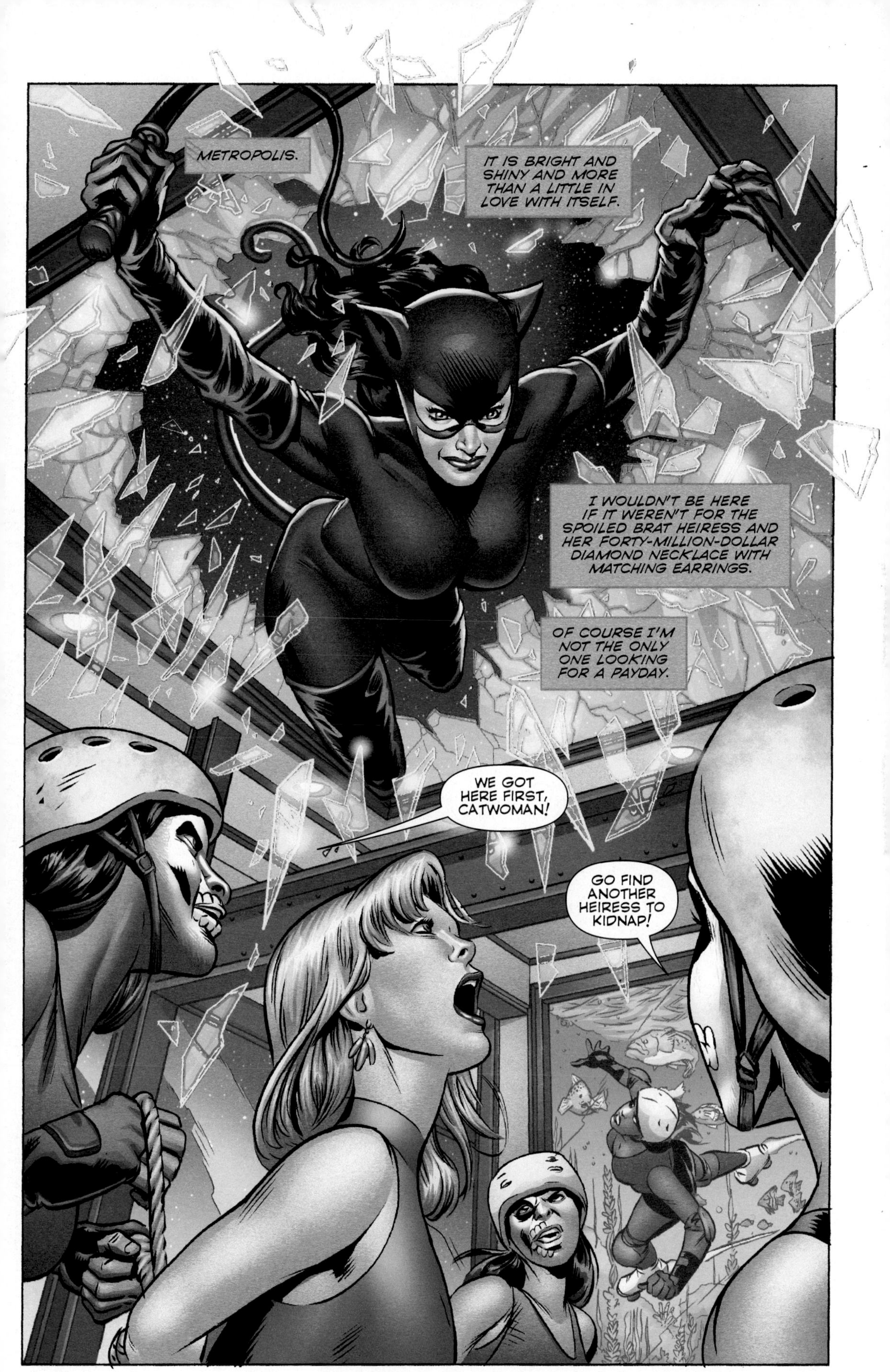
METROPOLIS.
IT IS BRIGHT AND SHINY AND MORE THAN A LITTLE IN LOVE WITH ITSELF.
I WOULDN'T BE HERE IF IT WEREN'T FOR THE SPOILED BRAT HEIRESS AND HER FORTY-MILLION-DOLLAR DIAMOND NECKLACE WITH MATCHING EARRINGS.
OF COURSE I'M NOT THE ONLY ONE LOOKING FOR A PAYDAY.
WE GOT HERE FIRST, CATWOMAN!
GO FIND ANOTHER HEIRESS TO KIDNAP!

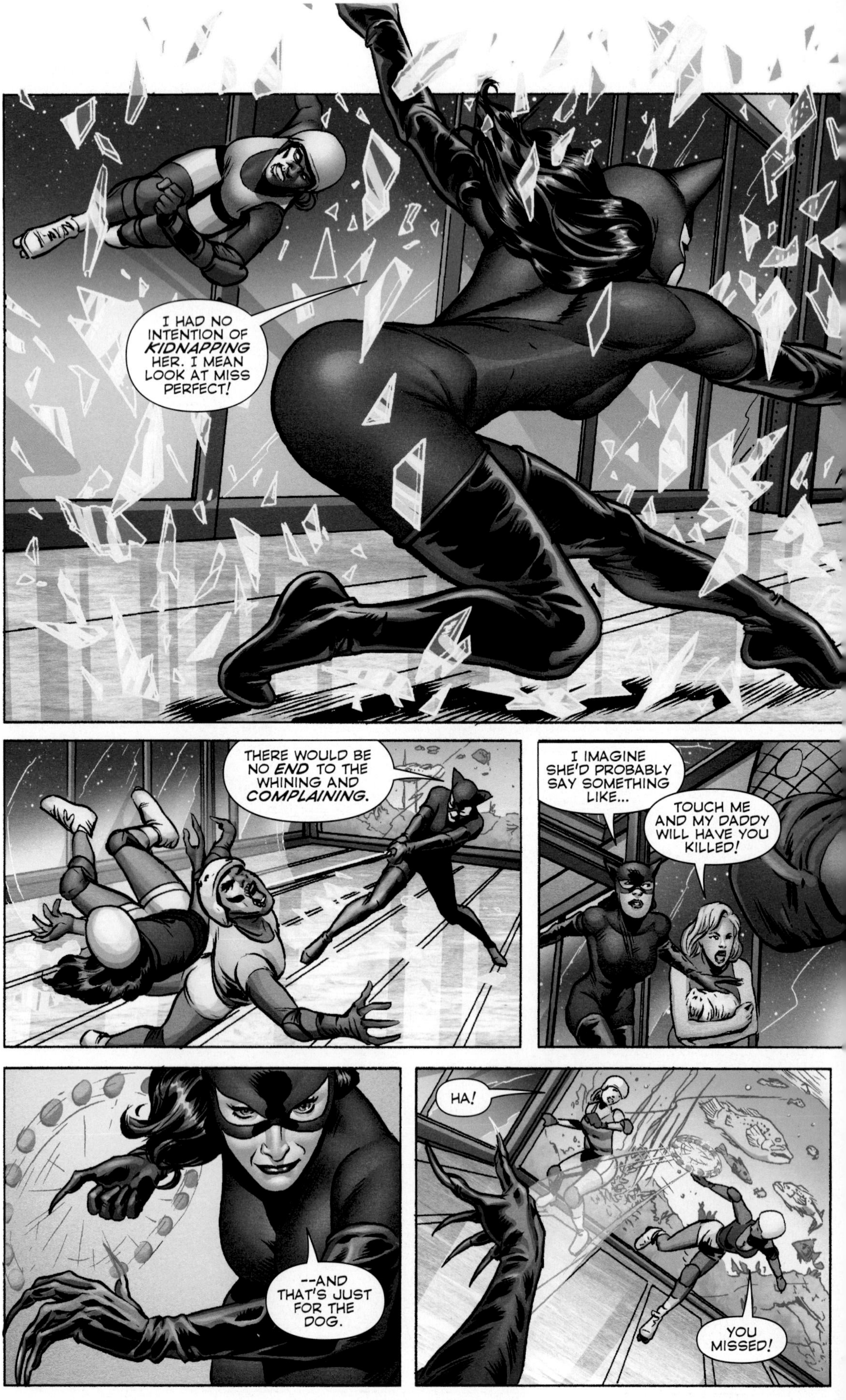
I HAD NO INTENTION OF KIDNAPPING HER. I MEAN LOOK AT MISS PERFECT!
THERE WOULD BE NO END TO THE WHINING AND COMPLAINING.
I IMAGINE SHE'D PROBABLY SAY SOMETHING LIKE...
TOUCH ME AND MY DADDY WILL HAVE YOU KILLED!
--AND THAT'S JUST FOR THE DOG.
HA!
YOU MISSED!

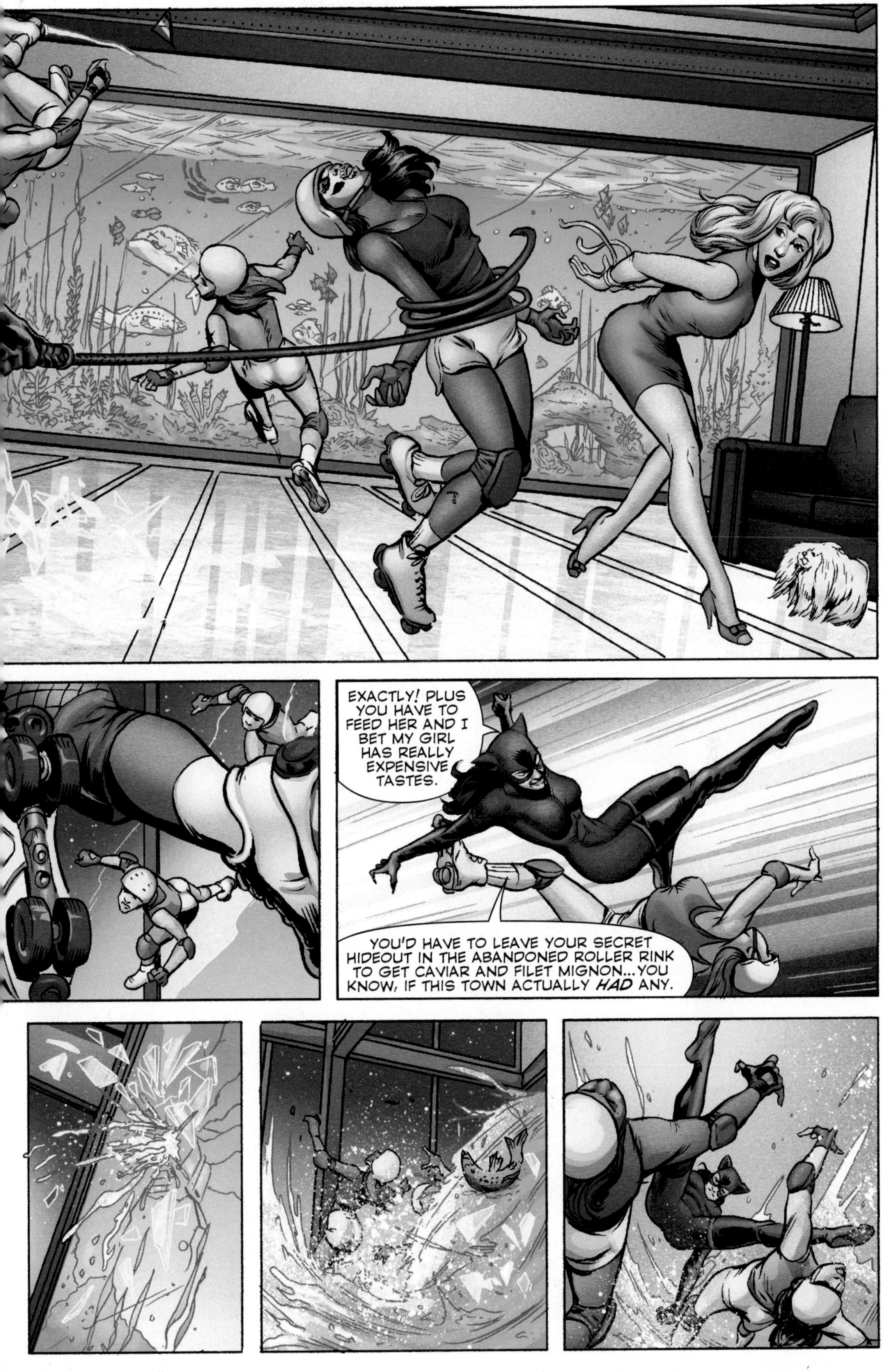
EXACTLY! PLUS YOU HAVE TO FEED HER AND I BET MY GIRL HAS REALLY EXPENSIVE TASTES.
YOU'D HAVE TO LEAVE YOUR SECRET HIDEOUT IN THE ABANDONED ROLLER RINK TO GET CAVIAR AND FILET MIGNON... YOU KNOW, IF THIS TOWN ACTUALLY *HAD* ANY.

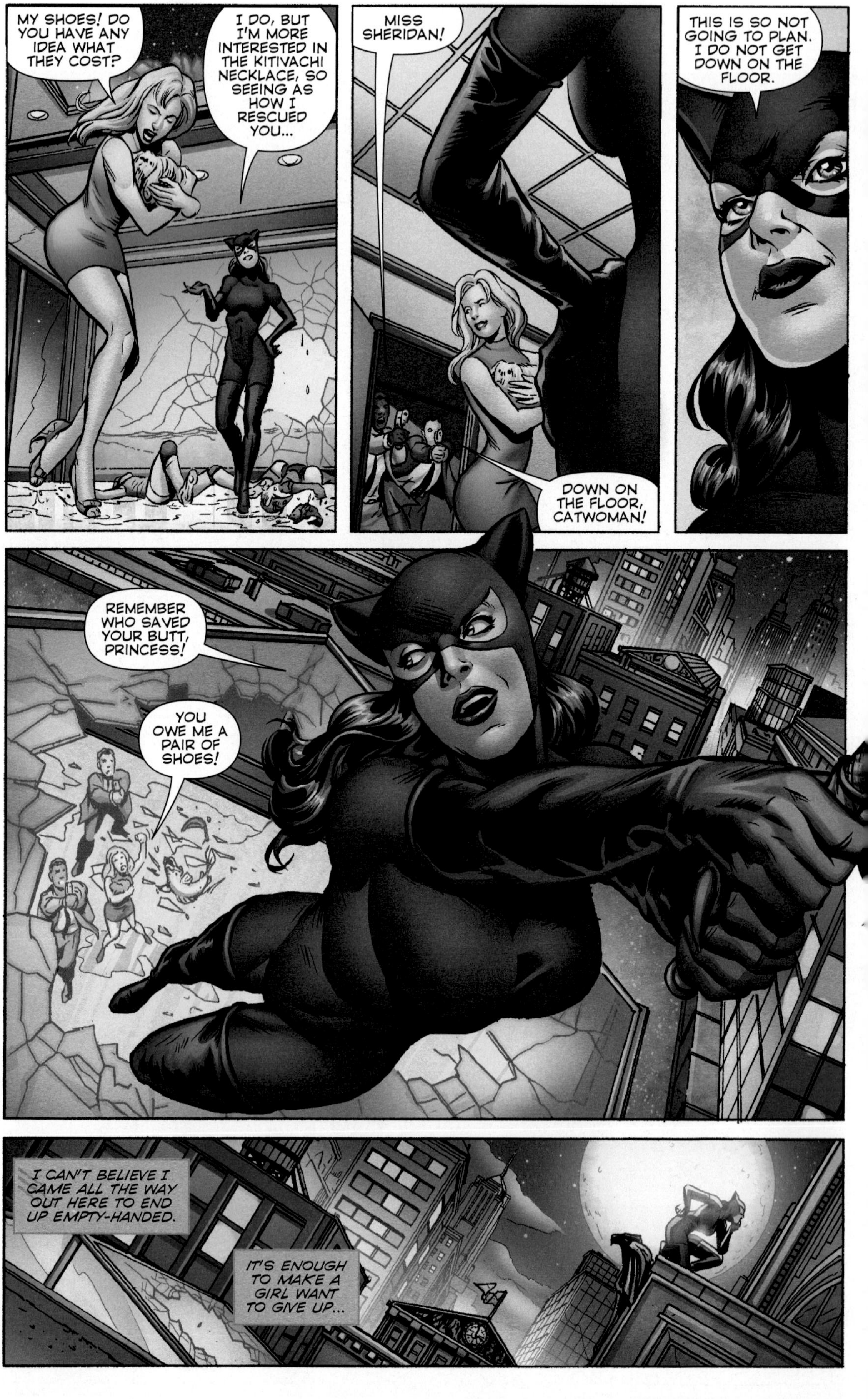

MY SHOES! DO YOU HAVE ANY IDEA WHAT THEY COST?
I DO, BUT I'M MORE INTERESTED IN THE KITIVACHI NECKLACE, SO SEEING AS HOW I RESCUED YOU...
MISS SHERIDAN!
DOWN ON THE FLOOR, CATWOMAN!
THIS IS SO NOT GOING TO PLAN. I DO NOT GET DOWN ON THE FLOOR.
REMEMBER WHO SAVED YOUR BUTT, PRINCESS!
YOU OWE ME A PAIR OF SHOES!
I CAN'T BELIEVE I CAME ALL THE WAY OUT HERE TO END UP EMPTY-HANDED.
IT'S ENOUGH TO MAKE A GIRL WANT TO GIVE UP...

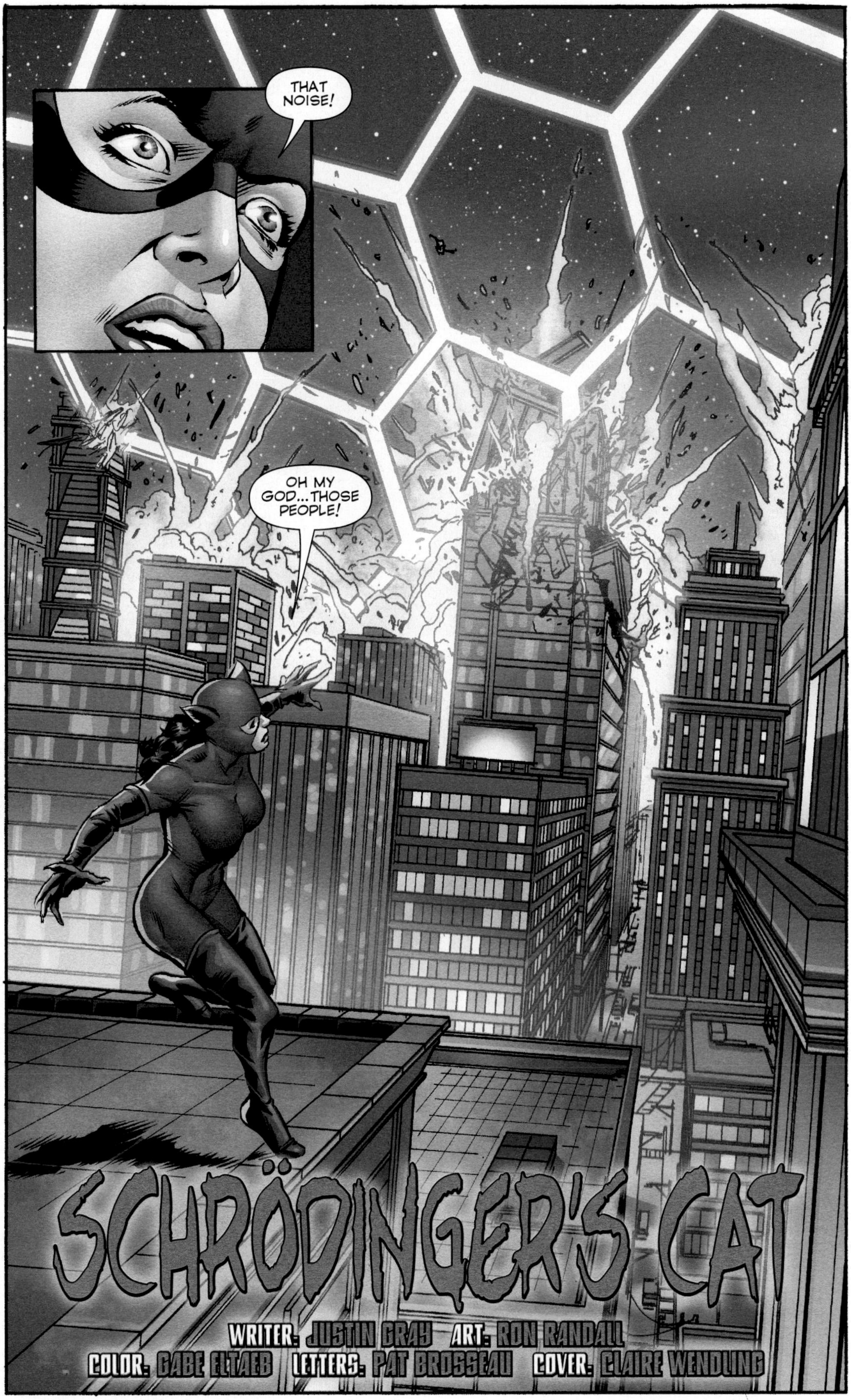
THAT NOISE!
OH MY GOD...THOSE PEOPLE!
SCHRÖDINGER'S CAT
WRITER: JUSTIN GRAY ART: RON RANDALL
COLOR: GABE ELTAEB LETTERS: PAT BROSSEAU COVER: CLAIRE WENDLING

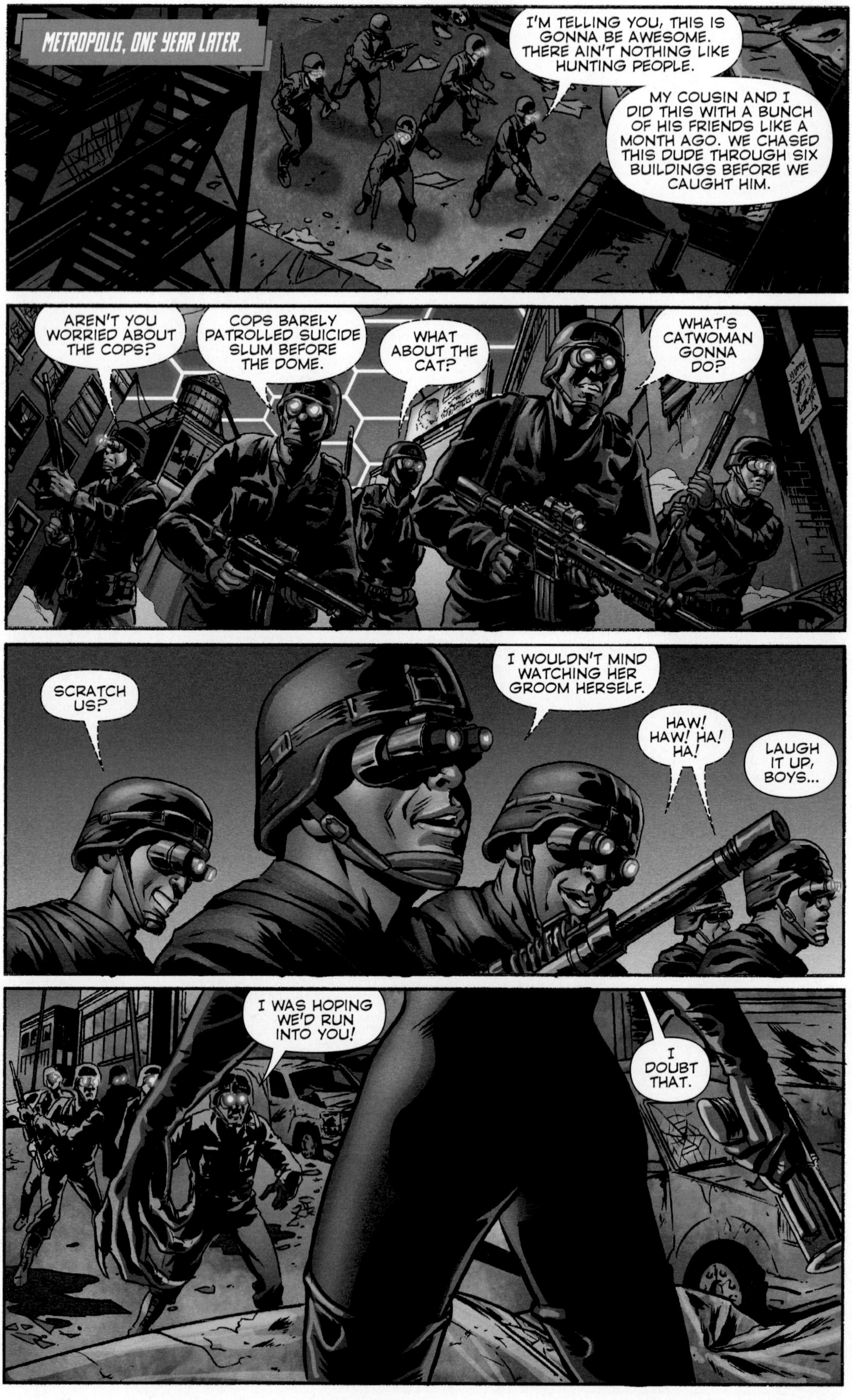
METROPOLIS, ONE YEAR LATER.
I'M TELLING YOU, THIS IS GONNA BE AWESOME. THERE AIN'T NOTHING LIKE HUNTING PEOPLE.
MY COUSIN AND I DID THIS WITH A BUNCH OF HIS FRIENDS LIKE A MONTH AGO. WE CHASED THIS DUDE THROUGH SIX BUILDINGS BEFORE WE CAUGHT HIM.
AREN'T YOU WORRIED ABOUT THE COPS?
COPS BARELY PATROLLED SUICIDE SLUM BEFORE THE DOME.
WHAT ABOUT THE CAT?
WHAT'S CATWOMAN GONNA DO?
SCRATCH US?
I WOULDN'T MIND WATCHING HER GROOM HERSELF.
HAW! HAW! HA! HA!
LAUGH IT UP, BOYS...
I WAS HOPING WE'D RUN INTO YOU!
I DOUBT THAT.

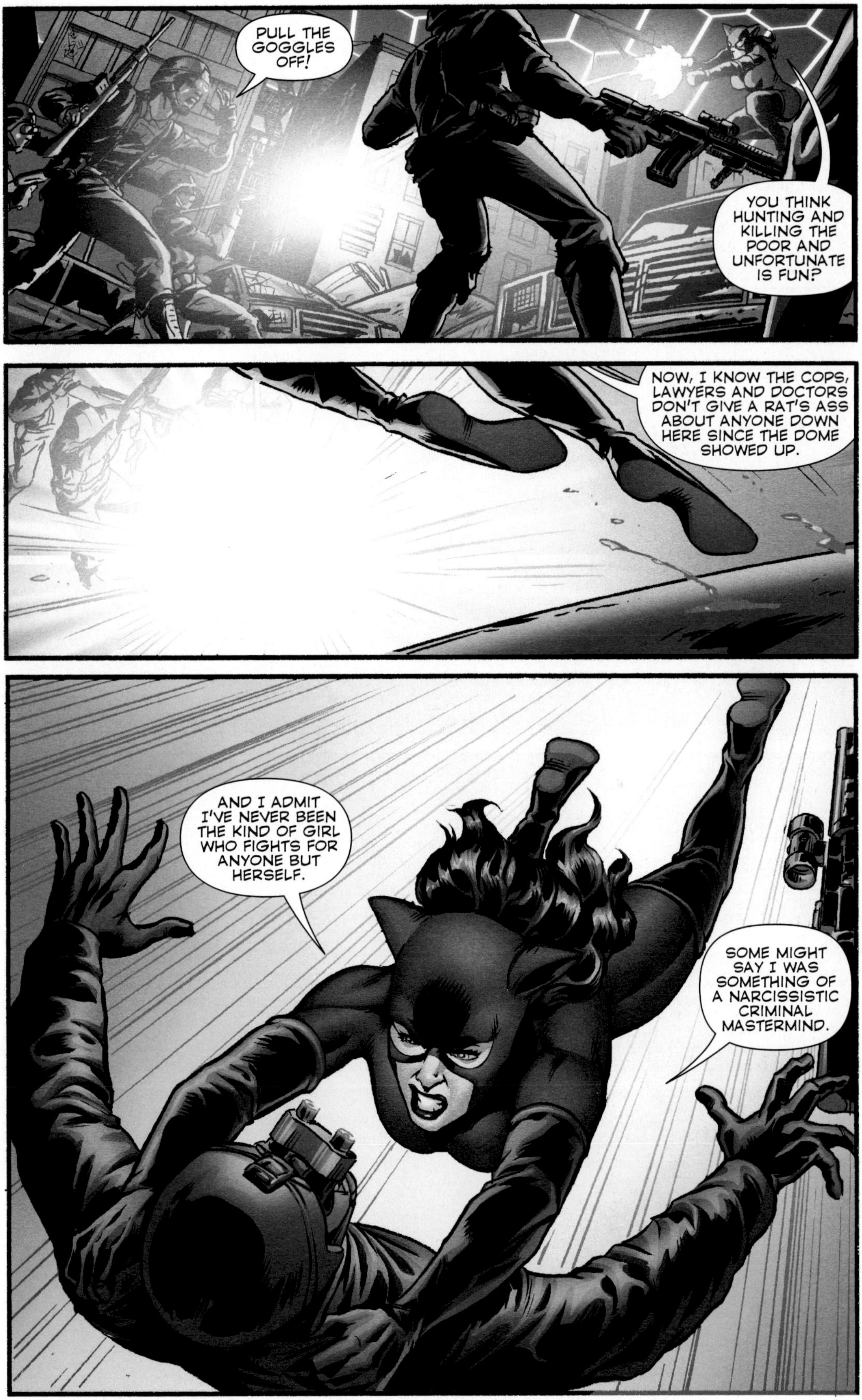
PULL THE GOGGLES OFF!
YOU THINK HUNTING AND KILLING THE POOR AND UNFORTUNATE IS FUN?
NOW, I KNOW THE COPS, LAWYERS AND DOCTORS DON'T GIVE A RAT'S ASS ABOUT ANYONE DOWN HERE SINCE THE DOME SHOWED UP.
AND I ADMIT I'VE NEVER BEEN THE KIND OF GIRL WHO FIGHTS FOR ANYONE BUT HERSELF.
SOME MIGHT SAY I WAS SOMETHING OF A NARCISSISTIC CRIMINAL MASTERMIND.

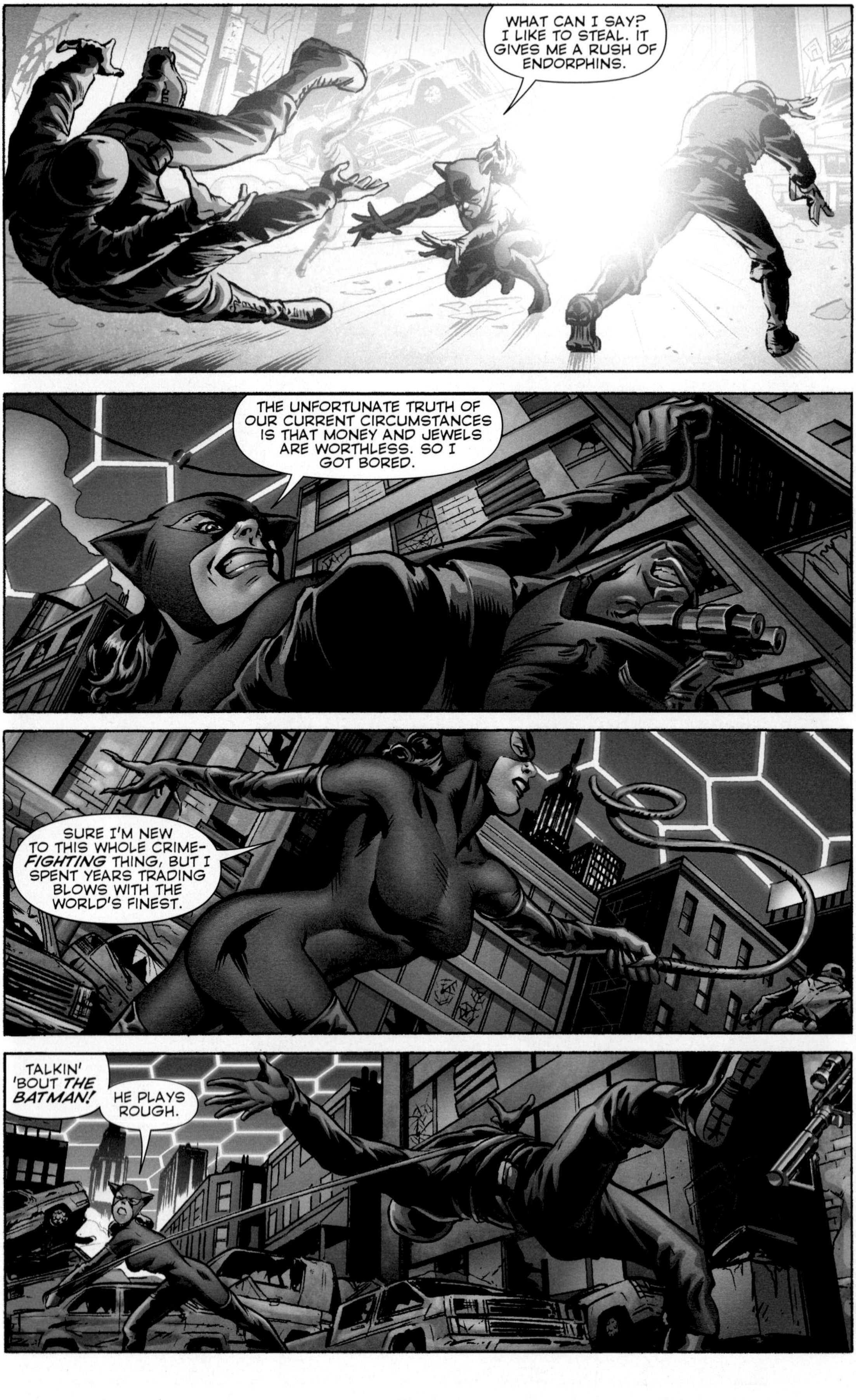
WHAT CAN I SAY? I LIKE TO STEAL. IT GIVES ME A RUSH OF ENDORPHINS.
THE UNFORTUNATE TRUTH OF OUR CURRENT CIRCUMSTANCES IS THAT MONEY AND JEWELS ARE WORTHLESS. SO I GOT BORED.
SURE I'M NEW TO THIS WHOLE CRIME-FIGHTING THING, BUT I SPENT YEARS TRADING BLOWS WITH THE WORLD'S FINEST.
TALKIN' 'BOUT THE BATMAN!
HE PLAYS ROUGH.

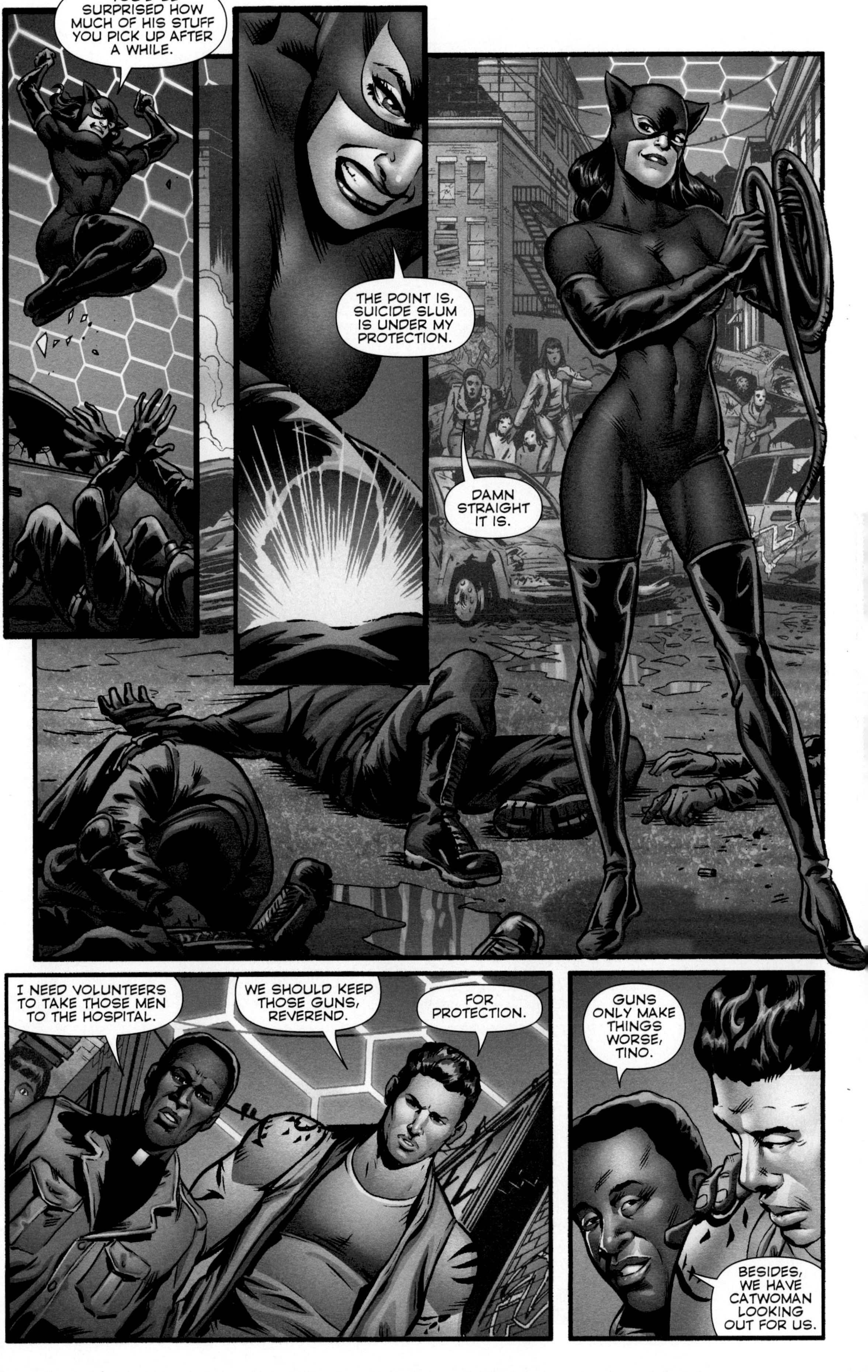
YOU'D BE SURPRISED HOW MUCH OF HIS STUFF YOU PICK UP AFTER A WHILE.
THE POINT IS, SUICIDE SLUM IS UNDER MY PROTECTION.
DAMN STRAIGHT IT IS.
I NEED VOLUNTEERS TO TAKE THOSE MEN TO THE HOSPITAL.
WE SHOULD KEEP THOSE GUNS, REVEREND.
FOR PROTECTION.
GUNS ONLY MAKE THINGS WORSE, TINO.
BESIDES, WE HAVE CATWOMAN LOOKING OUT FOR US.

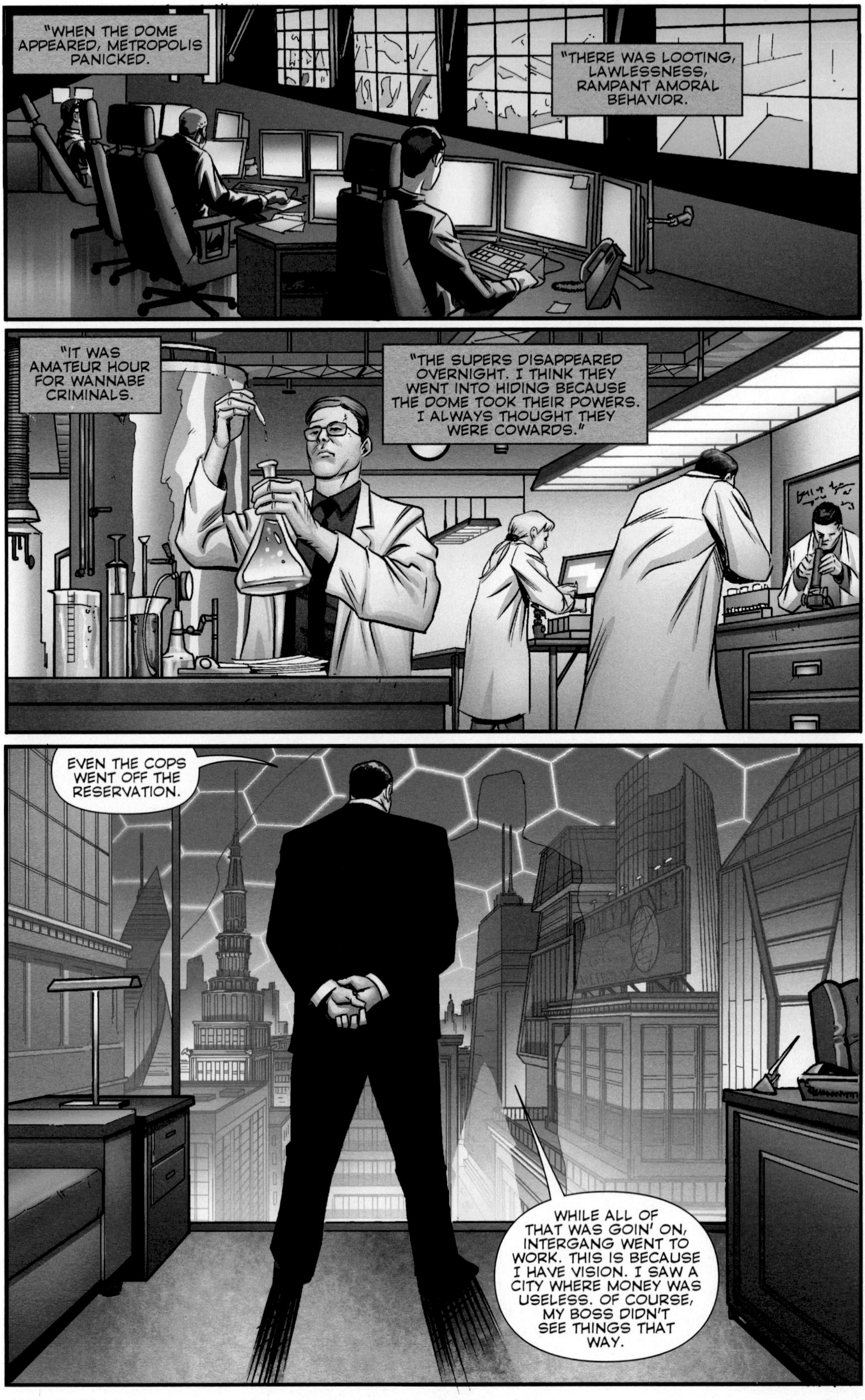
"WHEN THE DOME APPEARED, METROPOLIS PANICKED.
"THERE WAS LOOTING, LAWLESSNESS, RAMPANT AMORAL BEHAVIOR.
"IT WAS AMATEUR HOUR FOR WANNABE CRIMINALS.
"THE SUPERS DISAPPEARED OVERNIGHT. I THINK THEY WENT INTO HIDING BECAUSE THE DOME TOOK THEIR POWERS. I ALWAYS THOUGHT THEY WERE COWARDS."
EVEN THE COPS WENT OFF THE RESERVATION.
WHILE ALL OF THAT WAS GOIN' ON, INTERGANG WENT TO WORK. THIS IS BECAUSE I HAVE VISION. I SAW A CITY WHERE MONEY WAS USELESS. OF COURSE, MY BOSS DIDN'T SEE THINGS THAT WAY.

I SAW A CITY WHERE FOOD, ALCOHOL, DRUGS, AND MEDICINE WOULD BE WORTH MORE THAN GOLD. HE THOUGHT HE COULD RELY ON THE OLD WAYS.

I SAID THIS WAS A NEW WORLD WITH NO PLACE FOR OLD MEN AND OLD IDEAS. THEN I KILLED HIM.

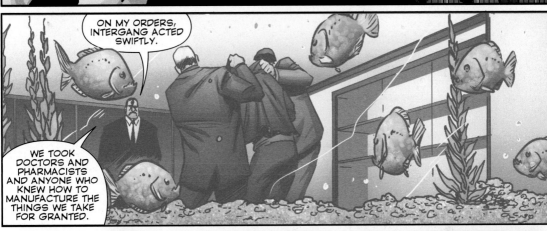

ON MY ORDERS, INTERGANG ACTED SWIFTLY.

WE TOOK DOCTORS AND PHARMACISTS AND ANYONE WHO KNEW HOW TO MANUFACTURE THE THINGS WE TAKE FOR GRANTED.

SURVIVAL IS PREDICATED ON THE ABILITY TO ADAPT QUICKLY TO EXTREME CHANGES.

ONE THING THAT NEVER, EVER SEEMS TO CHANGE IS WEAKNESS. PEOPLE LIKE YOU...

MISTER MANNHEIM, PLEASE! IT WON'T HAPPEN AGAIN!

I KNOW IT WON'T. NOT WITH YOU ANYWAY, BUT OTHERS NEED AN EXAMPLE BY WHICH TO AVOID MAKING THE SAME MISTAKES.

CRAKKK!

GHHHAAAHHH!!

YOU'RE A DRUG ADDICT AND A THIEF, THE LOWEST FORM OF CRIMINAL. THE KIND THAT MAKES LEGITIMATE MEN LIKE MYSELF LOOK BAD IN THE EYES OF OTHERS.

THERE'S NO PLACE FOR SCUM LIKE YOU IN METROPOLIS.

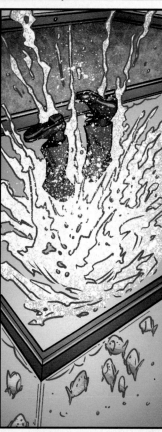

NOT IN *MY...*

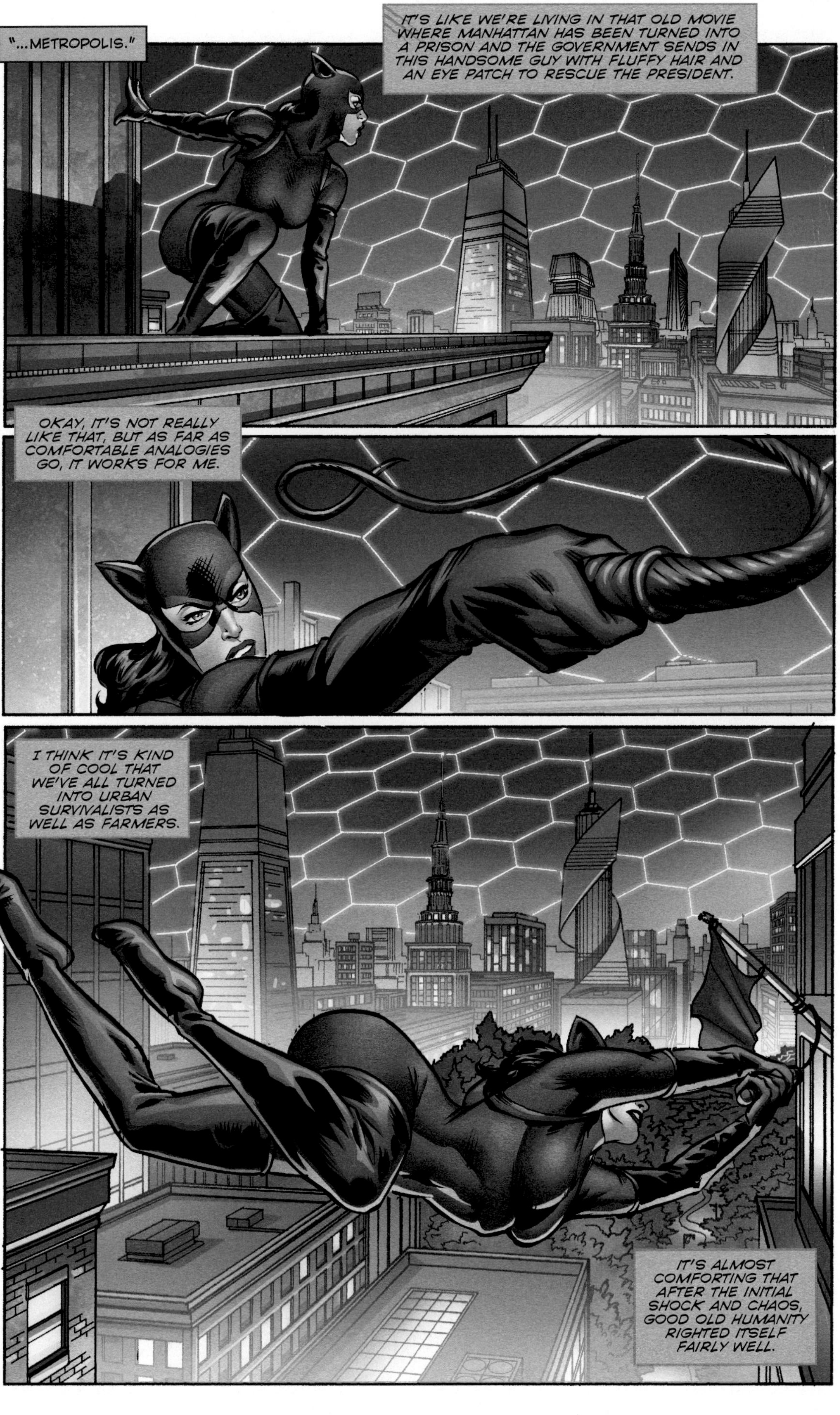
"...METROPOLIS."
IT'S LIKE WE'RE LIVING IN THAT OLD MOVIE WHERE MANHATTAN HAS BEEN TURNED INTO A PRISON AND THE GOVERNMENT SENDS IN THIS HANDSOME GUY WITH FLUFFY HAIR AND AN EYE PATCH TO RESCUE THE PRESIDENT.
OKAY, IT'S NOT REALLY LIKE THAT, BUT AS FAR AS COMFORTABLE ANALOGIES GO, IT WORKS FOR ME.
I THINK IT'S KIND OF COOL THAT WE'VE ALL TURNED INTO URBAN SURVIVALISTS AS WELL AS FARMERS.
IT'S ALMOST COMFORTING THAT AFTER THE INITIAL SHOCK AND CHAOS, GOOD OLD HUMANITY RIGHTED ITSELF FAIRLY WELL.

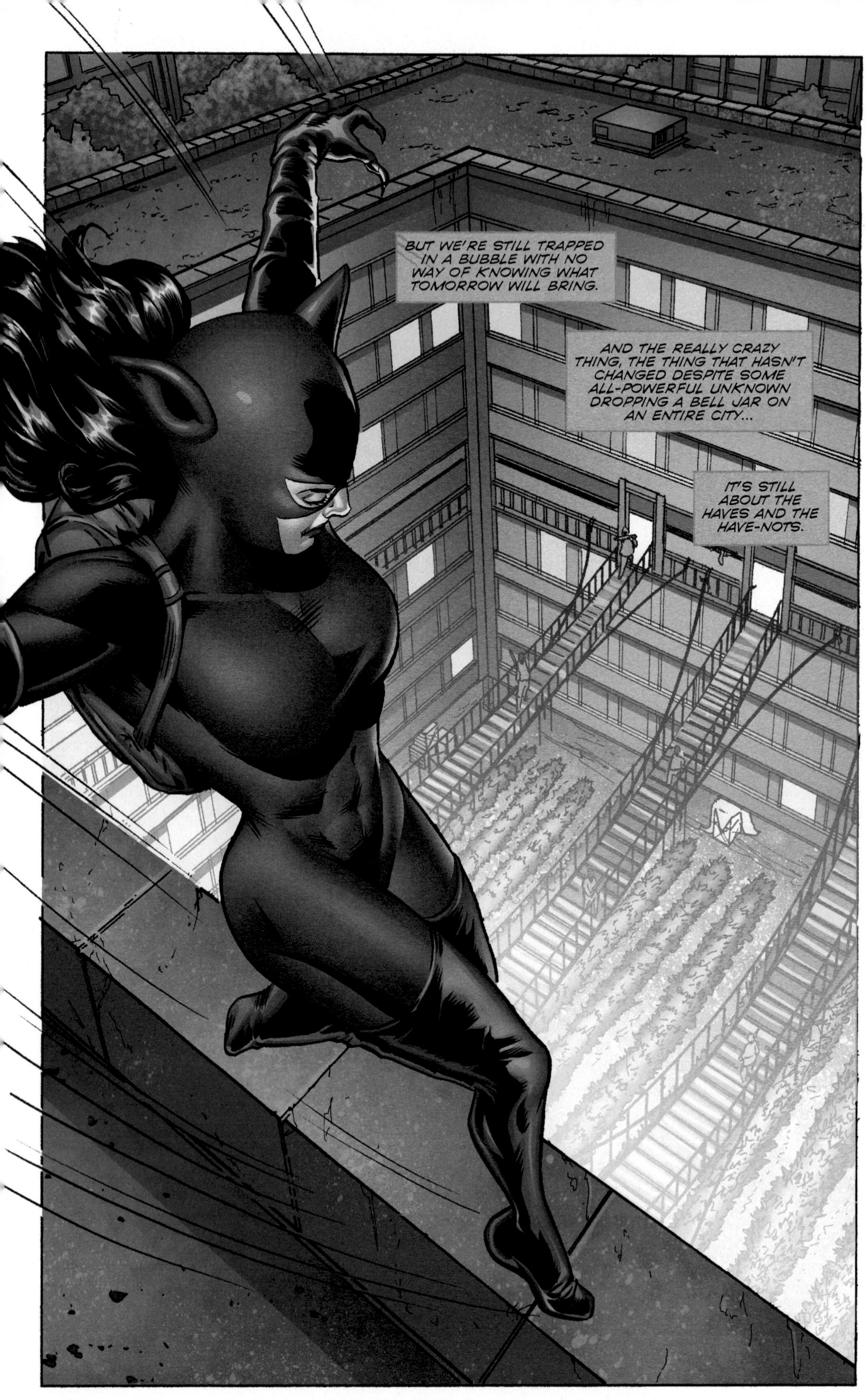
BUT WE'RE STILL TRAPPED IN A BUBBLE WITH NO WAY OF KNOWING WHAT TOMORROW WILL BRING.
AND THE REALLY CRAZY THING, THE THING THAT HASN'T CHANGED DESPITE SOME ALL-POWERFUL UNKNOWN DROPPING A BELL JAR ON AN ENTIRE CITY...
IT'S STILL ABOUT THE HAVES AND THE HAVE-NOTS.

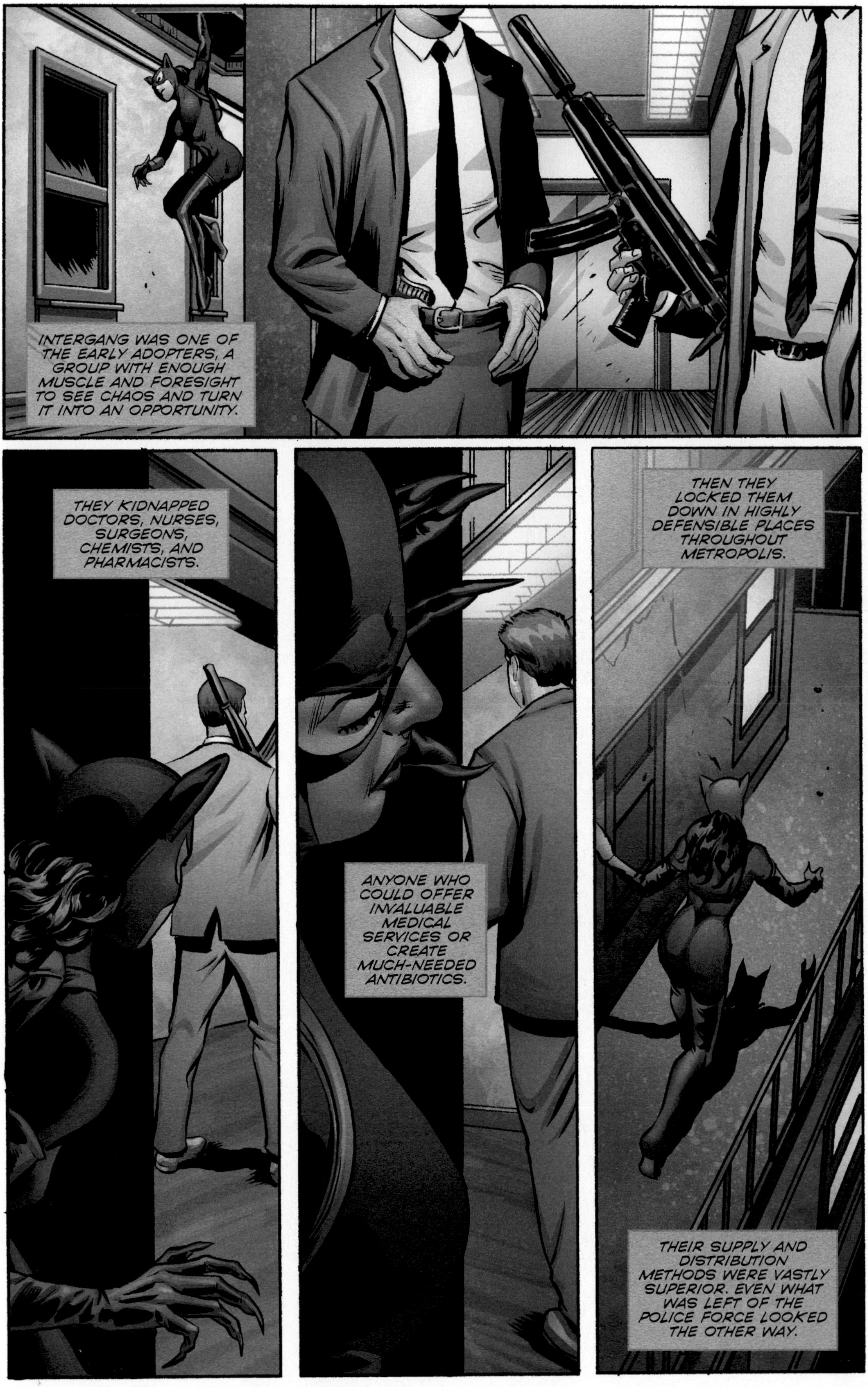
INTERGANG WAS ONE OF THE EARLY ADOPTERS, A GROUP WITH ENOUGH MUSCLE AND FORESIGHT TO SEE CHAOS AND TURN IT INTO AN OPPORTUNITY.
THEY KIDNAPPED DOCTORS, NURSES, SURGEONS, CHEMISTS, AND PHARMACISTS.
ANYONE WHO COULD OFFER INVALUABLE MEDICAL SERVICES OR CREATE MUCH-NEEDED ANTIBIOTICS.
THEN THEY LOCKED THEM DOWN IN HIGHLY DEFENSIBLE PLACES THROUGHOUT METROPOLIS.
THEIR SUPPLY AND DISTRIBUTION METHODS WERE VASTLY SUPERIOR. EVEN WHAT WAS LEFT OF THE POLICE FORCE LOOKED THE OTHER WAY.

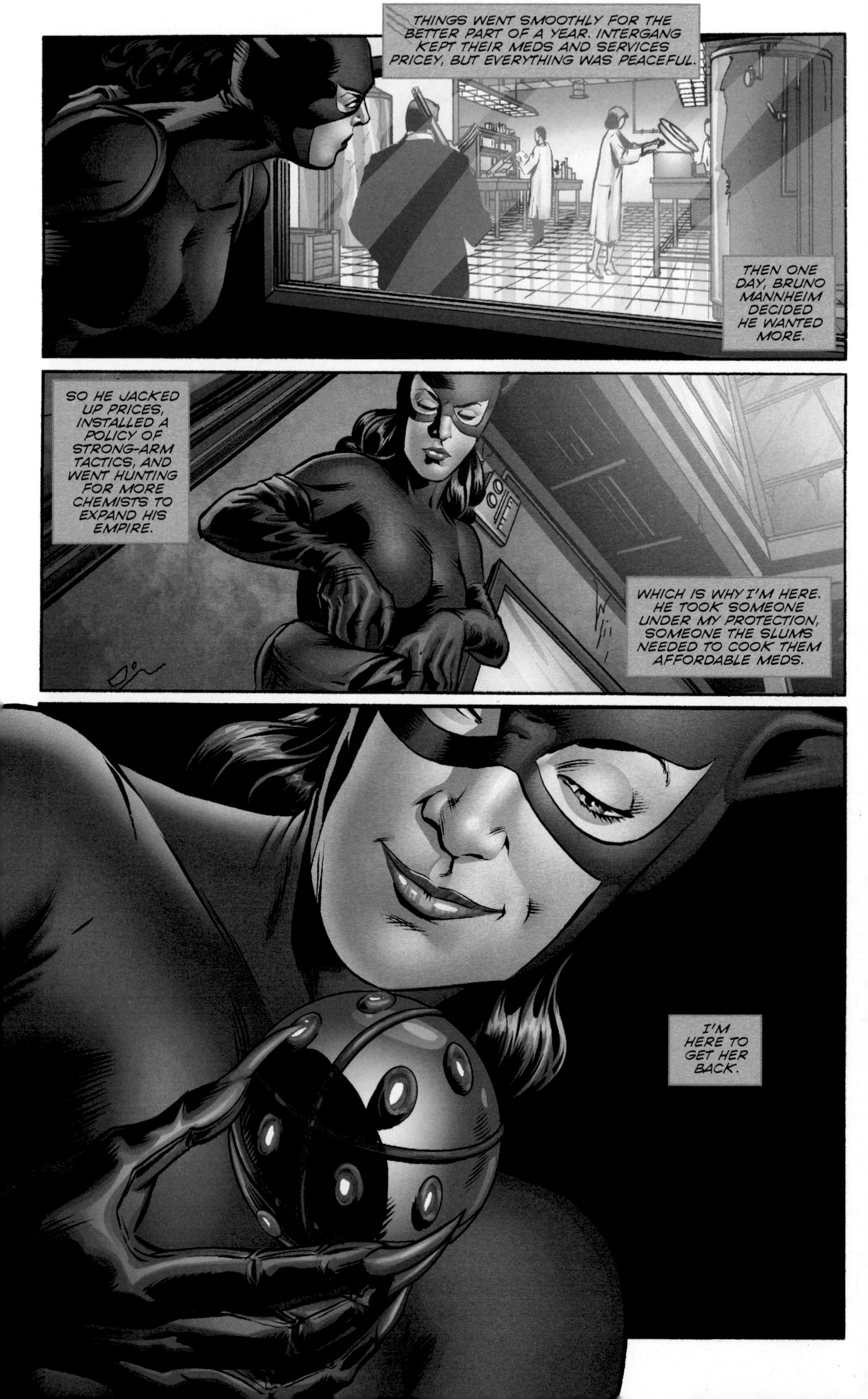
THINGS WENT SMOOTHLY FOR THE BETTER PART OF A YEAR. INTERGANG KEPT THEIR MEDS AND SERVICES PRICEY, BUT EVERYTHING WAS PEACEFUL.
THEN ONE DAY, BRUNO MANNHEIM DECIDED HE WANTED MORE.
SO HE JACKED UP PRICES, INSTALLED A POLICY OF STRONG-ARM TACTICS, AND WENT HUNTING FOR MORE CHEMISTS TO EXPAND HIS EMPIRE.
WHICH IS WHY I'M HERE. HE TOOK SOMEONE UNDER MY PROTECTION, SOMEONE THE SLUMS NEEDED TO COOK THEM AFFORDABLE MEDS.
I'M HERE TO GET HER BACK.

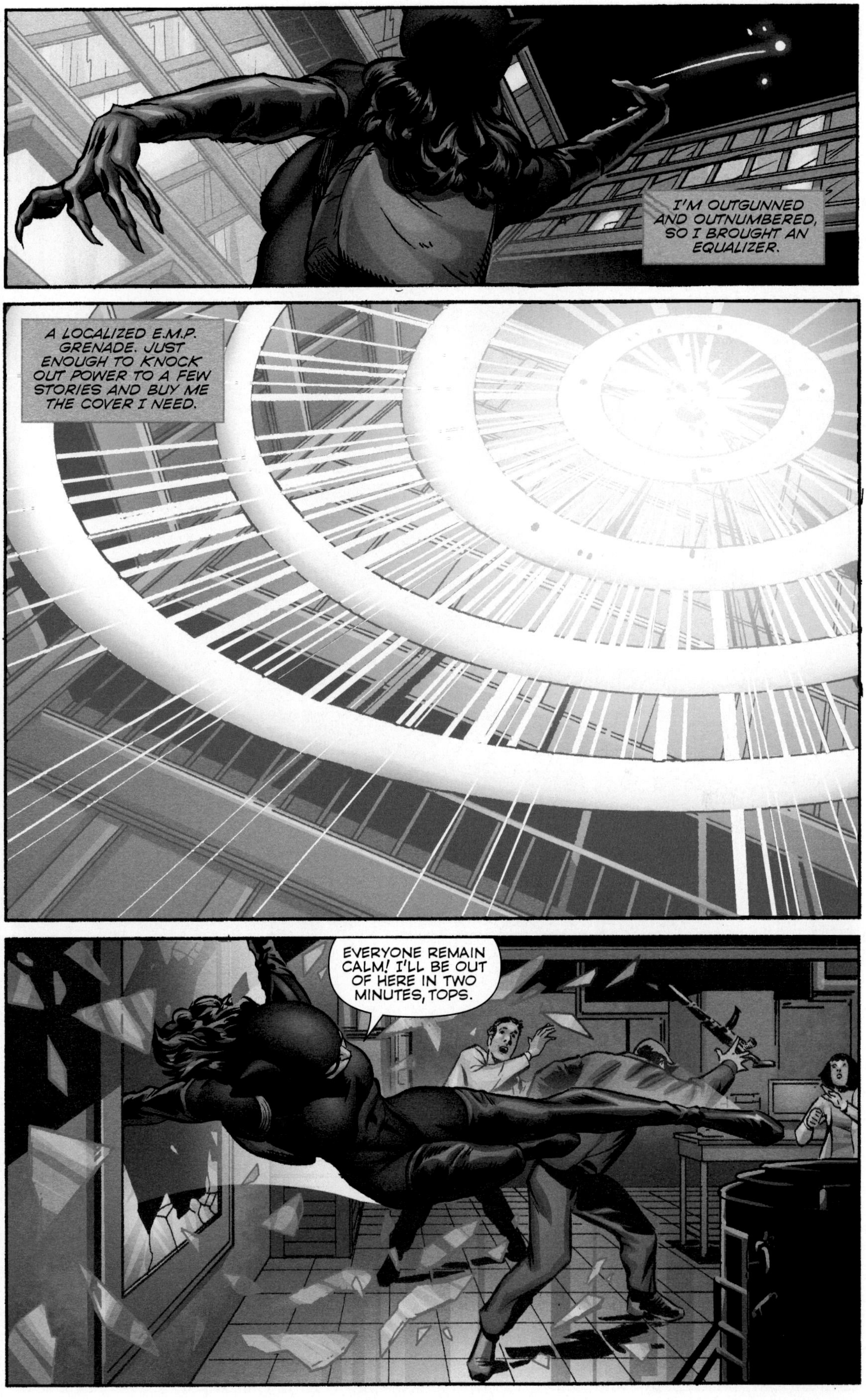
I'M OUTGUNNED AND OUTNUMBERED, SO I BROUGHT AN EQUALIZER.
A LOCALIZED E.M.P. GRENADE. JUST ENOUGH TO KNOCK OUT POWER TO A FEW STORIES AND BUY ME THE COVER I NEED.
EVERYONE REMAIN CALM! I'LL BE OUT OF HERE IN TWO MINUTES, TOPS.

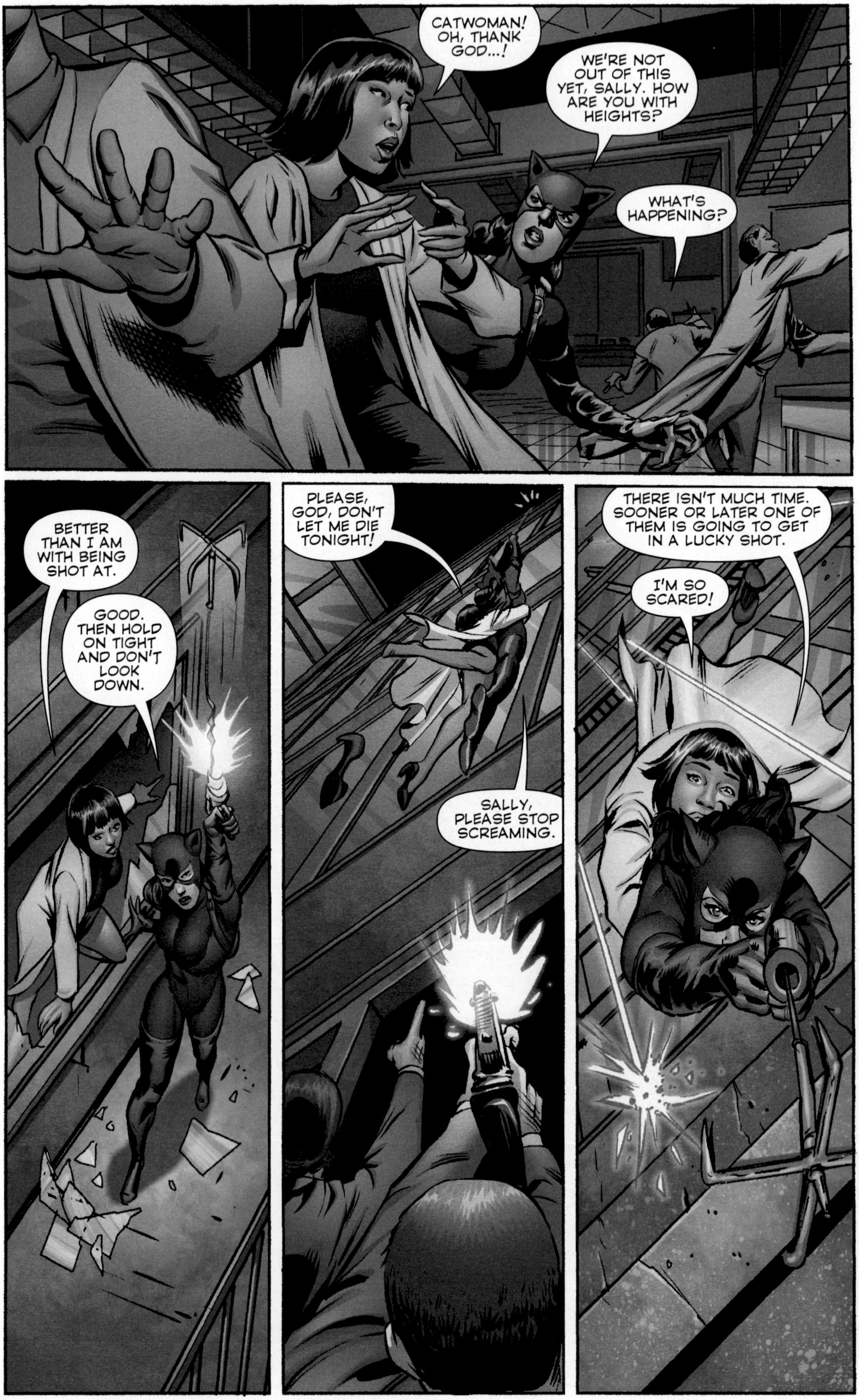
CATWOMAN! OH, THANK GOD...!
WE'RE NOT OUT OF THIS YET, SALLY. HOW ARE YOU WITH HEIGHTS?
WHAT'S HAPPENING?
BETTER THAN I AM WITH BEING SHOT AT.
GOOD. THEN HOLD ON TIGHT AND DON'T LOOK DOWN.
PLEASE, GOD, DON'T LET ME DIE TONIGHT!
SALLY, PLEASE STOP SCREAMING.
THERE ISN'T MUCH TIME. SOONER OR LATER ONE OF THEM IS GOING TO GET IN A LUCKY SHOT.
I'M SO SCARED!

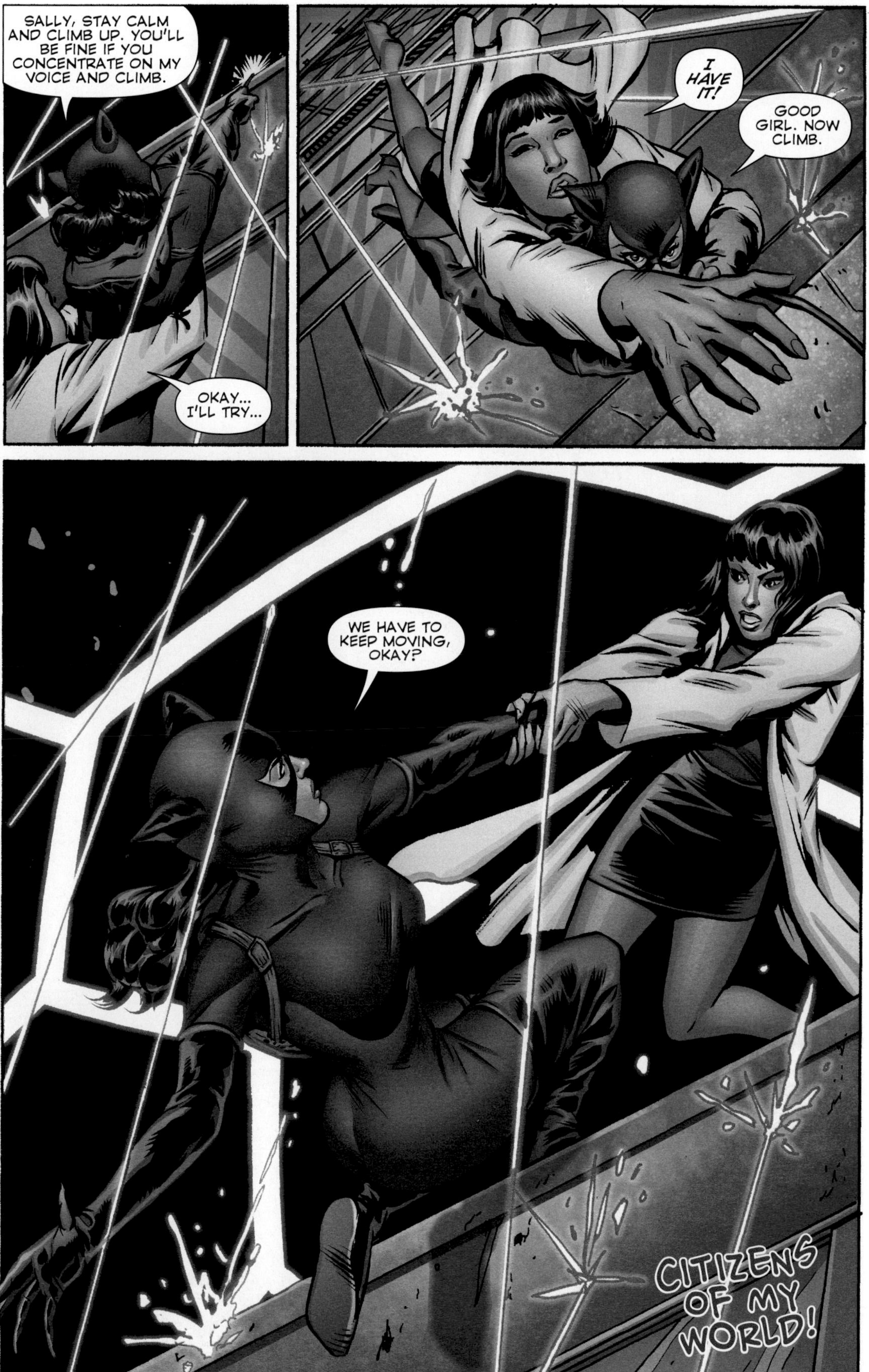
SALLY, STAY CALM AND CLIMB UP. YOU'LL BE FINE IF YOU CONCENTRATE ON MY VOICE AND CLIMB.
OKAY... I'LL TRY...
I HAVE IT!
GOOD GIRL. NOW CLIMB.
WE HAVE TO KEEP MOVING, OKAY?
CITIZENS OF MY WORLD!

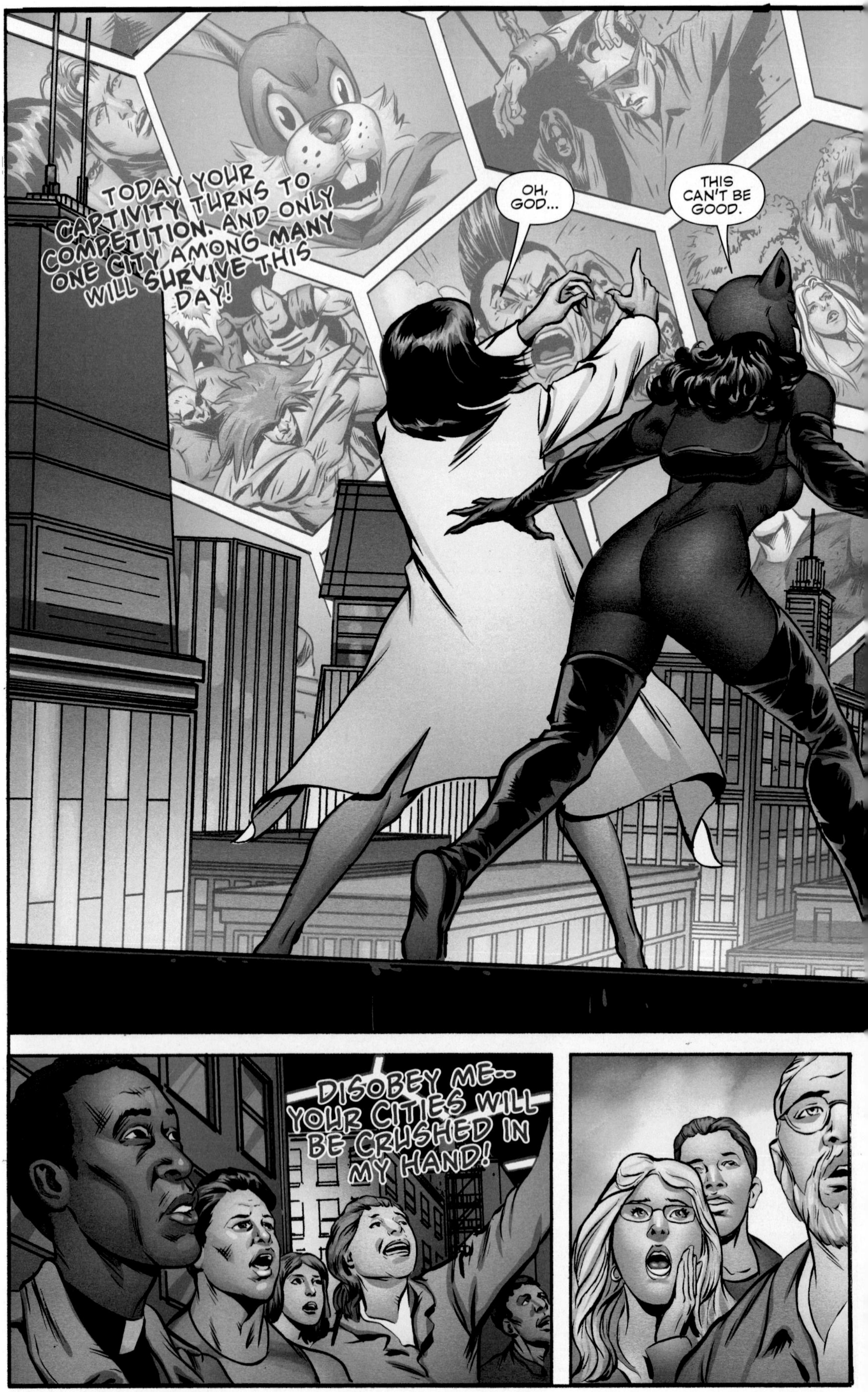
TODAY YOUR CAPTIVITY TURNS TO COMPETITION. AND ONLY ONE CITY AMONG MANY WILL SURVIVE THIS DAY!
OH, GOD...
THIS CAN'T BE GOOD.
DISOBEY ME-- YOUR CITIES WILL BE CRUSHED IN MY HAND!

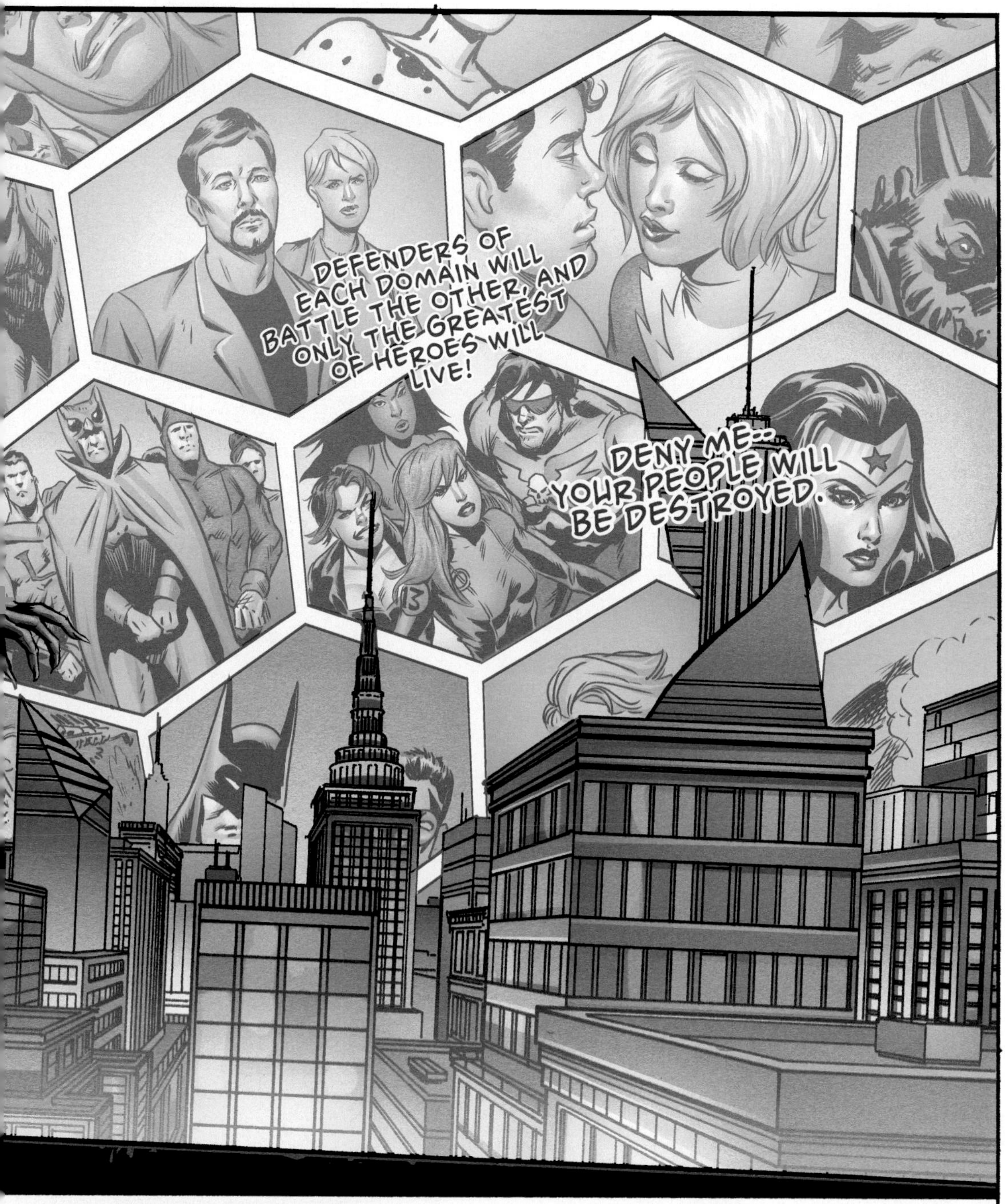
DEFENDERS OF EACH DOMAIN WILL BATTLE THE OTHER, AND ONLY THE GREATEST OF HEROES WILL LIVE!
DENY ME-- YOUR PEOPLE WILL BE DESTROYED.

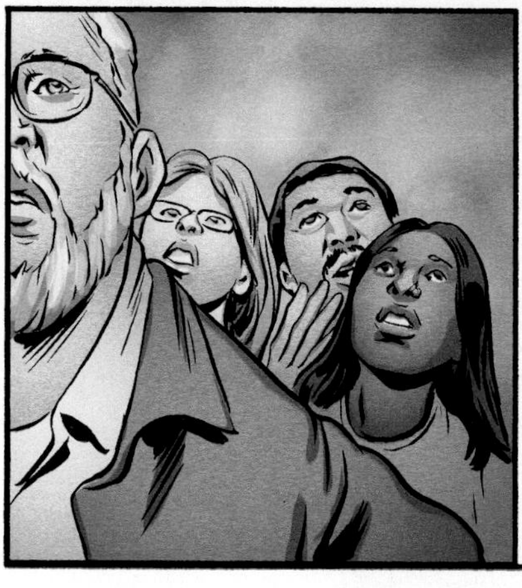

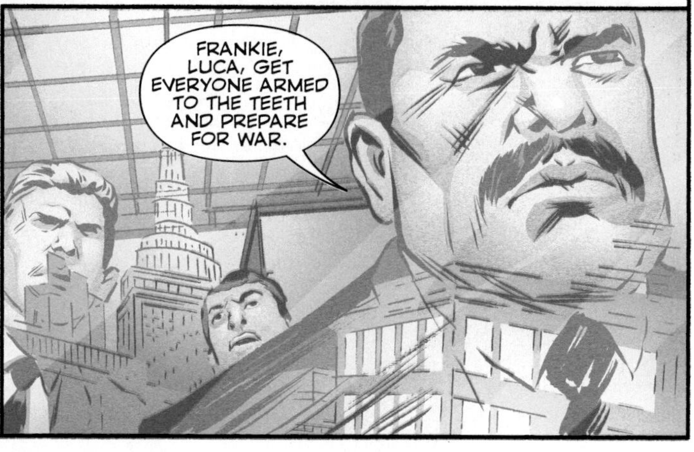
FRANKIE, LUCA, GET EVERYONE ARMED TO THE TEETH AND PREPARE FOR WAR.

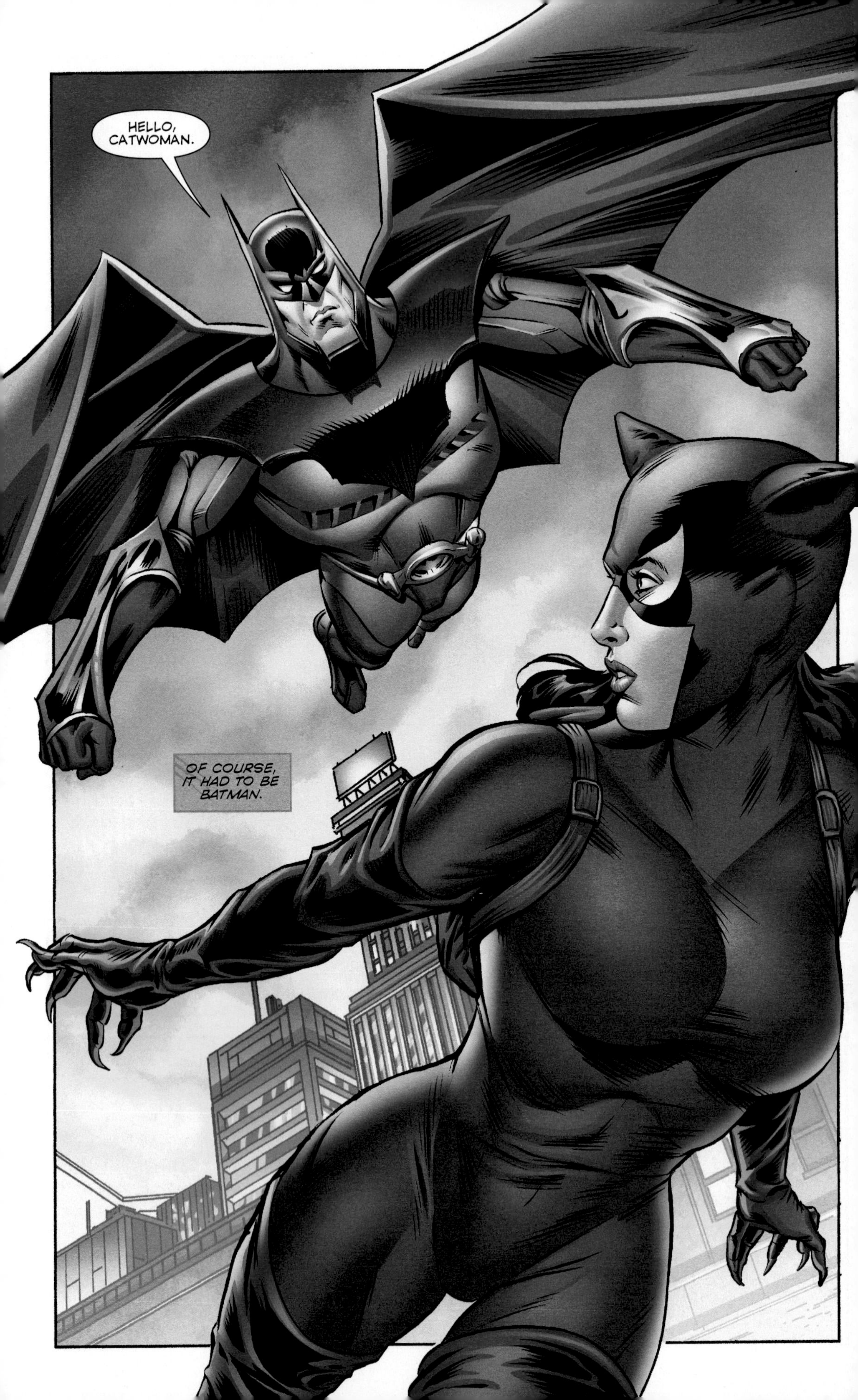
HELLO, CATWOMAN.
OF COURSE, IT HAD TO BE BATMAN.

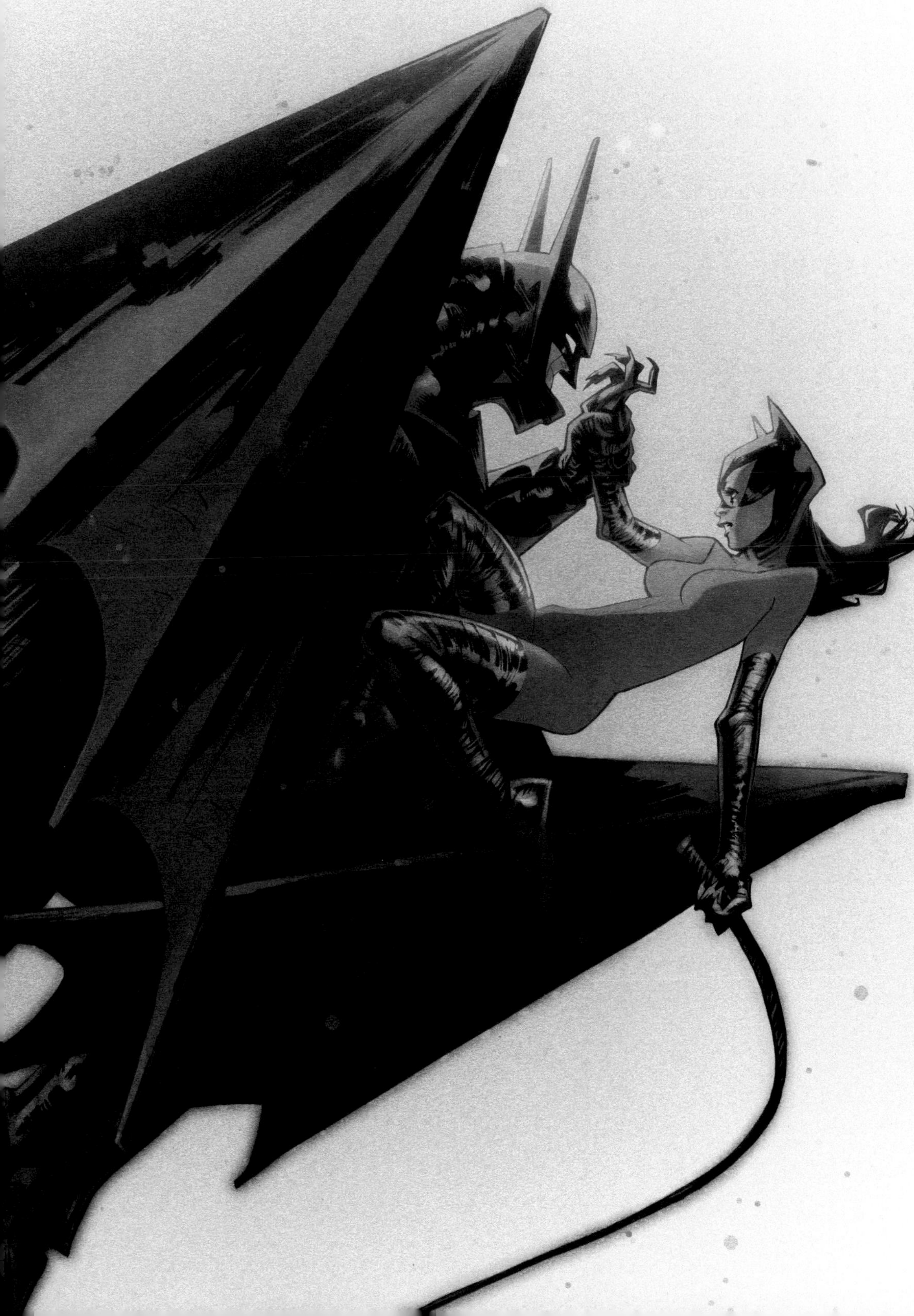

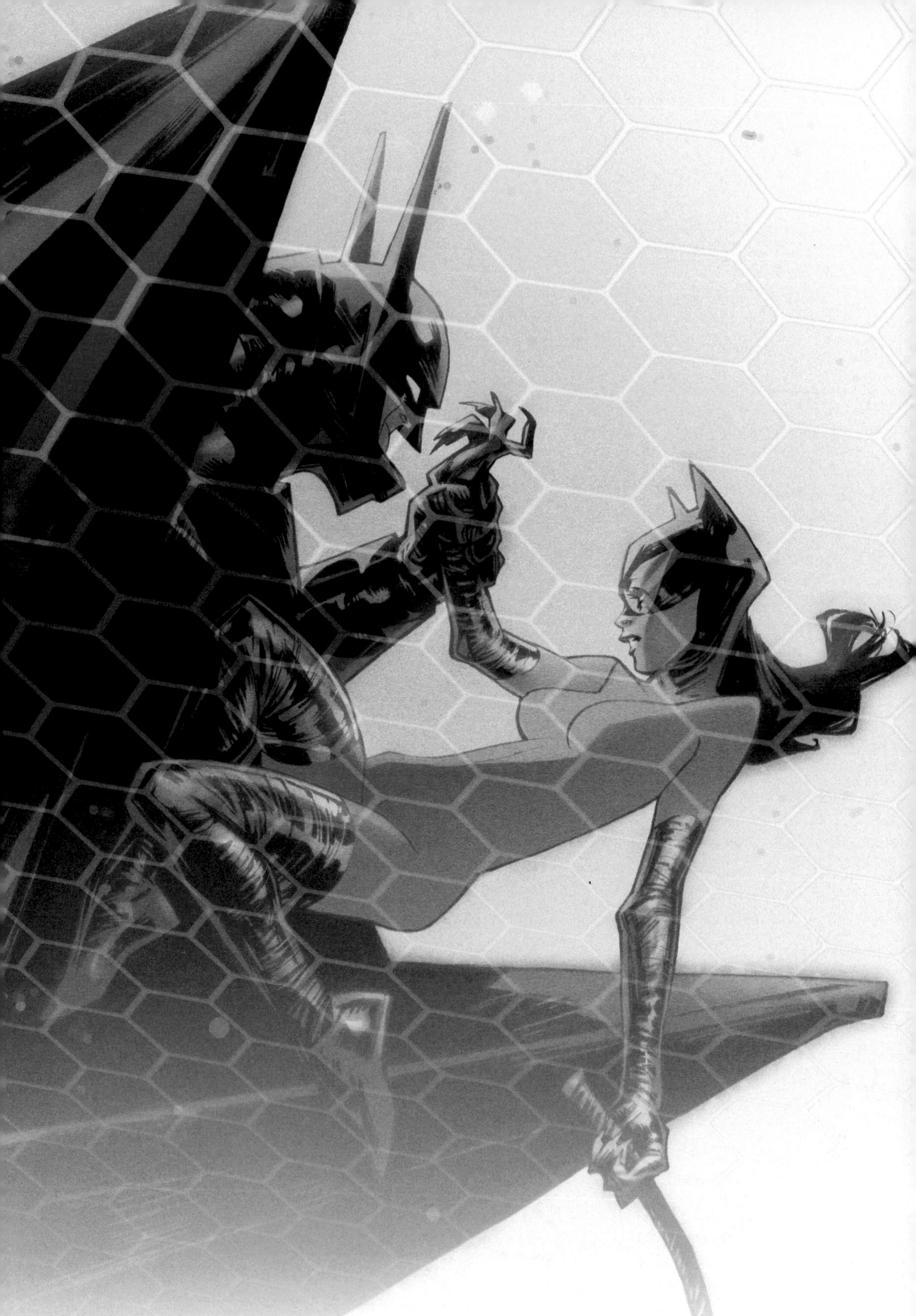

BATMAN IN A SUIT OF ARMOR. AS USUAL, HE'S PREPARED FOR ANYTHING.

BATMAN?

THIS ISN'T RIGHT.

WHAT'S WITH THE ARMOR?

ME, NOT SO MUCH.

I NEED TO GET SALLY TO *SAFETY* BEFORE I WORRY ABOUT WHAT TO DO *NEXT.*

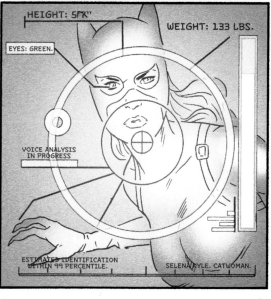

HEIGHT: 5'8"

WEIGHT: 133 LBS.

EYES: GREEN.

VOICE ANALYSIS IN PROGRESS

ESTIMATED IDENTIFICATION WITHIN 99 PERCENTILE.

SELENA KYLE. CATWOMAN.

CATWOMAN IS HALF MY AGE AND I'VE NEVER SEEN THAT SUIT.

THIS IS METROPOLIS, BUT THERE ARE ARCHITECTURAL AND TECHNOLOGICAL DIFFERENCES.

I'M NOT PICKING UP ANY DATA CLOUDS, AND THERE'S MINIMAL WIRELESS ACTIVITY.

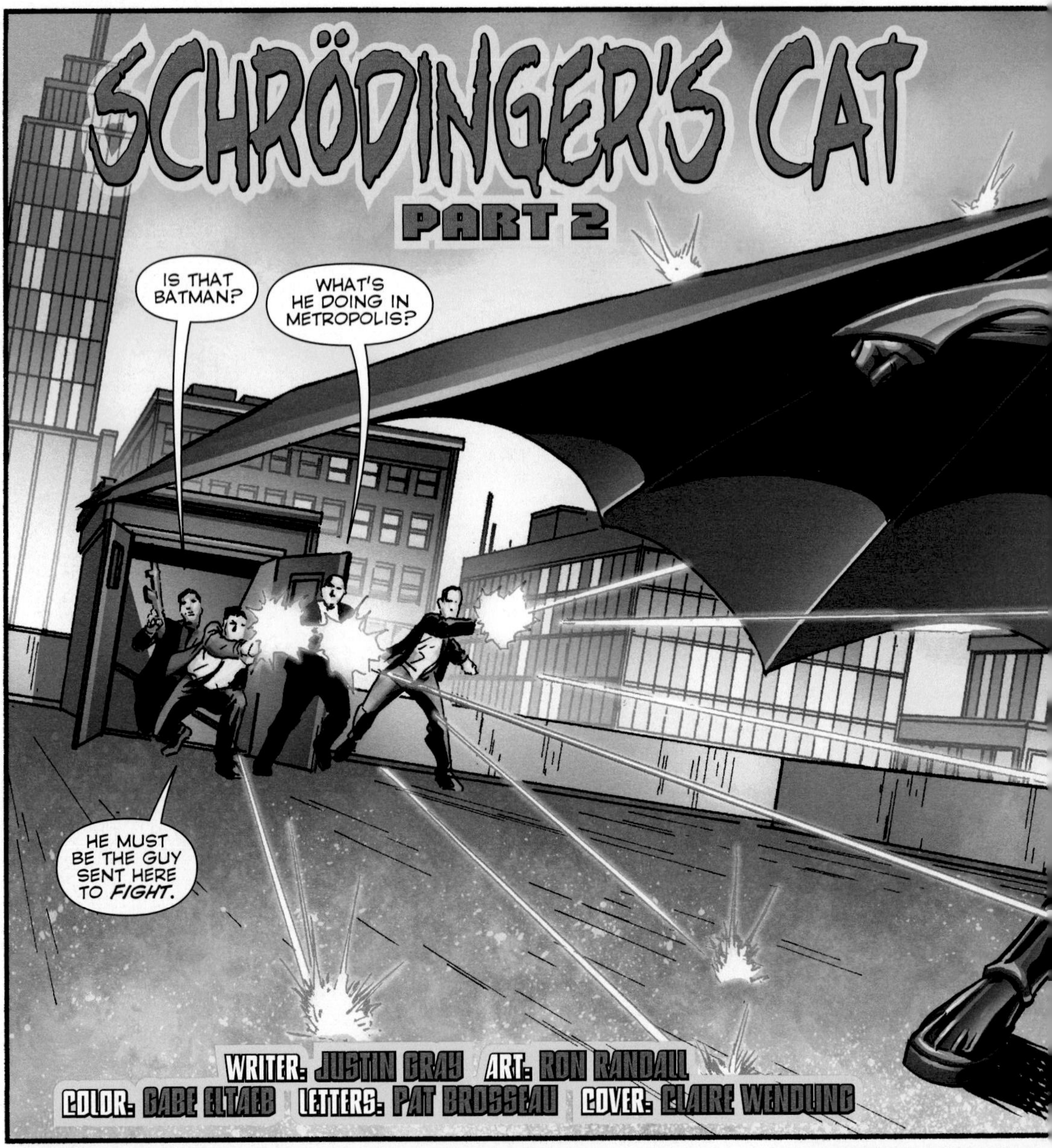
SCHRÖDINGER'S CAT
PART 2
IS THAT BATMAN?
WHAT'S HE DOING IN METROPOLIS?
HE MUST BE THE GUY SENT HERE TO FIGHT.
WRITER: JUSTIN GRAY ART: RON RANDALL
COLOR: GABE ELTAEB LETTERS: PAT BROSSEAU COVER: CLAIRE WENDLING

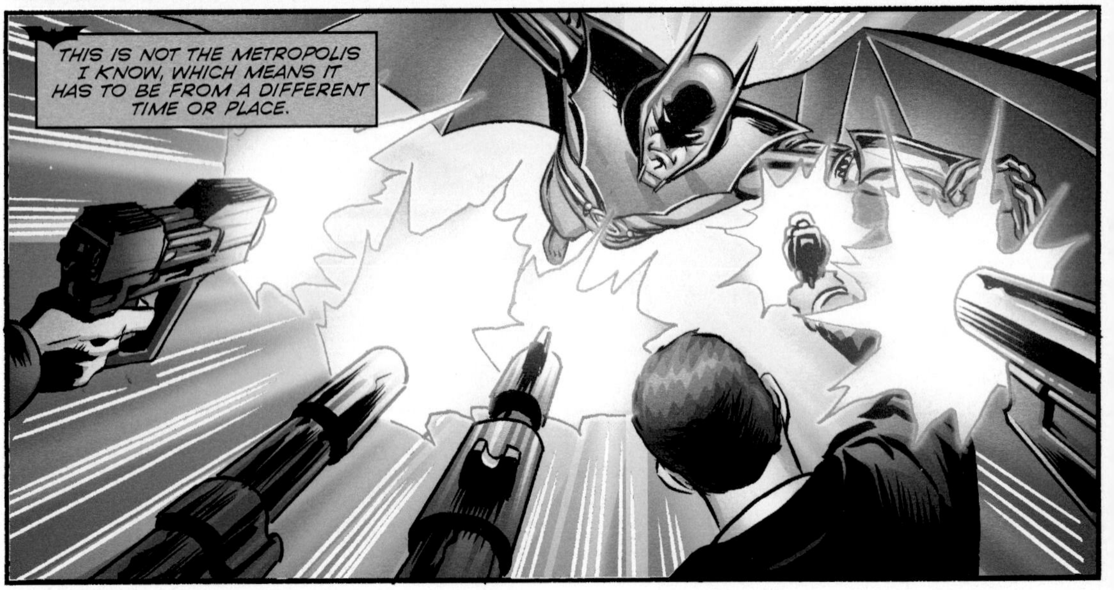
THIS IS NOT THE METROPOLIS I KNOW, WHICH MEANS IT HAS TO BE FROM A DIFFERENT TIME OR PLACE.

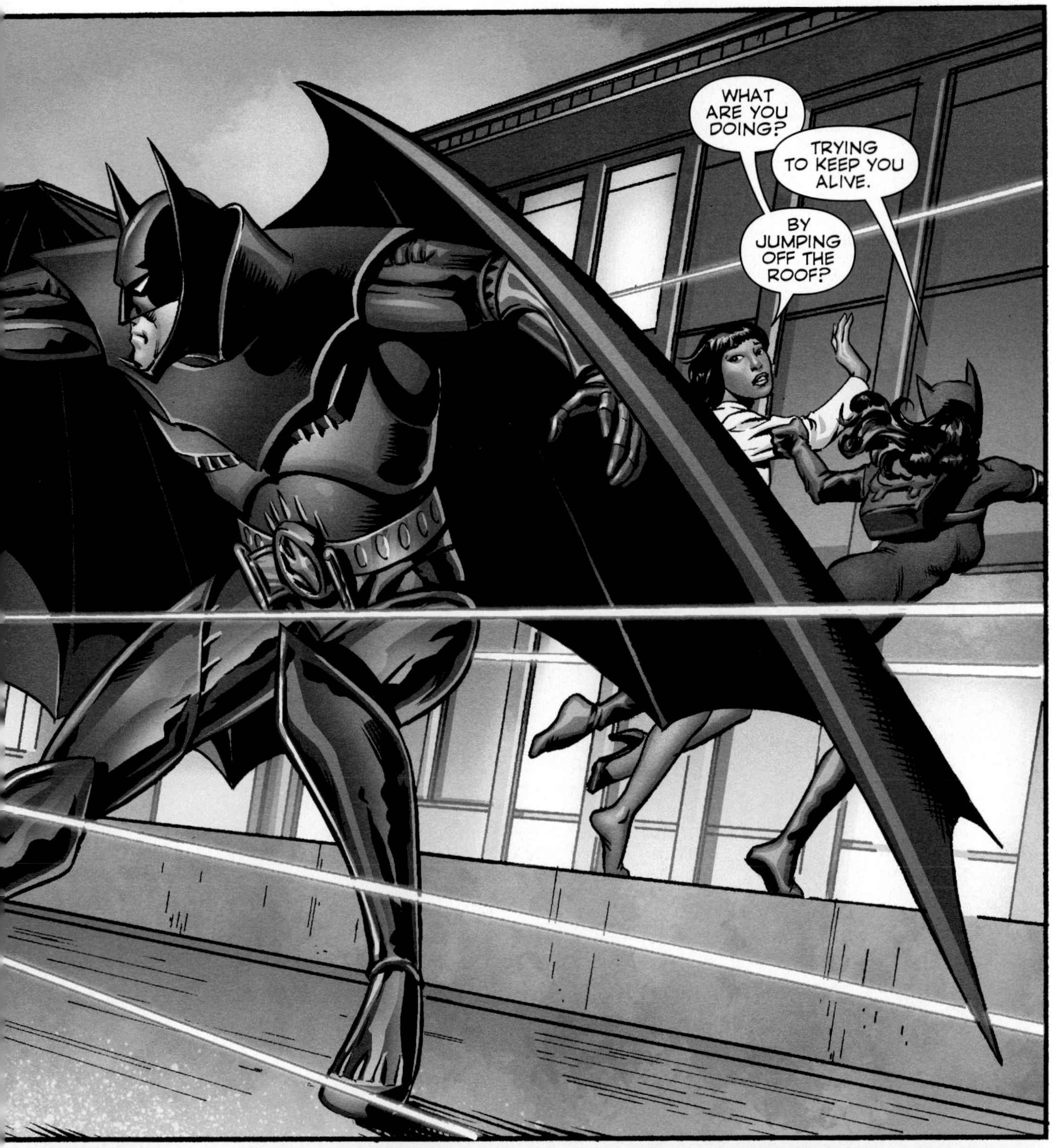
WHAT ARE YOU DOING?
TRYING TO KEEP YOU ALIVE.
BY JUMPING OFF THE ROOF?

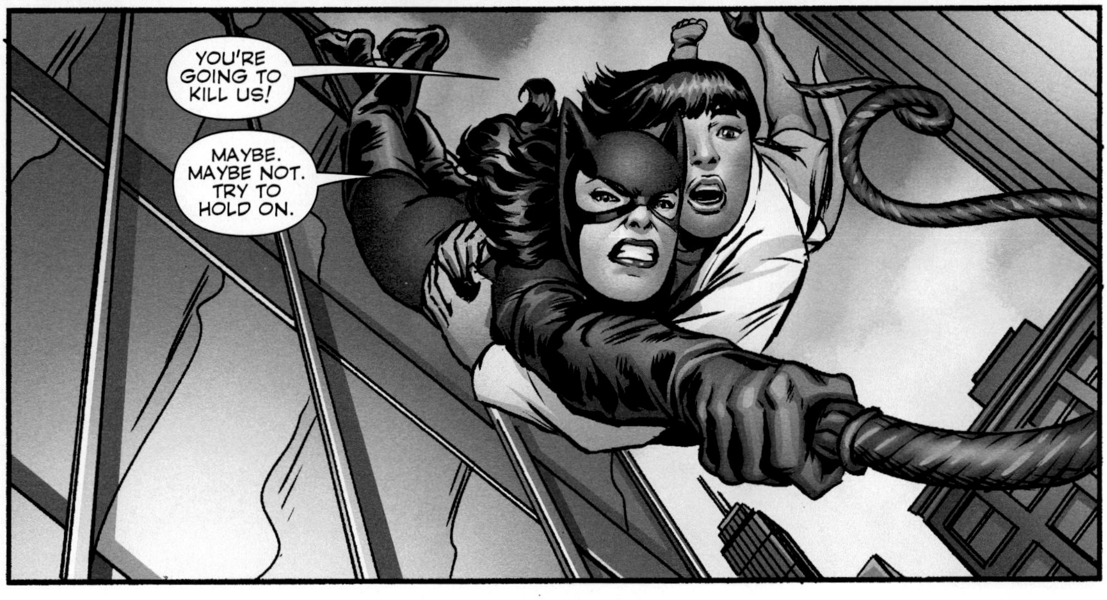
YOU'RE GOING TO KILL US!
MAYBE. MAYBE NOT. TRY TO HOLD ON.

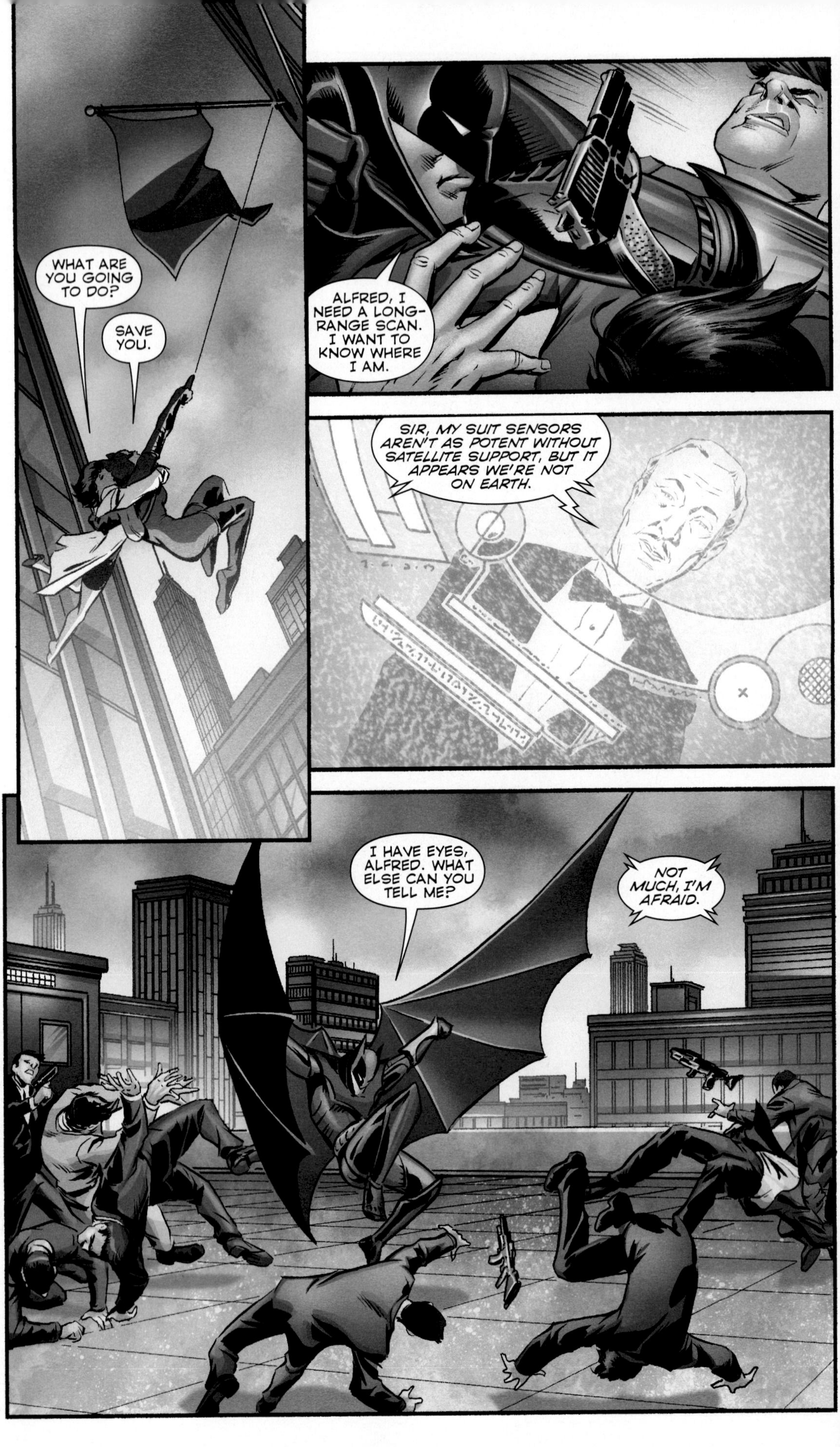
WHAT ARE YOU GOING TO DO?
SAVE YOU.
ALFRED, I NEED A LONG-RANGE SCAN. I WANT TO KNOW WHERE I AM.
SIR, MY SUIT SENSORS AREN'T AS POTENT WITHOUT SATELLITE SUPPORT, BUT IT APPEARS WE'RE NOT ON EARTH.
I HAVE EYES, ALFRED. WHAT ELSE CAN YOU TELL ME?
NOT MUCH, I'M AFRAID.

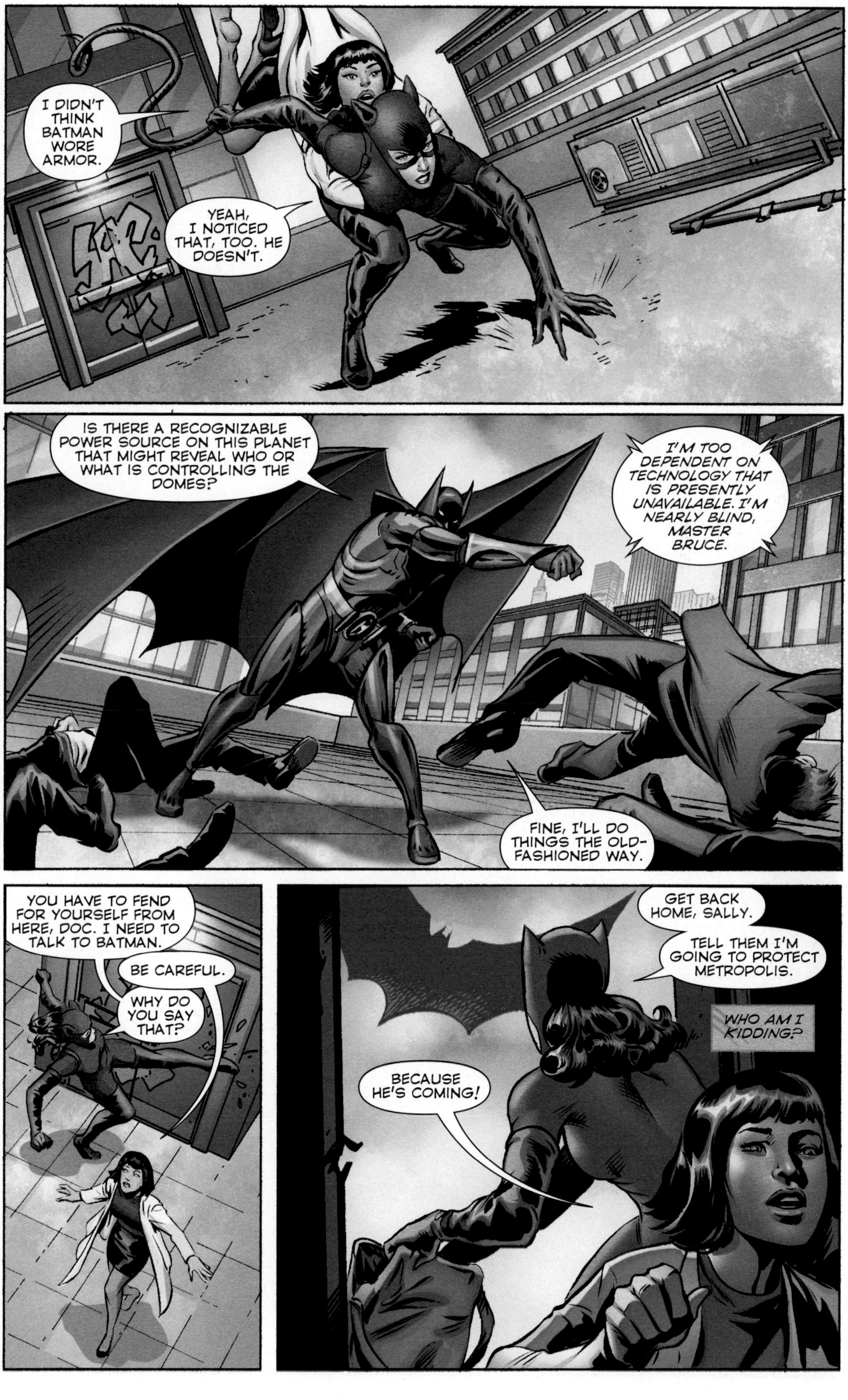

I DIDN'T THINK BATMAN WORE ARMOR.
YEAH, I NOTICED THAT, TOO. HE DOESN'T.
IS THERE A RECOGNIZABLE POWER SOURCE ON THIS PLANET THAT MIGHT REVEAL WHO OR WHAT IS CONTROLLING THE DOMES?
I'M TOO DEPENDENT ON TECHNOLOGY THAT IS PRESENTLY UNAVAILABLE. I'M NEARLY BLIND, MASTER BRUCE.
FINE, I'LL DO THINGS THE OLD-FASHIONED WAY.
YOU HAVE TO FEND FOR YOURSELF FROM HERE, DOC. I NEED TO TALK TO BATMAN.
BE CAREFUL.
WHY DO YOU SAY THAT?
BECAUSE HE'S COMING!
GET BACK HOME, SALLY.
TELL THEM I'M GOING TO PROTECT METROPOLIS.
WHO AM I KIDDING?

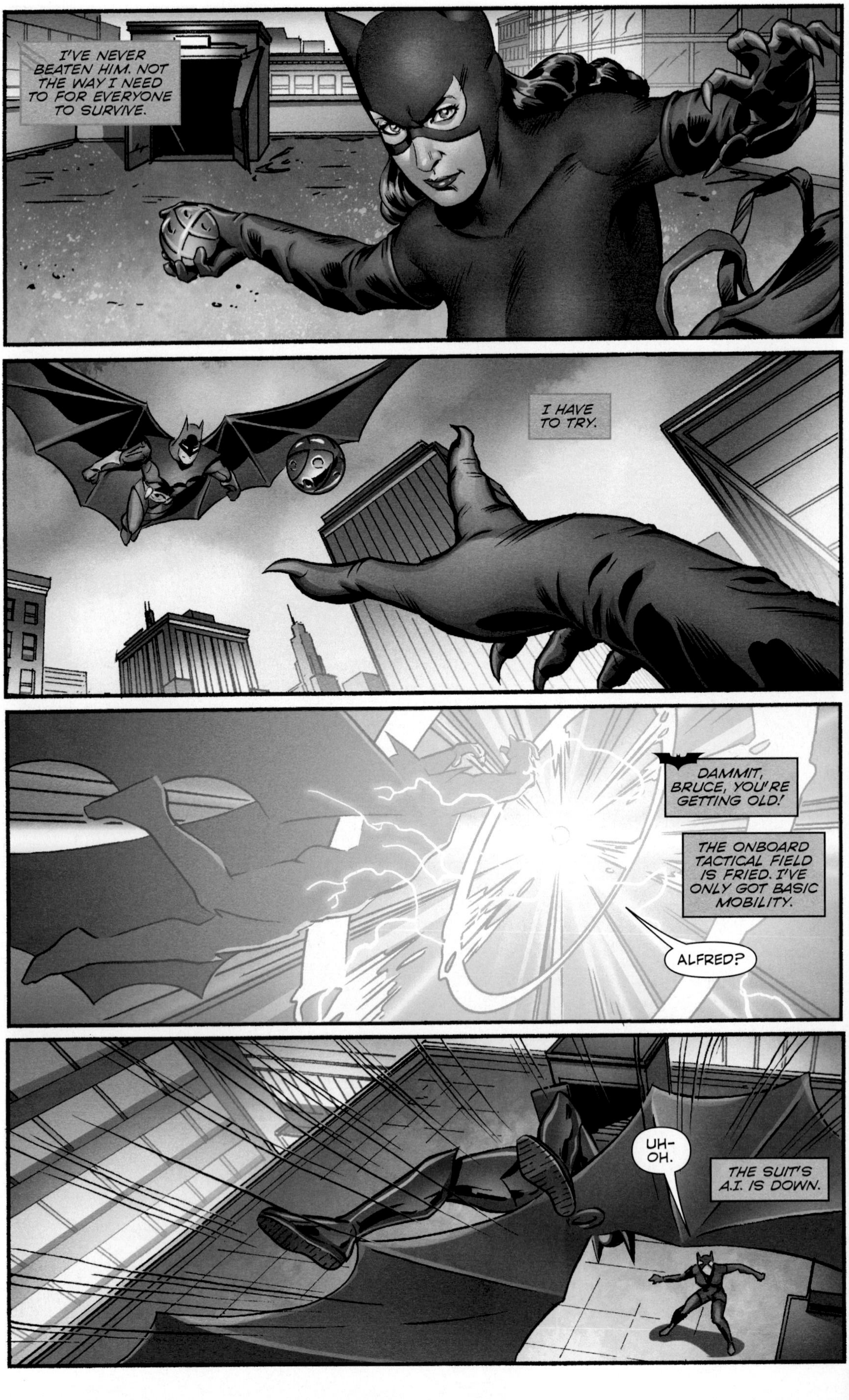
I'VE NEVER BEATEN HIM. NOT THE WAY I NEED TO FOR EVERYONE TO SURVIVE.
I HAVE TO TRY.
DAMMIT, BRUCE, YOU'RE GETTING OLD!
THE ONBOARD TACTICAL FIELD IS FRIED. I'VE ONLY GOT BASIC MOBILITY.
ALFRED?
UH-OH.
THE SUIT'S A.I. IS DOWN.

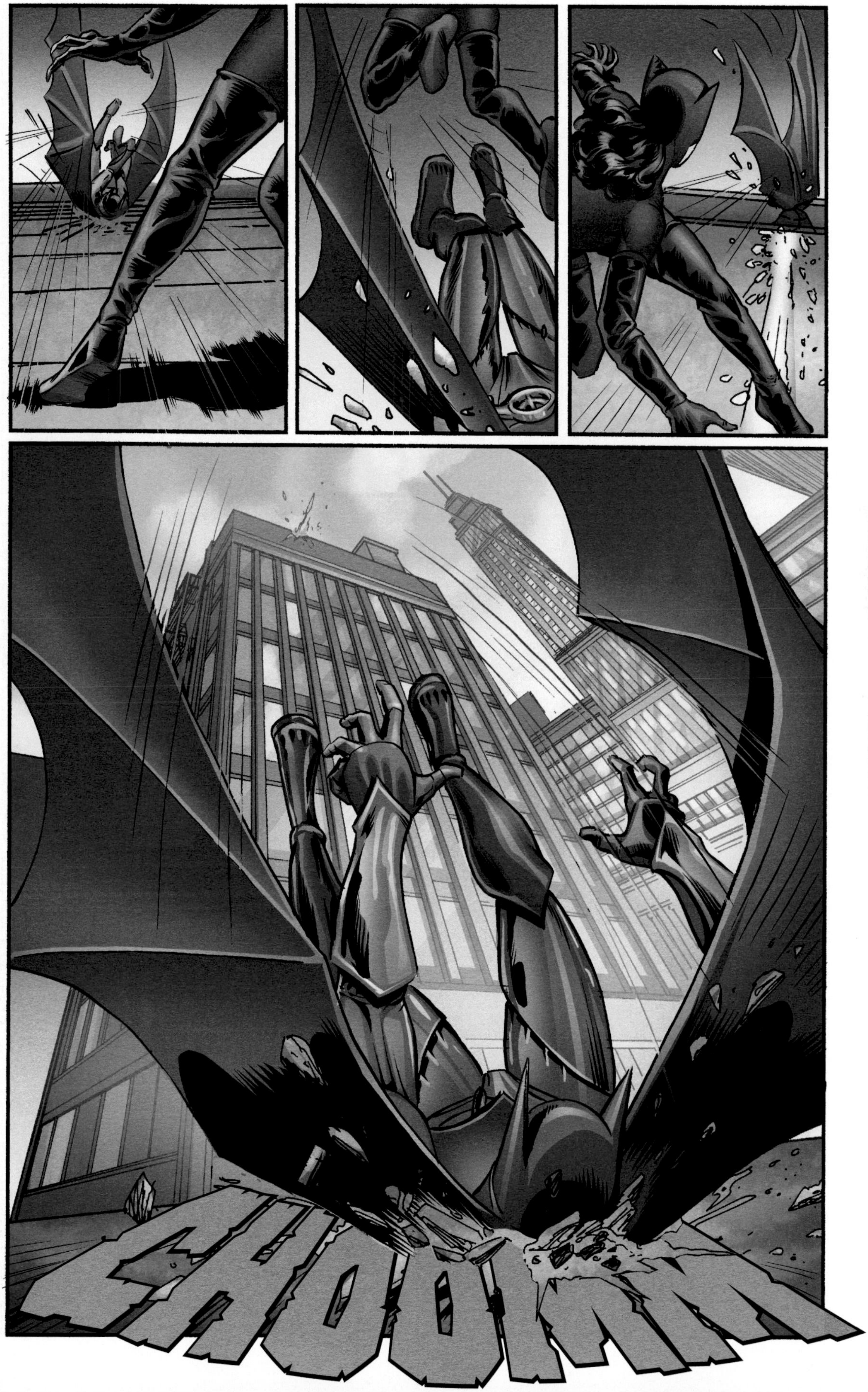
CHOOM

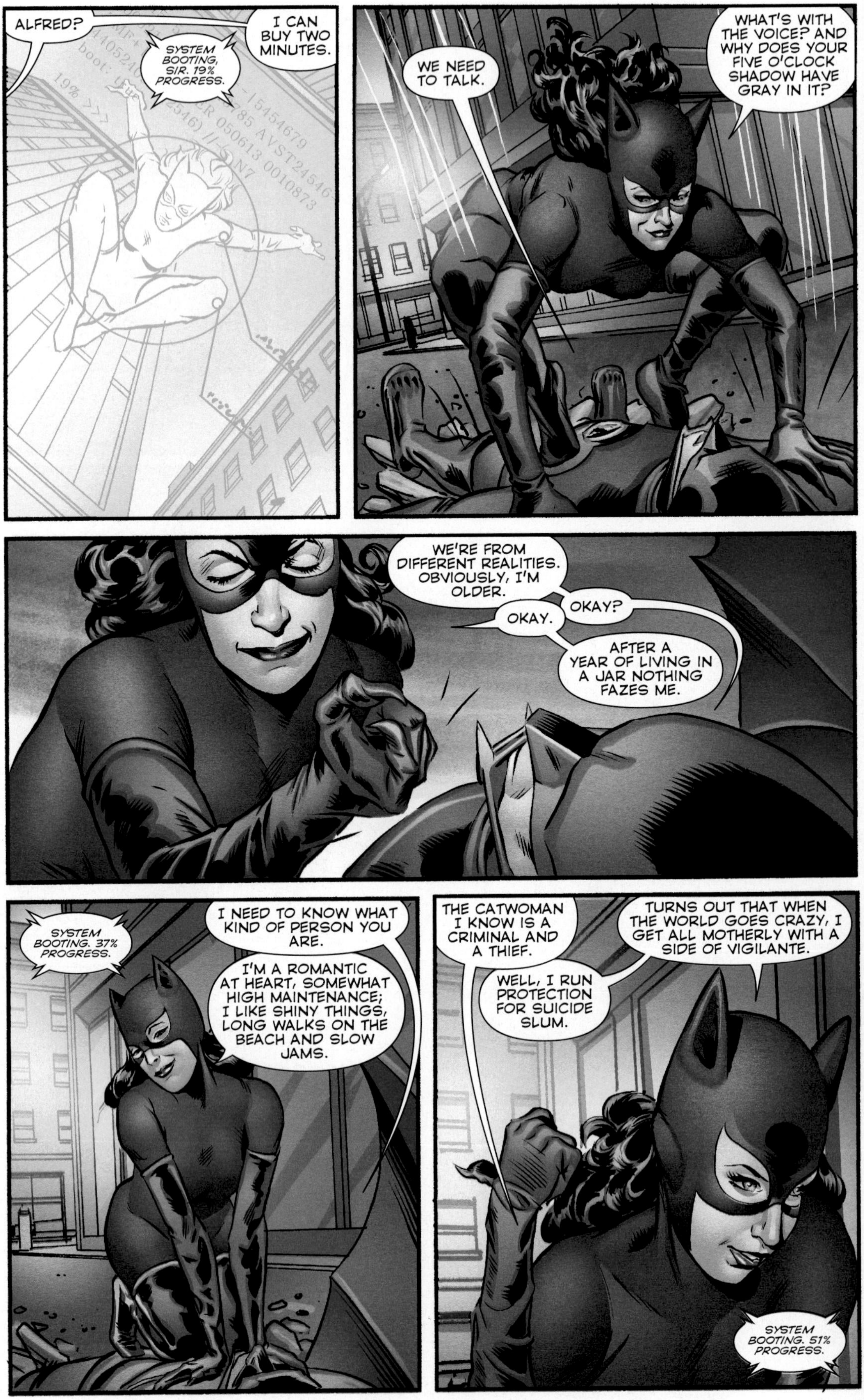
ALFRED?
SYSTEM BOOTING, SIR. 19% PROGRESS.
I CAN BUY TWO MINUTES.
WE NEED TO TALK.
WHAT'S WITH THE VOICE? AND WHY DOES YOUR FIVE O'CLOCK SHADOW HAVE GRAY IN IT?
WE'RE FROM DIFFERENT REALITIES. OBVIOUSLY, I'M OLDER.
OKAY?
OKAY.
AFTER A YEAR OF LIVING IN A JAR NOTHING FAZES ME.
SYSTEM BOOTING. 37% PROGRESS.
I NEED TO KNOW WHAT KIND OF PERSON YOU ARE.
I'M A ROMANTIC AT HEART, SOMEWHAT HIGH MAINTENANCE; I LIKE SHINY THINGS, LONG WALKS ON THE BEACH AND SLOW JAMS.
THE CATWOMAN I KNOW IS A CRIMINAL AND A THIEF.
WELL, I RUN PROTECTION FOR SUICIDE SLUM.
TURNS OUT THAT WHEN THE WORLD GOES CRAZY, I GET ALL MOTHERLY WITH A SIDE OF VIGILANTE.
SYSTEM BOOTING. 51% PROGRESS.

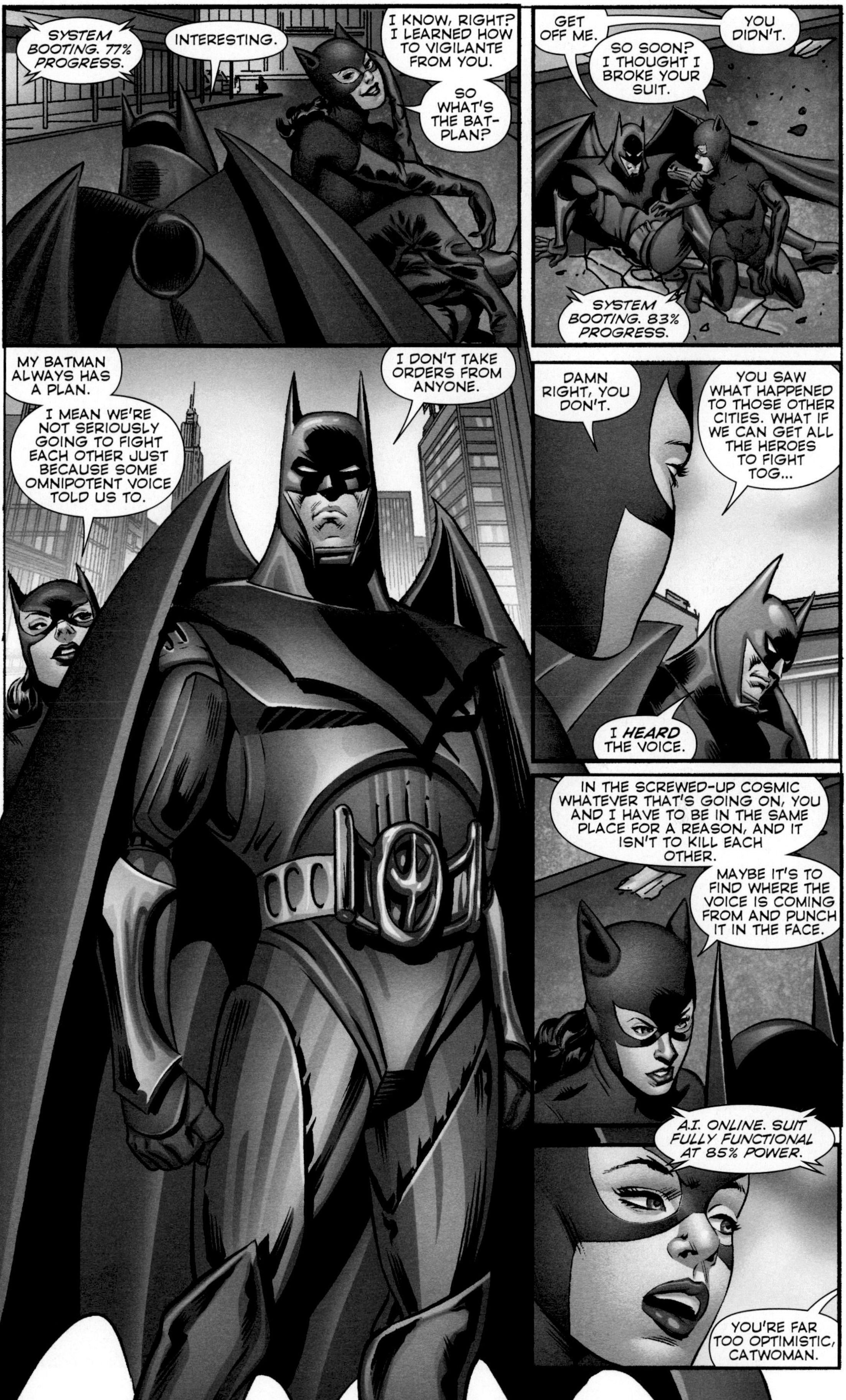

SYSTEM BOOTING. 77% PROGRESS.
INTERESTING.
I KNOW, RIGHT? I LEARNED HOW TO VIGILANTE FROM YOU.
SO WHAT'S THE BAT-PLAN?
GET OFF ME.
YOU DIDN'T.
SO SOON? I THOUGHT I BROKE YOUR SUIT.
SYSTEM BOOTING. 83% PROGRESS.
MY BATMAN ALWAYS HAS A PLAN.
I MEAN WE'RE NOT SERIOUSLY GOING TO FIGHT EACH OTHER JUST BECAUSE SOME OMNIPOTENT VOICE TOLD US TO.
I DON'T TAKE ORDERS FROM ANYONE.
DAMN RIGHT, YOU DON'T.
YOU SAW WHAT HAPPENED TO THOSE OTHER CITIES. WHAT IF WE CAN GET ALL THE HEROES TO FIGHT TOG...
I *HEARD* THE VOICE.
IN THE SCREWED-UP COSMIC WHATEVER THAT'S GOING ON, YOU AND I HAVE TO BE IN THE SAME PLACE FOR A REASON, AND IT ISN'T TO KILL EACH OTHER.
MAYBE IT'S TO FIND WHERE THE VOICE IS COMING FROM AND PUNCH IT IN THE FACE.
A.I. ONLINE. SUIT FULLY FUNCTIONAL AT 85% POWER.
YOU'RE FAR TOO OPTIMISTIC, CATWOMAN.

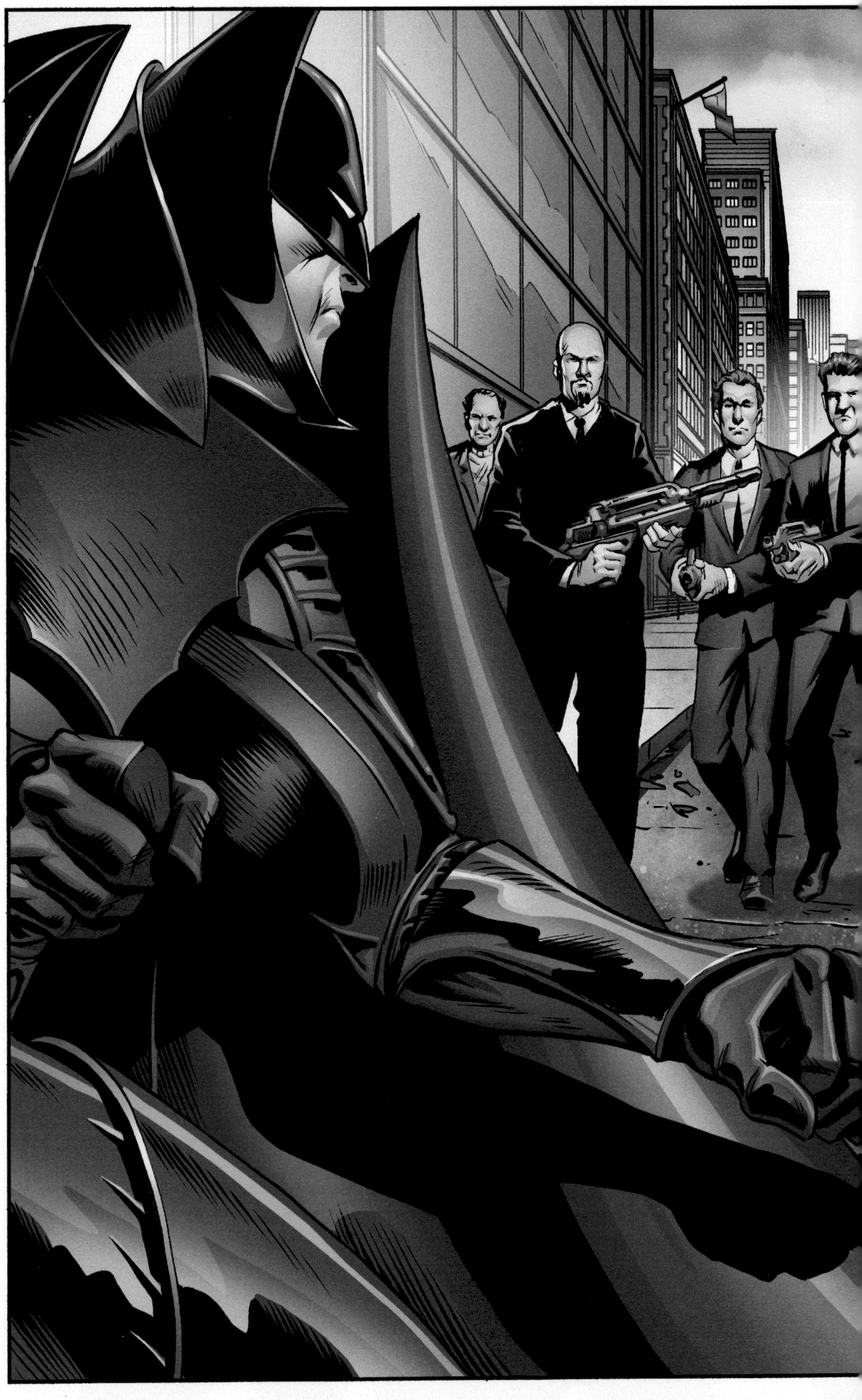

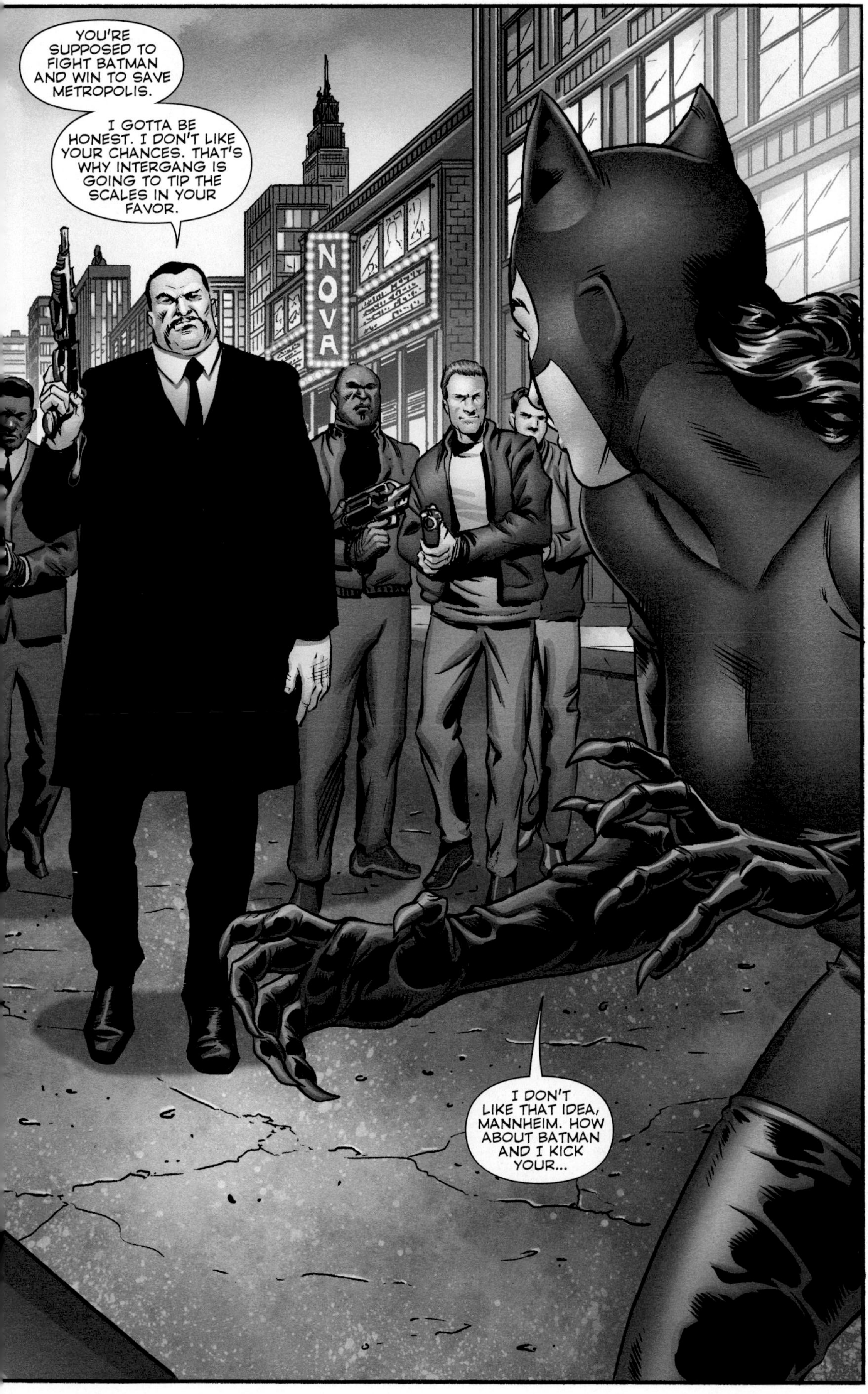
YOU'RE SUPPOSED TO FIGHT BATMAN AND WIN TO SAVE METROPOLIS.
I GOTTA BE HONEST. I DON'T LIKE YOUR CHANCES. THAT'S WHY INTERGANG IS GOING TO TIP THE SCALES IN YOUR FAVOR.
NOVA
I DON'T LIKE THAT IDEA, MANNHEIM. HOW ABOUT BATMAN AND I KICK YOUR...

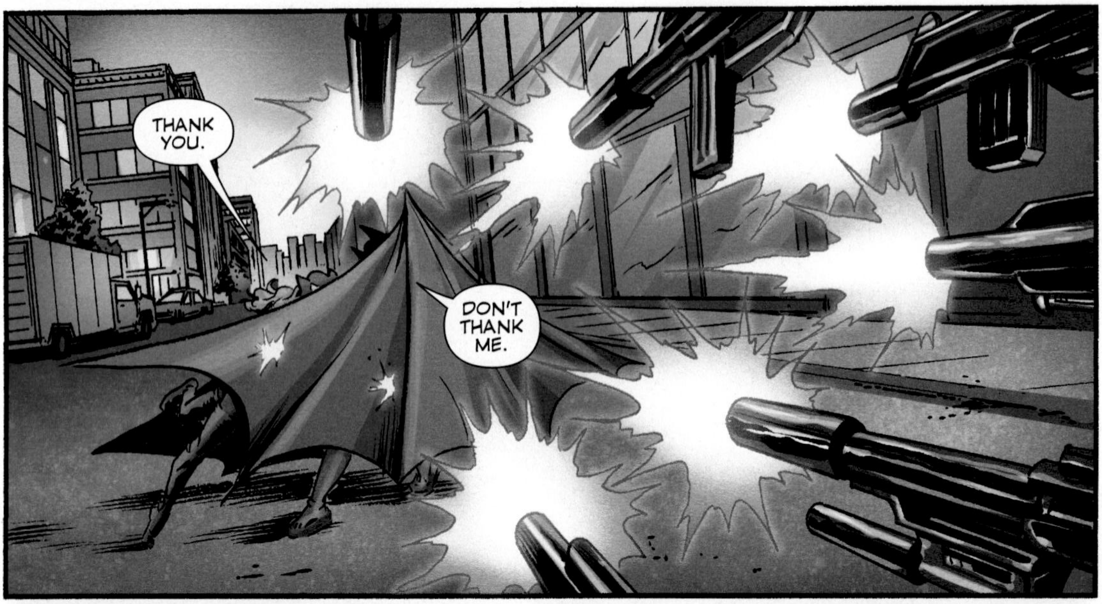
THANK YOU.
DON'T THANK ME.
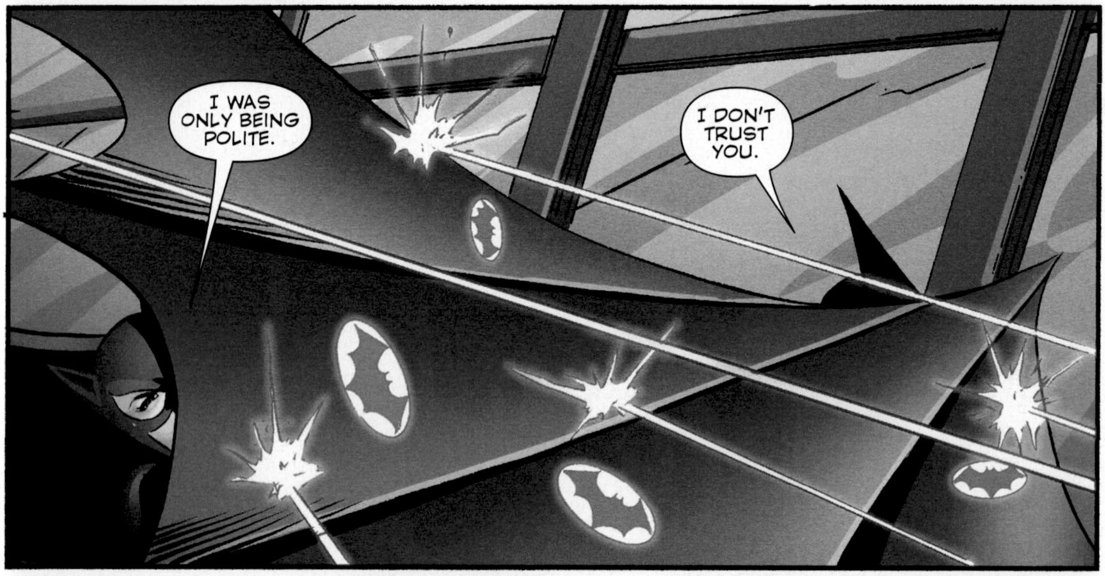
I WAS ONLY BEING POLITE.
I DON'T TRUST YOU.
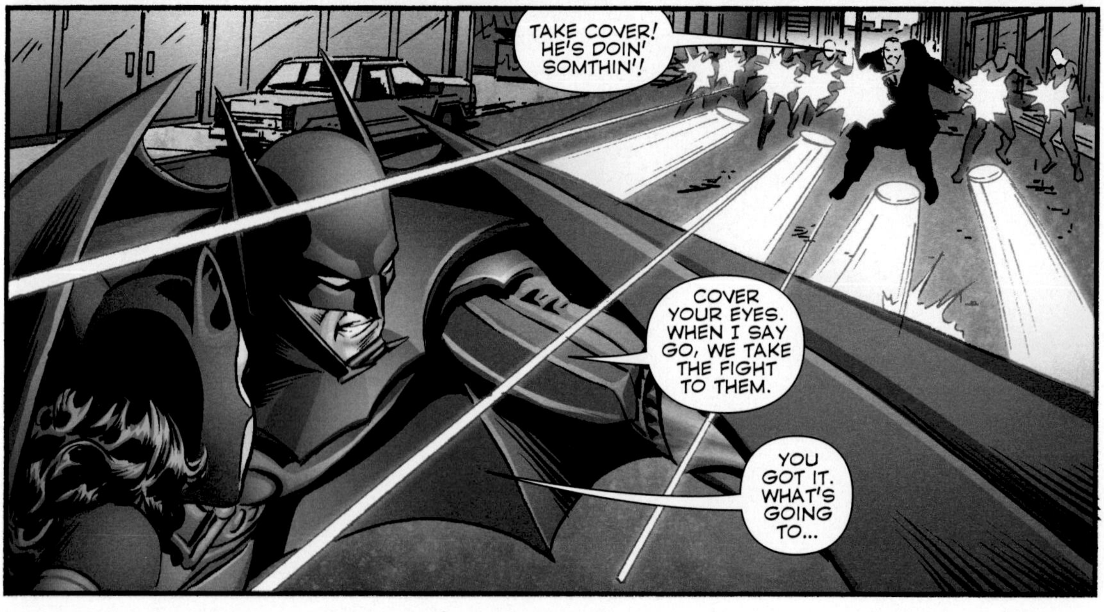
TAKE COVER! HE'S DOIN' SOMTHIN'!
COVER YOUR EYES. WHEN I SAY GO, WE TAKE THE FIGHT TO THEM.
YOU GOT IT. WHAT'S GOING TO...

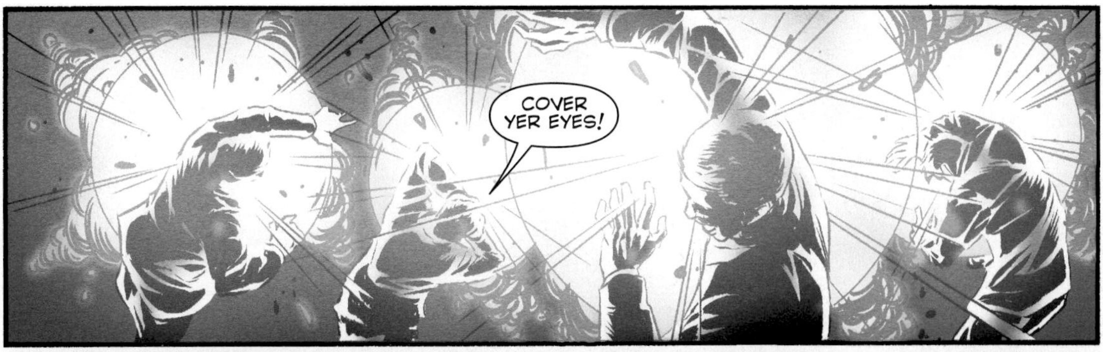
COVER YER EYES!

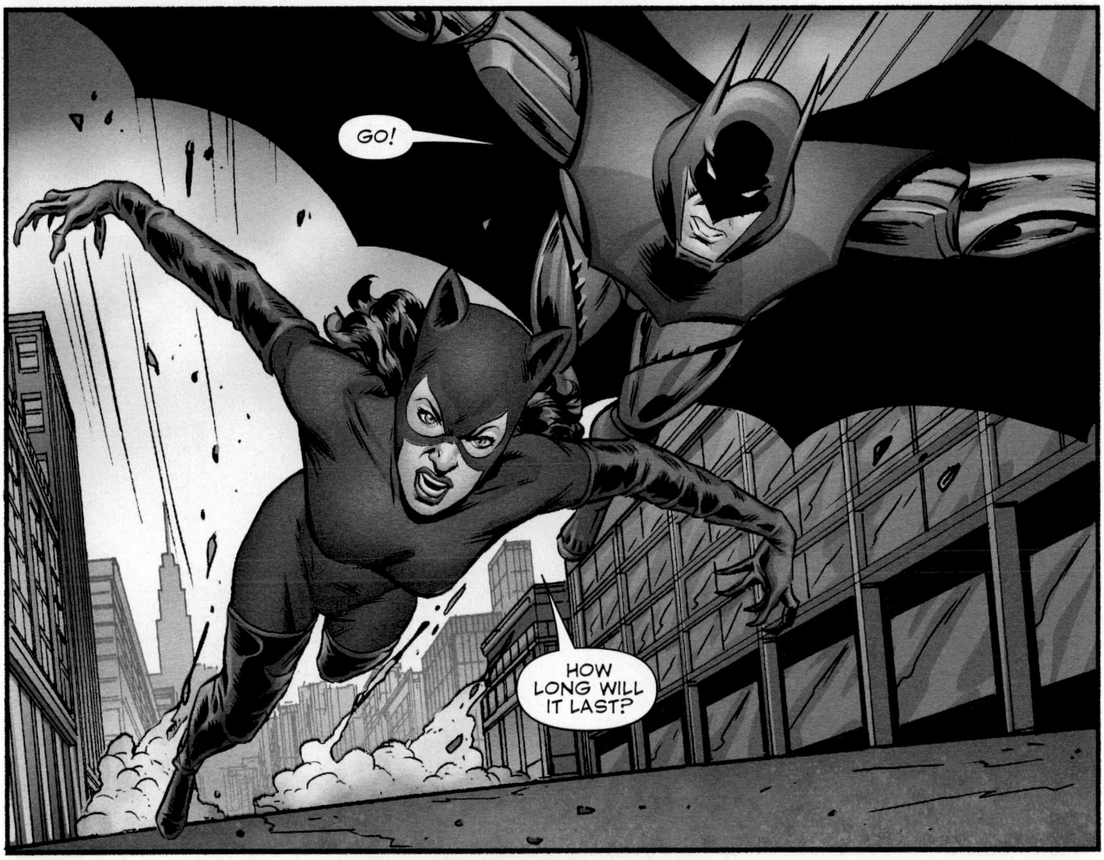
GO!
HOW LONG WILL IT LAST?

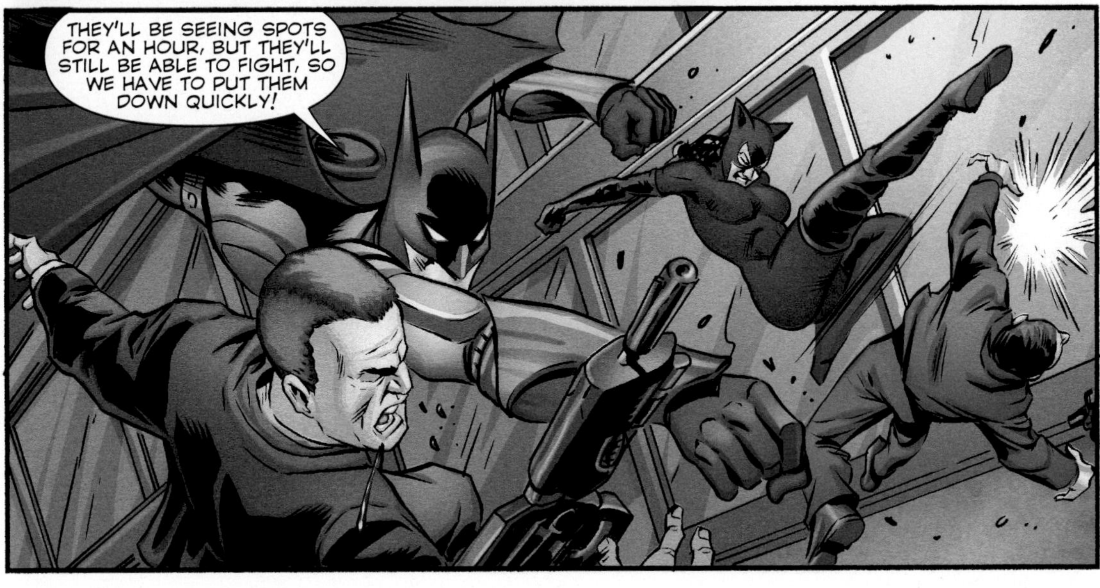
THEY'LL BE SEEING SPOTS FOR AN HOUR, BUT THEY'LL STILL BE ABLE TO FIGHT, SO WE HAVE TO PUT THEM DOWN QUICKLY!

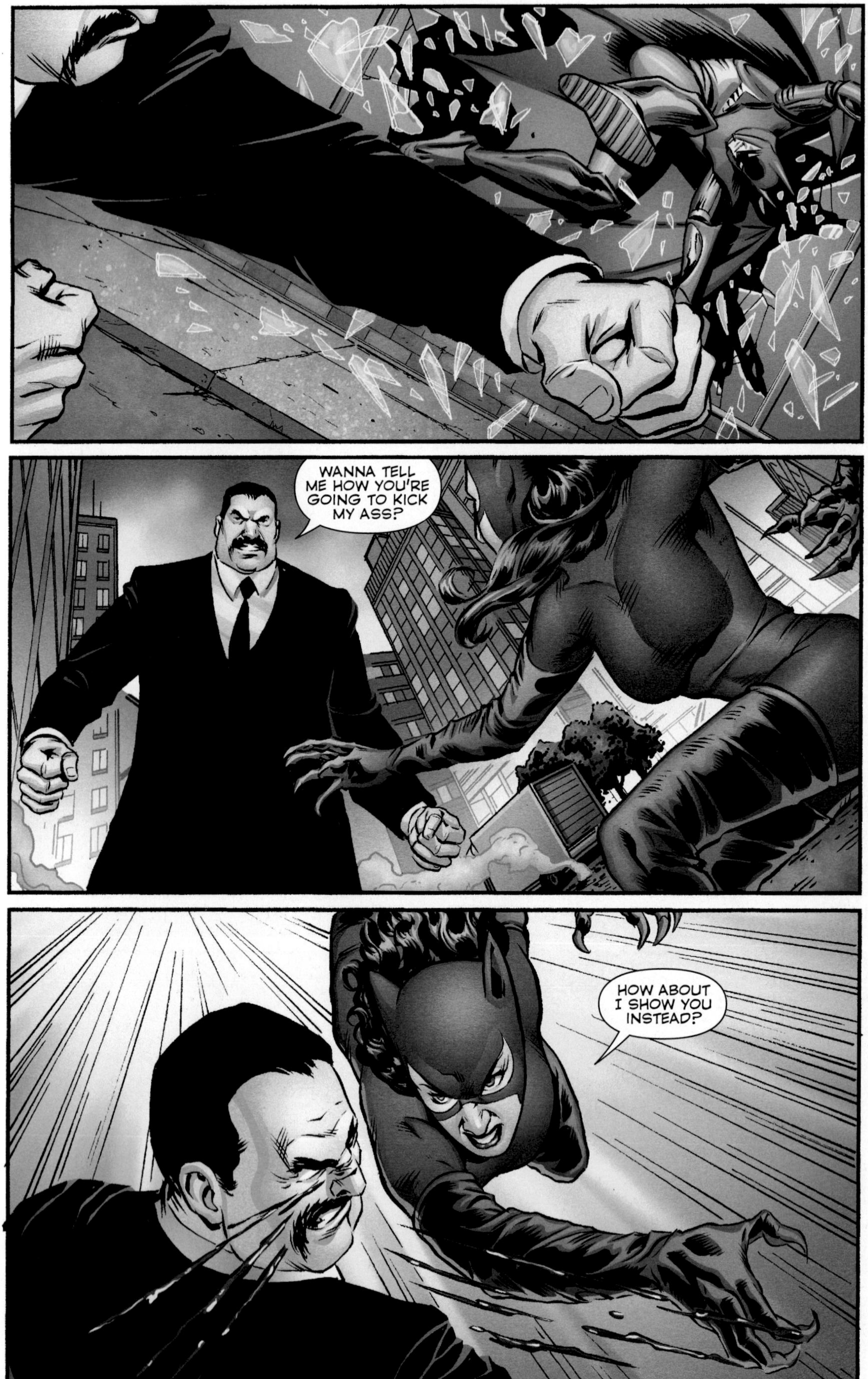
WANNA TELL ME HOW YOU'RE GOING TO KICK MY ASS?
HOW ABOUT I SHOW YOU INSTEAD?

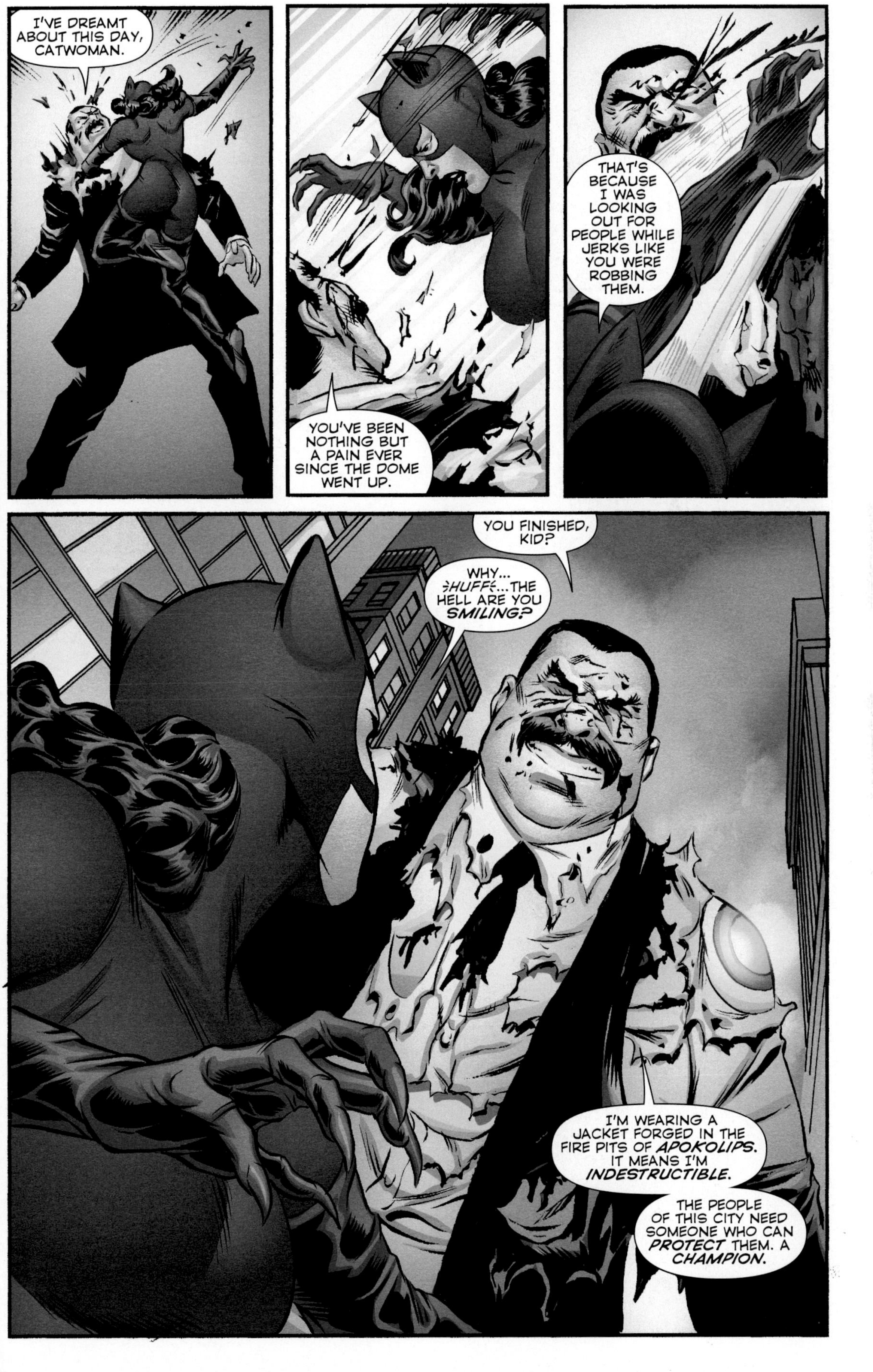
I'VE DREAMT ABOUT THIS DAY, CATWOMAN.
YOU'VE BEEN NOTHING BUT A PAIN EVER SINCE THE DOME WENT UP.
THAT'S BECAUSE I WAS LOOKING OUT FOR PEOPLE WHILE JERKS LIKE YOU WERE ROBBING THEM.
YOU FINISHED, KID?
WHY... HUFF...THE HELL ARE YOU SMILING?
I'M WEARING A JACKET FORGED IN THE FIRE PITS OF APOKOLIPS. IT MEANS I'M INDESTRUCTIBLE.
THE PEOPLE OF THIS CITY NEED SOMEONE WHO CAN PROTECT THEM. A CHAMPION.

THAT AIN'T YOU, SWEETHEART!

THRAK!

GO LIE DOWN WHILE I FINISH OFF THE...

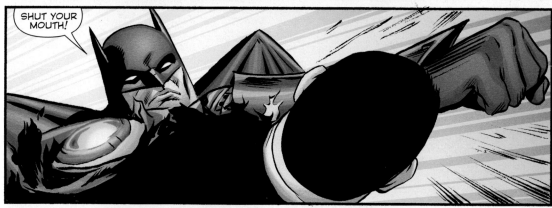

SHUT YOUR MOUTH!

I'M TOO OLD TO BE FIGHTING MORONS LIKE YOU.

YOU'RE RIGHT, BATMAN.

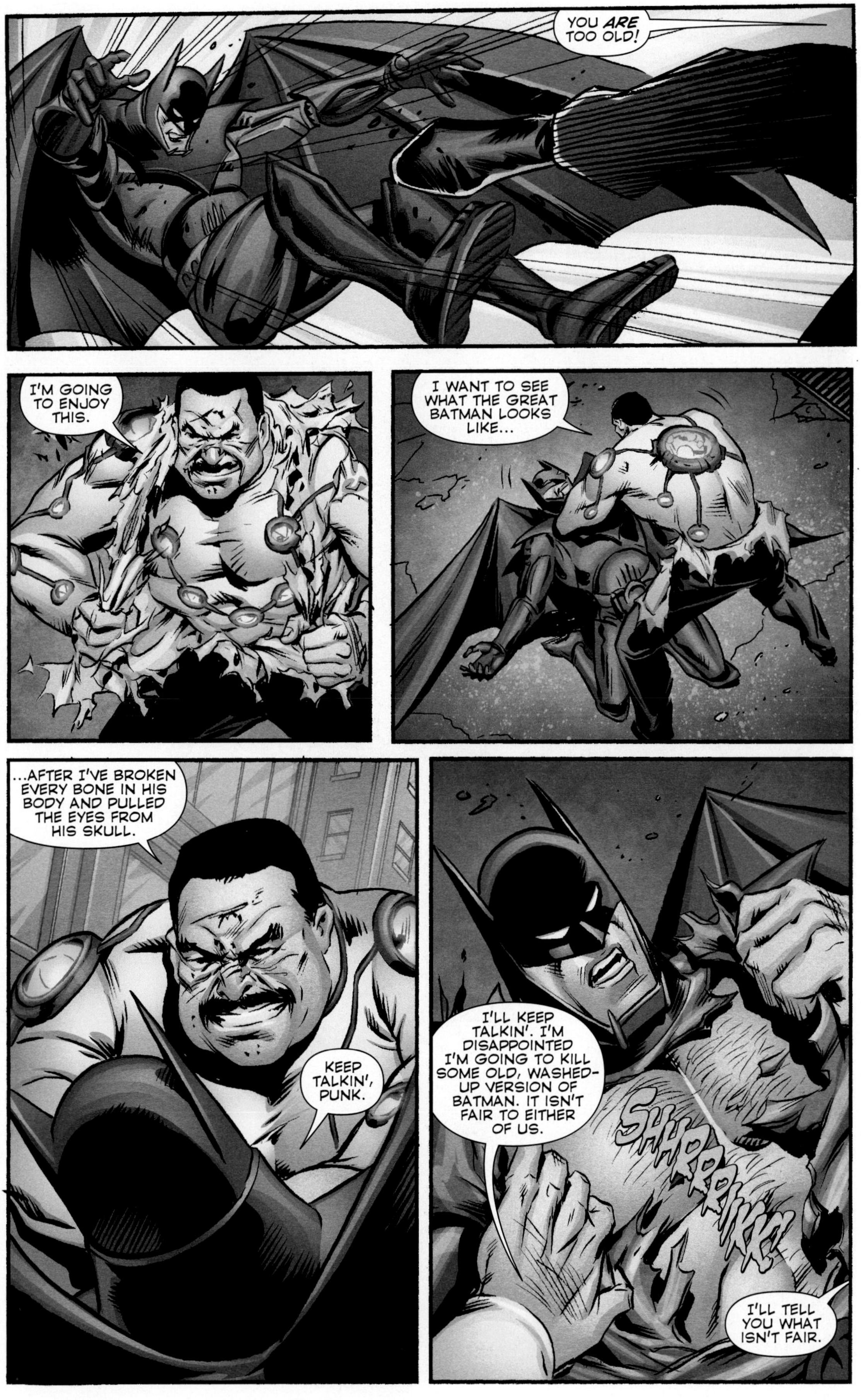
YOU *ARE* TOO OLD!
I'M GOING TO ENJOY THIS.
I WANT TO SEE WHAT THE GREAT BATMAN LOOKS LIKE...
...AFTER I'VE BROKEN EVERY BONE IN HIS BODY AND PULLED THE EYES FROM HIS SKULL.
KEEP TALKIN', PUNK.
I'LL KEEP TALKIN'. I'M DISAPPOINTED I'M GOING TO KILL SOME OLD, WASHED-UP VERSION OF BATMAN. IT ISN'T FAIR TO EITHER OF US.
SHRRIKK!
I'LL TELL YOU WHAT ISN'T FAIR.

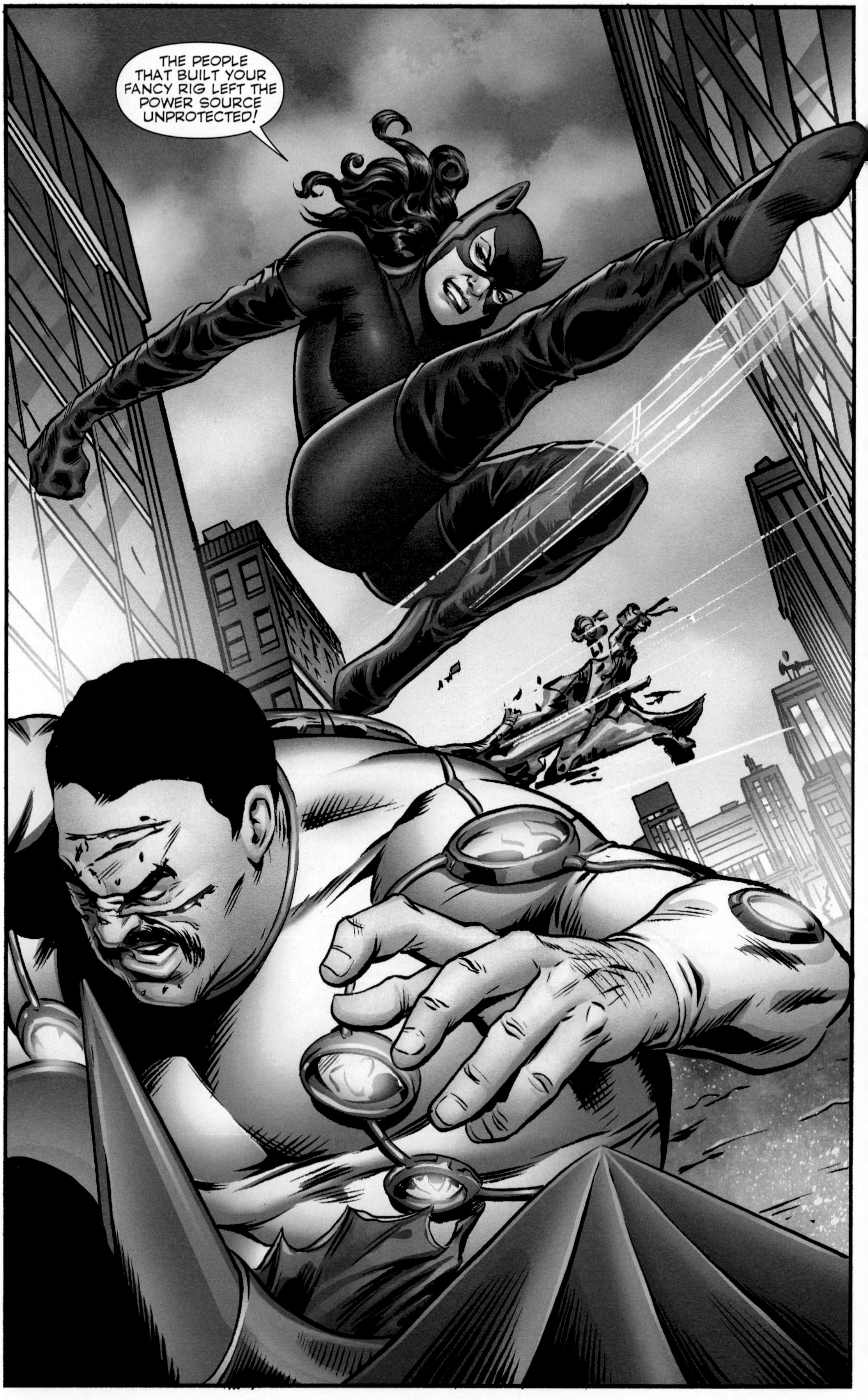
THE PEOPLE THAT BUILT YOUR FANCY RIG LEFT THE POWER SOURCE UNPROTECTED!

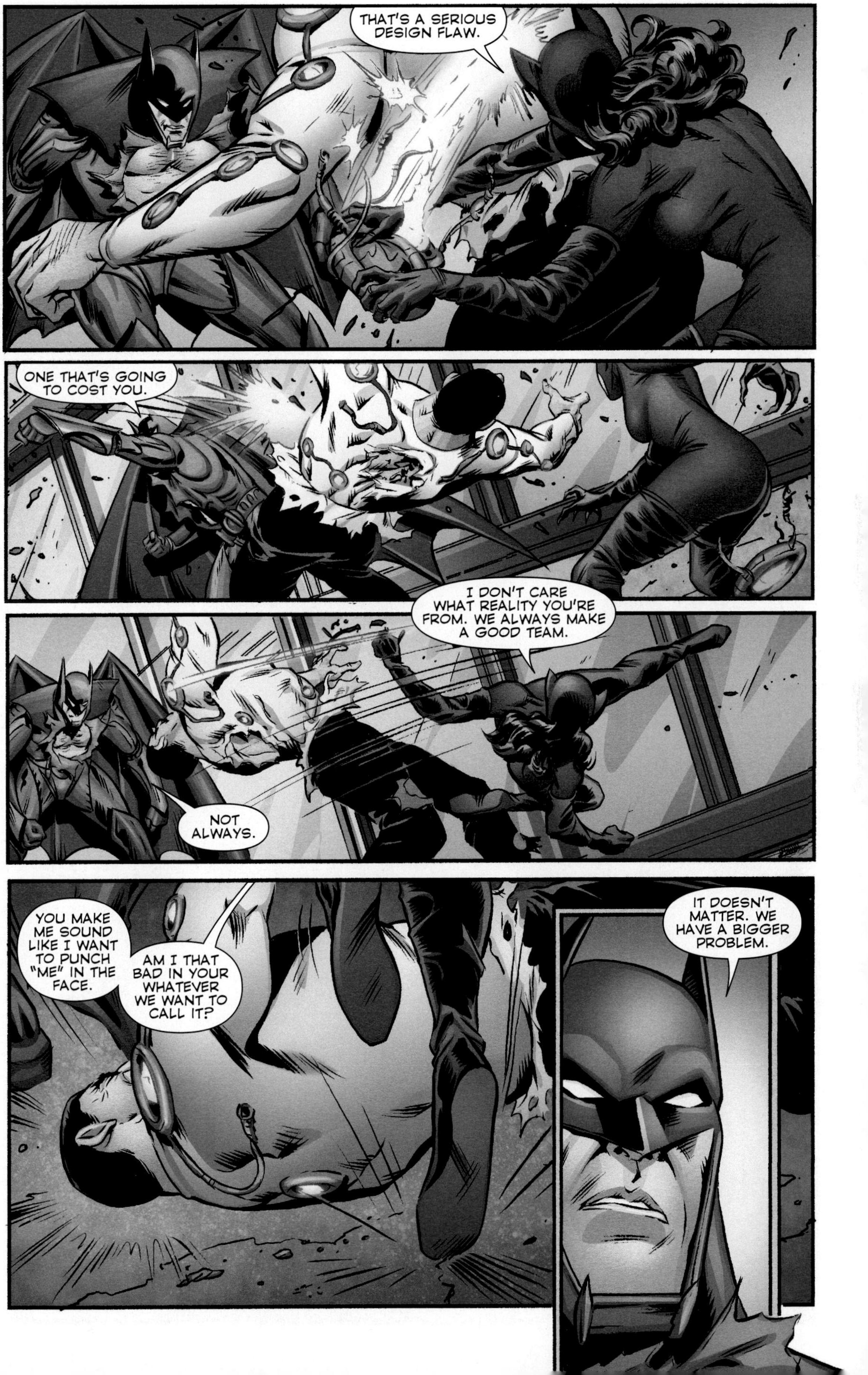
THAT'S A SERIOUS DESIGN FLAW.
ONE THAT'S GOING TO COST YOU.
I DON'T CARE WHAT REALITY YOU'RE FROM. WE ALWAYS MAKE A GOOD TEAM.
NOT ALWAYS.
YOU MAKE ME SOUND LIKE I WANT TO PUNCH "ME" IN THE FACE.
AM I THAT BAD IN YOUR WHATEVER WE WANT TO CALL IT?
IT DOESN'T MATTER. WE HAVE A BIGGER PROBLEM.

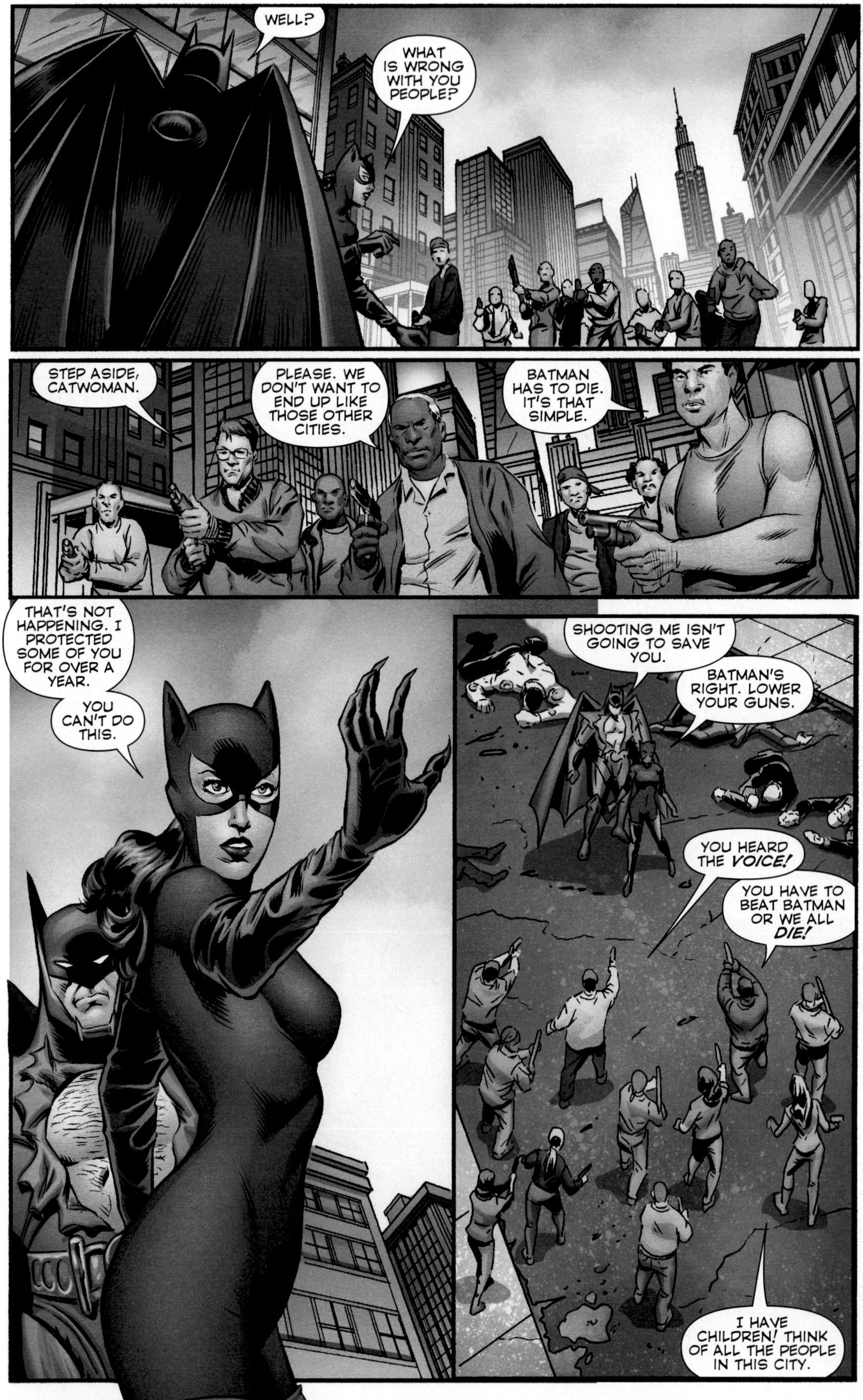
WELL?
WHAT IS WRONG WITH YOU PEOPLE?
STEP ASIDE, CATWOMAN.
PLEASE. WE DON'T WANT TO END UP LIKE THOSE OTHER CITIES.
BATMAN HAS TO DIE. IT'S THAT SIMPLE.
THAT'S NOT HAPPENING. I PROTECTED SOME OF YOU FOR OVER A YEAR.
YOU CAN'T DO THIS.
SHOOTING ME ISN'T GOING TO SAVE YOU.
BATMAN'S RIGHT. LOWER YOUR GUNS.
YOU HEARD THE *VOICE!*
YOU HAVE TO BEAT BATMAN OR WE ALL *DIE!*
I HAVE CHILDREN! THINK OF ALL THE PEOPLE IN THIS CITY.

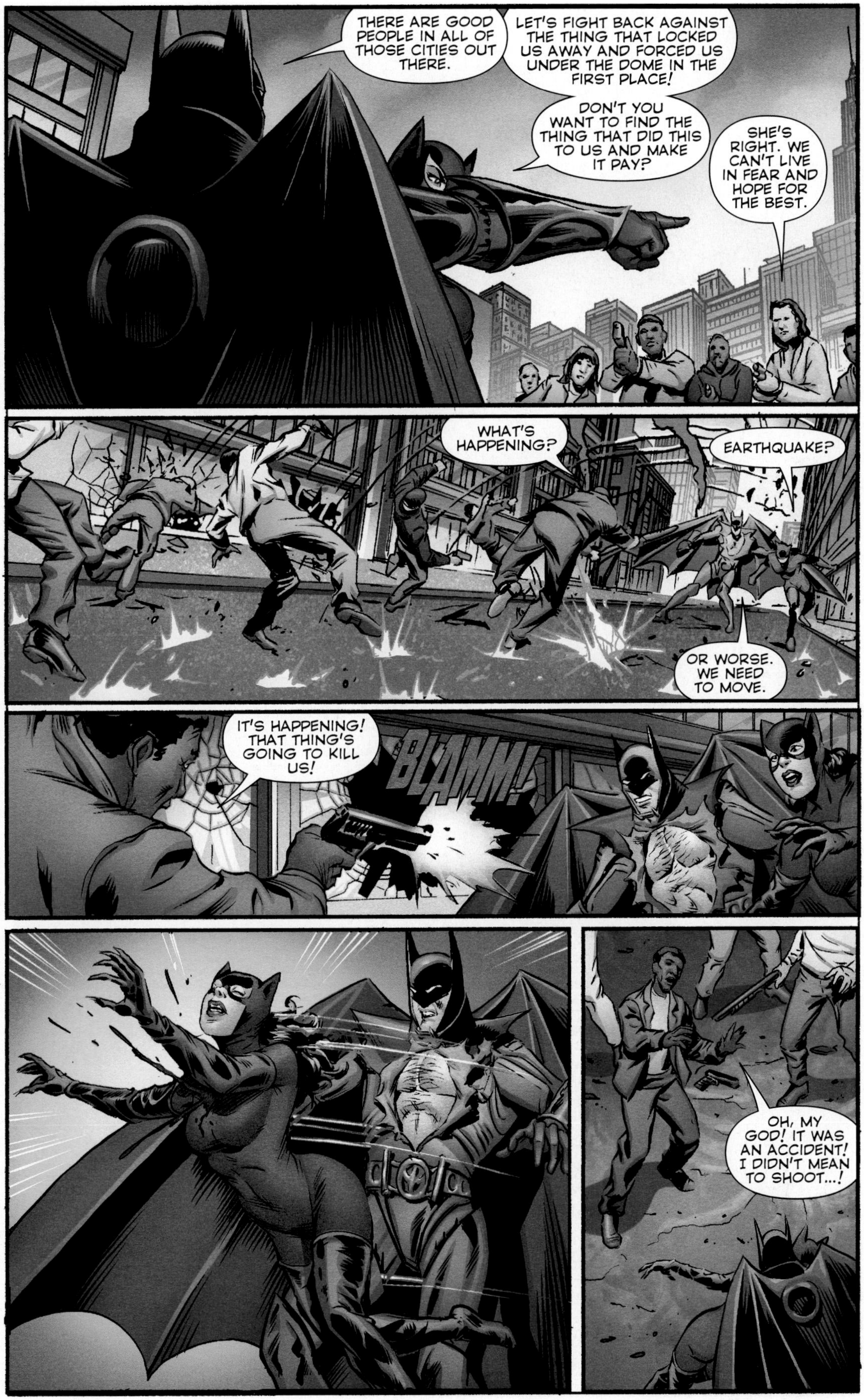
THERE ARE GOOD PEOPLE IN ALL OF THOSE CITIES OUT THERE.
LET'S FIGHT BACK AGAINST THE THING THAT LOCKED US AWAY AND FORCED US UNDER THE DOME IN THE FIRST PLACE!
DON'T YOU WANT TO FIND THE THING THAT DID THIS TO US AND MAKE IT PAY?
SHE'S RIGHT. WE CAN'T LIVE IN FEAR AND HOPE FOR THE BEST.
WHAT'S HAPPENING?
EARTHQUAKE?
OR WORSE. WE NEED TO MOVE.
IT'S HAPPENING! THAT THING'S GOING TO KILL US!
BLAMM!
OH, MY GOD! IT WAS AN ACCIDENT! I DIDN'T MEAN TO SHOOT...!

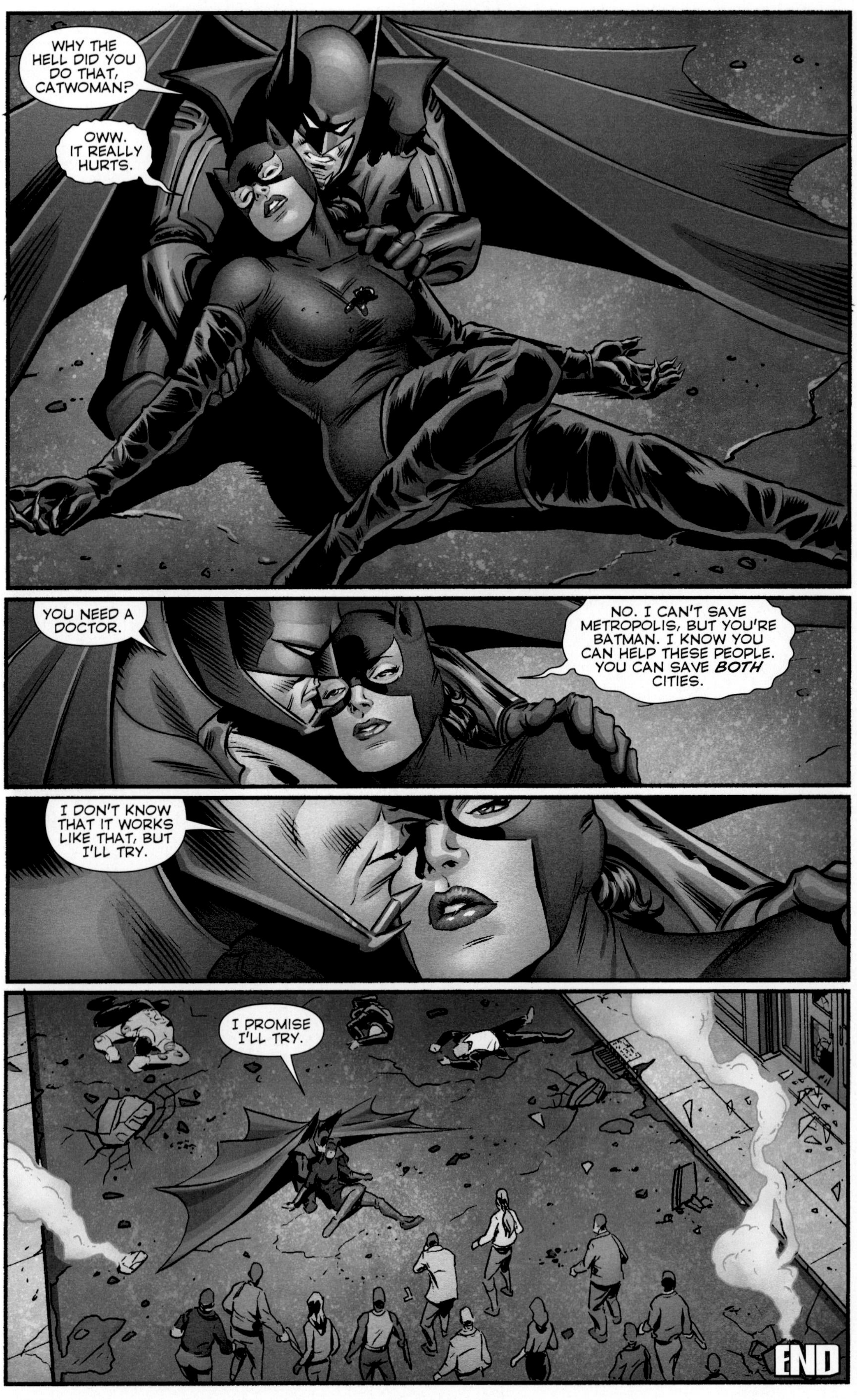
WHY THE HELL DID YOU DO THAT, CATWOMAN?
OWW. IT REALLY HURTS.
YOU NEED A DOCTOR.
NO. I CAN'T SAVE METROPOLIS, BUT YOU'RE BATMAN. I KNOW YOU CAN HELP THESE PEOPLE. YOU CAN SAVE *BOTH* CITIES.
I DON'T KNOW THAT IT WORKS LIKE THAT, BUT I'LL TRY.
I PROMISE I'LL TRY.
END

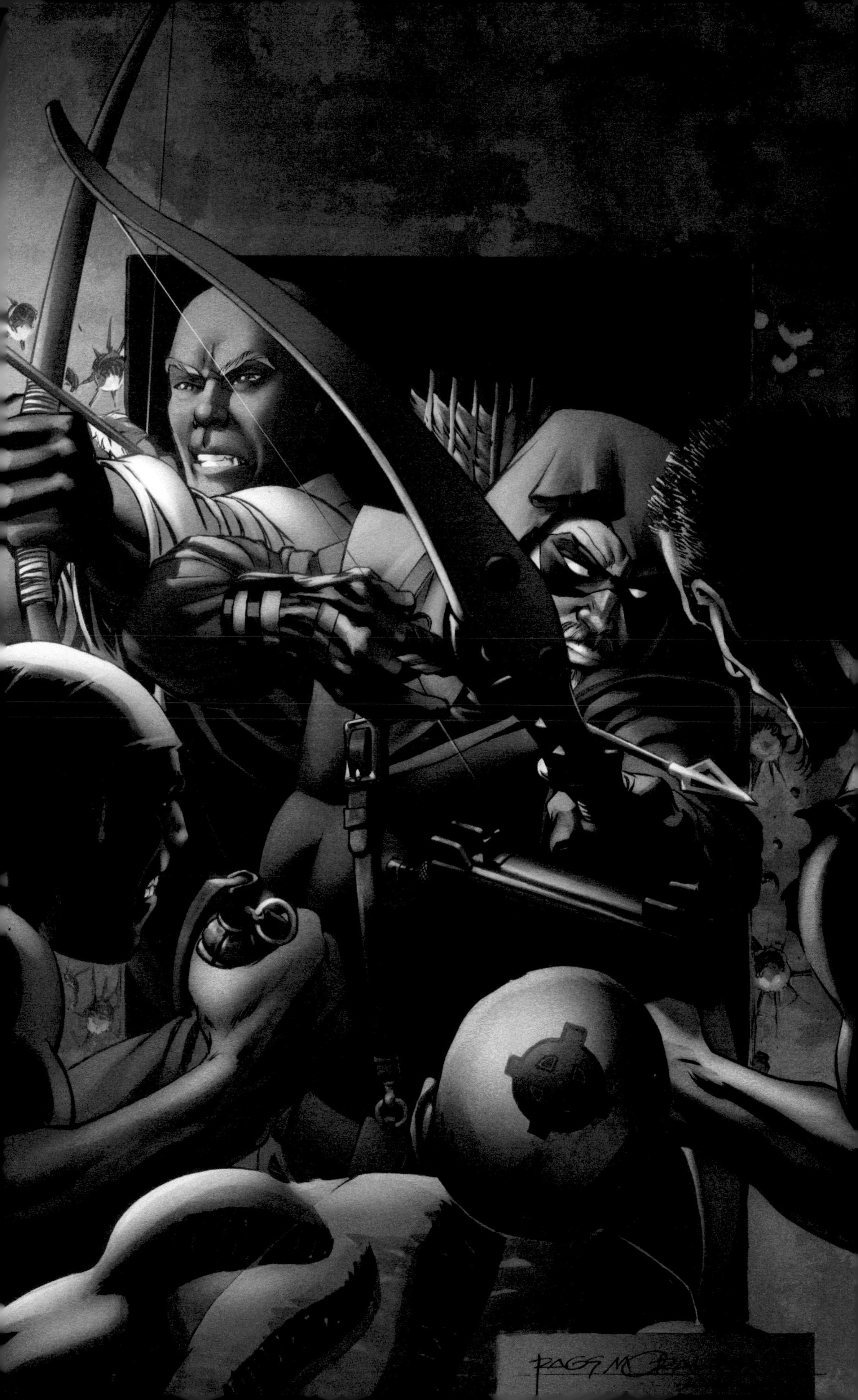

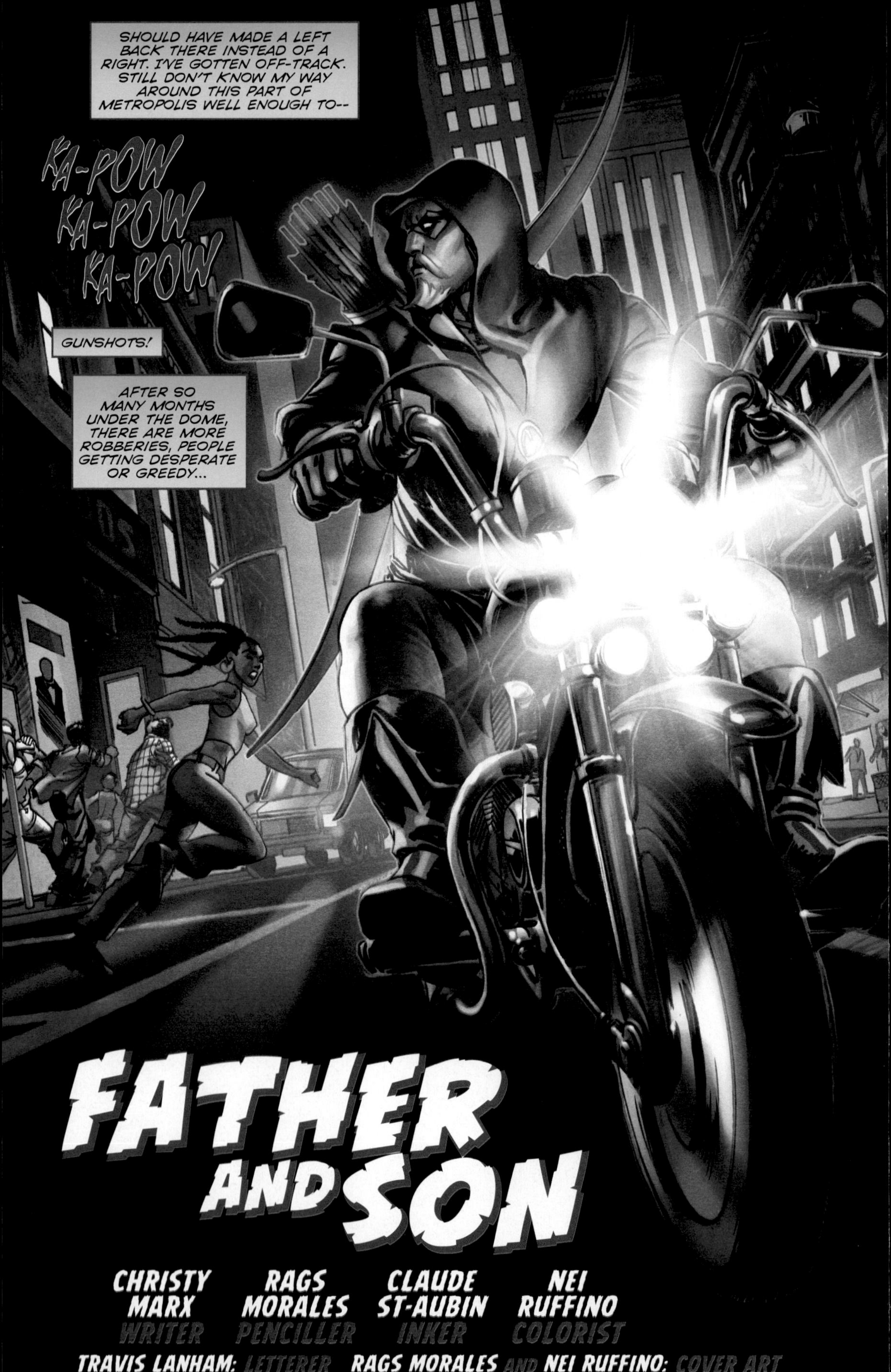
SHOULD HAVE MADE A LEFT BACK THERE INSTEAD OF A RIGHT. I'VE GOTTEN OFF-TRACK. STILL DON'T KNOW MY WAY AROUND THIS PART OF METROPOLIS WELL ENOUGH TO--
KA-POW
KA-POW
KA-POW
GUNSHOTS!
AFTER SO MANY MONTHS UNDER THE DOME, THERE ARE MORE ROBBERIES, PEOPLE GETTING DESPERATE OR GREEDY...
FATHER AND SON
CHRISTY MARX WRITER
RAGS MORALES PENCILLER
CLAUDE ST-AUBIN INKER
NEI RUFFINO COLORIST
TRAVIS LANHAM: LETTERER RAGS MORALES AND NEI RUFFINO: COVER ART

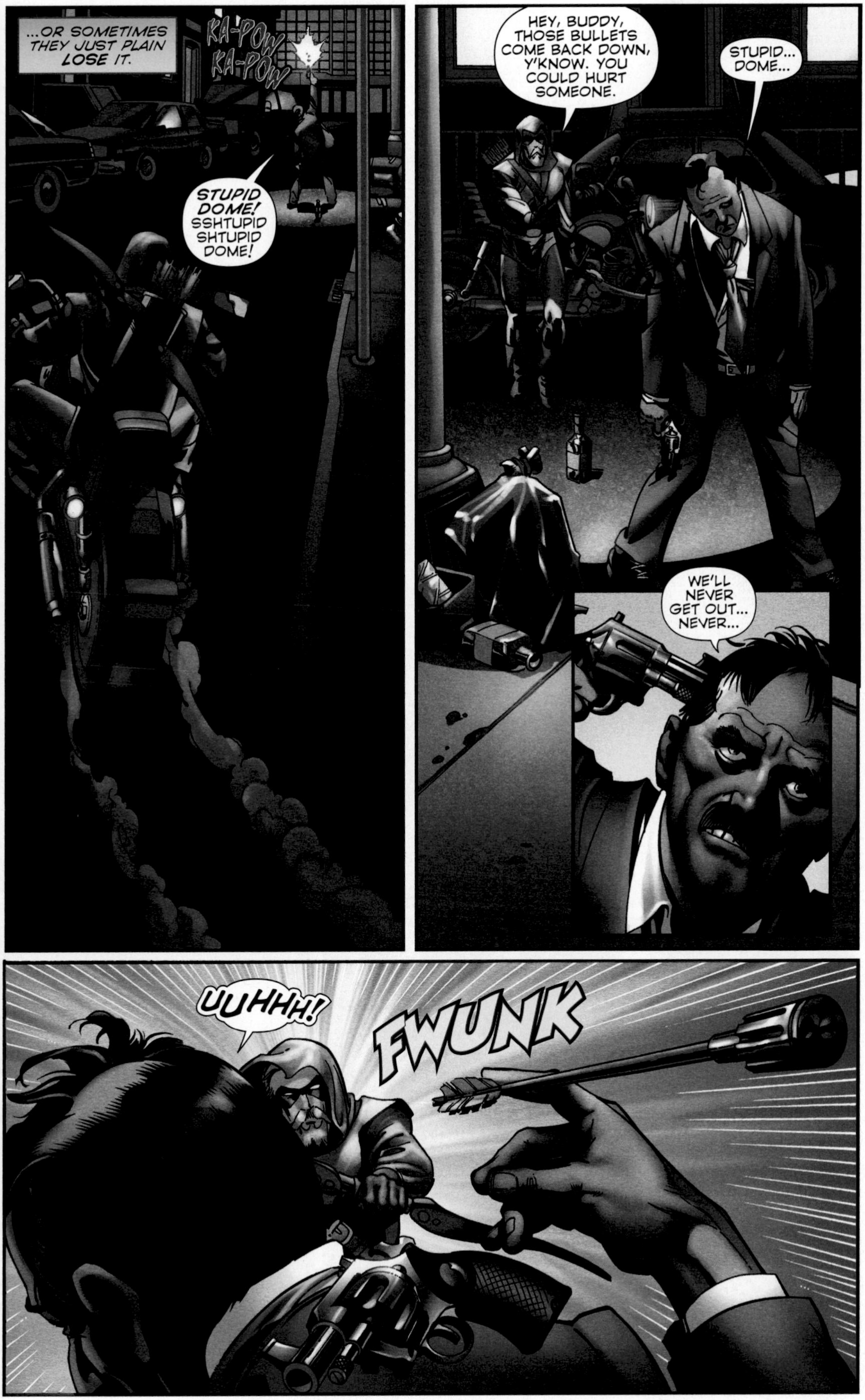
...OR SOMETIMES THEY JUST PLAIN LOSE IT.
KA-POW KA-POW
STUPID DOME! SSHTUPID SHTUPID DOME!
HEY, BUDDY, THOSE BULLETS COME BACK DOWN, Y'KNOW. YOU COULD HURT SOMEONE.
STUPID... DOME...
WE'LL NEVER GET OUT... NEVER...
UUHHH!
FWUNK

OKAY, CALM DOWN. TAKING POTSHOTS AT THE DOME ISN'T GOING TO CHANGE ANYTHING.

HE'S DRUNK AS A SKUNK. JUST ANOTHER GUY WHO'S SNAPPED. SEEMS LIKE I'M SEEING MORE OF THEM EACH WEEK.

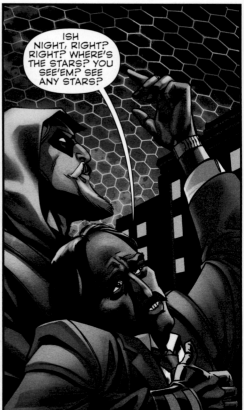

ISH NIGHT, RIGHT? RIGHT? WHERE'S THE STARS? YOU SEE 'EM? SEE ANY STARS?

YOU LIVE AROUND HERE? LET ME GET YOU HOME.

CAME HERE FOR A CONFERENCE. MY FAMILY'S IN BANGALORE. I'LL NEVER SEE 'EM AGAIN. I'LL NEVER GET OUT OF HERE.

I WAS AN ASHATRO...ASTROMO... ASTRONOMER. WHAT'M'I SUPPOS'D TO DO NOW, WHEN YOU CAN'T EVEN SEE THE STARS? WHASSA POINT OF LIVING?

THERE'S NO STARS...

I MAY AS WELL LET HIM SLEEP IT OFF HERE. THIS IS THE PART WHERE I SHOULD SAY SOMETHING ENCOURAGING.

"DON'T WORRY, THINGS'LL LOOK BETTER IN THE MORNING."

BUT WE DON'T HAVE MORNINGS ANYMORE.

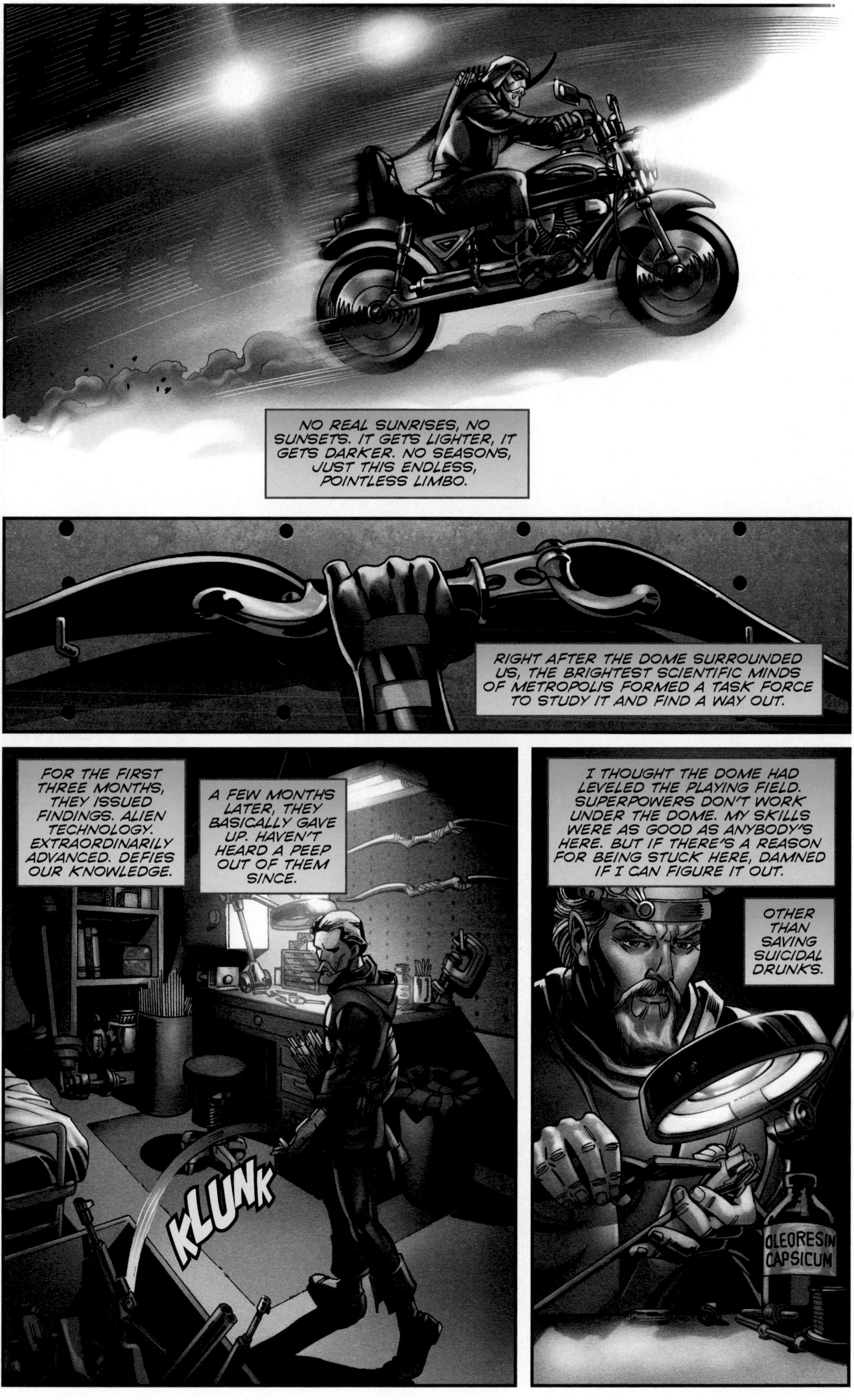
NO REAL SUNRISES, NO SUNSETS. IT GETS LIGHTER, IT GETS DARKER. NO SEASONS, JUST THIS ENDLESS, POINTLESS LIMBO.
RIGHT AFTER THE DOME SURROUNDED US, THE BRIGHTEST SCIENTIFIC MINDS OF METROPOLIS FORMED A TASK FORCE TO STUDY IT AND FIND A WAY OUT.
FOR THE FIRST THREE MONTHS, THEY ISSUED FINDINGS. ALIEN TECHNOLOGY. EXTRAORDINARILY ADVANCED. DEFIES OUR KNOWLEDGE.
A FEW MONTHS LATER, THEY BASICALLY GAVE UP. HAVEN'T HEARD A PEEP OUT OF THEM SINCE.
KLUNK
I THOUGHT THE DOME HAD LEVELED THE PLAYING FIELD. SUPERPOWERS DON'T WORK UNDER THE DOME. MY SKILLS WERE AS GOOD AS ANYBODY'S HERE. BUT IF THERE'S A REASON FOR BEING STUCK HERE, DAMNED IF I CAN FIGURE IT OUT.
OTHER THAN SAVING SUICIDAL DRUNKS.
OLEORESIN CAPSICUM

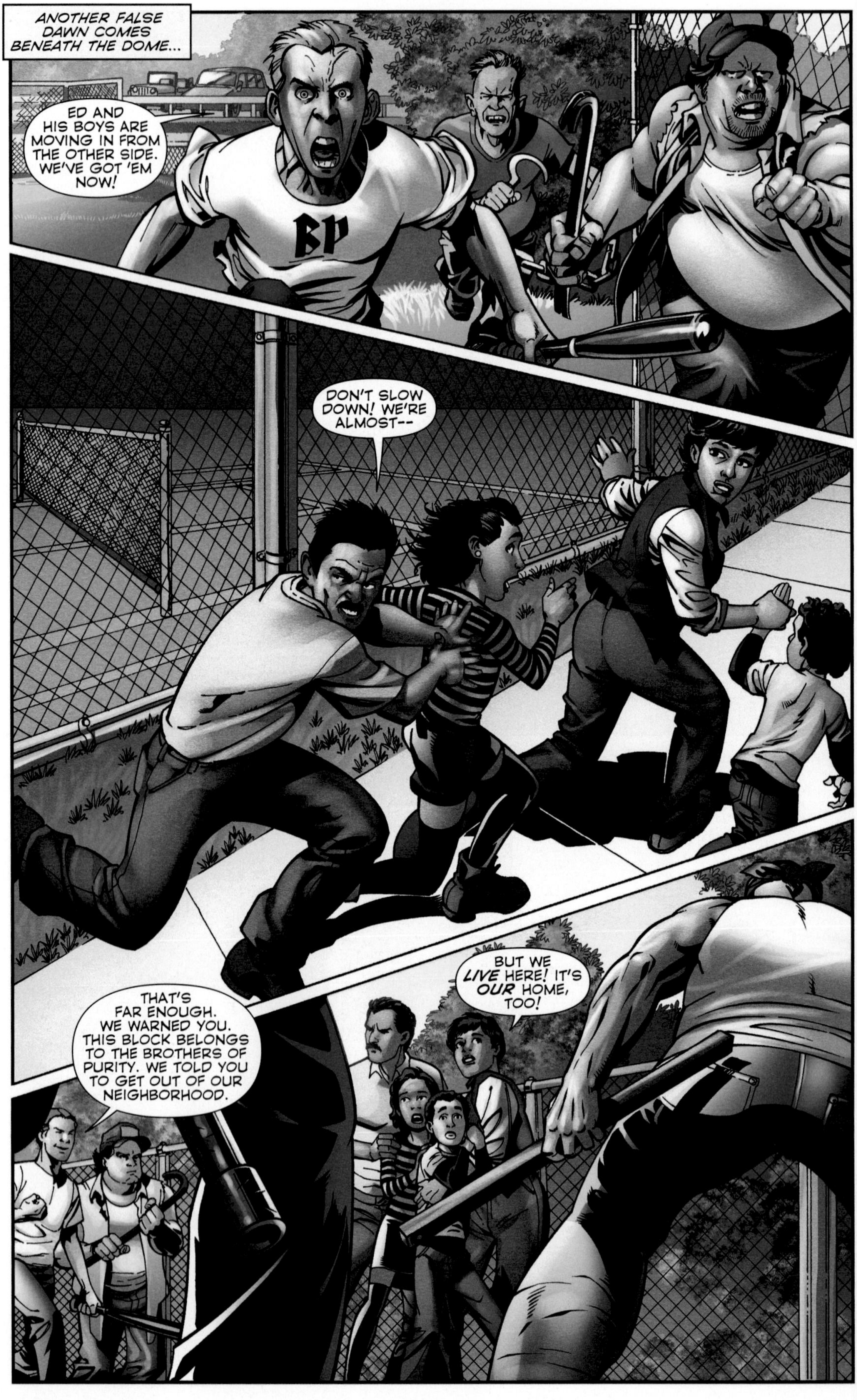
ANOTHER FALSE DAWN COMES BENEATH THE DOME...
ED AND HIS BOYS ARE MOVING IN FROM THE OTHER SIDE. WE'VE GOT 'EM NOW!
DON'T SLOW DOWN! WE'RE ALMOST--
BUT WE *LIVE* HERE! IT'S *OUR* HOME, TOO!
THAT'S FAR ENOUGH. WE WARNED YOU. THIS BLOCK BELONGS TO THE BROTHERS OF PURITY. WE TOLD YOU TO GET OUT OF OUR NEIGHBORHOOD.

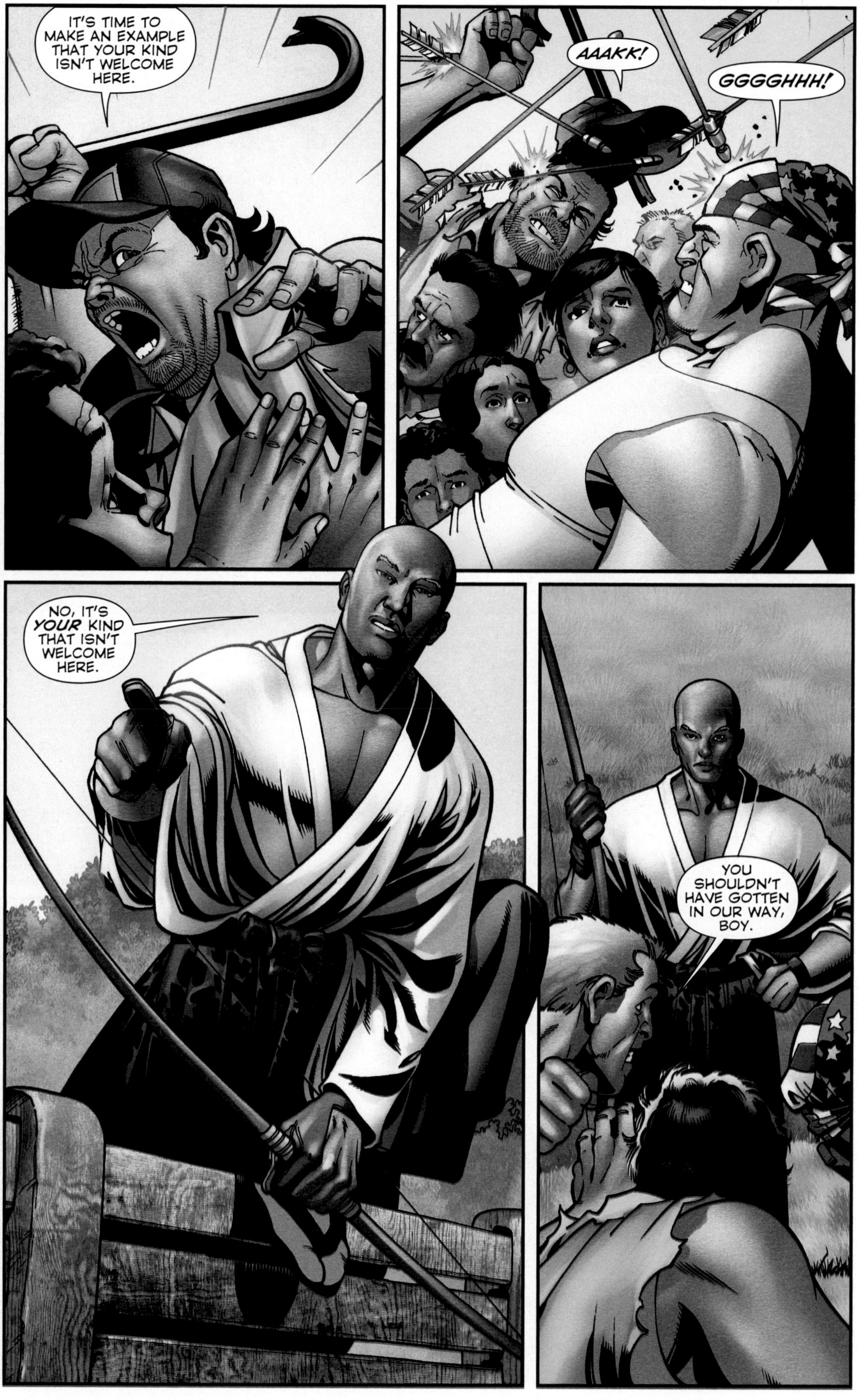
IT'S TIME TO MAKE AN EXAMPLE THAT YOUR KIND ISN'T WELCOME HERE.
AAAKK!
GGGGHHH!
NO, IT'S YOUR KIND THAT ISN'T WELCOME HERE.
YOU SHOULDN'T HAVE GOTTEN IN OUR WAY, BOY.

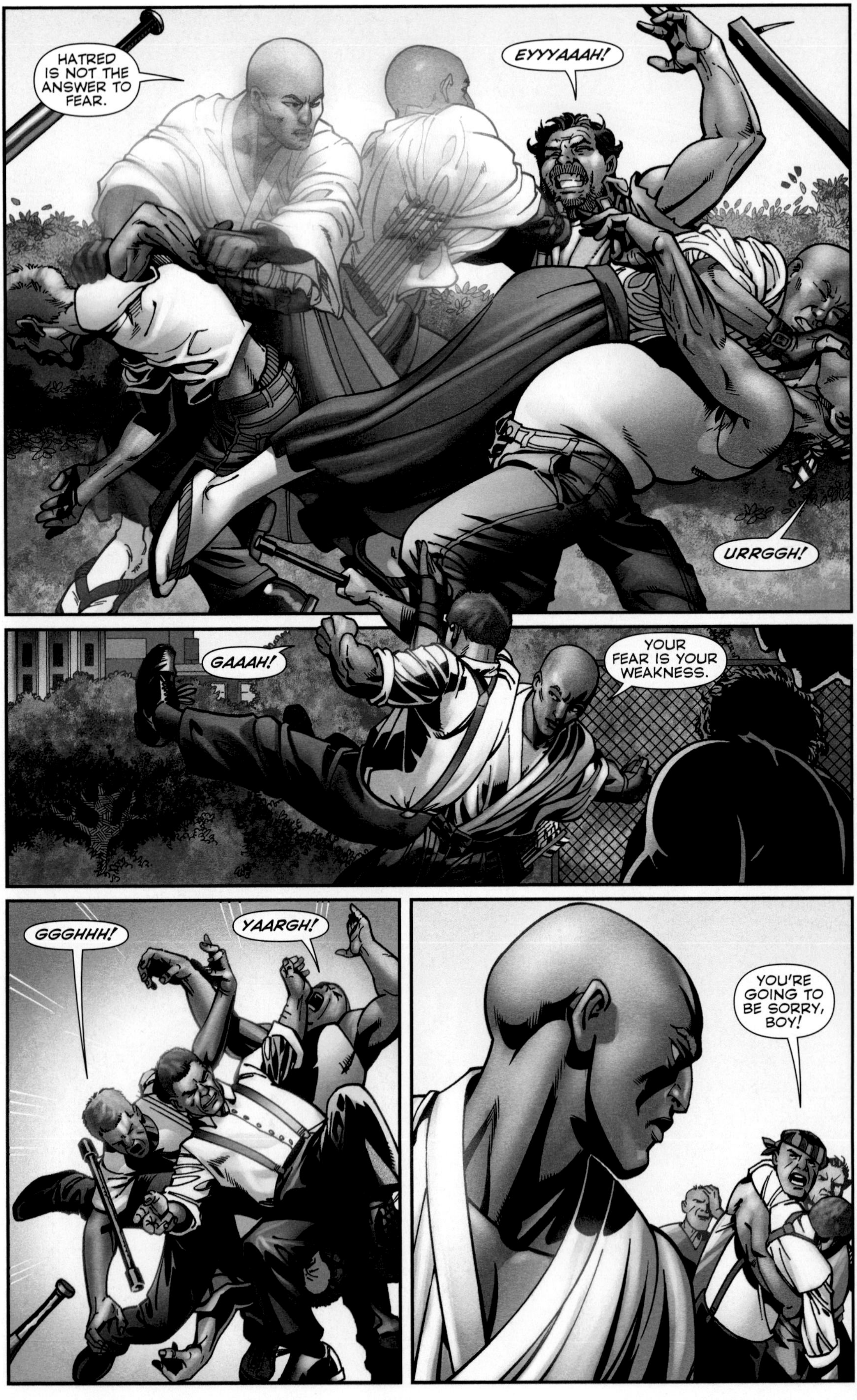
HATRED IS NOT THE ANSWER TO FEAR.
EYYYAAAH!
URRGGH!
GAAAH!
YOUR FEAR IS YOUR WEAKNESS.
GGGHHH!
YAARGH!
YOU'RE GOING TO BE SORRY, BOY!

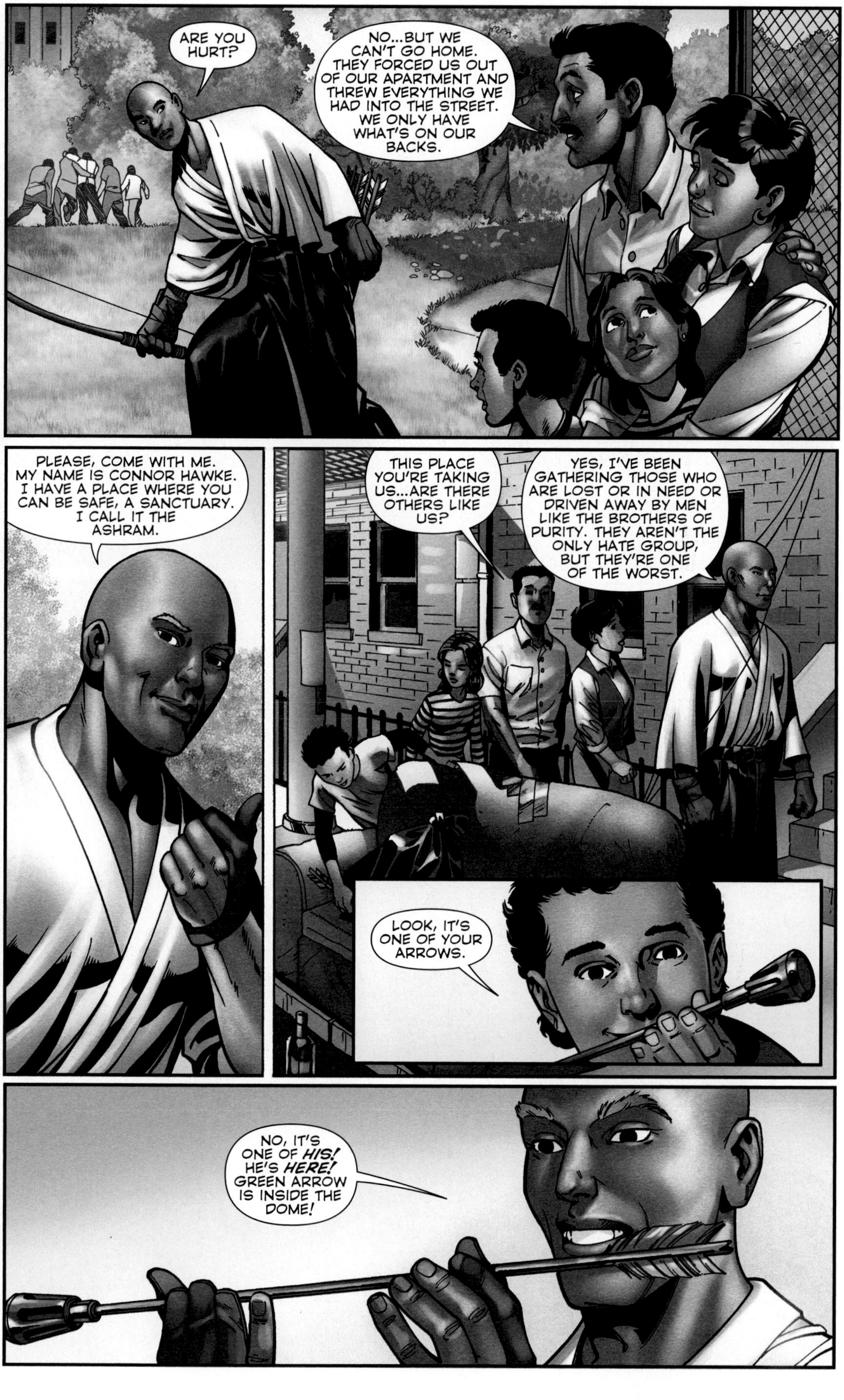
ARE YOU HURT?
NO...BUT WE CAN'T GO HOME. THEY FORCED US OUT OF OUR APARTMENT AND THREW EVERYTHING WE HAD INTO THE STREET. WE ONLY HAVE WHAT'S ON OUR BACKS.
PLEASE, COME WITH ME. MY NAME IS CONNOR HAWKE. I HAVE A PLACE WHERE YOU CAN BE SAFE, A SANCTUARY. I CALL IT THE ASHRAM.
THIS PLACE YOU'RE TAKING US...ARE THERE OTHERS LIKE US?
YES, I'VE BEEN GATHERING THOSE WHO ARE LOST OR IN NEED OR DRIVEN AWAY BY MEN LIKE THE BROTHERS OF PURITY. THEY AREN'T THE ONLY HATE GROUP, BUT THEY'RE ONE OF THE WORST.
LOOK, IT'S ONE OF YOUR ARROWS.
NO, IT'S ONE OF *HIS!* HE'S ***HERE!*** GREEN ARROW IS INSIDE THE DOME!

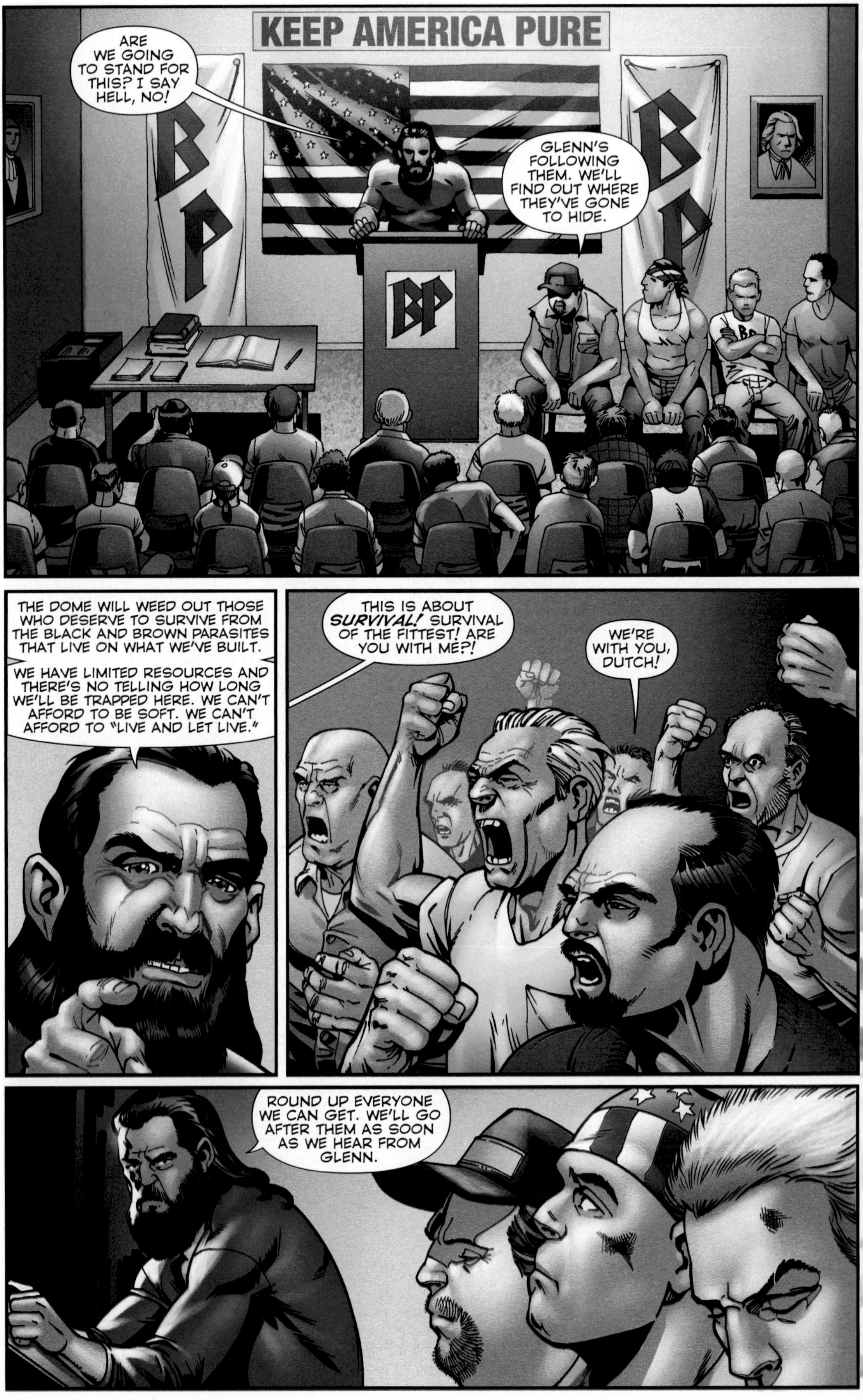
KEEP AMERICA PURE
ARE WE GOING TO STAND FOR THIS? I SAY HELL, NO!
GLENN'S FOLLOWING THEM. WE'LL FIND OUT WHERE THEY'VE GONE TO HIDE.
BP
THE DOME WILL WEED OUT THOSE WHO DESERVE TO SURVIVE FROM THE BLACK AND BROWN PARASITES THAT LIVE ON WHAT WE'VE BUILT.
WE HAVE LIMITED RESOURCES AND THERE'S NO TELLING HOW LONG WE'LL BE TRAPPED HERE. WE CAN'T AFFORD TO BE SOFT. WE CAN'T AFFORD TO "LIVE AND LET LIVE."
THIS IS ABOUT *SURVIVAL!* SURVIVAL OF THE FITTEST! ARE YOU WITH ME?!
WE'RE WITH YOU, DUTCH!
ROUND UP EVERYONE WE CAN GET. WE'LL GO AFTER THEM AS SOON AS WE HEAR FROM GLENN.

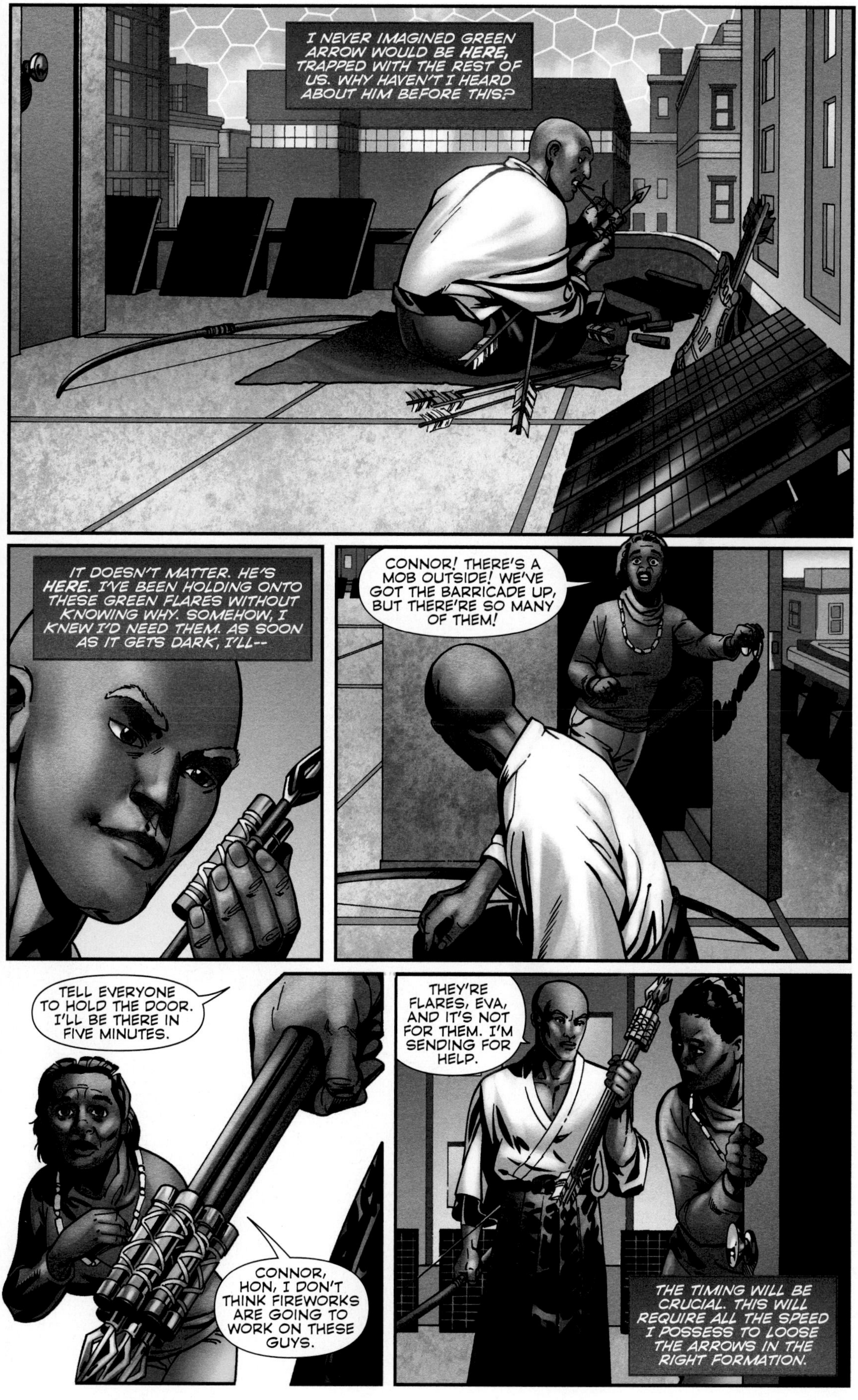

I NEVER IMAGINED GREEN ARROW WOULD BE HERE, TRAPPED WITH THE REST OF US. WHY HAVEN'T I HEARD ABOUT HIM BEFORE THIS?
IT DOESN'T MATTER. HE'S HERE. I'VE BEEN HOLDING ONTO THESE GREEN FLARES WITHOUT KNOWING WHY. SOMEHOW, I KNEW I'D NEED THEM. AS SOON AS IT GETS DARK, I'LL--
CONNOR! THERE'S A MOB OUTSIDE! WE'VE GOT THE BARRICADE UP, BUT THERE'RE SO MANY OF THEM!
TELL EVERYONE TO HOLD THE DOOR. I'LL BE THERE IN FIVE MINUTES.
CONNOR, HON, I DON'T THINK FIREWORKS ARE GOING TO WORK ON THESE GUYS.
THEY'RE FLARES, EVA, AND IT'S NOT FOR THEM. I'M SENDING FOR HELP.
THE TIMING WILL BE CRUCIAL. THIS WILL REQUIRE ALL THE SPEED I POSSESS TO LOOSE THE ARROWS IN THE RIGHT FORMATION.

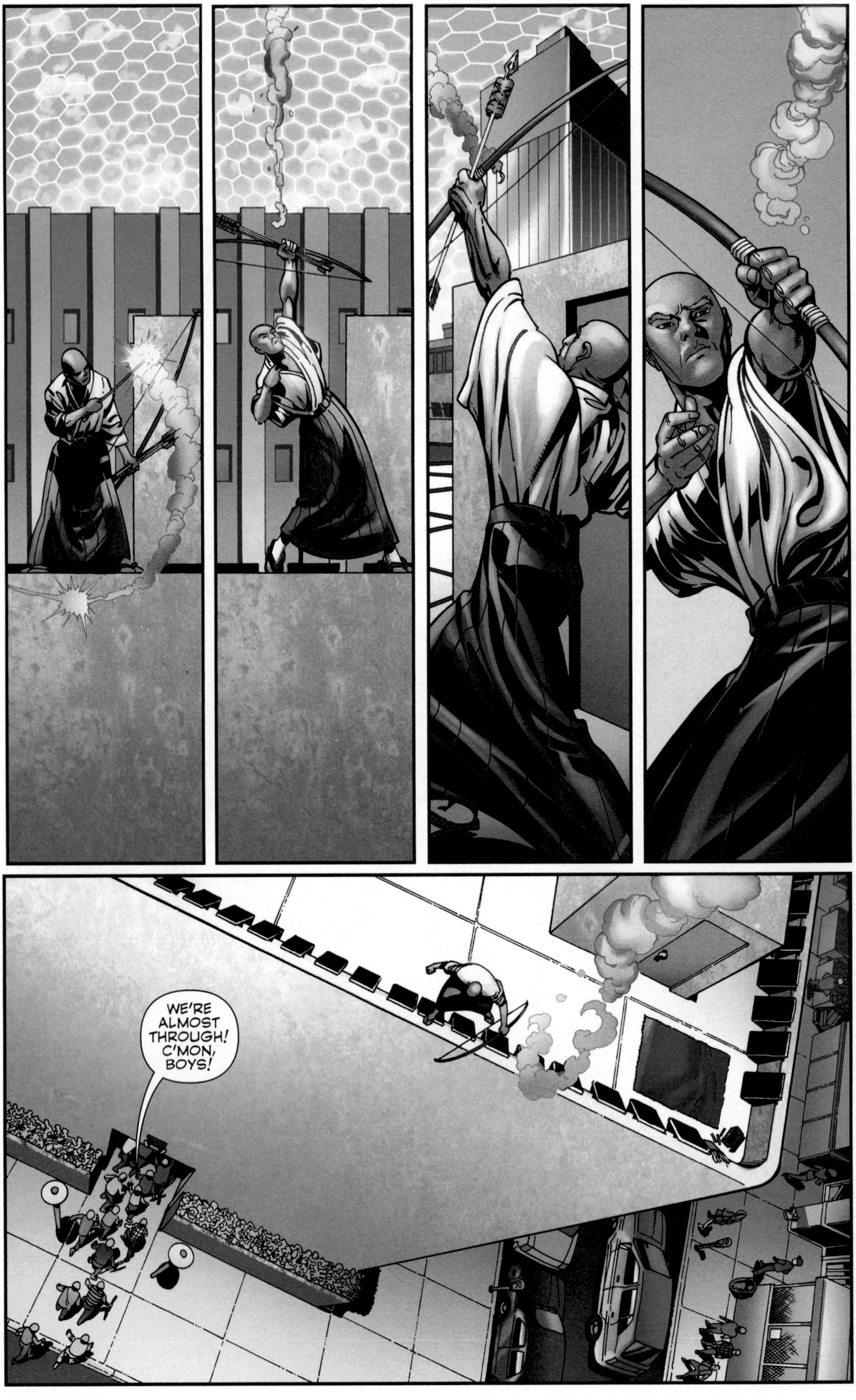
WE'RE ALMOST THROUGH! C'MON, BOYS!

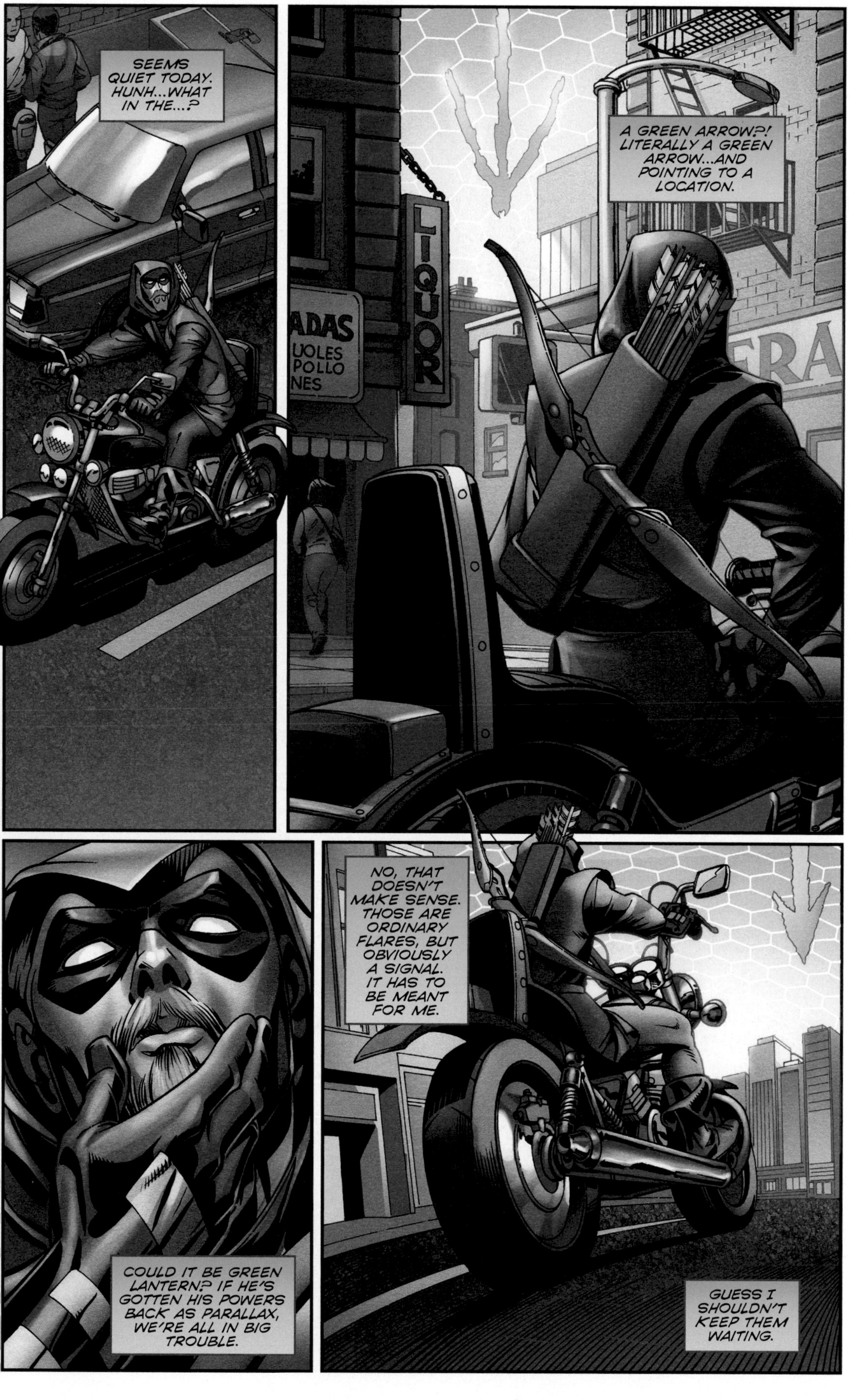
SEEMS QUIET TODAY. HUNH...WHAT IN THE...?
LIQUOR
A GREEN ARROW?! LITERALLY A GREEN ARROW...AND POINTING TO A LOCATION.
COULD IT BE GREEN LANTERN? IF HE'S GOTTEN HIS POWERS BACK AS PARALLAX, WE'RE ALL IN BIG TROUBLE.
NO, THAT DOESN'T MAKE SENSE. THOSE ARE ORDINARY FLARES, BUT OBVIOUSLY A SIGNAL. IT HAS TO BE MEANT FOR ME.
GUESS I SHOULDN'T KEEP THEM WAITING.

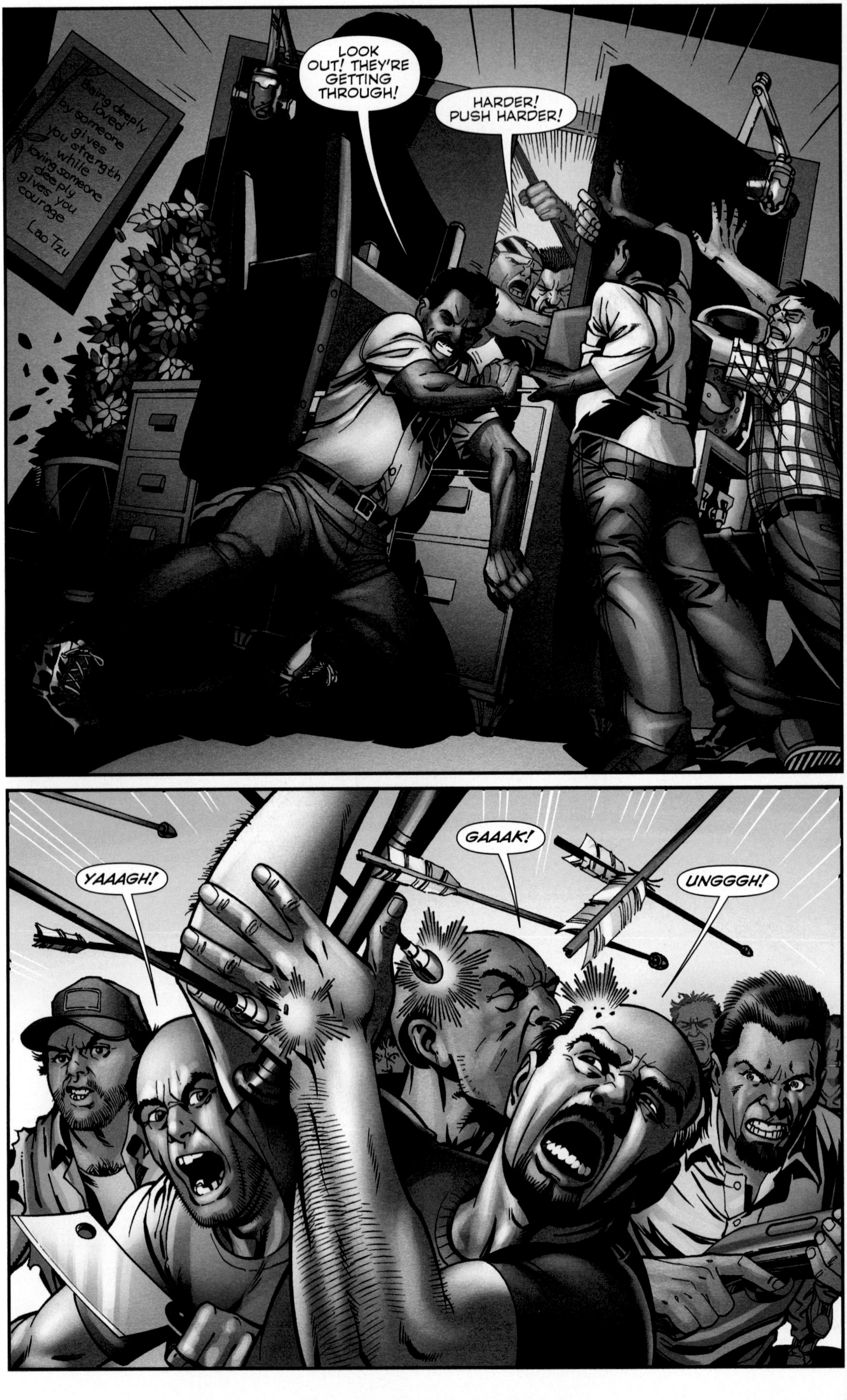
Being deeply loved by someone gives you strength while loving someone deeply gives you courage
Lao Tzu
LOOK OUT! THEY'RE GETTING THROUGH!
HARDER! PUSH HARDER!
YAAAGH!
GAAAK!
UNGGGH!

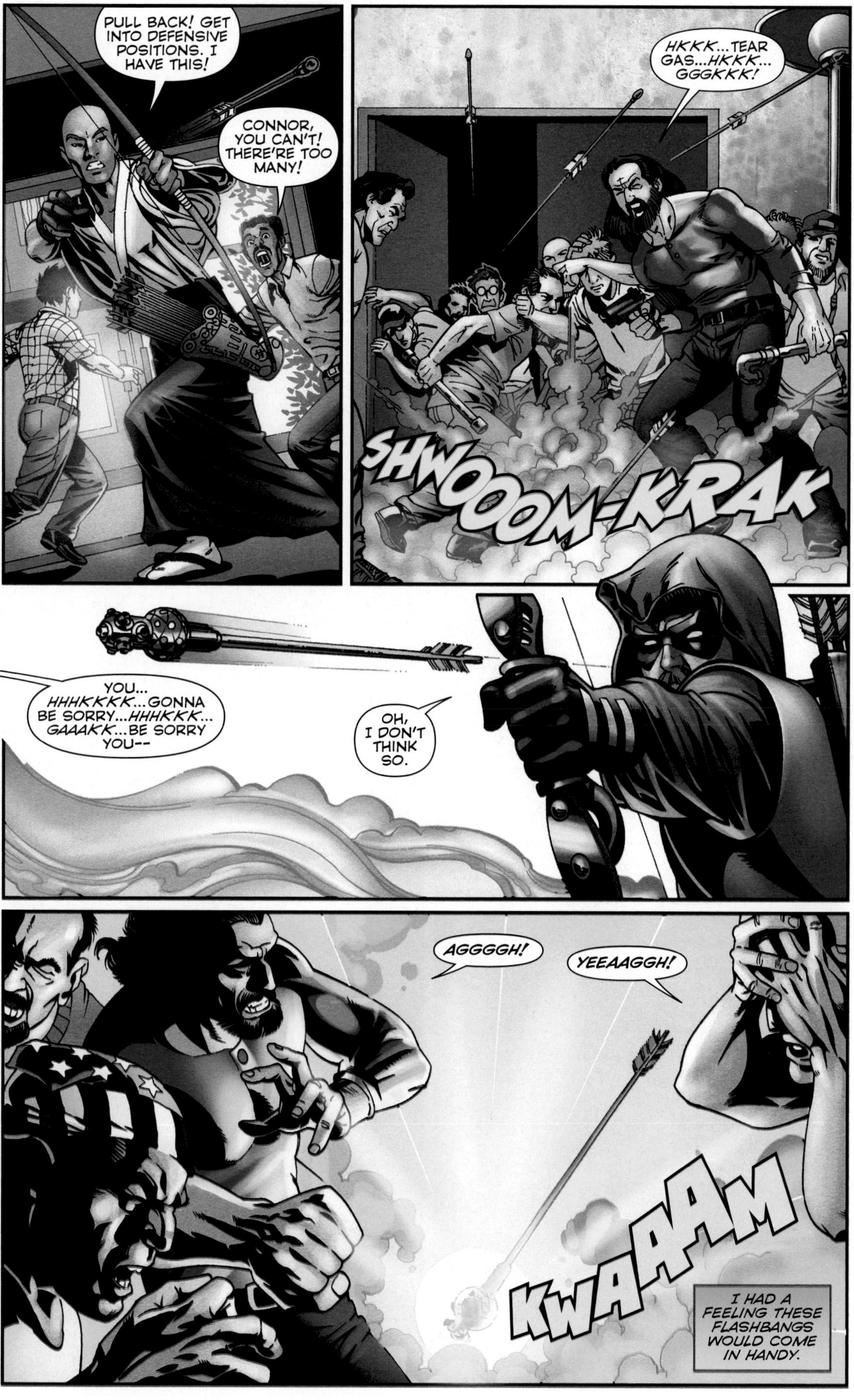
PULL BACK! GET INTO DEFENSIVE POSITIONS. I HAVE THIS!
CONNOR, YOU CAN'T! THERE'RE TOO MANY!
HKKK...TEAR GAS...HKKK... GGGKKK!
SHWOOOM-KRAK
YOU... HHHKKKK...GONNA BE SORRY...HHHKKK... GAAAKK...BE SORRY YOU--
OH, I DON'T THINK SO.
AGGGGH!
YEEAAGGH!
KWAAAAM
I HAD A FEELING THESE FLASHBANGS WOULD COME IN HANDY.

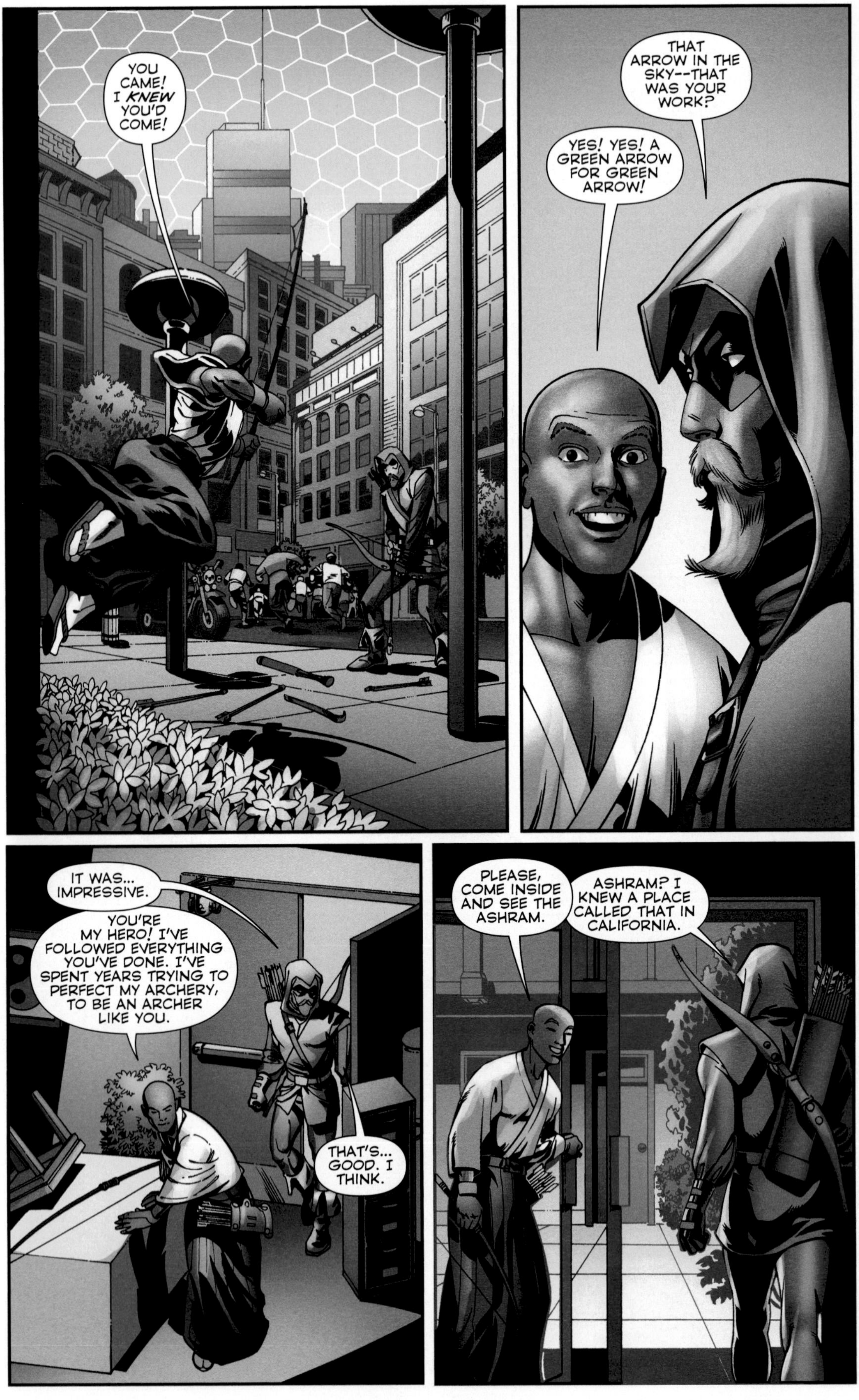

YOU CAME! I KNEW YOU'D COME!
THAT ARROW IN THE SKY--THAT WAS YOUR WORK?
YES! YES! A GREEN ARROW FOR GREEN ARROW!
IT WAS... IMPRESSIVE.
YOU'RE MY HERO! I'VE FOLLOWED EVERYTHING YOU'VE DONE. I'VE SPENT YEARS TRYING TO PERFECT MY ARCHERY, TO BE AN ARCHER LIKE YOU.
THAT'S... GOOD. I THINK.
PLEASE, COME INSIDE AND SEE THE ASHRAM.
ASHRAM? I KNEW A PLACE CALLED THAT IN CALIFORNIA.

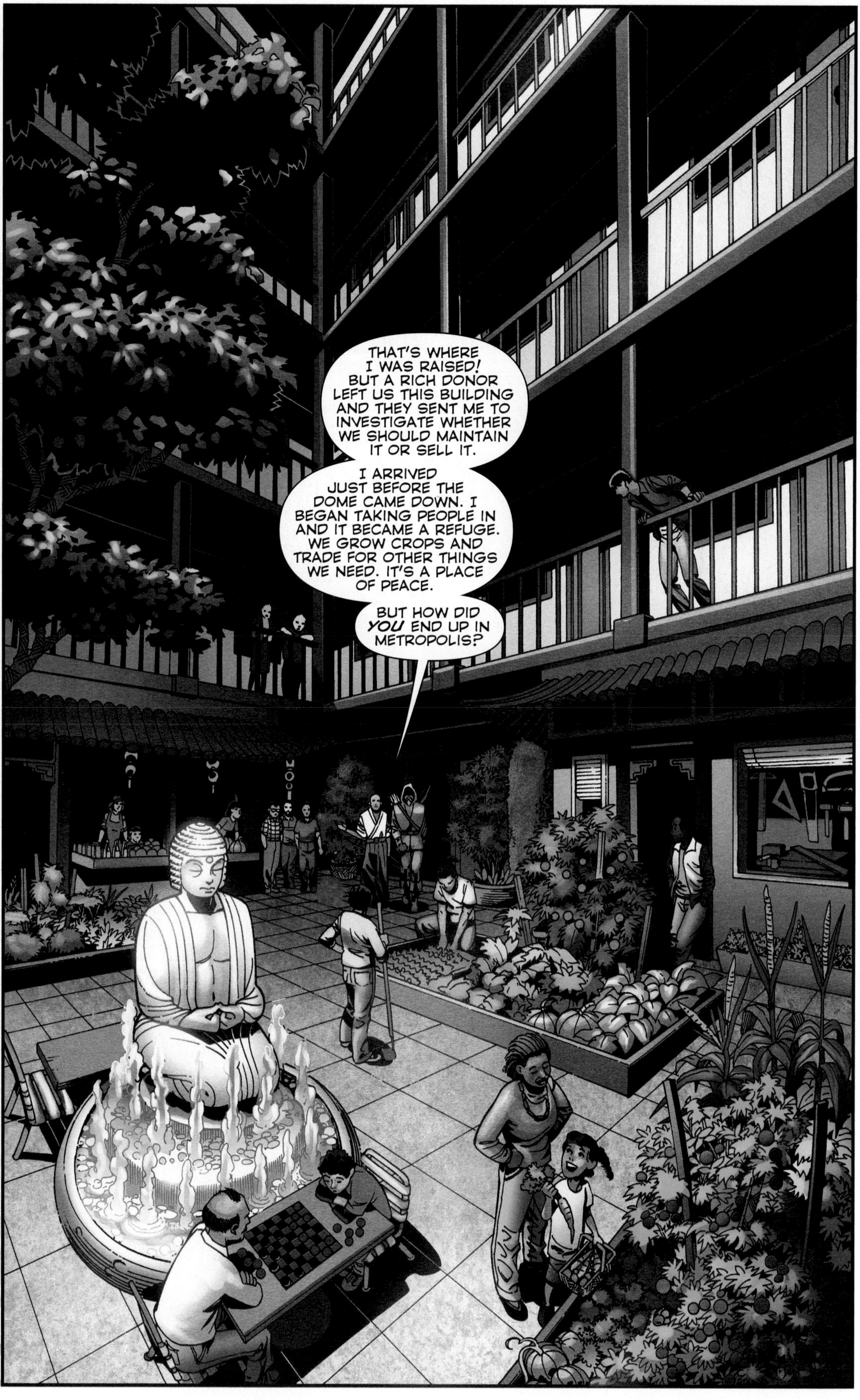
THAT'S WHERE I WAS RAISED! BUT A RICH DONOR LEFT US THIS BUILDING AND THEY SENT ME TO INVESTIGATE WHETHER WE SHOULD MAINTAIN IT OR SELL IT.
I ARRIVED JUST BEFORE THE DOME CAME DOWN. I BEGAN TAKING PEOPLE IN AND IT BECAME A REFUGE. WE GROW CROPS AND TRADE FOR OTHER THINGS WE NEED. IT'S A PLACE OF PEACE.
BUT HOW DID *YOU* END UP IN METROPOLIS?

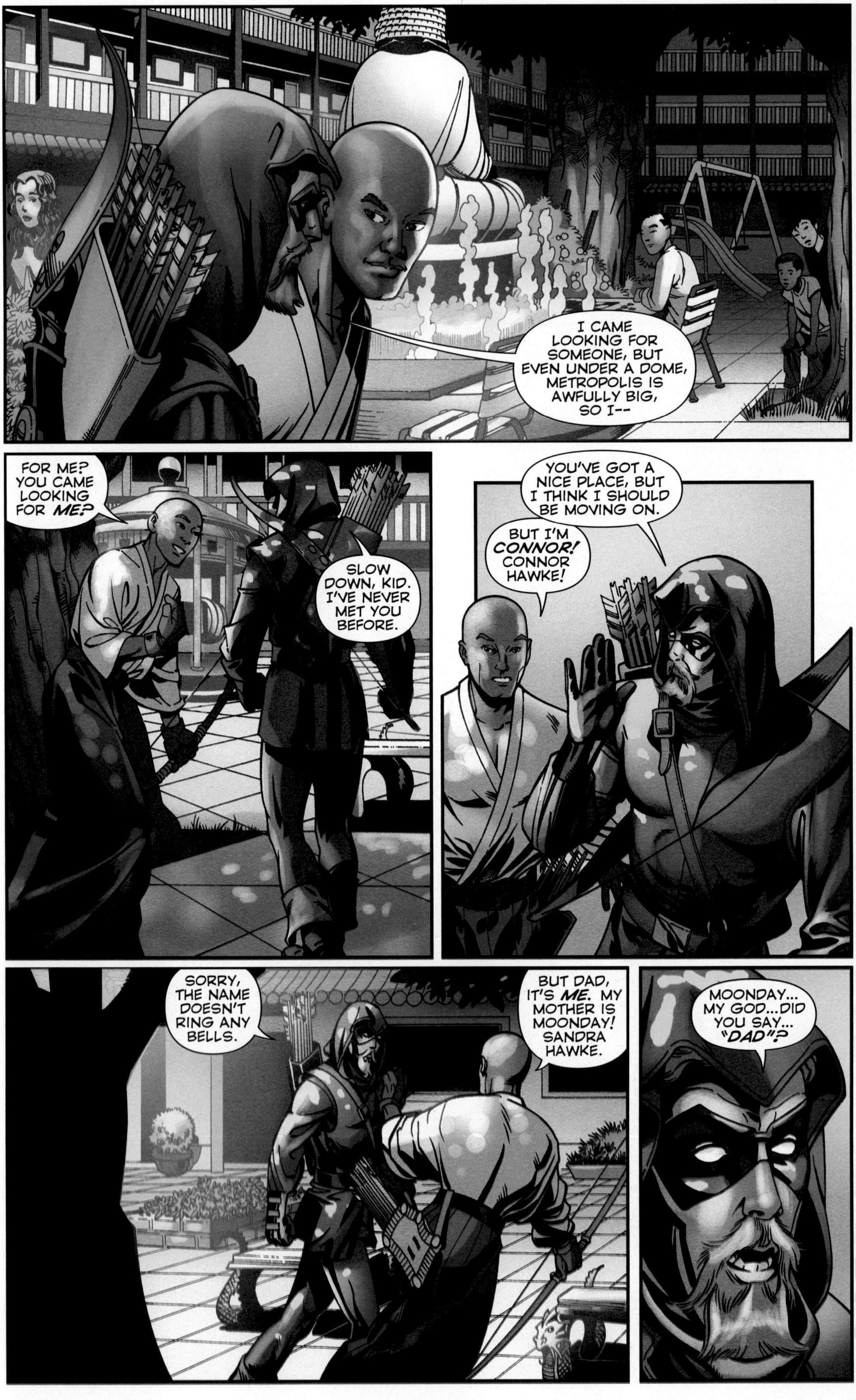
I CAME LOOKING FOR SOMEONE, BUT EVEN UNDER A DOME, METROPOLIS IS AWFULLY BIG, SO I--
FOR ME? YOU CAME LOOKING FOR *ME?*
SLOW DOWN, KID. I'VE NEVER MET YOU BEFORE.
YOU'VE GOT A NICE PLACE, BUT I THINK I SHOULD BE MOVING ON.
BUT I'M *CONNOR!* CONNOR HAWKE!
SORRY, THE NAME DOESN'T RING ANY BELLS.
BUT DAD, IT'S *ME.* MY MOTHER IS MOONDAY! SANDRA HAWKE.
MOONDAY... MY GOD...DID YOU SAY... *"DAD"?*

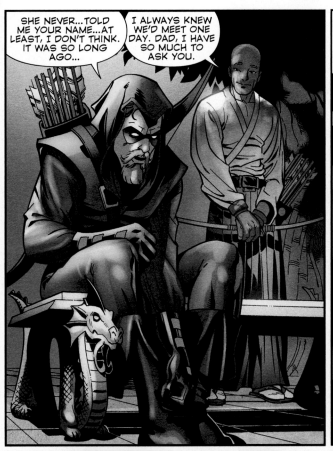

SHE NEVER...TOLD ME YOUR NAME...AT LEAST, I DON'T THINK. IT WAS SO LONG AGO...

I ALWAYS KNEW WE'D MEET ONE DAY. DAD, I HAVE SO MUCH TO ASK YOU.

LISTEN, THIS ISN'T GOING TO WORK. I'M BARELY ANY KIND OF HERO, LET ALONE A FATHER.

BUT YOU'RE HERE AND I'M HERE UNDER THIS DOME. WHAT ARE THE CHANCES OF THAT? I BELIEVE THE UNIVERSE MEANT FOR IT TO HAPPEN THIS WAY. IT'S DESTINY!

AND THERE'S SO MUCH YOU CAN TEACH ME ABOUT ARCHERY AND... AND OTHER THINGS.

NO, IT'S TOO LATE FOR THAT.

IS IT BECAUSE OF THIS--MY EYES? MY SKIN?

WHAT? GOD, NO. HOW COULD YOU EVEN...LOOK, I'M DOING YOU A FAVOR, TRUST ME.

THAT MAKES NO SENSE! HOW IS RUNNING AWAY FROM ME HELPING ME?

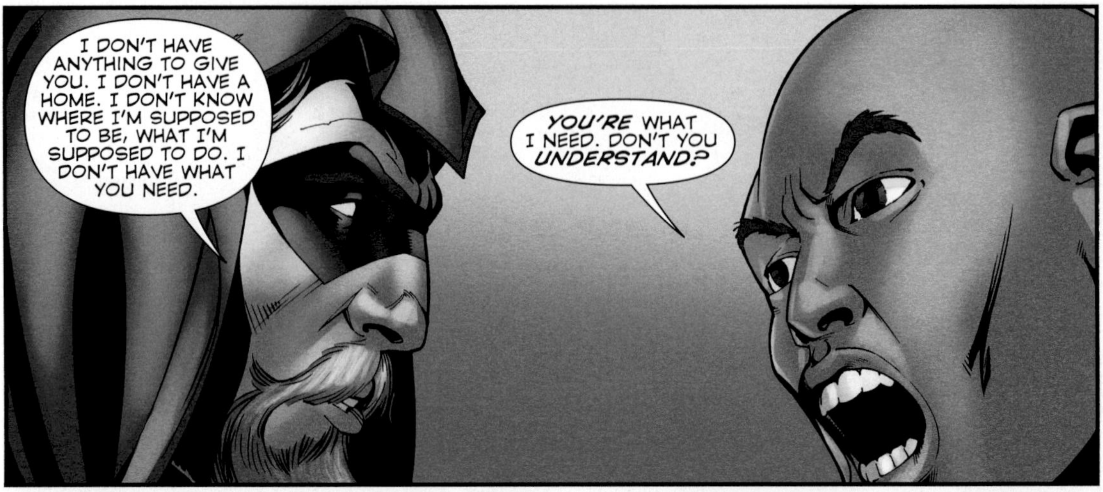
I DON'T HAVE ANYTHING TO GIVE YOU. I DON'T HAVE A HOME. I DON'T KNOW WHERE I'M SUPPOSED TO BE, WHAT I'M SUPPOSED TO DO. I DON'T HAVE WHAT YOU NEED.
YOU'RE WHAT I NEED. DON'T YOU UNDERSTAND?

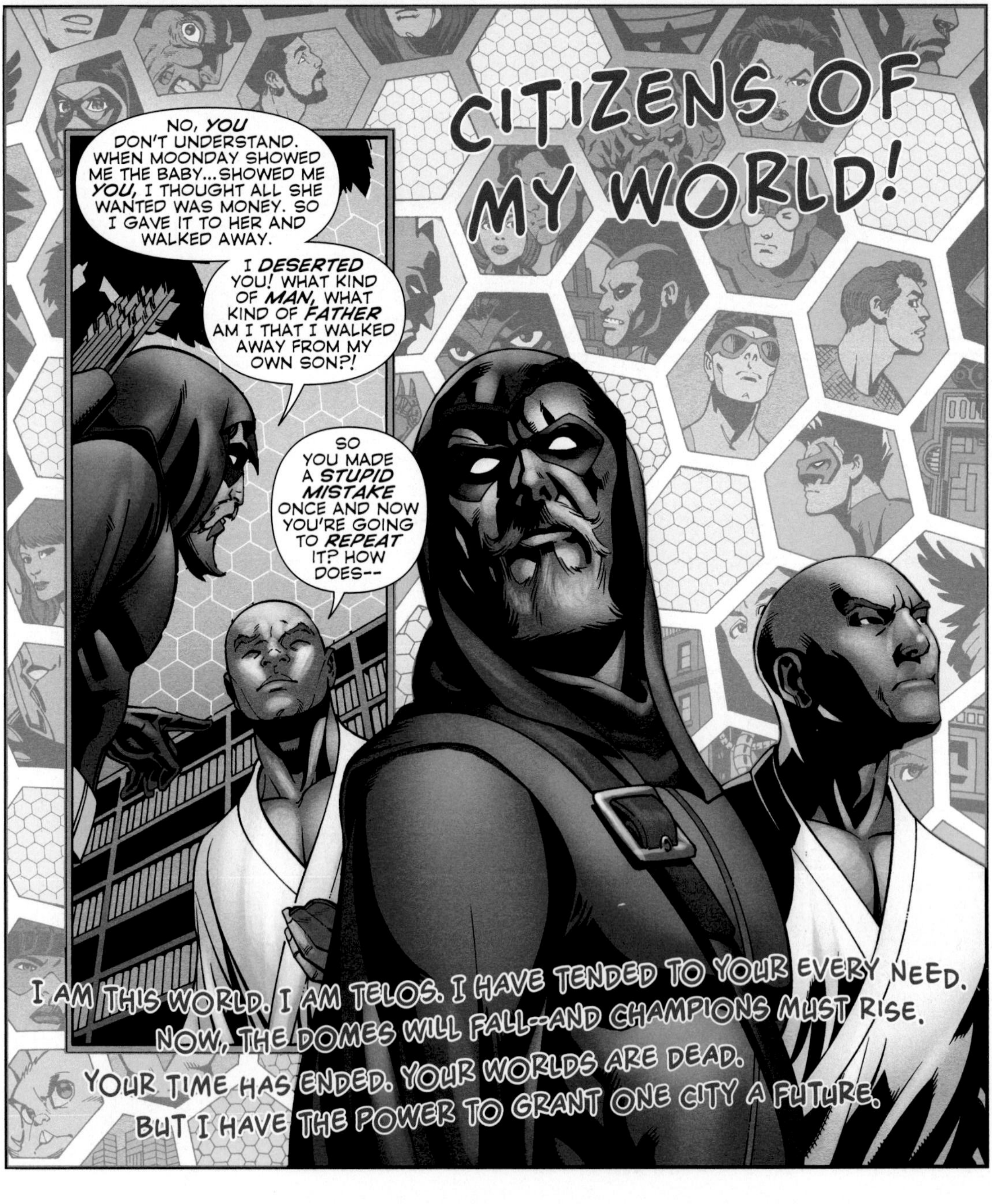
CITIZENS OF MY WORLD!
NO, YOU DON'T UNDERSTAND. WHEN MOONDAY SHOWED ME THE BABY...SHOWED ME YOU, I THOUGHT ALL SHE WANTED WAS MONEY. SO I GAVE IT TO HER AND WALKED AWAY.
I DESERTED YOU! WHAT KIND OF MAN, WHAT KIND OF FATHER AM I THAT I WALKED AWAY FROM MY OWN SON?!
SO YOU MADE A STUPID MISTAKE ONCE AND NOW YOU'RE GOING TO REPEAT IT? HOW DOES--
I AM THIS WORLD. I AM TELOS. I HAVE TENDED TO YOUR EVERY NEED.
NOW, THE DOMES WILL FALL--AND CHAMPIONS MUST RISE.
YOUR TIME HAS ENDED. YOUR WORLDS ARE DEAD.
BUT I HAVE THE POWER TO GRANT ONE CITY A FUTURE.

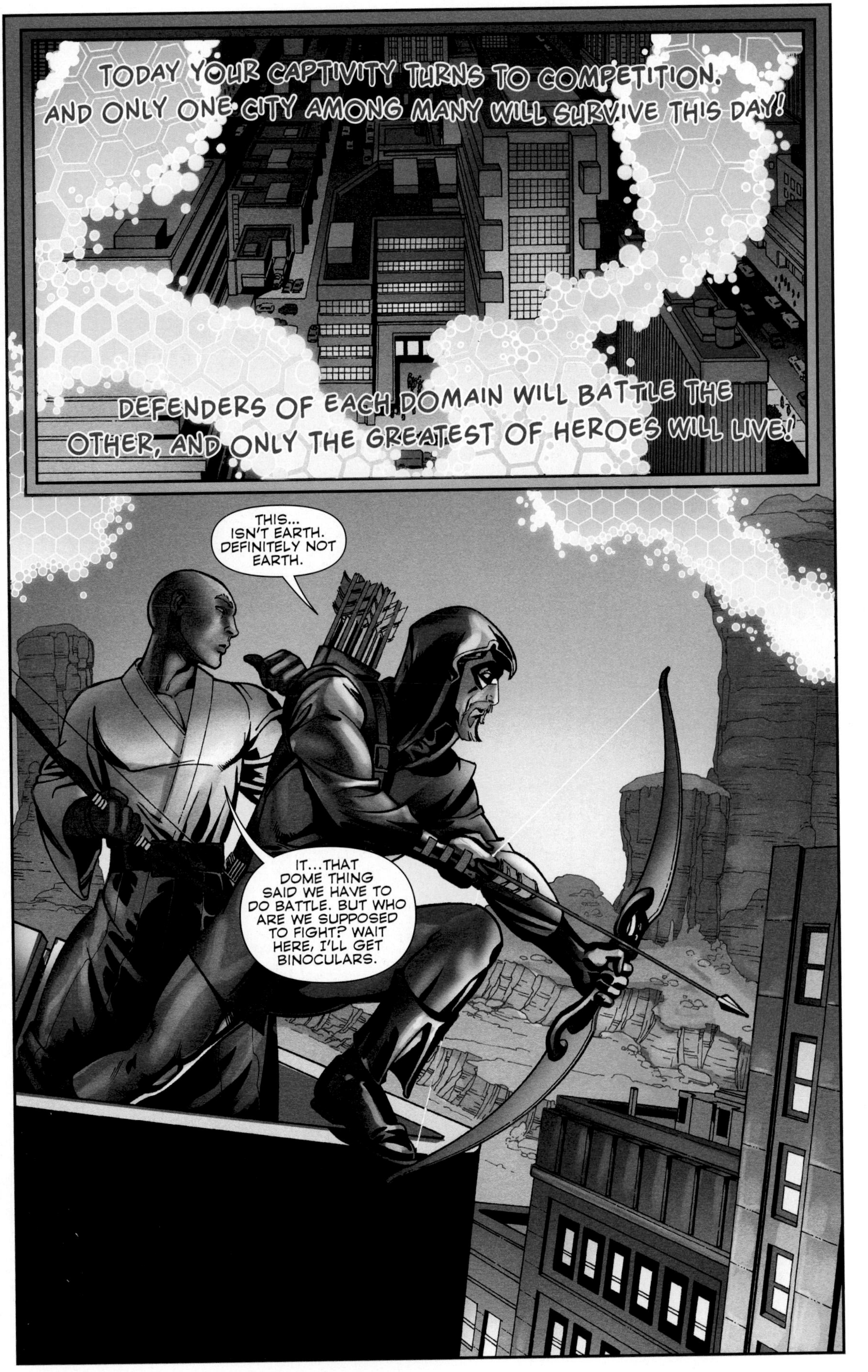
TODAY YOUR CAPTIVITY TURNS TO COMPETITION. AND ONLY ONE CITY AMONG MANY WILL SURVIVE THIS DAY!
DEFENDERS OF EACH DOMAIN WILL BATTLE THE OTHER, AND ONLY THE GREATEST OF HEROES WILL LIVE!
THIS... ISN'T EARTH. DEFINITELY NOT EARTH.
IT...THAT DOME THING SAID WE HAVE TO DO BATTLE. BUT WHO ARE WE SUPPOSED TO FIGHT? WAIT HERE, I'LL GET BINOCULARS.

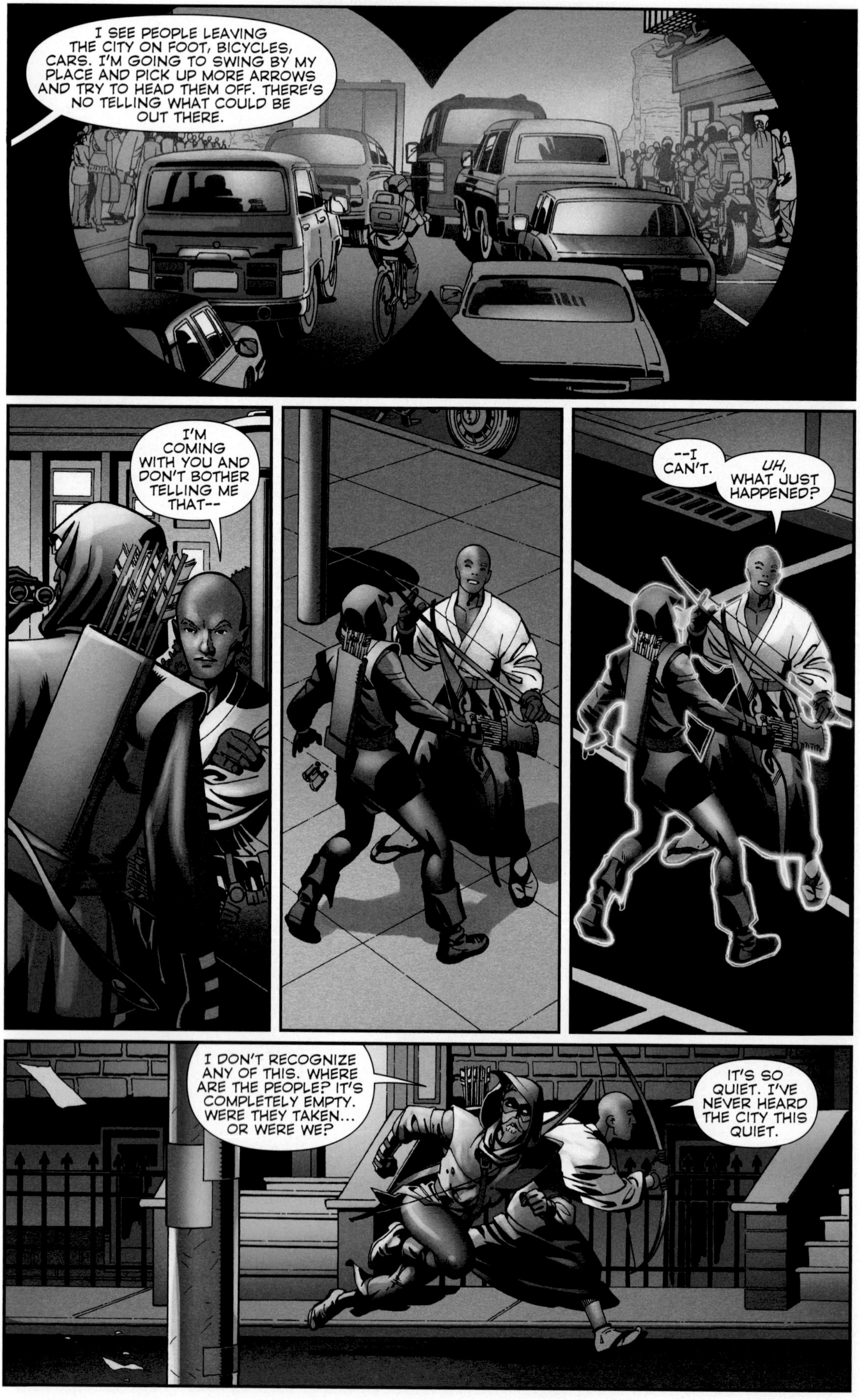
I SEE PEOPLE LEAVING THE CITY ON FOOT, BICYCLES, CARS. I'M GOING TO SWING BY MY PLACE AND PICK UP MORE ARROWS AND TRY TO HEAD THEM OFF. THERE'S NO TELLING WHAT COULD BE OUT THERE.
I'M COMING WITH YOU AND DON'T BOTHER TELLING ME THAT--
--I CAN'T.
UH, WHAT JUST HAPPENED?
I DON'T RECOGNIZE ANY OF THIS. WHERE ARE THE PEOPLE? IT'S COMPLETELY EMPTY. WERE THEY TAKEN... OR WERE WE?
IT'S SO QUIET. I'VE NEVER HEARD THE CITY THIS QUIET.

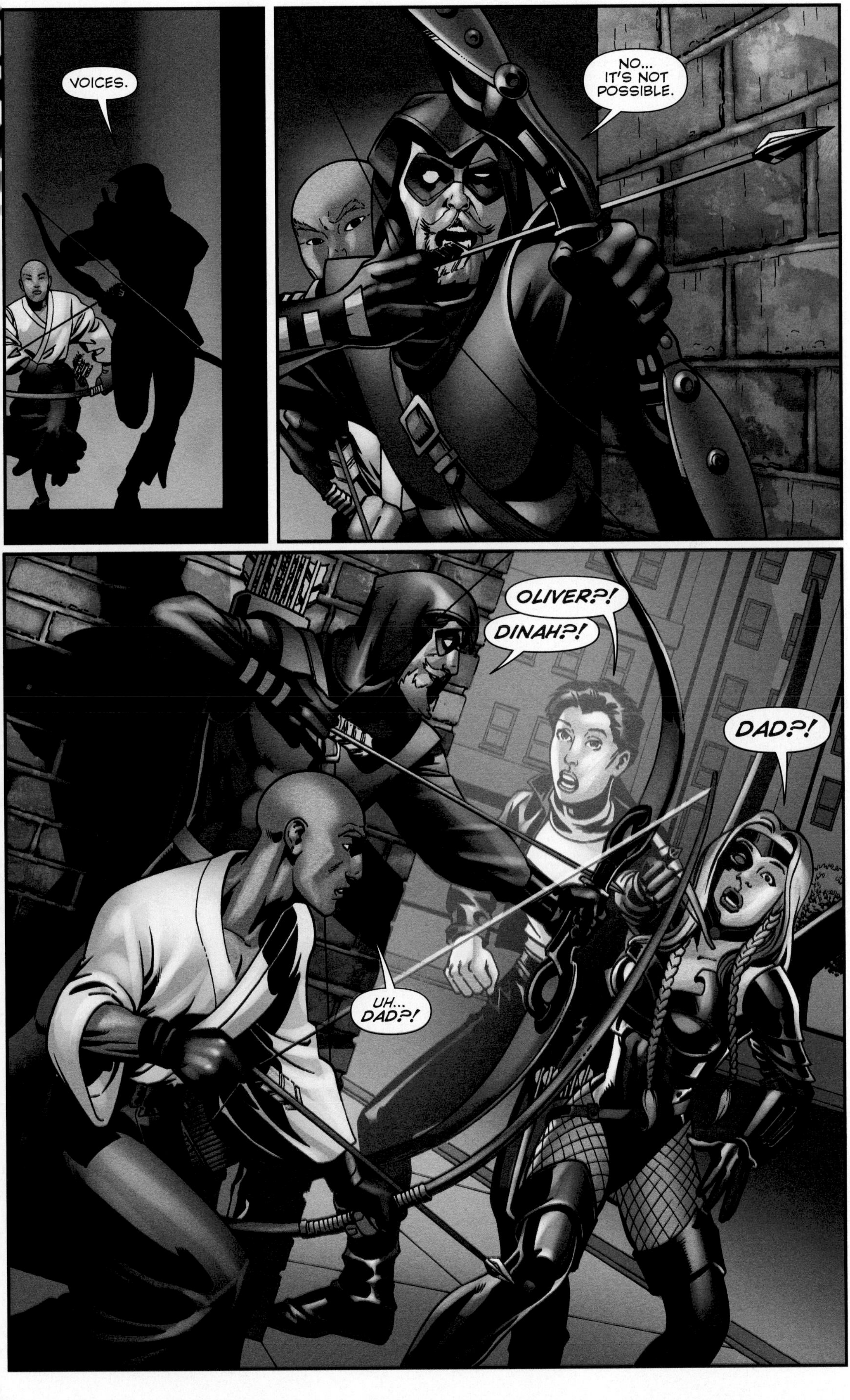
VOICES.
NO... IT'S NOT POSSIBLE.
OLIVER?!
DINAH?!
DAD?!
UH... DAD?!

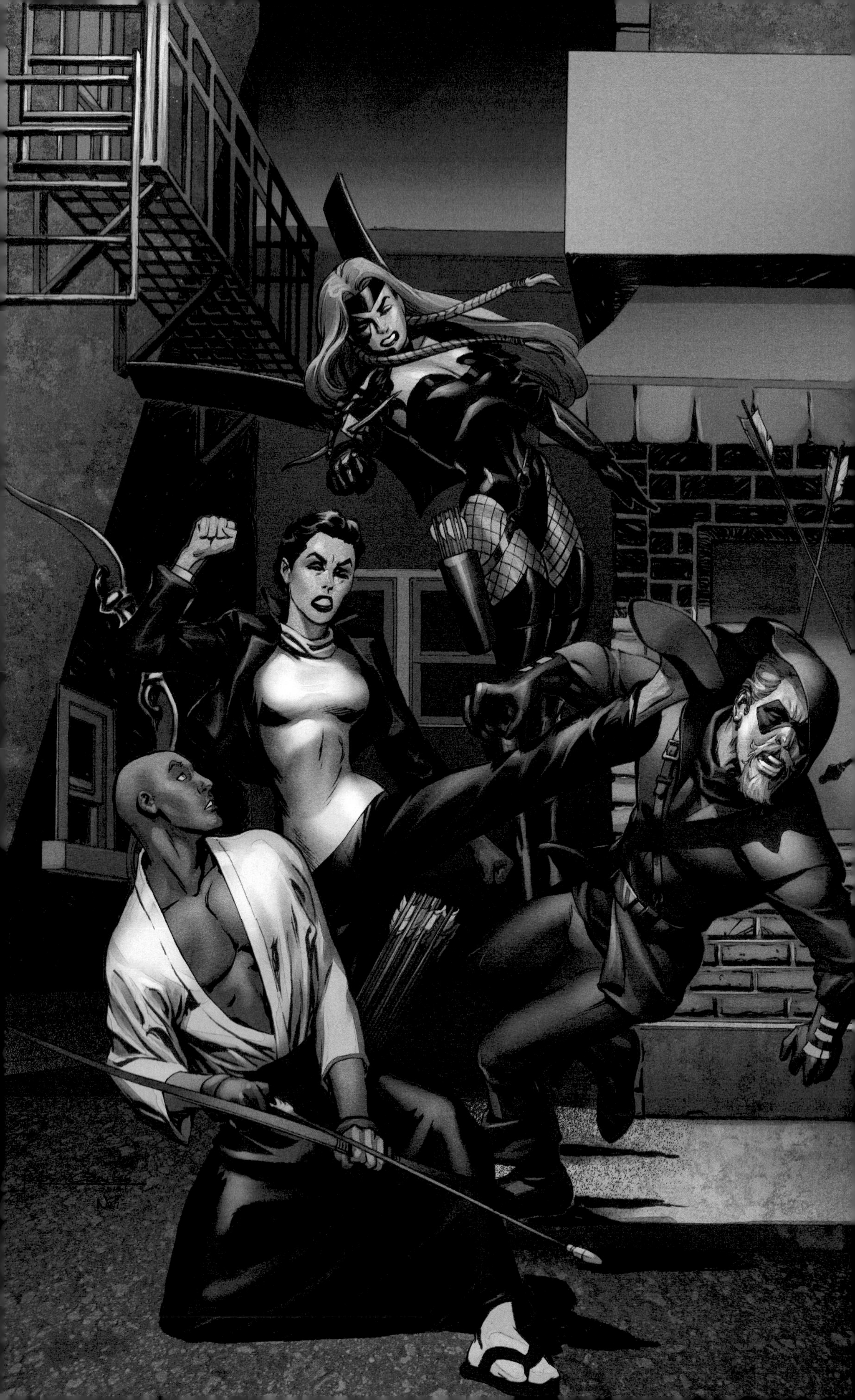

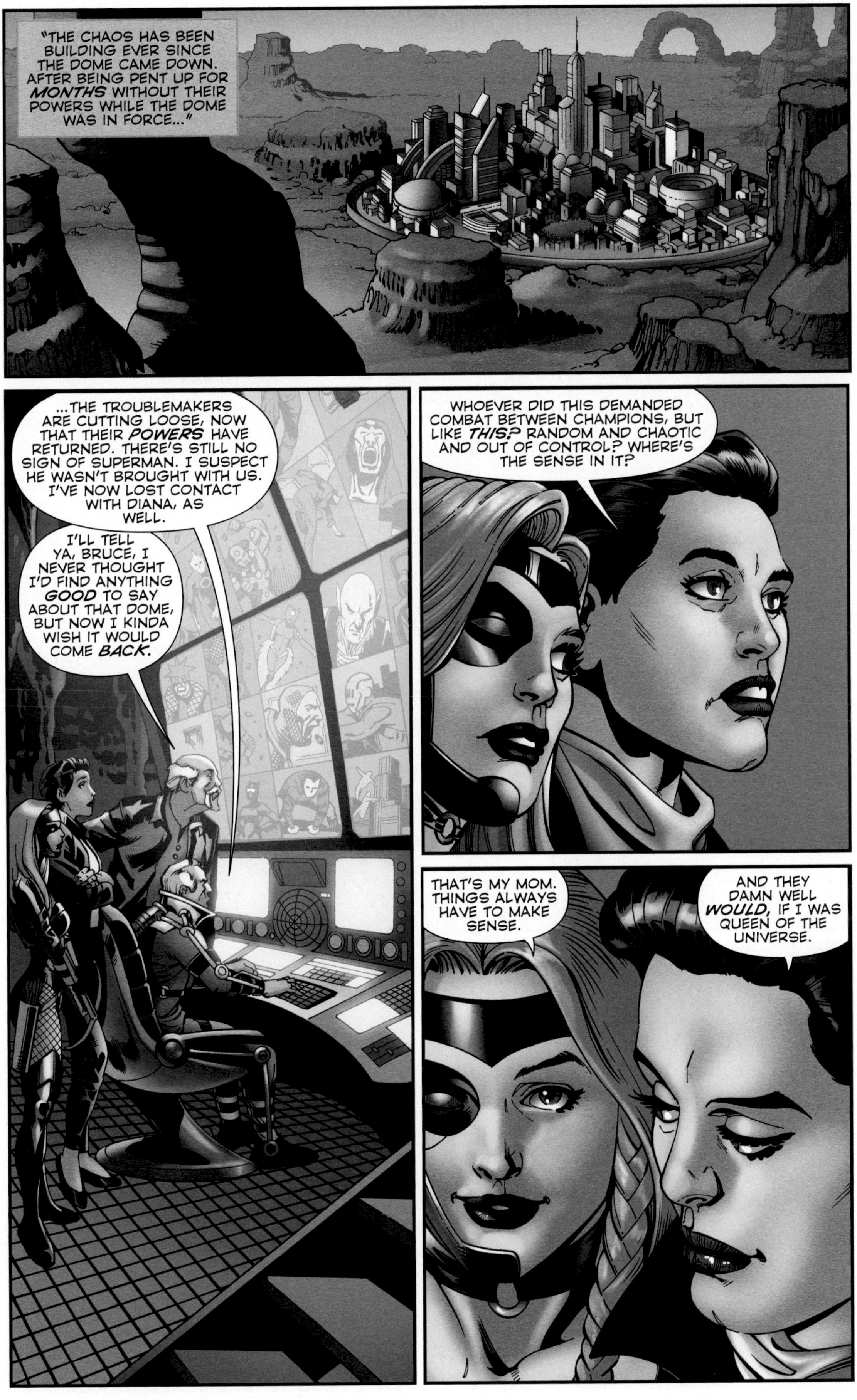
"THE CHAOS HAS BEEN BUILDING EVER SINCE THE DOME CAME DOWN. AFTER BEING PENT UP FOR MONTHS WITHOUT THEIR POWERS WHILE THE DOME WAS IN FORCE..."
...THE TROUBLEMAKERS ARE CUTTING LOOSE, NOW THAT THEIR POWERS HAVE RETURNED. THERE'S STILL NO SIGN OF SUPERMAN. I SUSPECT HE WASN'T BROUGHT WITH US. I'VE NOW LOST CONTACT WITH DIANA, AS WELL.
I'LL TELL YA, BRUCE, I NEVER THOUGHT I'D FIND ANYTHING GOOD TO SAY ABOUT THAT DOME, BUT NOW I KINDA WISH IT WOULD COME BACK.
WHOEVER DID THIS DEMANDED COMBAT BETWEEN CHAMPIONS, BUT LIKE THIS? RANDOM AND CHAOTIC AND OUT OF CONTROL? WHERE'S THE SENSE IN IT?
THAT'S MY MOM. THINGS ALWAYS HAVE TO MAKE SENSE.
AND THEY DAMN WELL WOULD, IF I WAS QUEEN OF THE UNIVERSE.

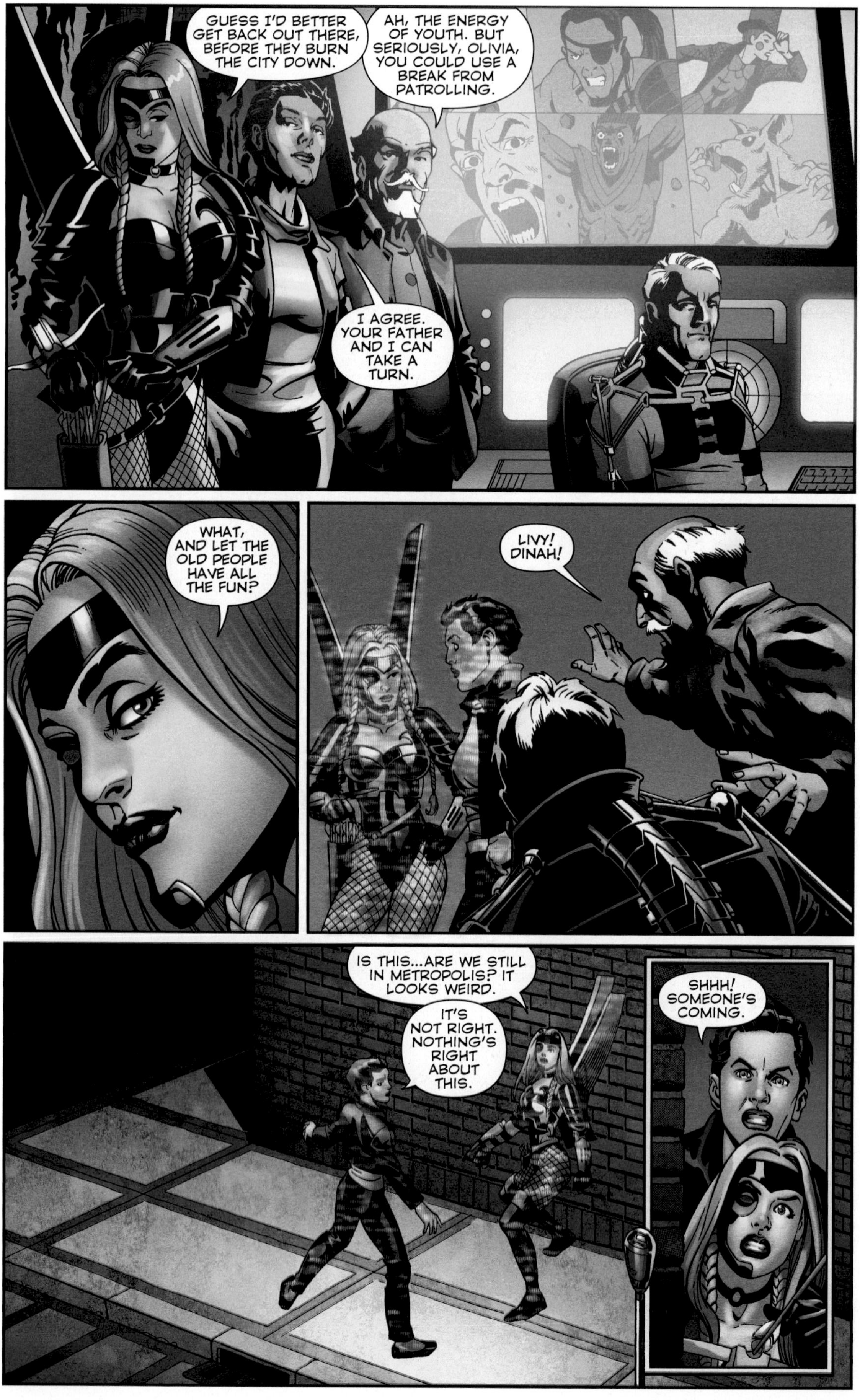
GUESS I'D BETTER GET BACK OUT THERE, BEFORE THEY BURN THE CITY DOWN.
AH, THE ENERGY OF YOUTH. BUT SERIOUSLY, OLIVIA, YOU COULD USE A BREAK FROM PATROLLING.
I AGREE. YOUR FATHER AND I CAN TAKE A TURN.
WHAT, AND LET THE OLD PEOPLE HAVE ALL THE FUN?
LIVY! DINAH!
IS THIS...ARE WE STILL IN METROPOLIS? IT LOOKS WEIRD.
IT'S NOT RIGHT. NOTHING'S RIGHT ABOUT THIS.
SHHH! SOMEONE'S COMING.

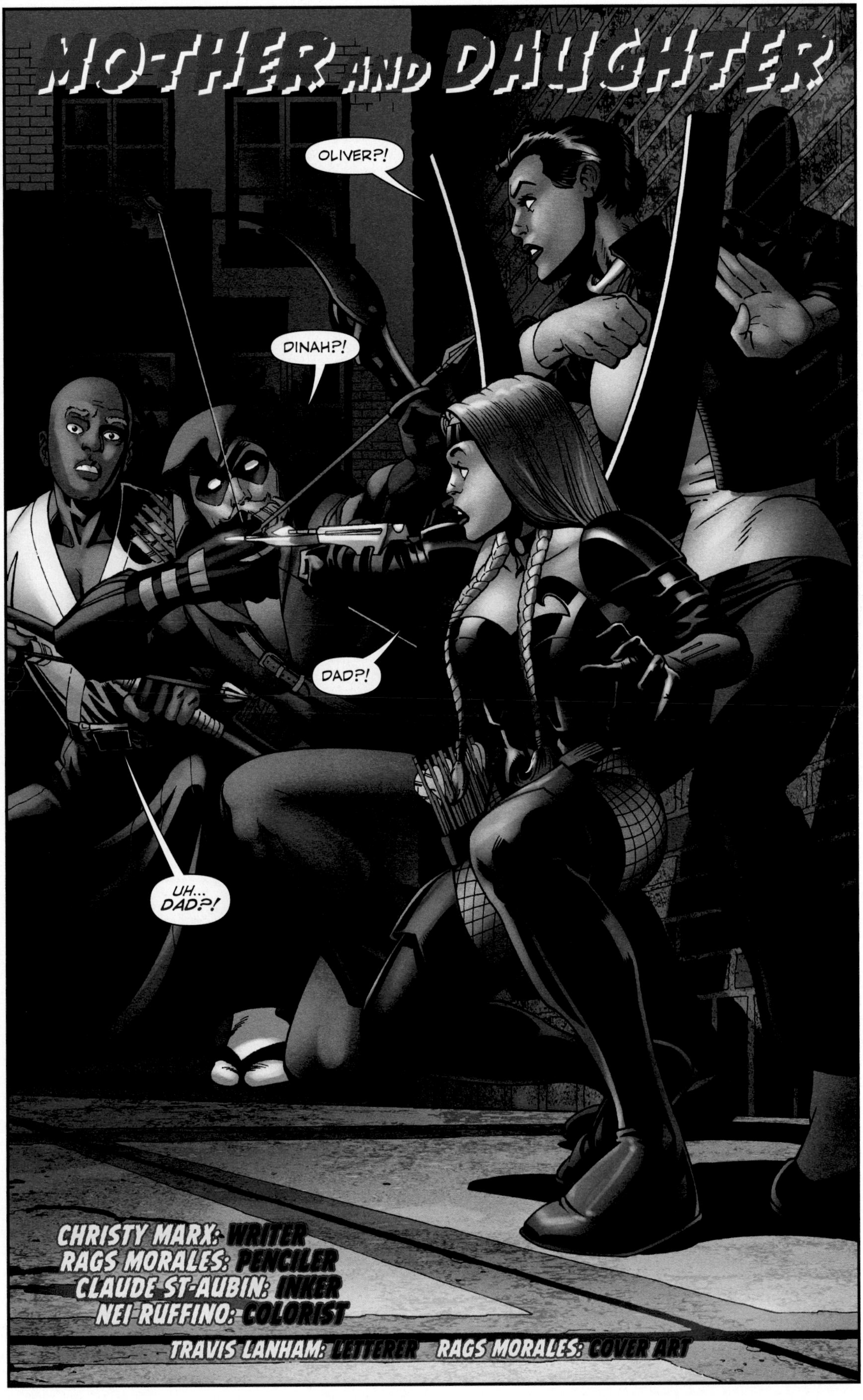
MOTHER AND DAUGHTER
OLIVER?!
DINAH?!
DAD?!
UH... DAD?!
CHRISTY MARX: WRITER
RAGS MORALES: PENCILER
CLAUDE ST-AUBIN: INKER
NEI RUFFINO: COLORIST
TRAVIS LANHAM: LETTERER RAGS MORALES: COVER ART

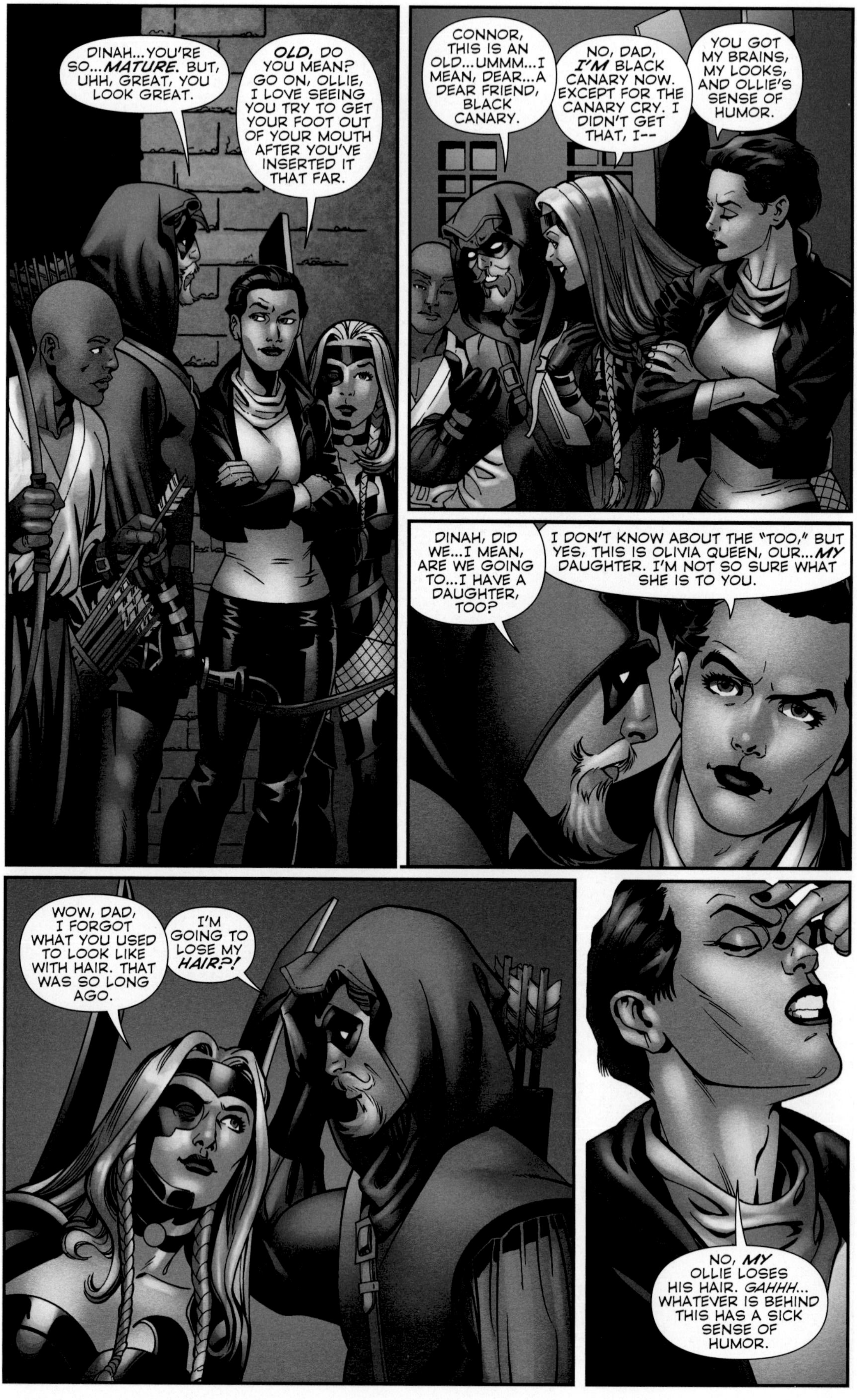
DINAH...YOU'RE SO...MATURE. BUT, UHH, GREAT, YOU LOOK GREAT.
OLD, DO YOU MEAN? GO ON, OLLIE, I LOVE SEEING YOU TRY TO GET YOUR FOOT OUT OF YOUR MOUTH AFTER YOU'VE INSERTED IT THAT FAR.
CONNOR, THIS IS AN OLD...UMMM...I MEAN, DEAR...A DEAR FRIEND, BLACK CANARY.
NO, DAD, I'M BLACK CANARY NOW. EXCEPT FOR THE CANARY CRY. I DIDN'T GET THAT, I--
YOU GOT MY BRAINS, MY LOOKS, AND OLLIE'S SENSE OF HUMOR.
DINAH, DID WE...I MEAN, ARE WE GOING TO...I HAVE A DAUGHTER, TOO?
I DON'T KNOW ABOUT THE "TOO," BUT YES, THIS IS OLIVIA QUEEN, OUR...MY DAUGHTER. I'M NOT SO SURE WHAT SHE IS TO YOU.
WOW, DAD, I FORGOT WHAT YOU USED TO LOOK LIKE WITH HAIR. THAT WAS SO LONG AGO.
I'M GOING TO LOSE MY HAIR?!
NO, MY OLLIE LOSES HIS HAIR. GAHHH... WHATEVER IS BEHIND THIS HAS A SICK SENSE OF HUMOR.

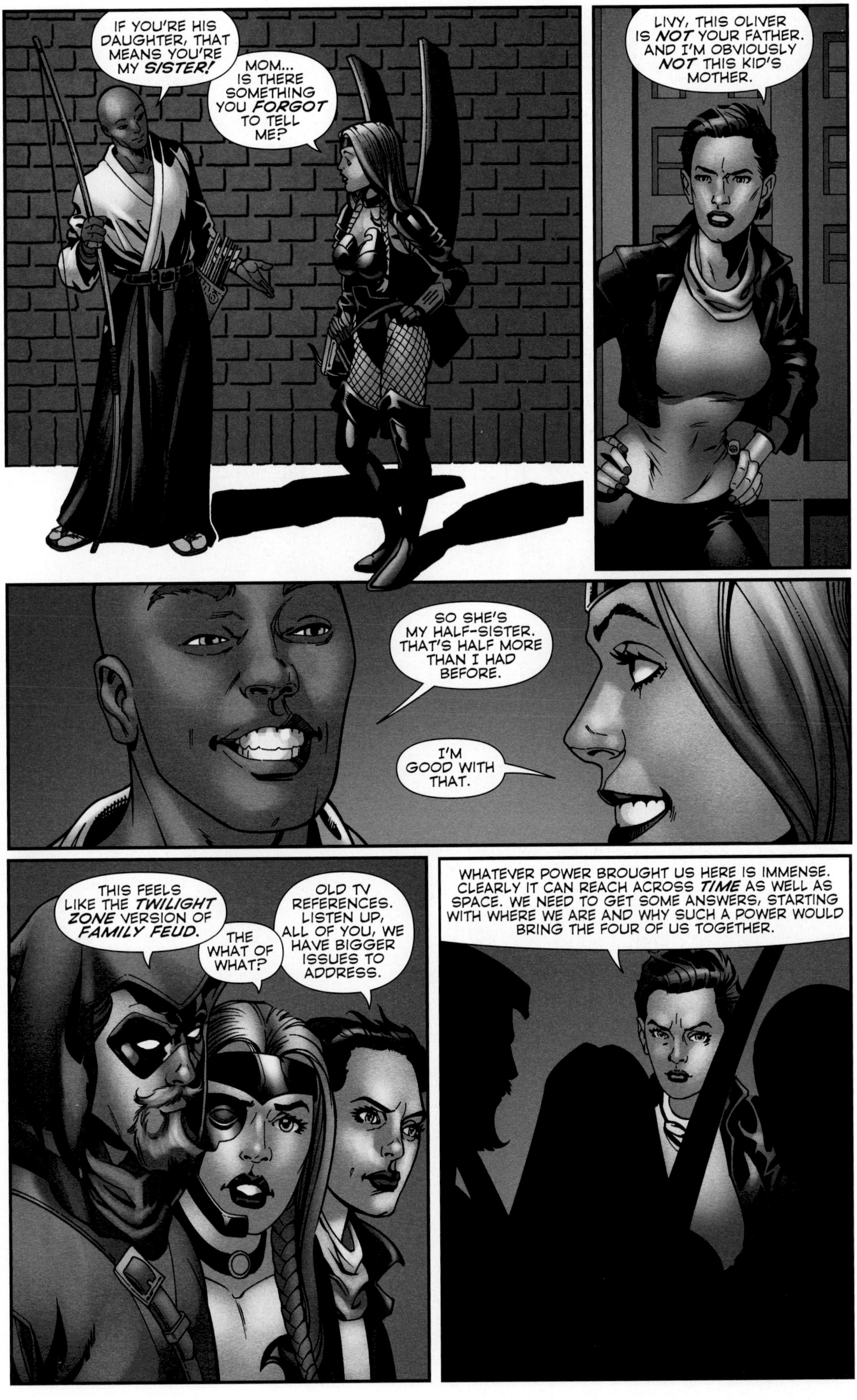
IF YOU'RE HIS DAUGHTER, THAT MEANS YOU'RE MY SISTER!
MOM... IS THERE SOMETHING YOU FORGOT TO TELL ME?
LIVY, THIS OLIVER IS NOT YOUR FATHER. AND I'M OBVIOUSLY NOT THIS KID'S MOTHER.
SO SHE'S MY HALF-SISTER. THAT'S HALF MORE THAN I HAD BEFORE.
I'M GOOD WITH THAT.
THIS FEELS LIKE THE TWILIGHT ZONE VERSION OF FAMILY FEUD.
THE WHAT OF WHAT?
OLD TV REFERENCES. LISTEN UP, ALL OF YOU, WE HAVE BIGGER ISSUES TO ADDRESS.
WHATEVER POWER BROUGHT US HERE IS IMMENSE. CLEARLY IT CAN REACH ACROSS TIME AS WELL AS SPACE. WE NEED TO GET SOME ANSWERS, STARTING WITH WHERE WE ARE AND WHY SUCH A POWER WOULD BRING THE FOUR OF US TOGETHER.

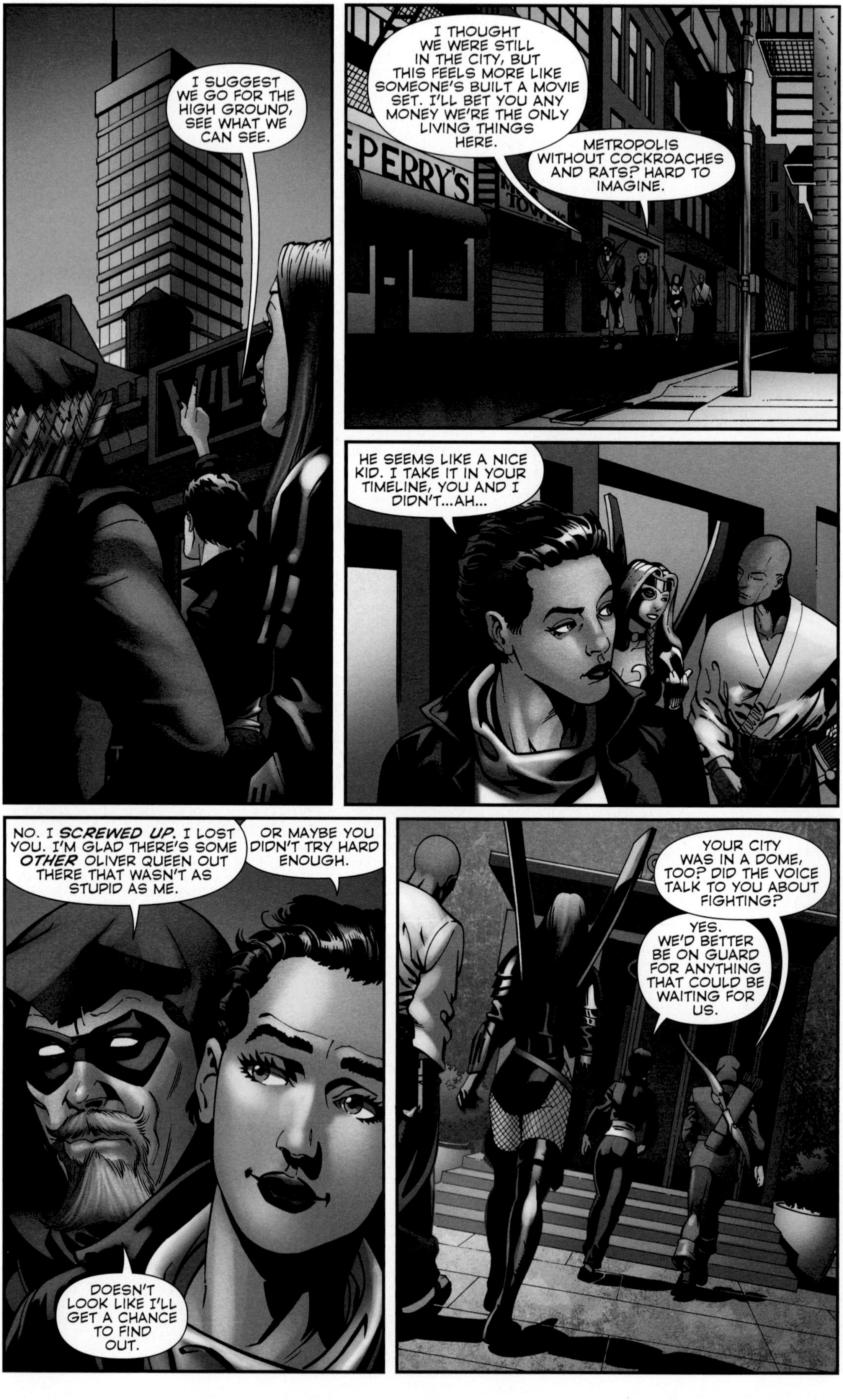
I SUGGEST WE GO FOR THE HIGH GROUND, SEE WHAT WE CAN SEE.
I THOUGHT WE WERE STILL IN THE CITY, BUT THIS FEELS MORE LIKE SOMEONE'S BUILT A MOVIE SET. I'LL BET YOU ANY MONEY WE'RE THE ONLY LIVING THINGS HERE.
METROPOLIS WITHOUT COCKROACHES AND RATS? HARD TO IMAGINE.
PERRY'S
HE SEEMS LIKE A NICE KID. I TAKE IT IN YOUR TIMELINE, YOU AND I DIDN'T...AH...
NO. I *SCREWED UP*. I LOST YOU. I'M GLAD THERE'S SOME *OTHER* OLIVER QUEEN OUT THERE THAT WASN'T AS STUPID AS ME.
OR MAYBE YOU DIDN'T TRY HARD ENOUGH.
DOESN'T LOOK LIKE I'LL GET A CHANCE TO FIND OUT.
YOUR CITY WAS IN A DOME, TOO? DID THE VOICE TALK TO YOU ABOUT FIGHTING?
YES. WE'D BETTER BE ON GUARD FOR ANYTHING THAT COULD BE WAITING FOR US.

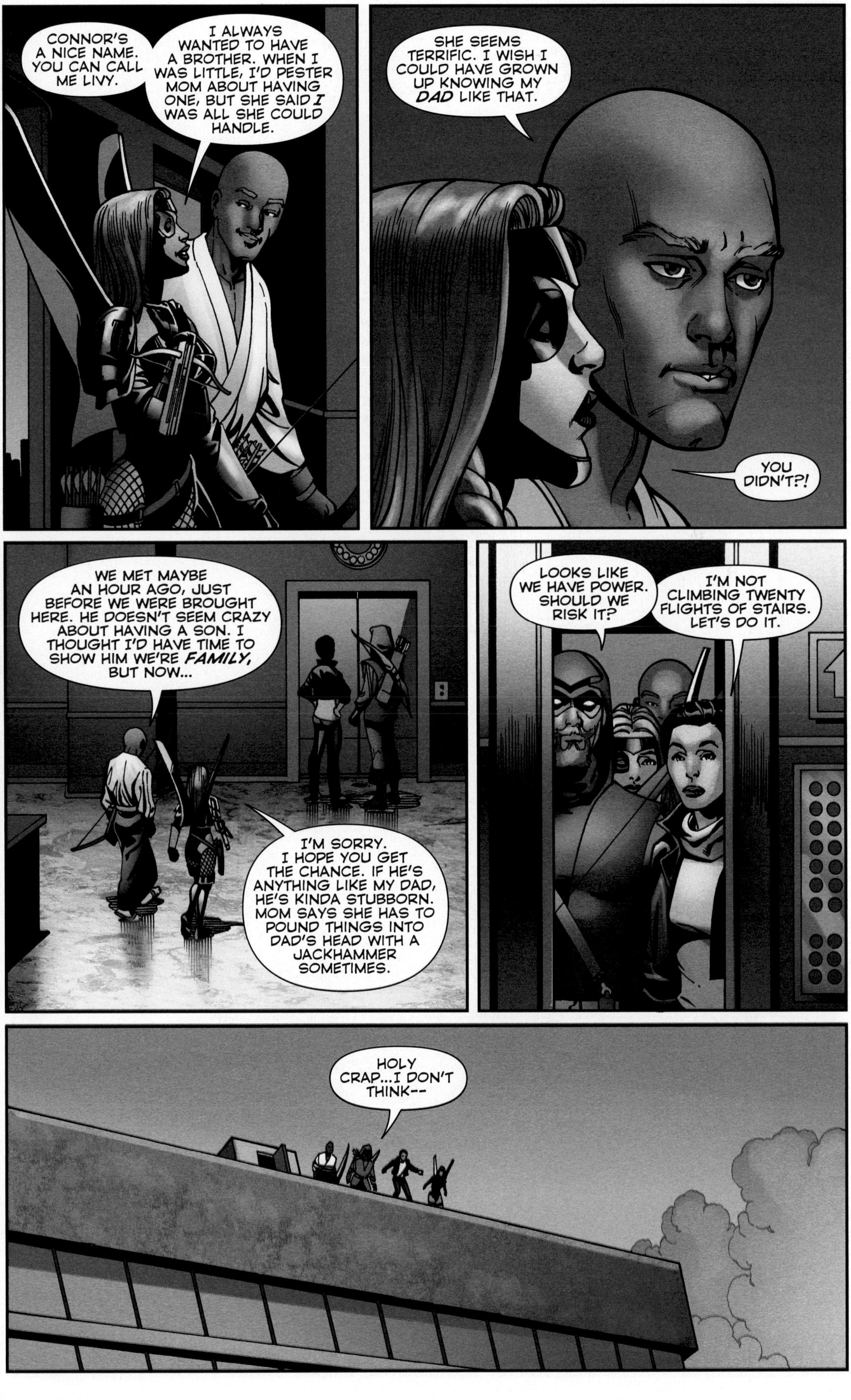

CONNOR'S A NICE NAME. YOU CAN CALL ME LIVY.
I ALWAYS WANTED TO HAVE A BROTHER. WHEN I WAS LITTLE, I'D PESTER MOM ABOUT HAVING ONE, BUT SHE SAID *I* WAS ALL SHE COULD HANDLE.
SHE SEEMS TERRIFIC. I WISH I COULD HAVE GROWN UP KNOWING MY *DAD* LIKE THAT.
YOU DIDN'T?!
WE MET MAYBE AN HOUR AGO, JUST BEFORE WE WERE BROUGHT HERE. HE DOESN'T SEEM CRAZY ABOUT HAVING A SON. I THOUGHT I'D HAVE TIME TO SHOW HIM WE'RE *FAMILY,* BUT NOW...
I'M SORRY. I HOPE YOU GET THE CHANCE. IF HE'S ANYTHING LIKE MY DAD, HE'S KINDA STUBBORN. MOM SAYS SHE HAS TO POUND THINGS INTO DAD'S HEAD WITH A JACKHAMMER SOMETIMES.
LOOKS LIKE WE HAVE POWER. SHOULD WE RISK IT?
I'M NOT CLIMBING TWENTY FLIGHTS OF STAIRS. LET'S DO IT.
HOLY CRAP...I DON'T THINK--

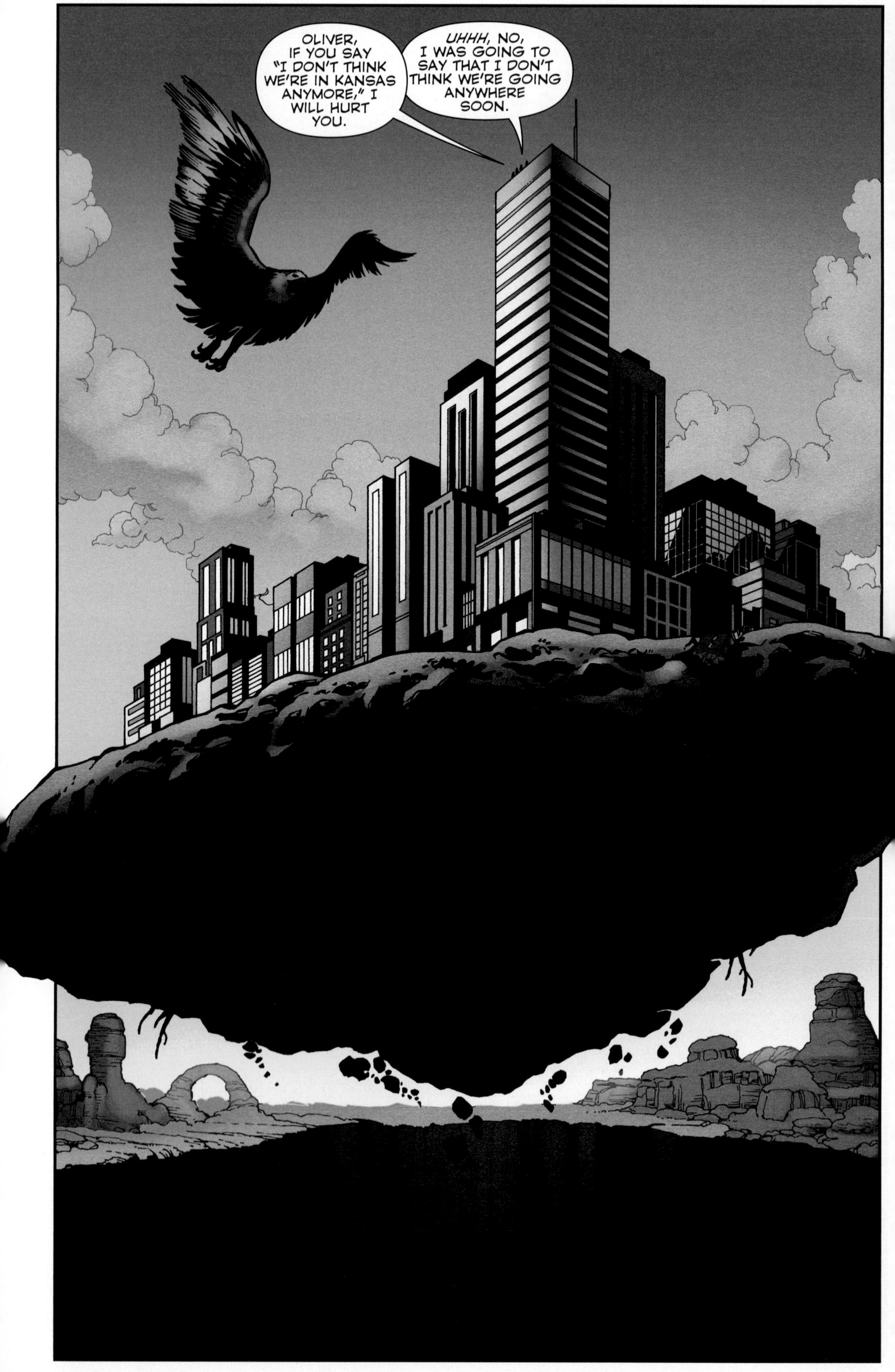
OLIVER, IF YOU SAY "I DON'T THINK WE'RE IN KANSAS ANYMORE," I WILL HURT YOU.
UHHH, NO, I WAS GOING TO SAY THAT I DON'T THINK WE'RE GOING ANYWHERE SOON.

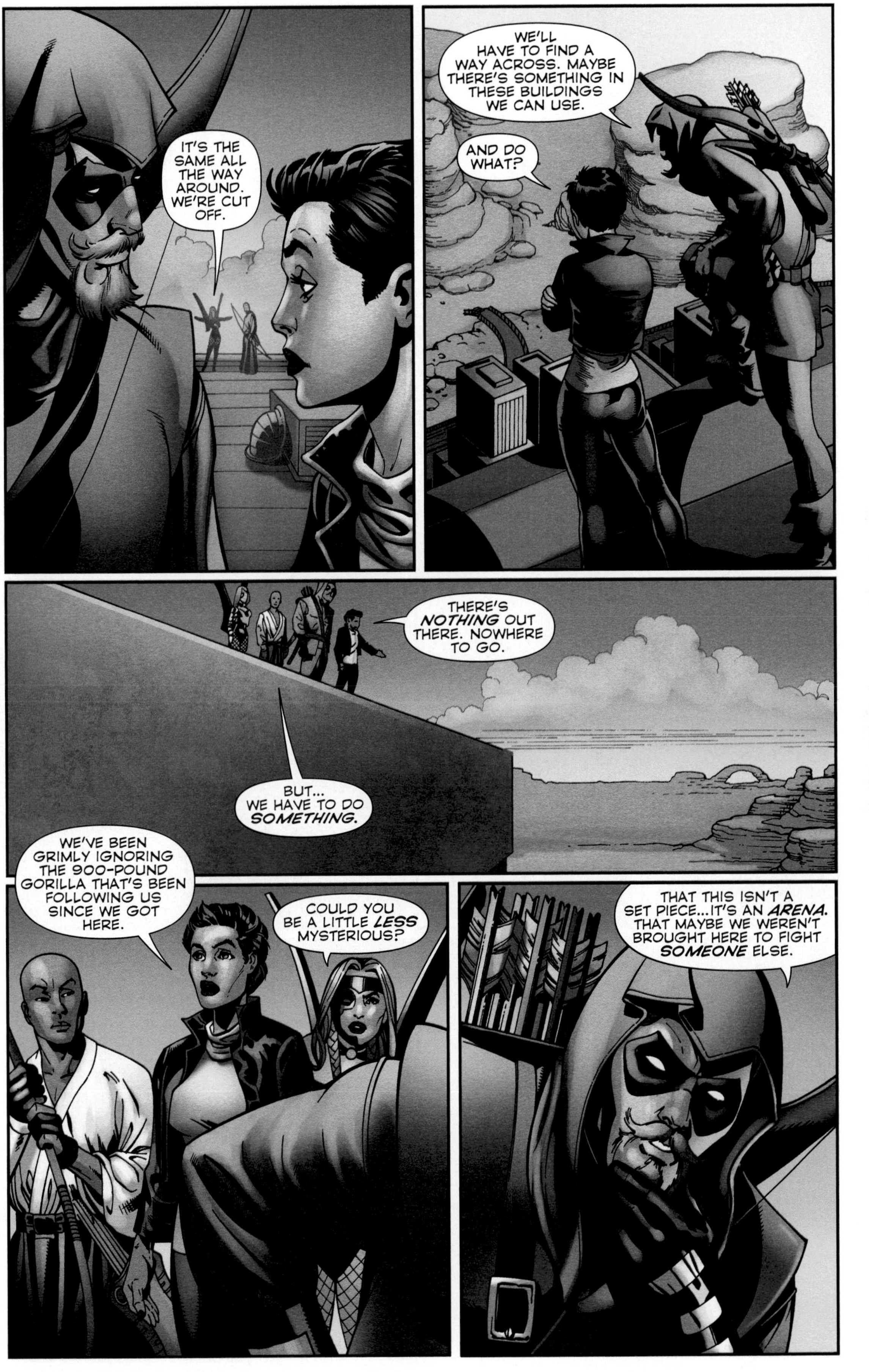
IT'S THE SAME ALL THE WAY AROUND. WE'RE CUT OFF.
WE'LL HAVE TO FIND A WAY ACROSS. MAYBE THERE'S SOMETHING IN THESE BUILDINGS WE CAN USE.
AND DO WHAT?
THERE'S *NOTHING* OUT THERE. NOWHERE TO GO.
BUT... WE HAVE TO DO *SOMETHING*.
WE'VE BEEN GRIMLY IGNORING THE 900-POUND GORILLA THAT'S BEEN FOLLOWING US SINCE WE GOT HERE.
COULD YOU BE A LITTLE *LESS* MYSTERIOUS?
THAT THIS ISN'T A SET PIECE...IT'S AN *ARENA*. THAT MAYBE WE WEREN'T BROUGHT HERE TO FIGHT *SOMEONE* ELSE.

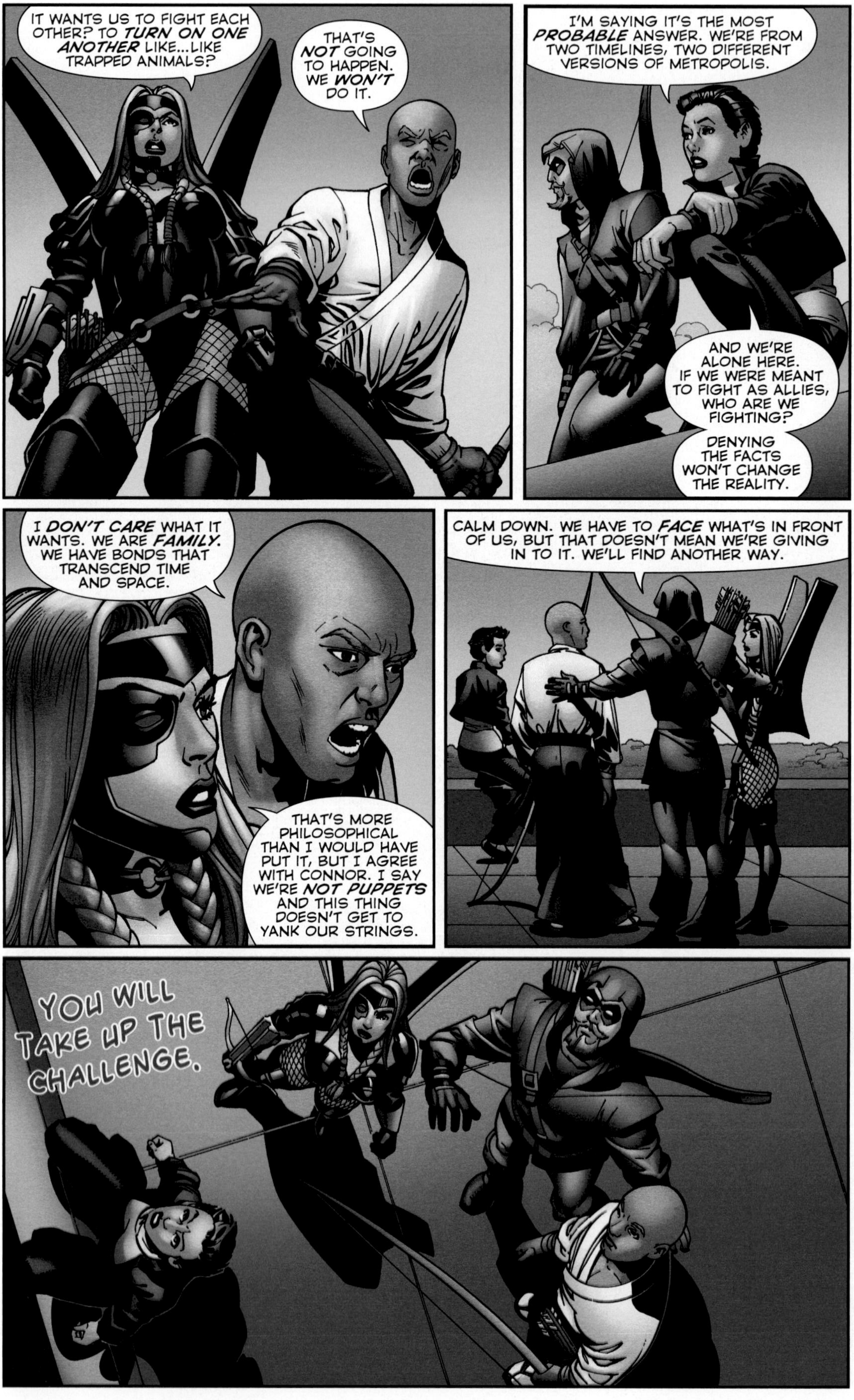

IT WANTS US TO FIGHT EACH OTHER? TO TURN ON ONE ANOTHER LIKE...LIKE TRAPPED ANIMALS?
THAT'S NOT GOING TO HAPPEN. WE WON'T DO IT.
I'M SAYING IT'S THE MOST PROBABLE ANSWER. WE'RE FROM TWO TIMELINES, TWO DIFFERENT VERSIONS OF METROPOLIS.
AND WE'RE ALONE HERE. IF WE WERE MEANT TO FIGHT AS ALLIES, WHO ARE WE FIGHTING?
DENYING THE FACTS WON'T CHANGE THE REALITY.
I DON'T CARE WHAT IT WANTS. WE ARE FAMILY. WE HAVE BONDS THAT TRANSCEND TIME AND SPACE.
THAT'S MORE PHILOSOPHICAL THAN I WOULD HAVE PUT IT, BUT I AGREE WITH CONNOR. I SAY WE'RE NOT PUPPETS AND THIS THING DOESN'T GET TO YANK OUR STRINGS.
CALM DOWN. WE HAVE TO FACE WHAT'S IN FRONT OF US, BUT THAT DOESN'T MEAN WE'RE GIVING IN TO IT. WE'LL FIND ANOTHER WAY.
YOU WILL TAKE UP THE CHALLENGE.

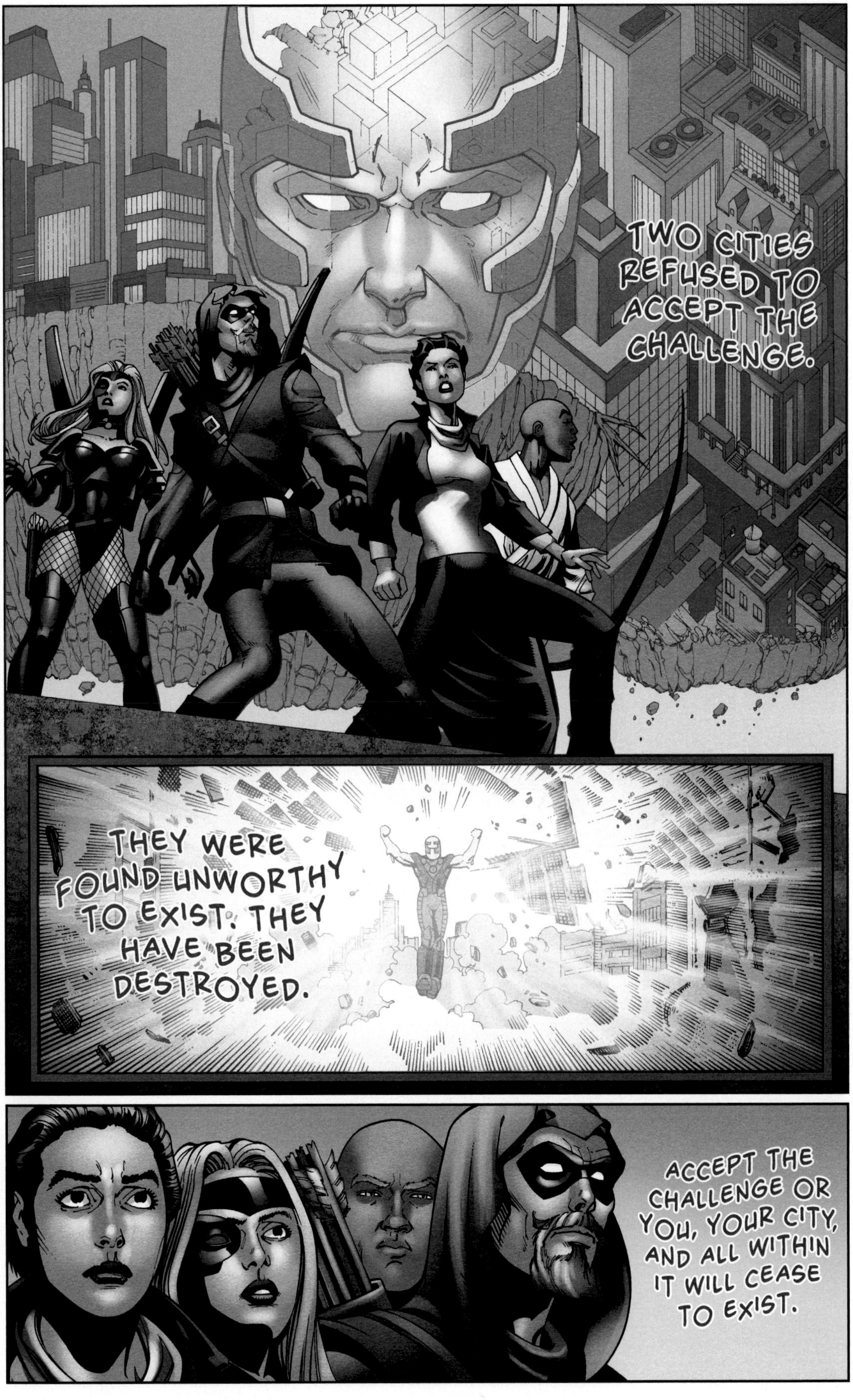
TWO CITIES REFUSED TO ACCEPT THE CHALLENGE.
THEY WERE FOUND UNWORTHY TO EXIST. THEY HAVE BEEN DESTROYED.
ACCEPT THE CHALLENGE OR YOU, YOUR CITY, AND ALL WITHIN IT WILL CEASE TO EXIST.

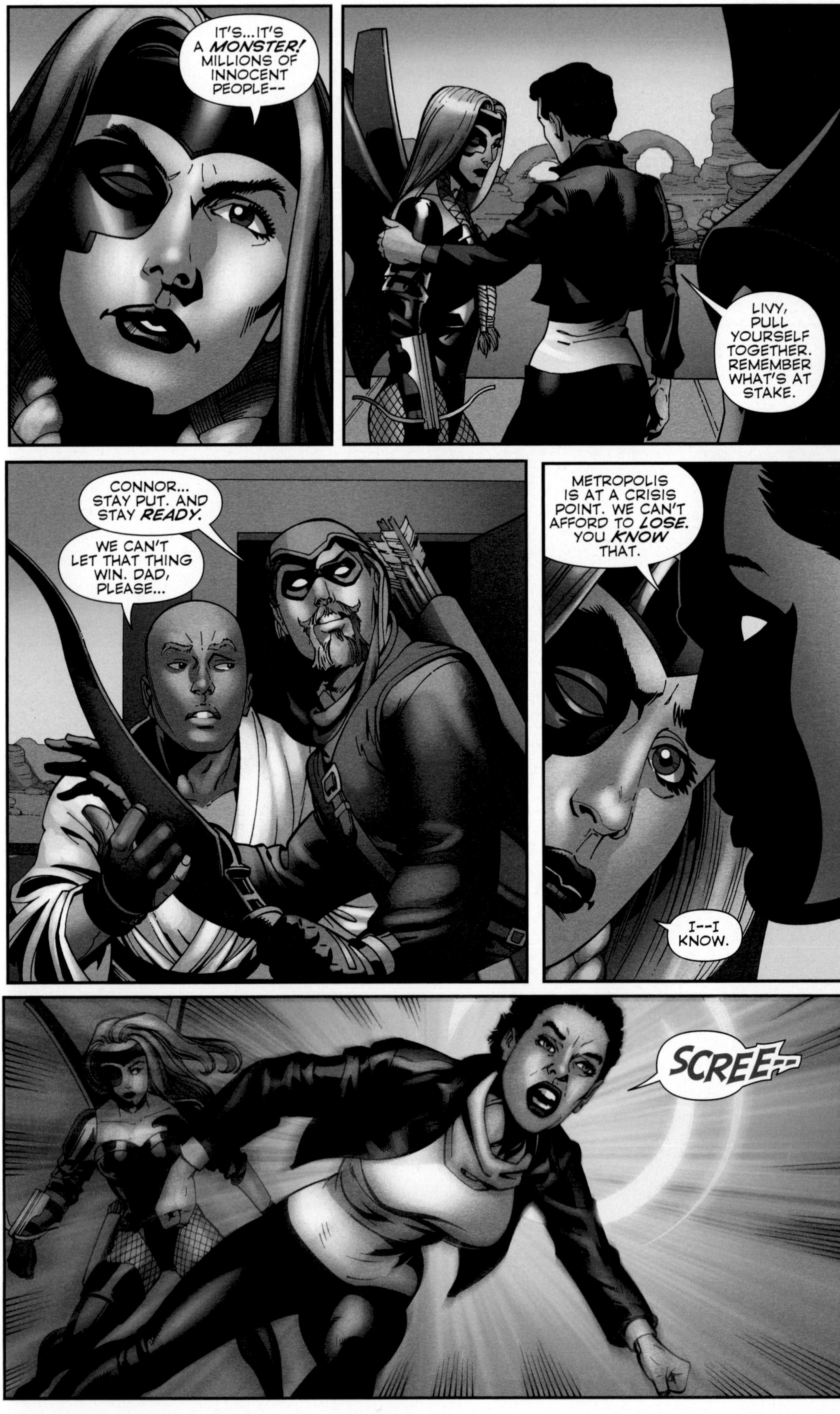
IT'S...IT'S A MONSTER! MILLIONS OF INNOCENT PEOPLE--
LIVY, PULL YOURSELF TOGETHER. REMEMBER WHAT'S AT STAKE.
CONNOR... STAY PUT. AND STAY READY.
WE CAN'T LET THAT THING WIN. DAD, PLEASE...
METROPOLIS IS AT A CRISIS POINT. WE CAN'T AFFORD TO LOSE. YOU KNOW THAT.
I--I KNOW.
SCREE--

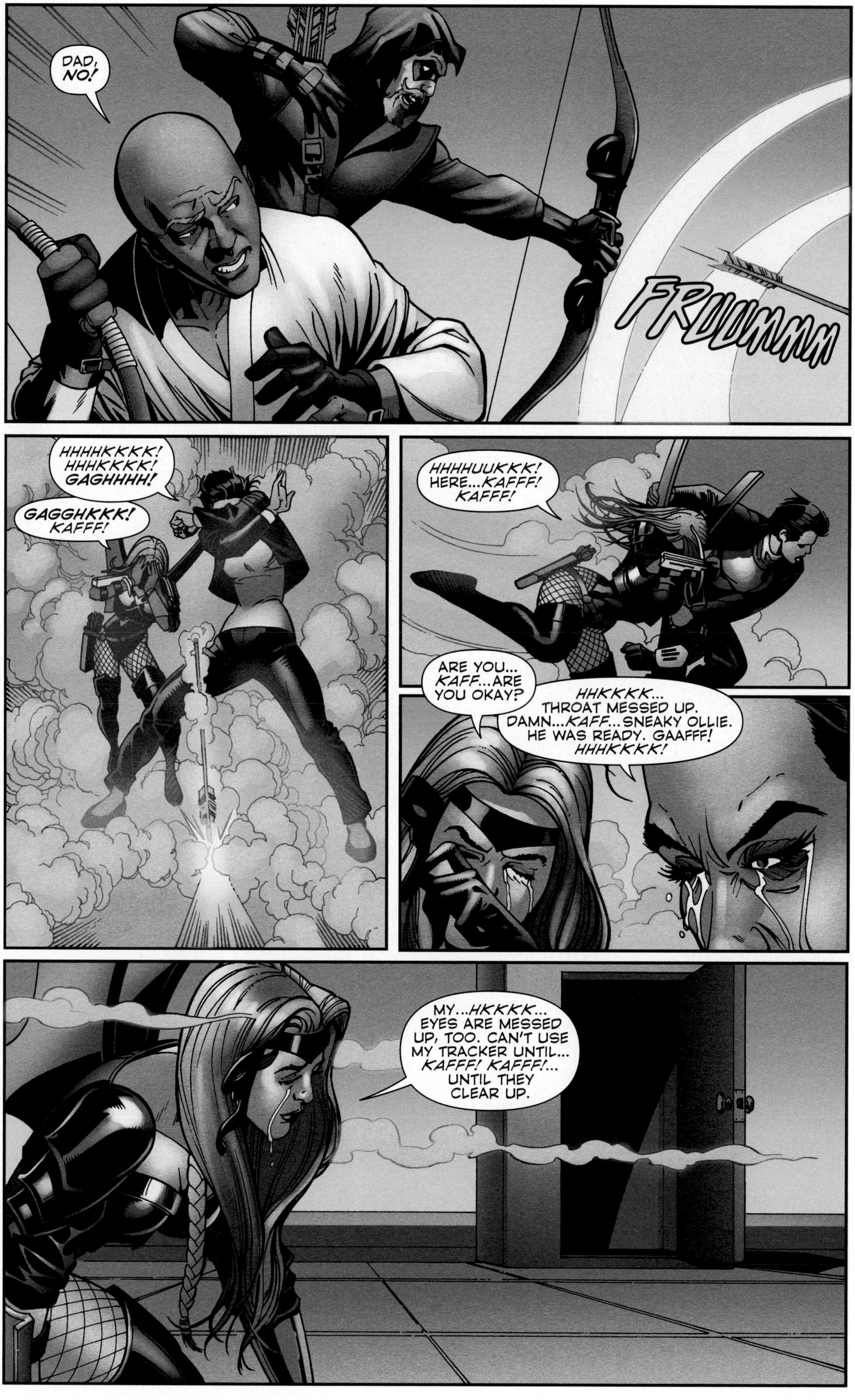
DAD, NO!
FRUUMMM
HHHHKKKK! HHHKKKK! GAGHHHH!
GAGGHKKK! KAFFF!
HHHHUUKKK! HERE...KAFFF! KAFFF!
ARE YOU... KAFF...ARE YOU OKAY?
HHKKKK... THROAT MESSED UP. DAMN...KAFF...SNEAKY OLLIE. HE WAS READY. GAAFFF! HHHKKKK!
MY...HKKKK... EYES ARE MESSED UP, TOO. CAN'T USE MY TRACKER UNTIL... KAFFF! KAFFF!... UNTIL THEY CLEAR UP.

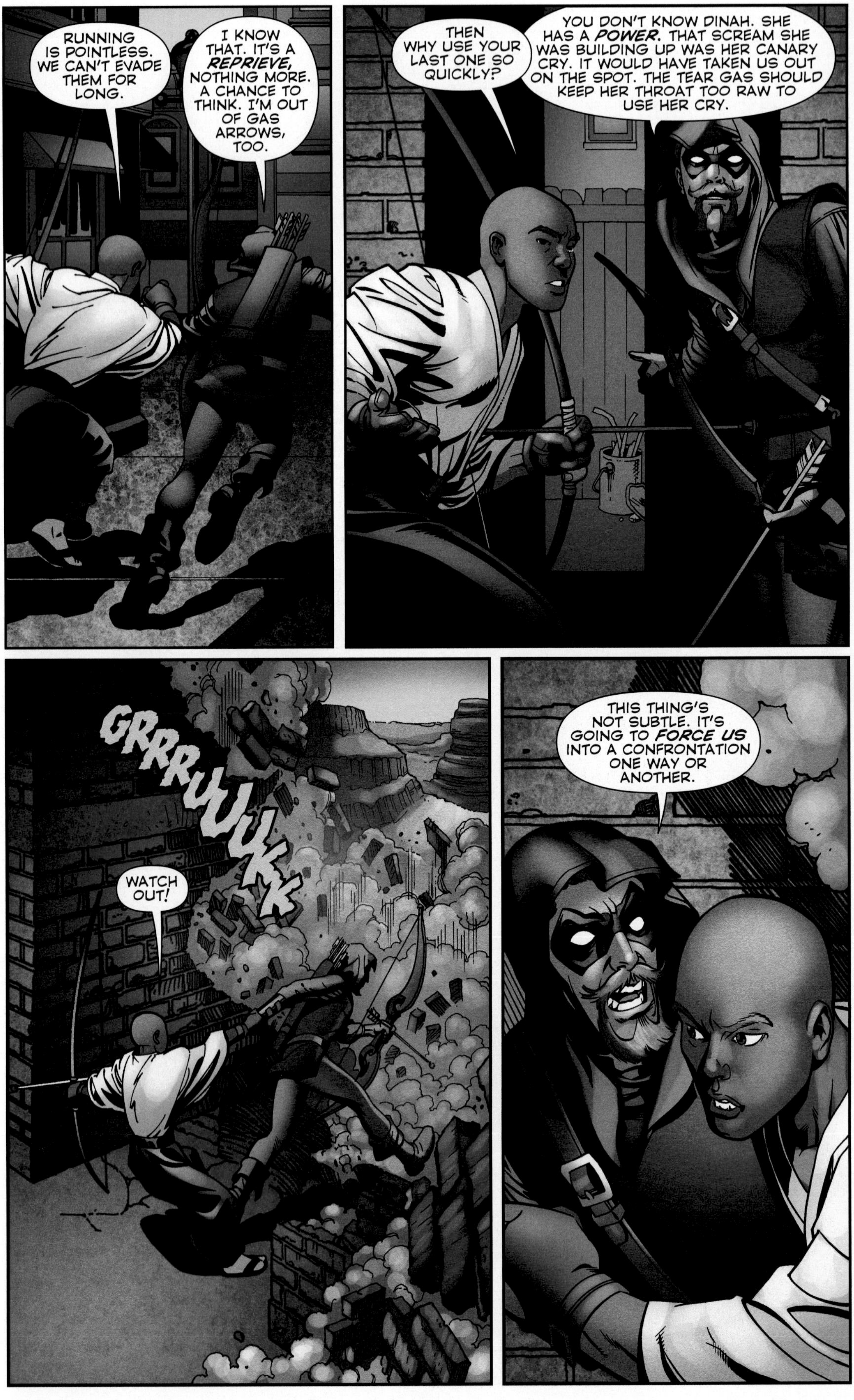
RUNNING IS POINTLESS. WE CAN'T EVADE THEM FOR LONG.
I KNOW THAT. IT'S A REPRIEVE, NOTHING MORE. A CHANCE TO THINK. I'M OUT OF GAS ARROWS, TOO.
THEN WHY USE YOUR LAST ONE SO QUICKLY?
YOU DON'T KNOW DINAH. SHE HAS A POWER. THAT SCREAM SHE WAS BUILDING UP WAS HER CANARY CRY. IT WOULD HAVE TAKEN US OUT ON THE SPOT. THE TEAR GAS SHOULD KEEP HER THROAT TOO RAW TO USE HER CRY.
GRRRUUUKK
WATCH OUT!
THIS THING'S NOT SUBTLE. IT'S GOING TO FORCE US INTO A CONFRONTATION ONE WAY OR ANOTHER.

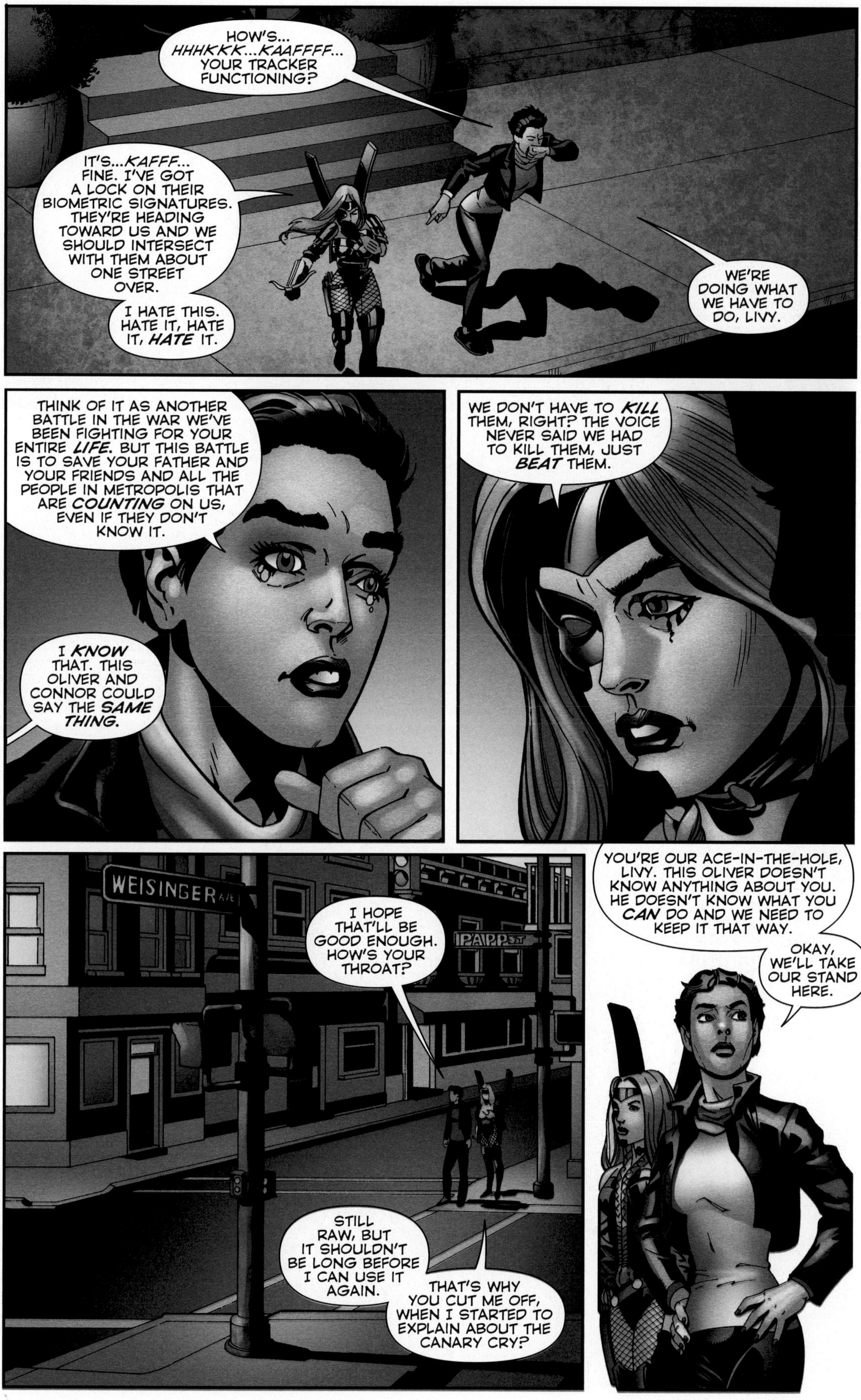
HOW'S... *HHHKKK...KAAFFFF...* YOUR TRACKER FUNCTIONING?
IT'S...*KAFFF...* FINE. I'VE GOT A LOCK ON THEIR BIOMETRIC SIGNATURES. THEY'RE HEADING TOWARD US AND WE SHOULD INTERSECT WITH THEM ABOUT ONE STREET OVER.
I HATE THIS. HATE IT, HATE IT, ***HATE*** IT.
WE'RE DOING WHAT WE HAVE TO DO, LIVY.
THINK OF IT AS ANOTHER BATTLE IN THE WAR WE'VE BEEN FIGHTING FOR YOUR ENTIRE ***LIFE.*** BUT THIS BATTLE IS TO SAVE YOUR FATHER AND YOUR FRIENDS AND ALL THE PEOPLE IN METROPOLIS THAT ARE ***COUNTING*** ON US, EVEN IF THEY DON'T KNOW IT.
I ***KNOW*** THAT. THIS OLIVER AND CONNOR COULD SAY THE ***SAME THING.***
WE DON'T HAVE TO ***KILL*** THEM, RIGHT? THE VOICE NEVER SAID WE HAD TO KILL THEM, JUST ***BEAT*** THEM.
WEISINGER
PAPP ST
I HOPE THAT'LL BE GOOD ENOUGH. HOW'S YOUR THROAT?
STILL RAW, BUT IT SHOULDN'T BE LONG BEFORE I CAN USE IT AGAIN.
THAT'S WHY YOU CUT ME OFF, WHEN I STARTED TO EXPLAIN ABOUT THE CANARY CRY?
YOU'RE OUR ACE-IN-THE-HOLE, LIVY. THIS OLIVER DOESN'T KNOW ANYTHING ABOUT YOU. HE DOESN'T KNOW WHAT YOU ***CAN*** DO AND WE NEED TO KEEP IT THAT WAY.
OKAY, WE'LL TAKE OUR STAND HERE.

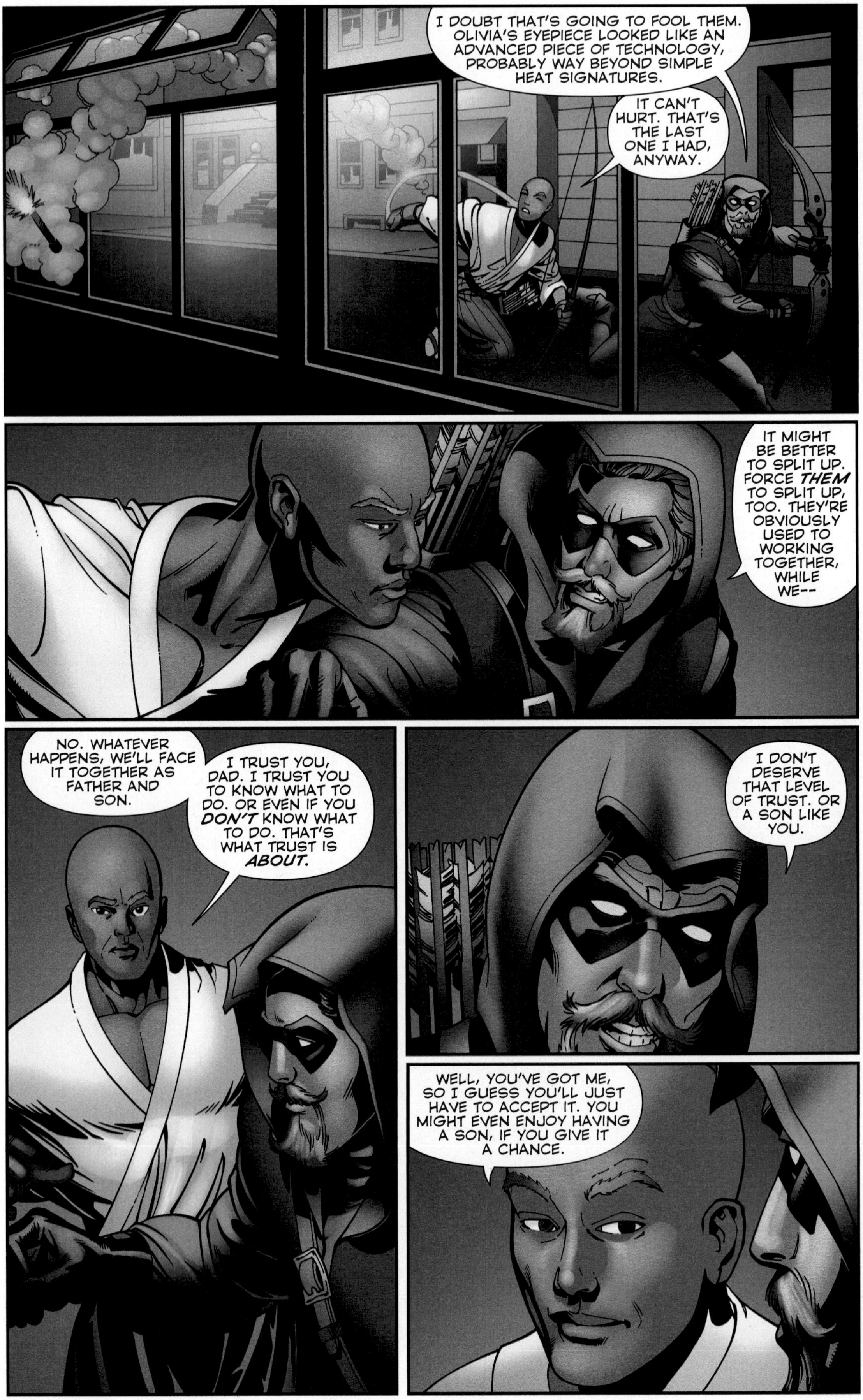
I DOUBT THAT'S GOING TO FOOL THEM. OLIVIA'S EYEPIECE LOOKED LIKE AN ADVANCED PIECE OF TECHNOLOGY, PROBABLY WAY BEYOND SIMPLE HEAT SIGNATURES.
IT CAN'T HURT. THAT'S THE LAST ONE I HAD, ANYWAY.
IT MIGHT BE BETTER TO SPLIT UP. FORCE *THEM* TO SPLIT UP, TOO. THEY'RE OBVIOUSLY USED TO WORKING TOGETHER, WHILE WE--
NO. WHATEVER HAPPENS, WE'LL FACE IT TOGETHER AS FATHER AND SON.
I TRUST YOU, DAD. I TRUST YOU TO KNOW WHAT TO DO. OR EVEN IF YOU *DON'T* KNOW WHAT TO DO. THAT'S WHAT TRUST IS *ABOUT.*
I DON'T DESERVE THAT LEVEL OF TRUST. OR A SON LIKE YOU.
WELL, YOU'VE GOT ME, SO I GUESS YOU'LL JUST HAVE TO ACCEPT IT. YOU MIGHT EVEN ENJOY HAVING A SON, IF YOU GIVE IT A CHANCE.

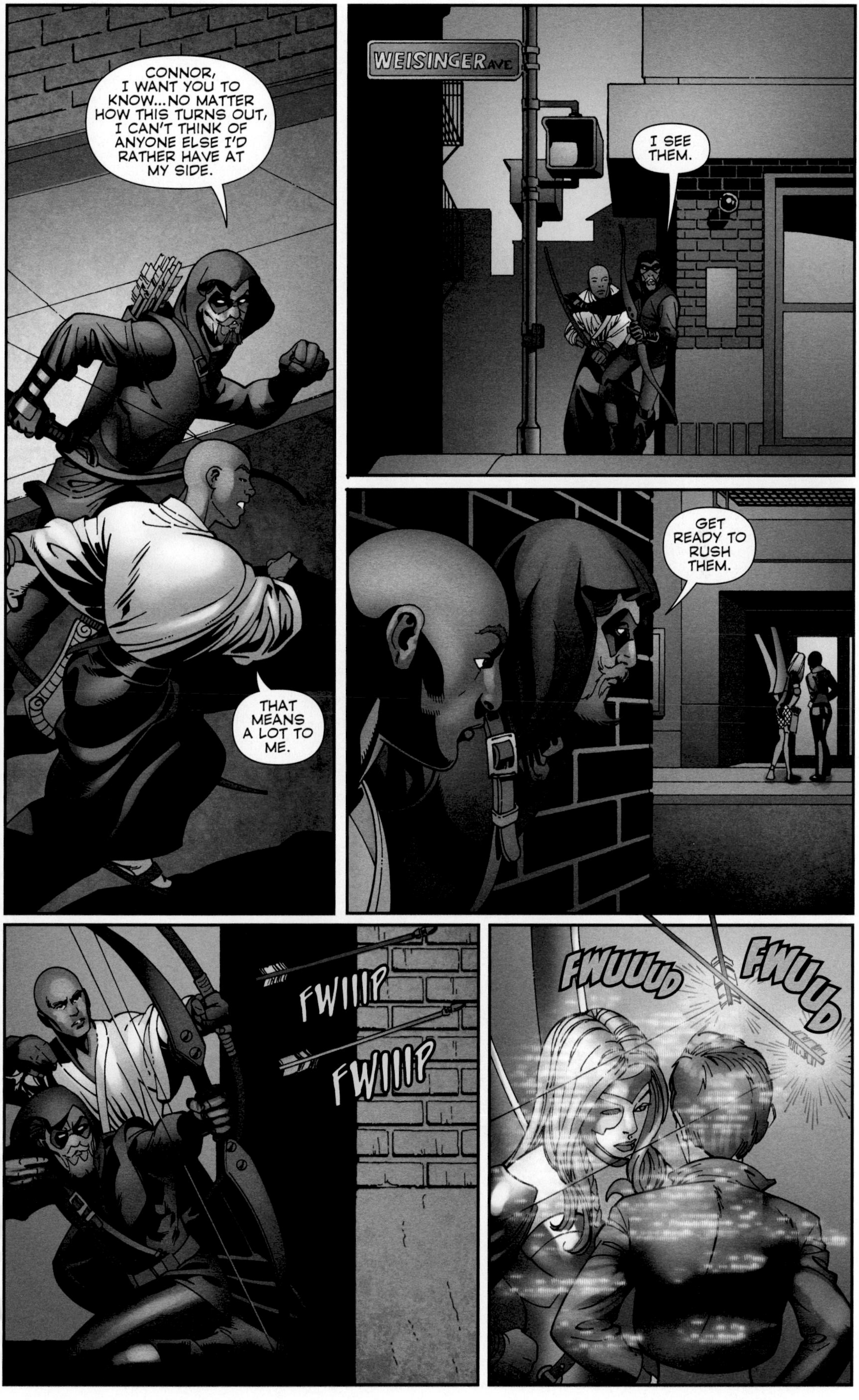
CONNOR, I WANT YOU TO KNOW...NO MATTER HOW THIS TURNS OUT, I CAN'T THINK OF ANYONE ELSE I'D RATHER HAVE AT MY SIDE.
THAT MEANS A LOT TO ME.
WEISINGER AVE
I SEE THEM.
GET READY TO RUSH THEM.
FWIIIP
FWIIIP
FWUUUD
FWUUD

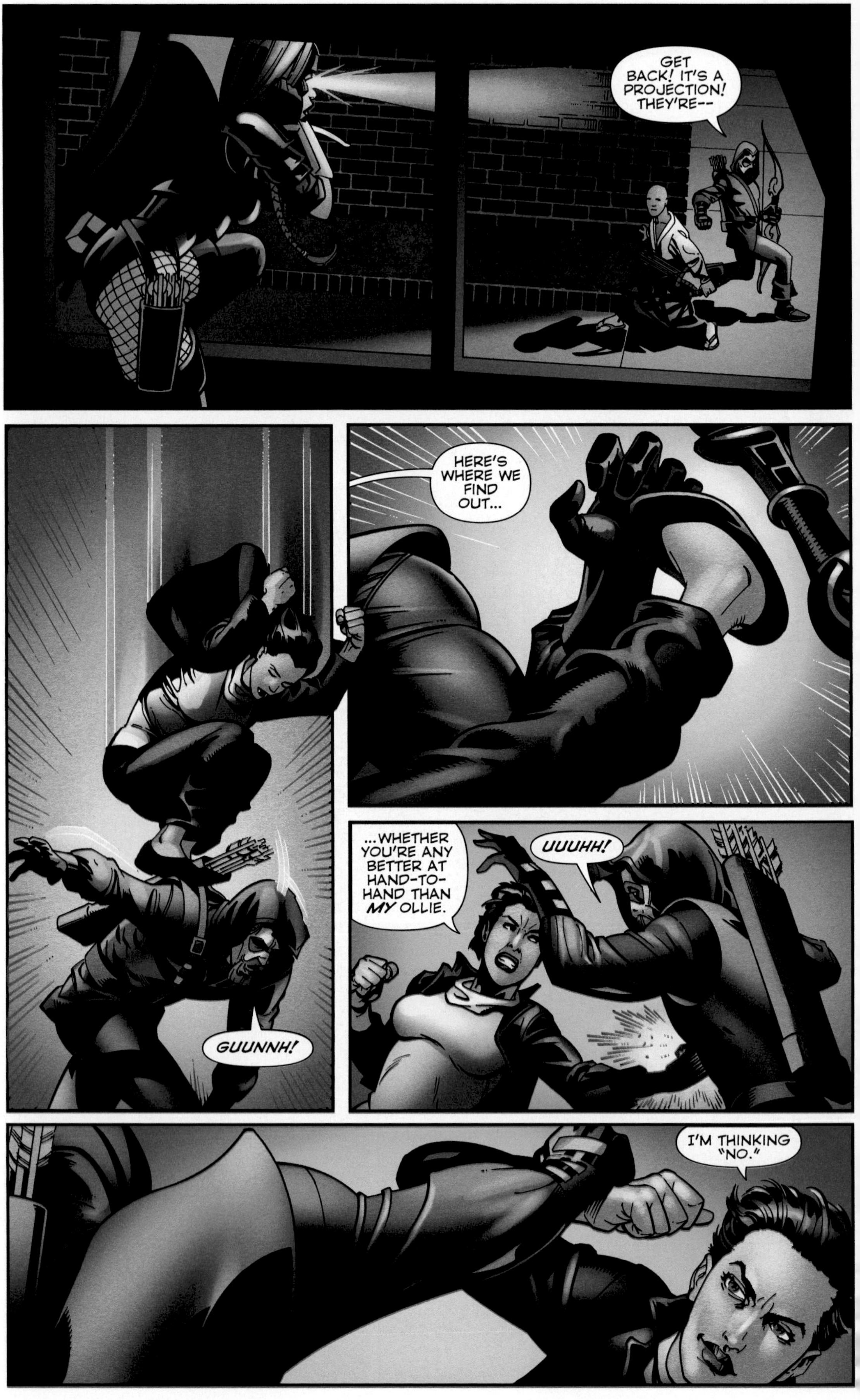
GET BACK! IT'S A PROJECTION! THEY'RE--
HERE'S WHERE WE FIND OUT...
GUUNNH!
...WHETHER YOU'RE ANY BETTER AT HAND-TO-HAND THAN MY OLLIE.
UUUHH!
I'M THINKING "NO."

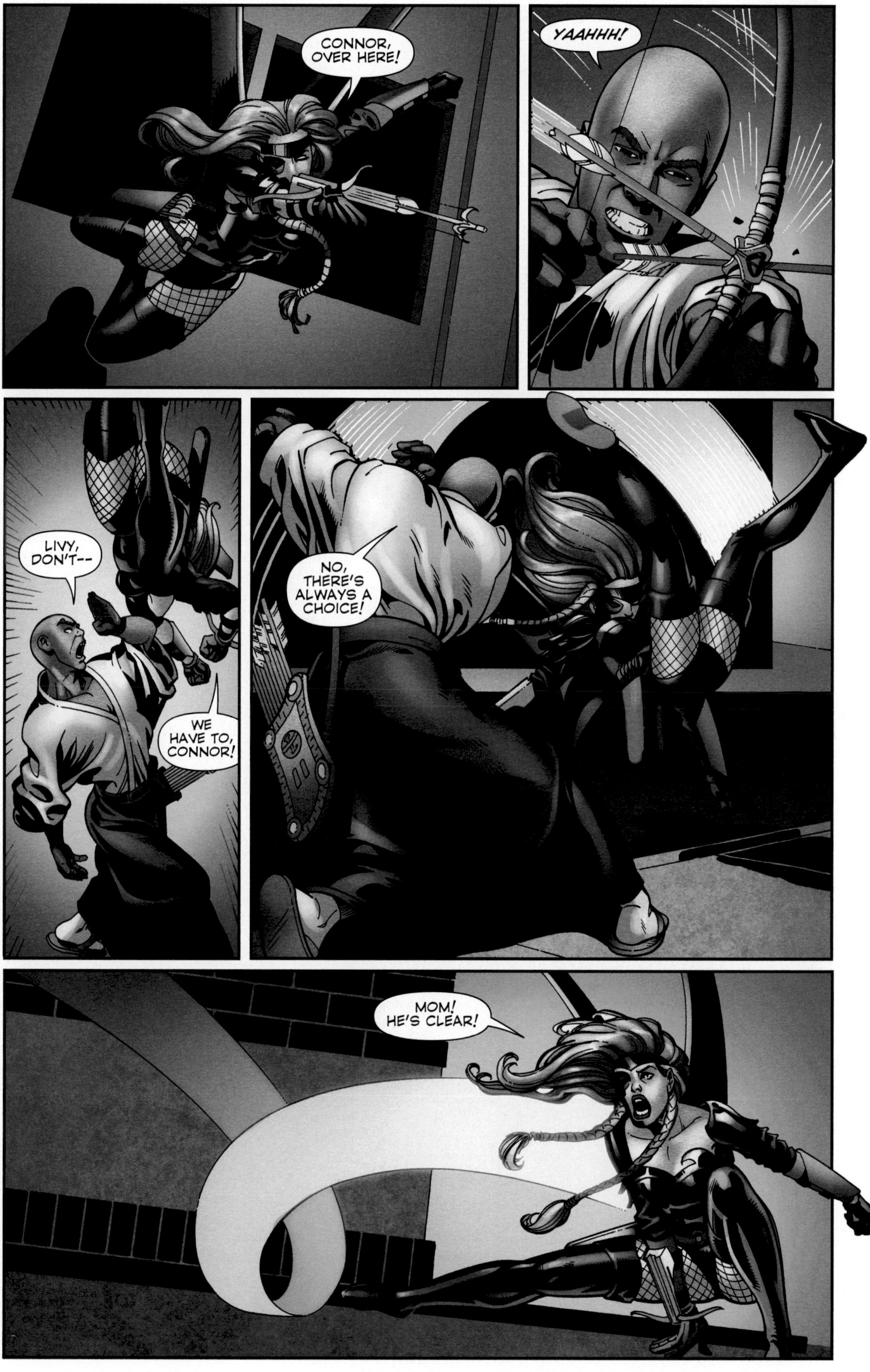
CONNOR, OVER HERE!
YAAHHH!
LIVY, DON'T--
WE HAVE TO, CONNOR!
NO, THERE'S ALWAYS A CHOICE!
MOM! HE'S CLEAR!

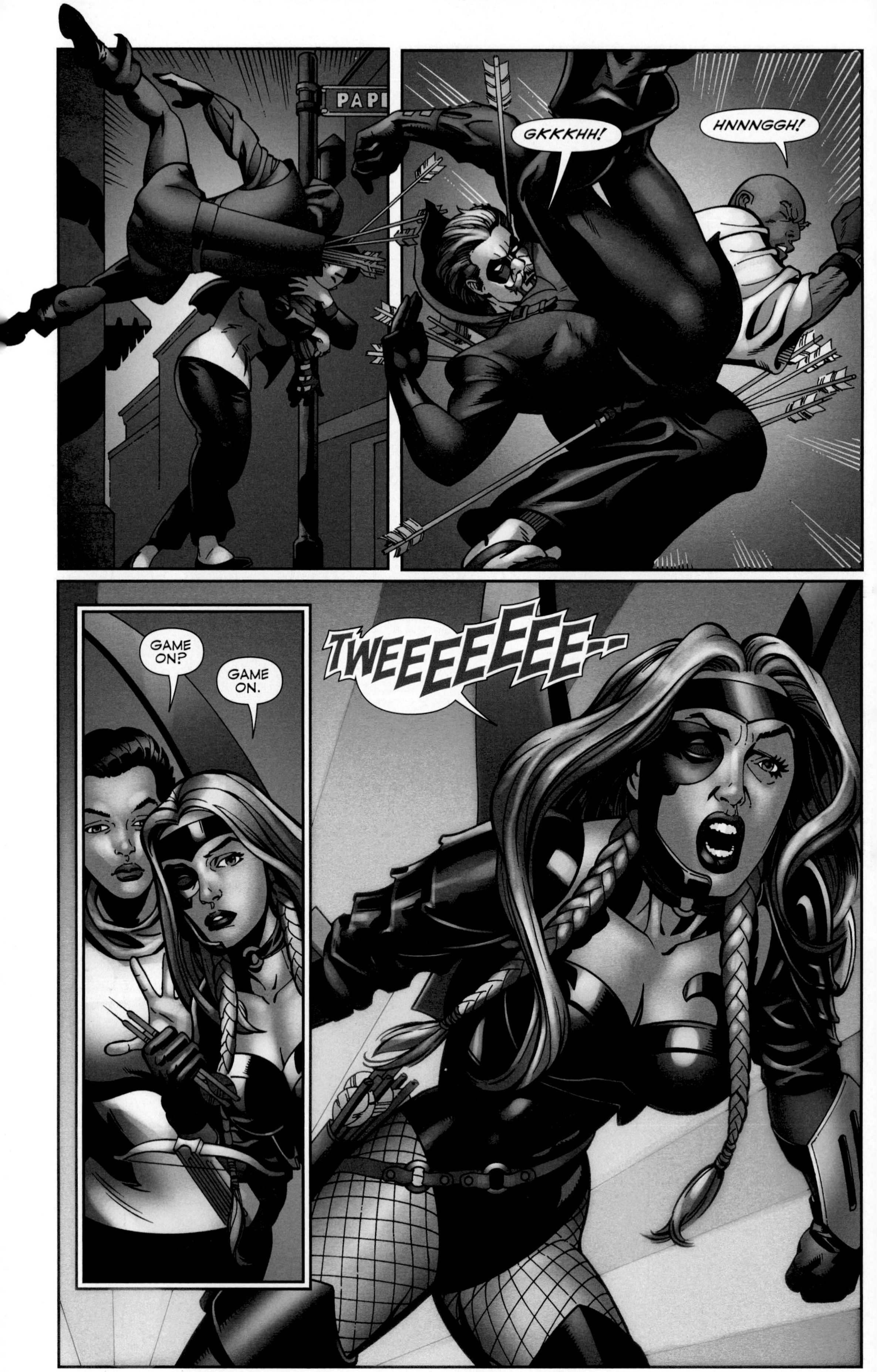
PAPI
GKKKHH!
HNNNGGH!
GAME ON?
GAME ON.
TWEEEEEEE--

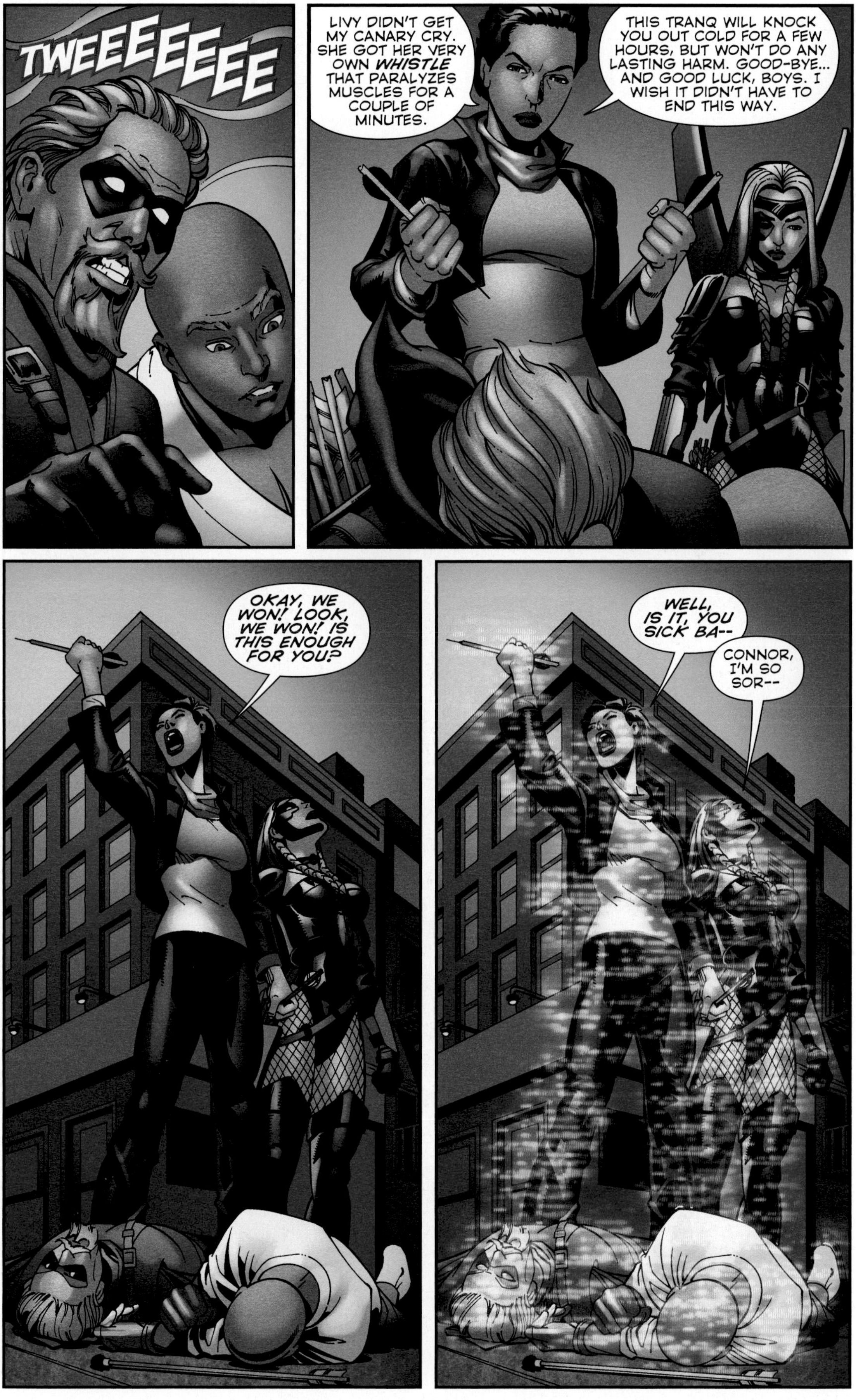
TWEEEEEEE
LIVY DIDN'T GET MY CANARY CRY. SHE GOT HER VERY OWN *WHISTLE* THAT PARALYZES MUSCLES FOR A COUPLE OF MINUTES.
THIS TRANQ WILL KNOCK YOU OUT COLD FOR A FEW HOURS, BUT WON'T DO ANY LASTING HARM. GOOD-BYE... AND GOOD LUCK, BOYS. I WISH IT DIDN'T HAVE TO END THIS WAY.
OKAY, WE WON! LOOK, WE WON! IS THIS ENOUGH FOR YOU?
WELL, IS IT, YOU SICK BA--
CONNOR, I'M SO SOR--

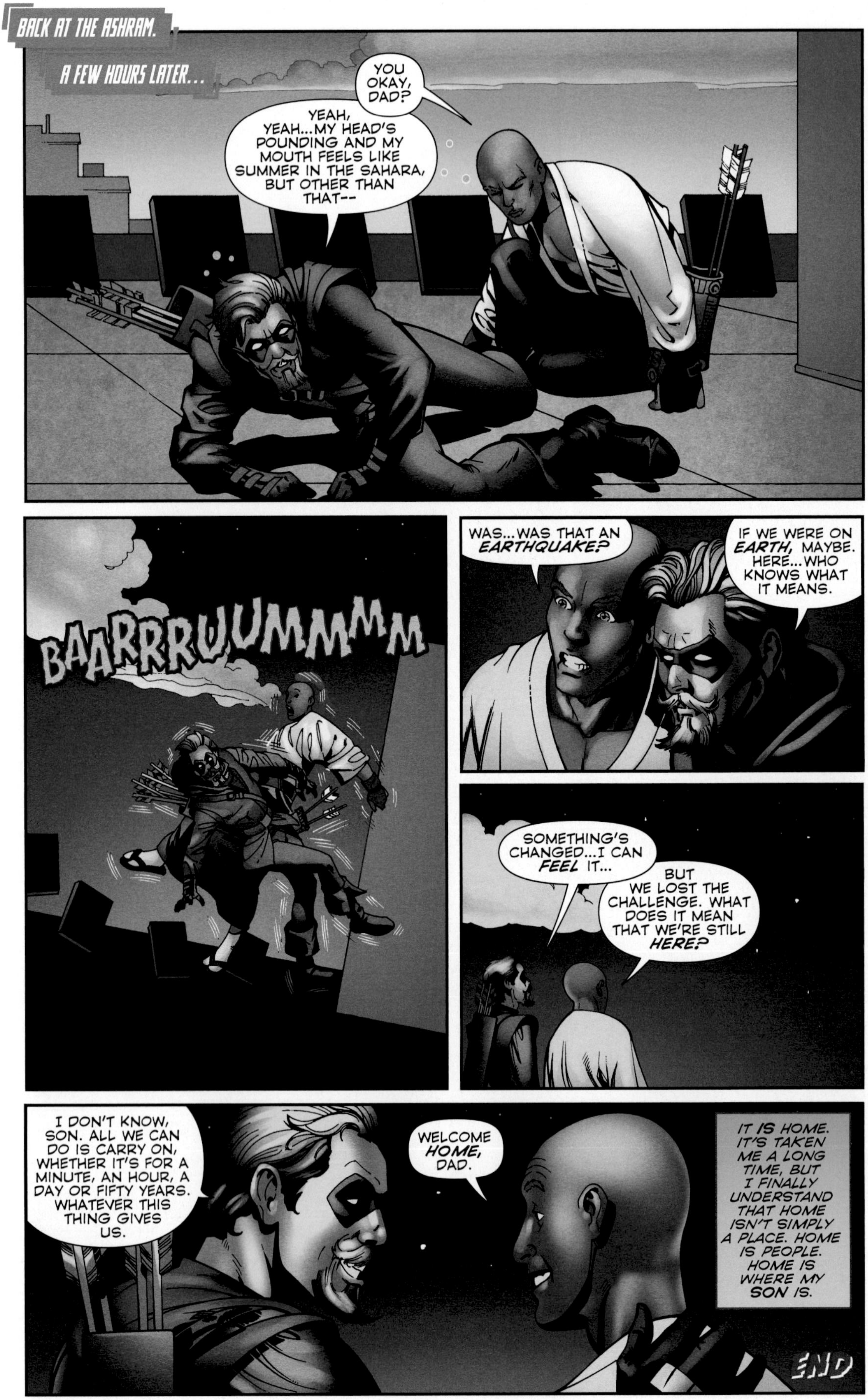
BACK AT THE ASHRAM.
A FEW HOURS LATER...
YOU OKAY, DAD?
YEAH, YEAH...MY HEAD'S POUNDING AND MY MOUTH FEELS LIKE SUMMER IN THE SAHARA, BUT OTHER THAN THAT--
BAARRRUUMMMMM
WAS...WAS THAT AN EARTHQUAKE?
IF WE WERE ON EARTH, MAYBE. HERE...WHO KNOWS WHAT IT MEANS.
SOMETHING'S CHANGED...I CAN FEEL IT...
BUT WE LOST THE CHALLENGE. WHAT DOES IT MEAN THAT WE'RE STILL HERE?
I DON'T KNOW, SON. ALL WE CAN DO IS CARRY ON, WHETHER IT'S FOR A MINUTE, AN HOUR, A DAY OR FIFTY YEARS. WHATEVER THIS THING GIVES US.
WELCOME HOME, DAD.
IT IS HOME. IT'S TAKEN ME A LONG TIME, BUT I FINALLY UNDERSTAND THAT HOME ISN'T SIMPLY A PLACE. HOME IS PEOPLE. HOME IS WHERE MY SON IS.
END

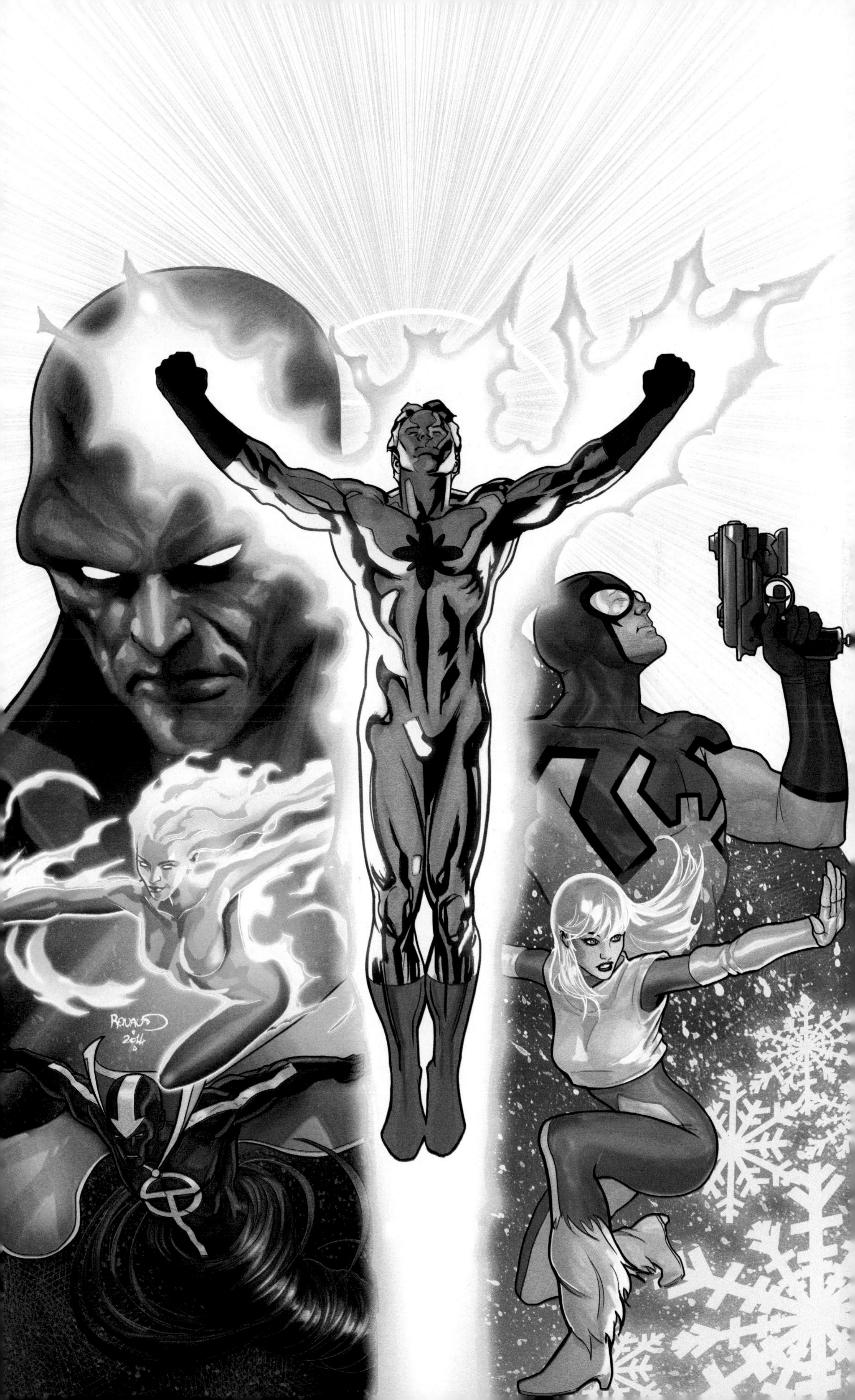

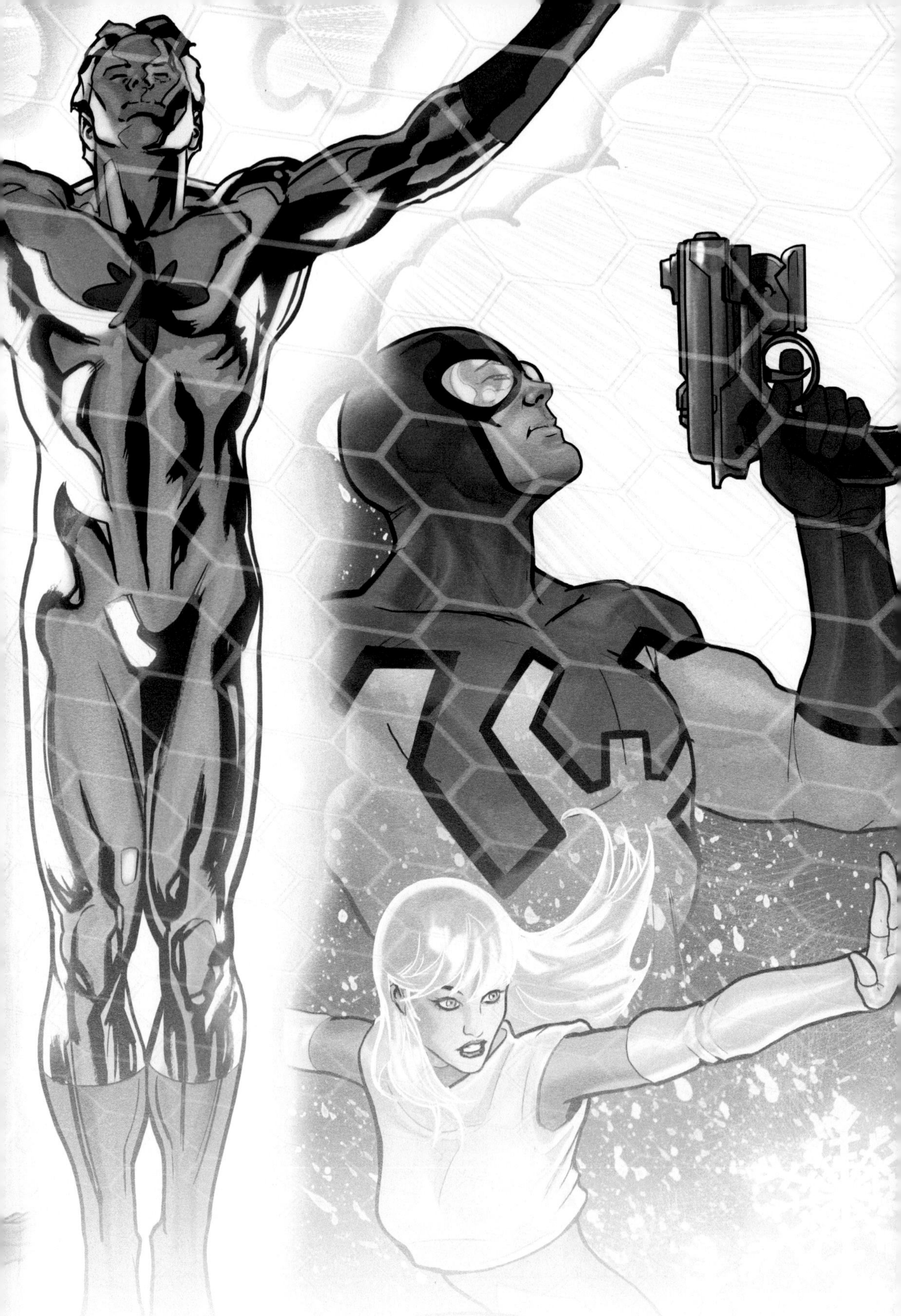

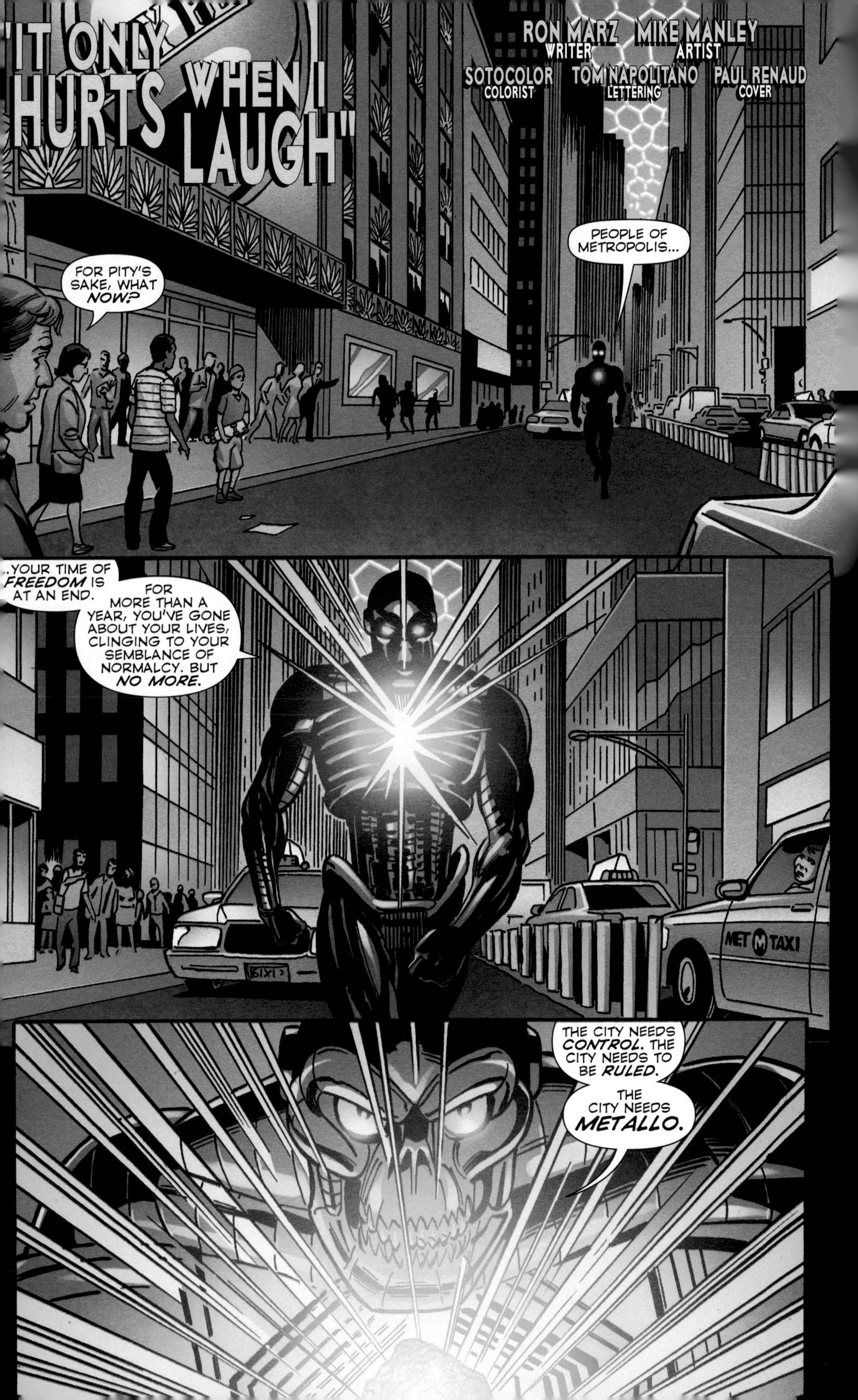
"IT ONLY HURTS WHEN I LAUGH"
RON MARZ WRITER
MIKE MANLEY ARTIST
SOTOCOLOR COLORIST
TOM NAPOLITANO LETTERING
PAUL RENAUD COVER
FOR PITY'S SAKE, WHAT NOW?
PEOPLE OF METROPOLIS...
...YOUR TIME OF FREEDOM IS AT AN END.
FOR MORE THAN A YEAR, YOU'VE GONE ABOUT YOUR LIVES, CLINGING TO YOUR SEMBLANCE OF NORMALCY. BUT NO MORE.
MET TAXI
THE CITY NEEDS CONTROL. THE CITY NEEDS TO BE RULED.
THE CITY NEEDS METALLO.

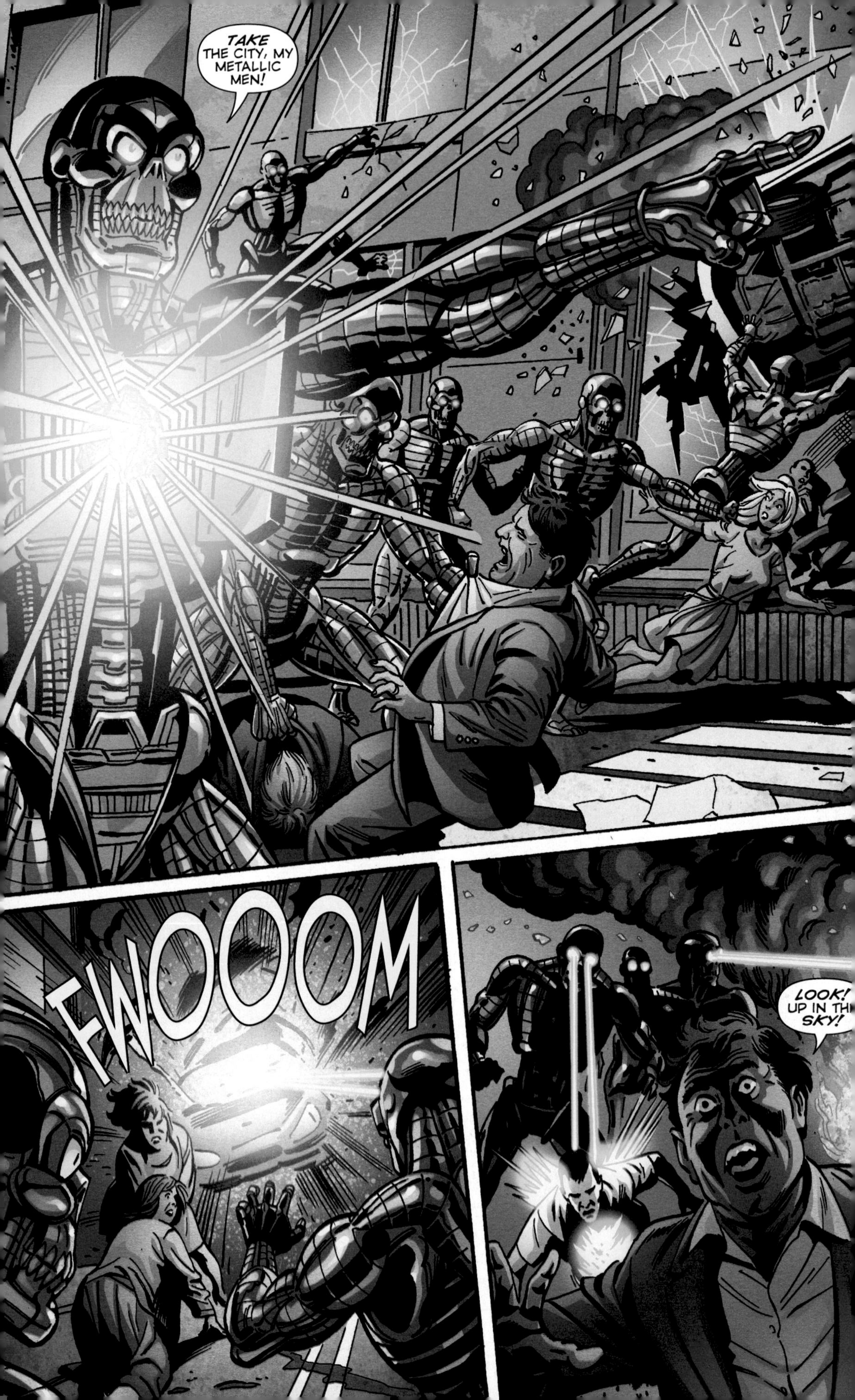
TAKE THE CITY, MY METALLIC MEN!
FWOOOM
LOOK! UP IN TH SKY!

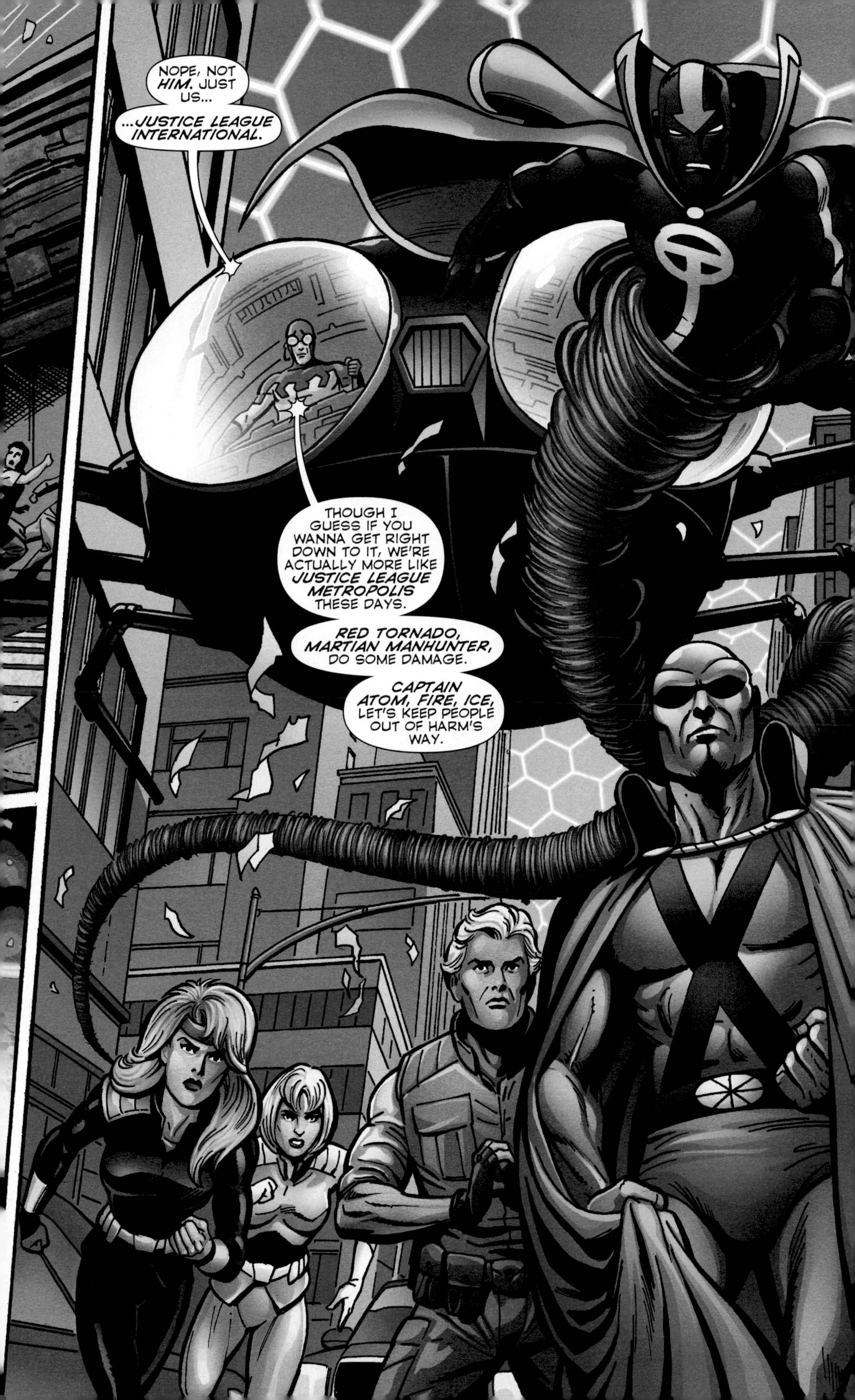
NOPE, NOT *HIM*. JUST US...
...*JUSTICE LEAGUE INTERNATIONAL*.
THOUGH I GUESS IF YOU WANNA GET RIGHT DOWN TO IT, WE'RE ACTUALLY MORE LIKE *JUSTICE LEAGUE METROPOLIS* THESE DAYS.
RED TORNADO, MARTIAN MANHUNTER, DO SOME DAMAGE.
CAPTAIN ATOM, FIRE, ICE, LET'S KEEP PEOPLE OUT OF HARM'S WAY.

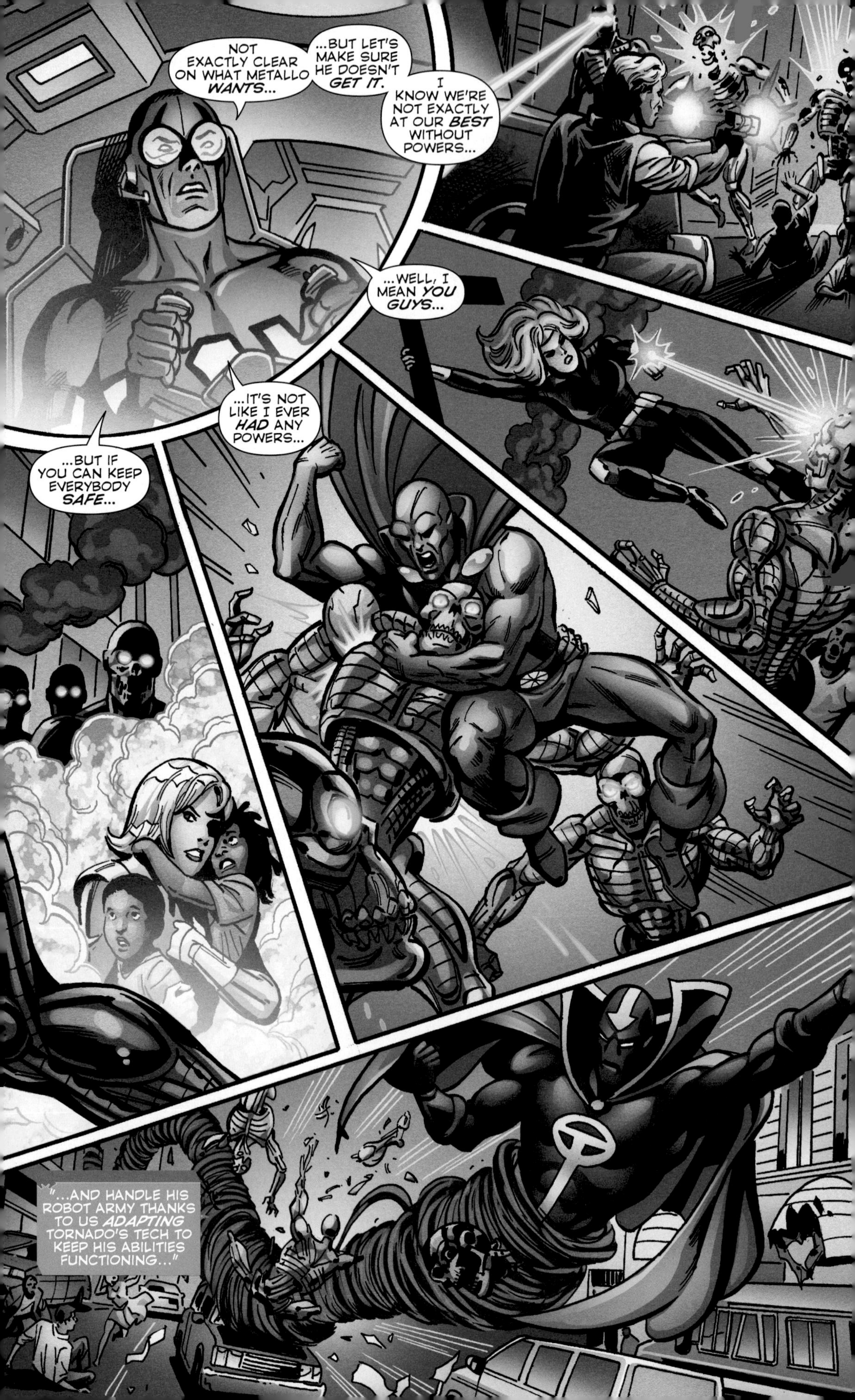
NOT EXACTLY CLEAR ON WHAT METALLO WANTS...
...BUT LET'S MAKE SURE HE DOESN'T GET IT.
I KNOW WE'RE NOT EXACTLY AT OUR BEST WITHOUT POWERS...
...WELL, I MEAN YOU GUYS...
...IT'S NOT LIKE I EVER HAD ANY POWERS...
...BUT IF YOU CAN KEEP EVERYBODY SAFE...
"...AND HANDLE HIS ROBOT ARMY THANKS TO US ADAPTING TORNADO'S TECH TO KEEP HIS ABILITIES FUNCTIONING..."

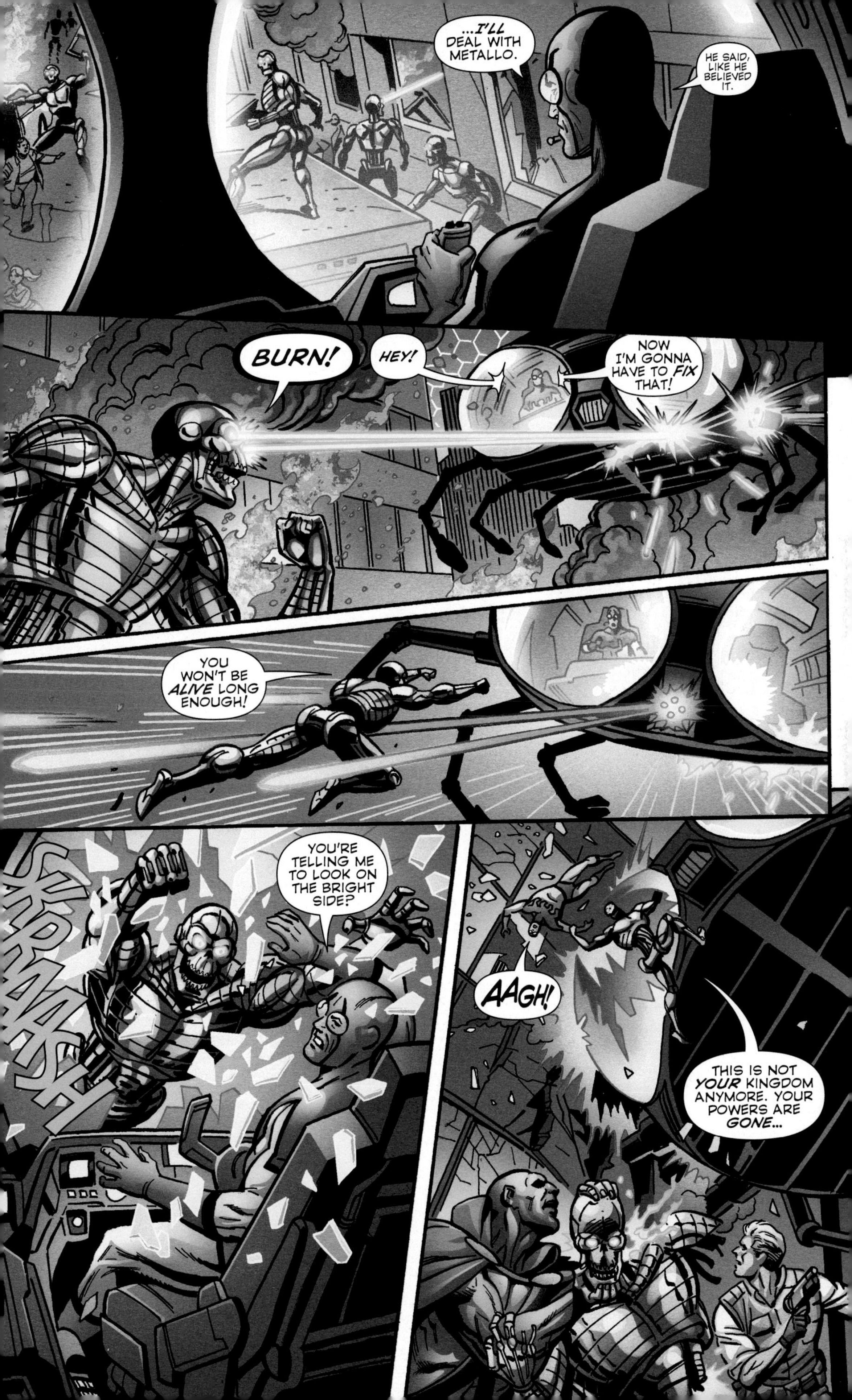

...I'LL DEAL WITH METALLO.
HE SAID, LIKE HE BELIEVED IT.
BURN!
HEY!
NOW I'M GONNA HAVE TO FIX THAT!
YOU WON'T BE ALIVE LONG ENOUGH!
SKRASH
YOU'RE TELLING ME TO LOOK ON THE BRIGHT SIDE?
AAGH!
THIS IS NOT YOUR KINGDOM ANYMORE. YOUR POWERS ARE GONE...

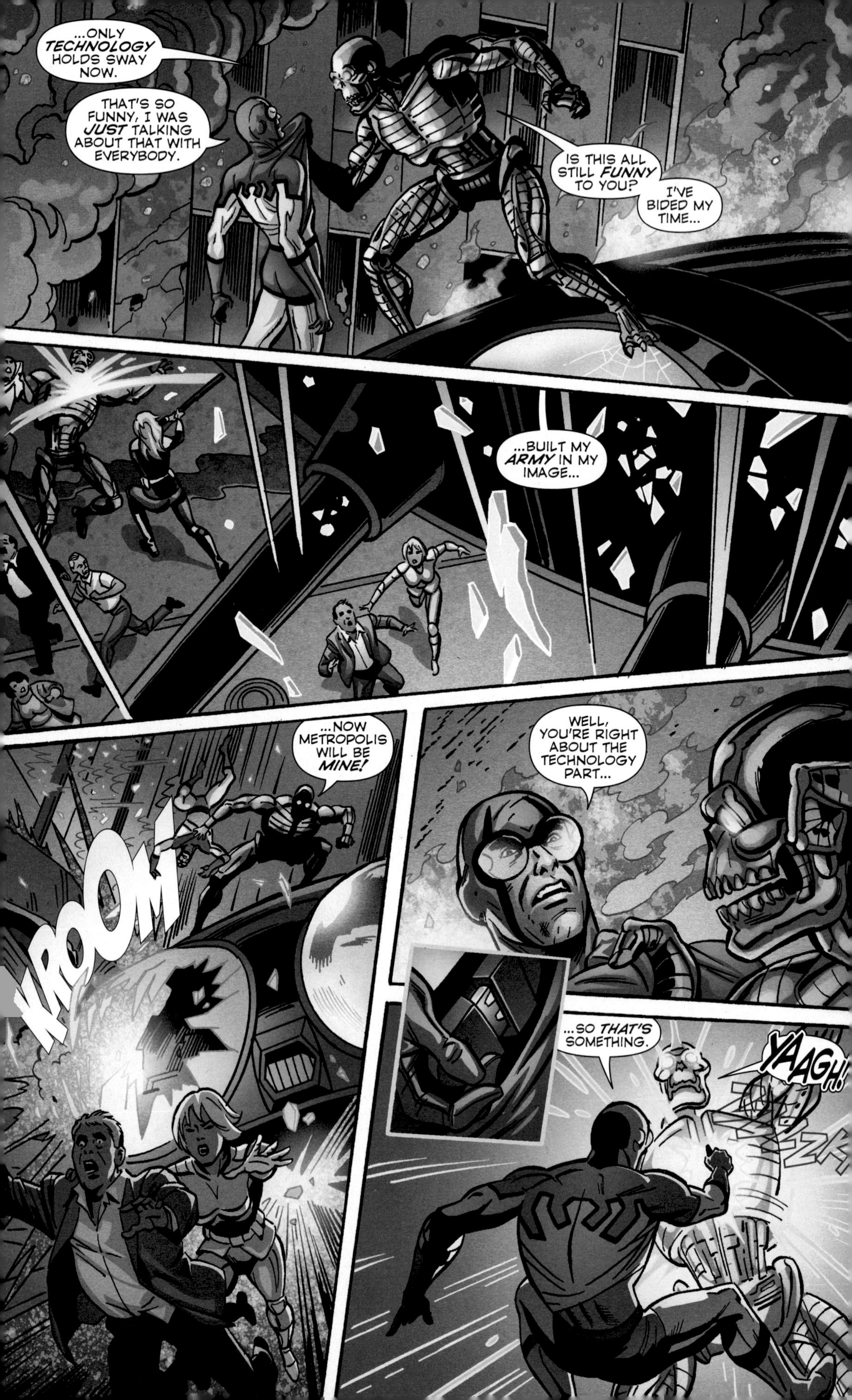
...ONLY TECHNOLOGY HOLDS SWAY NOW.
THAT'S SO FUNNY, I WAS JUST TALKING ABOUT THAT WITH EVERYBODY.
IS THIS ALL STILL FUNNY TO YOU?
I'VE BIDED MY TIME...
...BUILT MY ARMY IN MY IMAGE...
...NOW METROPOLIS WILL BE MINE!
KROOM
WELL, YOU'RE RIGHT ABOUT THE TECHNOLOGY PART...
...SO THAT'S SOMETHING.
YAAGH!

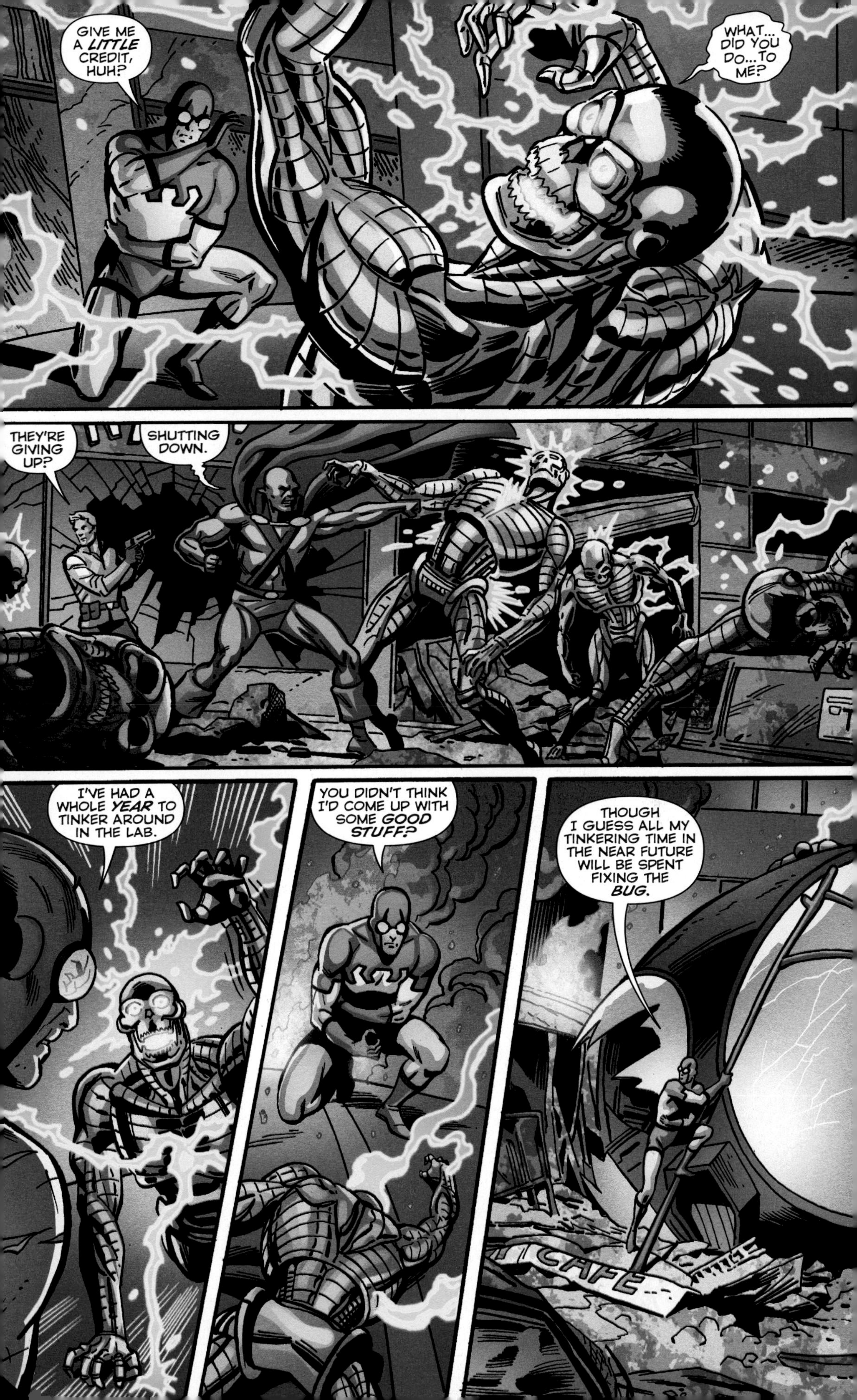
GIVE ME A *LITTLE* CREDIT, HUH?
WHAT... DID YOU DO... TO ME?
THEY'RE GIVING UP?
SHUTTING DOWN.
I'VE HAD A WHOLE *YEAR* TO TINKER AROUND IN THE LAB.
YOU DIDN'T THINK I'D COME UP WITH SOME *GOOD STUFF?*
THOUGH I GUESS ALL MY TINKERING TIME IN THE NEAR FUTURE WILL BE SPENT FIXING THE *BUG*.
CAFE

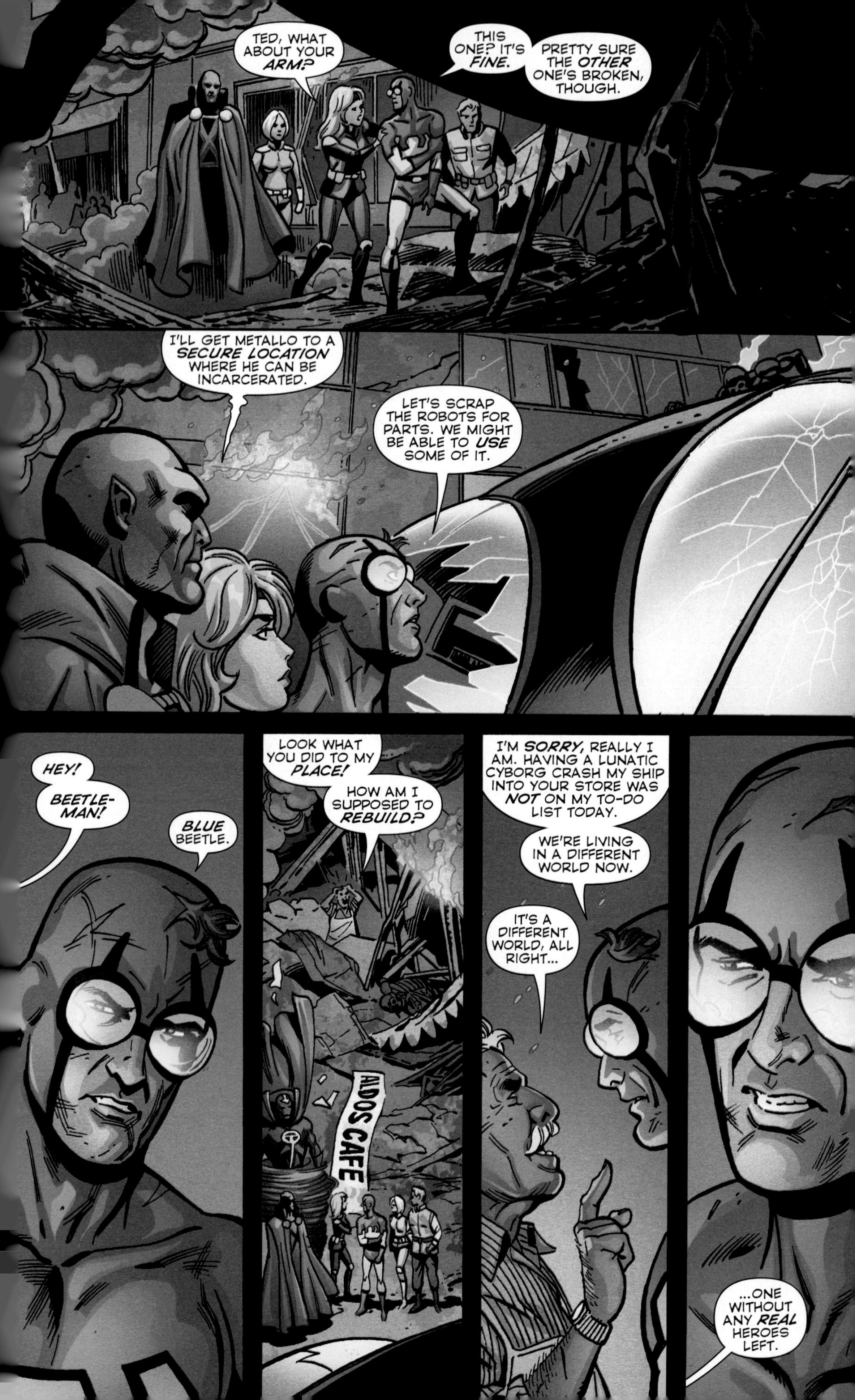
TED, WHAT ABOUT YOUR ARM?
THIS ONE? IT'S FINE.
PRETTY SURE THE OTHER ONE'S BROKEN, THOUGH.
I'LL GET METALLO TO A SECURE LOCATION WHERE HE CAN BE INCARCERATED.
LET'S SCRAP THE ROBOTS FOR PARTS. WE MIGHT BE ABLE TO USE SOME OF IT.
HEY!
BEETLE-MAN!
BLUE BEETLE.
LOOK WHAT YOU DID TO MY PLACE!
HOW AM I SUPPOSED TO REBUILD?
ALDOS CAFE
I'M SORRY, REALLY I AM. HAVING A LUNATIC CYBORG CRASH MY SHIP INTO YOUR STORE WAS NOT ON MY TO-DO LIST TODAY.
WE'RE LIVING IN A DIFFERENT WORLD NOW.
IT'S A DIFFERENT WORLD, ALL RIGHT...
...ONE WITHOUT ANY REAL HEROES LEFT.

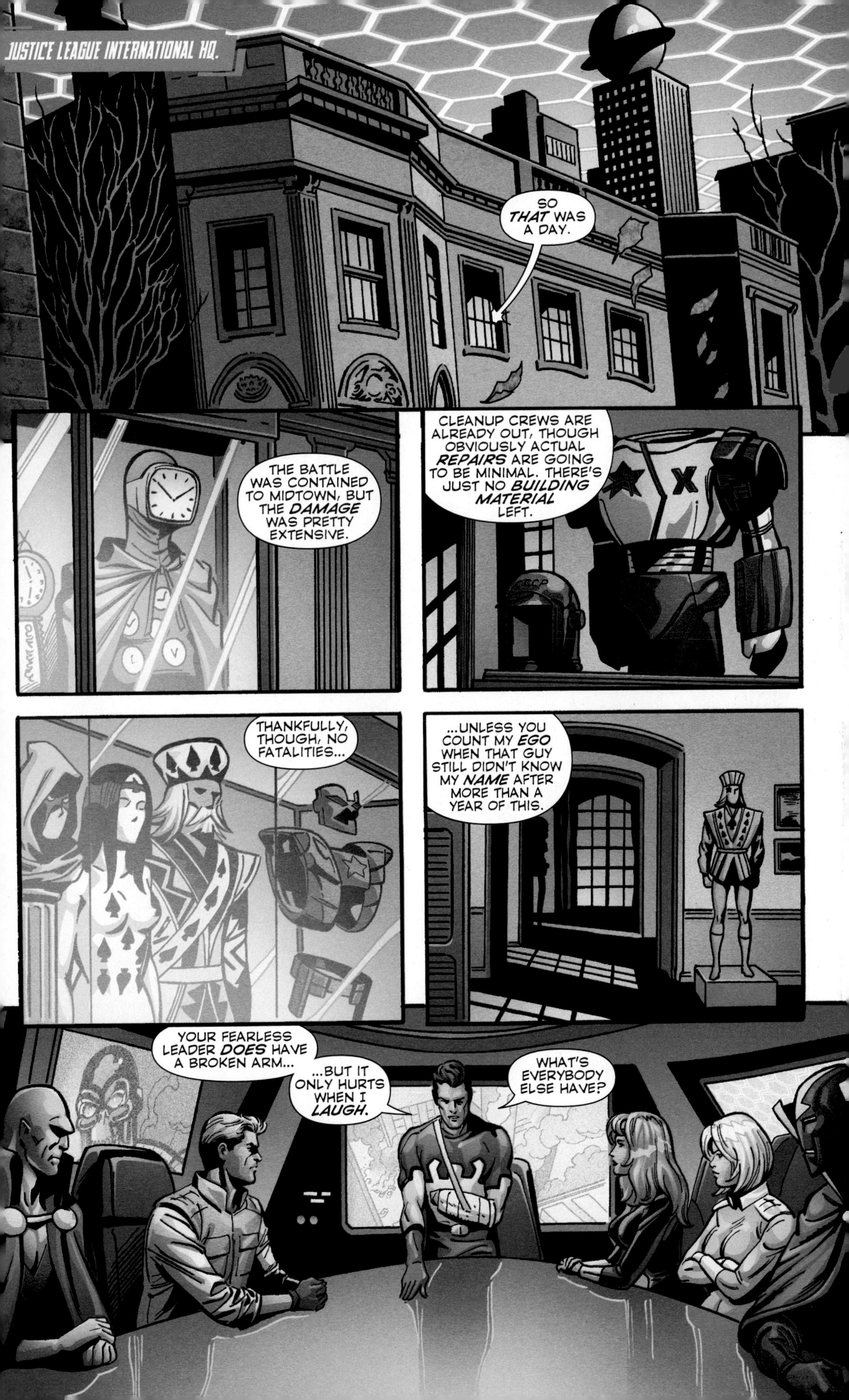
JUSTICE LEAGUE INTERNATIONAL HQ.
SO THAT WAS A DAY.
THE BATTLE WAS CONTAINED TO MIDTOWN, BUT THE DAMAGE WAS PRETTY EXTENSIVE.
CLEANUP CREWS ARE ALREADY OUT, THOUGH OBVIOUSLY ACTUAL REPAIRS ARE GOING TO BE MINIMAL. THERE'S JUST NO BUILDING MATERIAL LEFT.
THANKFULLY, THOUGH, NO FATALITIES...
...UNLESS YOU COUNT MY EGO WHEN THAT GUY STILL DIDN'T KNOW MY NAME AFTER MORE THAN A YEAR OF THIS.
YOUR FEARLESS LEADER DOES HAVE A BROKEN ARM...
...BUT IT ONLY HURTS WHEN I LAUGH.
WHAT'S EVERYBODY ELSE HAVE?

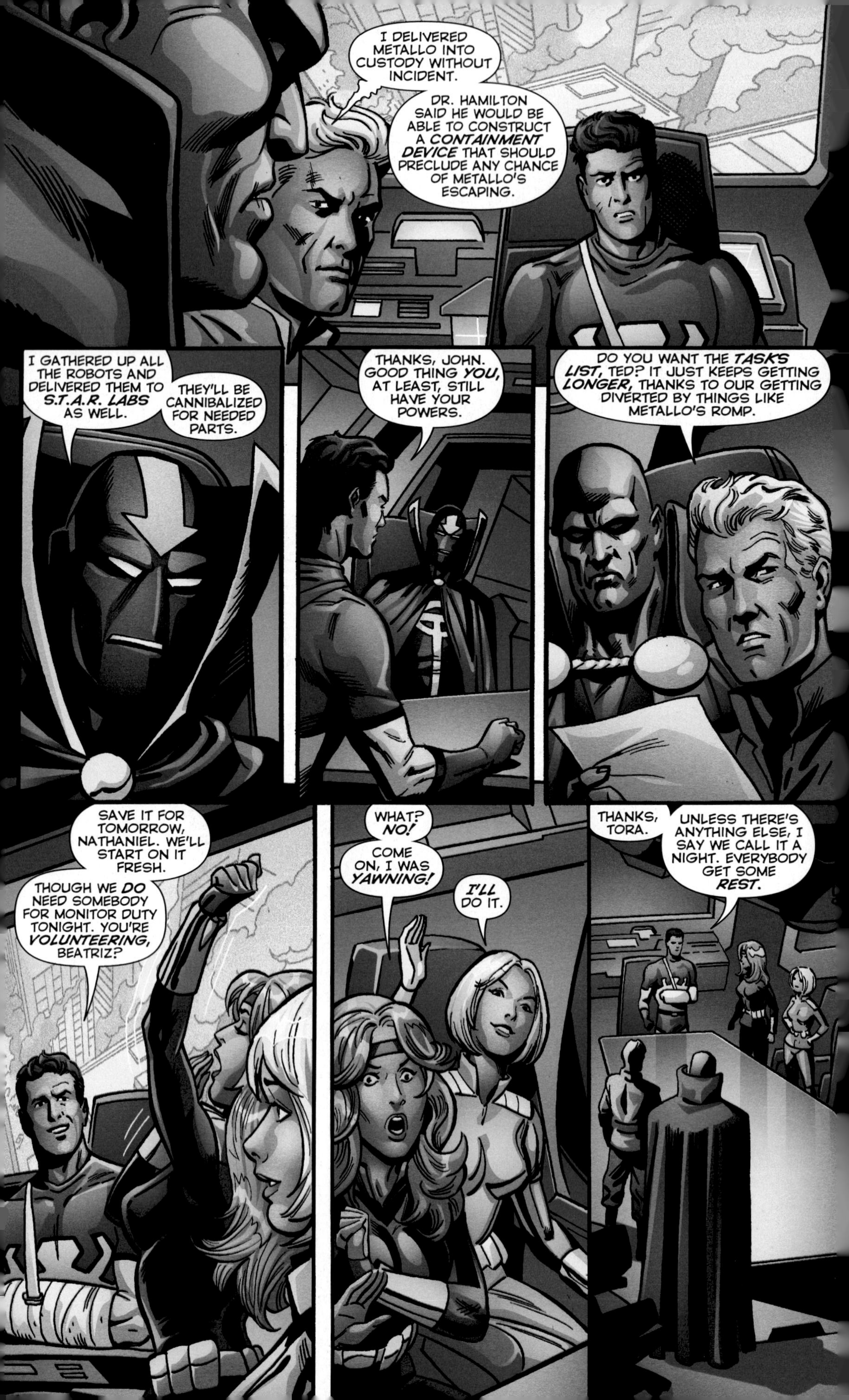
I DELIVERED METALLO INTO CUSTODY WITHOUT INCIDENT.
DR. HAMILTON SAID HE WOULD BE ABLE TO CONSTRUCT A CONTAINMENT DEVICE THAT SHOULD PRECLUDE ANY CHANCE OF METALLO'S ESCAPING.
I GATHERED UP ALL THE ROBOTS AND DELIVERED THEM TO S.T.A.R. LABS AS WELL.
THEY'LL BE CANNIBALIZED FOR NEEDED PARTS.
THANKS, JOHN. GOOD THING YOU, AT LEAST, STILL HAVE YOUR POWERS.
DO YOU WANT THE TASKS LIST, TED? IT JUST KEEPS GETTING LONGER, THANKS TO OUR GETTING DIVERTED BY THINGS LIKE METALLO'S ROMP.
SAVE IT FOR TOMORROW, NATHANIEL. WE'LL START ON IT FRESH.
THOUGH WE DO NEED SOMEBODY FOR MONITOR DUTY TONIGHT. YOU'RE VOLUNTEERING, BEATRIZ?
WHAT? NO!
COME ON, I WAS YAWNING!
I'LL DO IT.
THANKS, TORA.
UNLESS THERE'S ANYTHING ELSE, I SAY WE CALL IT A NIGHT. EVERYBODY GET SOME REST.

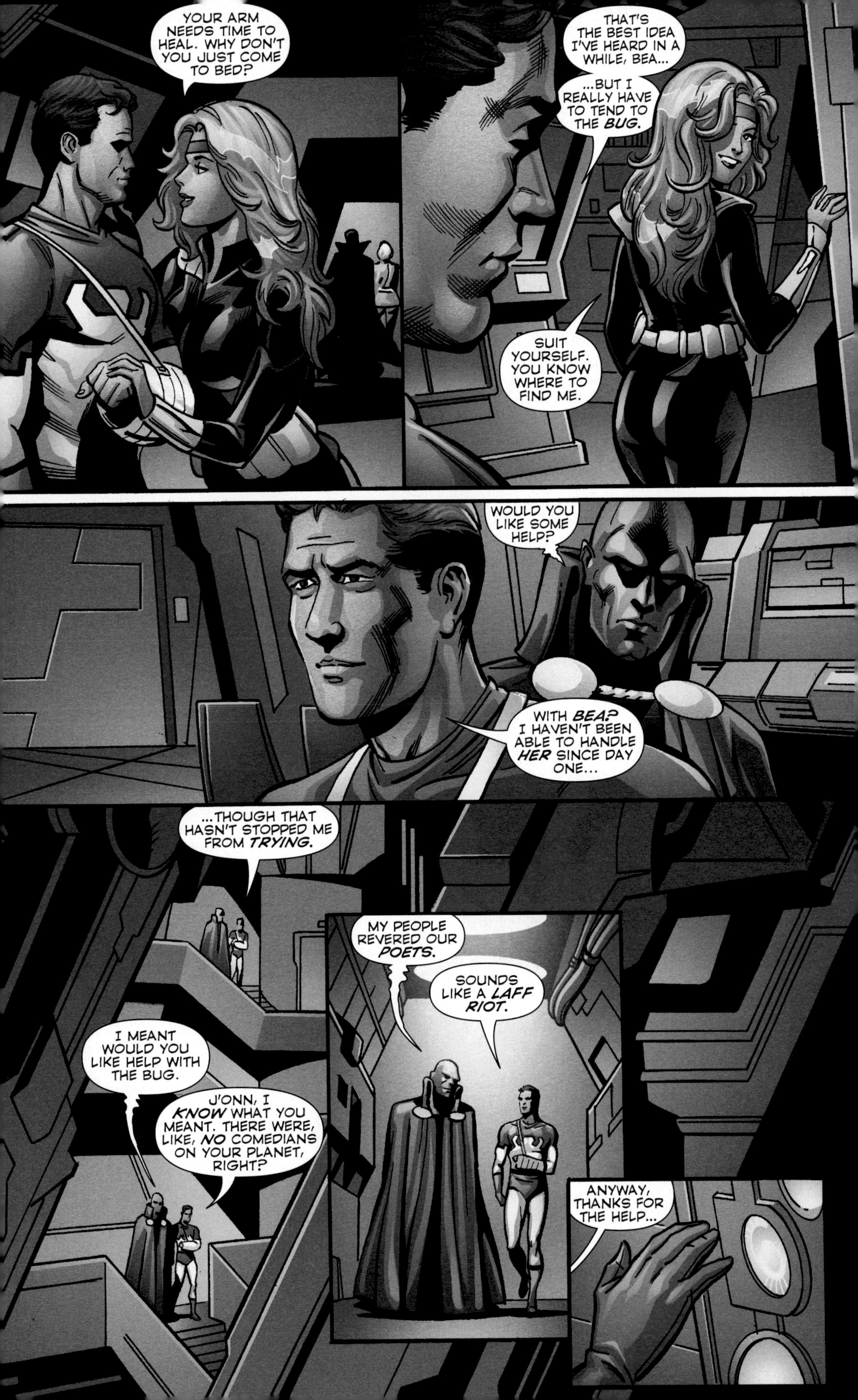
YOUR ARM NEEDS TIME TO HEAL. WHY DON'T YOU JUST COME TO BED?
THAT'S THE BEST IDEA I'VE HEARD IN A WHILE, BEA...
...BUT I REALLY HAVE TO TEND TO THE BUG.
SUIT YOURSELF. YOU KNOW WHERE TO FIND ME.
WOULD YOU LIKE SOME HELP?
WITH BEA? I HAVEN'T BEEN ABLE TO HANDLE HER SINCE DAY ONE...
...THOUGH THAT HASN'T STOPPED ME FROM TRYING.
I MEANT WOULD YOU LIKE HELP WITH THE BUG.
J'ONN, I KNOW WHAT YOU MEANT. THERE WERE, LIKE, NO COMEDIANS ON YOUR PLANET, RIGHT?
MY PEOPLE REVERED OUR POETS.
SOUNDS LIKE A LAFF RIOT.
ANYWAY, THANKS FOR THE HELP...

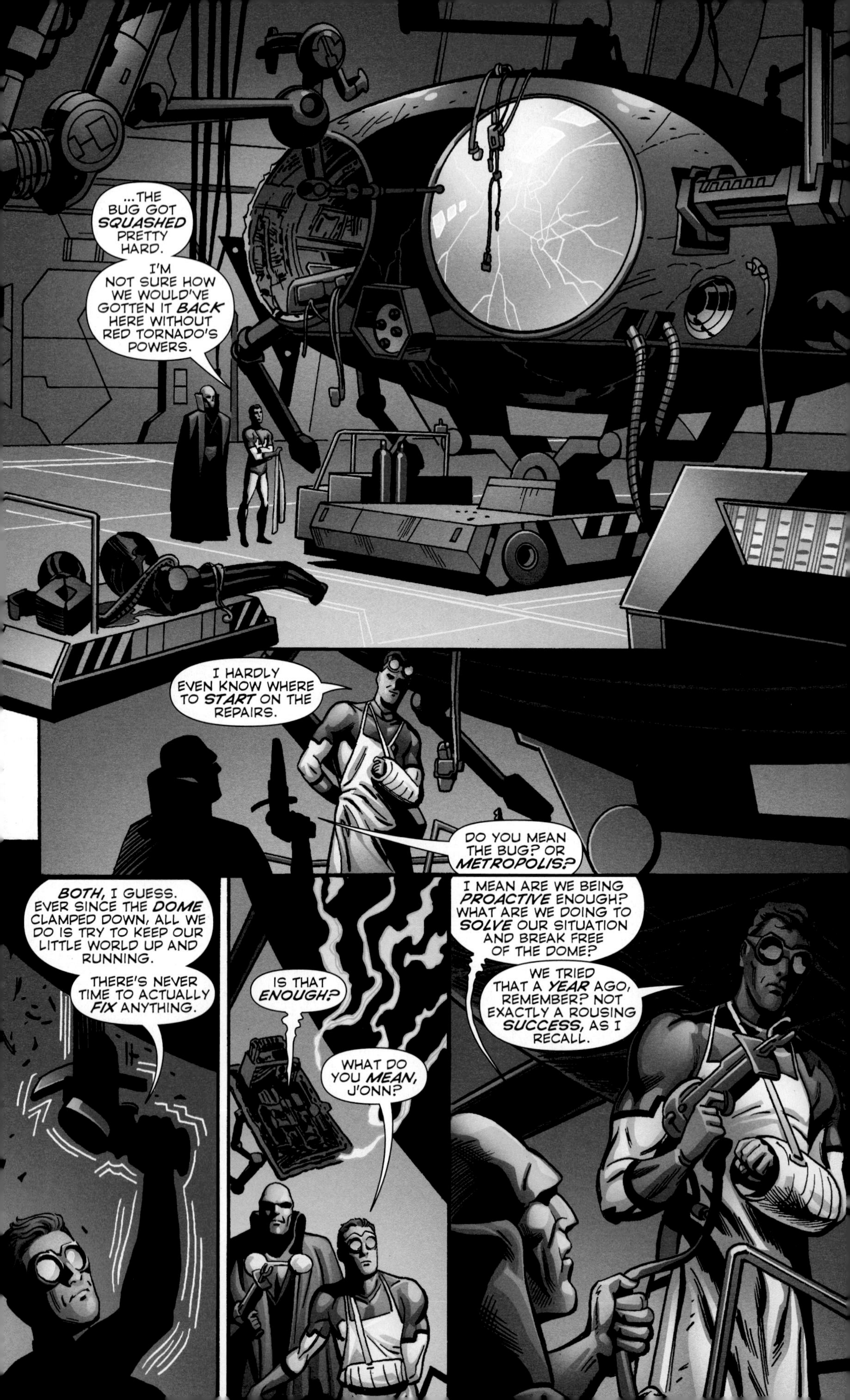
...THE BUG GOT *SQUASHED* PRETTY HARD.
I'M NOT SURE HOW WE WOULD'VE GOTTEN IT *BACK* HERE WITHOUT RED TORNADO'S POWERS.
I HARDLY EVEN KNOW WHERE TO *START* ON THE REPAIRS.
DO YOU MEAN THE BUG? OR *METROPOLIS?*
BOTH, I GUESS. EVER SINCE THE *DOME* CLAMPED DOWN, ALL WE DO IS TRY TO KEEP OUR LITTLE WORLD UP AND RUNNING.
THERE'S NEVER TIME TO ACTUALLY *FIX* ANYTHING.
IS THAT *ENOUGH?*
WHAT DO YOU *MEAN,* J'ONN?
I MEAN ARE WE BEING *PROACTIVE* ENOUGH? WHAT ARE WE DOING TO *SOLVE* OUR SITUATION AND BREAK FREE OF THE DOME?
WE TRIED THAT A *YEAR* AGO, REMEMBER? NOT EXACTLY A ROUSING *SUCCESS,* AS I RECALL.

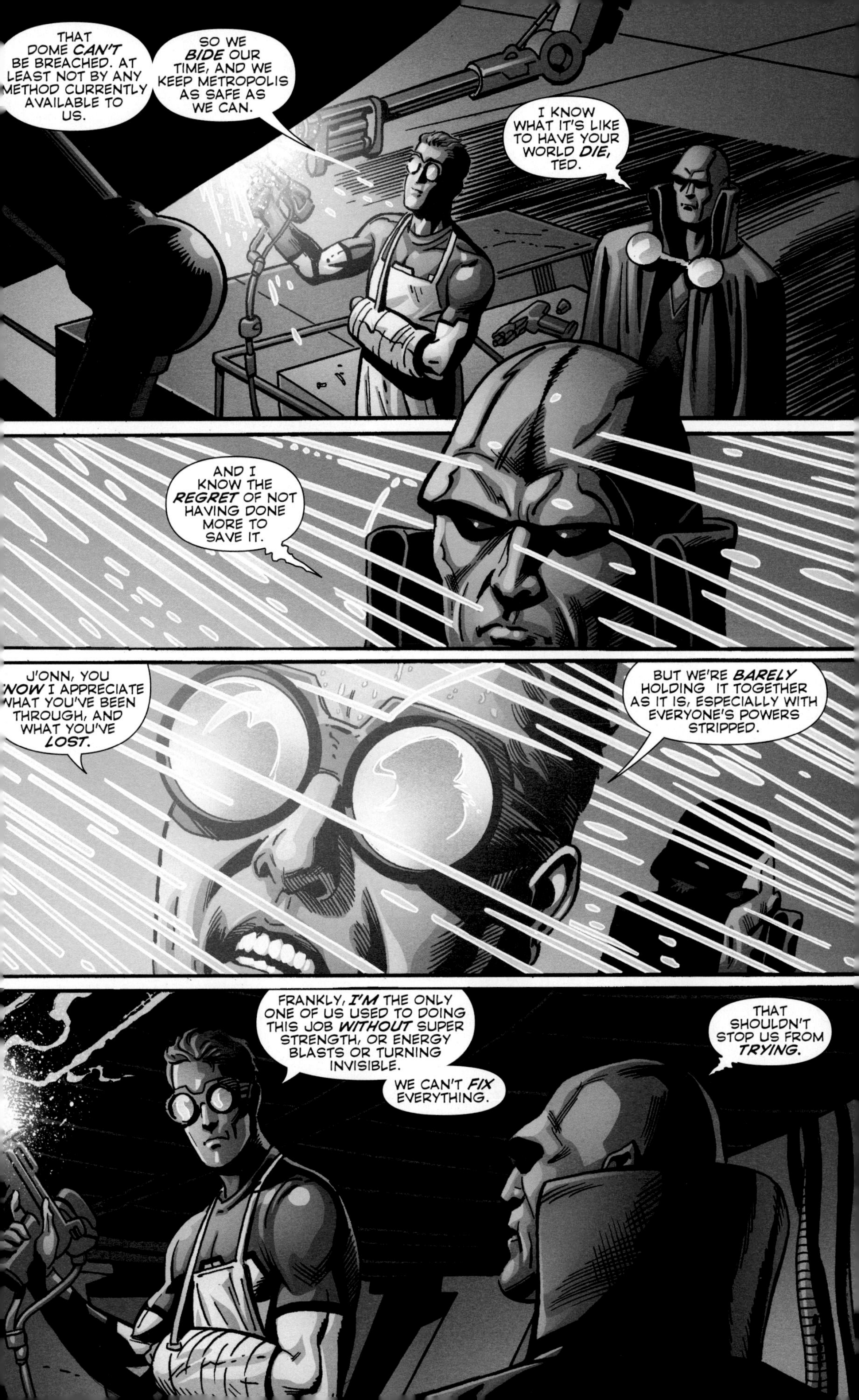
THAT DOME CAN'T BE BREACHED. AT LEAST NOT BY ANY METHOD CURRENTLY AVAILABLE TO US.
SO WE BIDE OUR TIME, AND WE KEEP METROPOLIS AS SAFE AS WE CAN.
I KNOW WHAT IT'S LIKE TO HAVE YOUR WORLD DIE, TED.
AND I KNOW THE REGRET OF NOT HAVING DONE MORE TO SAVE IT.
J'ONN, YOU KNOW I APPRECIATE WHAT YOU'VE BEEN THROUGH, AND WHAT YOU'VE LOST.
BUT WE'RE BARELY HOLDING IT TOGETHER AS IT IS, ESPECIALLY WITH EVERYONE'S POWERS STRIPPED.
FRANKLY, I'M THE ONLY ONE OF US USED TO DOING THIS JOB WITHOUT SUPER STRENGTH, OR ENERGY BLASTS OR TURNING INVISIBLE.
WE CAN'T FIX EVERYTHING.
THAT SHOULDN'T STOP US FROM TRYING.

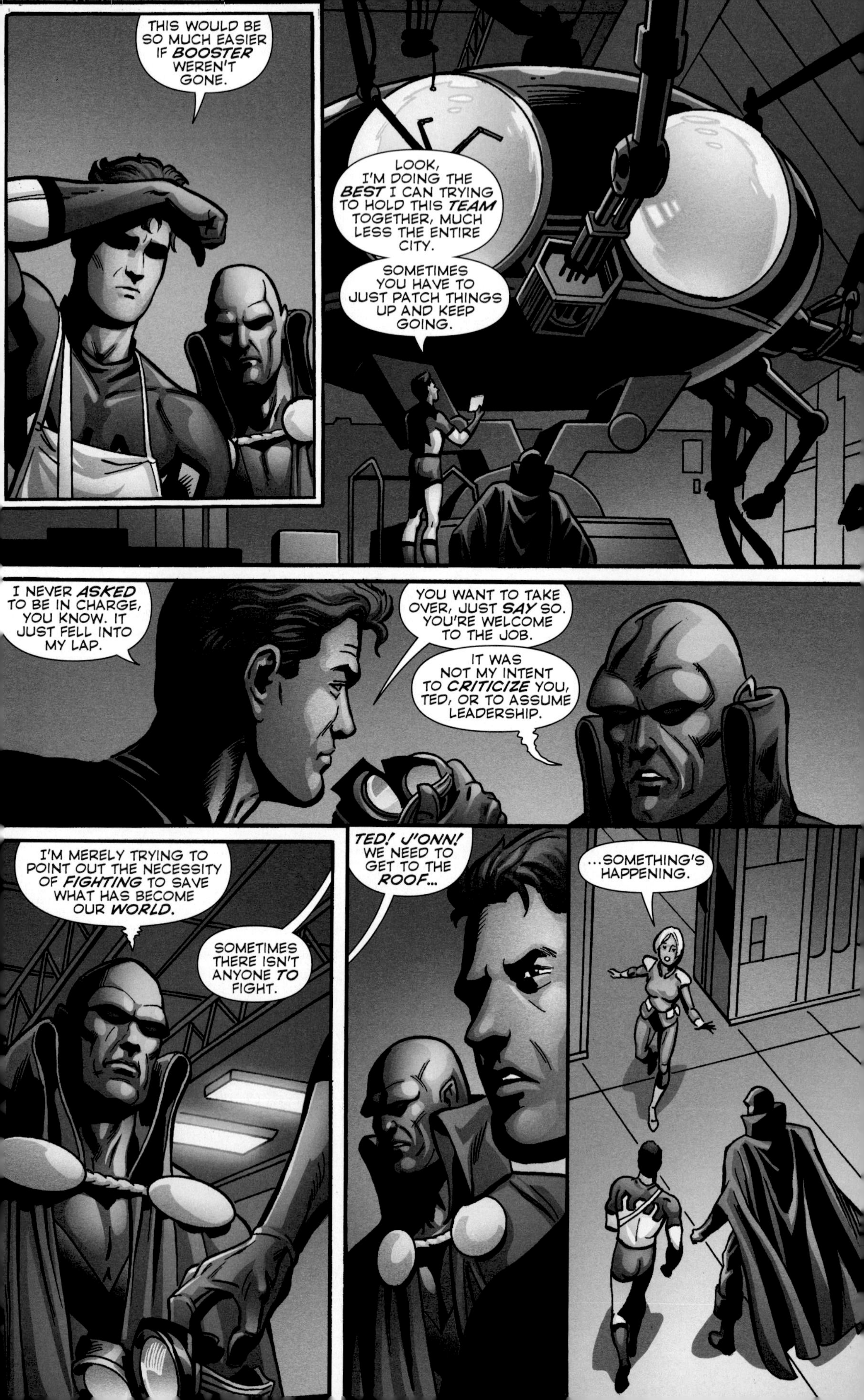
THIS WOULD BE SO MUCH EASIER IF BOOSTER WEREN'T GONE.
LOOK, I'M DOING THE BEST I CAN TRYING TO HOLD THIS TEAM TOGETHER, MUCH LESS THE ENTIRE CITY.
SOMETIMES YOU HAVE TO JUST PATCH THINGS UP AND KEEP GOING.
I NEVER ASKED TO BE IN CHARGE, YOU KNOW. IT JUST FELL INTO MY LAP.
YOU WANT TO TAKE OVER, JUST SAY SO. YOU'RE WELCOME TO THE JOB.
IT WAS NOT MY INTENT TO CRITICIZE YOU, TED, OR TO ASSUME LEADERSHIP.
I'M MERELY TRYING TO POINT OUT THE NECESSITY OF FIGHTING TO SAVE WHAT HAS BECOME OUR WORLD.
SOMETIMES THERE ISN'T ANYONE TO FIGHT.
TED! J'ONN! WE NEED TO GET TO THE ROOF...
...SOMETHING'S HAPPENING.

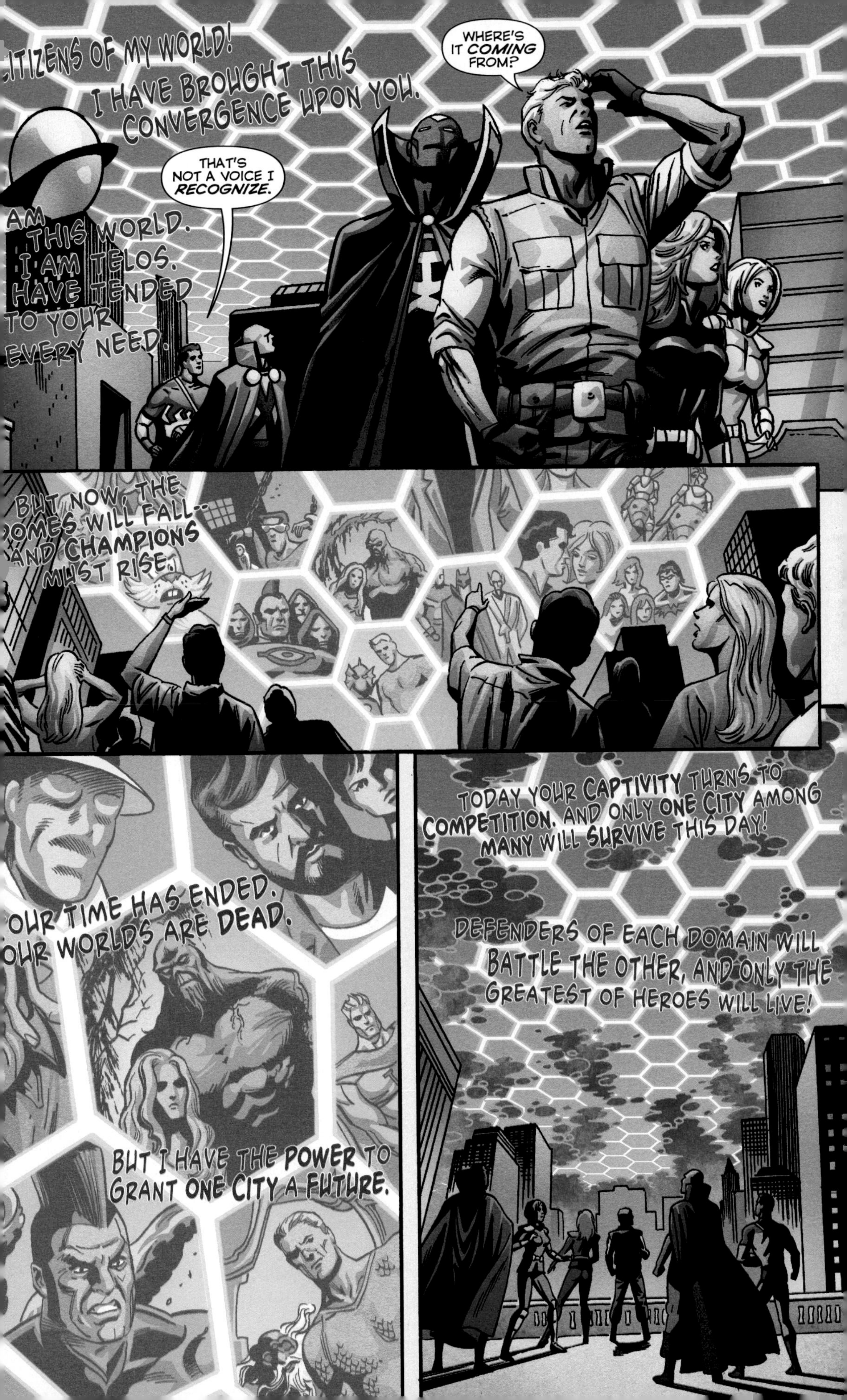
CITIZENS OF MY WORLD!
I HAVE BROUGHT THIS CONVERGENCE UPON YOU.
WHERE'S IT COMING FROM?
THAT'S NOT A VOICE I RECOGNIZE.
I AM THIS WORLD. I AM TELOS. I HAVE TENDED TO YOUR EVERY NEED.
BUT NOW, THE DOMES WILL FALL-- AND CHAMPIONS MUST RISE.
YOUR TIME HAS ENDED. YOUR WORLDS ARE DEAD.
BUT I HAVE THE POWER TO GRANT ONE CITY A FUTURE.
TODAY YOUR CAPTIVITY TURNS TO COMPETITION. AND ONLY ONE CITY AMONG MANY WILL SURVIVE THIS DAY!
DEFENDERS OF EACH DOMAIN WILL BATTLE THE OTHER, AND ONLY THE GREATEST OF HEROES WILL LIVE!

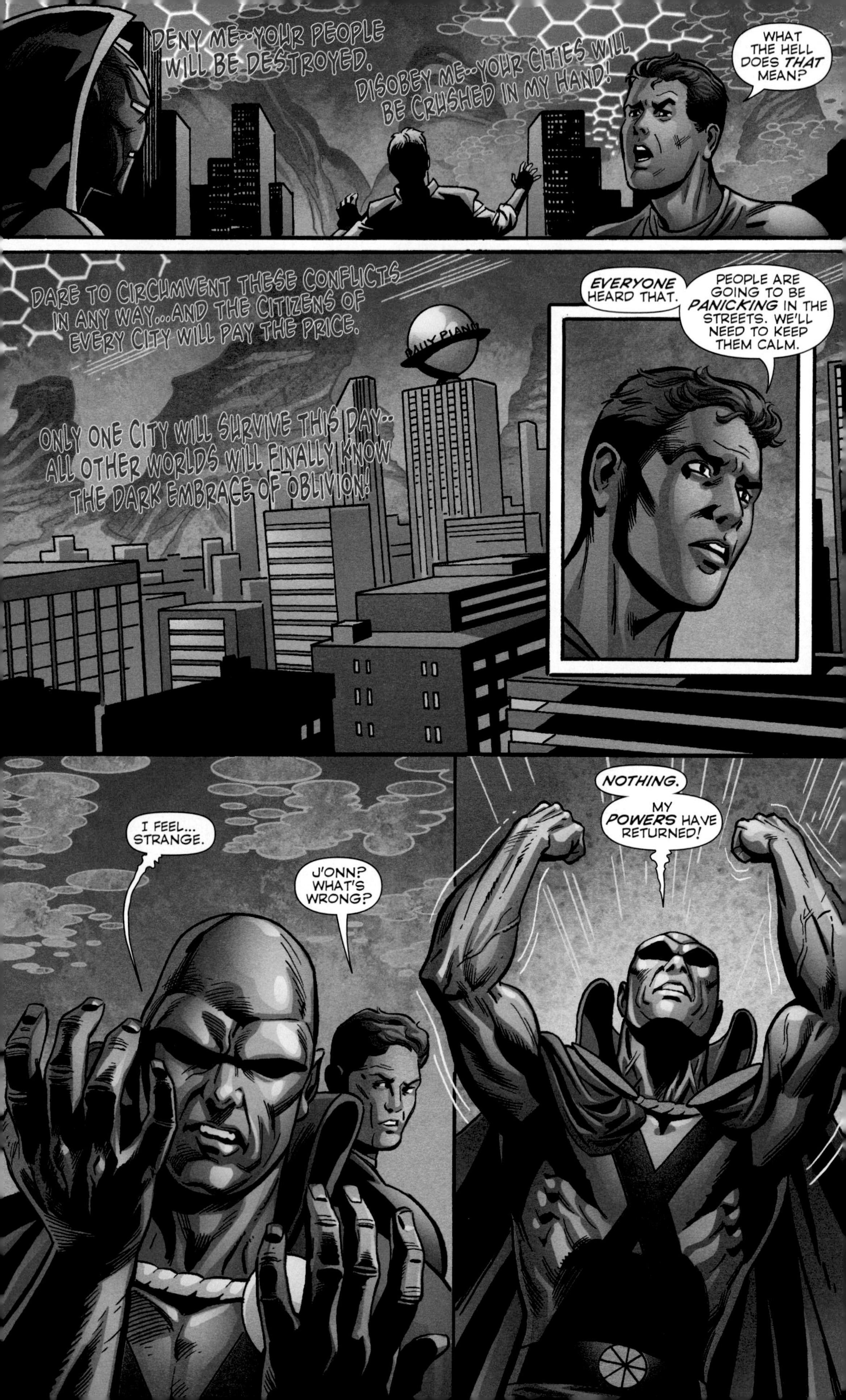
DENY ME...YOUR PEOPLE WILL BE DESTROYED.
DISOBEY ME...YOUR CITIES WILL BE CRUSHED IN MY HAND!
WHAT THE HELL DOES *THAT* MEAN?
DARE TO CIRCUMVENT THESE CONFLICTS IN ANY WAY...AND THE CITIZENS OF EVERY CITY WILL PAY THE PRICE.
ONLY ONE CITY WILL SURVIVE THIS DAY... ALL OTHER WORLDS WILL FINALLY KNOW THE DARK EMBRACE OF OBLIVION!
EVERYONE HEARD THAT.
PEOPLE ARE GOING TO BE *PANICKING* IN THE STREETS. WE'LL NEED TO KEEP THEM CALM.
I FEEL... STRANGE.
J'ONN? WHAT'S WRONG?
NOTHING.
MY *POWERS* HAVE RETURNED!

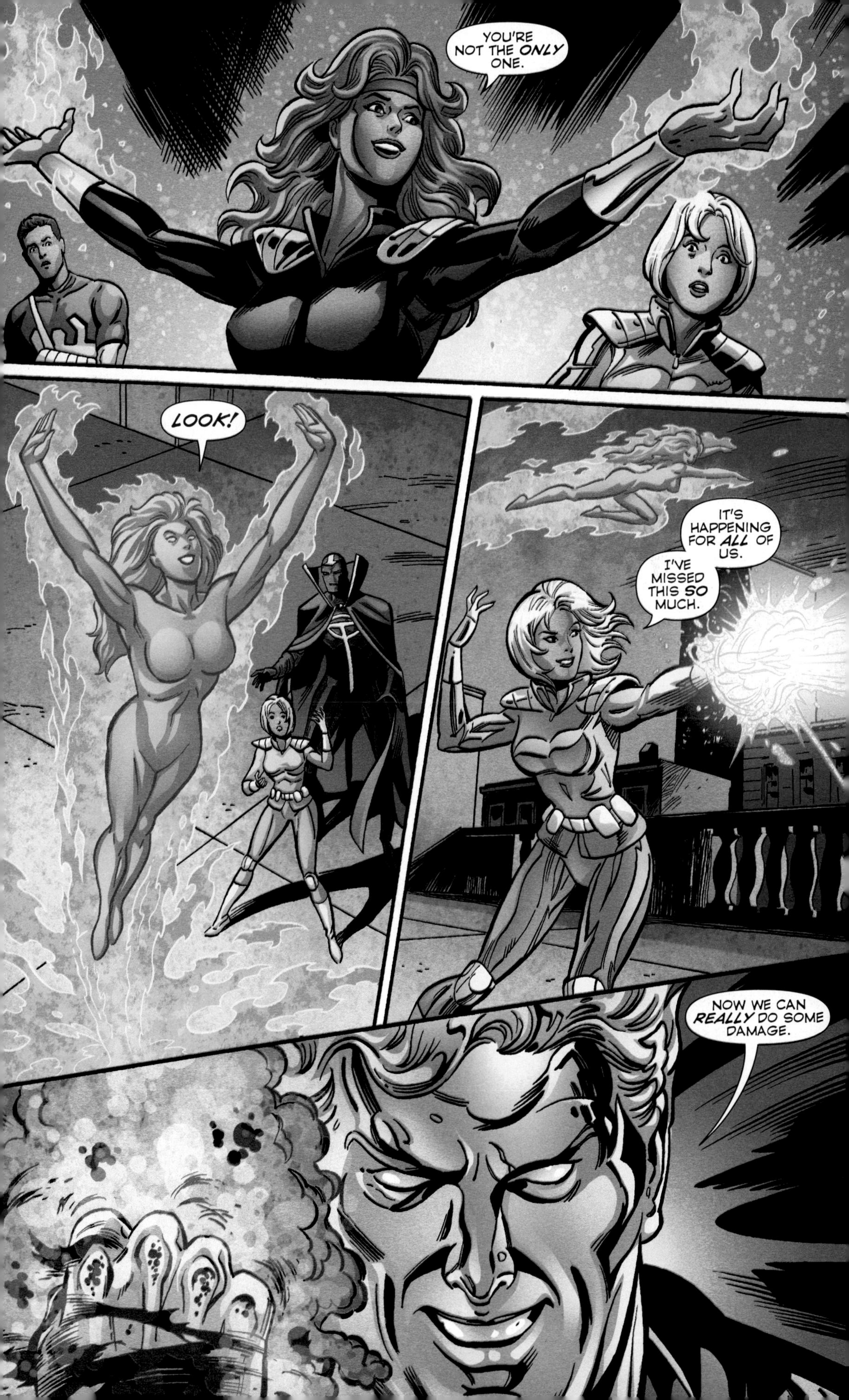
YOU'RE NOT THE ONLY ONE.
LOOK!
IT'S HAPPENING FOR ALL OF US.
I'VE MISSED THIS SO MUCH.
NOW WE CAN REALLY DO SOME DAMAGE.

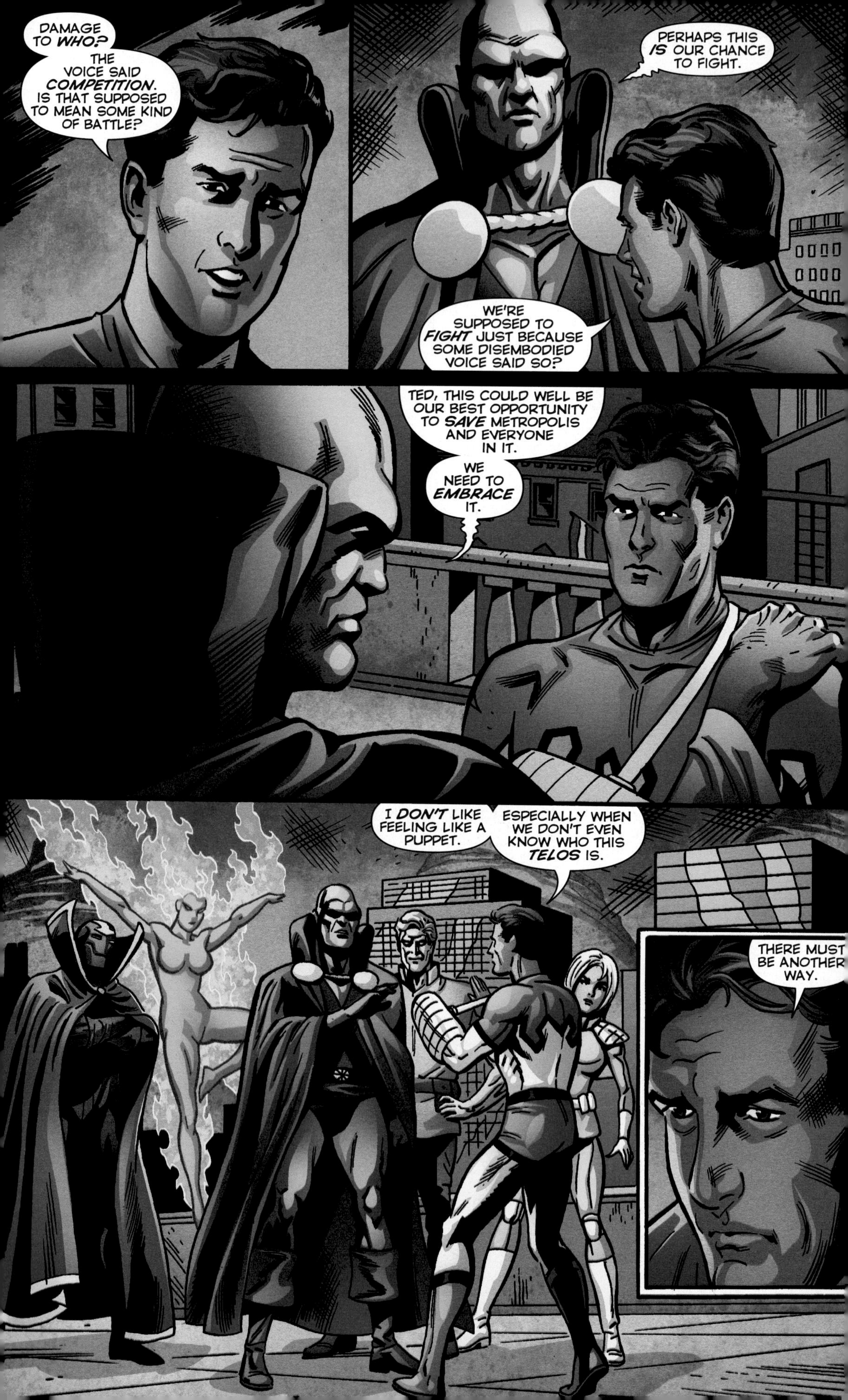
DAMAGE TO WHO? THE VOICE SAID COMPETITION. IS THAT SUPPOSED TO MEAN SOME KIND OF BATTLE?
PERHAPS THIS IS OUR CHANCE TO FIGHT.
WE'RE SUPPOSED TO FIGHT JUST BECAUSE SOME DISEMBODIED VOICE SAID SO?
TED, THIS COULD WELL BE OUR BEST OPPORTUNITY TO SAVE METROPOLIS AND EVERYONE IN IT.
WE NEED TO EMBRACE IT.
I DON'T LIKE FEELING LIKE A PUPPET.
ESPECIALLY WHEN WE DON'T EVEN KNOW WHO THIS TELOS IS.
THERE MUST BE ANOTHER WAY.

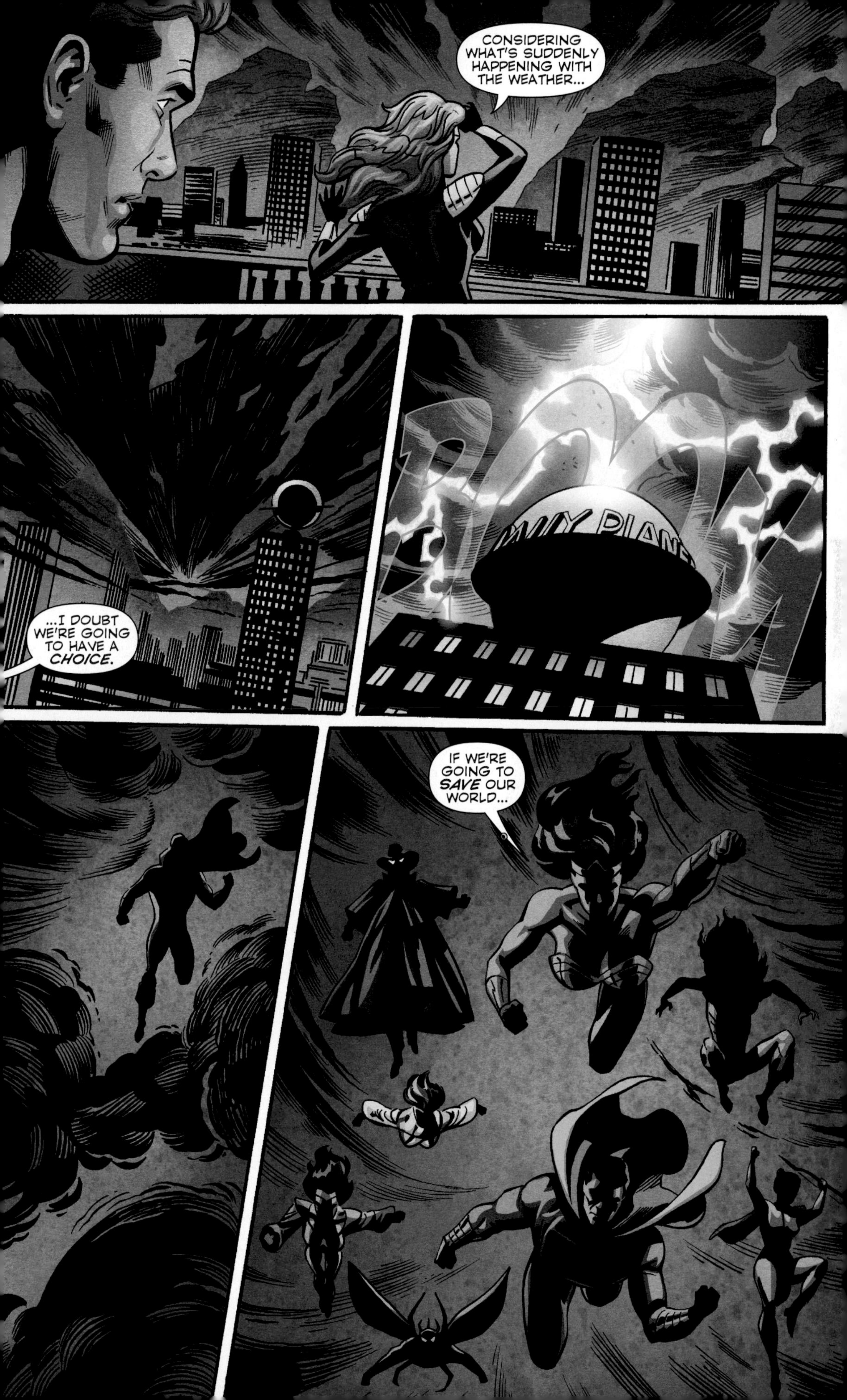
CONSIDERING WHAT'S SUDDENLY HAPPENING WITH THE WEATHER...
...I DOUBT WE'RE GOING TO HAVE A *CHOICE*.
IF WE'RE GOING TO *SAVE* OUR WORLD...

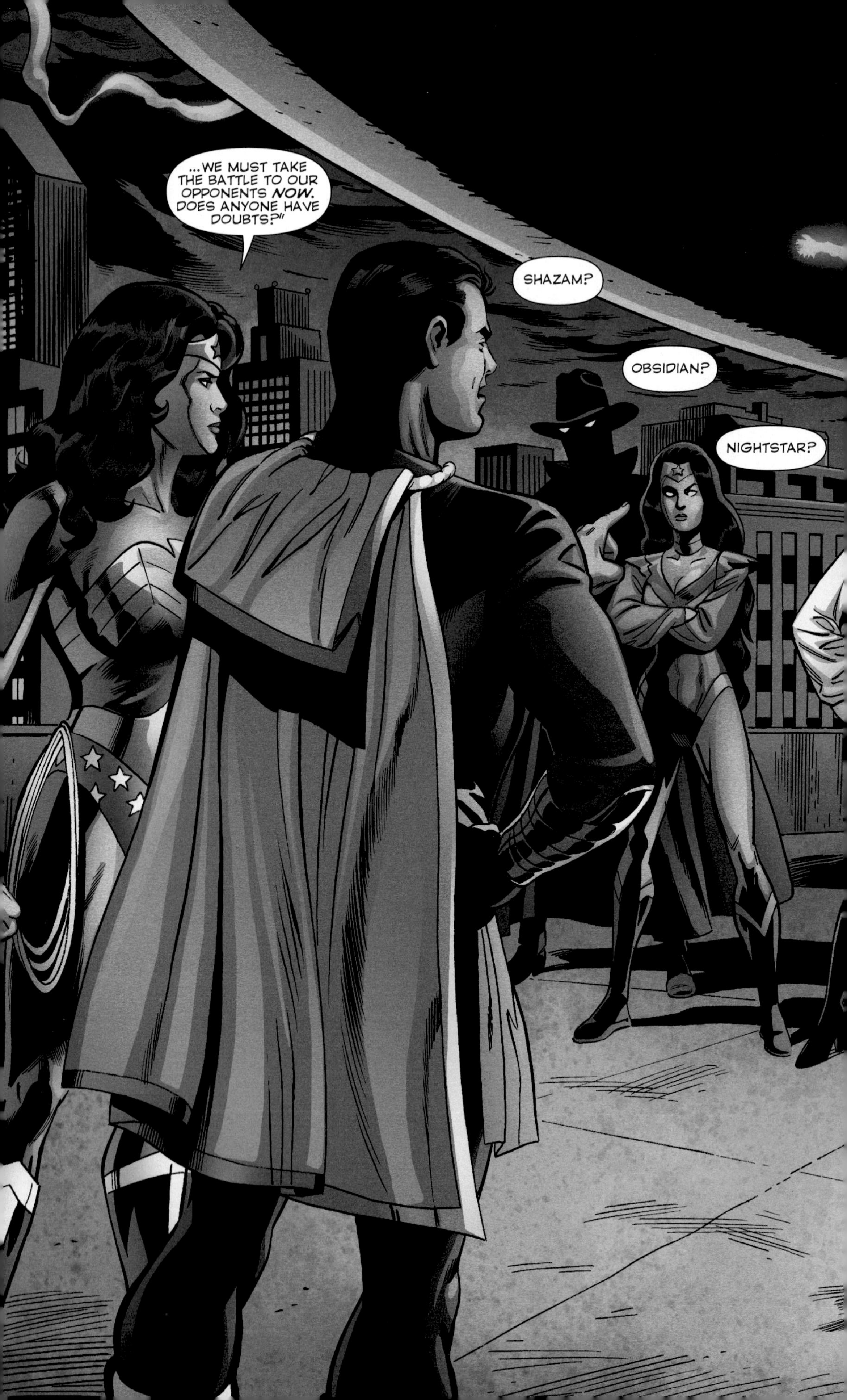
...WE MUST TAKE THE BATTLE TO OUR OPPONENTS NOW. DOES ANYONE HAVE DOUBTS?"
SHAZAM?
OBSIDIAN?
NIGHTSTAR?

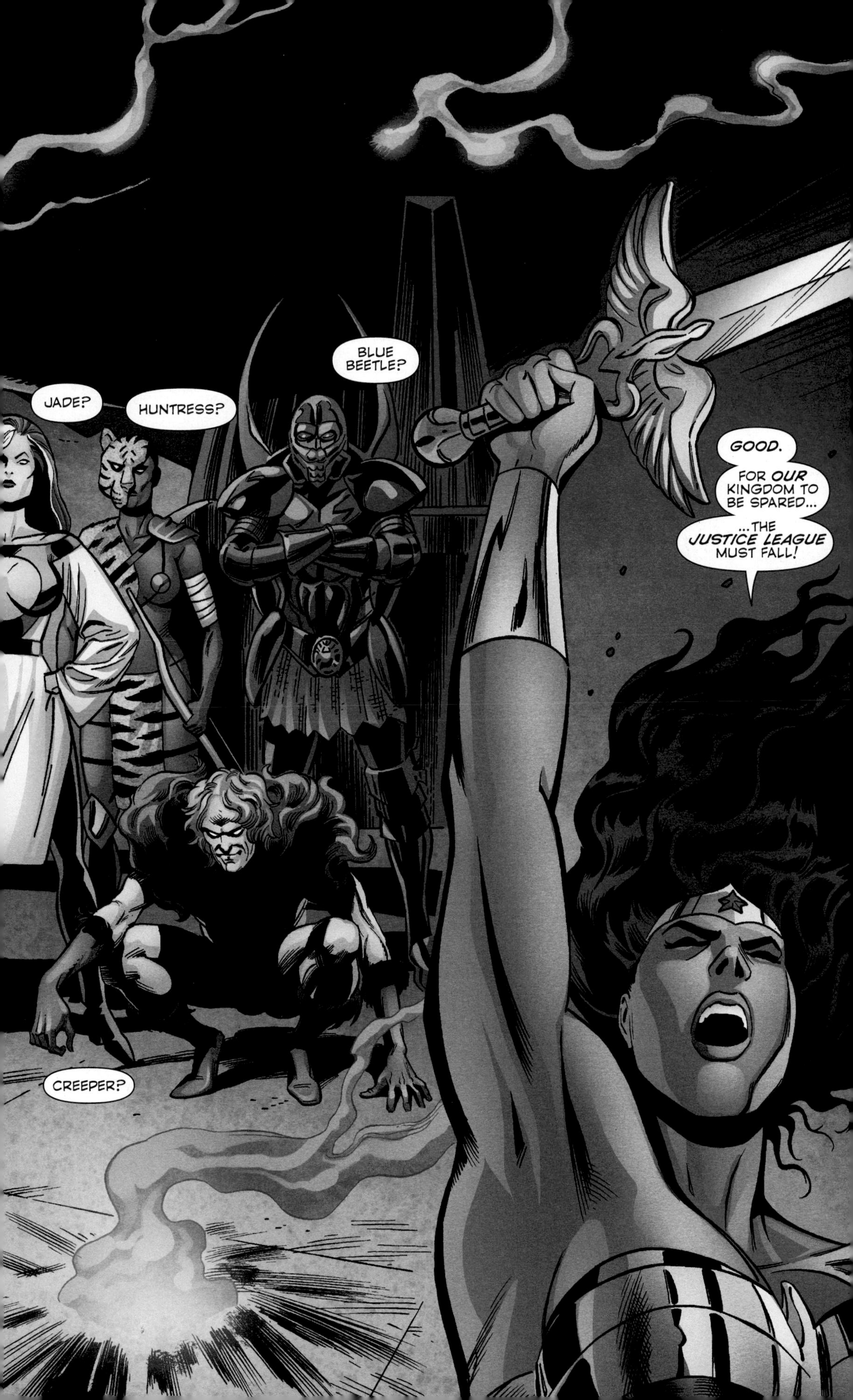
JADE?
HUNTRESS?
BLUE BEETLE?
CREEPER?
GOOD.
FOR OUR KINGDOM TO BE SPARED...
...THE JUSTICE LEAGUE MUST FALL!

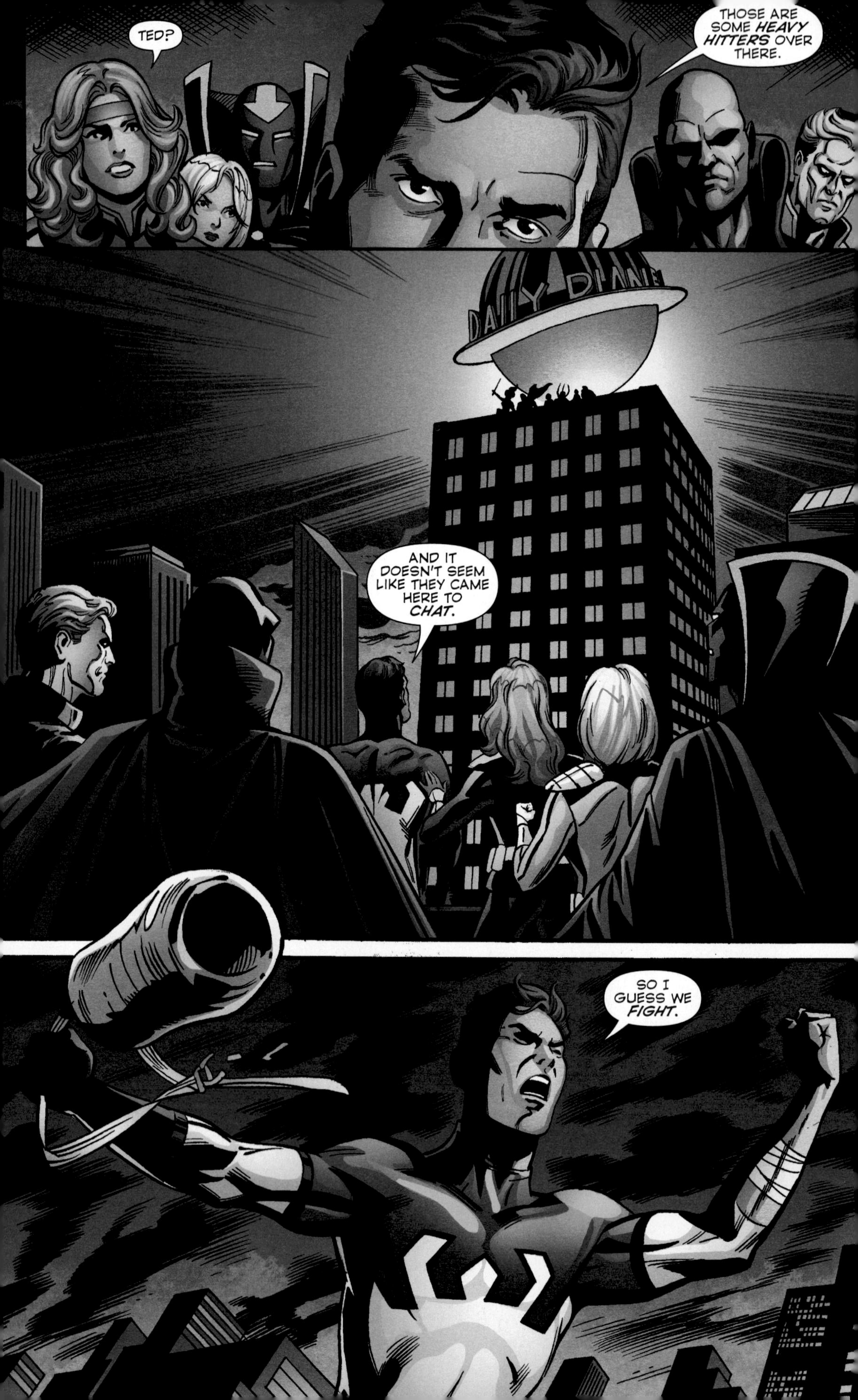
TED?
THOSE ARE SOME HEAVY HITTERS OVER THERE.
DAILY PLANET
AND IT DOESN'T SEEM LIKE THEY CAME HERE TO CHAT.
SO I GUESS WE FIGHT.

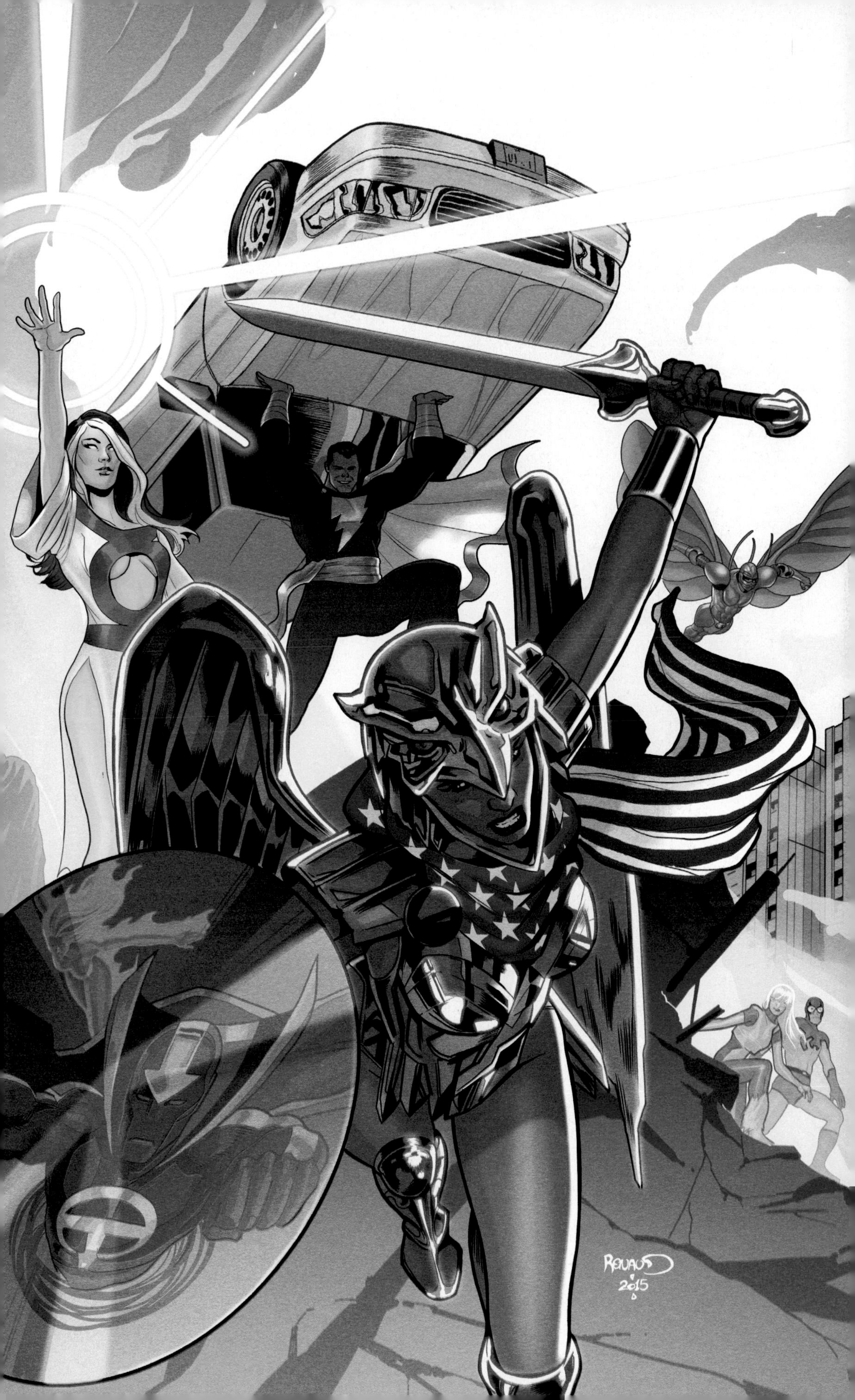

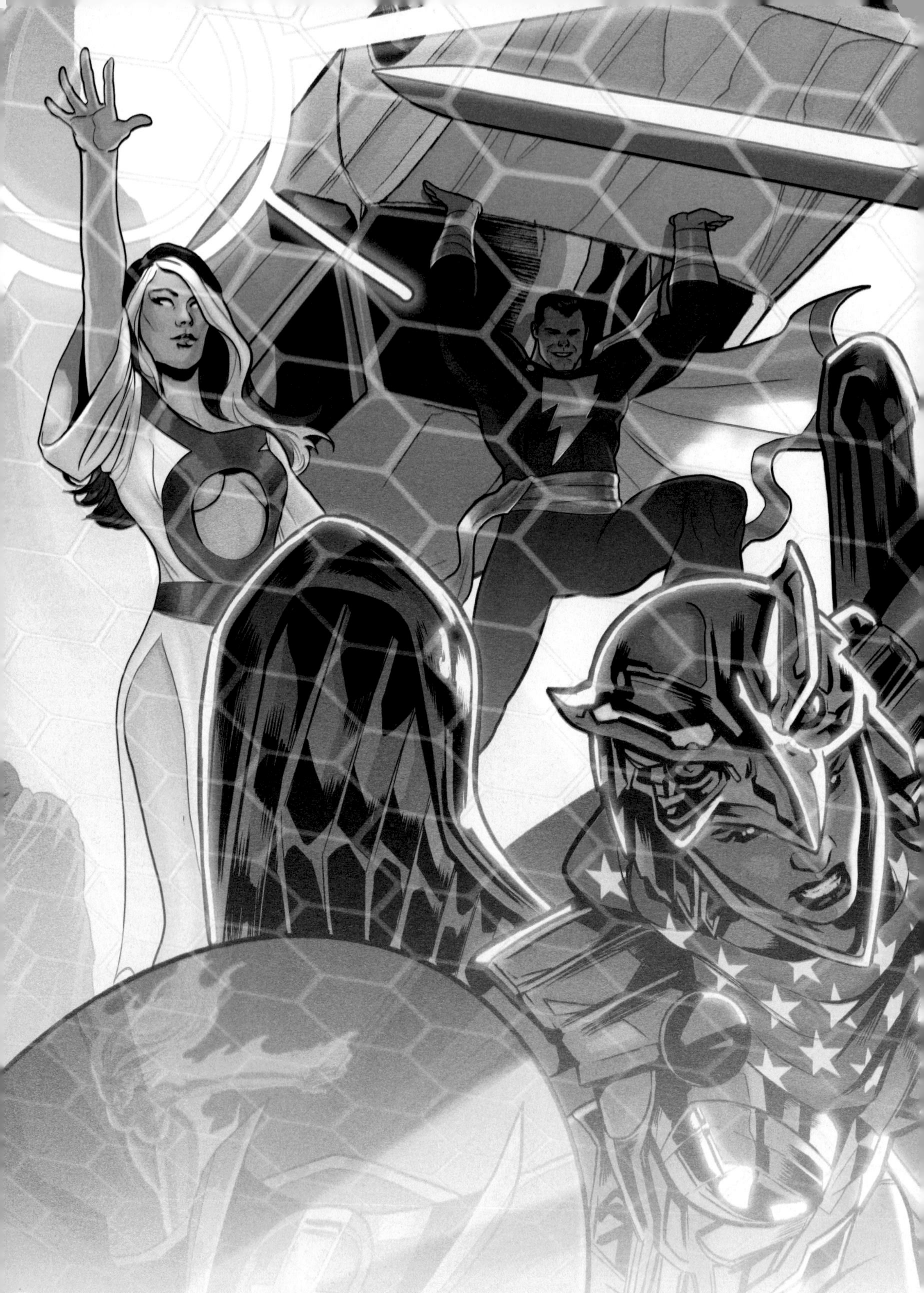

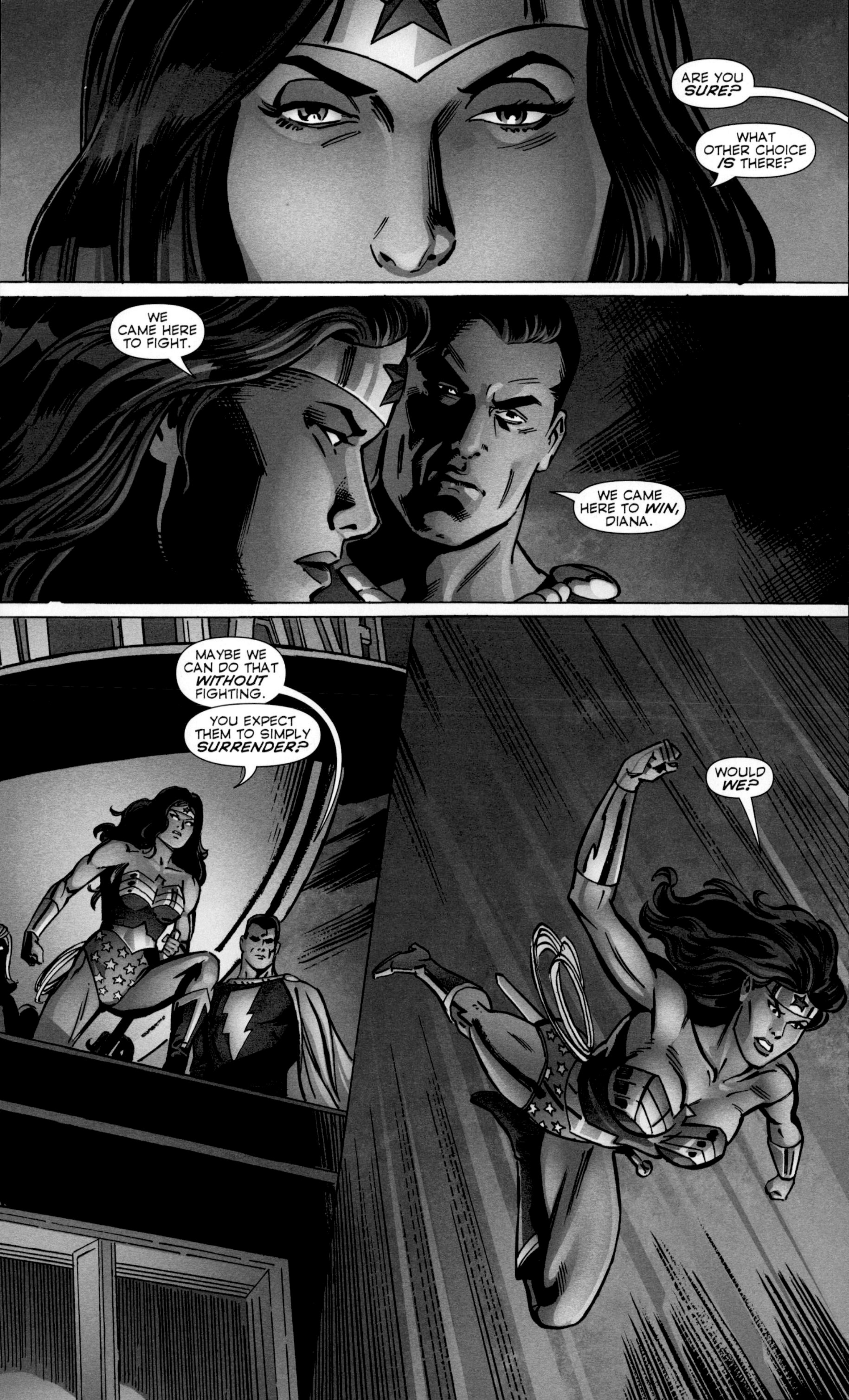

ARE YOU SURE?
WHAT OTHER CHOICE IS THERE?
WE CAME HERE TO FIGHT.
WE CAME HERE TO WIN, DIANA.
MAYBE WE CAN DO THAT WITHOUT FIGHTING.
YOU EXPECT THEM TO SIMPLY SURRENDER?
WOULD WE?

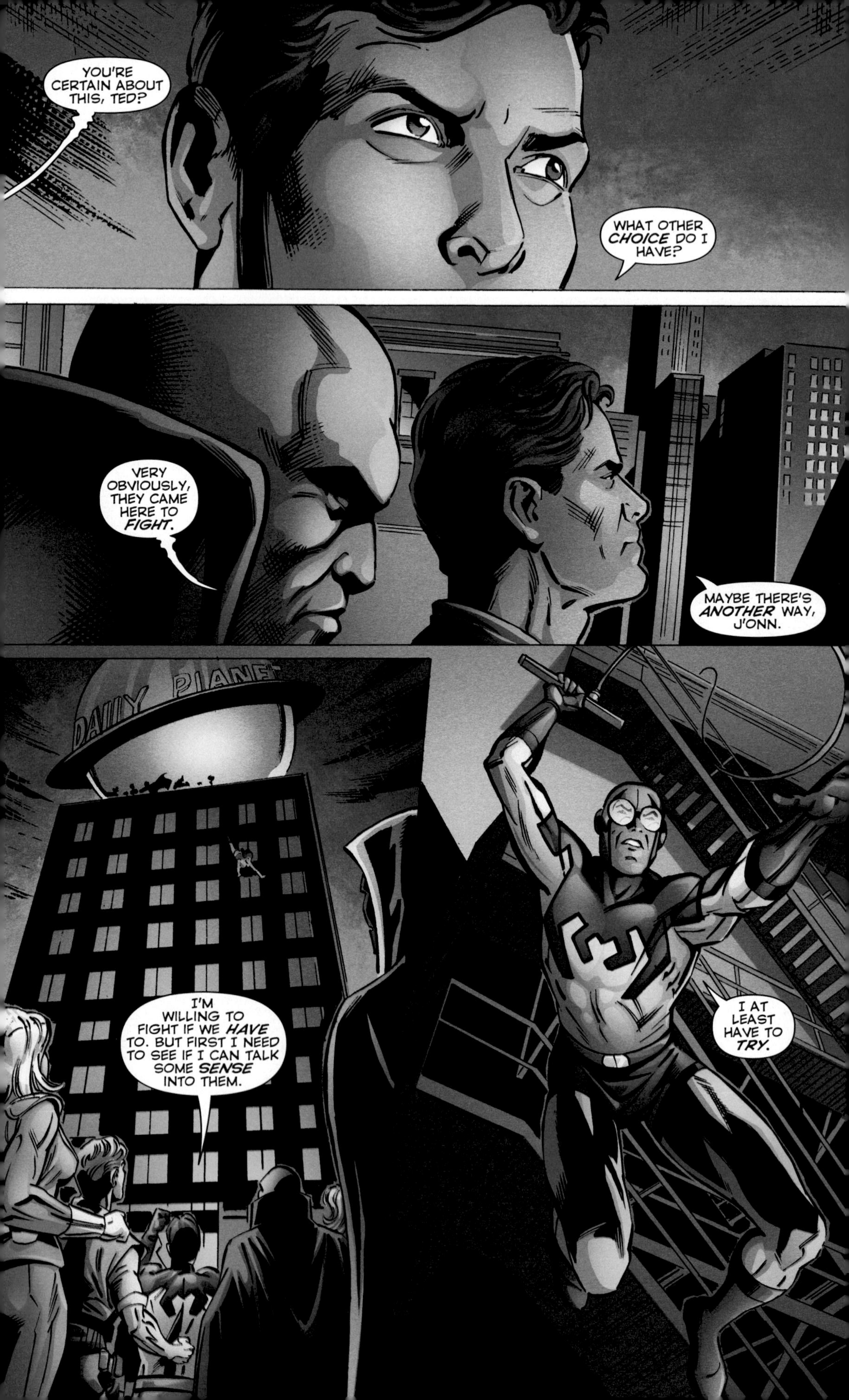
YOU'RE CERTAIN ABOUT THIS, TED?
WHAT OTHER CHOICE DO I HAVE?
VERY OBVIOUSLY, THEY CAME HERE TO FIGHT.
MAYBE THERE'S ANOTHER WAY, J'ONN.
DAILY PLANET
I'M WILLING TO FIGHT IF WE HAVE TO. BUT FIRST I NEED TO SEE IF I CAN TALK SOME SENSE INTO THEM.
I AT LEAST HAVE TO TRY.

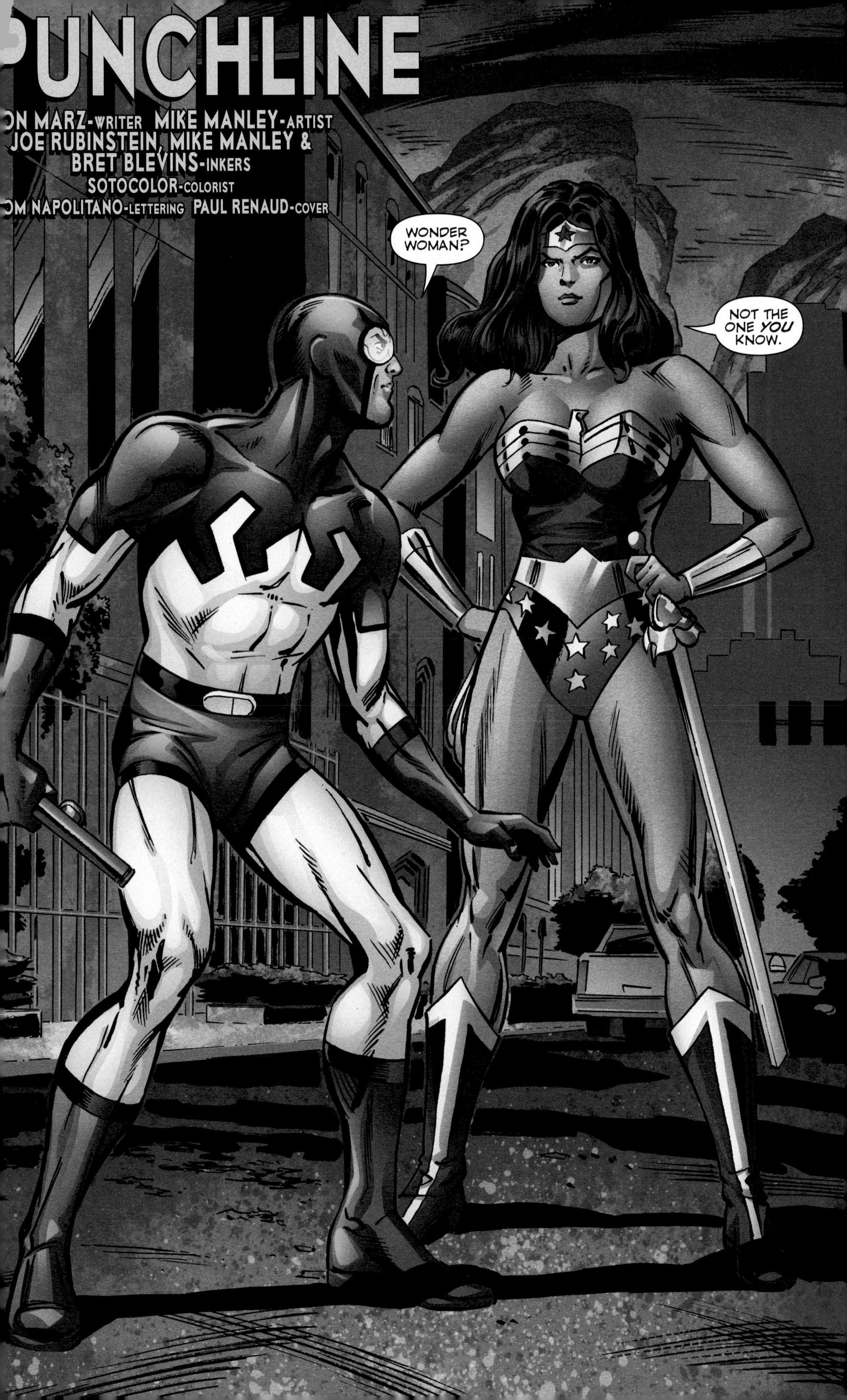
PUNCHLINE
ON MARZ-WRITER MIKE MANLEY-ARTIST
JOE RUBINSTEIN, MIKE MANLEY &
BRET BLEVINS-INKERS
SOTOCOLOR-COLORIST
OM NAPOLITANO-LETTERING PAUL RENAUD-COVER
WONDER WOMAN?
NOT THE ONE YOU KNOW.

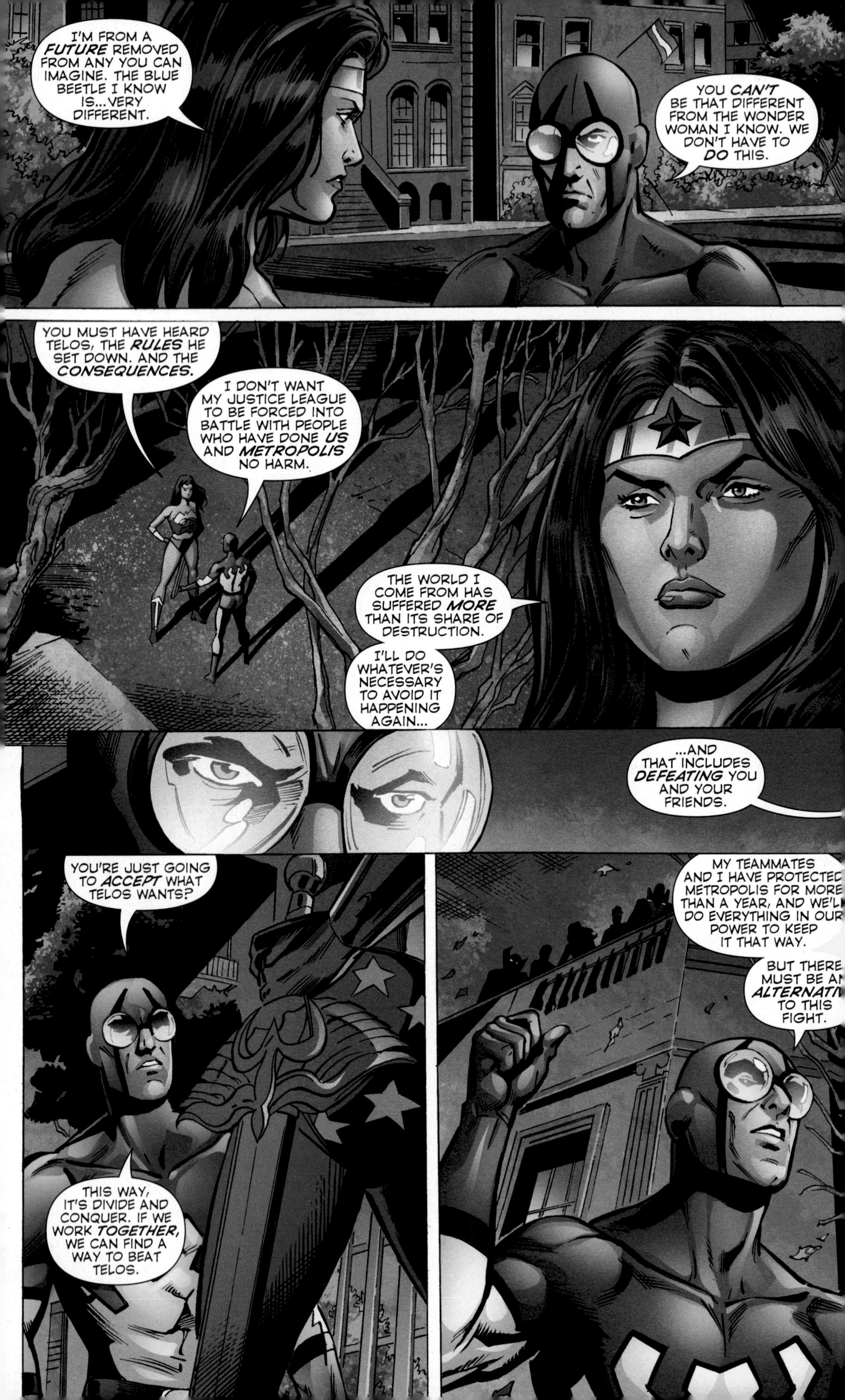

I'M FROM A FUTURE REMOVED FROM ANY YOU CAN IMAGINE. THE BLUE BEETLE I KNOW IS...VERY DIFFERENT.
YOU CAN'T BE THAT DIFFERENT FROM THE WONDER WOMAN I KNOW. WE DON'T HAVE TO DO THIS.
YOU MUST HAVE HEARD TELOS, THE RULES HE SET DOWN. AND THE CONSEQUENCES.
I DON'T WANT MY JUSTICE LEAGUE TO BE FORCED INTO BATTLE WITH PEOPLE WHO HAVE DONE US AND METROPOLIS NO HARM.
THE WORLD I COME FROM HAS SUFFERED MORE THAN ITS SHARE OF DESTRUCTION.
I'LL DO WHATEVER'S NECESSARY TO AVOID IT HAPPENING AGAIN...
...AND THAT INCLUDES DEFEATING YOU AND YOUR FRIENDS.
YOU'RE JUST GOING TO ACCEPT WHAT TELOS WANTS?
THIS WAY, IT'S DIVIDE AND CONQUER. IF WE WORK TOGETHER, WE CAN FIND A WAY TO BEAT TELOS.
MY TEAMMATES AND I HAVE PROTECTED METROPOLIS FOR MORE THAN A YEAR, AND WE'LL DO EVERYTHING IN OUR POWER TO KEEP IT THAT WAY.
BUT THERE MUST BE AN ALTERNATIVE TO THIS FIGHT.

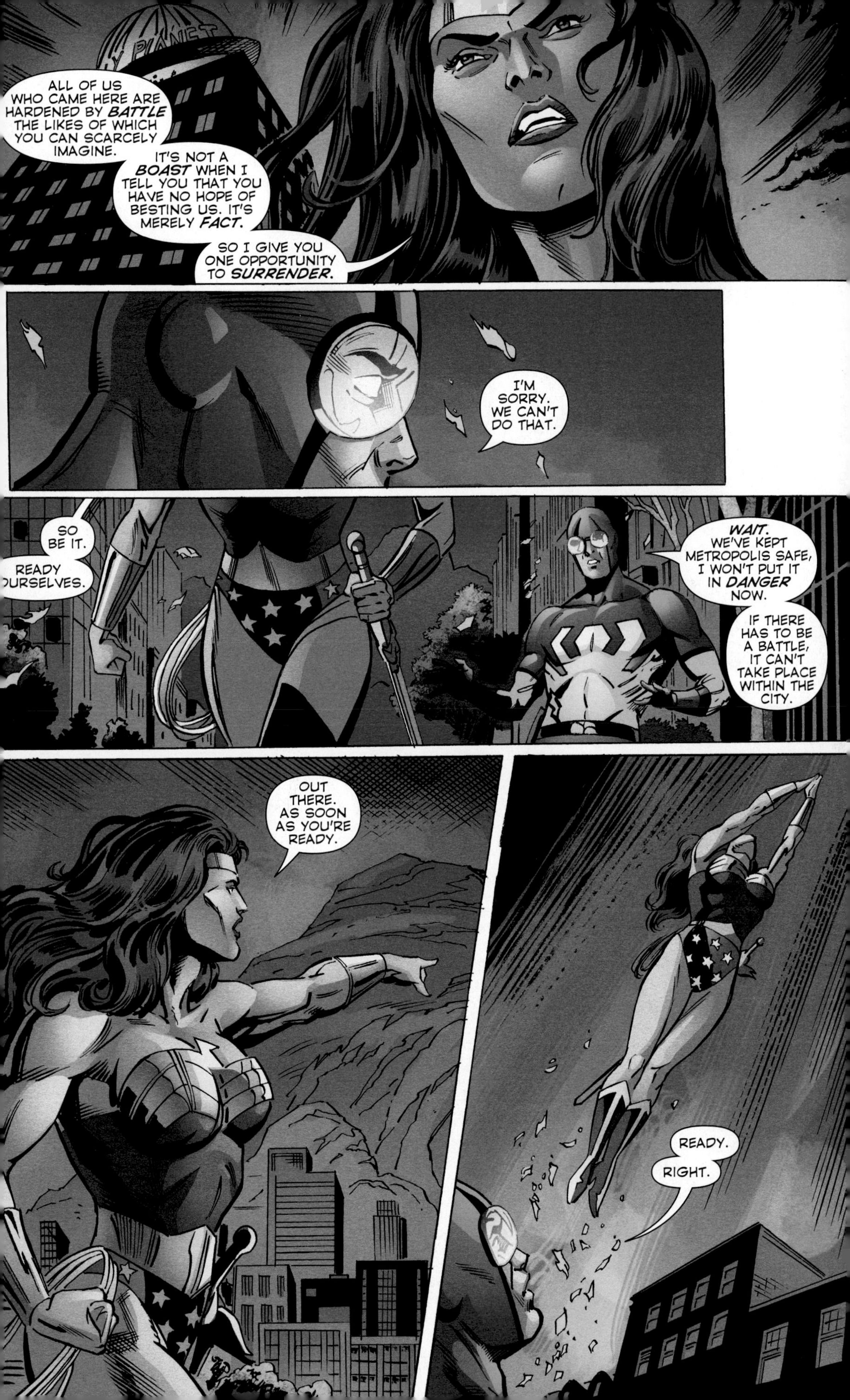
ALL OF US WHO CAME HERE ARE HARDENED BY BATTLE THE LIKES OF WHICH YOU CAN SCARCELY IMAGINE.
IT'S NOT A BOAST WHEN I TELL YOU THAT YOU HAVE NO HOPE OF BESTING US. IT'S MERELY FACT.
SO I GIVE YOU ONE OPPORTUNITY TO SURRENDER.
I'M SORRY. WE CAN'T DO THAT.
SO BE IT.
READY OURSELVES.
WAIT. WE'VE KEPT METROPOLIS SAFE, I WON'T PUT IT IN DANGER NOW.
IF THERE HAS TO BE A BATTLE, IT CAN'T TAKE PLACE WITHIN THE CITY.
OUT THERE. AS SOON AS YOU'RE READY.
READY.
RIGHT.

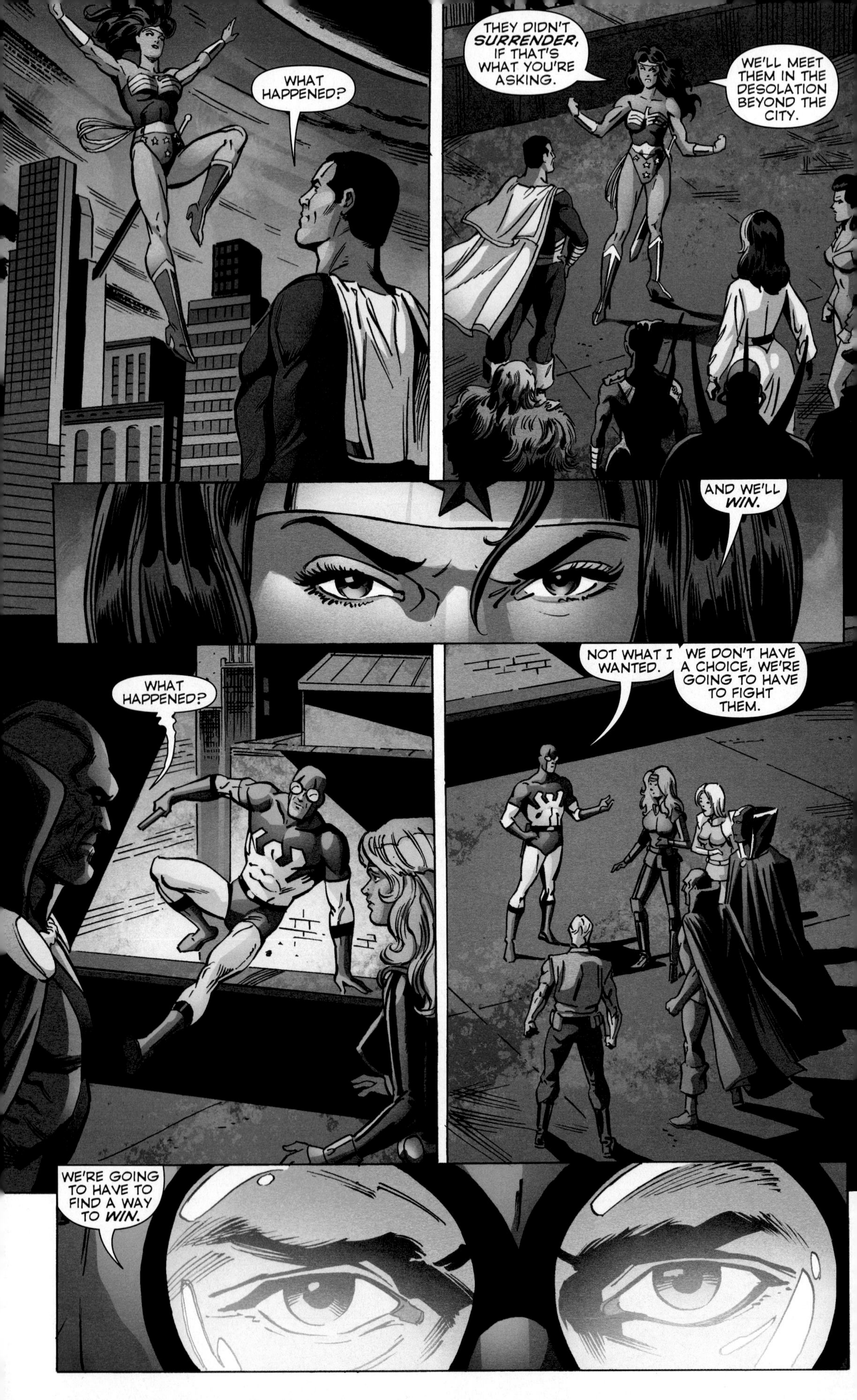
WHAT HAPPENED?
THEY DIDN'T SURRENDER, IF THAT'S WHAT YOU'RE ASKING.
WE'LL MEET THEM IN THE DESOLATION BEYOND THE CITY.
AND WE'LL WIN.
WHAT HAPPENED?
NOT WHAT I WANTED.
WE DON'T HAVE A CHOICE, WE'RE GOING TO HAVE TO FIGHT THEM.
WE'RE GOING TO HAVE TO FIND A WAY TO WIN.

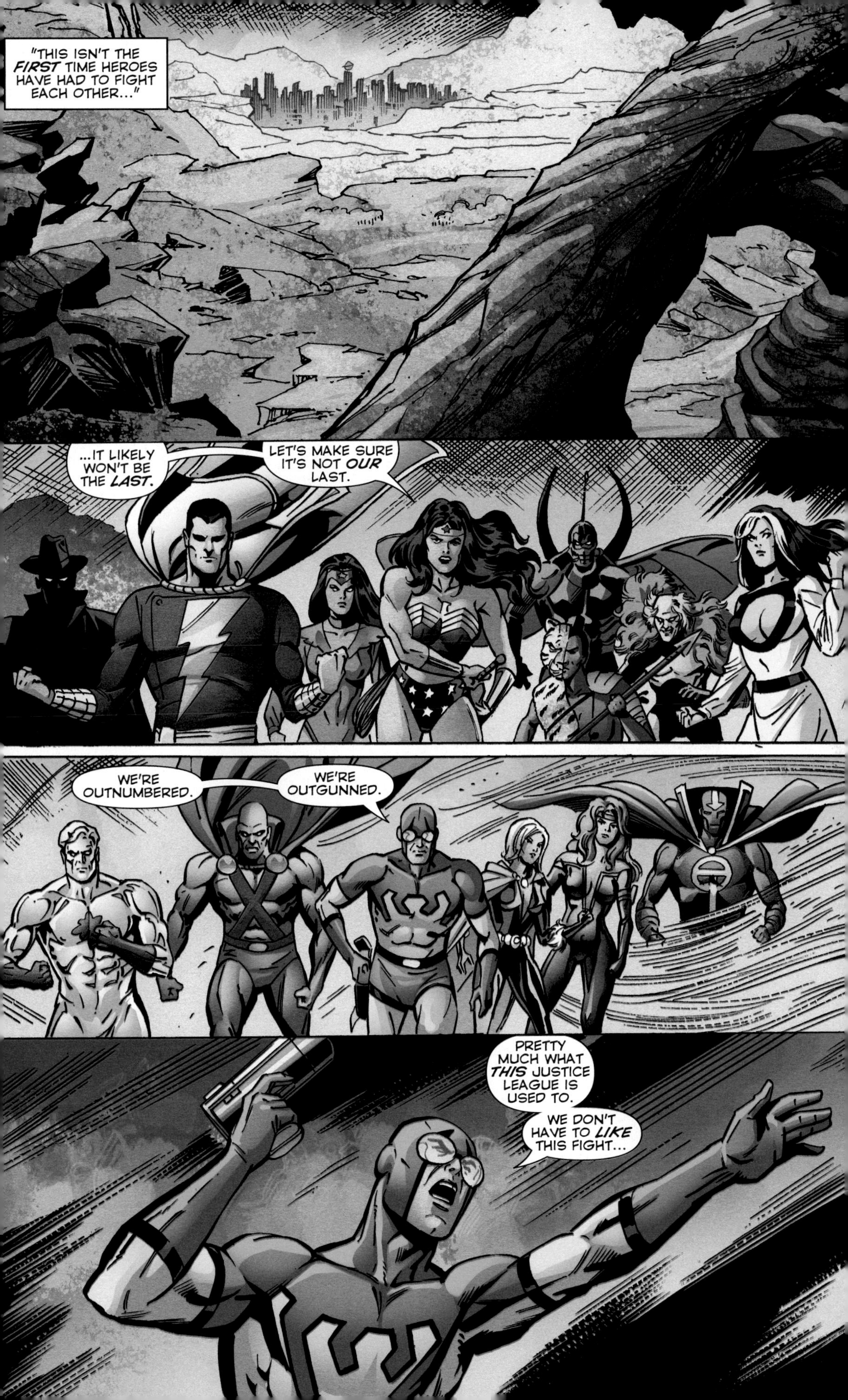
"THIS ISN'T THE FIRST TIME HEROES HAVE HAD TO FIGHT EACH OTHER..."
...IT LIKELY WON'T BE THE LAST.
LET'S MAKE SURE IT'S NOT OUR LAST.
WE'RE OUTNUMBERED.
WE'RE OUTGUNNED.
PRETTY MUCH WHAT THIS JUSTICE LEAGUE IS USED TO.
WE DON'T HAVE TO LIKE THIS FIGHT...

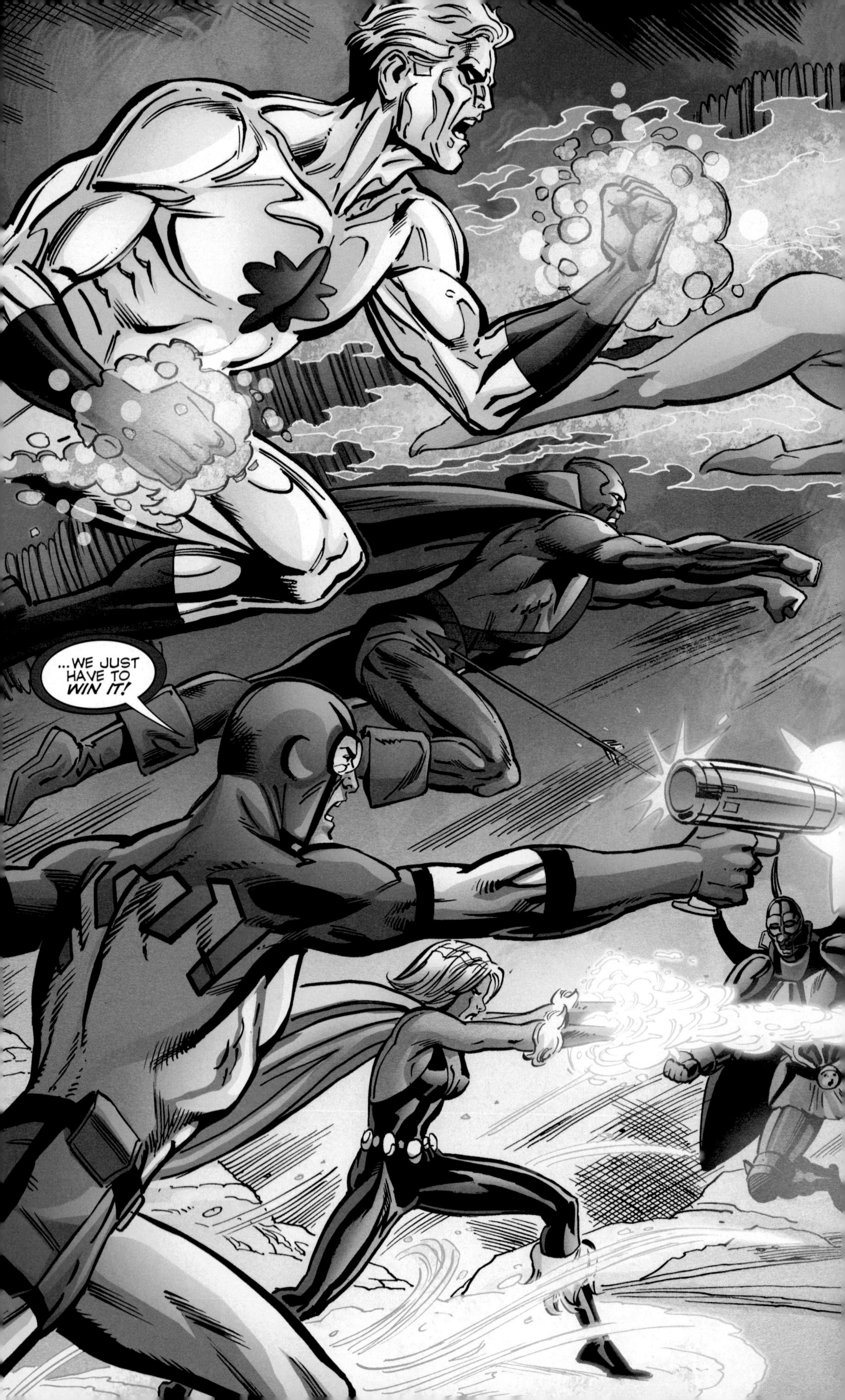
...WE JUST HAVE TO WIN IT!

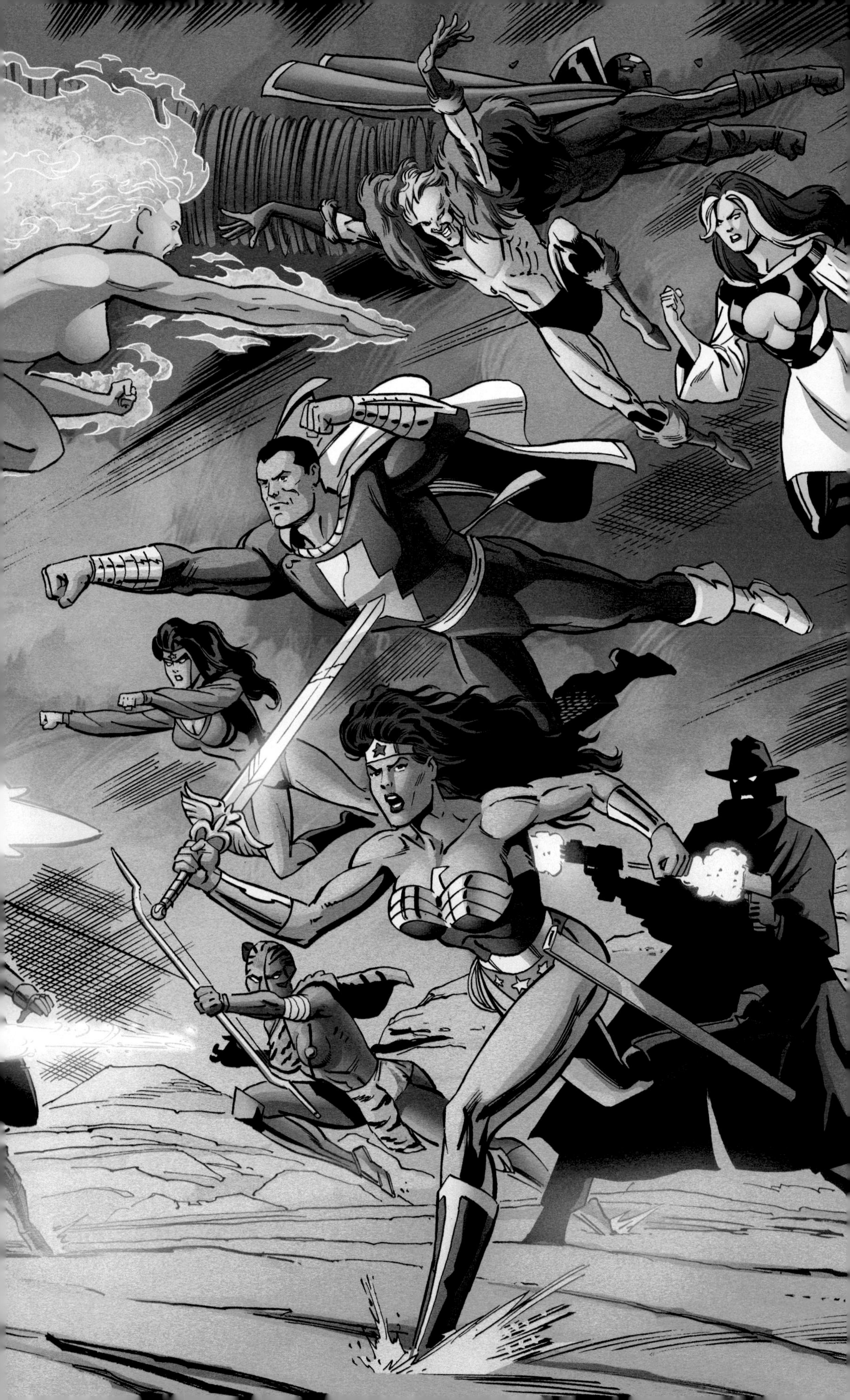

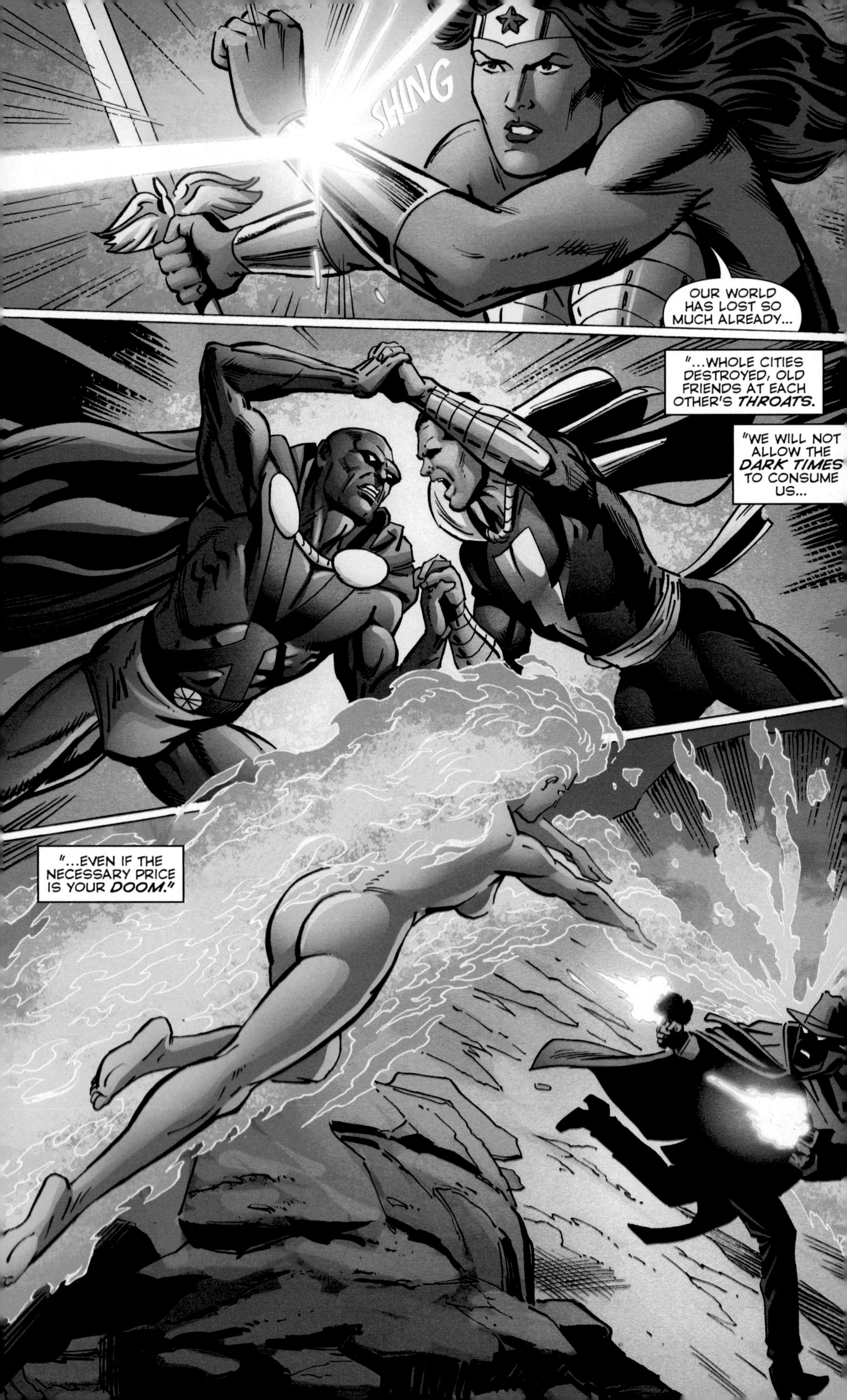
SHING
OUR WORLD HAS LOST SO MUCH ALREADY...
"...WHOLE CITIES DESTROYED, OLD FRIENDS AT EACH OTHER'S *THROATS*.
"WE WILL NOT ALLOW THE *DARK TIMES* TO CONSUME US...
"...EVEN IF THE NECESSARY PRICE IS YOUR *DOOM*."

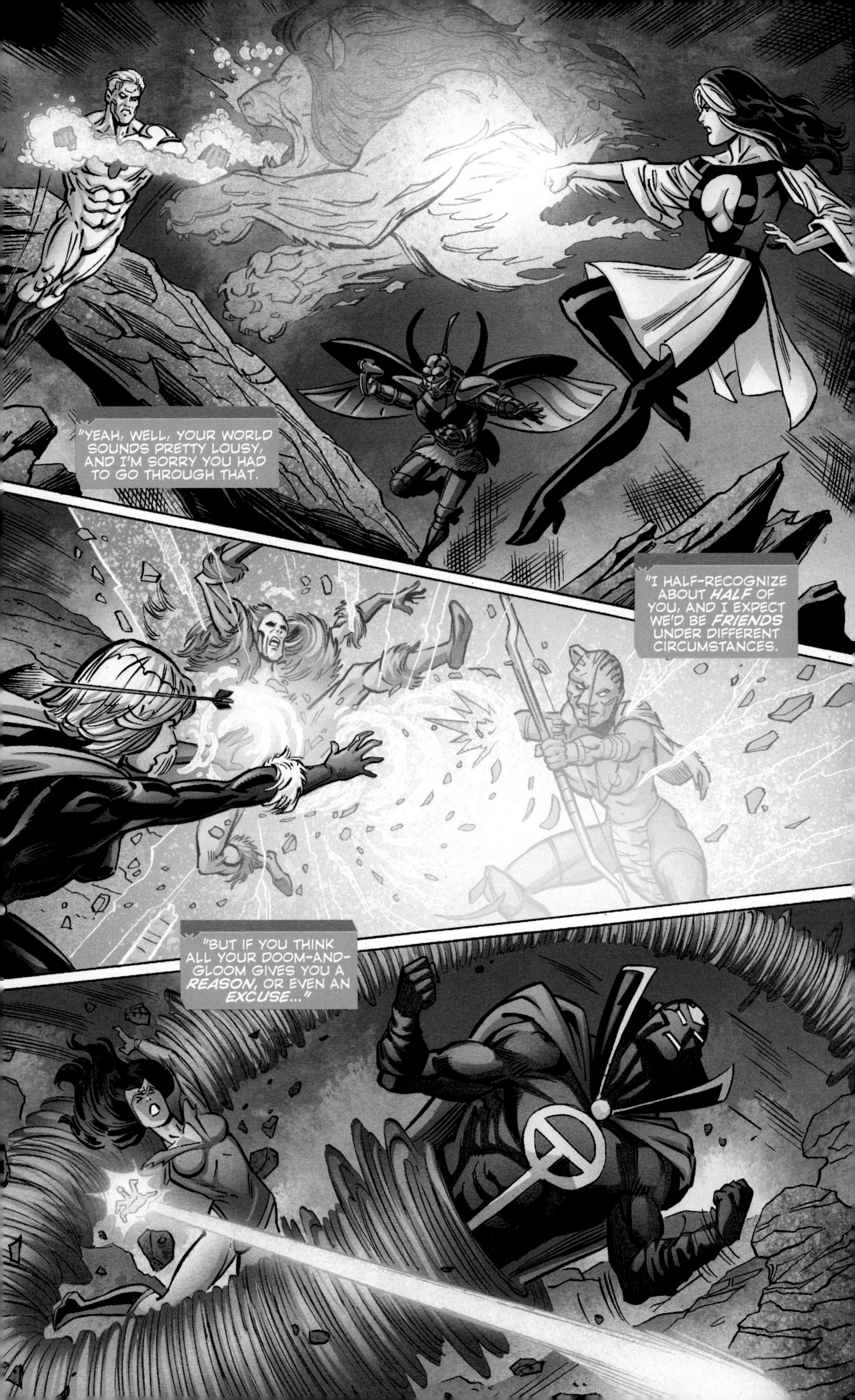
"YEAH, WELL, YOUR WORLD SOUNDS PRETTY LOUSY, AND I'M SORRY YOU HAD TO GO THROUGH THAT.
"I HALF-RECOGNIZE ABOUT HALF OF YOU, AND I EXPECT WE'D BE FRIENDS UNDER DIFFERENT CIRCUMSTANCES.
"BUT IF YOU THINK ALL YOUR DOOM-AND-GLOOM GIVES YOU A REASON, OR EVEN AN EXCUSE..."

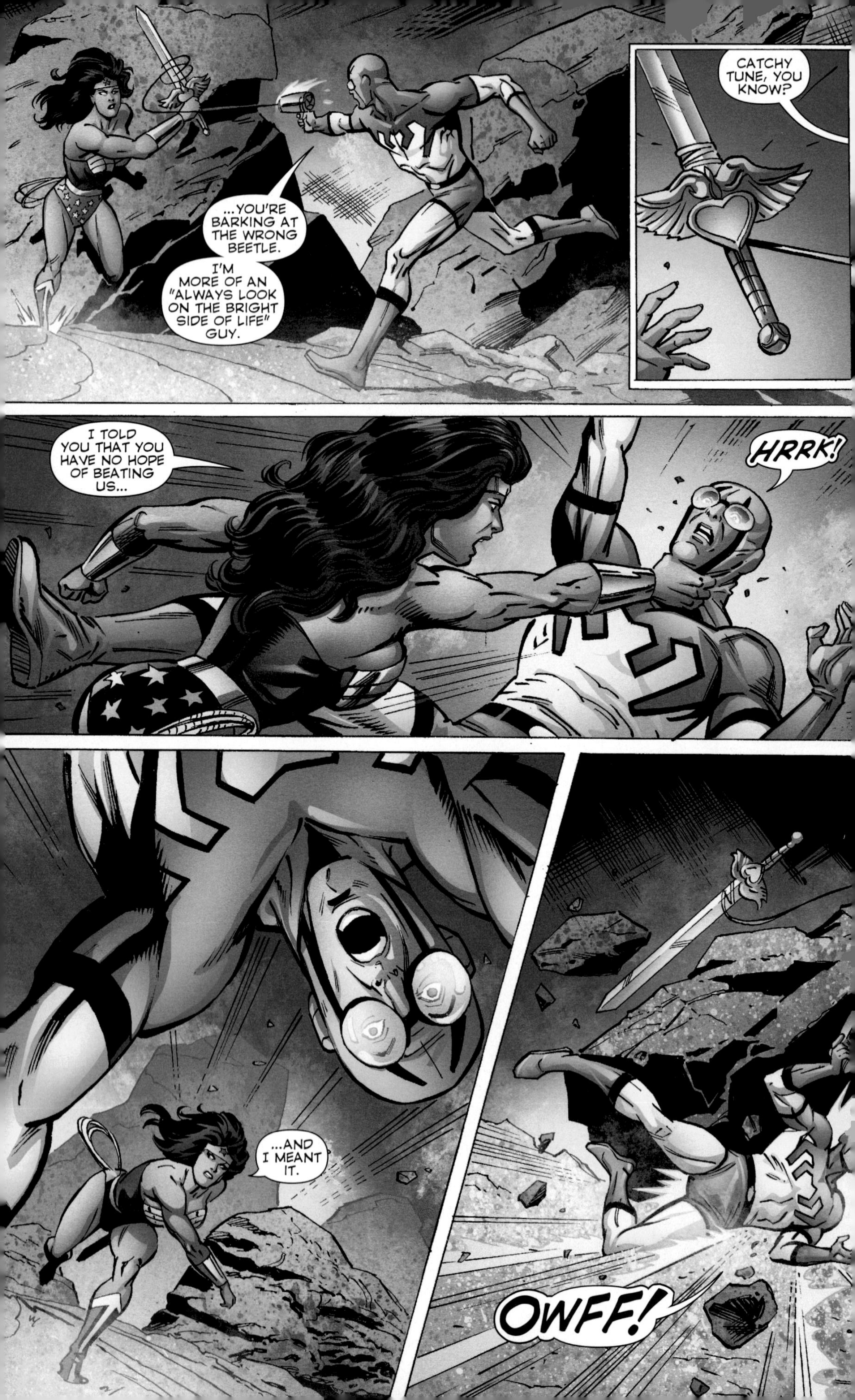

...YOU'RE BARKING AT THE WRONG BEETLE.
I'M MORE OF AN "ALWAYS LOOK ON THE BRIGHT SIDE OF LIFE" GUY.
CATCHY TUNE, YOU KNOW?
I TOLD YOU THAT YOU HAVE NO HOPE OF BEATING US...
HRRK!
...AND I MEANT IT.
OWFF!

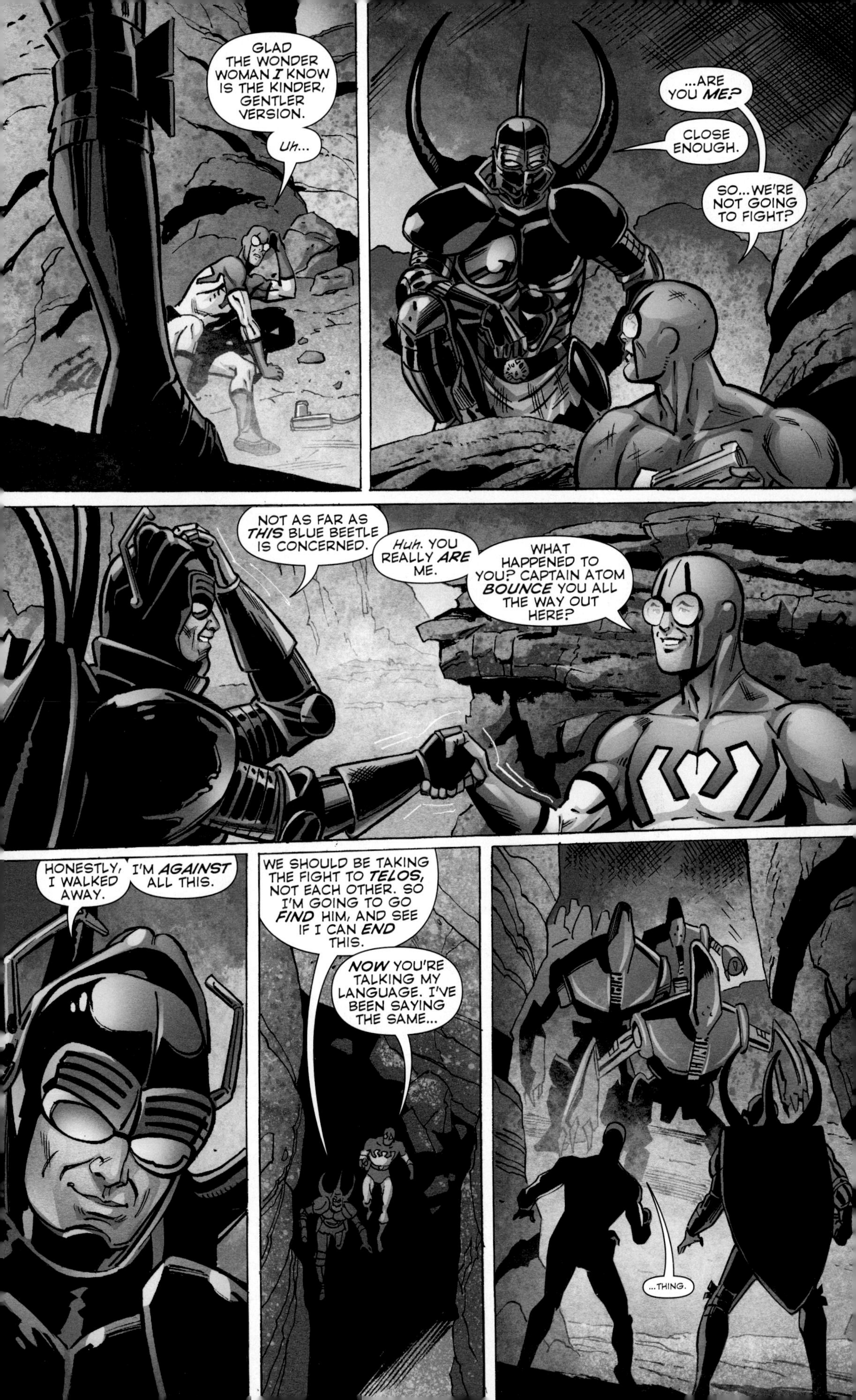
GLAD THE WONDER WOMAN *I* KNOW IS THE KINDER, GENTLER VERSION.
Uh...
...ARE YOU *ME?*
CLOSE ENOUGH.
SO... WE'RE NOT GOING TO FIGHT?
NOT AS FAR AS *THIS* BLUE BEETLE IS CONCERNED.
Huh. YOU REALLY *ARE* ME.
WHAT HAPPENED TO YOU? CAPTAIN ATOM *BOUNCE* YOU ALL THE WAY OUT HERE?
HONESTLY, I WALKED AWAY.
I'M *AGAINST* ALL THIS.
WE SHOULD BE TAKING THE FIGHT TO *TELOS,* NOT EACH OTHER. SO I'M GOING TO GO *FIND* HIM, AND SEE IF I CAN *END* THIS.
NOW YOU'RE TALKING MY LANGUAGE. I'VE BEEN SAYING THE SAME...
...THING.

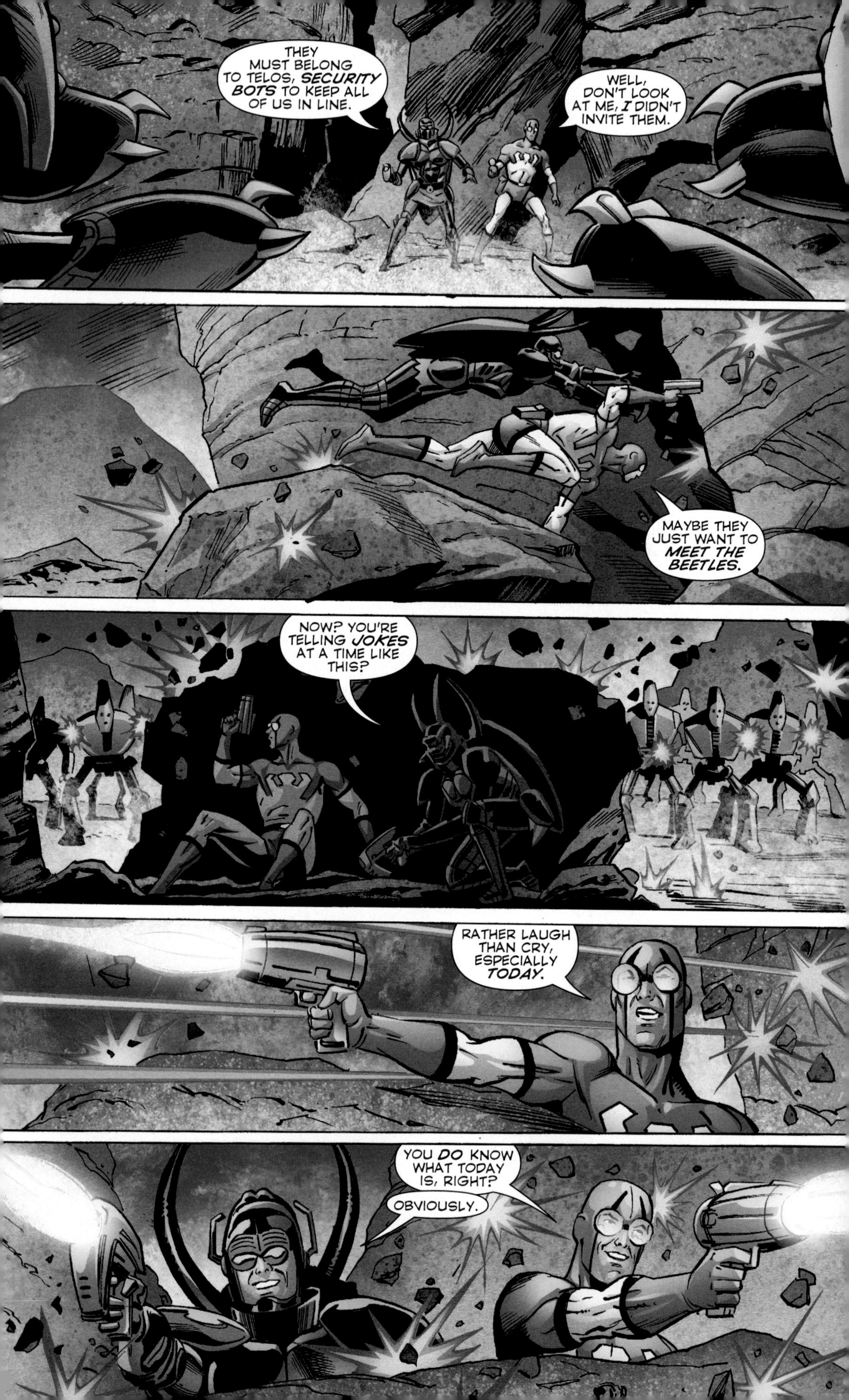
THEY MUST BELONG TO TELOS, SECURITY BOTS TO KEEP ALL OF US IN LINE.
WELL, DON'T LOOK AT ME, I DIDN'T INVITE THEM.
MAYBE THEY JUST WANT TO MEET THE BEETLES.
NOW? YOU'RE TELLING JOKES AT A TIME LIKE THIS?
RATHER LAUGH THAN CRY, ESPECIALLY TODAY.
YOU DO KNOW WHAT TODAY IS, RIGHT?
OBVIOUSLY.

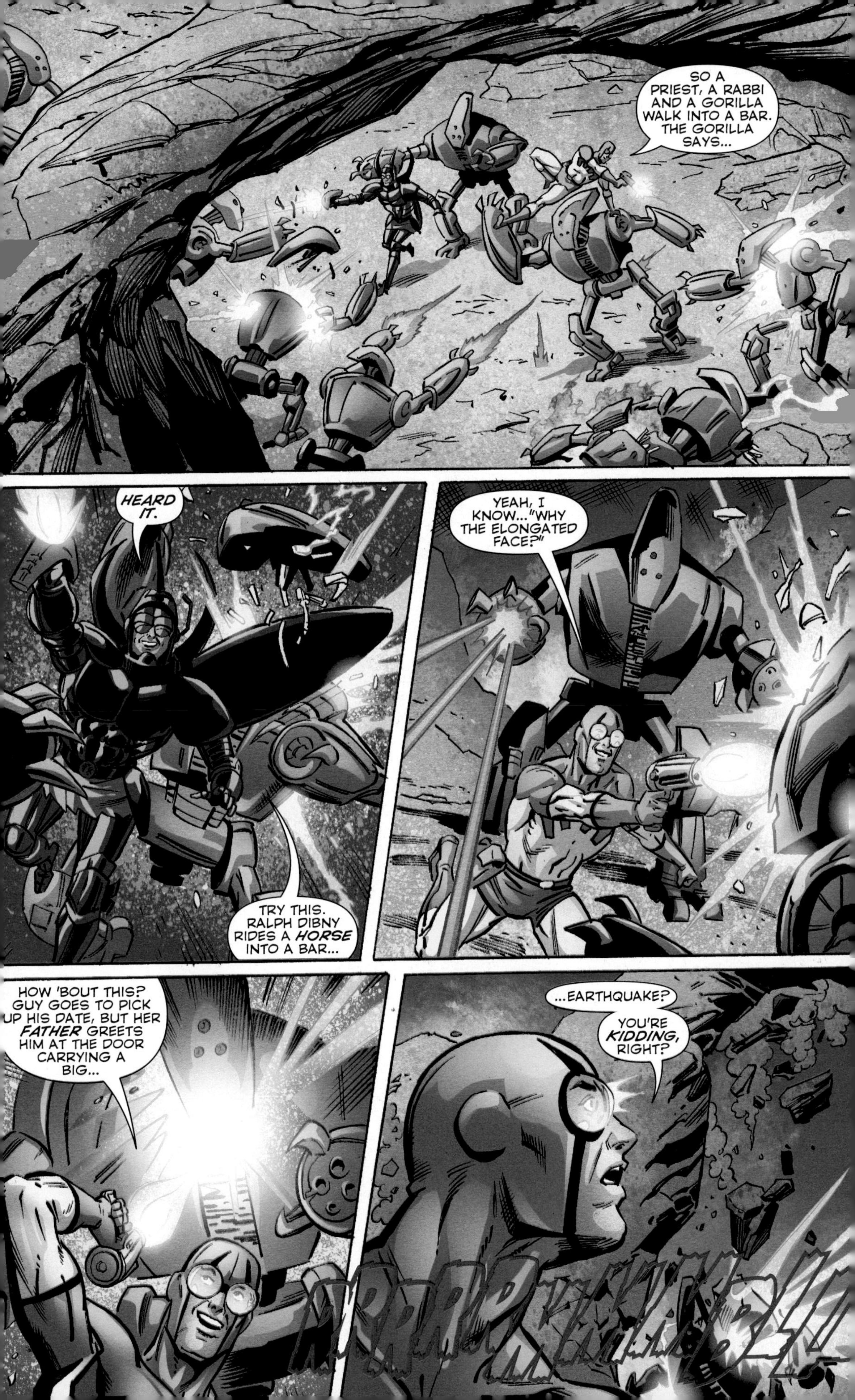
SO A PRIEST, A RABBI AND A GORILLA WALK INTO A BAR. THE GORILLA SAYS...
HEARD IT.
TRY THIS. RALPH DIBNY RIDES A HORSE INTO A BAR...
YEAH, I KNOW... "WHY THE ELONGATED FACE?"
HOW 'BOUT THIS? GUY GOES TO PICK UP HIS DATE, BUT HER FATHER GREETS HIM AT THE DOOR CARRYING A BIG...
...EARTHQUAKE?
YOU'RE KIDDING, RIGHT?

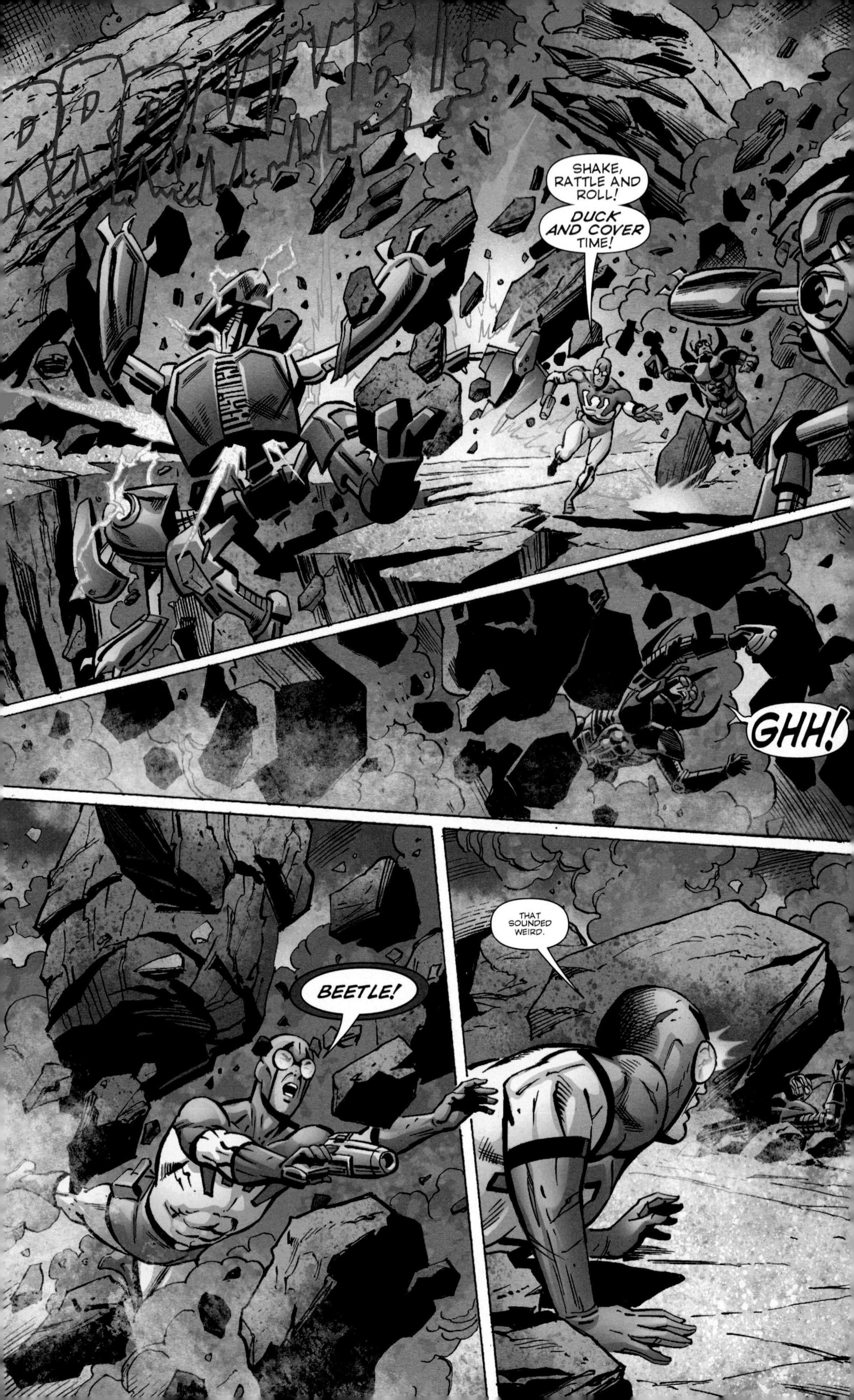
SHAKE, RATTLE AND ROLL!
DUCK AND COVER TIME!
GHH!
BEETLE!
THAT SOUNDED WEIRD.

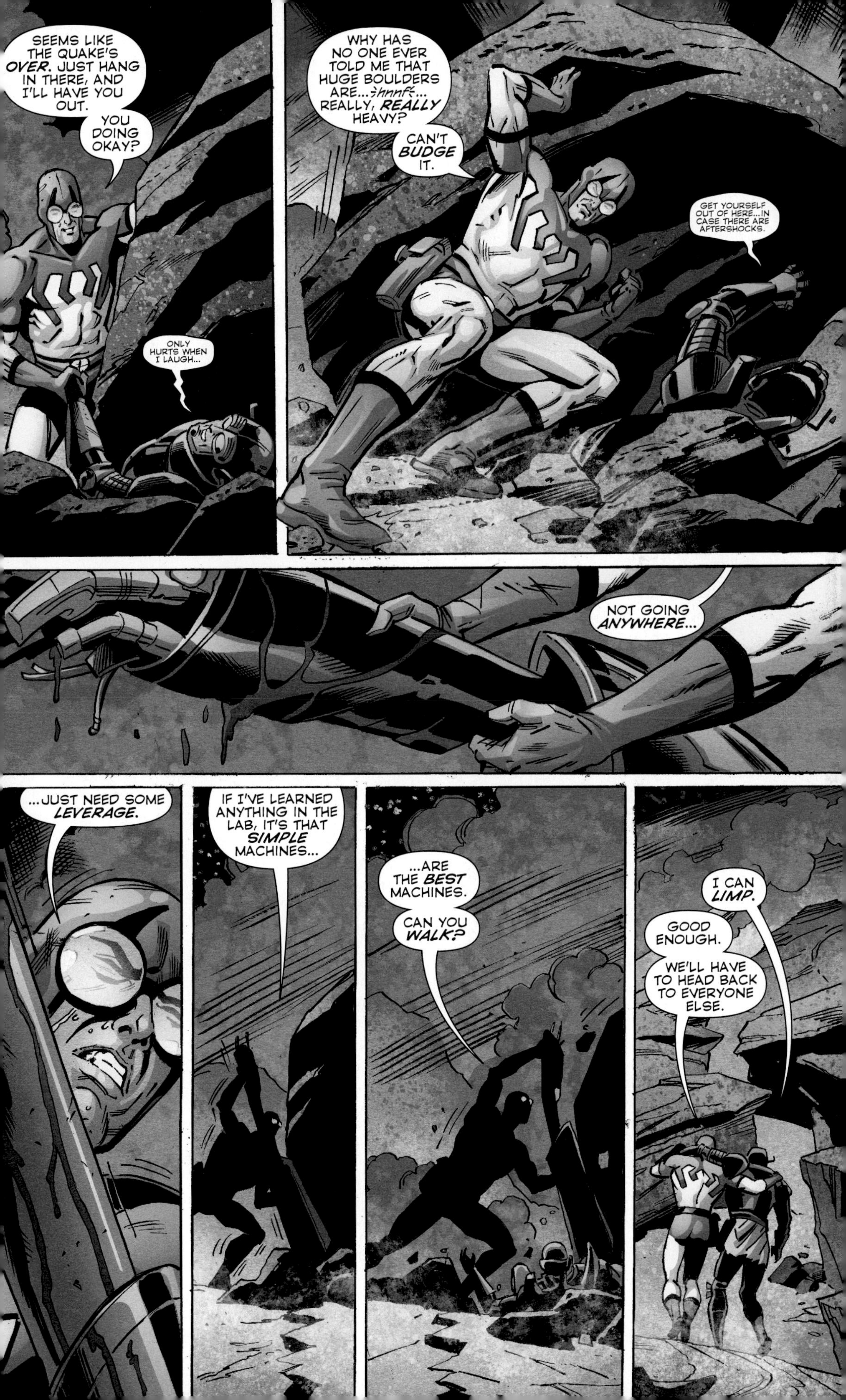
SEEMS LIKE THE QUAKE'S **OVER.** JUST HANG IN THERE, AND I'LL HAVE YOU OUT.
YOU DOING OKAY?
ONLY HURTS WHEN I LAUGH...
WHY HAS NO ONE EVER TOLD ME THAT HUGE BOULDERS ARE...*hnnf*... REALLY, ***REALLY*** HEAVY?
CAN'T ***BUDGE*** IT.
GET YOURSELF OUT OF HERE...IN CASE THERE ARE AFTERSHOCKS.
NOT GOING ***ANYWHERE...***
...JUST NEED SOME ***LEVERAGE.***
IF I'VE LEARNED ANYTHING IN THE LAB, IT'S THAT ***SIMPLE*** MACHINES...
...ARE THE ***BEST*** MACHINES.
CAN YOU ***WALK?***
I CAN ***LIMP.***
GOOD ENOUGH.
WE'LL HAVE TO HEAD BACK TO EVERYONE ELSE.

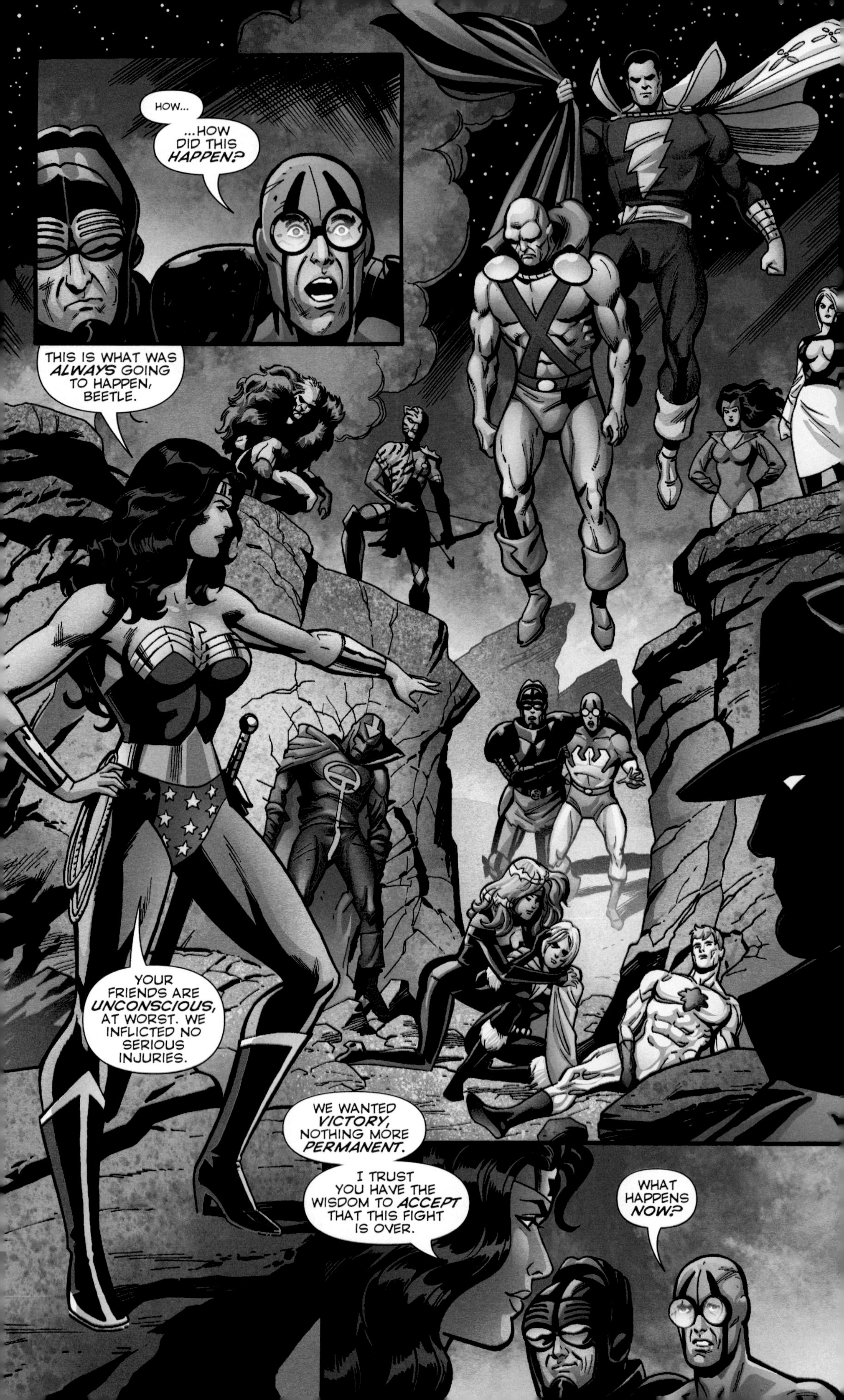
HOW...
...HOW DID THIS HAPPEN?
THIS IS WHAT WAS ALWAYS GOING TO HAPPEN, BEETLE.
YOUR FRIENDS ARE UNCONSCIOUS, AT WORST. WE INFLICTED NO SERIOUS INJURIES.
WE WANTED VICTORY, NOTHING MORE PERMANENT.
I TRUST YOU HAVE THE WISDOM TO ACCEPT THAT THIS FIGHT IS OVER.
WHAT HAPPENS NOW?

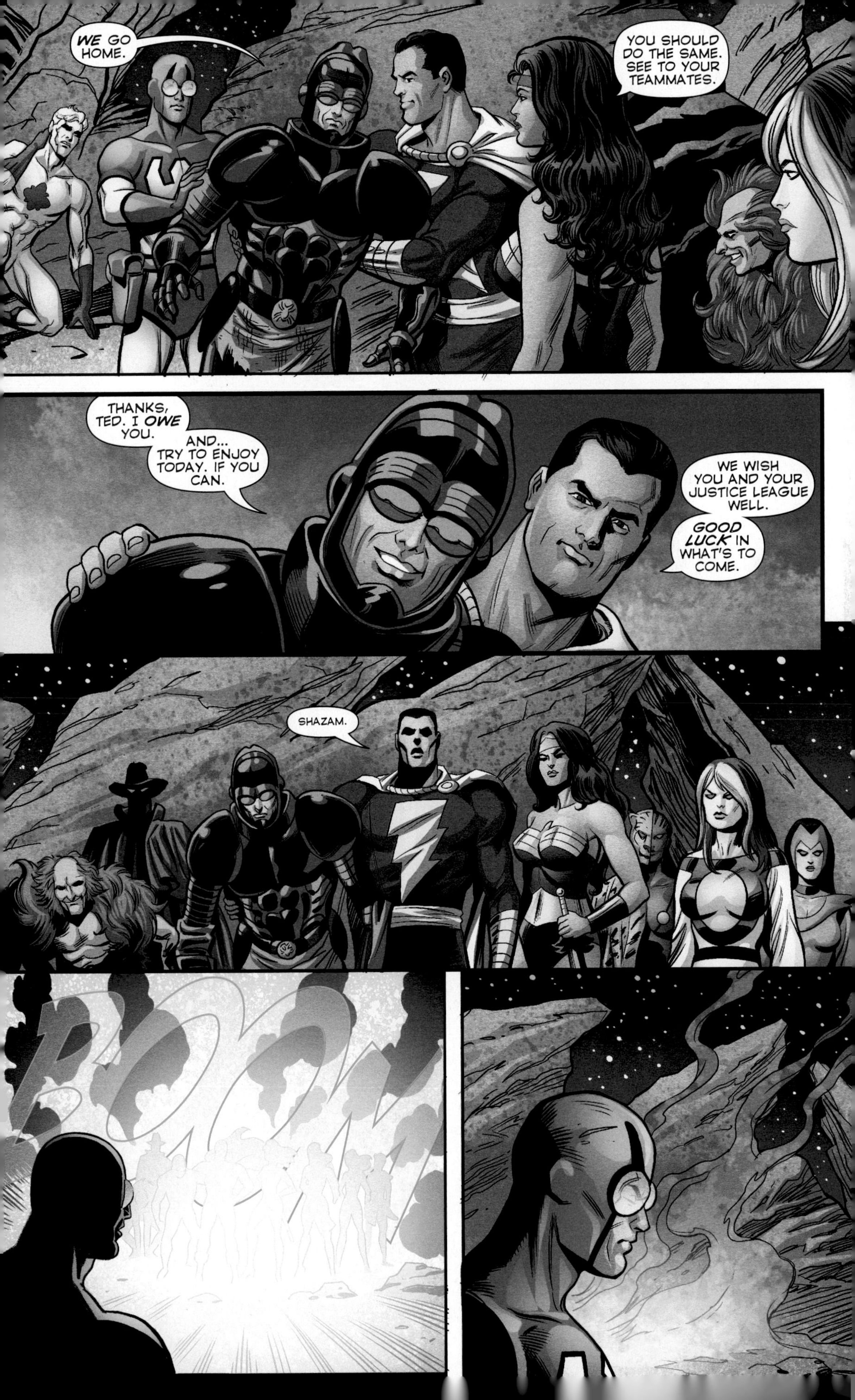
WE GO HOME.
YOU SHOULD DO THE SAME. SEE TO YOUR TEAMMATES.
THANKS, TED. I OWE YOU.
AND... TRY TO ENJOY TODAY. IF YOU CAN.
WE WISH YOU AND YOUR JUSTICE LEAGUE WELL.
GOOD LUCK IN WHAT'S TO COME.
SHAZAM.

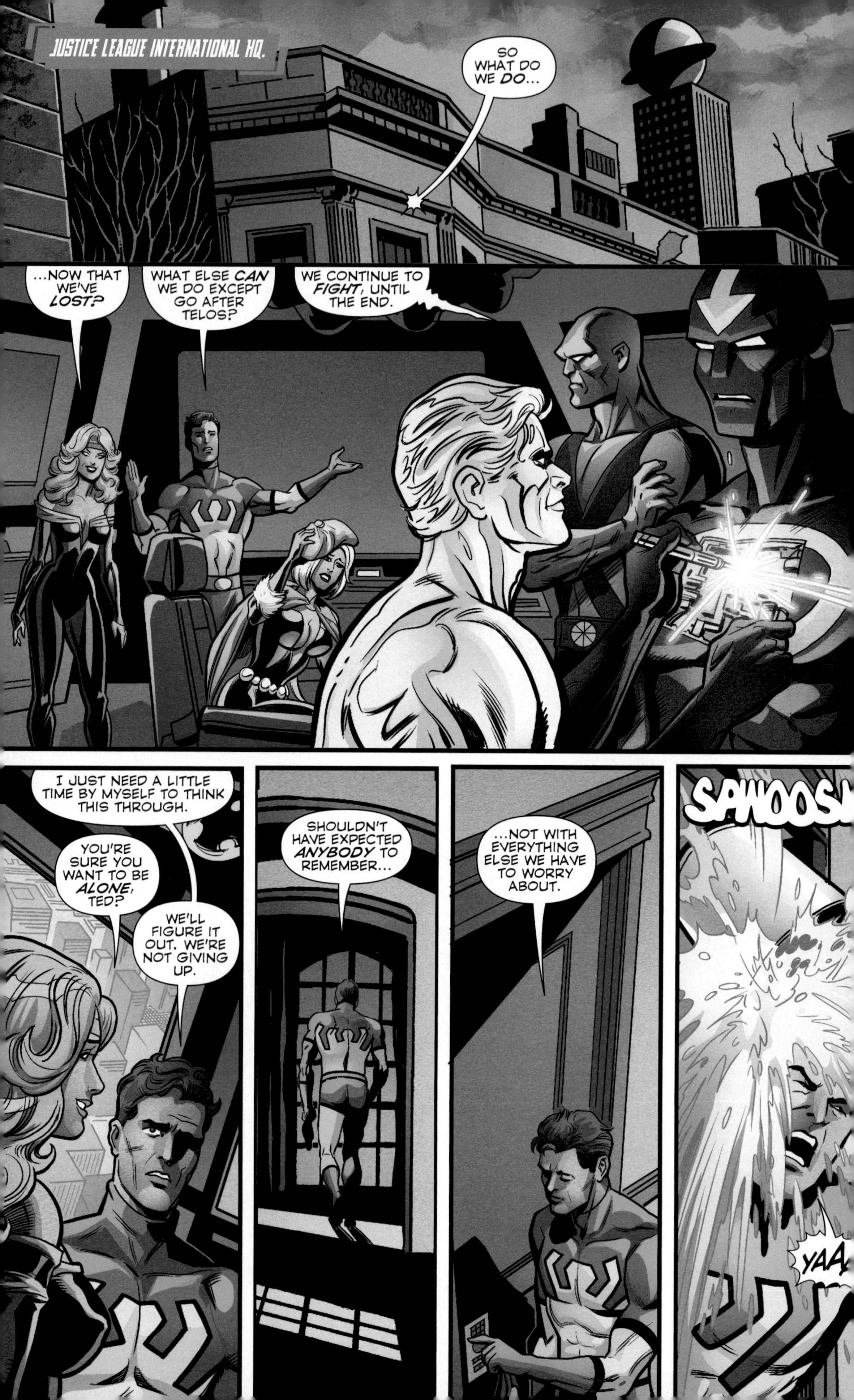
JUSTICE LEAGUE INTERNATIONAL HQ.
SO WHAT DO WE DO...
...NOW THAT WE'VE LOST?
WHAT ELSE CAN WE DO EXCEPT GO AFTER TELOS?
WE CONTINUE TO FIGHT, UNTIL THE END.
I JUST NEED A LITTLE TIME BY MYSELF TO THINK THIS THROUGH.
YOU'RE SURE YOU WANT TO BE ALONE, TED?
WE'LL FIGURE IT OUT. WE'RE NOT GIVING UP.
SHOULDN'T HAVE EXPECTED ANYBODY TO REMEMBER...
...NOT WITH EVERYTHING ELSE WE HAVE TO WORRY ABOUT.
YAA

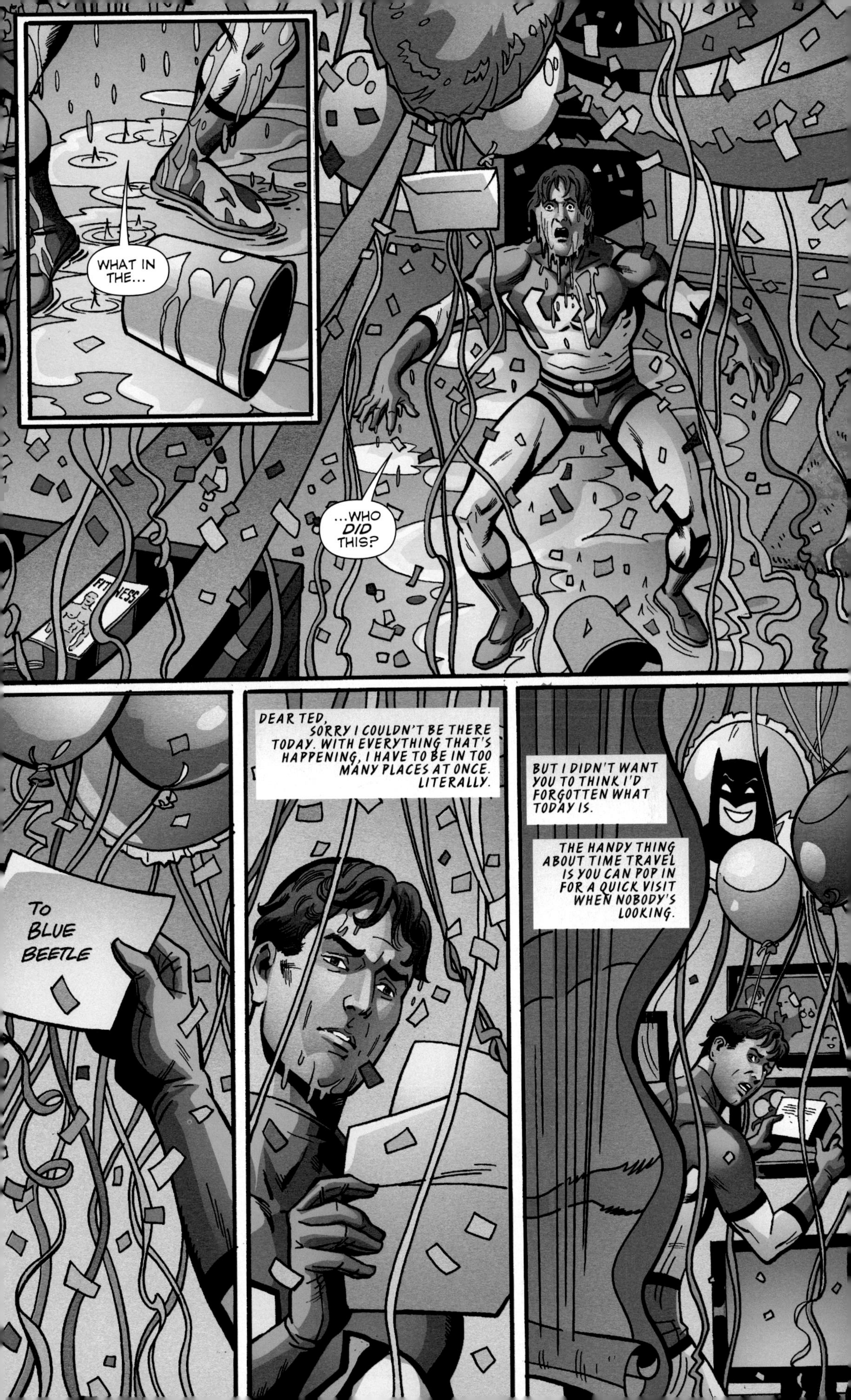

WHAT IN THE...
...WHO DID THIS?
FITNESS
TO BLUE BEETLE
DEAR TED, SORRY I COULDN'T BE THERE TODAY. WITH EVERYTHING THAT'S HAPPENING, I HAVE TO BE IN TOO MANY PLACES AT ONCE. LITERALLY.
BUT I DIDN'T WANT YOU TO THINK I'D FORGOTTEN WHAT TODAY IS.
THE HANDY THING ABOUT TIME TRAVEL IS YOU CAN POP IN FOR A QUICK VISIT WHEN NOBODY'S LOOKING.

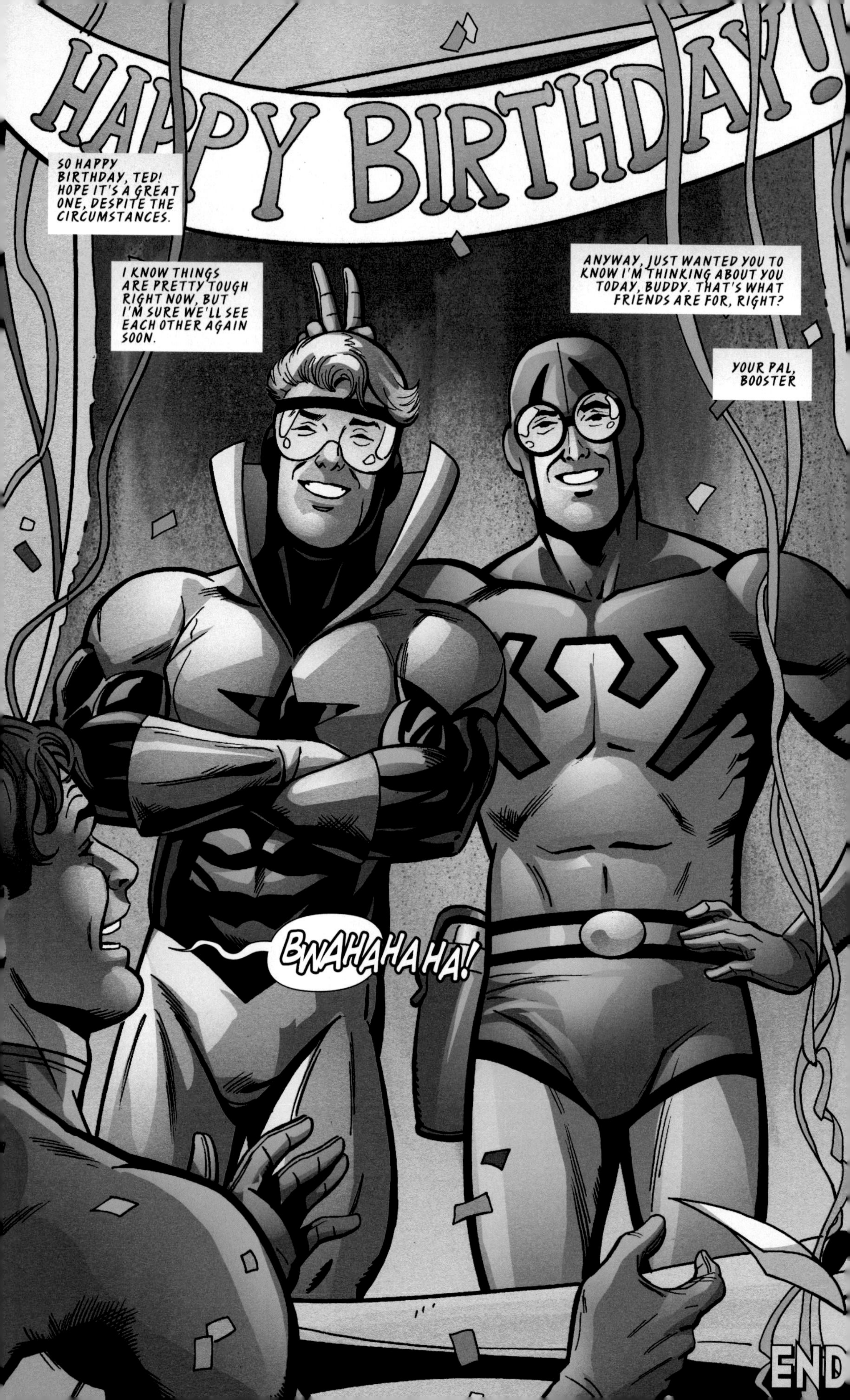
HAPPY BIRTHDAY!
SO HAPPY BIRTHDAY, TED! HOPE IT'S A GREAT ONE, DESPITE THE CIRCUMSTANCES.
I KNOW THINGS ARE PRETTY TOUGH RIGHT NOW, BUT I'M SURE WE'LL SEE EACH OTHER AGAIN SOON.
ANYWAY, JUST WANTED YOU TO KNOW I'M THINKING ABOUT YOU TODAY, BUDDY. THAT'S WHAT FRIENDS ARE FOR, RIGHT?
YOUR PAL, BOOSTER
BWAHAHAHAHA!
END

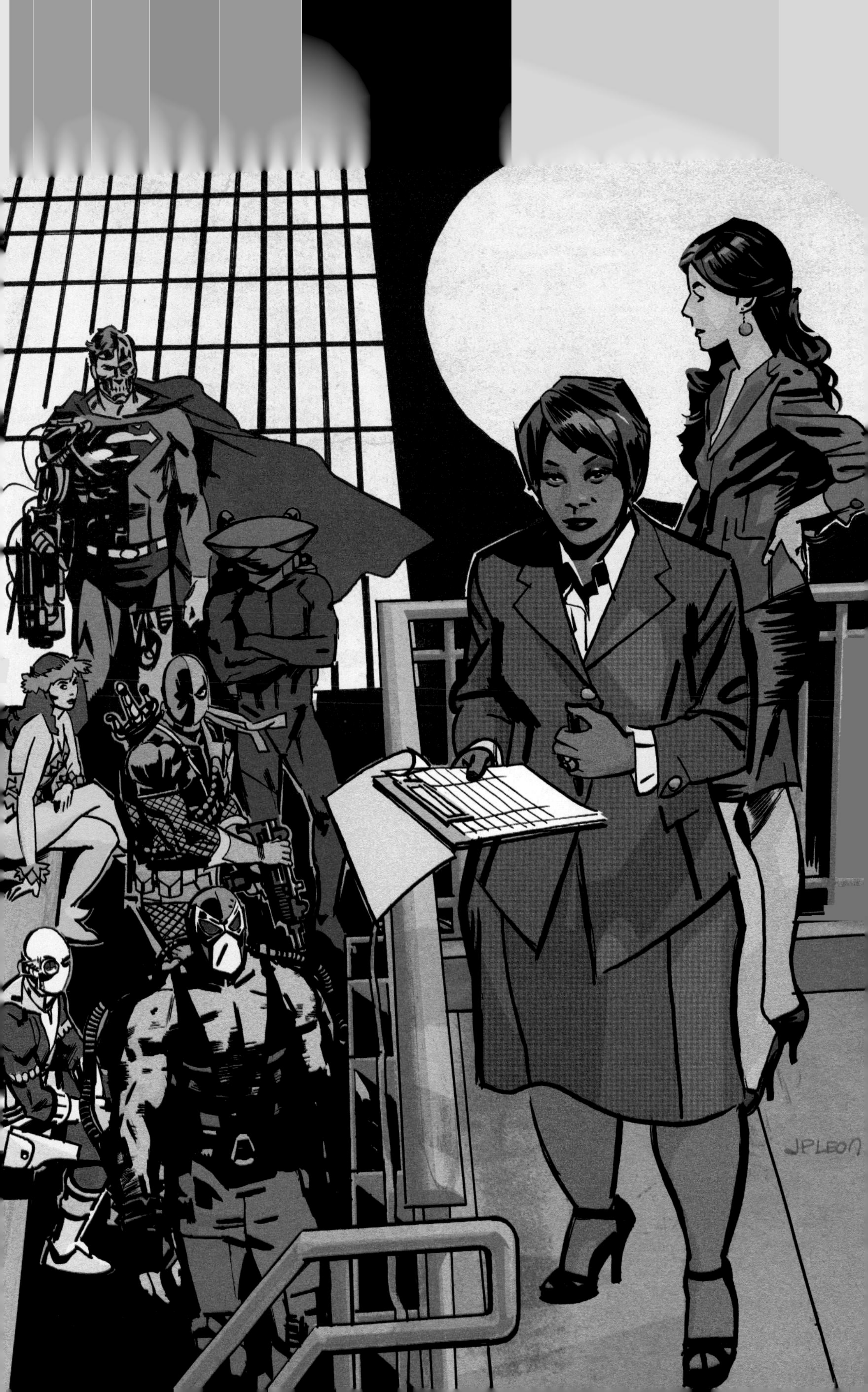
JPLEON

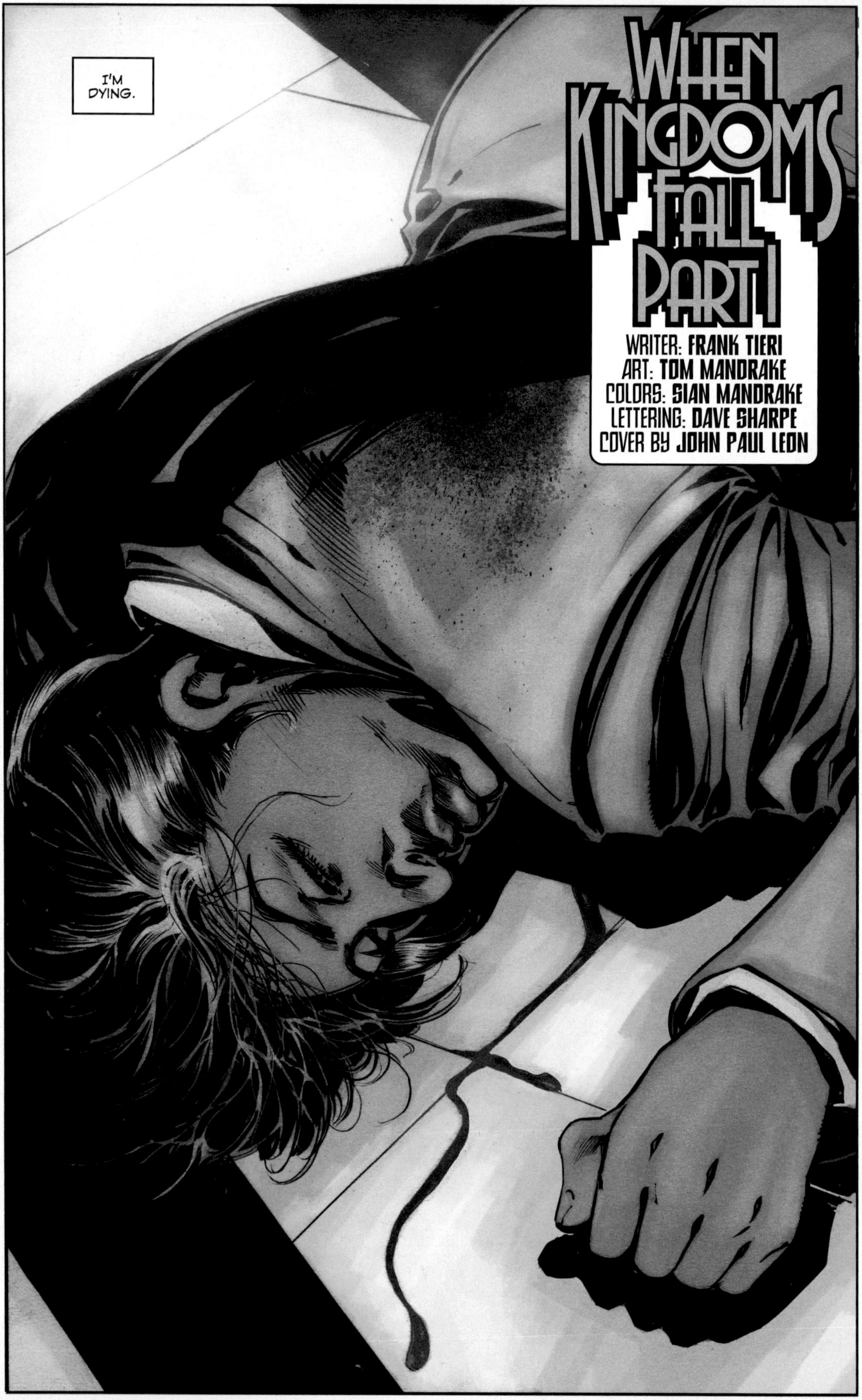
I'M DYING.
WHEN KINGDOMS FALL PART I
WRITER: FRANK TIERI
ART: TOM MANDRAKE
COLORS: SIAN MANDRAKE
LETTERING: DAVE SHARPE
COVER BY JOHN PAUL LEON

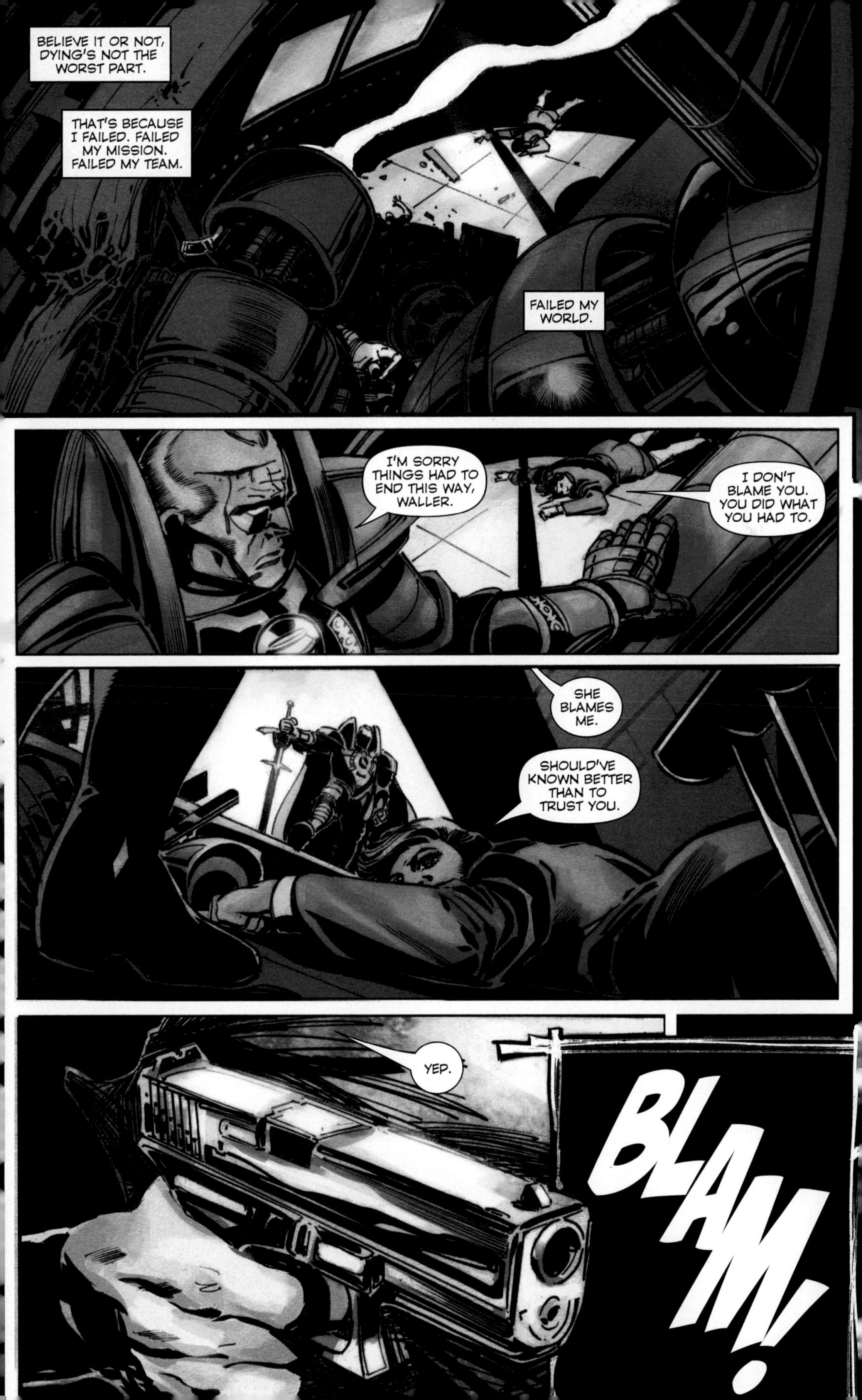

BELIEVE IT OR NOT, DYING'S NOT THE WORST PART.
THAT'S BECAUSE I FAILED. FAILED MY MISSION. FAILED MY TEAM.
FAILED MY WORLD.
I'M SORRY THINGS HAD TO END THIS WAY, WALLER.
I DON'T BLAME YOU. YOU DID WHAT YOU HAD TO.
SHE BLAMES ME.
SHOULD'VE KNOWN BETTER THAN TO TRUST YOU.
YEP.
BLAM!

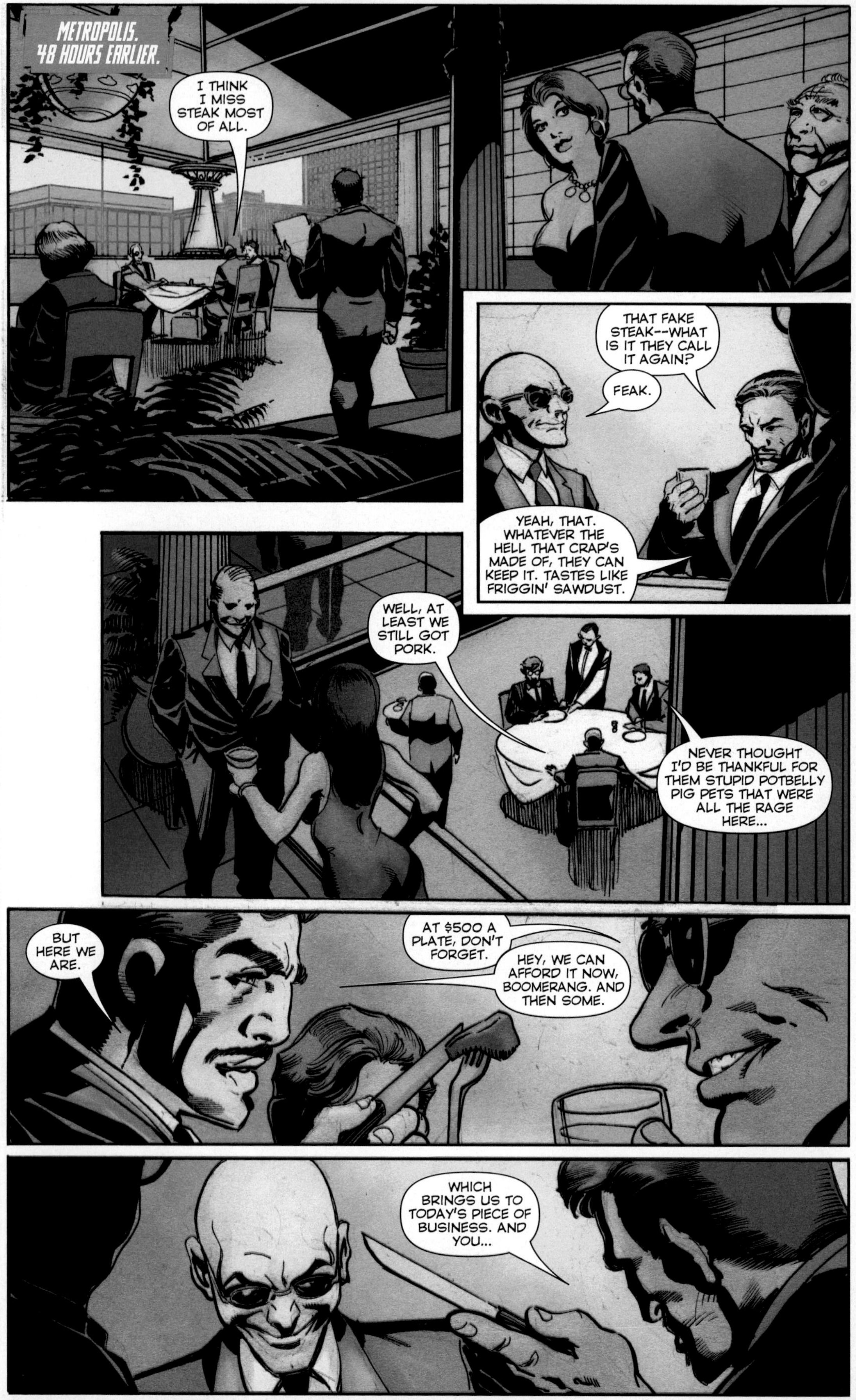
METROPOLIS. 48 HOURS EARLIER.
I THINK I MISS STEAK MOST OF ALL.
THAT FAKE STEAK--WHAT IS IT THEY CALL IT AGAIN?
FEAK.
YEAH, THAT. WHATEVER THE HELL THAT CRAP'S MADE OF, THEY CAN KEEP IT. TASTES LIKE FRIGGIN' SAWDUST.
WELL, AT LEAST WE STILL GOT PORK.
NEVER THOUGHT I'D BE THANKFUL FOR THEM STUPID POTBELLY PIG PETS THAT WERE ALL THE RAGE HERE...
BUT HERE WE ARE.
AT $500 A PLATE, DON'T FORGET.
HEY, WE CAN AFFORD IT NOW, BOOMERANG. AND THEN SOME.
WHICH BRINGS US TO TODAY'S PIECE OF BUSINESS. AND YOU...

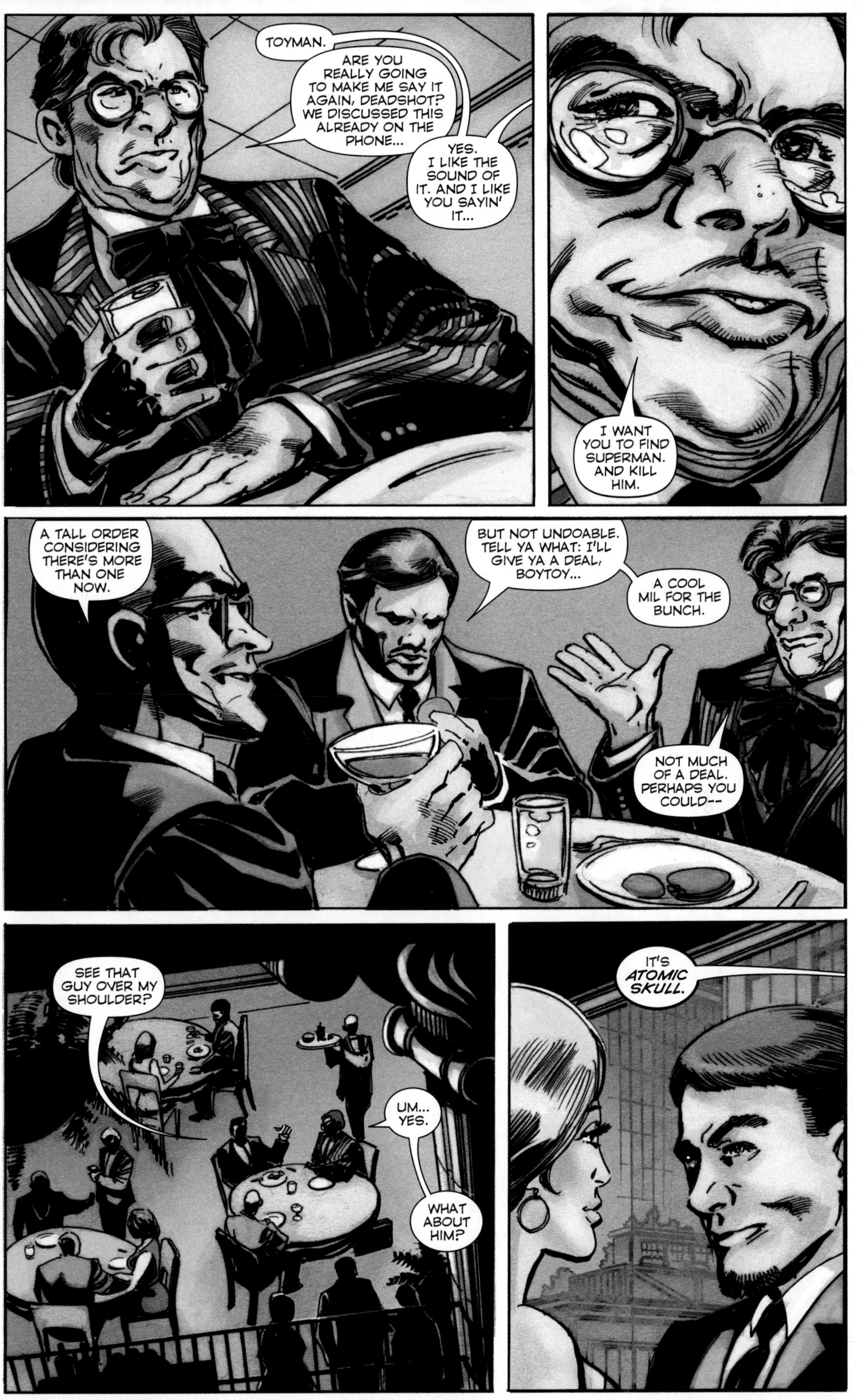
TOYMAN.
ARE YOU REALLY GOING TO MAKE ME SAY IT AGAIN, DEADSHOT? WE DISCUSSED THIS ALREADY ON THE PHONE...
YES. I LIKE THE SOUND OF IT. AND I LIKE YOU SAYIN' IT...
I WANT YOU TO FIND SUPERMAN. AND KILL HIM.
A TALL ORDER CONSIDERING THERE'S MORE THAN ONE NOW.
BUT NOT UNDOABLE. TELL YA WHAT: I'LL GIVE YA A DEAL, BOYTOY...
A COOL MIL FOR THE BUNCH.
NOT MUCH OF A DEAL. PERHAPS YOU COULD--
SEE THAT GUY OVER MY SHOULDER?
UM... YES.
WHAT ABOUT HIM?
IT'S *ATOMIC SKULL.*

IT IS? I DIDN'T RECOGNIZE HIM.

RIGHT. BECAUSE I SHOULD SAY HE *WAS* ATOMIC SKULL.

NOW? JUST AN ORDINARY SCHMOE.

TIME WAS YOU'D BE SUCKING UP TO HIM RIGHT NOW. OR METALLO. OR WHOEVER THE NEW SUPER TOUGH GUY FLAVOR OF THE MONTH WAS.

BUT NOT ME AND BOOM HERE.

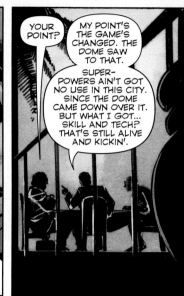

YOUR POINT?

MY POINT'S THE GAME'S CHANGED. THE DOME SAW TO THAT. SUPER-POWERS AIN'T GOT NO USE IN THIS CITY. SINCE THE DOME CAME DOWN OVER IT. BUT WHAT I GOT... SKILL AND TECH? THAT'S STILL ALIVE AND KICKIN'.

AND IT'S A COOL MIL IF YA WANT THE CLOWNS WITH THE ESSES ON THEIR CHESTS NOT TO BE.

〈SIGH〉

FINE.

THAT'S MY BOY. NOW HOW ABOUT WE HAVE ANOTHER DRINK TO CELEBRATE. I HEAR THEY GOT A HUNDRED-BUCK BOTTLE OF ORANGE SODA THAT--

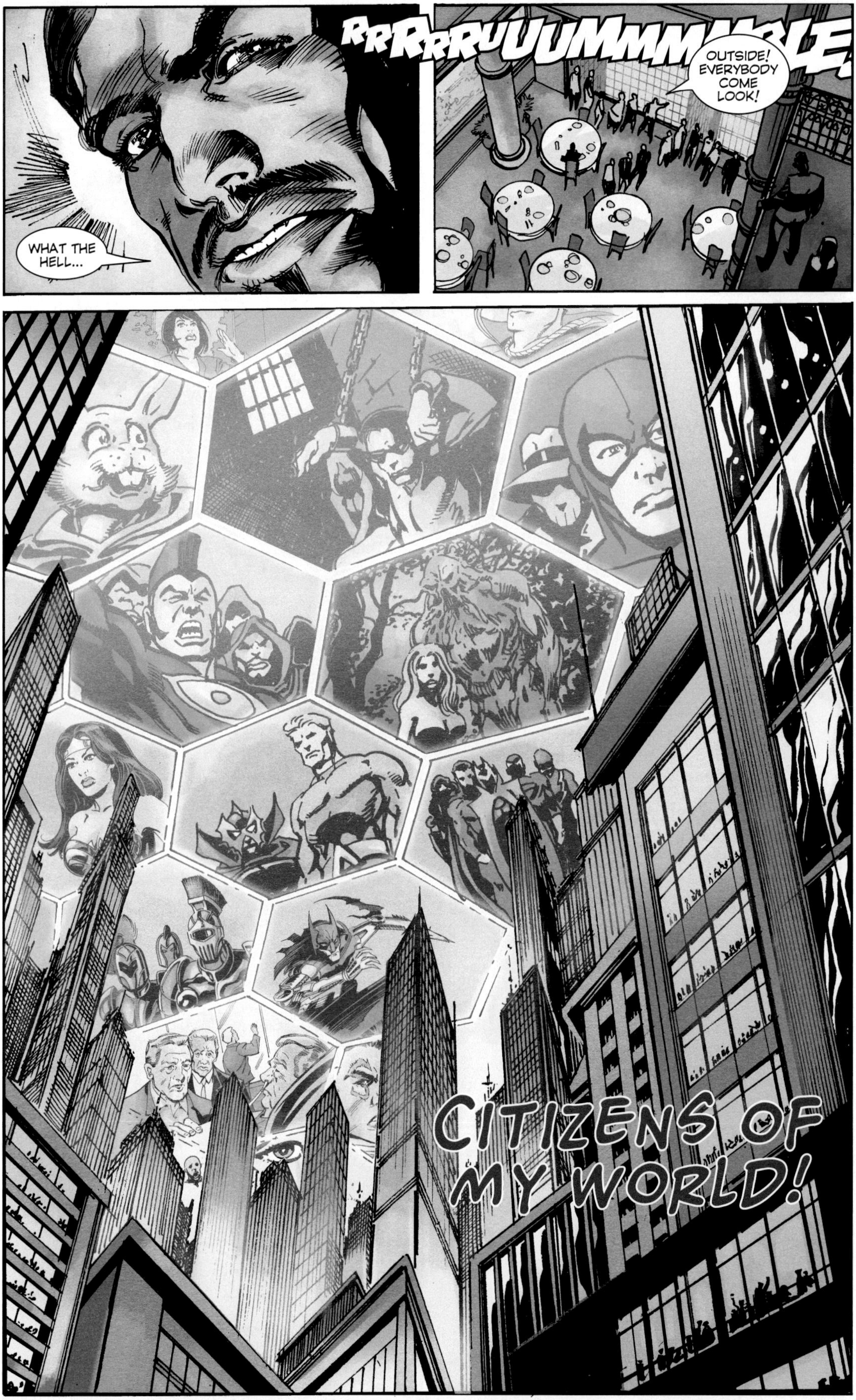
WHAT THE HELL...
RRRRRRUUUUMMMMMBLE
OUTSIDE! EVERYBODY COME LOOK!
CITIZENS OF MY WORLD!

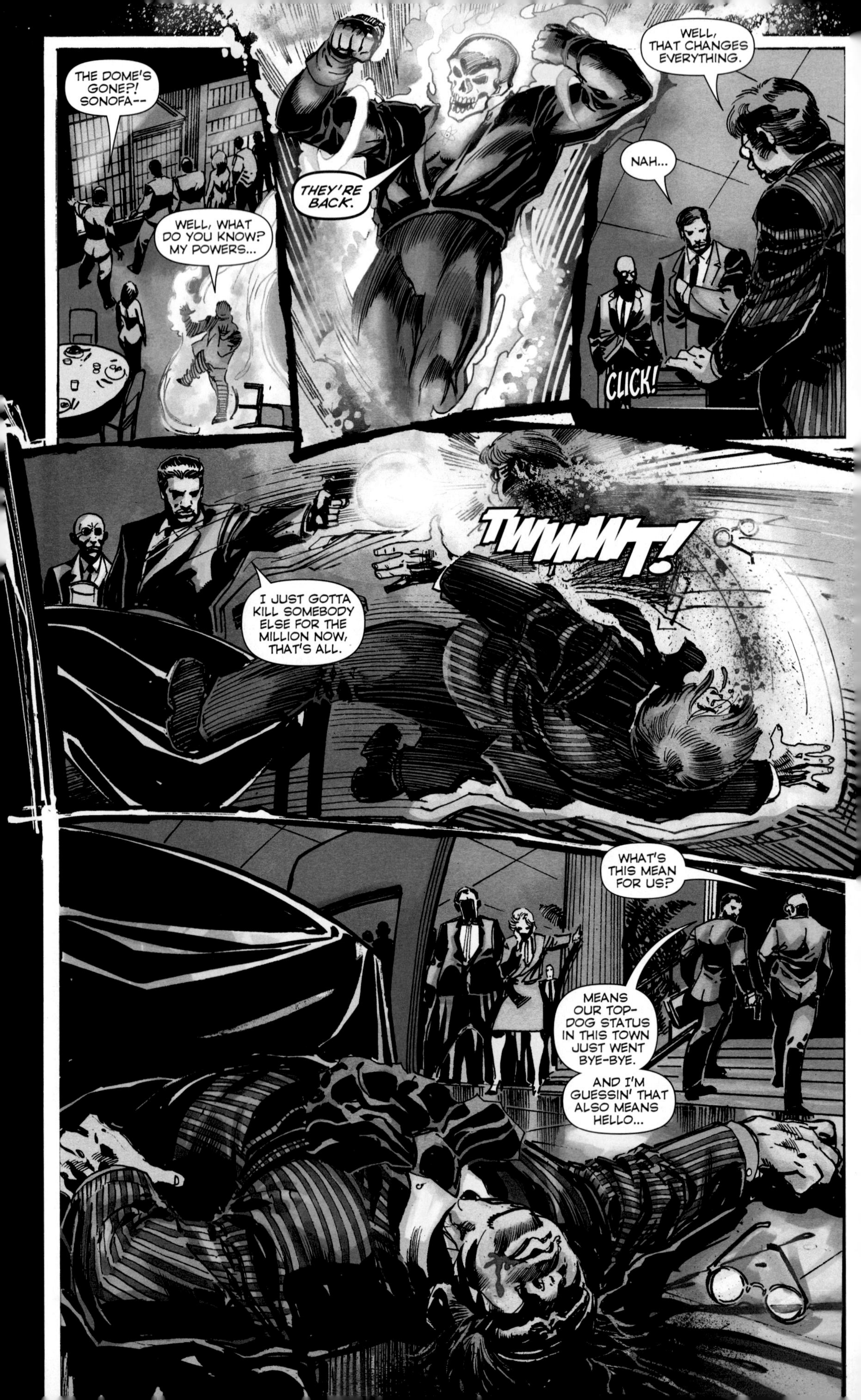
THE DOME'S GONE?! SONOFA--
WELL, WHAT DO YOU KNOW? MY POWERS...
THEY'RE BACK.
WELL, THAT CHANGES EVERYTHING.
NAH...
CLICK!
TWWWT!
I JUST GOTTA KILL SOMEBODY ELSE FOR THE MILLION NOW, THAT'S ALL.
WHAT'S THIS MEAN FOR US?
MEANS OUR TOP-DOG STATUS IN THIS TOWN JUST WENT BYE-BYE.
AND I'M GUESSIN' THAT ALSO MEANS HELLO...

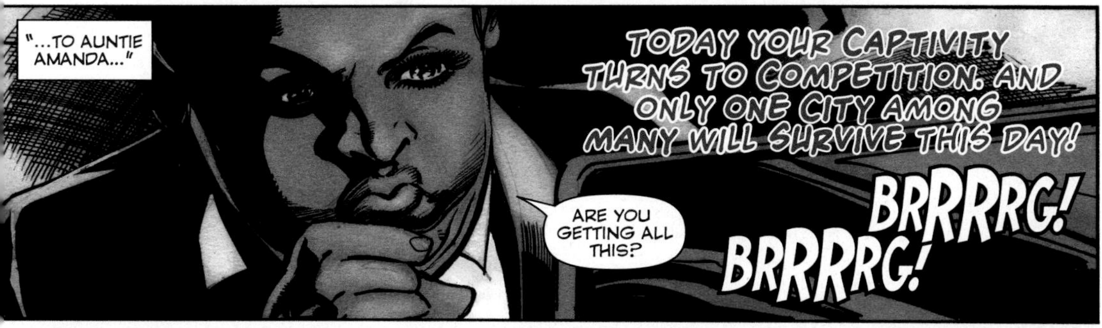
"...TO AUNTIE AMANDA..."
TODAY YOUR CAPTIVITY TURNS TO COMPETITION. AND ONLY ONE CITY AMONG MANY WILL SURVIVE THIS DAY!
ARE YOU GETTING ALL THIS?
BRRRRG!
BRRRRG!

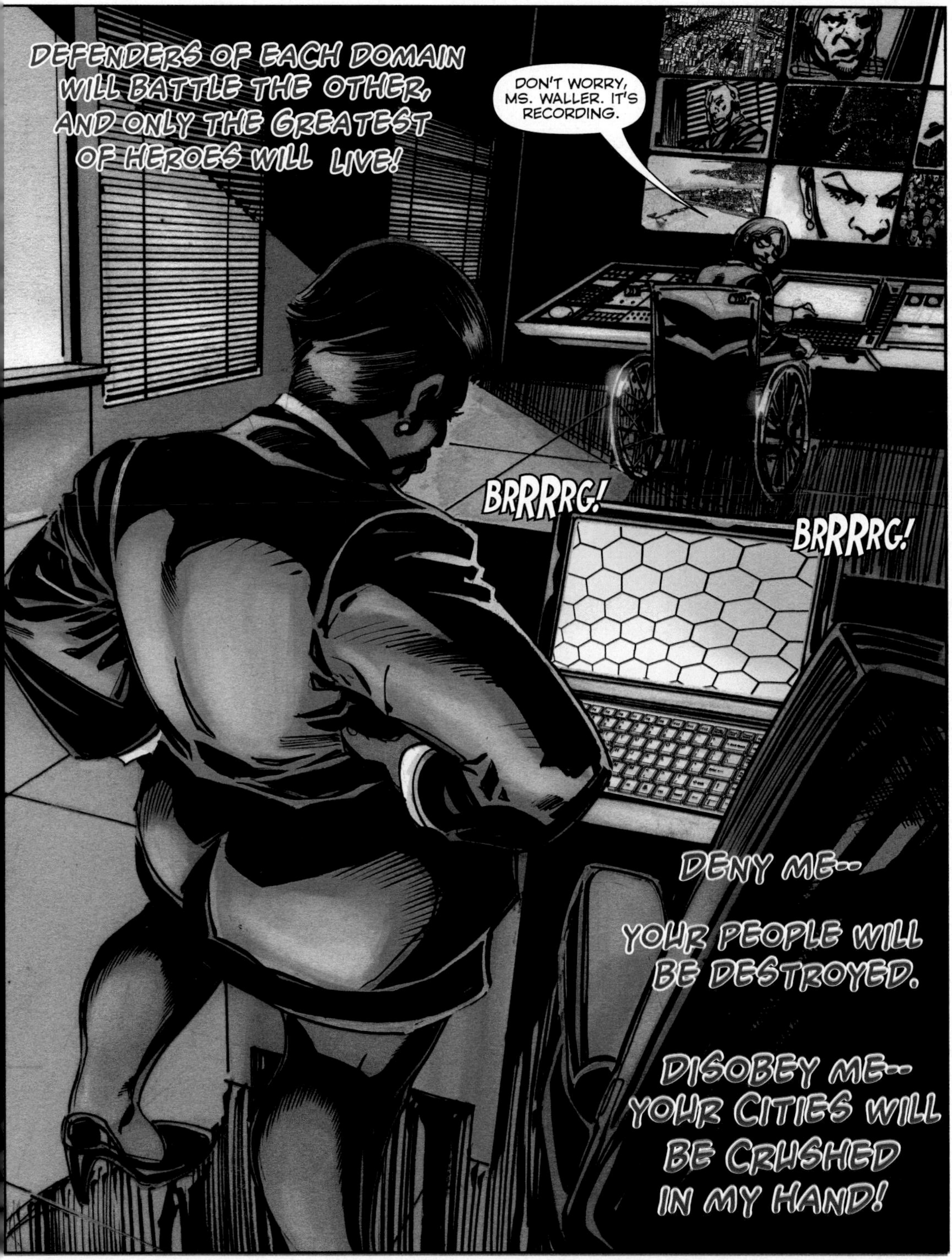
DEFENDERS OF EACH DOMAIN WILL BATTLE THE OTHER, AND ONLY THE GREATEST OF HEROES WILL LIVE!
DON'T WORRY, MS. WALLER. IT'S RECORDING.
BRRRRG!
BRRRRG!
DENY ME--
YOUR PEOPLE WILL BE DESTROYED.
DISOBEY ME--
YOUR CITIES WILL BE CRUSHED IN MY HAND!

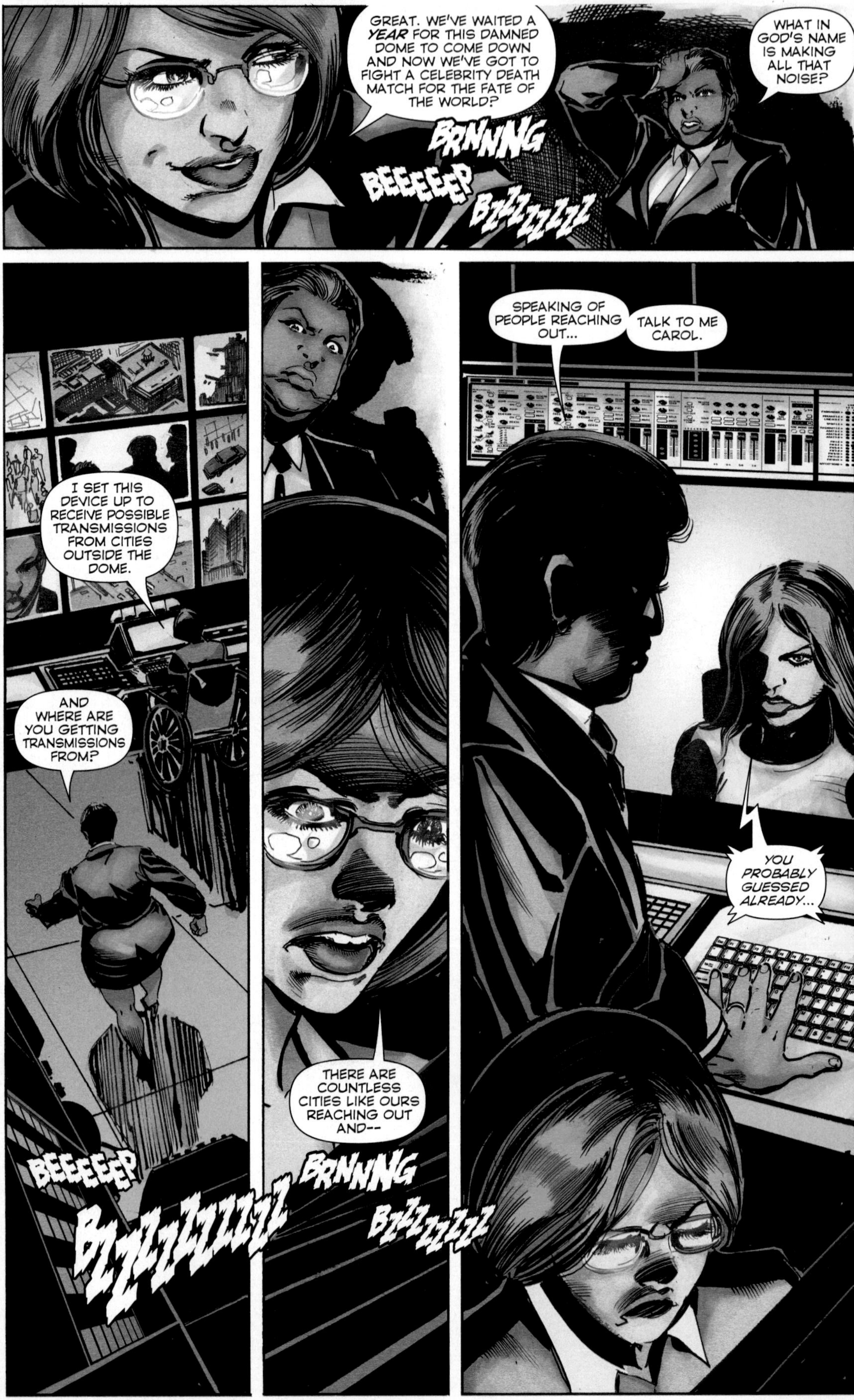
GREAT. WE'VE WAITED A *YEAR* FOR THIS DAMNED DOME TO COME DOWN AND NOW WE'VE GOT TO FIGHT A CELEBRITY DEATH MATCH FOR THE FATE OF THE WORLD?
WHAT IN GOD'S NAME IS MAKING ALL THAT NOISE?
BRNNNG
BEEEEEEP
BZZZZZZZZ
I SET THIS DEVICE UP TO RECEIVE POSSIBLE TRANSMISSIONS FROM CITIES OUTSIDE THE DOME.
AND WHERE ARE YOU GETTING TRANSMISSIONS FROM?
THERE ARE COUNTLESS CITIES LIKE OURS REACHING OUT AND--
BEEEEEEP
BZZZZZZZZZZ
BRNNNG
BZZZZZZZZ
SPEAKING OF PEOPLE REACHING OUT...
TALK TO ME CAROL.
YOU PROBABLY GUESSED ALREADY...

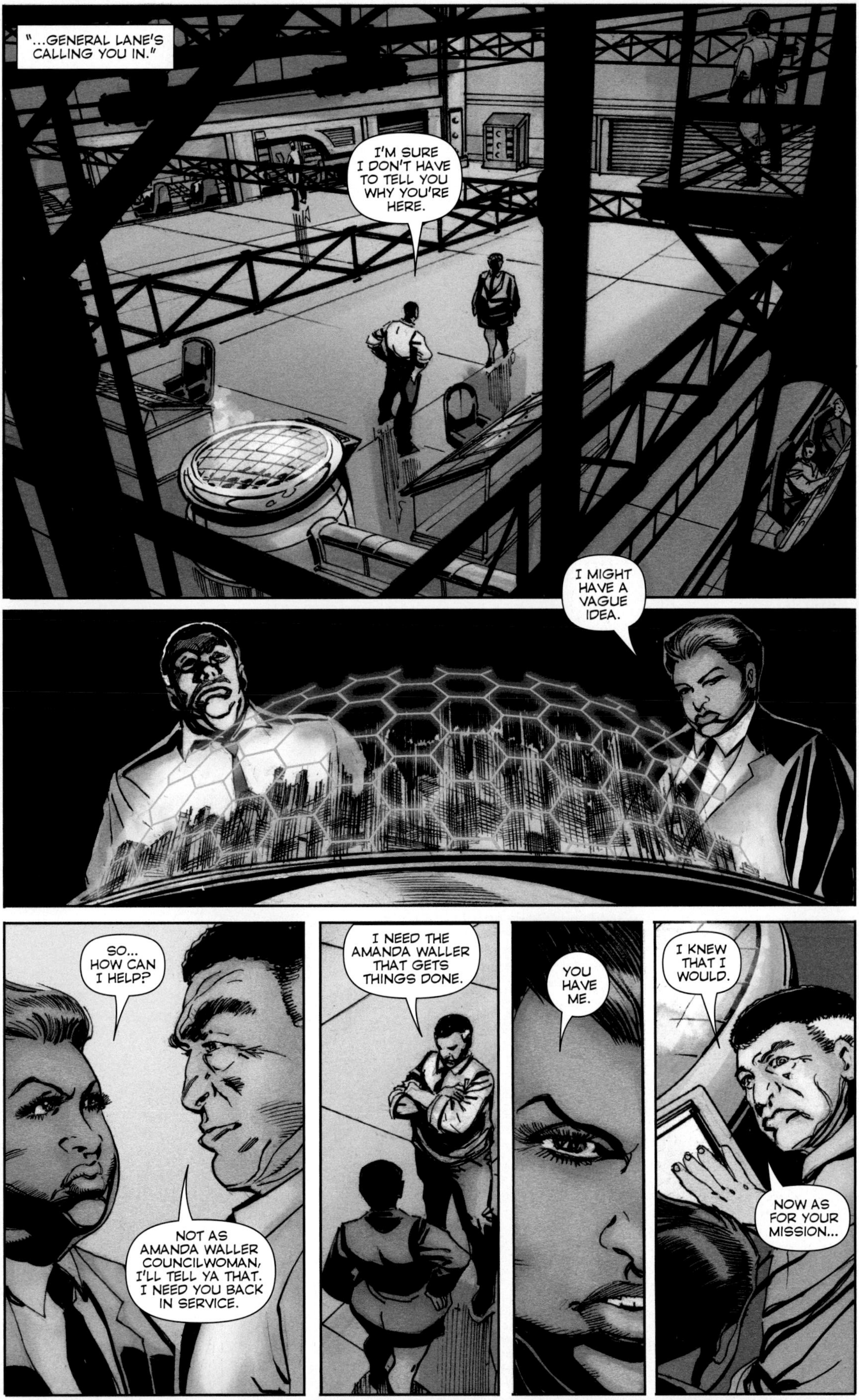
"...GENERAL LANE'S CALLING YOU IN."
I'M SURE I DON'T HAVE TO TELL YOU WHY YOU'RE HERE.
I MIGHT HAVE A VAGUE IDEA.
SO... HOW CAN I HELP?
NOT AS AMANDA WALLER COUNCILWOMAN, I'LL TELL YA THAT. I NEED YOU BACK IN SERVICE.
I NEED THE AMANDA WALLER THAT GETS THINGS DONE.
YOU HAVE ME.
I KNEW THAT I WOULD.
NOW AS FOR YOUR MISSION...

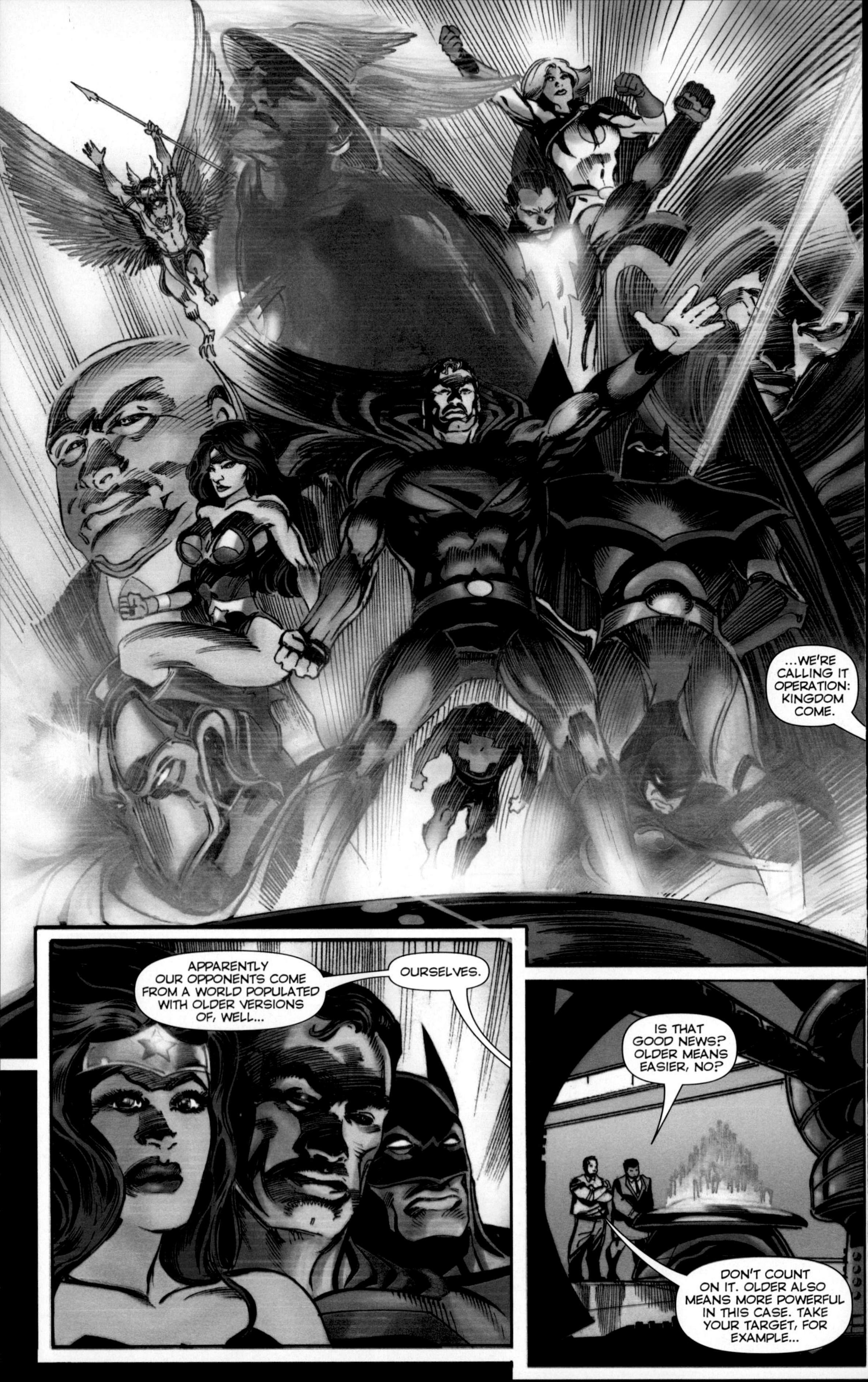
...WE'RE CALLING IT OPERATION: KINGDOM COME.
APPARENTLY OUR OPPONENTS COME FROM A WORLD POPULATED WITH OLDER VERSIONS OF, WELL...
OURSELVES.
IS THAT GOOD NEWS? OLDER MEANS EASIER, NO?
DON'T COUNT ON IT. OLDER ALSO MEANS MORE POWERFUL IN THIS CASE. TAKE YOUR TARGET, FOR EXAMPLE...

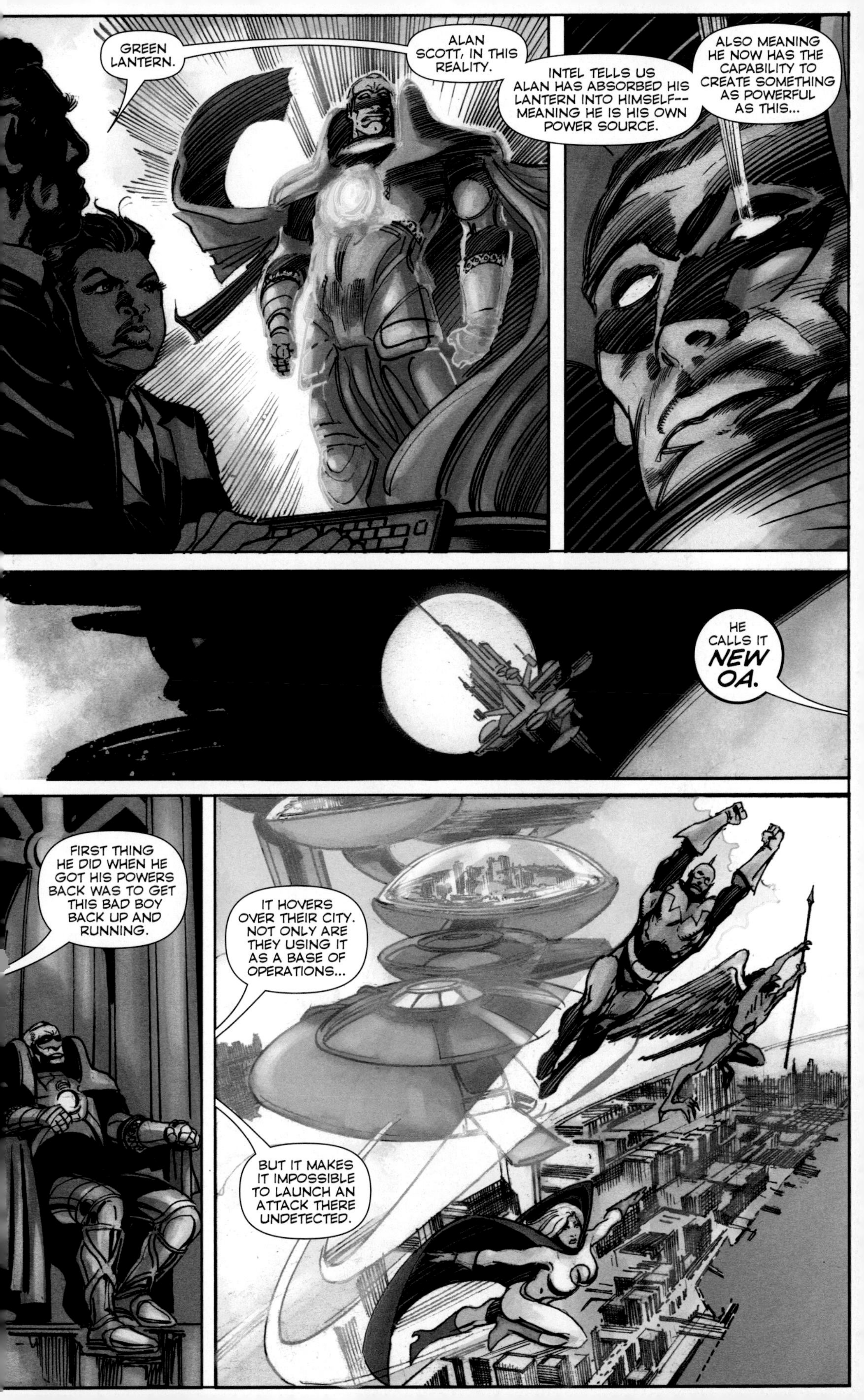
GREEN LANTERN.
ALAN SCOTT, IN THIS REALITY.
INTEL TELLS US ALAN HAS ABSORBED HIS LANTERN INTO HIMSELF-- MEANING HE IS HIS OWN POWER SOURCE.
ALSO MEANING HE NOW HAS THE CAPABILITY TO CREATE SOMETHING AS POWERFUL AS THIS...
HE CALLS IT NEW OA.
FIRST THING HE DID WHEN HE GOT HIS POWERS BACK WAS TO GET THIS BAD BOY BACK UP AND RUNNING.
IT HOVERS OVER THEIR CITY. NOT ONLY ARE THEY USING IT AS A BASE OF OPERATIONS...
BUT IT MAKES IT IMPOSSIBLE TO LAUNCH AN ATTACK THERE UNDETECTED.

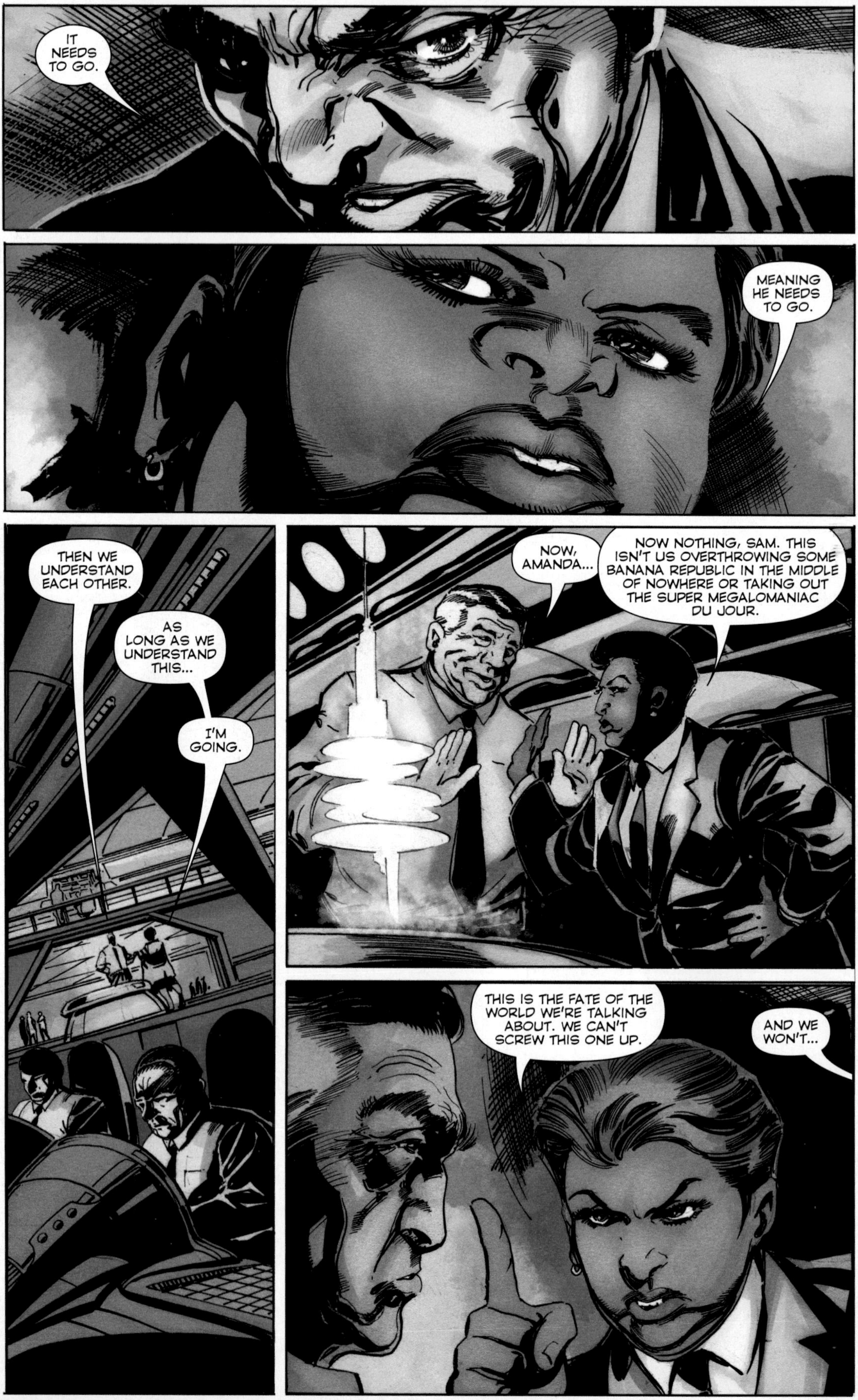
IT NEEDS TO GO.
MEANING HE NEEDS TO GO.
THEN WE UNDERSTAND EACH OTHER.
AS LONG AS WE UNDERSTAND THIS...
I'M GOING.
NOW, AMANDA...
NOW NOTHING, SAM. THIS ISN'T US OVERTHROWING SOME BANANA REPUBLIC IN THE MIDDLE OF NOWHERE OR TAKING OUT THE SUPER MEGALOMANIAC DU JOUR.
THIS IS THE FATE OF THE WORLD WE'RE TALKING ABOUT. WE CAN'T SCREW THIS ONE UP.
AND WE WON'T...

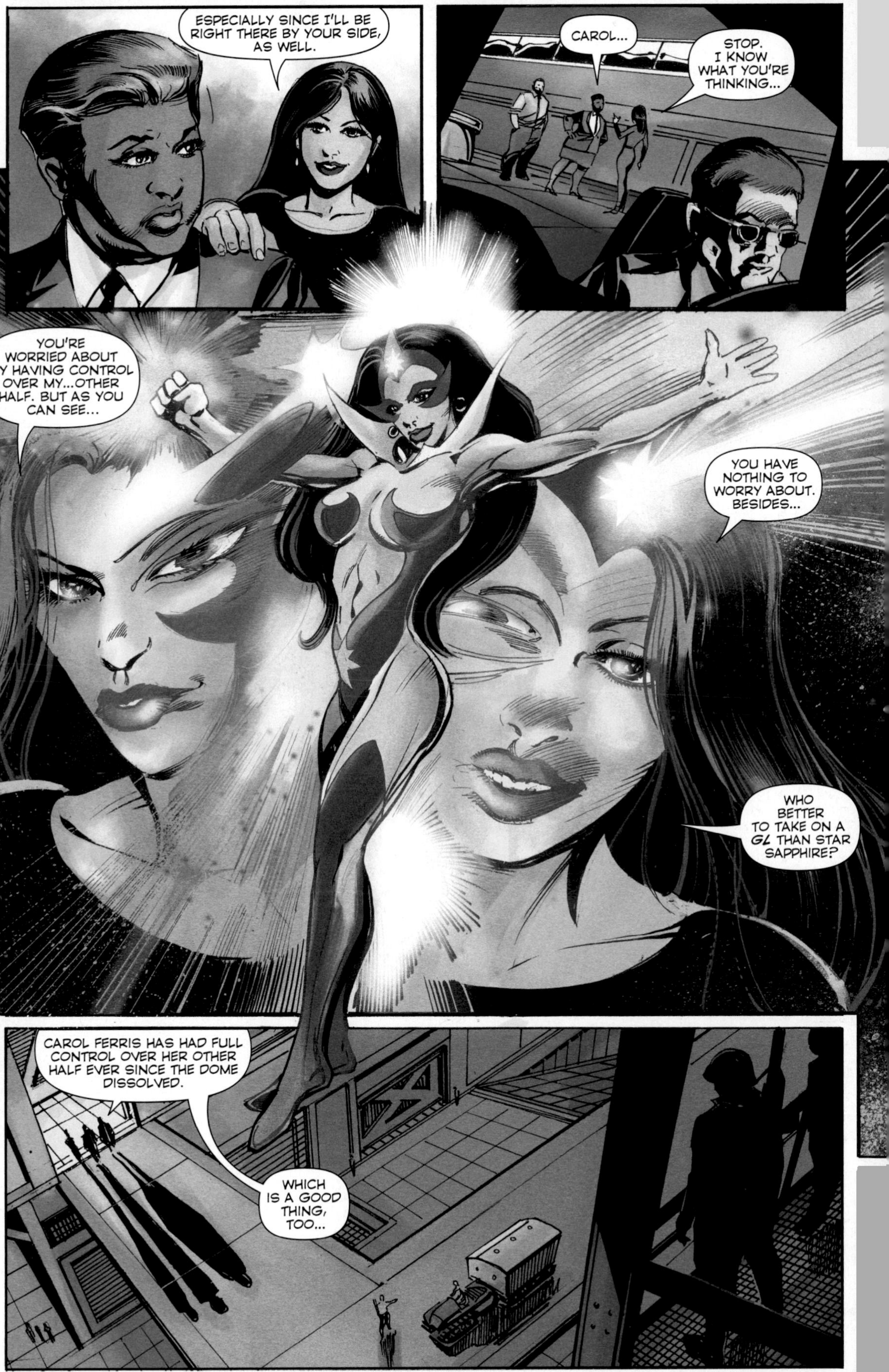
ESPECIALLY SINCE I'LL BE RIGHT THERE BY YOUR SIDE, AS WELL.
CAROL...
STOP. I KNOW WHAT YOU'RE THINKING...
YOU'RE WORRIED ABOUT MY HAVING CONTROL OVER MY...OTHER HALF. BUT AS YOU CAN SEE...
YOU HAVE NOTHING TO WORRY ABOUT. BESIDES...
WHO BETTER TO TAKE ON A *GL* THAN STAR SAPPHIRE?
CAROL FERRIS HAS HAD FULL CONTROL OVER HER OTHER HALF EVER SINCE THE DOME DISSOLVED.
WHICH IS A GOOD THING, TOO...

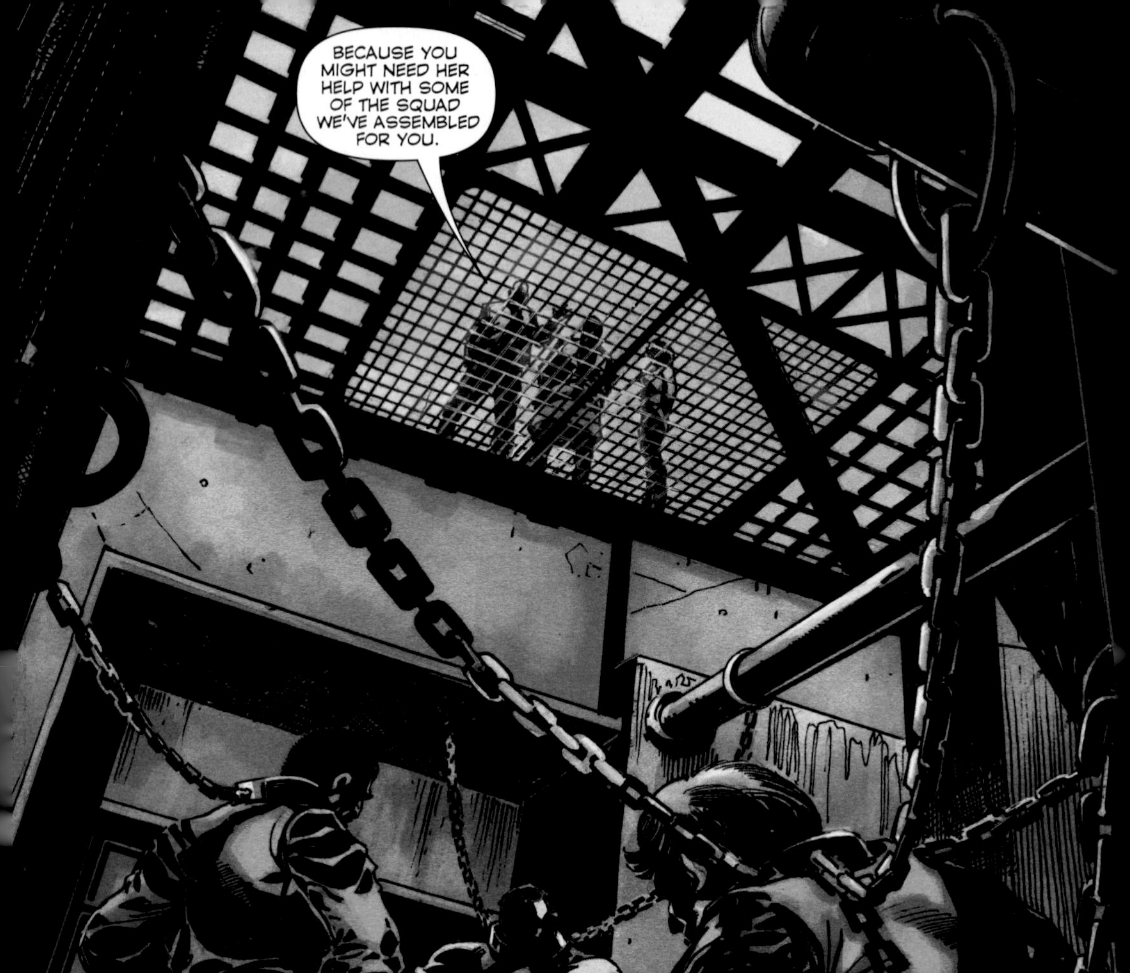
BECAUSE YOU MIGHT NEED HER HELP WITH SOME OF THE SQUAD WE'VE ASSEMBLED FOR YOU.

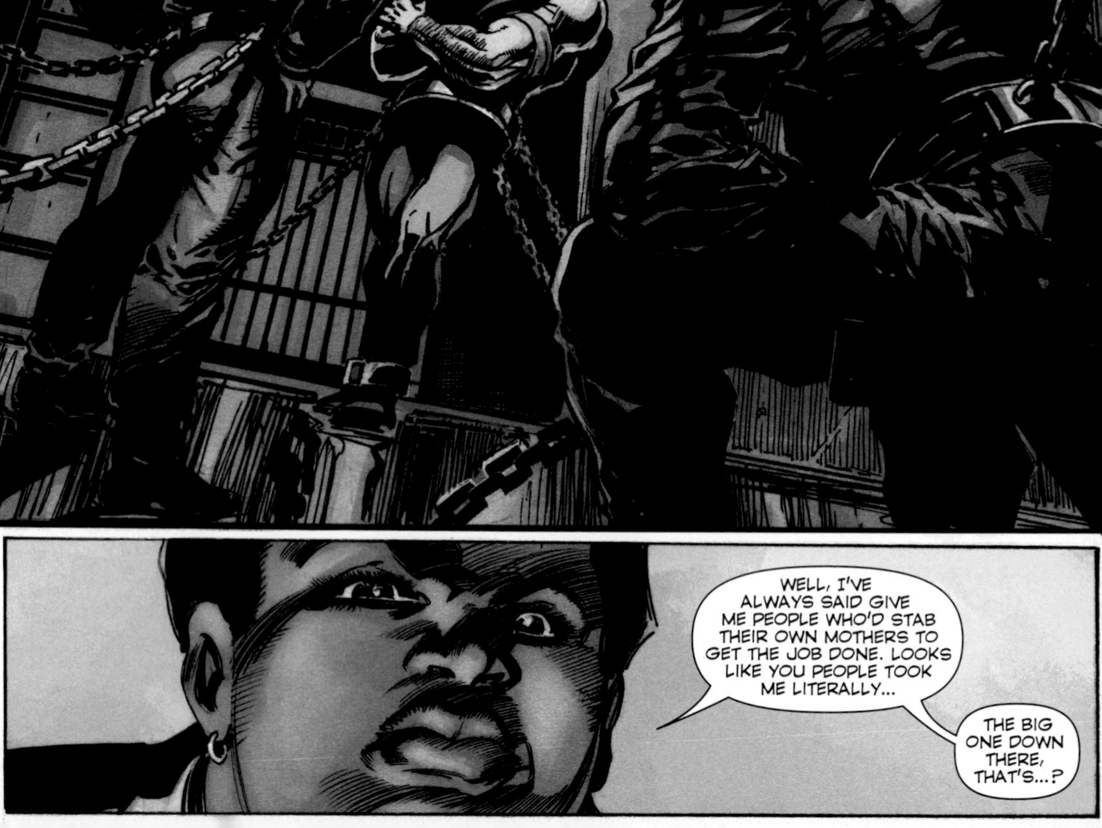
WELL, I'VE ALWAYS SAID GIVE ME PEOPLE WHO'D STAB THEIR OWN MOTHERS TO GET THE JOB DONE. LOOKS LIKE YOU PEOPLE TOOK ME LITERALLY...
THE BIG ONE DOWN THERE, THAT'S...?

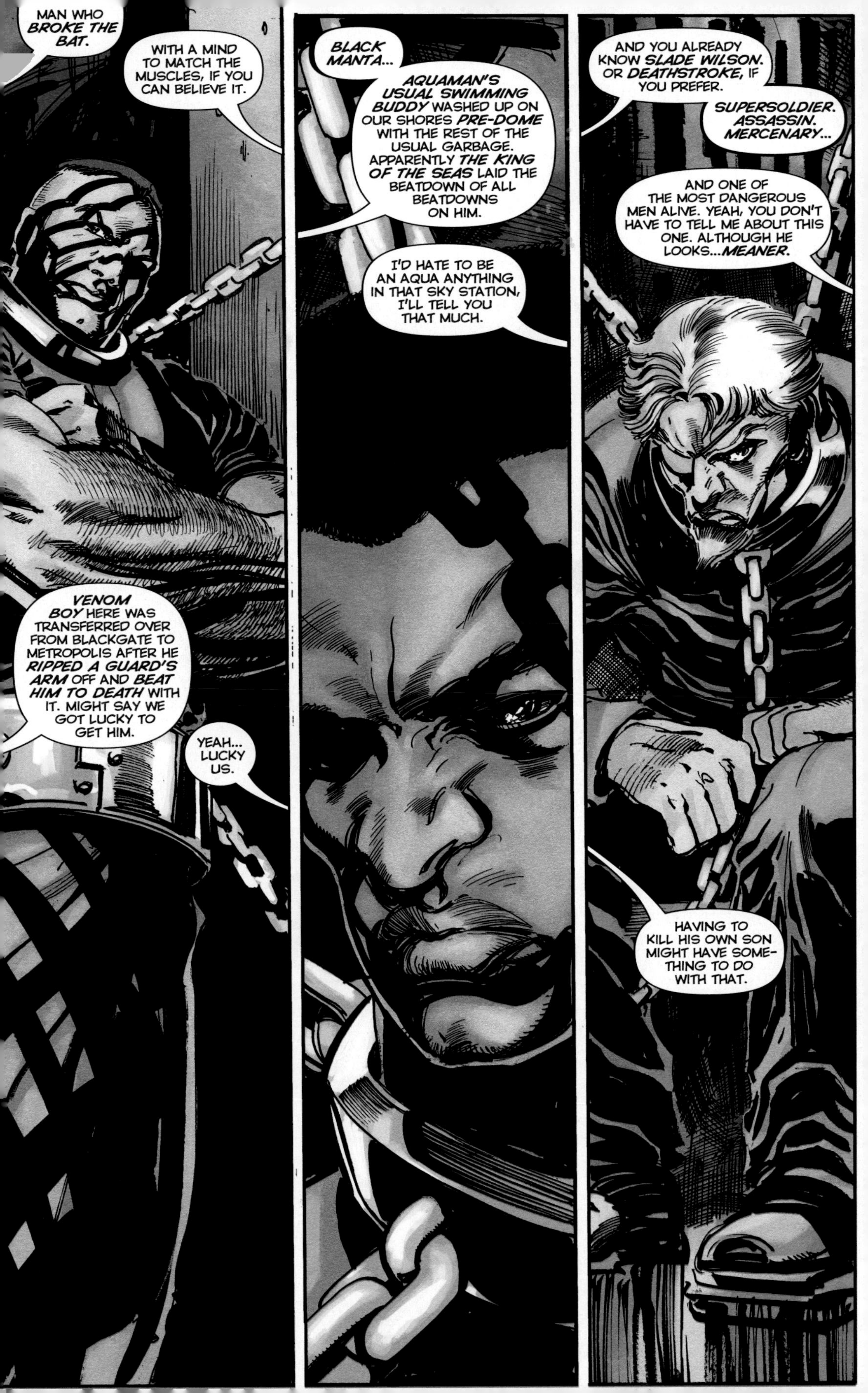

MAN WHO BROKE THE BAT.
WITH A MIND TO MATCH THE MUSCLES, IF YOU CAN BELIEVE IT.
VENOM BOY HERE WAS TRANSFERRED OVER FROM BLACKGATE TO METROPOLIS AFTER HE RIPPED A GUARD'S ARM OFF AND BEAT HIM TO DEATH WITH IT. MIGHT SAY WE GOT LUCKY TO GET HIM.
YEAH... LUCKY US.
BLACK MANTA...
AQUAMAN'S USUAL SWIMMING BUDDY WASHED UP ON OUR SHORES PRE-DOME WITH THE REST OF THE USUAL GARBAGE. APPARENTLY THE KING OF THE SEAS LAID THE BEATDOWN OF ALL BEATDOWNS ON HIM.
I'D HATE TO BE AN AQUA ANYTHING IN THAT SKY STATION, I'LL TELL YOU THAT MUCH.
AND YOU ALREADY KNOW SLADE WILSON. OR DEATHSTROKE, IF YOU PREFER.
SUPERSOLDIER. ASSASSIN. MERCENARY...
AND ONE OF THE MOST DANGEROUS MEN ALIVE. YEAH, YOU DON'T HAVE TO TELL ME ABOUT THIS ONE. ALTHOUGH HE LOOKS...MEANER.
HAVING TO KILL HIS OWN SON MIGHT HAVE SOME-THING TO DO WITH THAT.

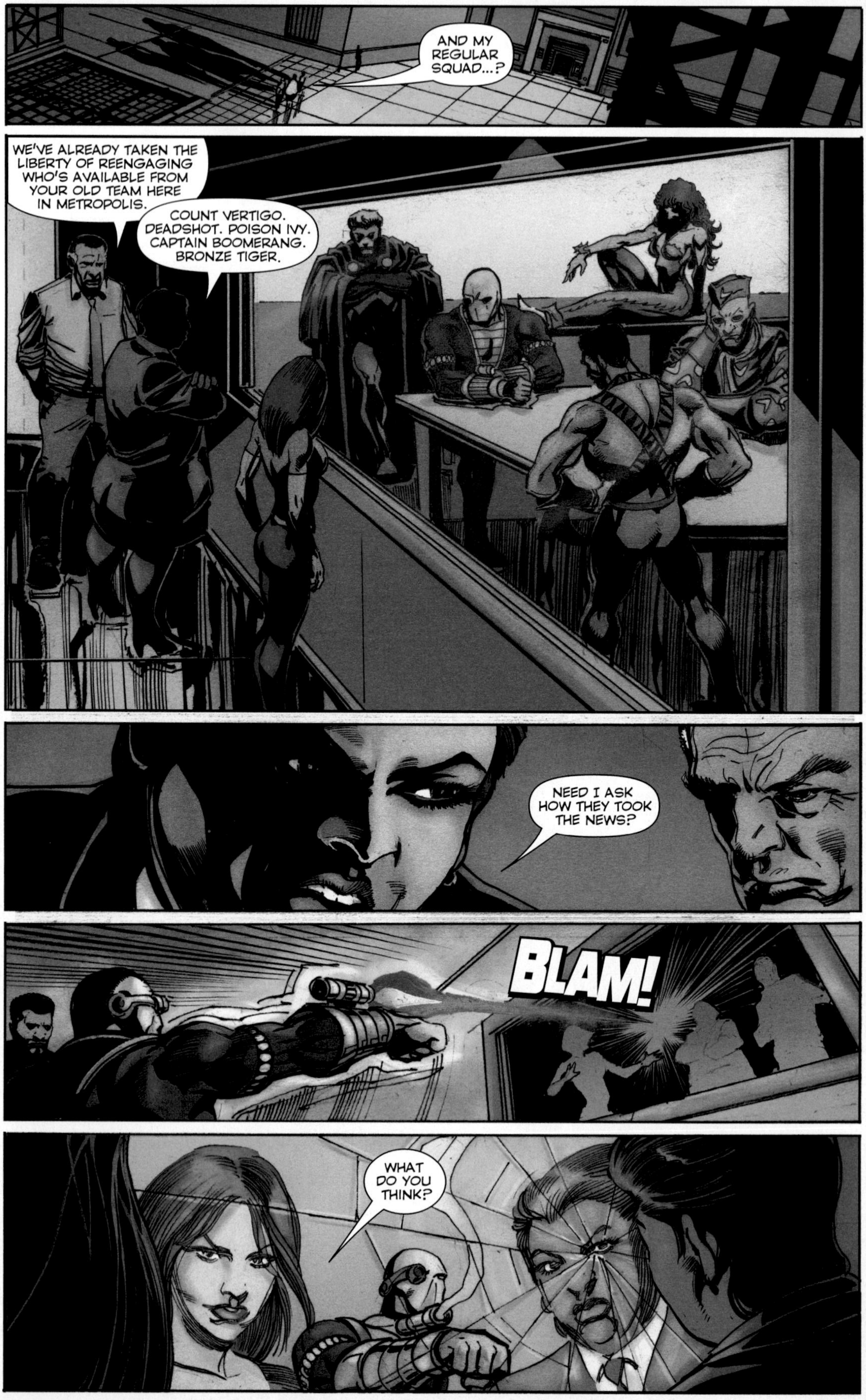
AND MY REGULAR SQUAD...?
WE'VE ALREADY TAKEN THE LIBERTY OF REENGAGING WHO'S AVAILABLE FROM YOUR OLD TEAM HERE IN METROPOLIS.
COUNT VERTIGO. DEADSHOT. POISON IVY. CAPTAIN BOOMERANG. BRONZE TIGER.
NEED I ASK HOW THEY TOOK THE NEWS?
BLAM!
WHAT DO YOU THINK?

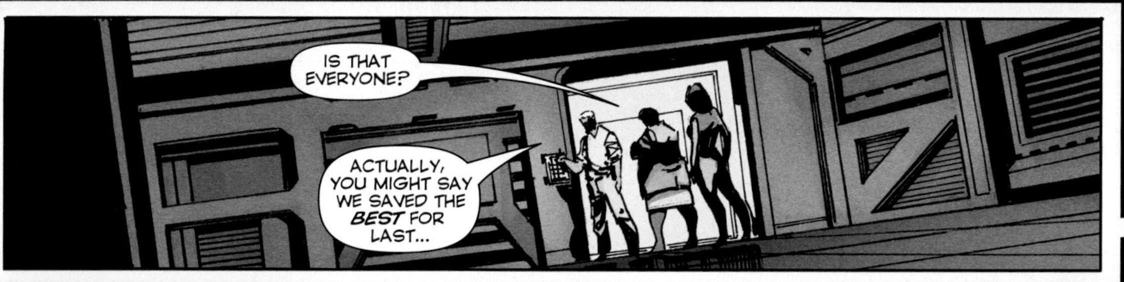
IS THAT EVERYONE?
ACTUALLY, YOU MIGHT SAY WE SAVED THE BEST FOR LAST...

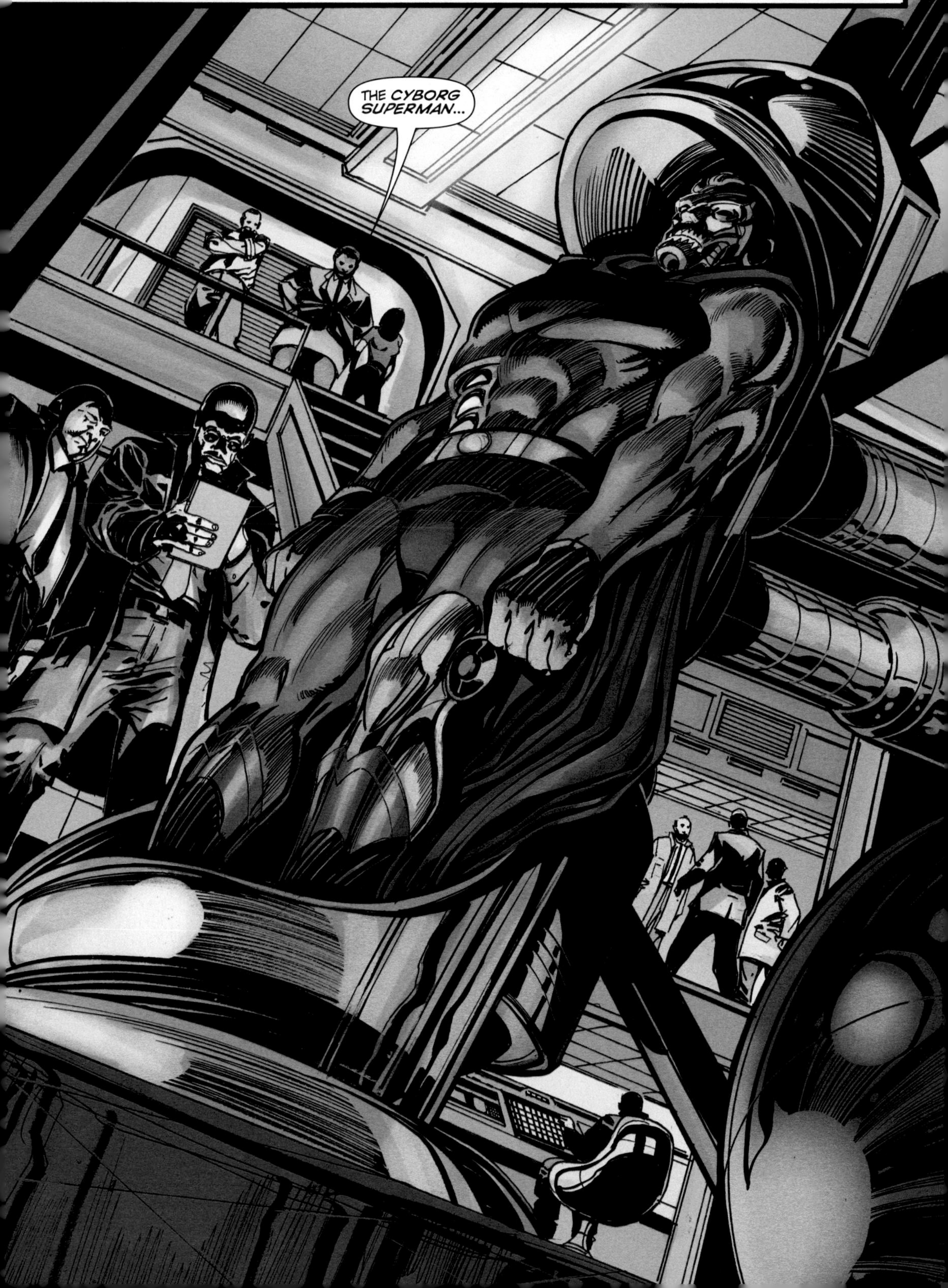
THE CYBORG SUPERMAN...

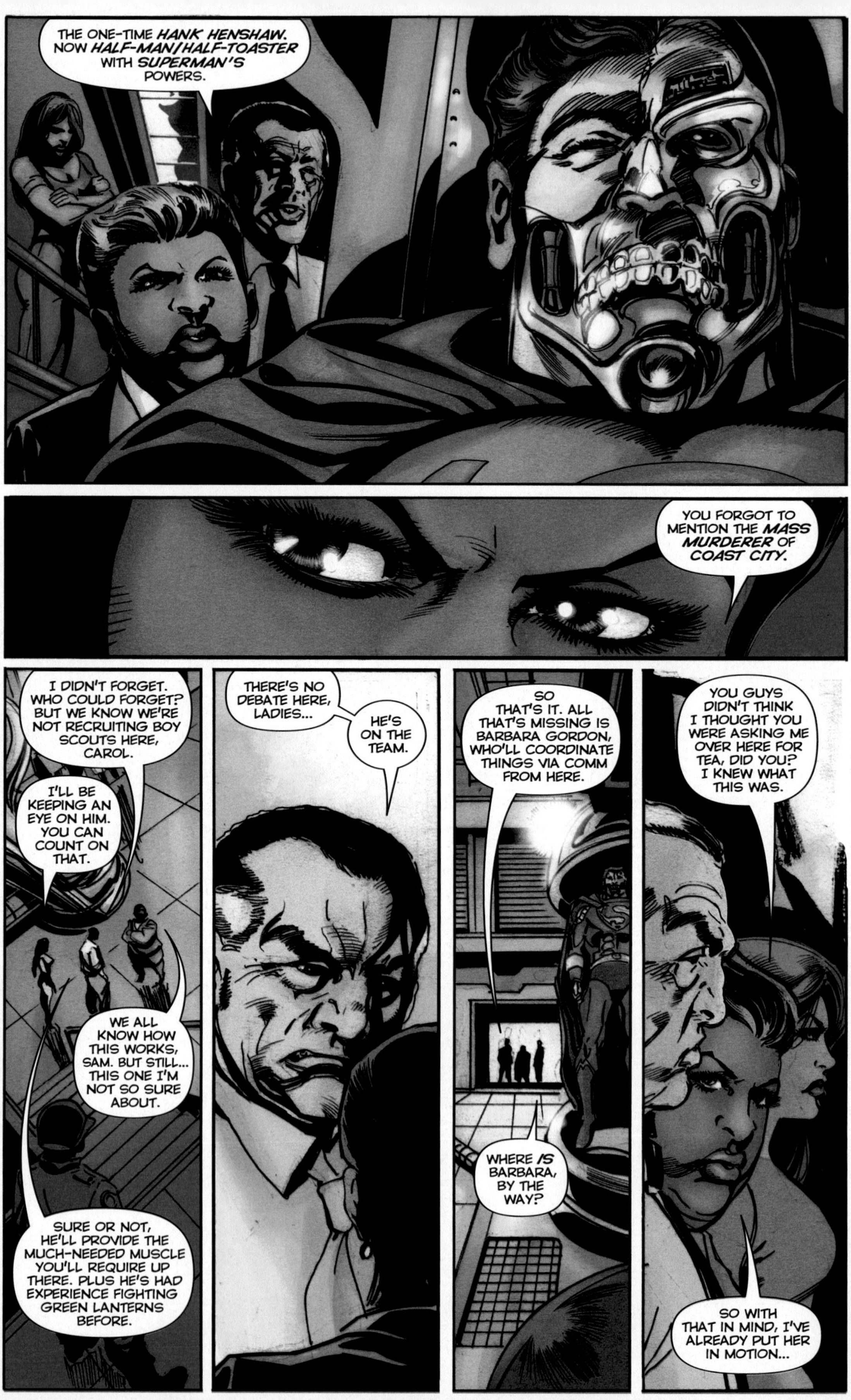
THE ONE-TIME HANK HENSHAW. NOW HALF-MAN/HALF-TOASTER WITH SUPERMAN'S POWERS.
YOU FORGOT TO MENTION THE MASS MURDERER OF COAST CITY.
I DIDN'T FORGET. WHO COULD FORGET? BUT WE KNOW WE'RE NOT RECRUITING BOY SCOUTS HERE, CAROL.
I'LL BE KEEPING AN EYE ON HIM. YOU CAN COUNT ON THAT.
WE ALL KNOW HOW THIS WORKS, SAM. BUT STILL... THIS ONE I'M NOT SO SURE ABOUT.
SURE OR NOT, HE'LL PROVIDE THE MUCH-NEEDED MUSCLE YOU'LL REQUIRE UP THERE. PLUS HE'S HAD EXPERIENCE FIGHTING GREEN LANTERNS BEFORE.
THERE'S NO DEBATE HERE, LADIES...
HE'S ON THE TEAM.
SO THAT'S IT. ALL THAT'S MISSING IS BARBARA GORDON, WHO'LL COORDINATE THINGS VIA COMM FROM HERE.
WHERE IS BARBARA, BY THE WAY?
YOU GUYS DIDN'T THINK I THOUGHT YOU WERE ASKING ME OVER HERE FOR TEA, DID YOU? I KNEW WHAT THIS WAS.
SO WITH THAT IN MIND, I'VE ALREADY PUT HER IN MOTION...

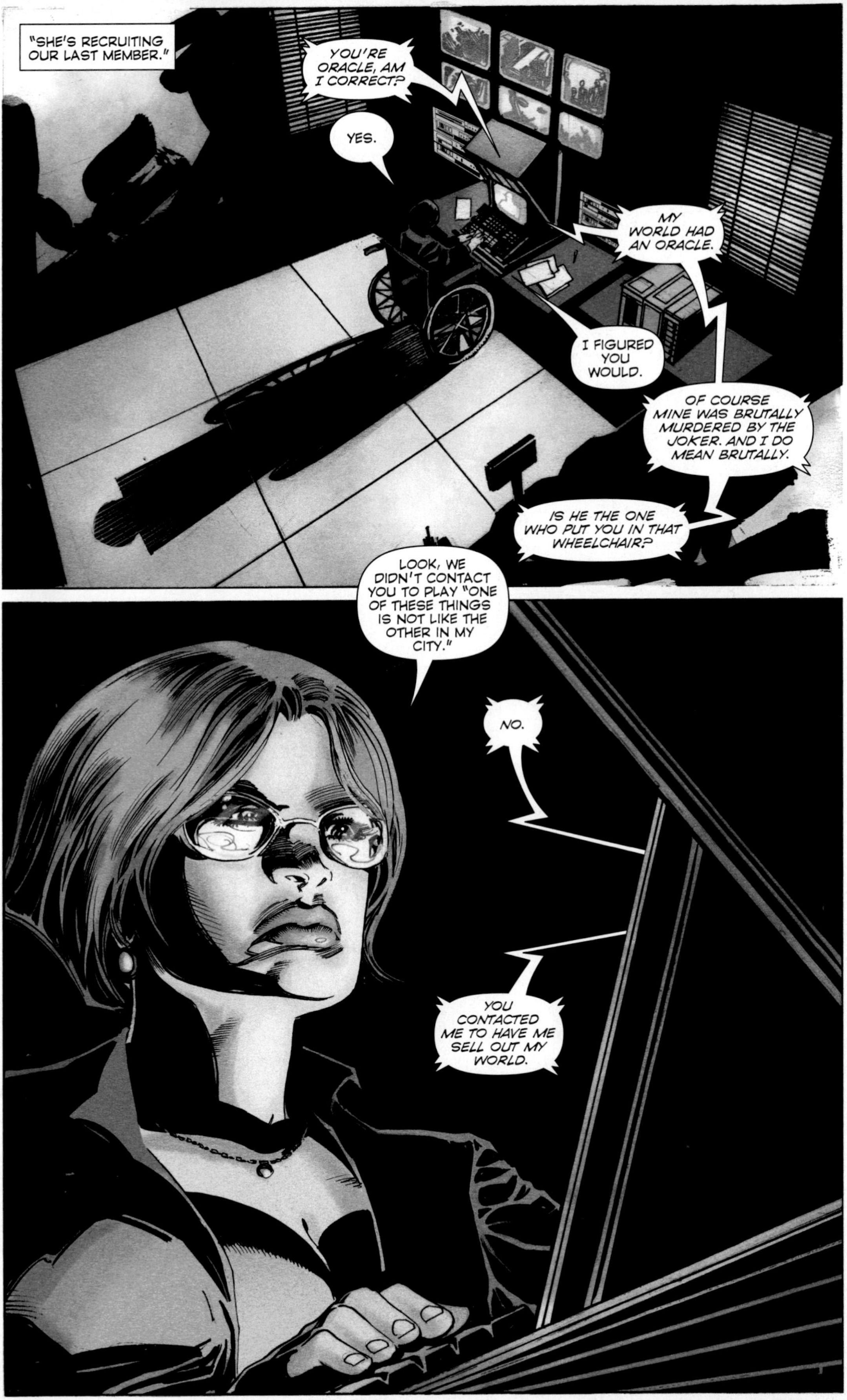
"SHE'S RECRUITING OUR LAST MEMBER."
YOU'RE ORACLE, AM I CORRECT?
YES.
MY WORLD HAD AN ORACLE.
I FIGURED YOU WOULD.
OF COURSE MINE WAS BRUTALLY MURDERED BY THE JOKER. AND I DO MEAN BRUTALLY.
IS HE THE ONE WHO PUT YOU IN THAT WHEELCHAIR?
LOOK, WE DIDN'T CONTACT YOU TO PLAY "ONE OF THESE THINGS IS NOT LIKE THE OTHER IN MY CITY."
NO.
YOU CONTACTED ME TO HAVE ME SELL OUT MY WORLD.

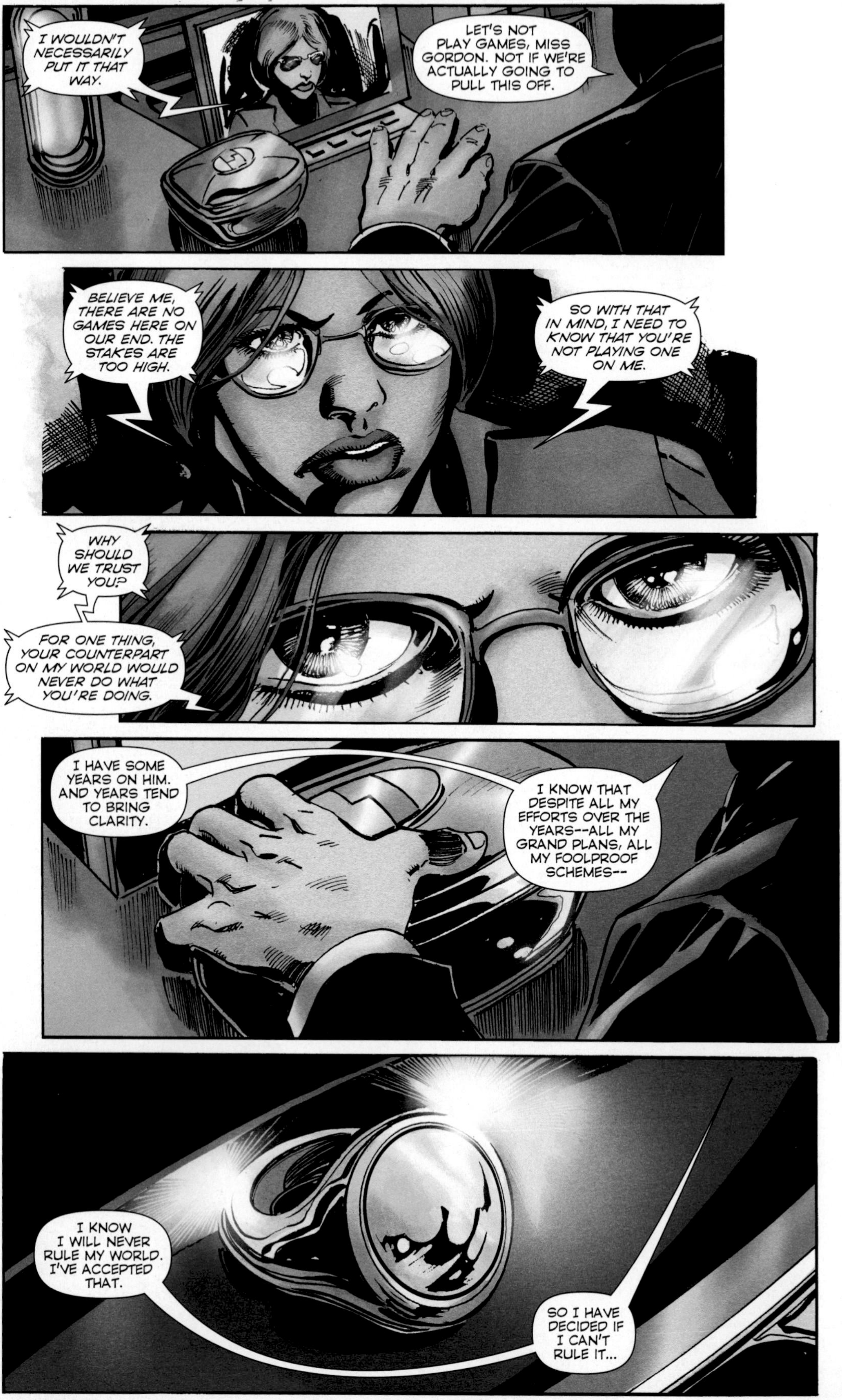
I WOULDN'T NECESSARILY PUT IT THAT WAY.
LET'S NOT PLAY GAMES, MISS GORDON. NOT IF WE'RE ACTUALLY GOING TO PULL THIS OFF.
BELIEVE ME, THERE ARE NO GAMES HERE ON OUR END. THE STAKES ARE TOO HIGH.
SO WITH THAT IN MIND, I NEED TO KNOW THAT YOU'RE NOT PLAYING ONE ON ME.
WHY SHOULD WE TRUST YOU?
FOR ONE THING, YOUR COUNTERPART ON MY WORLD WOULD NEVER DO WHAT YOU'RE DOING.
I HAVE SOME YEARS ON HIM. AND YEARS TEND TO BRING CLARITY.
I KNOW THAT DESPITE ALL MY EFFORTS OVER THE YEARS--ALL MY GRAND PLANS, ALL MY FOOLPROOF SCHEMES--
I KNOW I WILL NEVER RULE MY WORLD. I'VE ACCEPTED THAT.
SO I HAVE DECIDED IF I CAN'T RULE IT...

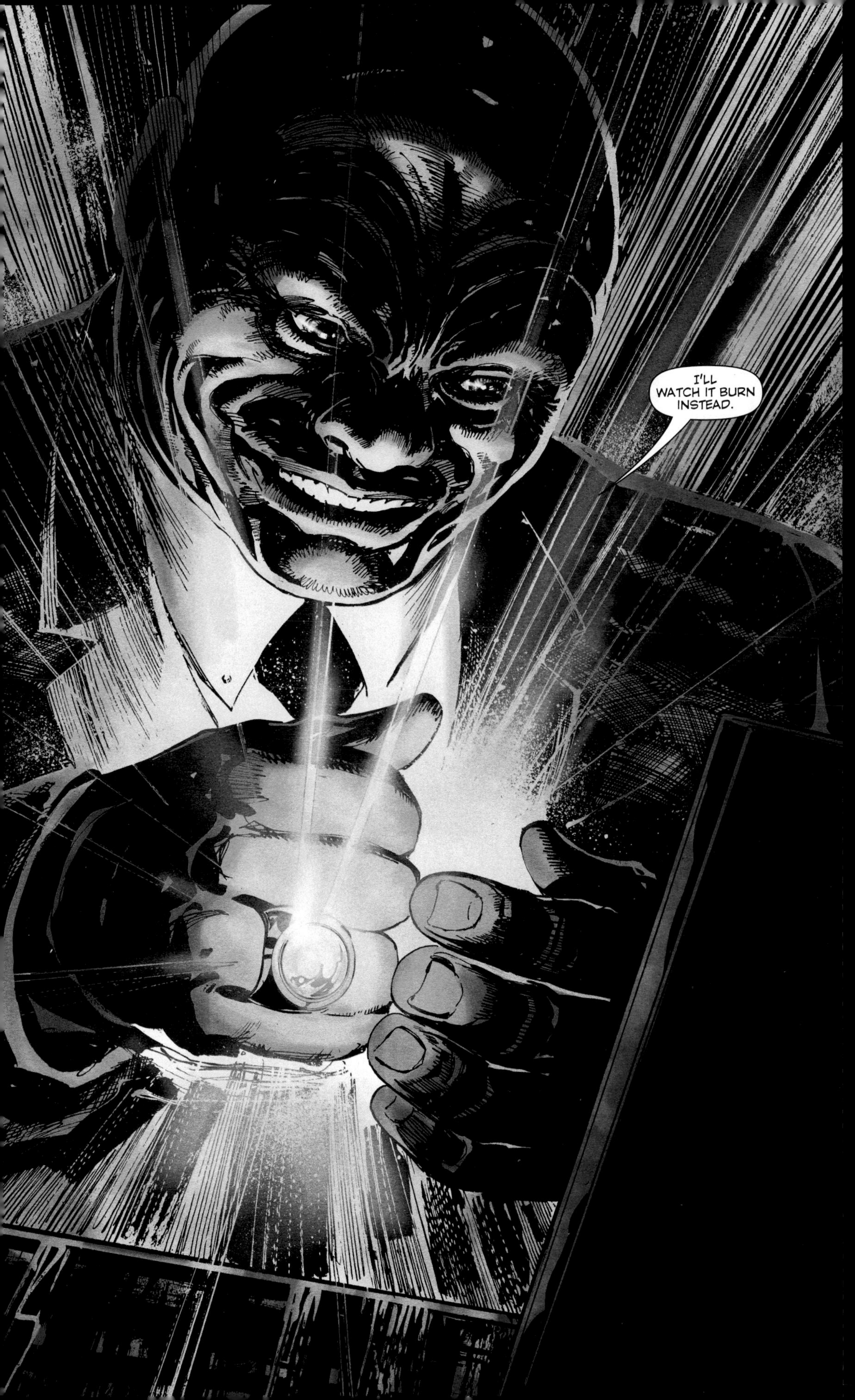
I'LL WATCH IT BURN INSTEAD.

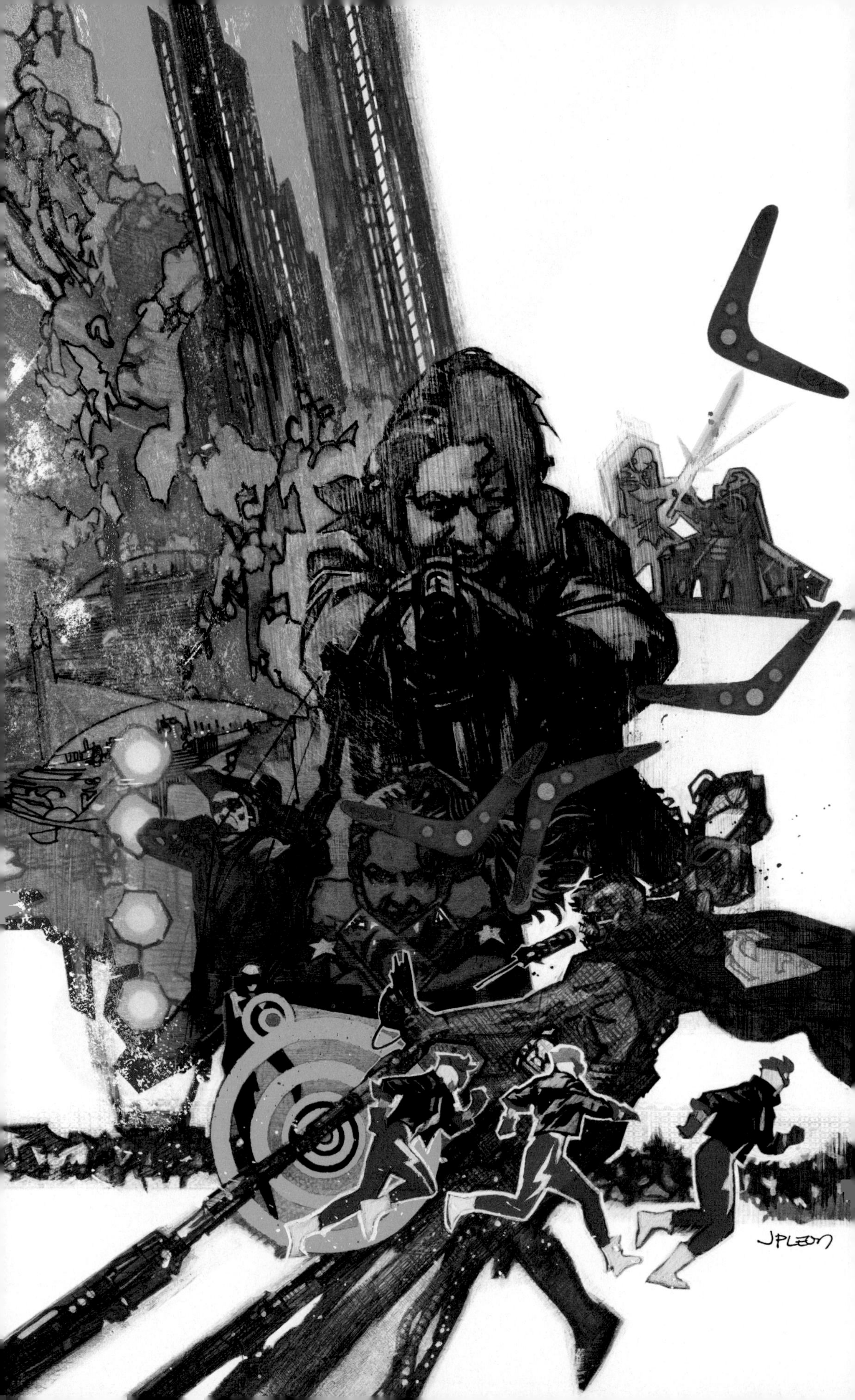
JPLEON

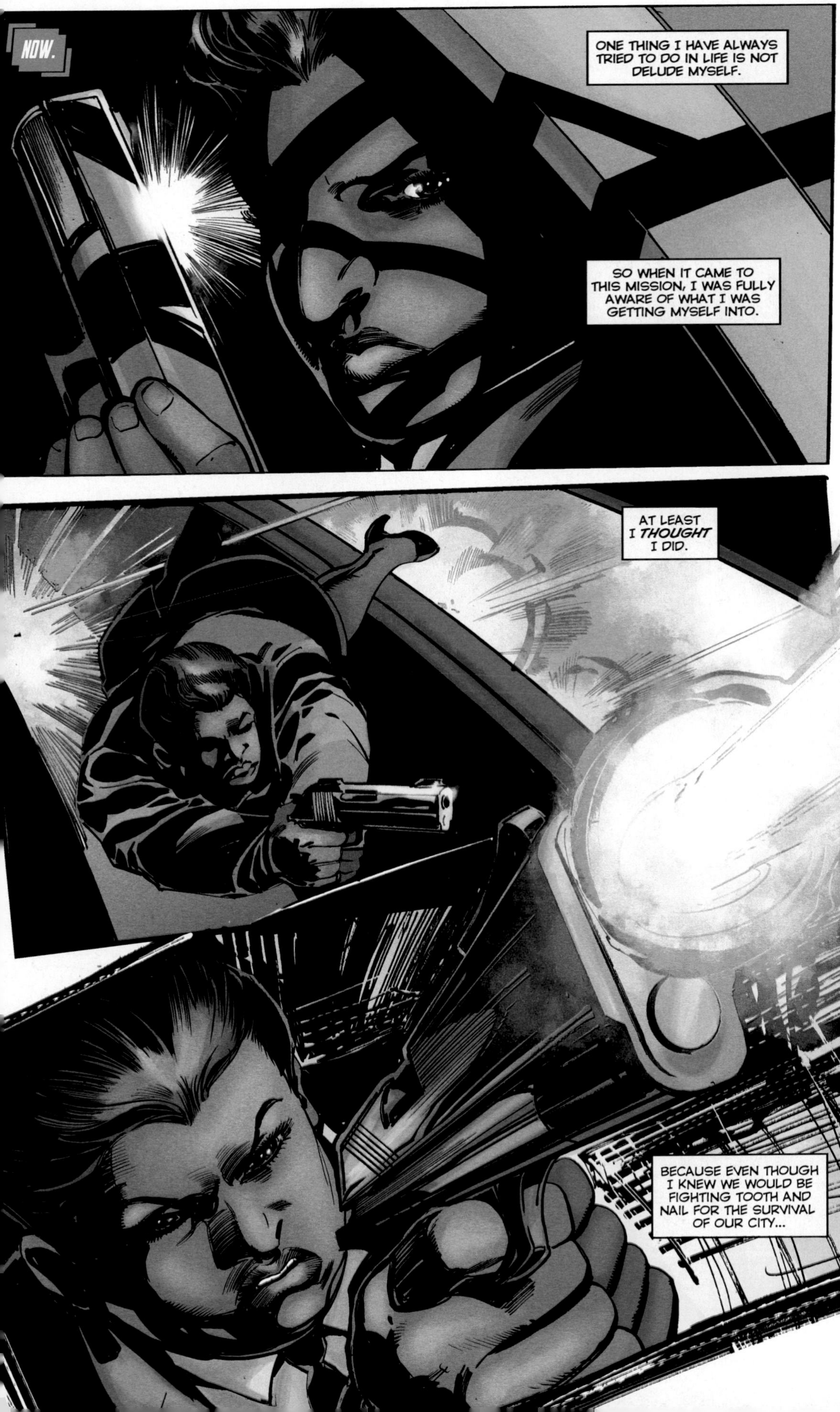
NOW.
ONE THING I HAVE ALWAYS TRIED TO DO IN LIFE IS NOT DELUDE MYSELF.
SO WHEN IT CAME TO THIS MISSION, I WAS FULLY AWARE OF WHAT I WAS GETTING MYSELF INTO.
AT LEAST I *THOUGHT* I DID.
BECAUSE EVEN THOUGH I KNEW WE WOULD BE FIGHTING TOOTH AND NAIL FOR THE SURVIVAL OF OUR CITY...

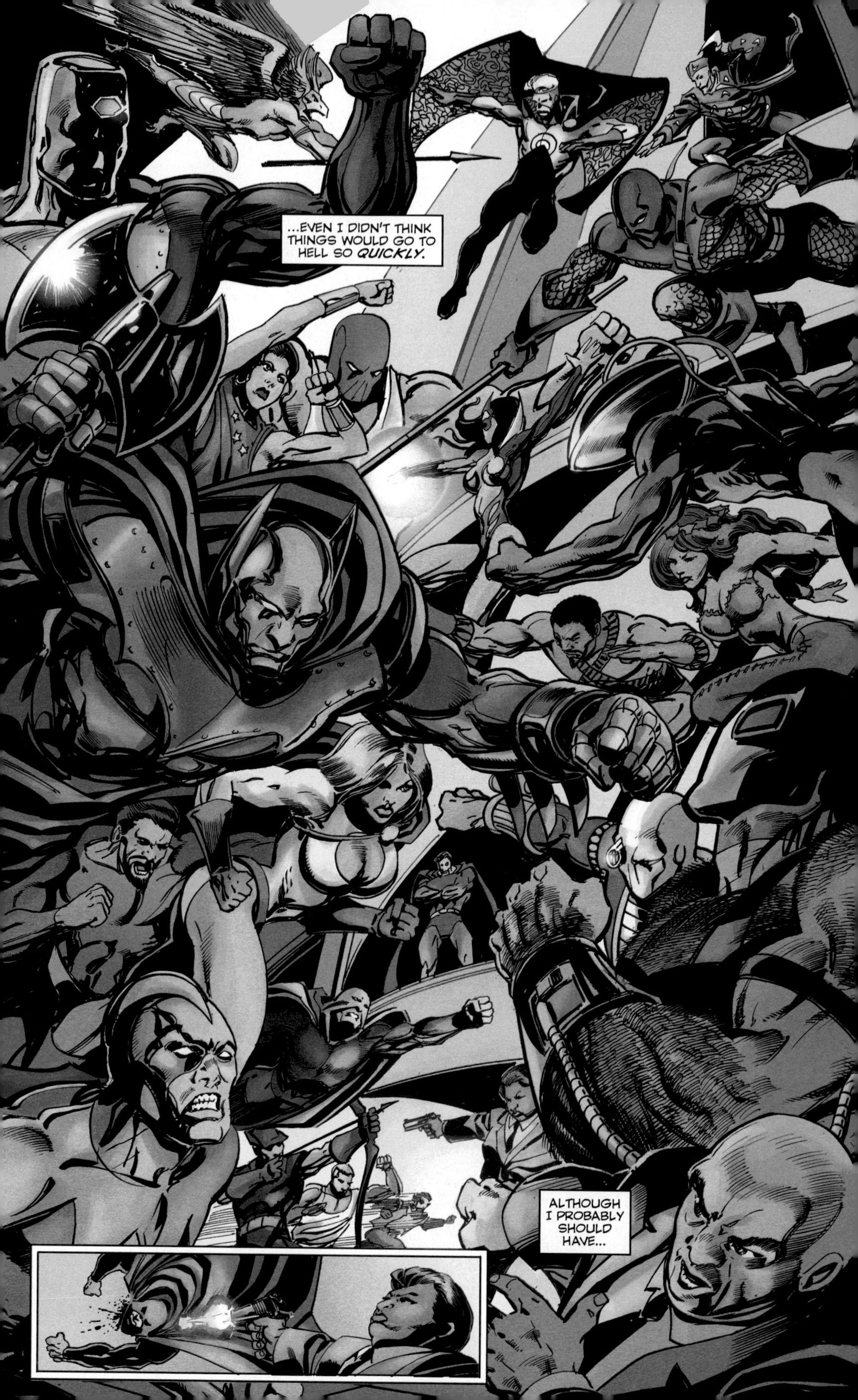
...EVEN I DIDN'T THINK THINGS WOULD GO TO HELL SO *QUICKLY*.
ALTHOUGH I PROBABLY SHOULD HAVE...

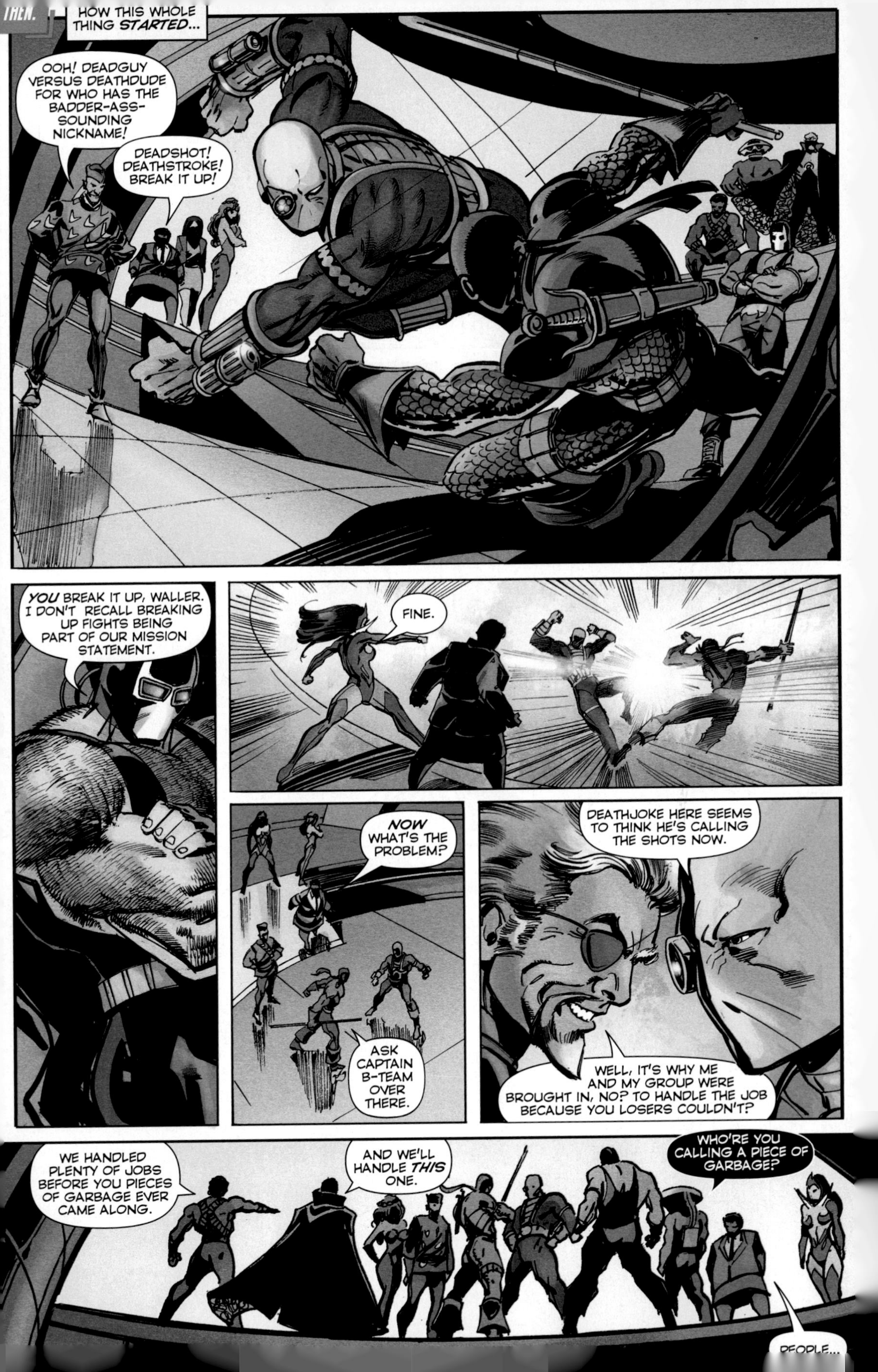
THEN.
HOW THIS WHOLE THING STARTED...
OOH! DEADGUY VERSUS DEATHDUDE FOR WHO HAS THE BADDER-ASS-SOUNDING NICKNAME!
DEADSHOT! DEATHSTROKE! BREAK IT UP!
YOU BREAK IT UP, WALLER. I DON'T RECALL BREAKING UP FIGHTS BEING PART OF OUR MISSION STATEMENT.
FINE.
NOW WHAT'S THE PROBLEM?
ASK CAPTAIN B-TEAM OVER THERE.
DEATHJOKE HERE SEEMS TO THINK HE'S CALLING THE SHOTS NOW.
WELL, IT'S WHY ME AND MY GROUP WERE BROUGHT IN, NO? TO HANDLE THE JOB BECAUSE YOU LOSERS COULDN'T?
WE HANDLED PLENTY OF JOBS BEFORE YOU PIECES OF GARBAGE EVER CAME ALONG.
AND WE'LL HANDLE THIS ONE.
WHO'RE YOU CALLING A PIECE OF GARBAGE?
PEOPLE...

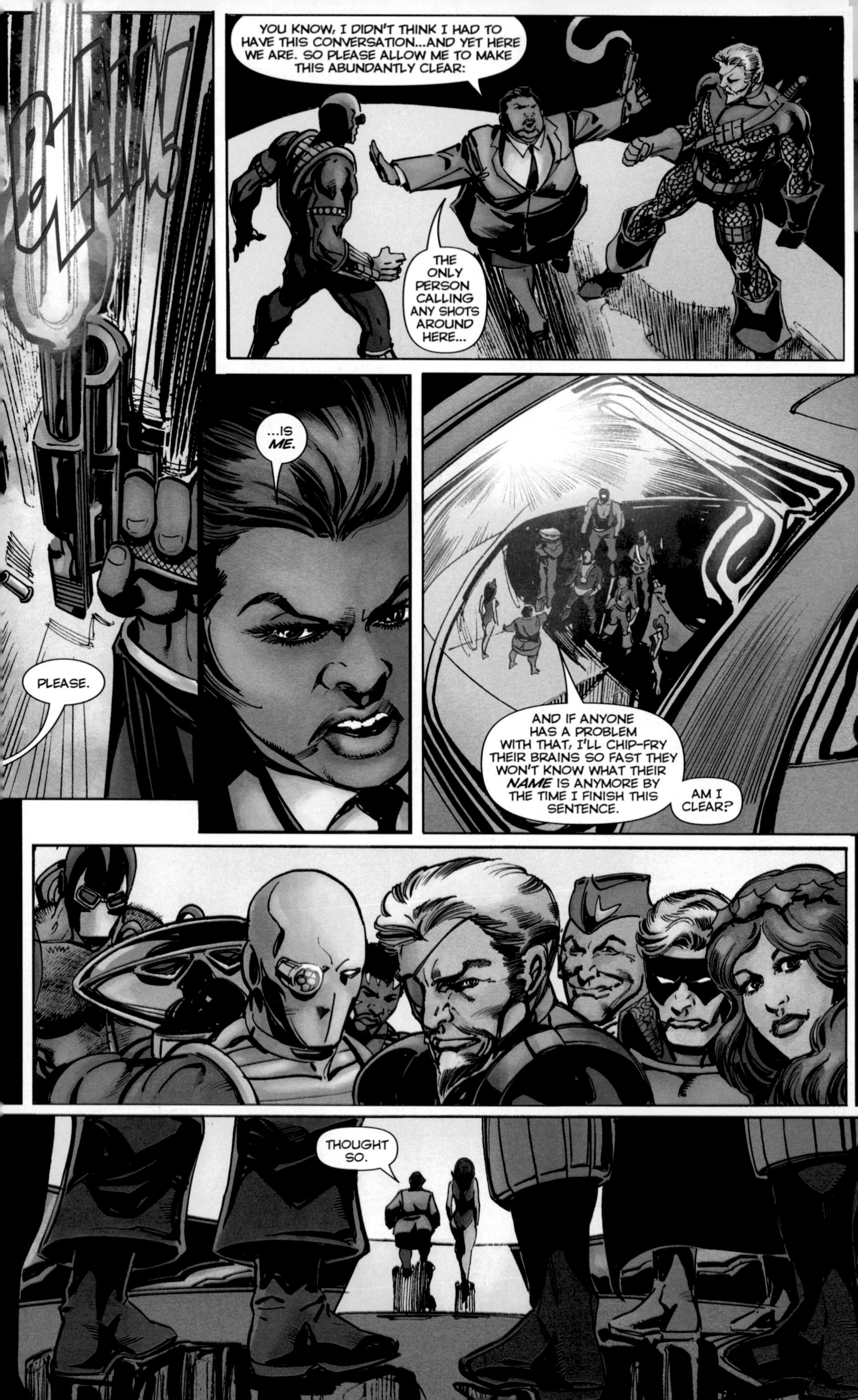
BLAM!
YOU KNOW, I DIDN'T THINK I HAD TO HAVE THIS CONVERSATION...AND YET HERE WE ARE. SO PLEASE ALLOW ME TO MAKE THIS ABUNDANTLY CLEAR:
THE ONLY PERSON CALLING ANY SHOTS AROUND HERE...
...IS ME.
PLEASE.
AND IF ANYONE HAS A PROBLEM WITH THAT, I'LL CHIP-FRY THEIR BRAINS SO FAST THEY WON'T KNOW WHAT THEIR NAME IS ANYMORE BY THE TIME I FINISH THIS SENTENCE.
AM I CLEAR?
THOUGHT SO.

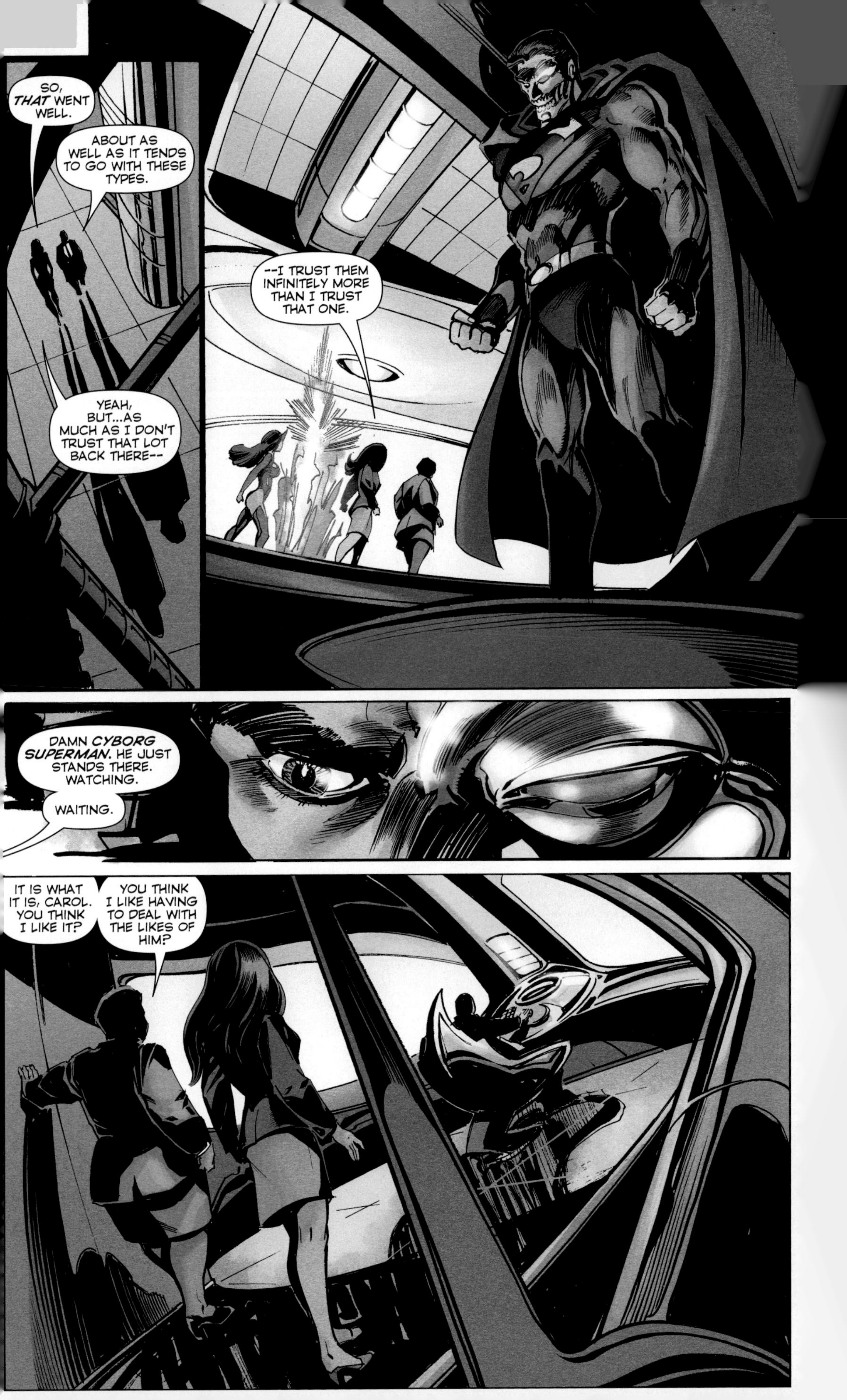
SO, *THAT* WENT WELL.
ABOUT AS WELL AS IT TENDS TO GO WITH THESE TYPES.
YEAH, BUT...AS MUCH AS I DON'T TRUST THAT LOT BACK THERE--
--I TRUST THEM INFINITELY MORE THAN I TRUST THAT ONE.
DAMN *CYBORG SUPERMAN*. HE JUST STANDS THERE. WATCHING.
WAITING.
IT IS WHAT IT IS, CAROL. YOU THINK I LIKE IT?
YOU THINK I LIKE HAVING TO DEAL WITH THE LIKES OF HIM?

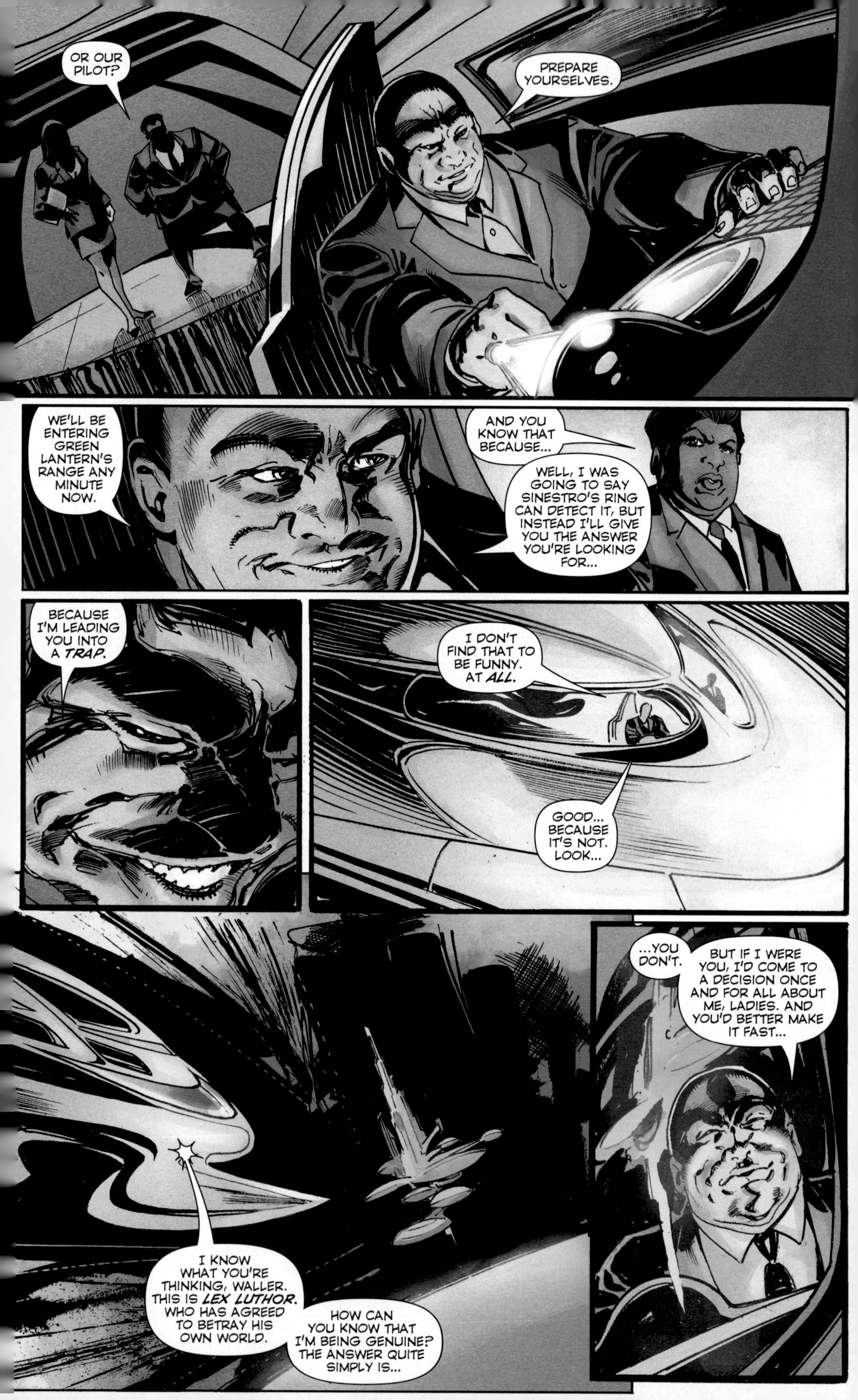
OR OUR PILOT?
PREPARE YOURSELVES.
WE'LL BE ENTERING GREEN LANTERN'S RANGE ANY MINUTE NOW.
AND YOU KNOW THAT BECAUSE...
WELL, I WAS GOING TO SAY SINESTRO'S RING CAN DETECT IT, BUT INSTEAD I'LL GIVE YOU THE ANSWER YOU'RE LOOKING FOR...
BECAUSE I'M LEADING YOU INTO A *TRAP*.
I DON'T FIND THAT TO BE FUNNY. AT *ALL*.
GOOD... BECAUSE IT'S NOT. LOOK...
I KNOW WHAT YOU'RE THINKING, WALLER. THIS IS *LEX LUTHOR*. WHO HAS AGREED TO BETRAY HIS OWN WORLD.
HOW CAN YOU KNOW THAT I'M BEING GENUINE? THE ANSWER QUITE SIMPLY IS...
...YOU DON'T.
BUT IF I WERE YOU, I'D COME TO A DECISION ONCE AND FOR ALL ABOUT ME, LADIES. AND YOU'D BETTER MAKE IT FAST...

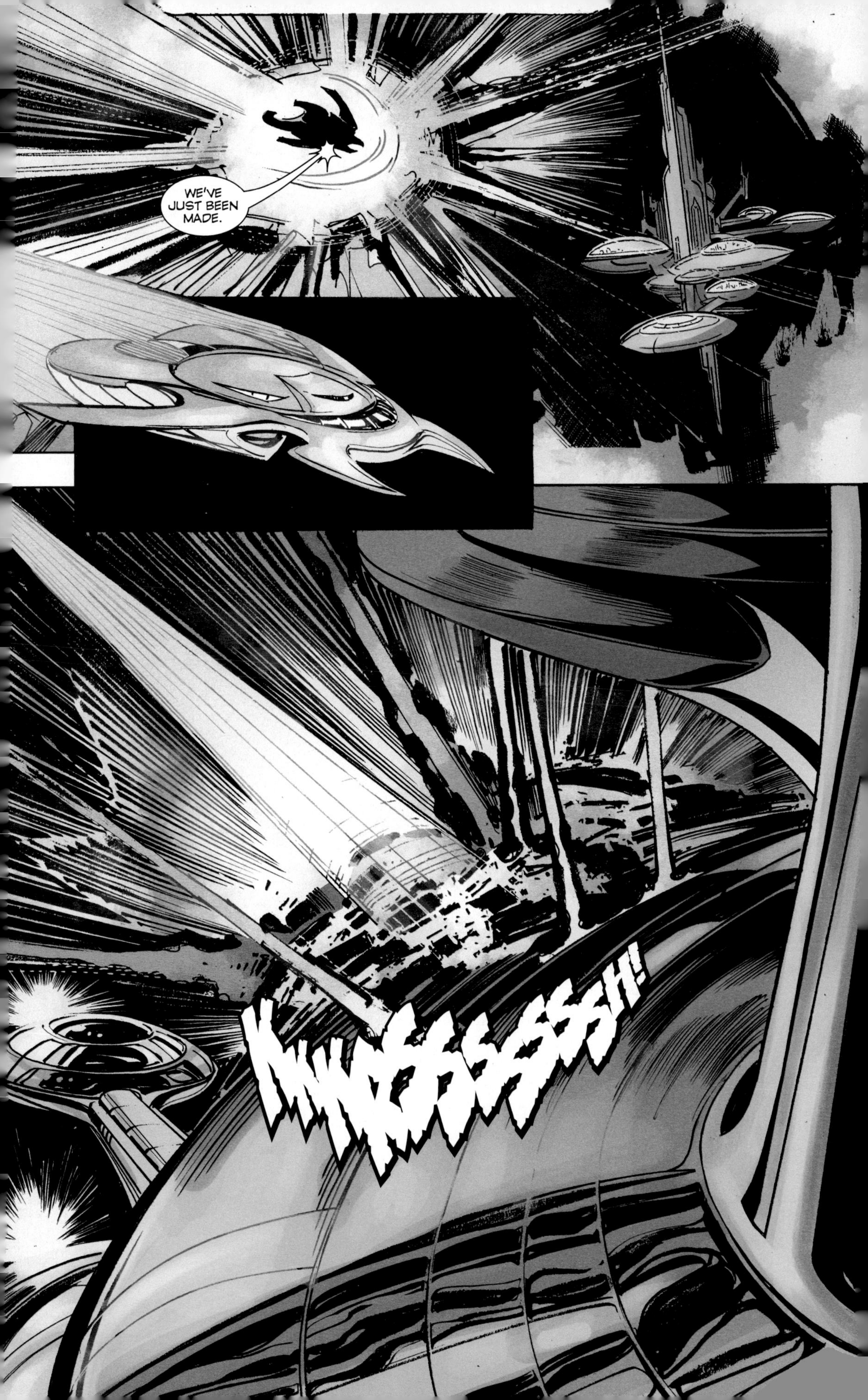
WE'VE JUST BEEN MADE.
KWOSSSSSSH!

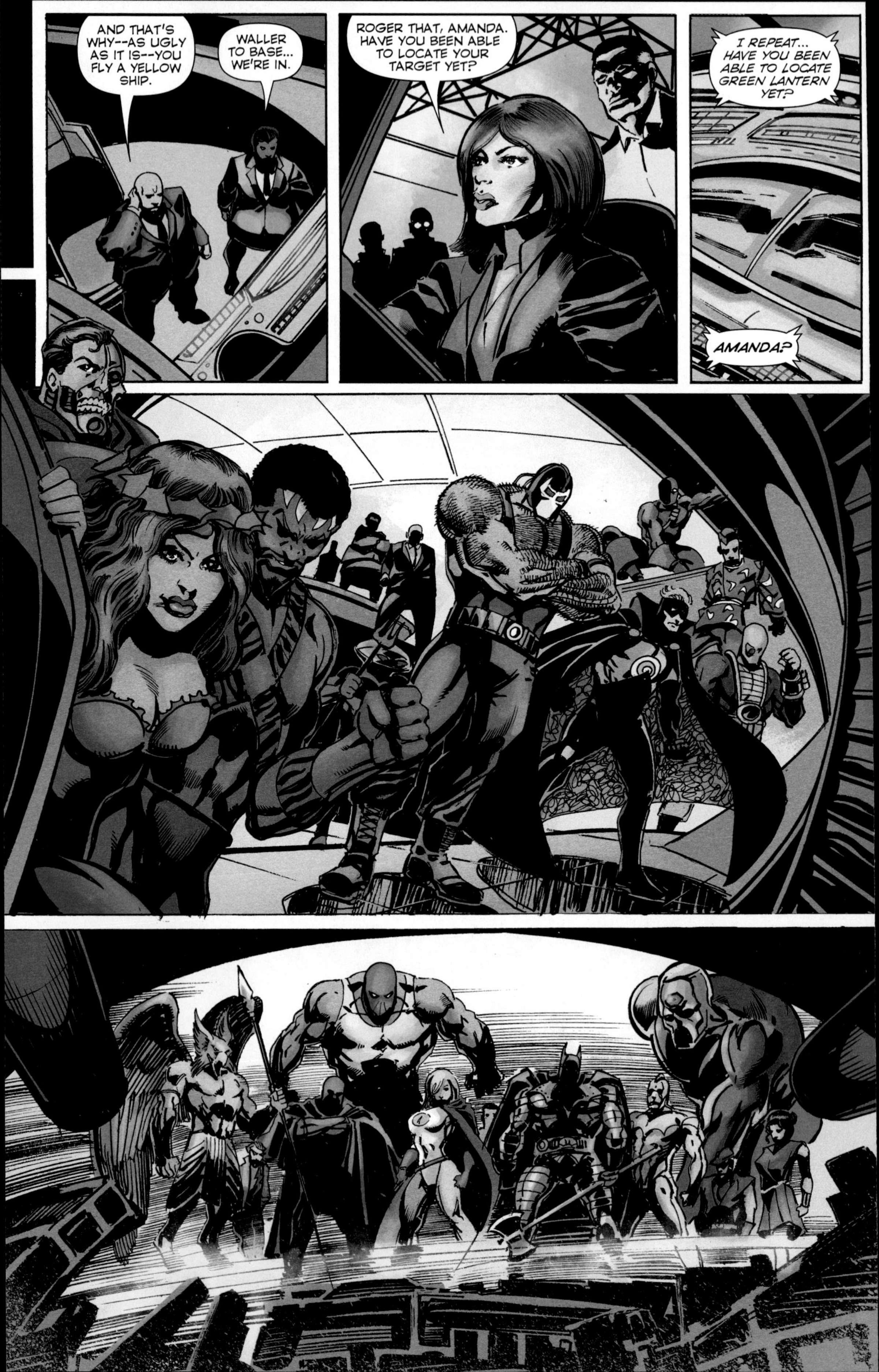
AND THAT'S WHY--AS UGLY AS IT IS--YOU FLY A YELLOW SHIP.
WALLER TO BASE... WE'RE IN.
ROGER THAT, AMANDA. HAVE YOU BEEN ABLE TO LOCATE YOUR TARGET YET?
I REPEAT... HAVE YOU BEEN ABLE TO LOCATE GREEN LANTERN YET?
AMANDA?

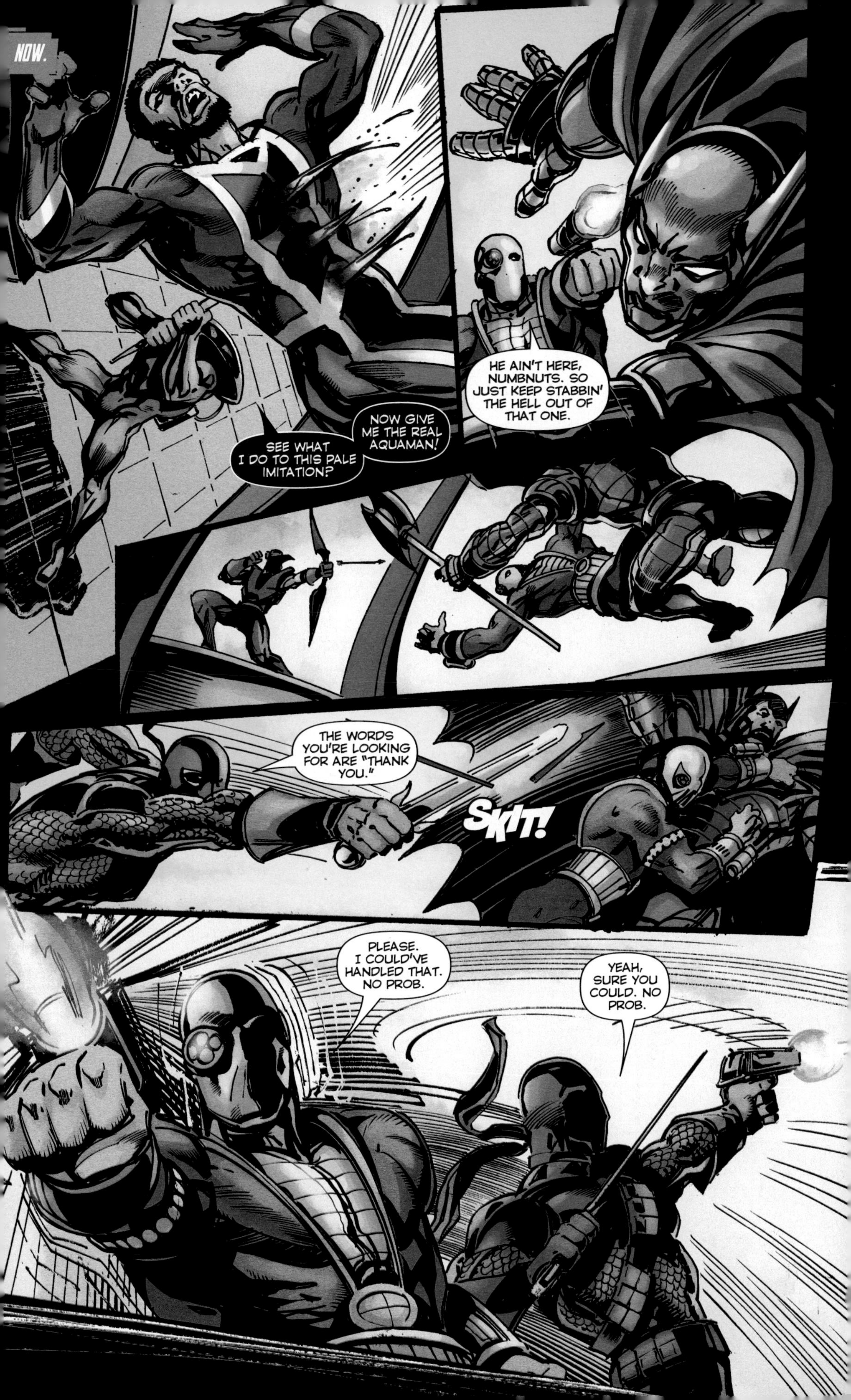
NOW.
HE AIN'T HERE, NUMBNUTS. SO JUST KEEP STABBIN' THE HELL OUT OF THAT ONE.
SEE WHAT I DO TO THIS PALE IMITATION?
NOW GIVE ME THE REAL AQUAMAN!
THE WORDS YOU'RE LOOKING FOR ARE "THANK YOU."
SKIT!
PLEASE. I COULD'VE HANDLED THAT. NO PROB.
YEAH, SURE YOU COULD. NO PROB.

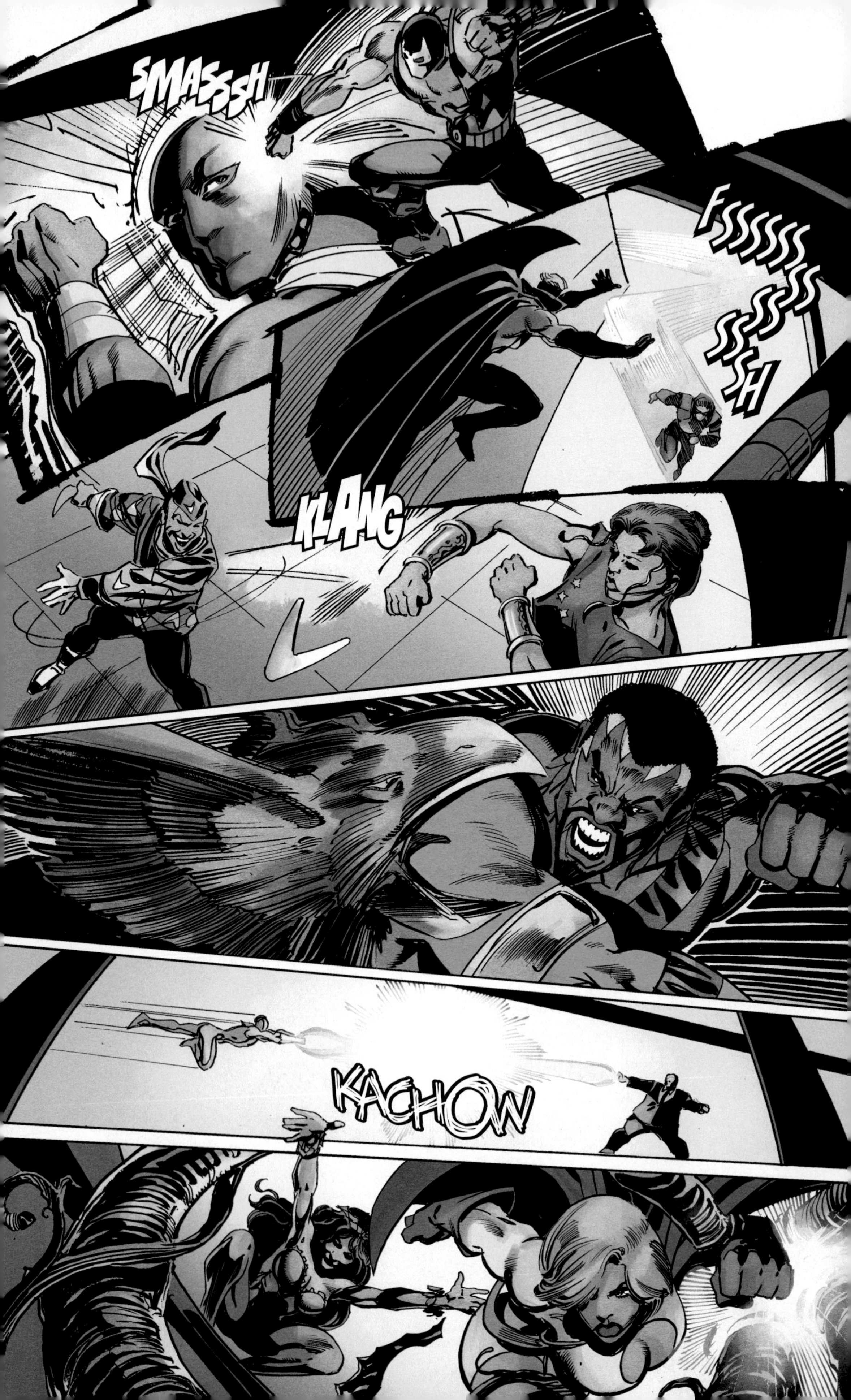
SMASSSH
FSSSSSSSSSSSH
KLANG
KACHOW

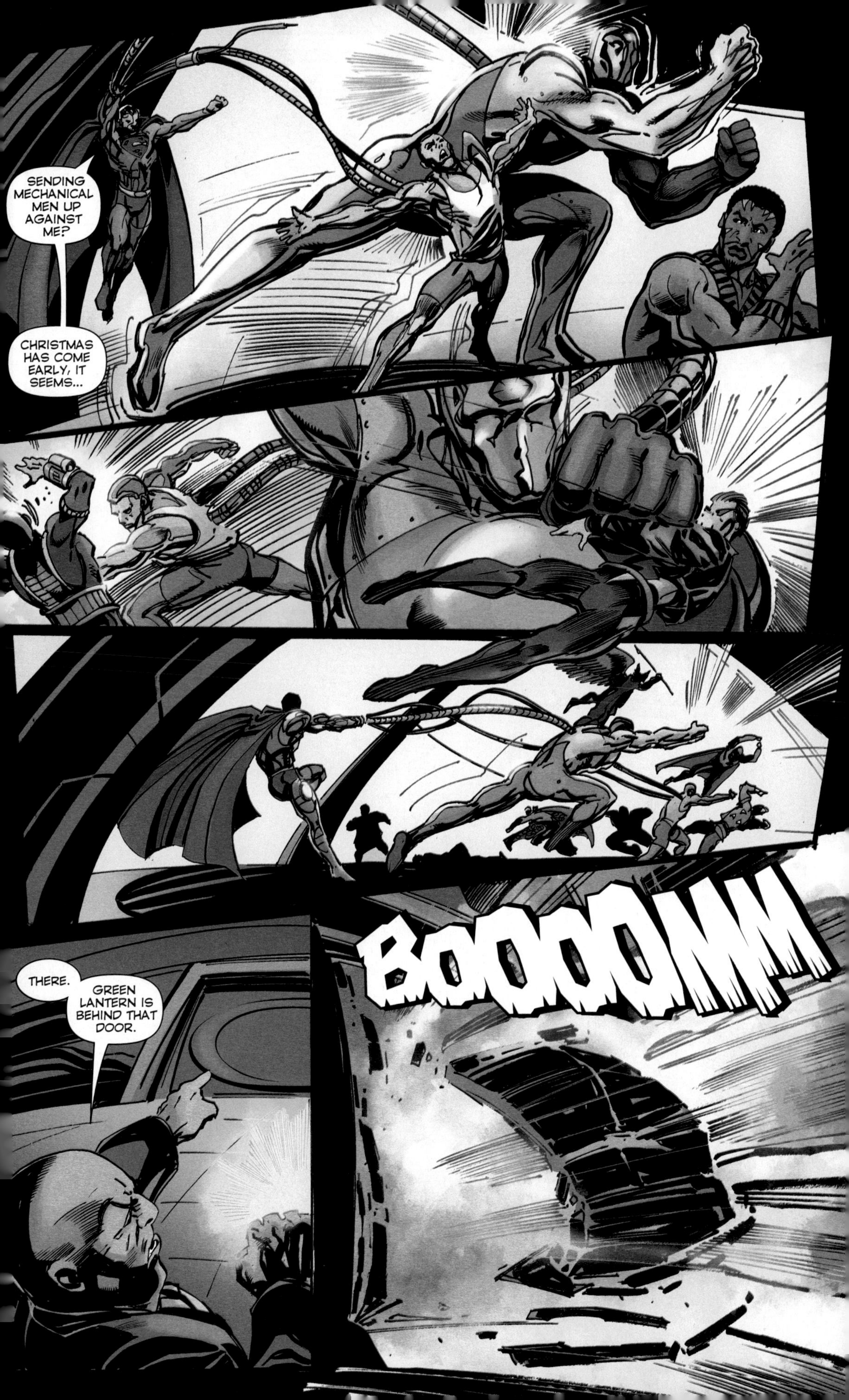
SENDING MECHANICAL MEN UP AGAINST ME?
CHRISTMAS HAS COME EARLY, IT SEEMS...
THERE.
GREEN LANTERN IS BEHIND THAT DOOR.
BOOOOOMM

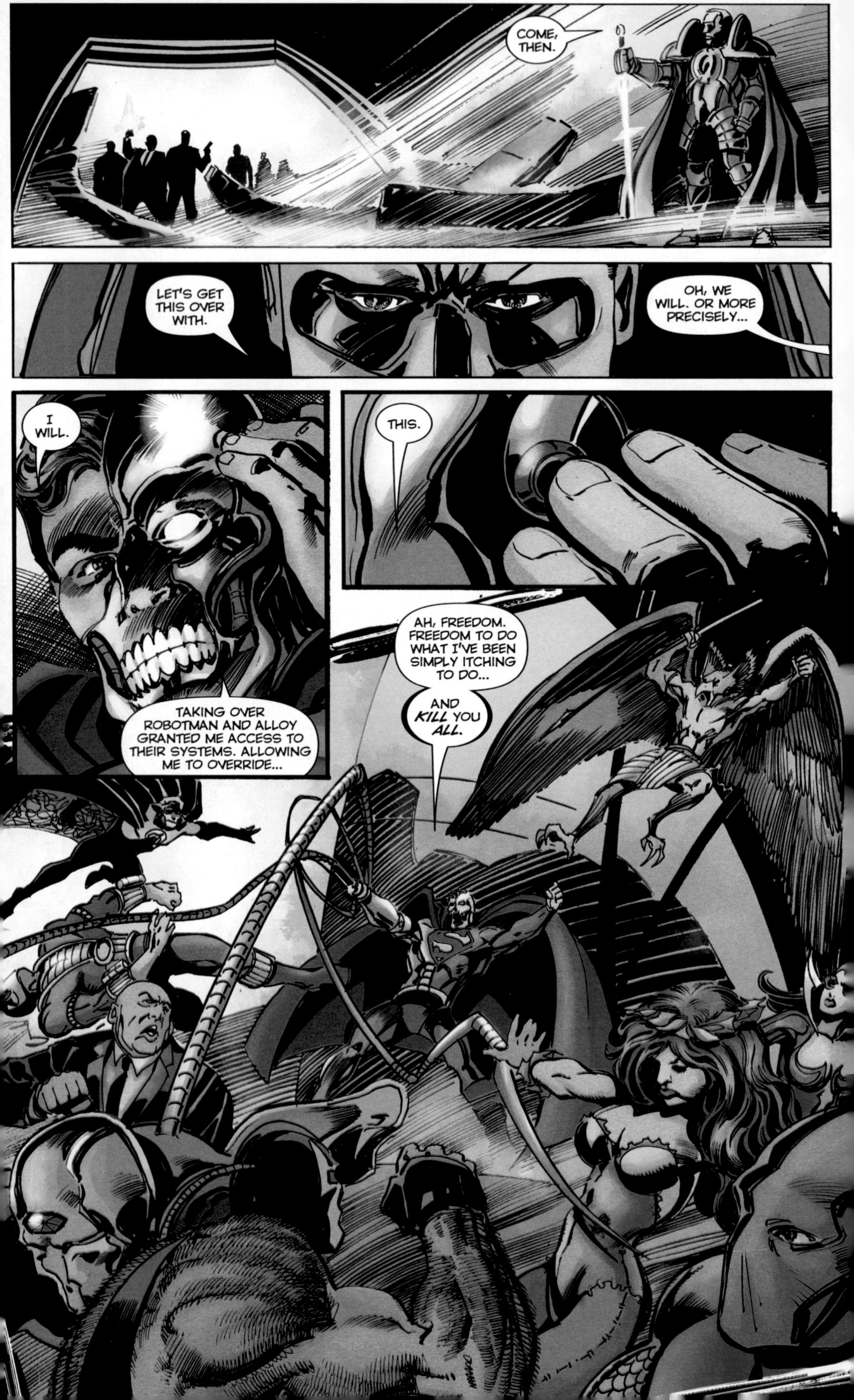
COME, THEN.
LET'S GET THIS OVER WITH.
OH, WE WILL. OR MORE PRECISELY...
I WILL.
THIS.
TAKING OVER ROBOTMAN AND ALLOY GRANTED ME ACCESS TO THEIR SYSTEMS. ALLOWING ME TO OVERRIDE...
AH, FREEDOM. FREEDOM TO DO WHAT I'VE BEEN SIMPLY ITCHING TO DO...
AND *KILL* YOU *ALL*.

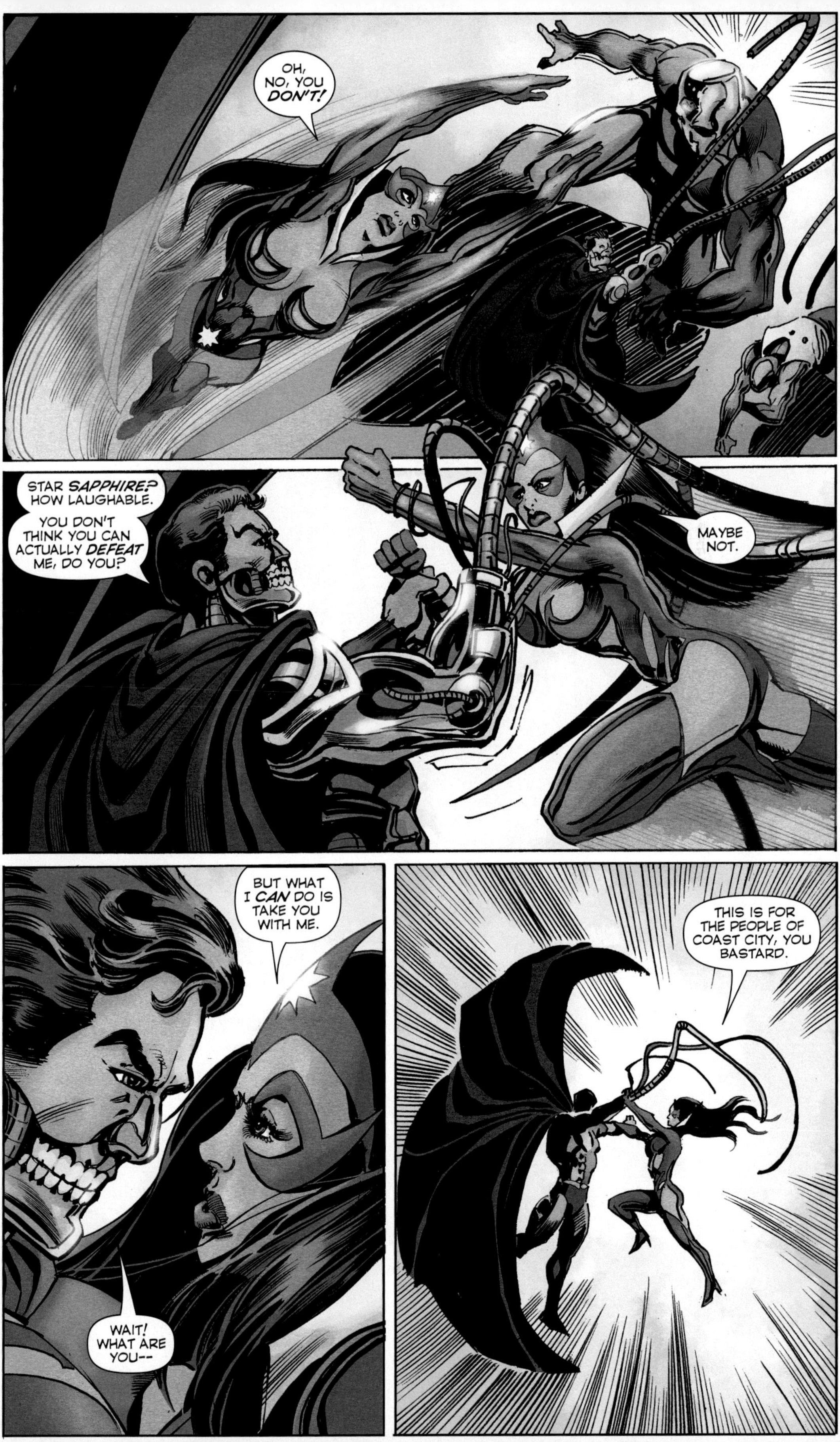
OH, NO, YOU DON'T!
STAR SAPPHIRE? HOW LAUGHABLE.
YOU DON'T THINK YOU CAN ACTUALLY DEFEAT ME, DO YOU?
MAYBE NOT.
BUT WHAT I CAN DO IS TAKE YOU WITH ME.
WAIT! WHAT ARE YOU--
THIS IS FOR THE PEOPLE OF COAST CITY, YOU BASTARD.

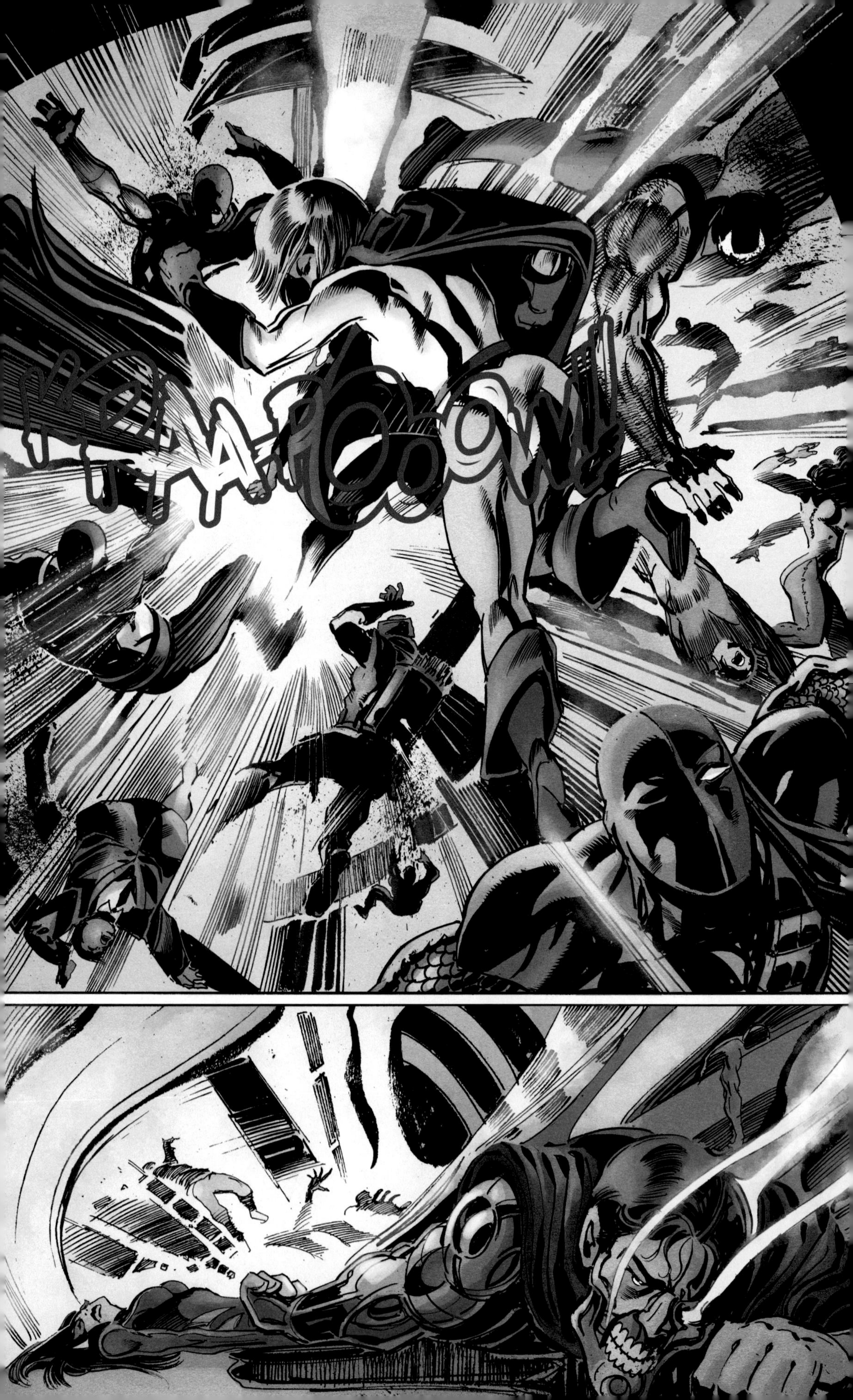
KRA-BOOOM!!

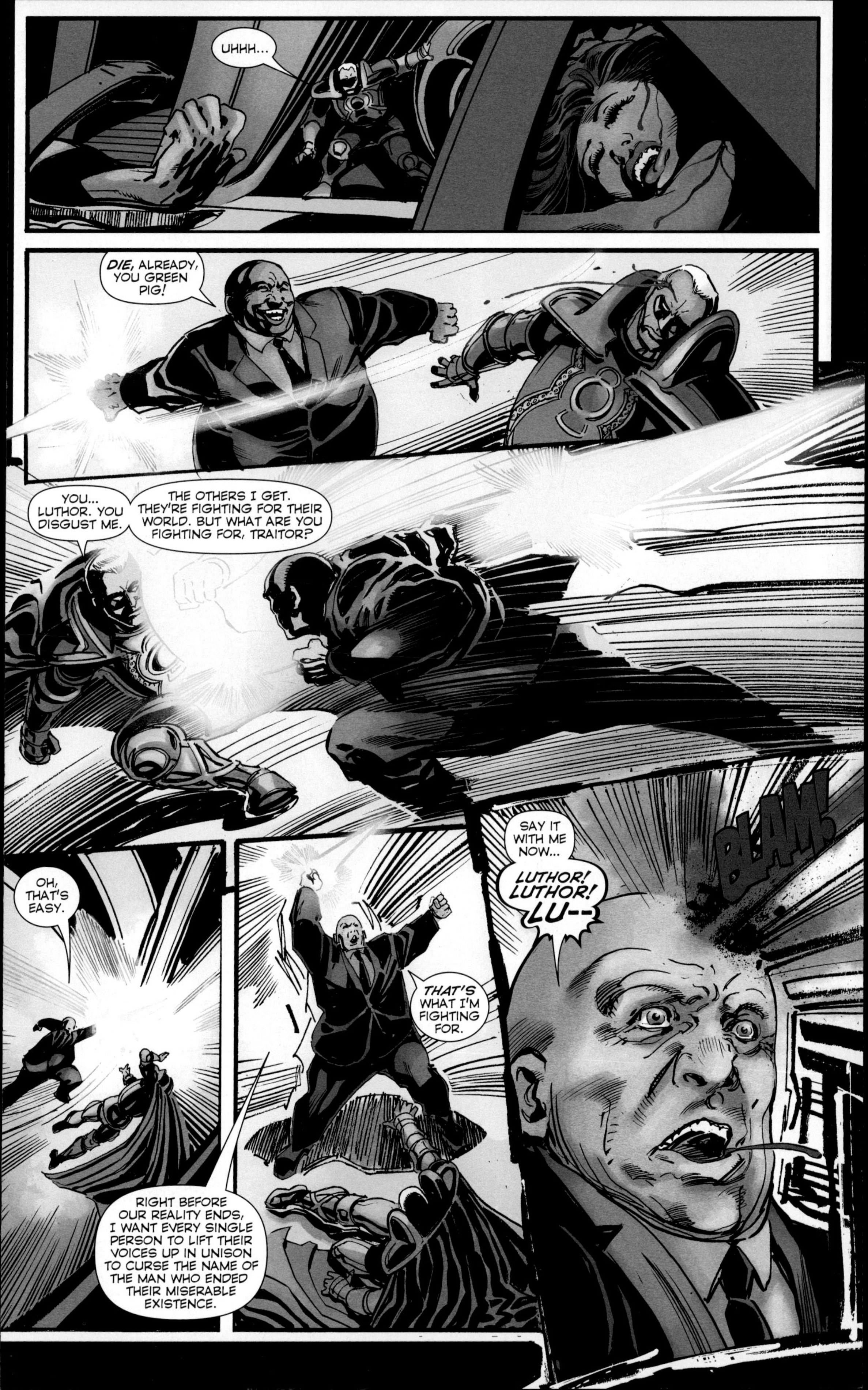
UHHH...
DIE, ALREADY, YOU GREEN PIG!
YOU... LUTHOR. YOU DISGUST ME.
THE OTHERS I GET. THEY'RE FIGHTING FOR THEIR WORLD. BUT WHAT ARE YOU FIGHTING FOR, TRAITOR?
OH, THAT'S EASY.
RIGHT BEFORE OUR REALITY ENDS, I WANT EVERY SINGLE PERSON TO LIFT THEIR VOICES UP IN UNISON TO CURSE THE NAME OF THE MAN WHO ENDED THEIR MISERABLE EXISTENCE.
THAT'S WHAT I'M FIGHTING FOR.
SAY IT WITH ME NOW...
LUTHOR! LUTHOR! LU--
BLAM!

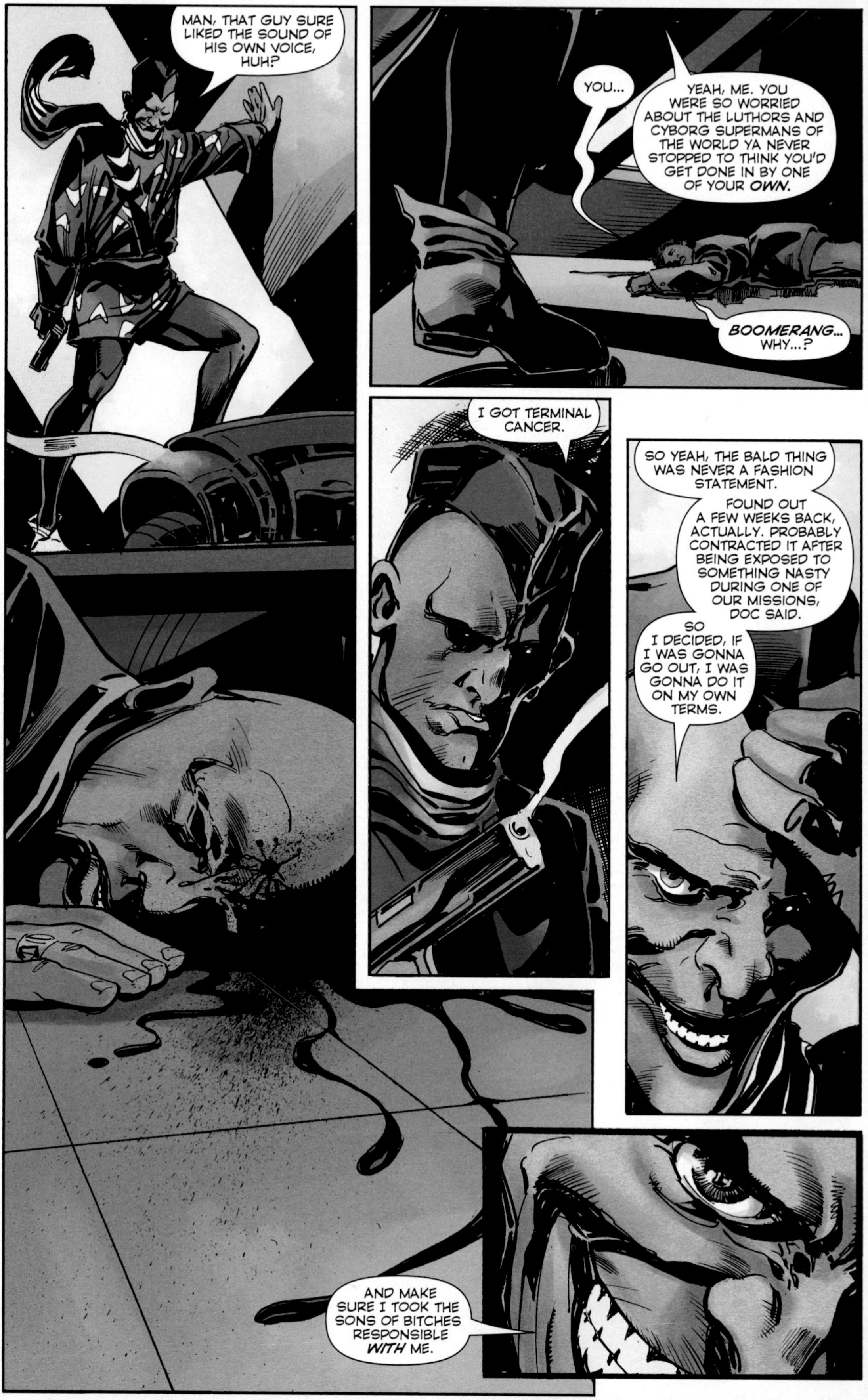
MAN, THAT GUY SURE LIKED THE SOUND OF HIS OWN VOICE, HUH?
YOU...
YEAH, ME. YOU WERE SO WORRIED ABOUT THE LUTHORS AND CYBORG SUPERMANS OF THE WORLD YA NEVER STOPPED TO THINK YOU'D GET DONE IN BY ONE OF YOUR *OWN.*
BOOMERANG... WHY...?
I GOT TERMINAL CANCER.
SO YEAH, THE BALD THING WAS NEVER A FASHION STATEMENT.
FOUND OUT A FEW WEEKS BACK, ACTUALLY. PROBABLY CONTRACTED IT AFTER BEING EXPOSED TO SOMETHING NASTY DURING ONE OF OUR MISSIONS, DOC SAID.
SO I DECIDED, IF I WAS GONNA GO OUT, I WAS GONNA DO IT ON MY OWN TERMS.
AND MAKE SURE I TOOK THE SONS OF BITCHES RESPONSIBLE *WITH* ME.

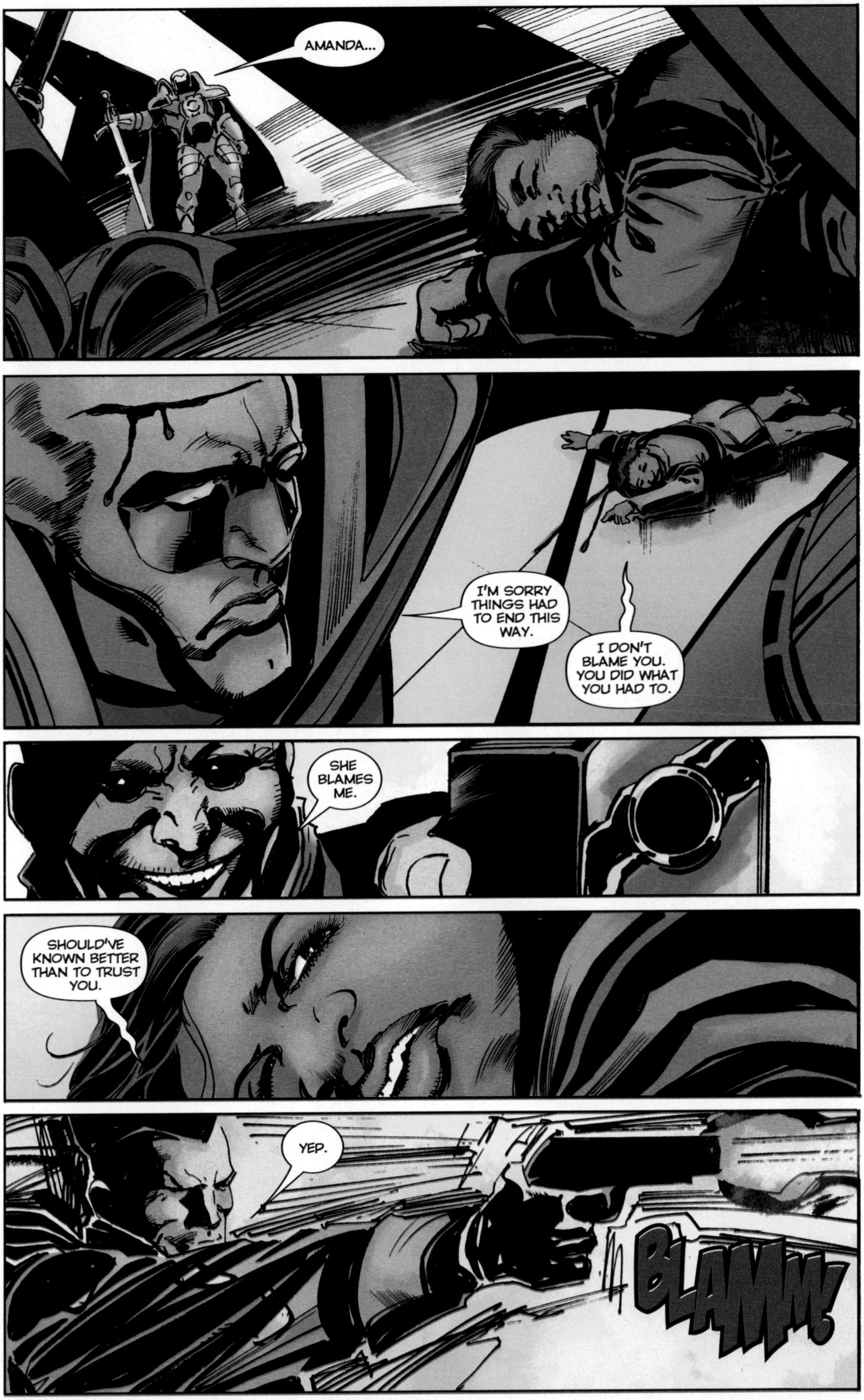
AMANDA...
I'M SORRY THINGS HAD TO END THIS WAY.
I DON'T BLAME YOU. YOU DID WHAT YOU HAD TO.
SHE BLAMES ME.
SHOULD'VE KNOWN BETTER THAN TO TRUST YOU.
YEP.
BLAMM!

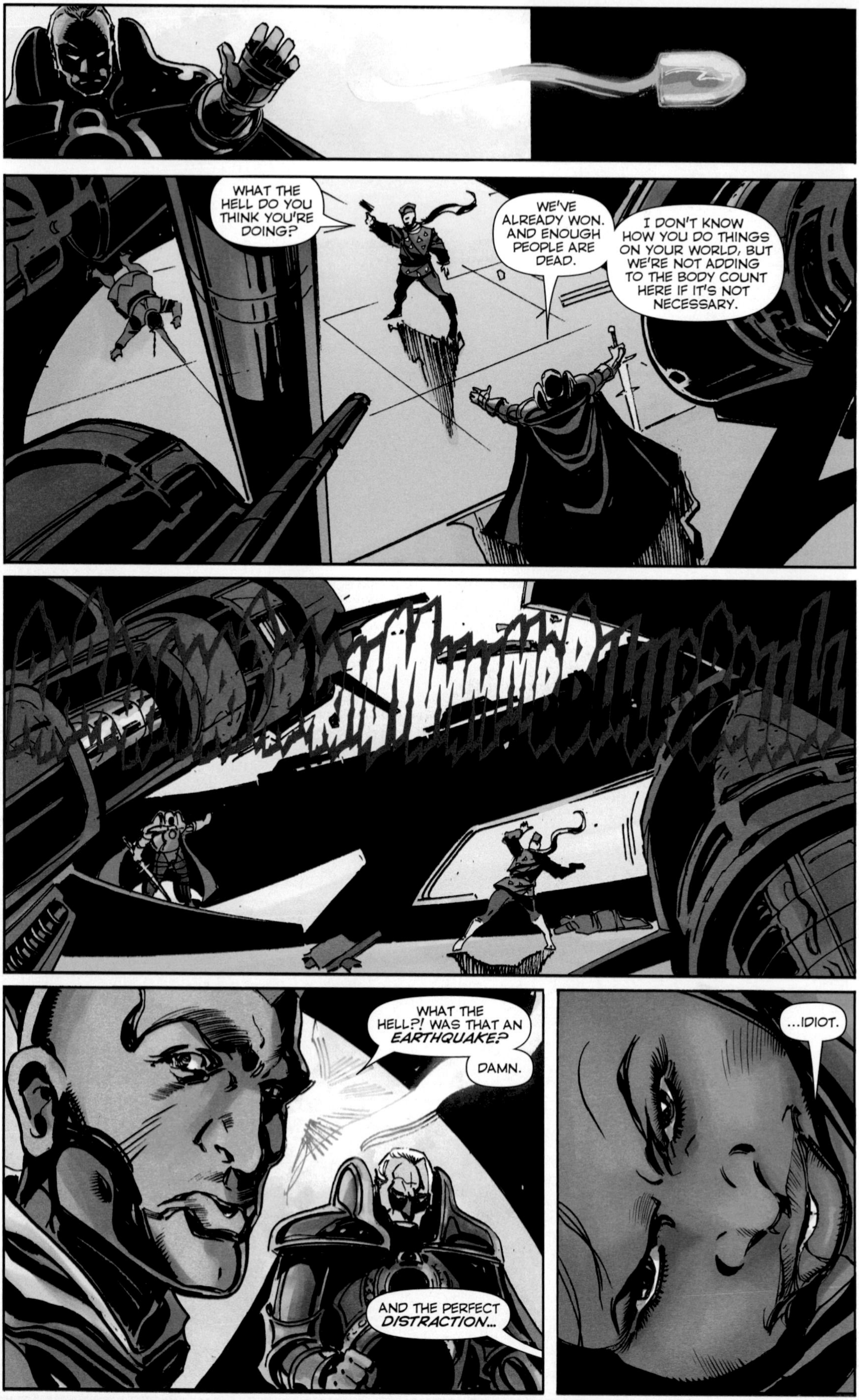
WHAT THE HELL DO YOU THINK YOU'RE DOING?
WE'VE ALREADY WON. AND ENOUGH PEOPLE ARE DEAD.
I DON'T KNOW HOW YOU DO THINGS ON YOUR WORLD, BUT WE'RE NOT ADDING TO THE BODY COUNT HERE IF IT'S NOT NECESSARY.
WHAT THE HELL?! WAS THAT AN *EARTHQUAKE?*
DAMN.
AND THE PERFECT *DISTRACTION*...
...IDIOT.

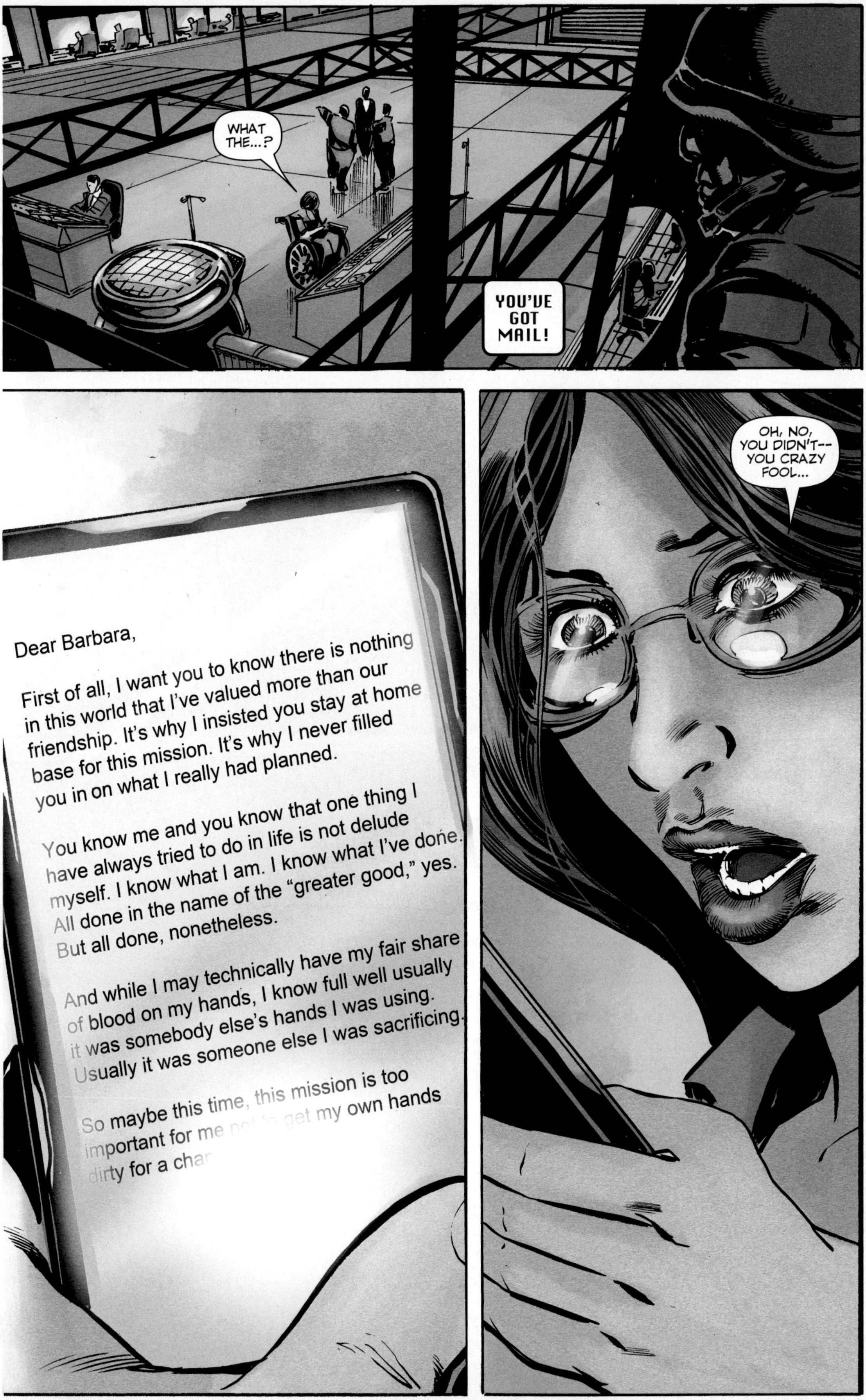
WHAT THE...?
YOU'VE GOT MAIL!
Dear Barbara,
First of all, I want you to know there is nothing in this world that I've valued more than our friendship. It's why I insisted you stay at home base for this mission. It's why I never filled you in on what I really had planned.
You know me and you know that one thing I have always tried to do in life is not delude myself. I know what I am. I know what I've done. All done in the name of the "greater good," yes. But all done, nonetheless.
And while I may technically have my fair share of blood on my hands, I know full well usually it was somebody else's hands I was using. Usually it was someone else I was sacrificing.
So maybe this time, this mission is too important for me
dirty for a
OH, NO, YOU DIDN'T-- YOU CRAZY FOOL...

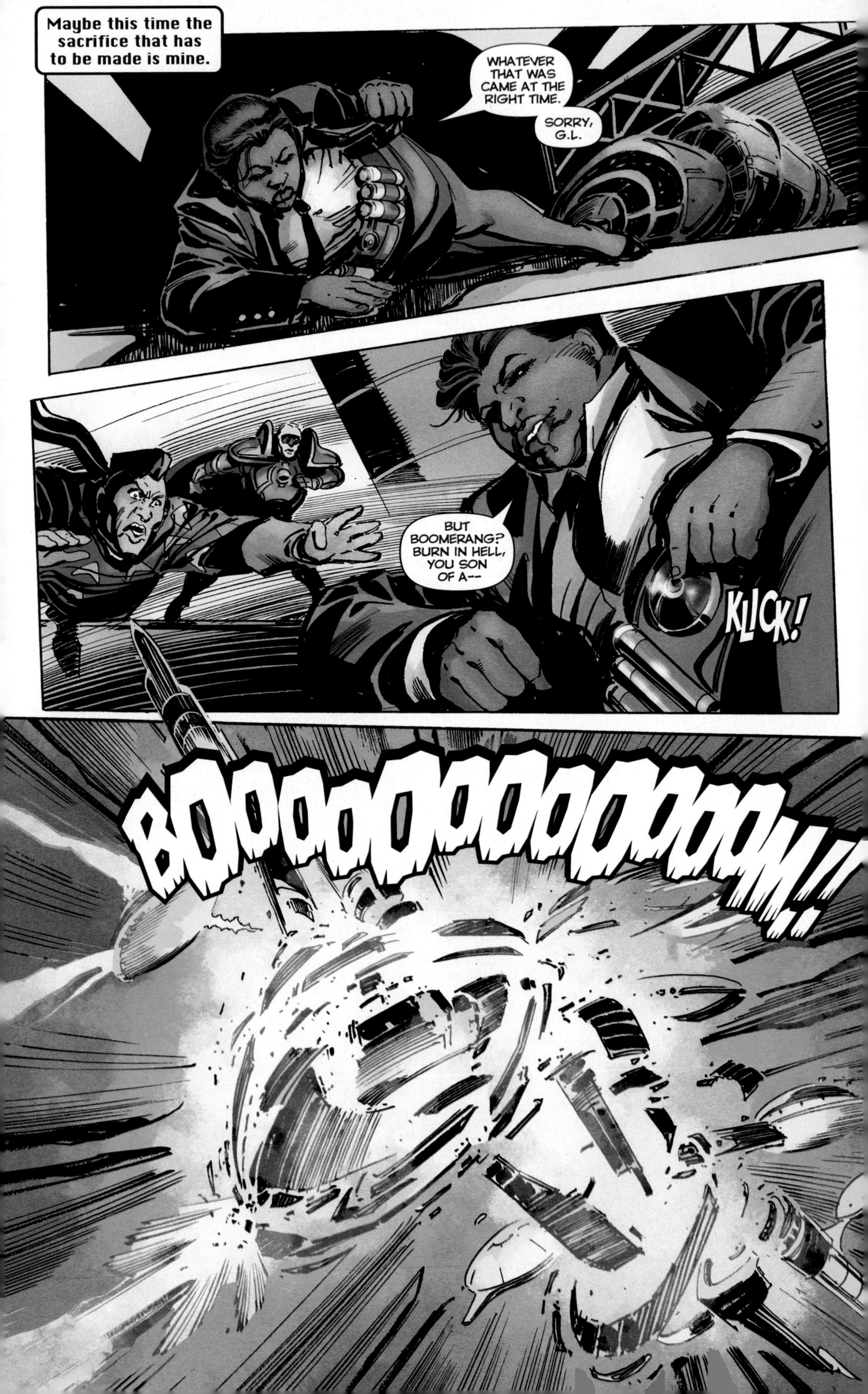

Maybe this time the sacrifice that has to be made is mine.
WHATEVER THAT WAS CAME AT THE RIGHT TIME.
SORRY, G.L.
BUT BOOMERANG? BURN IN HELL, YOU SON OF A--
KLICK!
BOOOOOOOOOOOOM!!

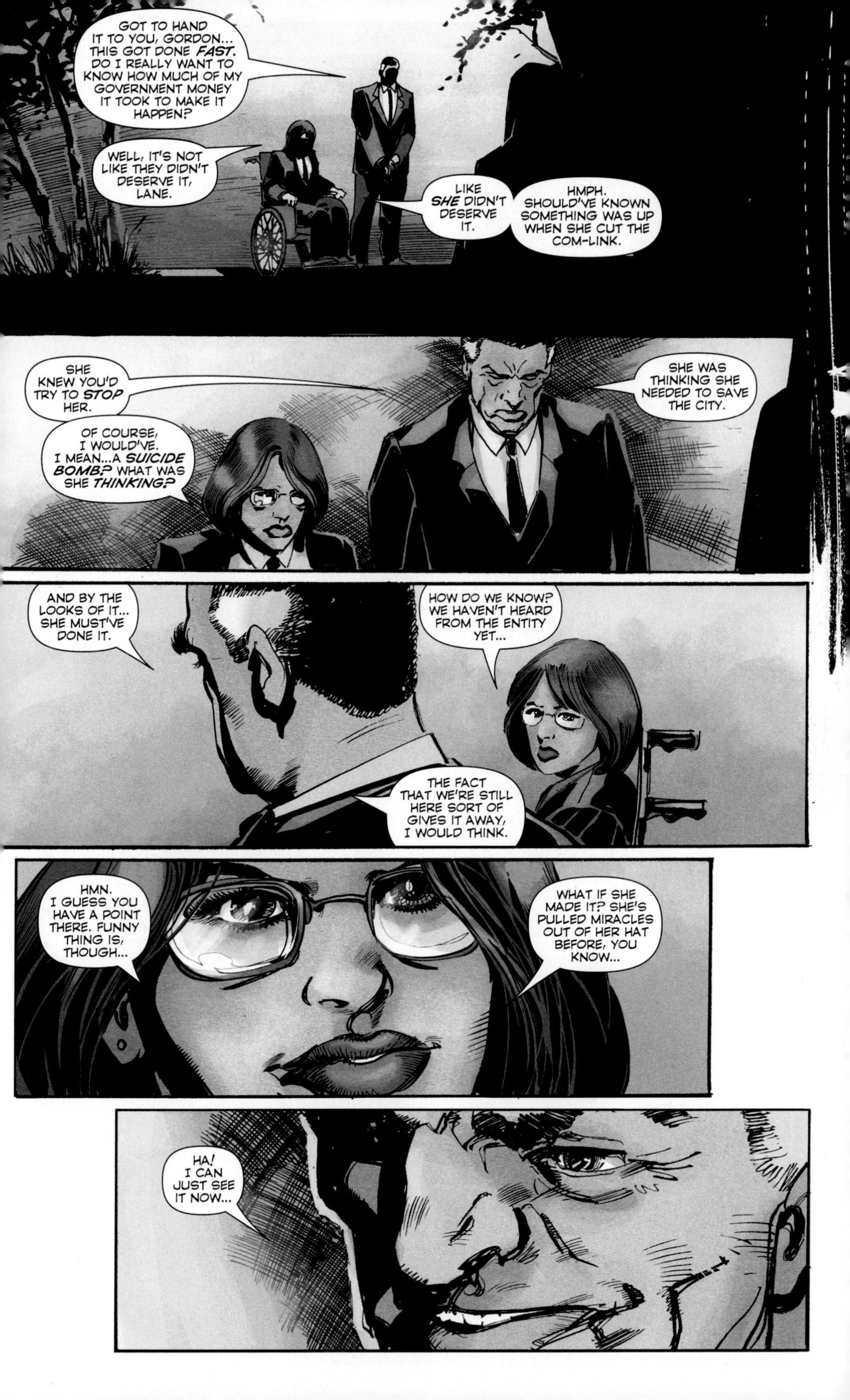
GOT TO HAND IT TO YOU, GORDON... THIS GOT DONE FAST. DO I REALLY WANT TO KNOW HOW MUCH OF MY GOVERNMENT MONEY IT TOOK TO MAKE IT HAPPEN?
WELL, IT'S NOT LIKE THEY DIDN'T DESERVE IT, LANE.
LIKE SHE DIDN'T DESERVE IT.
HMPH. SHOULD'VE KNOWN SOMETHING WAS UP WHEN SHE CUT THE COM-LINK.
SHE KNEW YOU'D TRY TO STOP HER.
OF COURSE, I WOULD'VE. I MEAN...A SUICIDE BOMB? WHAT WAS SHE THINKING?
SHE WAS THINKING SHE NEEDED TO SAVE THE CITY.
AND BY THE LOOKS OF IT... SHE MUST'VE DONE IT.
HOW DO WE KNOW? WE HAVEN'T HEARD FROM THE ENTITY YET...
THE FACT THAT WE'RE STILL HERE SORT OF GIVES IT AWAY, I WOULD THINK.
HMN. I GUESS YOU HAVE A POINT THERE. FUNNY THING IS, THOUGH...
WHAT IF SHE MADE IT? SHE'S PULLED MIRACLES OUT OF HER HAT BEFORE, YOU KNOW...
HA! I CAN JUST SEE IT NOW...

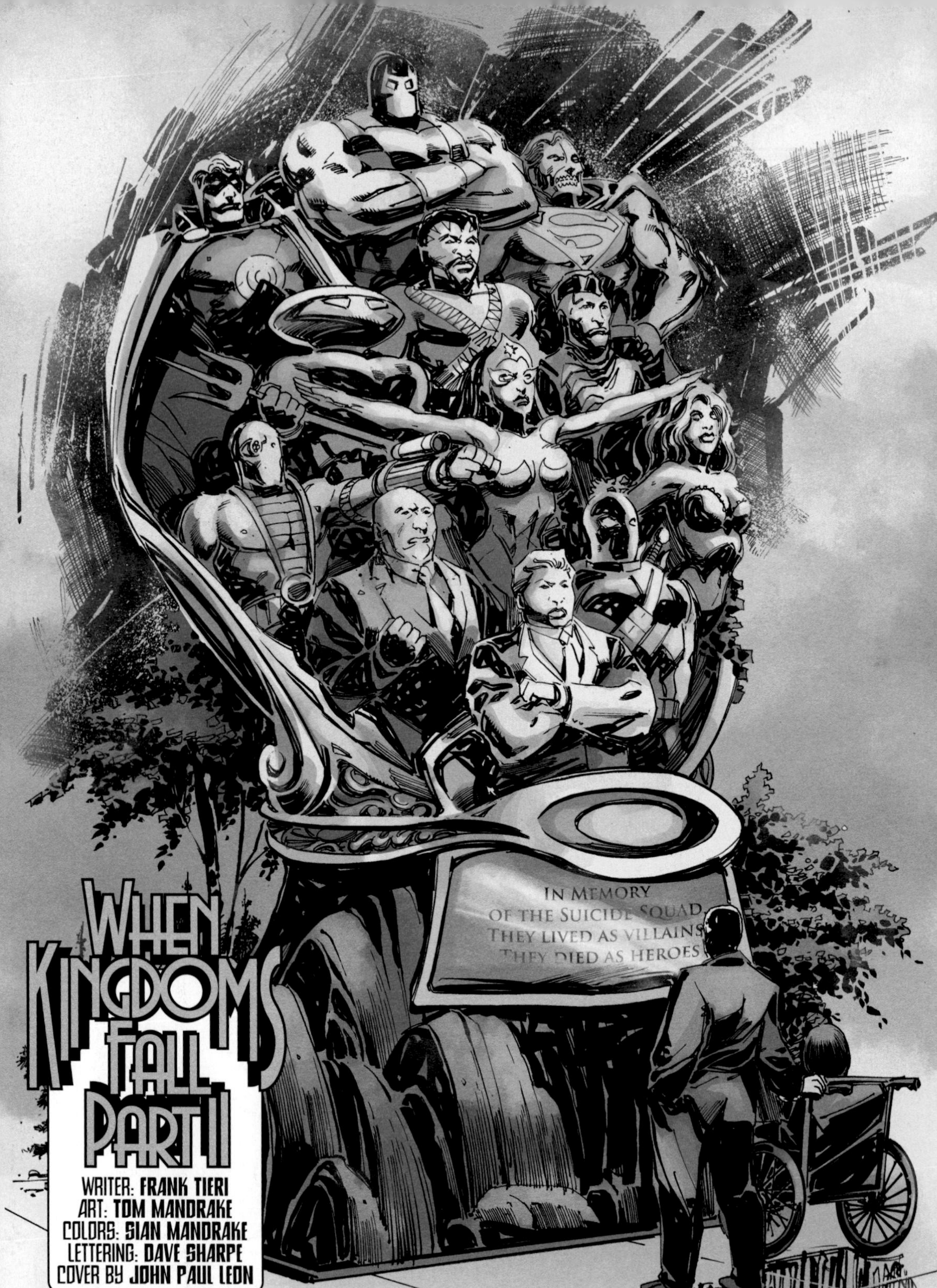
IN MEMORY
OF THE SUICIDE SQUAD.
THEY LIVED AS VILLAINS
THEY DIED AS HEROES
WHEN KINGDOMS FALL PART II
WRITER: FRANK TIERI
ART: TOM MANDRAKE
COLORS: SIAN MANDRAKE
LETTERING: DAVE SHARPE
COVER BY JOHN PAUL LEON

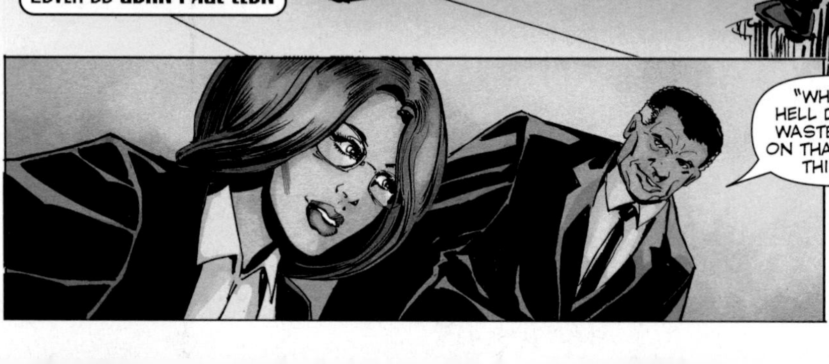
"WHY THE HELL DID YOU WASTE MONEY ON THAT STUPID THING?"

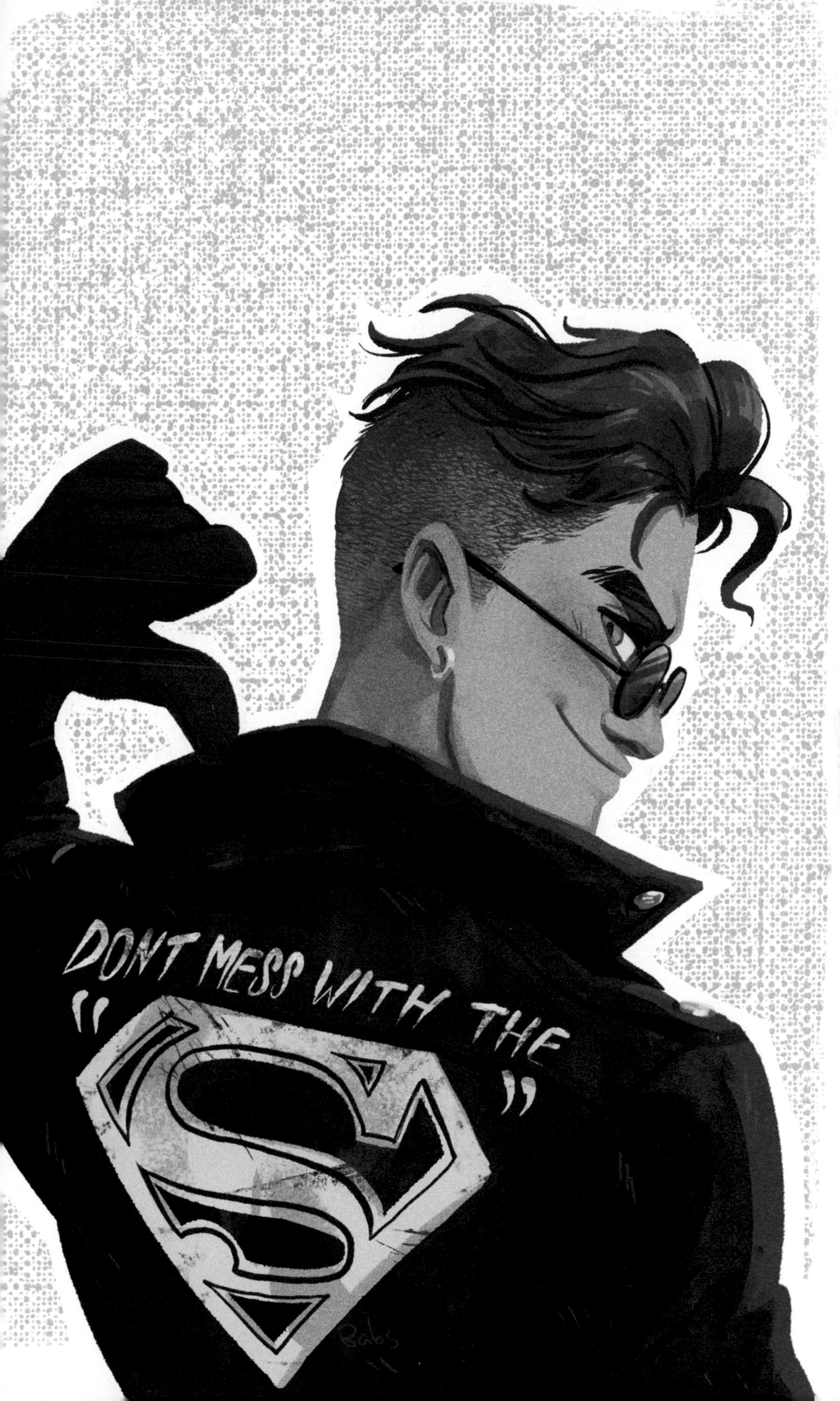
DONT MESS WITH THE

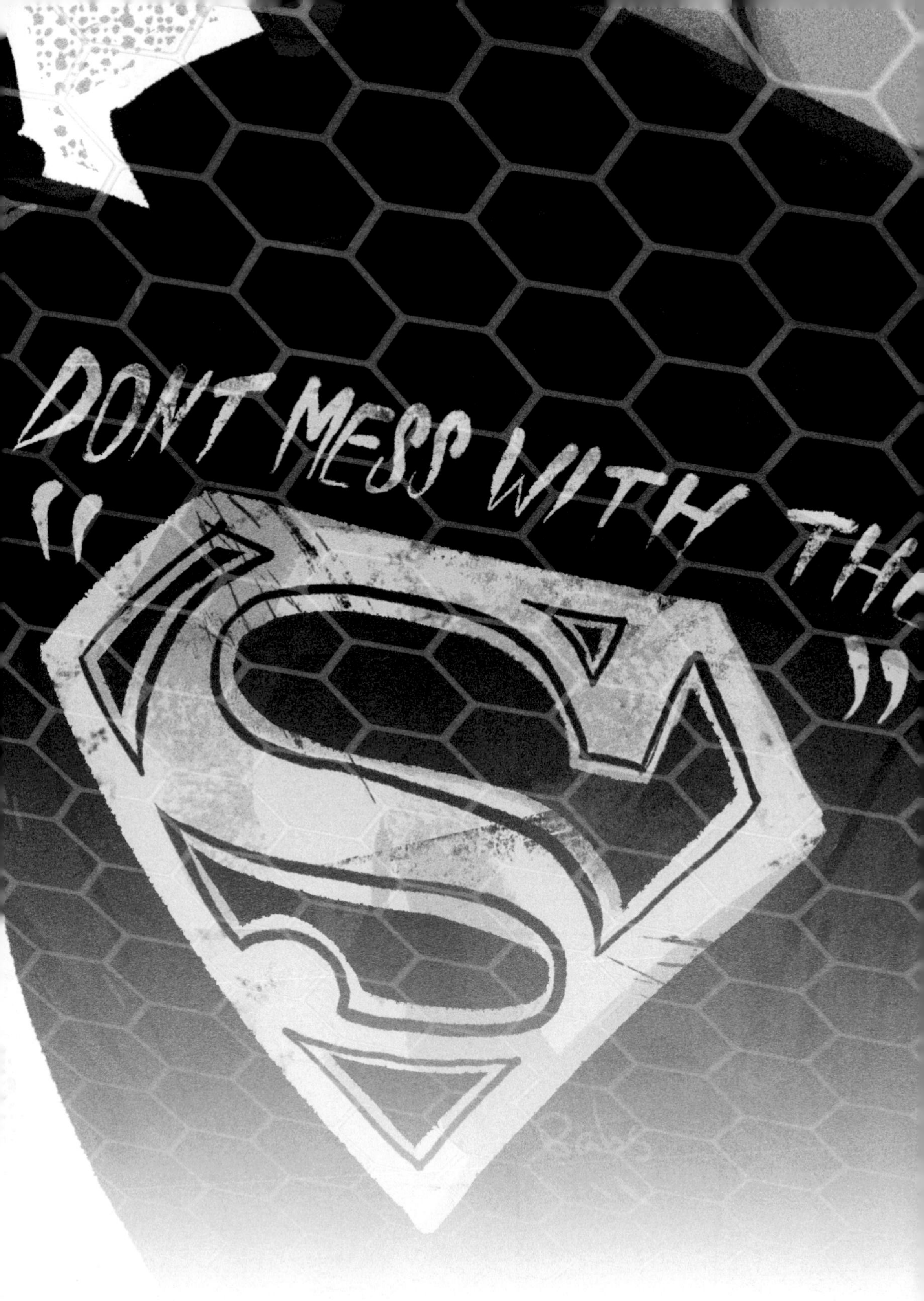

DONT MESS WITH TH

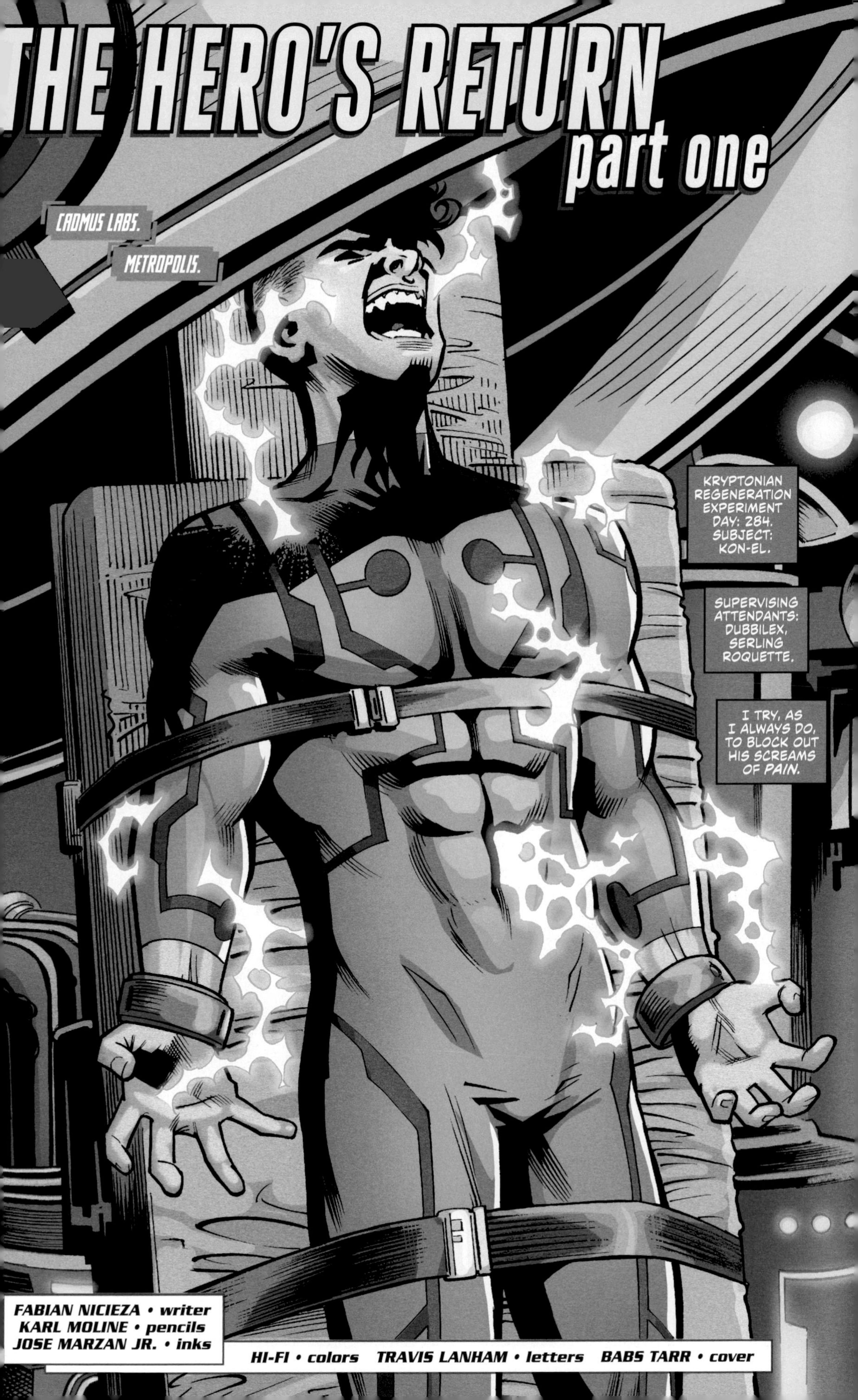
THE HERO'S RETURN
part one
CADMUS LABS.
METROPOLIS.
KRYPTONIAN REGENERATION EXPERIMENT DAY: 284. SUBJECT: KON-EL.
SUPERVISING ATTENDANTS: DUBBILEX, SERLING ROQUETTE.
I TRY, AS I ALWAYS DO, TO BLOCK OUT HIS SCREAMS OF *PAIN*.
FABIAN NICIEZA • writer
KARL MOLINE • pencils
JOSE MARZAN JR. • inks
HI-FI • colors TRAVIS LANHAM • letters BABS TARR • cover

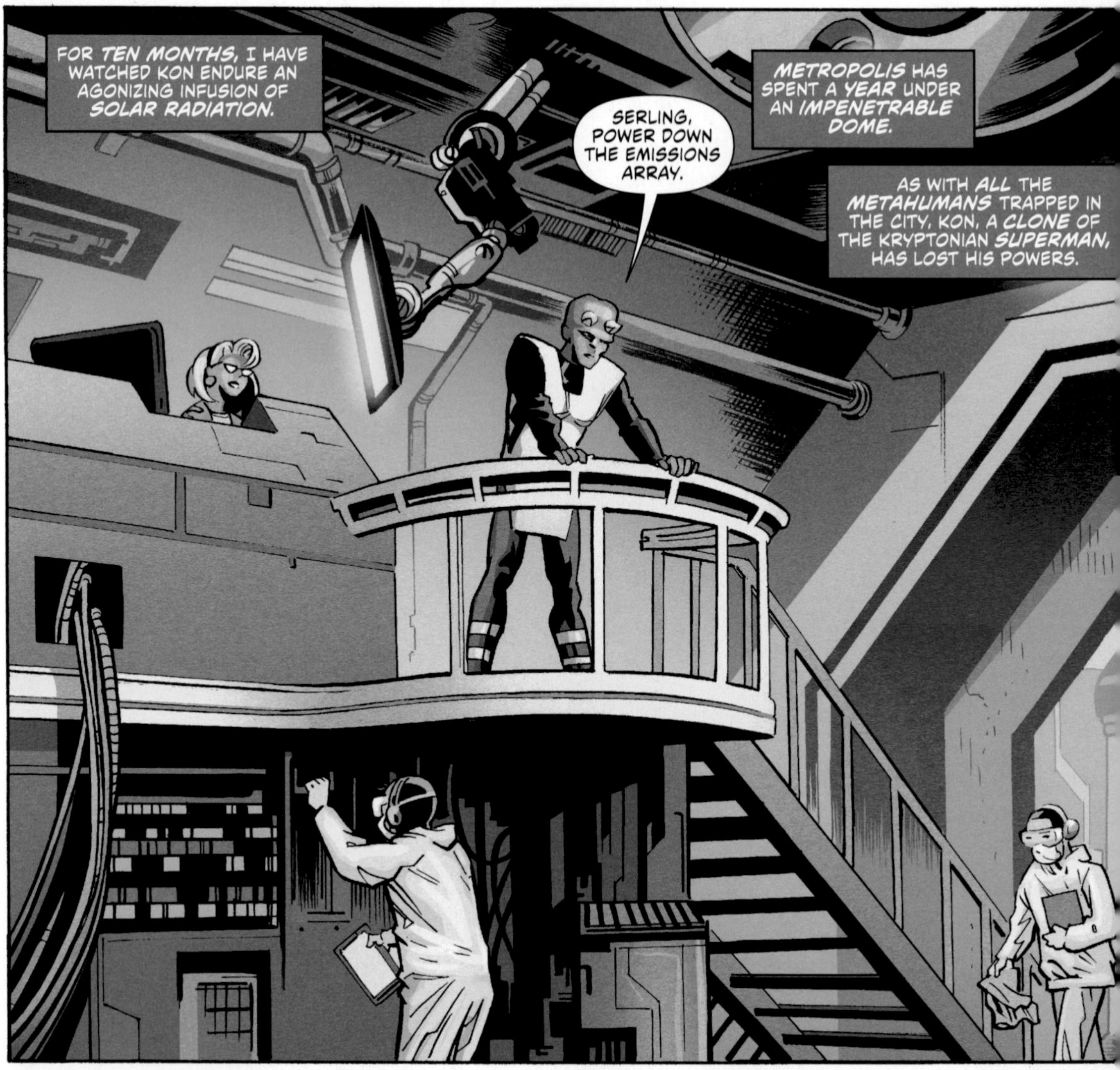
FOR TEN MONTHS, I HAVE WATCHED KON ENDURE AN AGONIZING INFUSION OF SOLAR RADIATION.
SERLING, POWER DOWN THE EMISSIONS ARRAY.
METROPOLIS HAS SPENT A YEAR UNDER AN IMPENETRABLE DOME.
AS WITH ALL THE METAHUMANS TRAPPED IN THE CITY, KON, A CLONE OF THE KRYPTONIAN SUPERMAN, HAS LOST HIS POWERS.

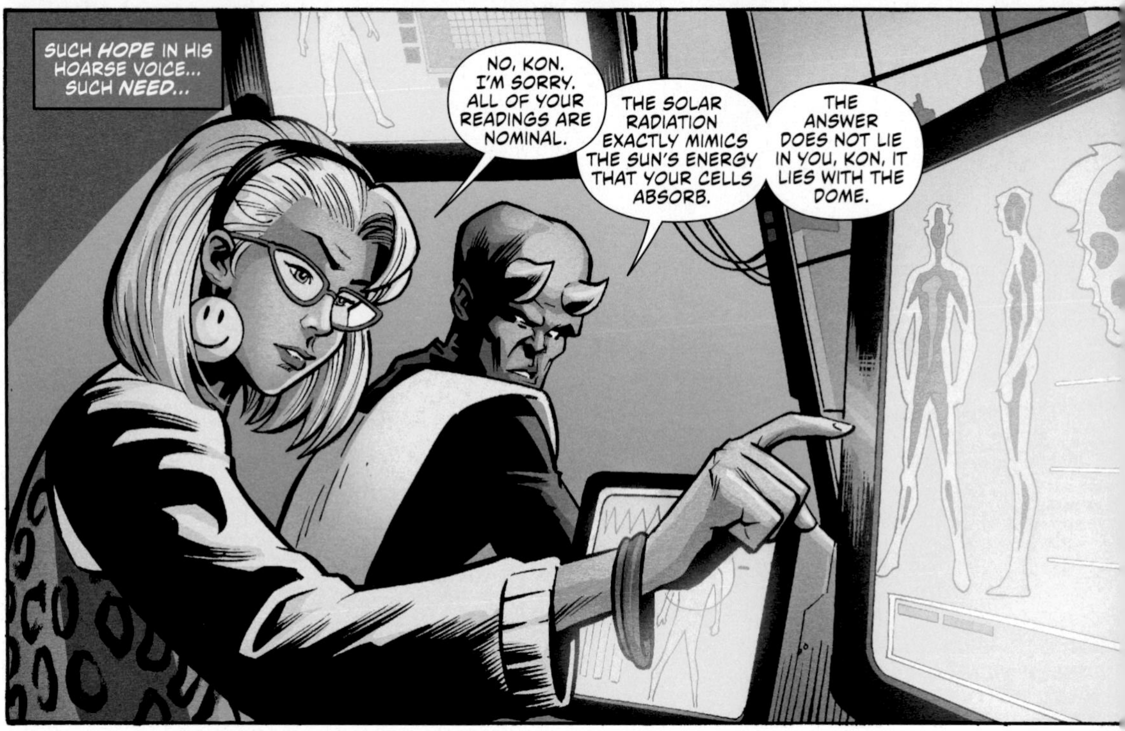
SUCH HOPE IN HIS HOARSE VOICE... SUCH NEED...
NO, KON. I'M SORRY. ALL OF YOUR READINGS ARE NOMINAL.
THE SOLAR RADIATION EXACTLY MIMICS THE SUN'S ENERGY THAT YOUR CELLS ABSORB.
THE ANSWER DOES NOT LIE IN YOU, KON, IT LIES WITH THE DOME.

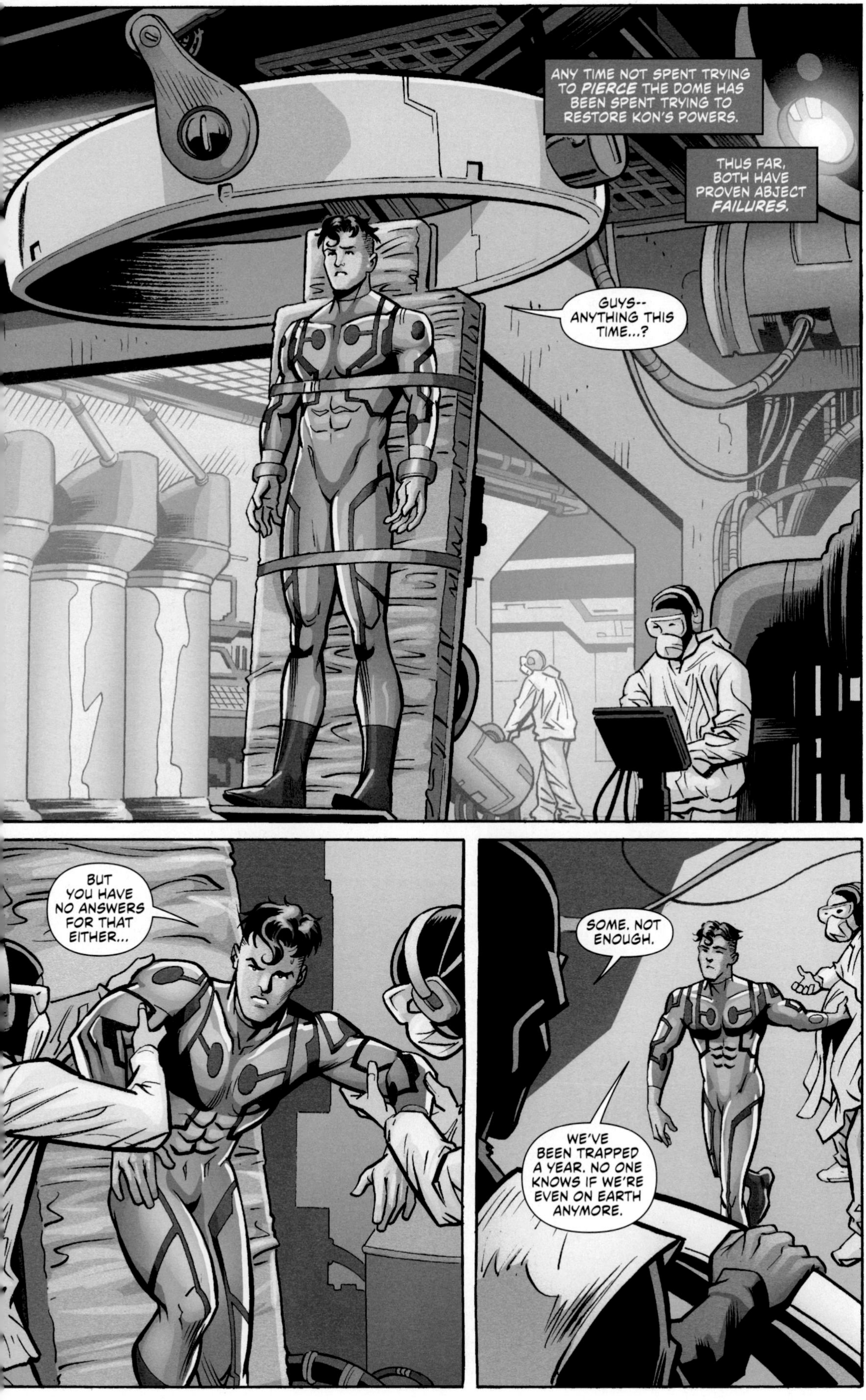
ANY TIME NOT SPENT TRYING TO *PIERCE* THE DOME HAS BEEN SPENT TRYING TO RESTORE KON'S POWERS.
THUS FAR, BOTH HAVE PROVEN ABJECT *FAILURES.*
GUYS-- ANYTHING THIS TIME...?
BUT YOU HAVE NO ANSWERS FOR THAT EITHER...
SOME. NOT ENOUGH.
WE'VE BEEN TRAPPED A YEAR. NO ONE KNOWS IF WE'RE EVEN ON EARTH ANYMORE.

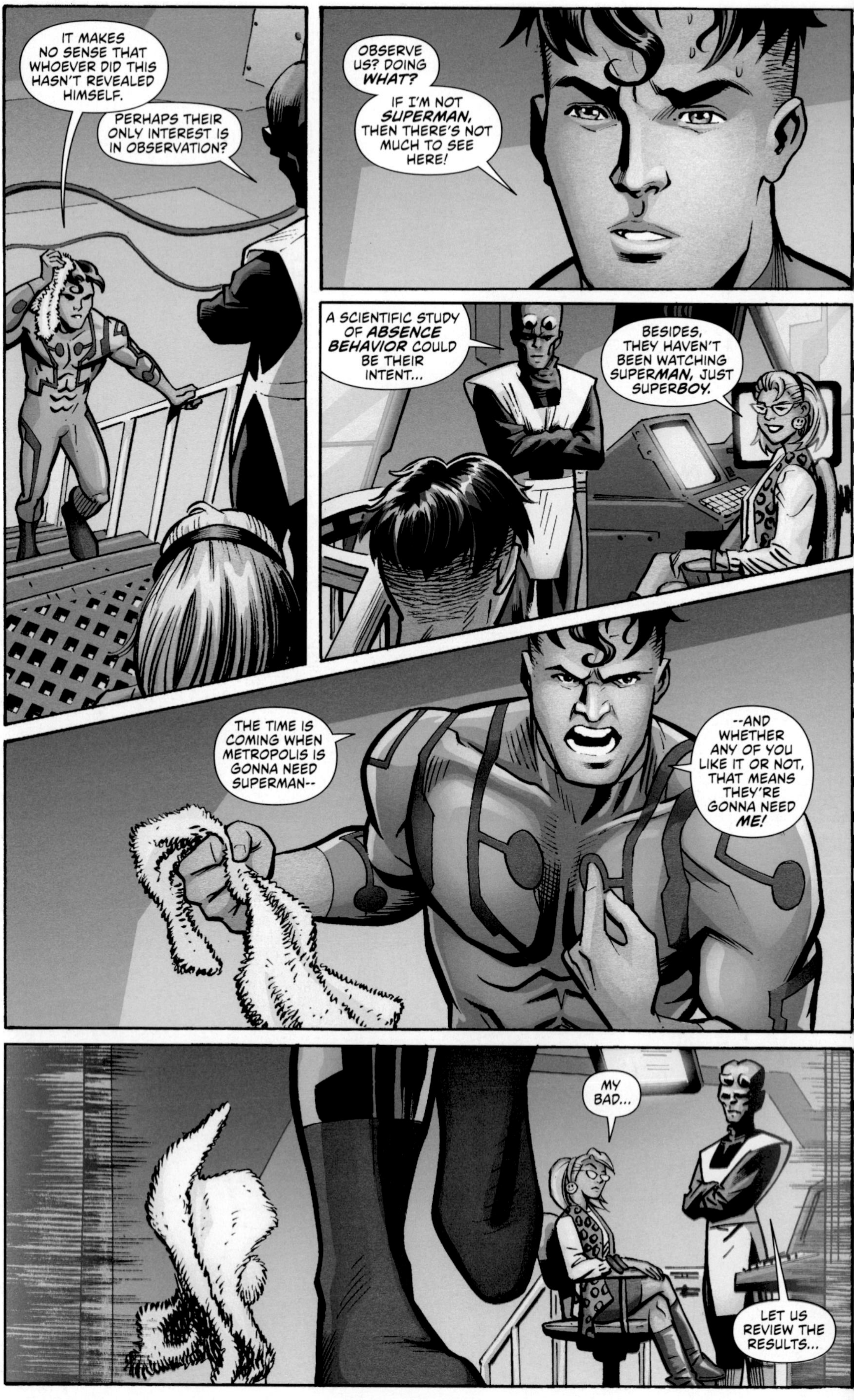
IT MAKES NO SENSE THAT WHOEVER DID THIS HASN'T REVEALED HIMSELF.
PERHAPS THEIR ONLY INTEREST IS IN OBSERVATION?
OBSERVE US? DOING WHAT?
IF I'M NOT SUPERMAN, THEN THERE'S NOT MUCH TO SEE HERE!
A SCIENTIFIC STUDY OF ABSENCE BEHAVIOR COULD BE THEIR INTENT...
BESIDES, THEY HAVEN'T BEEN WATCHING SUPERMAN, JUST SUPERBOY.
THE TIME IS COMING WHEN METROPOLIS IS GONNA NEED SUPERMAN--
--AND WHETHER ANY OF YOU LIKE IT OR NOT, THAT MEANS THEY'RE GONNA NEED ME!
MY BAD...
LET US REVIEW THE RESULTS...

THE LATEST SCAN CORROBORATES OUR THEORIES.

HIS CELLS *ARE* ABSORBING THE RADIATION.

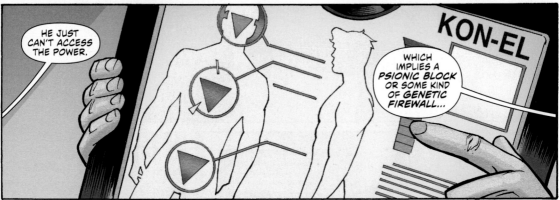

HE JUST CAN'T ACCESS THE POWER.

KON-EL

WHICH IMPLIES A *PSIONIC BLOCK* OR SOME KIND OF *GENETIC FIREWALL...*

BOTH OF WHICH ARE OPERATING ON LEVELS *FAR* BEYOND OUR KEN...

...JUST LIKE THE DOME ITSELF.

SIMULATES DAYLIGHT AND NIGHT, GENERATES ITS OWN ATMOSPHERE, WEATHER SYSTEMS... MAYBE EVEN GRAVITY, FOR ALL WE KNOW.

THERE ARE MANY WHO HAVE SUCH TECHNOLOGY...

...*BRAINIAC, KRONA, DARKSEID...*

...BUT IT IS UNLIKE *ANY* OF THEM NOT TO HAVE... *GLOATED...*ABOUT THEIR ACTIONS...

KON-EL IS CORRECT IN THAT ASSUMPTION.

AND IF ANYONE WOULD KNOW ABOUT THE DESIRE TO GLOAT OVER ONE'S ACCOMPLISHMENTS...

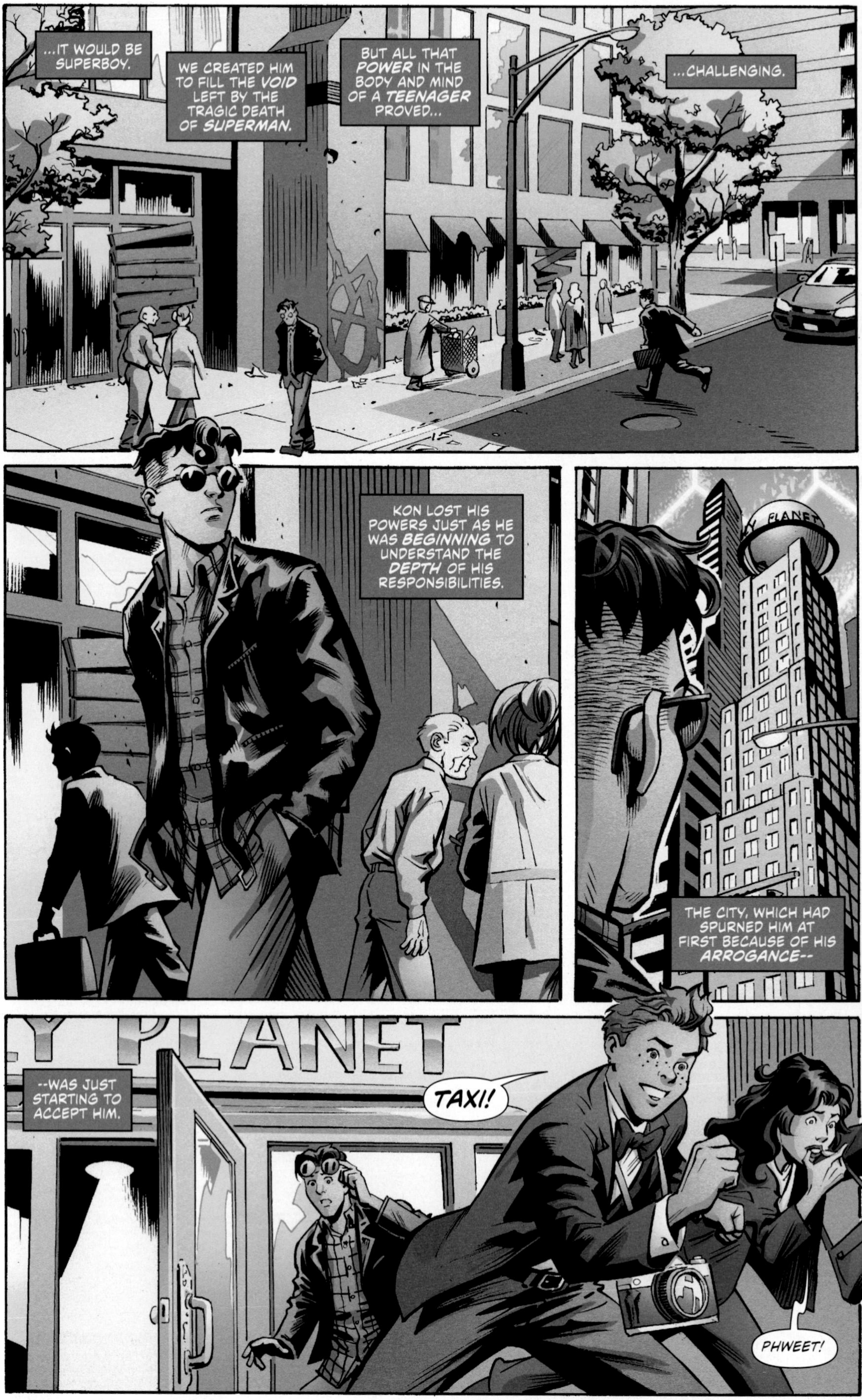
...IT WOULD BE SUPERBOY.
WE CREATED HIM TO FILL THE VOID LEFT BY THE TRAGIC DEATH OF SUPERMAN.
BUT ALL THAT POWER IN THE BODY AND MIND OF A TEENAGER PROVED...
...CHALLENGING.
KON LOST HIS POWERS JUST AS HE WAS BEGINNING TO UNDERSTAND THE DEPTH OF HIS RESPONSIBILITIES.
THE CITY, WHICH HAD SPURNED HIM AT FIRST BECAUSE OF HIS ARROGANCE--
PLANET
--WAS JUST STARTING TO ACCEPT HIM.
TAXI!
PHWEET!

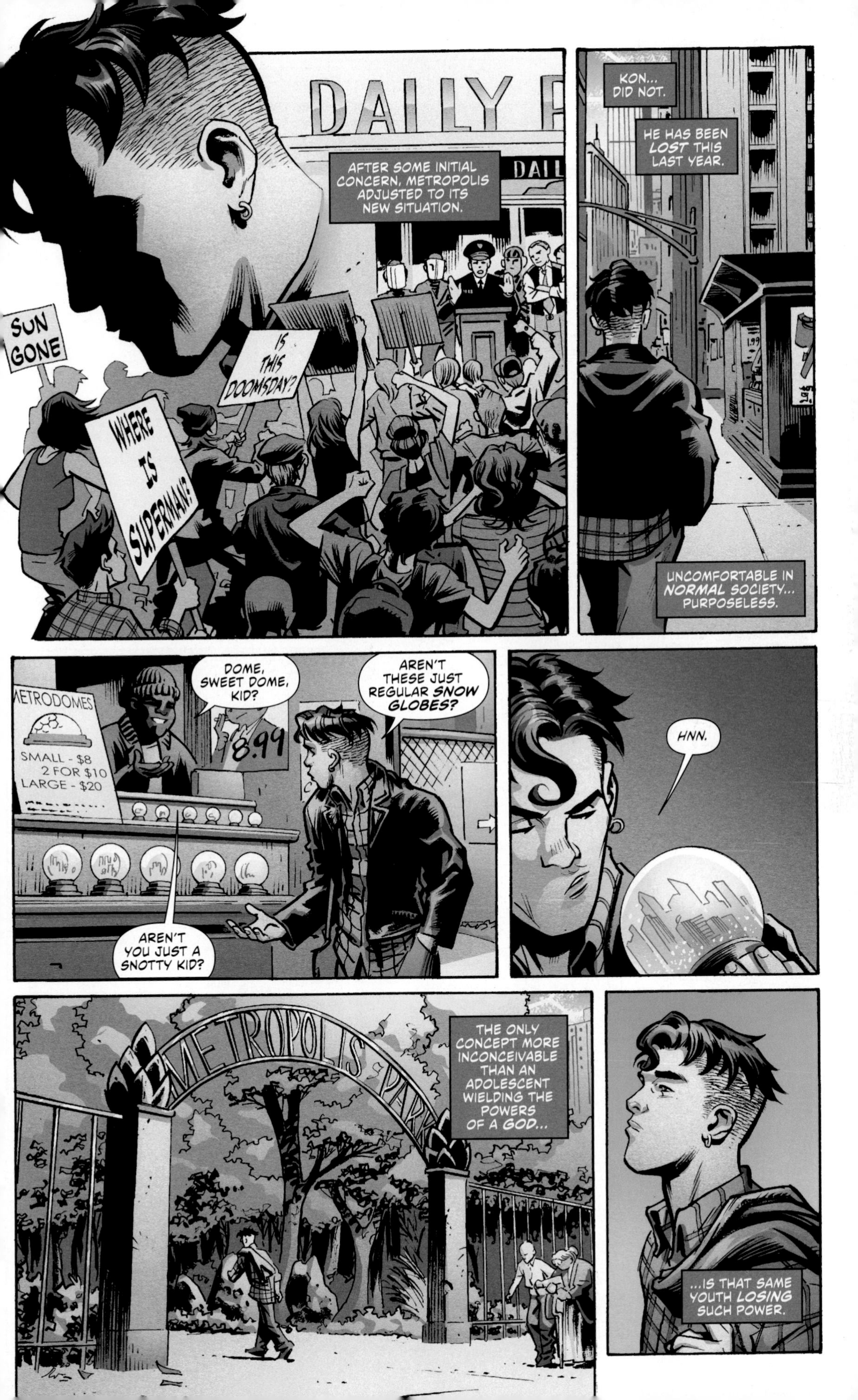
DAILY
DAIL
AFTER SOME INITIAL CONCERN, METROPOLIS ADJUSTED TO ITS NEW SITUATION.
SUN GONE
IS THIS DOOMSDAY?
WHERE IS SUPERMAN?
KON... DID NOT.
HE HAS BEEN LOST THIS LAST YEAR.
UNCOMFORTABLE IN NORMAL SOCIETY... PURPOSELESS.
METRODOMES
SMALL - $8
2 FOR $10
LARGE - $20
8.99
DOME, SWEET DOME, KID?
AREN'T THESE JUST REGULAR SNOW GLOBES?
AREN'T YOU JUST A SNOTTY KID?
HNN.
METROPOLIS PARK
THE ONLY CONCEPT MORE INCONCEIVABLE THAN AN ADOLESCENT WIELDING THE POWERS OF A GOD...
...IS THAT SAME YOUTH LOSING SUCH POWER.

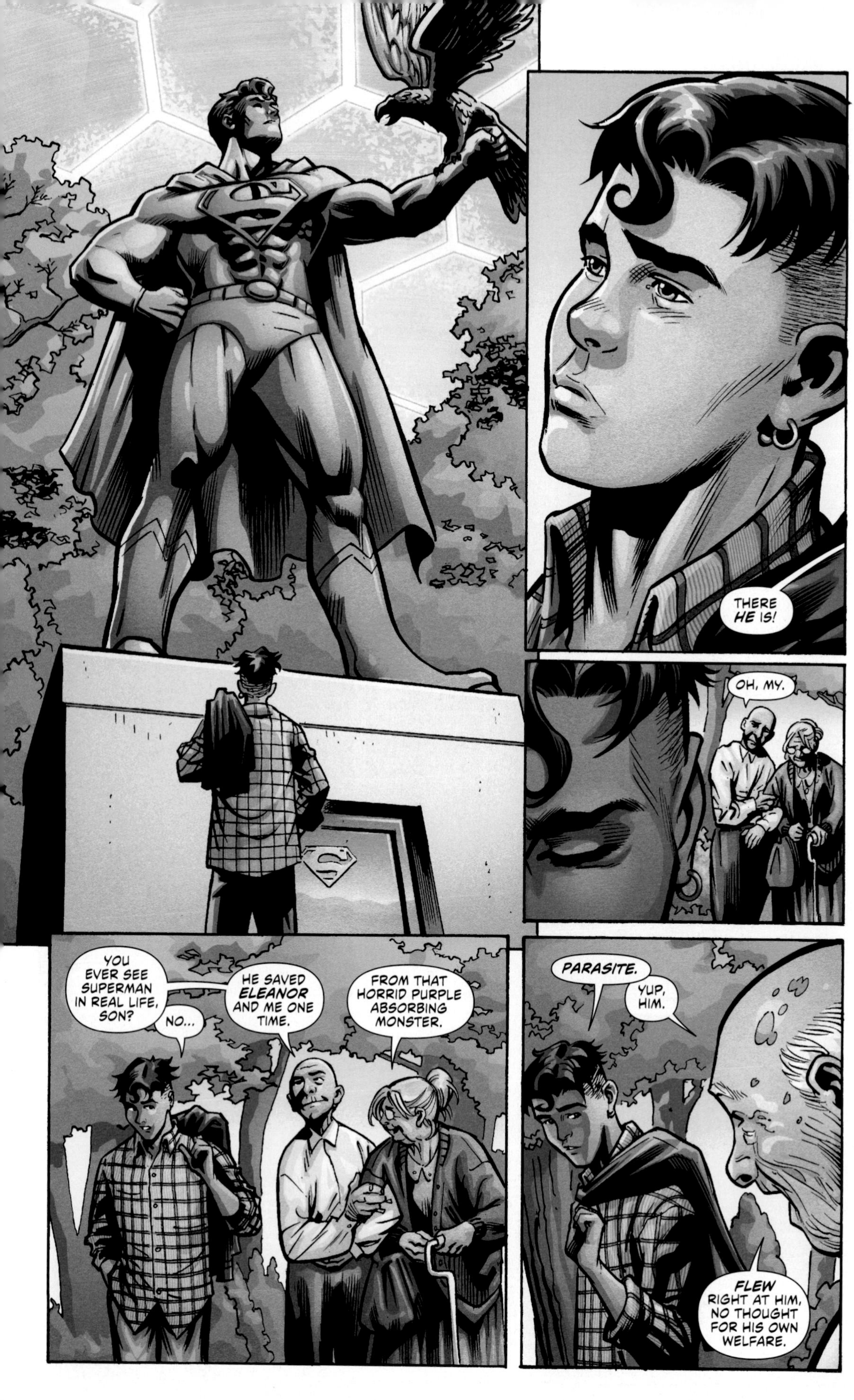
THERE HE IS!
OH, MY.
YOU EVER SEE SUPERMAN IN REAL LIFE, SON?
NO...
HE SAVED ELEANOR AND ME ONE TIME.
FROM THAT HORRID PURPLE ABSORBING MONSTER.
PARASITE.
YUP, HIM.
FLEW RIGHT AT HIM, NO THOUGHT FOR HIS OWN WELFARE.

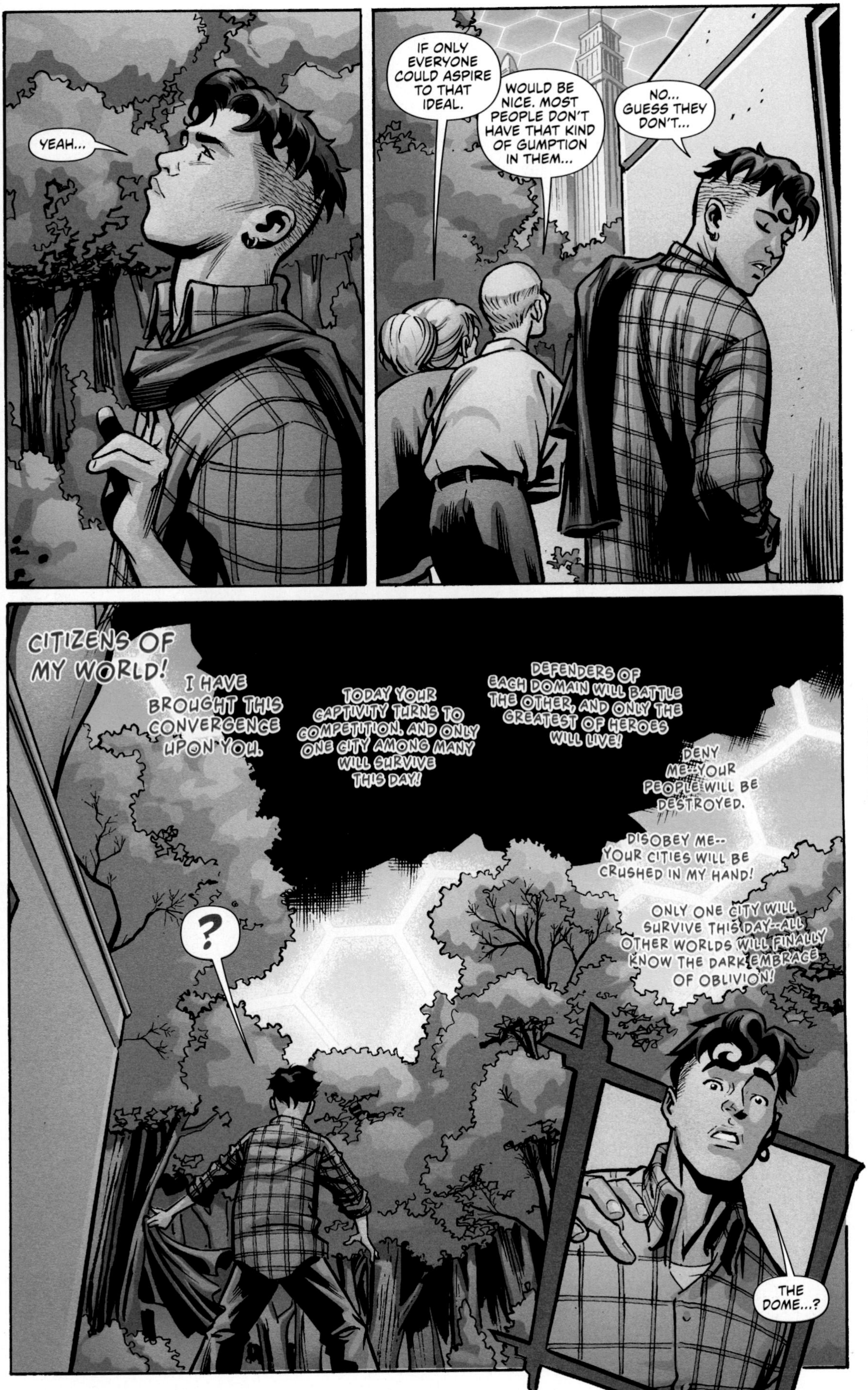
YEAH...
IF ONLY EVERYONE COULD ASPIRE TO THAT IDEAL.
WOULD BE NICE. MOST PEOPLE DON'T HAVE THAT KIND OF GUMPTION IN THEM...
NO... GUESS THEY DON'T...
CITIZENS OF MY WORLD!
I HAVE BROUGHT THIS CONVERGENCE UPON YOU.
TODAY YOUR CAPTIVITY TURNS TO COMPETITION, AND ONLY ONE CITY AMONG MANY WILL SURVIVE THIS DAY!
DEFENDERS OF EACH DOMAIN WILL BATTLE THE OTHER, AND ONLY THE GREATEST OF HEROES WILL LIVE!
DENY ME--YOUR PEOPLE WILL BE DESTROYED.
DISOBEY ME--YOUR CITIES WILL BE CRUSHED IN MY HAND!
ONLY ONE CITY WILL SURVIVE THIS DAY--ALL OTHER WORLDS WILL FINALLY KNOW THE DARK EMBRACE OF OBLIVION!
?
THE DOME...?

DO YOU GUYS HEAR THAT, TOO?

THE DOME IS DOWN!

AND...

...I FEEL...

DO YOU GUYS *HEAR* ANYTHING FUNNY?

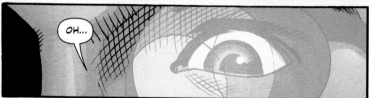

OH...

WHAT IS IT, SON?

YOU LOOK LIKE YOU'VE SEEN A GHOST.

NO... BETTER...

HE'S FLYING--?

...MUCH... *MUCH* BETTER--!

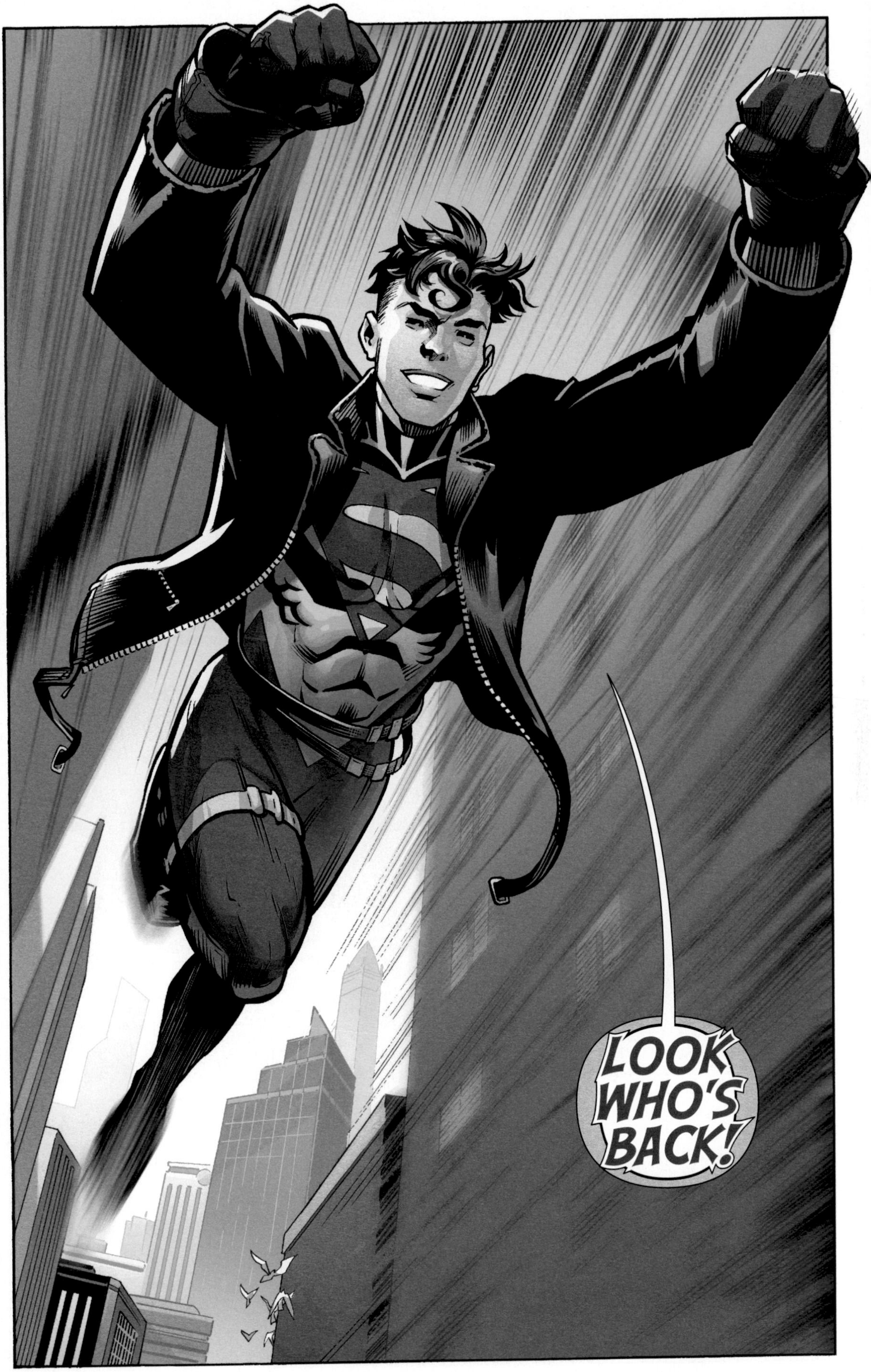
LOOK WHO'S BACK!

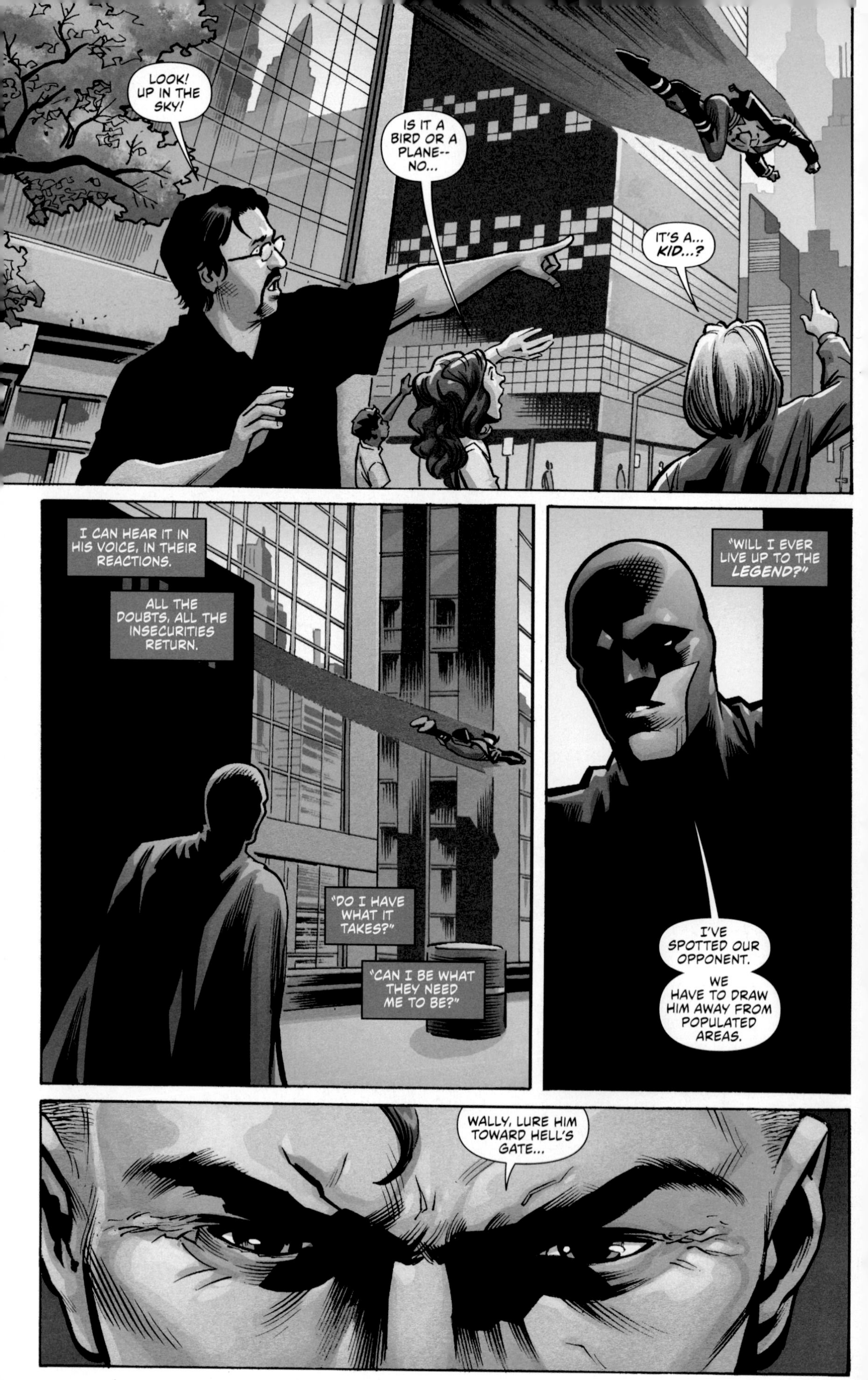
LOOK! UP IN THE SKY!
IS IT A BIRD OR A PLANE-- NO...
IT'S A... *KID...?*
I CAN HEAR IT IN HIS VOICE, IN THEIR REACTIONS.
ALL THE DOUBTS, ALL THE INSECURITIES RETURN.
"DO I HAVE WHAT IT TAKES?"
"CAN I BE WHAT THEY NEED ME TO BE?"
"WILL I EVER LIVE UP TO THE *LEGEND?*"
I'VE SPOTTED OUR OPPONENT.
WE HAVE TO DRAW HIM AWAY FROM POPULATED AREAS.
WALLY, LURE HIM TOWARD HELL'S GATE...

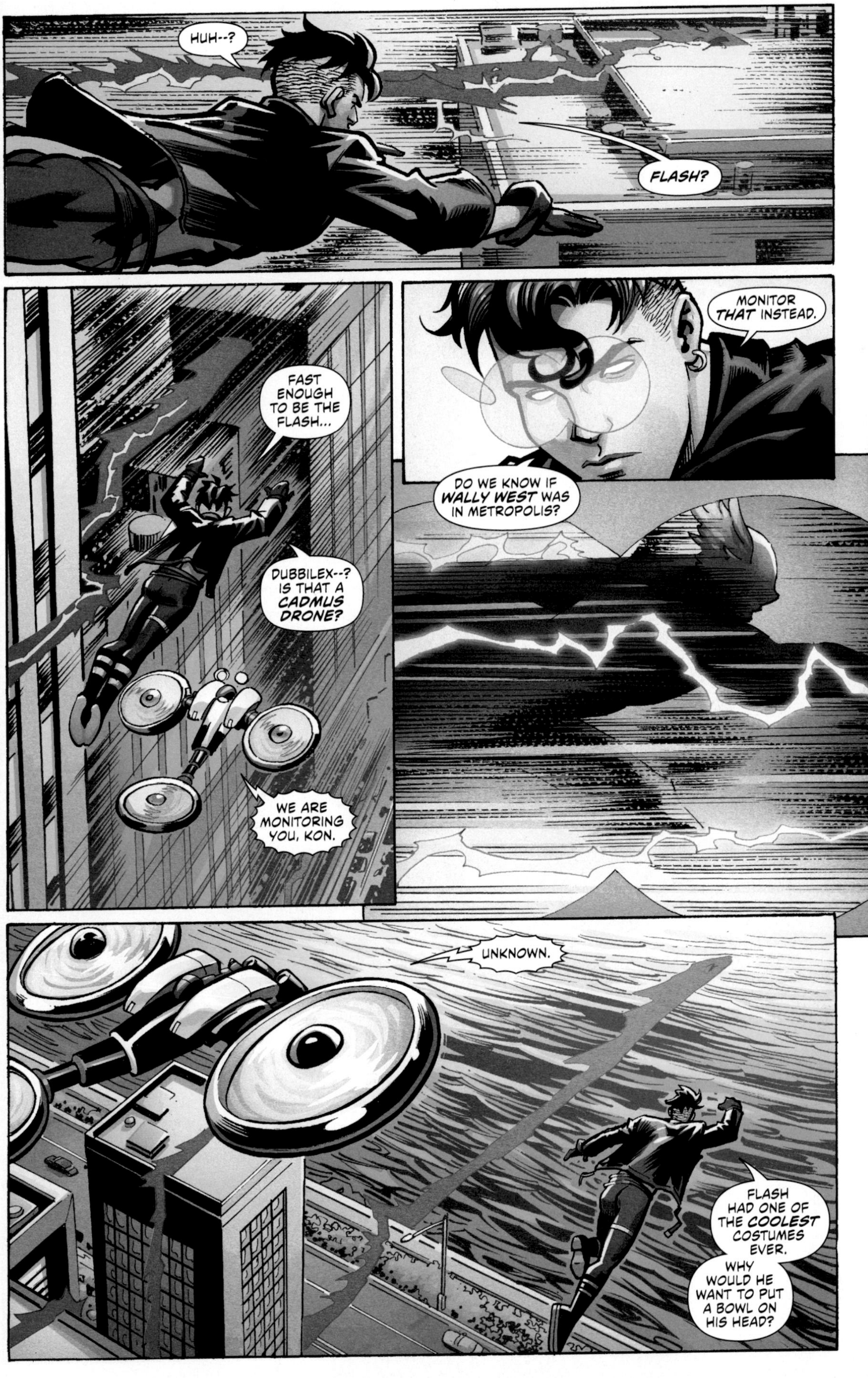
HUH--?
FLASH?
FAST ENOUGH TO BE THE FLASH...
DUBBILEX--? IS THAT A CADMUS DRONE?
WE ARE MONITORING YOU, KON.
MONITOR THAT INSTEAD.
DO WE KNOW IF WALLY WEST WAS IN METROPOLIS?
UNKNOWN.
FLASH HAD ONE OF THE COOLEST COSTUMES EVER.
WHY WOULD HE WANT TO PUT A BOWL ON HIS HEAD?

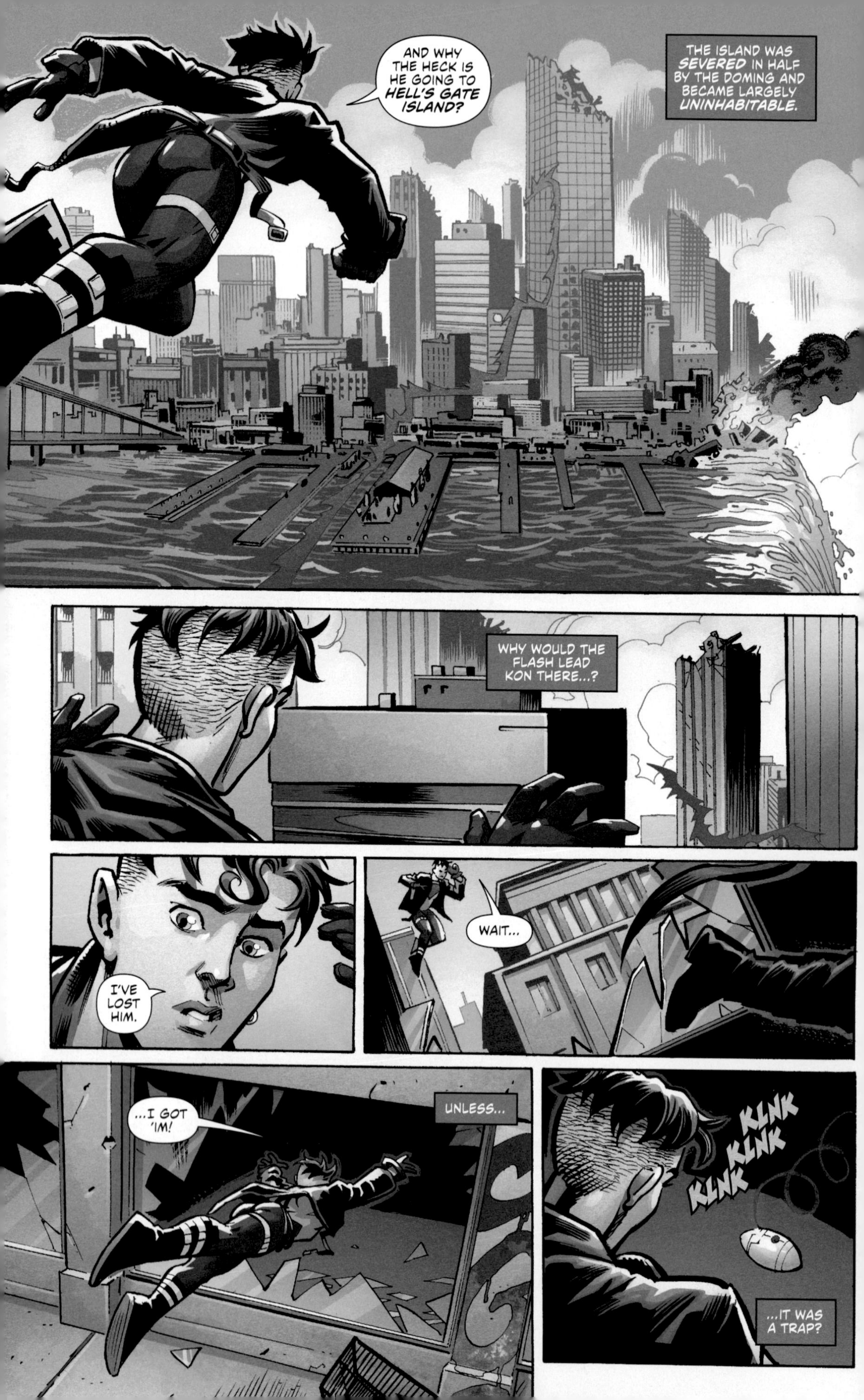
AND WHY THE HECK IS HE GOING TO HELL'S GATE ISLAND?
THE ISLAND WAS SEVERED IN HALF BY THE DOMING AND BECAME LARGELY UNINHABITABLE.
WHY WOULD THE FLASH LEAD KON THERE...?
I'VE LOST HIM.
WAIT...
...I GOT 'IM!
UNLESS...
KLNK KLNK KLNK
...IT WAS A TRAP?

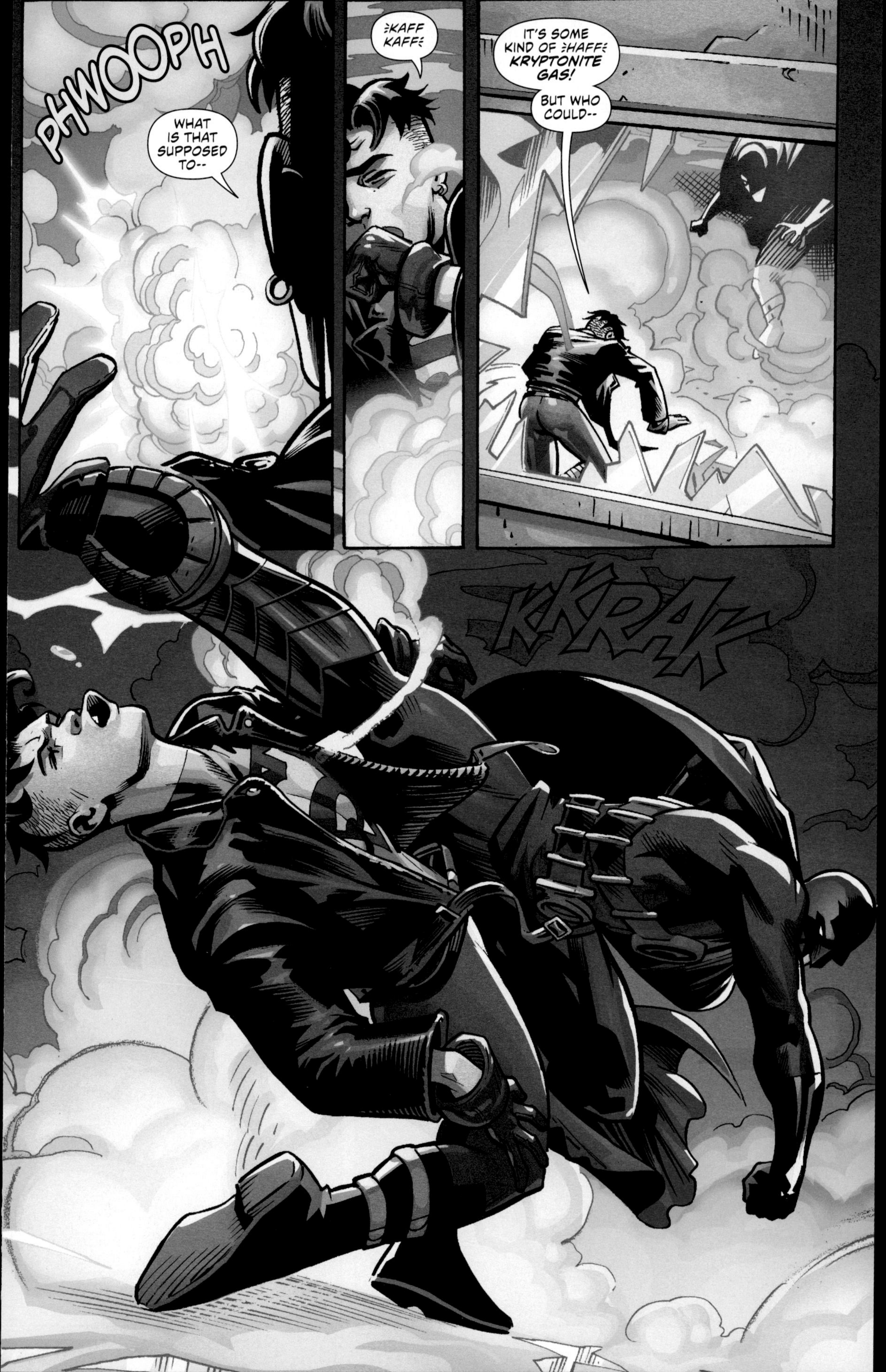
PHWOOPH
WHAT IS THAT SUPPOSED TO--
KAFF KAFF
IT'S SOME KIND OF HAFF KRYPTONITE GAS!
BUT WHO COULD--
KKRAK

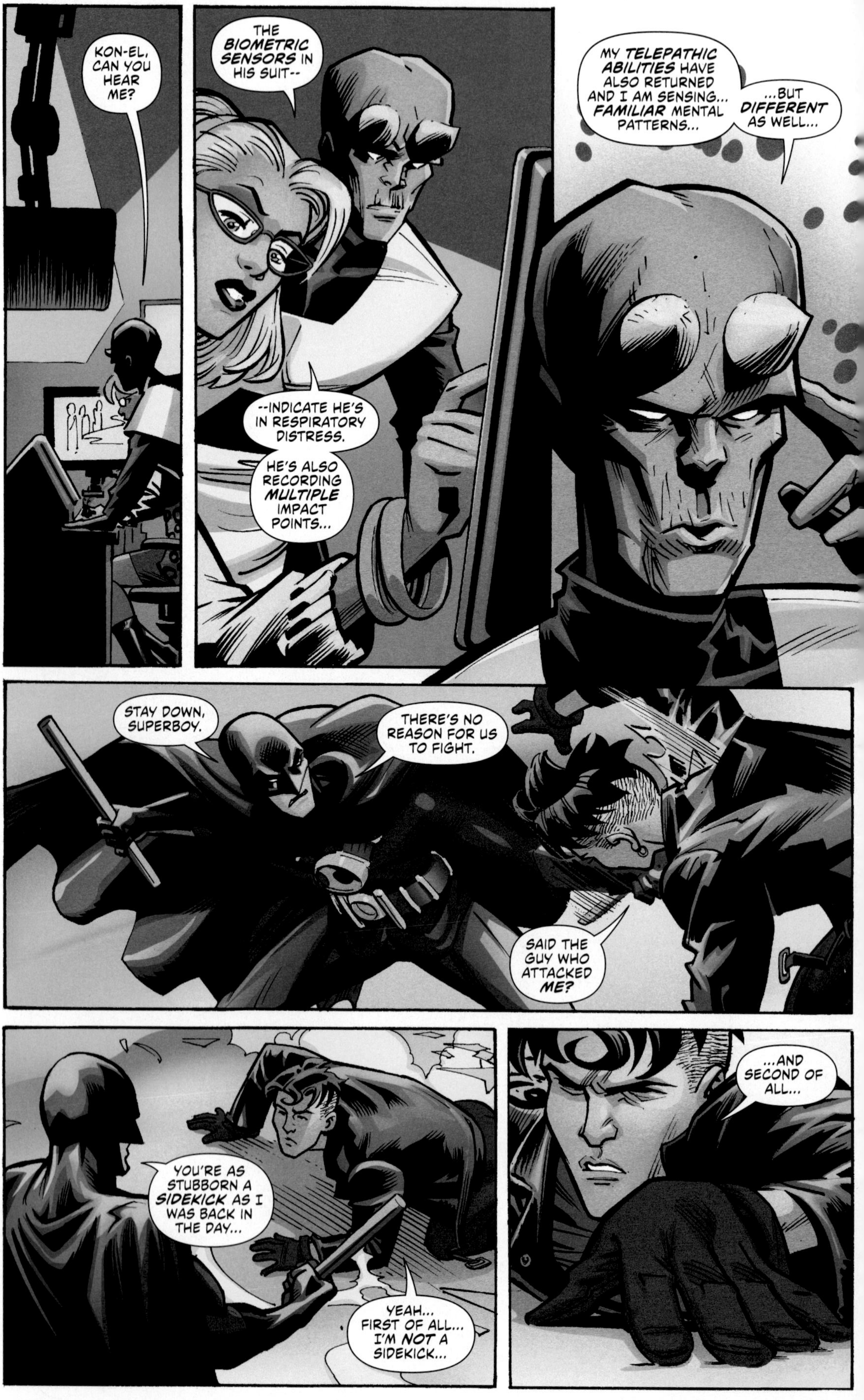
KON-EL, CAN YOU HEAR ME?
THE BIOMETRIC SENSORS IN HIS SUIT--
--INDICATE HE'S IN RESPIRATORY DISTRESS.
HE'S ALSO RECORDING MULTIPLE IMPACT POINTS...
MY TELEPATHIC ABILITIES HAVE ALSO RETURNED AND I AM SENSING... FAMILIAR MENTAL PATTERNS...
...BUT DIFFERENT AS WELL...
STAY DOWN, SUPERBOY.
THERE'S NO REASON FOR US TO FIGHT.
SAID THE GUY WHO ATTACKED ME?
YOU'RE AS STUBBORN A SIDEKICK AS I WAS BACK IN THE DAY...
YEAH... FIRST OF ALL... I'M NOT A SIDEKICK...
...AND SECOND OF ALL...

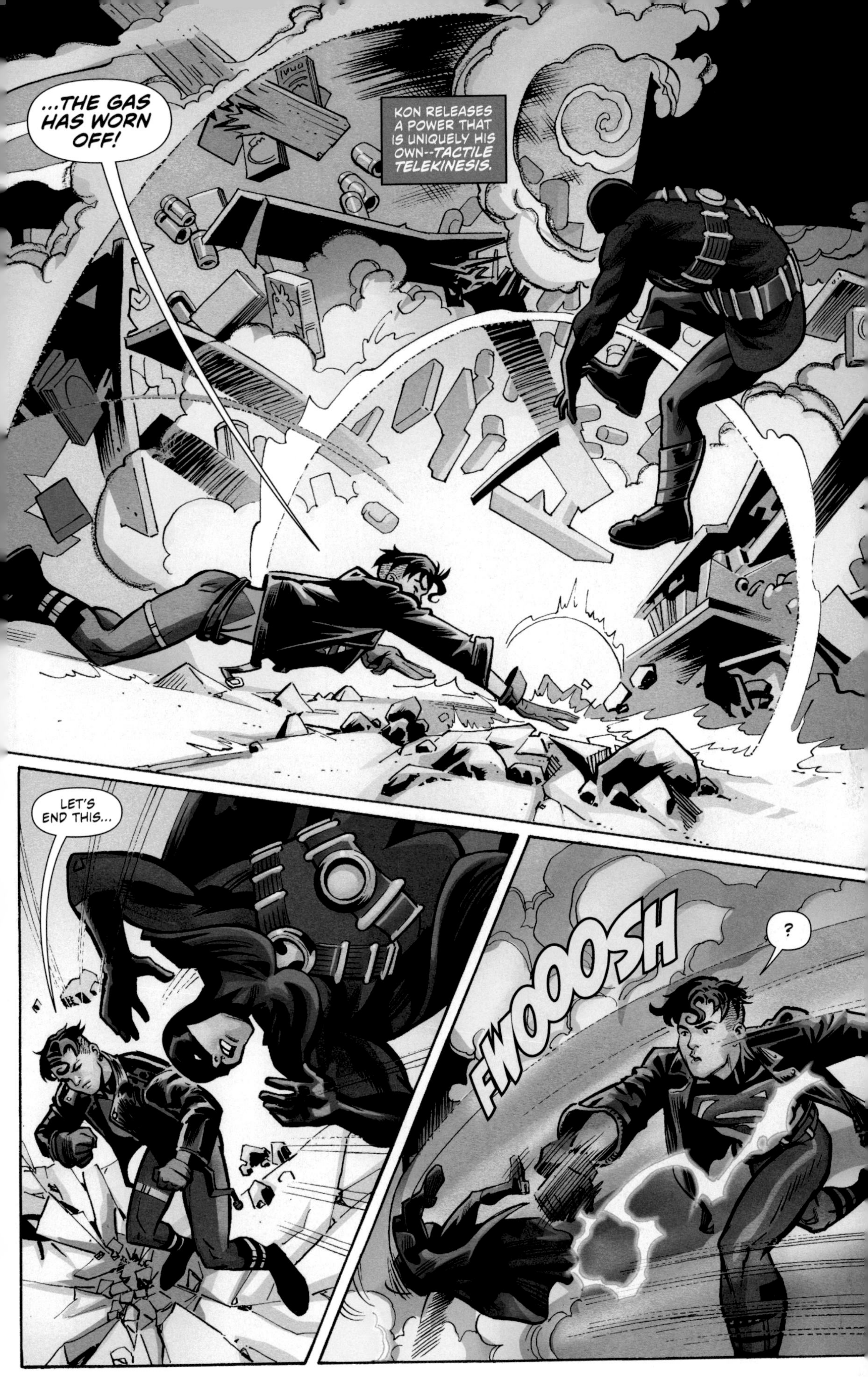

...THE GAS HAS WORN OFF!
KON RELEASES A POWER THAT IS UNIQUELY HIS OWN--TACTILE TELEKINESIS.
LET'S END THIS...
FWOOOSH
?

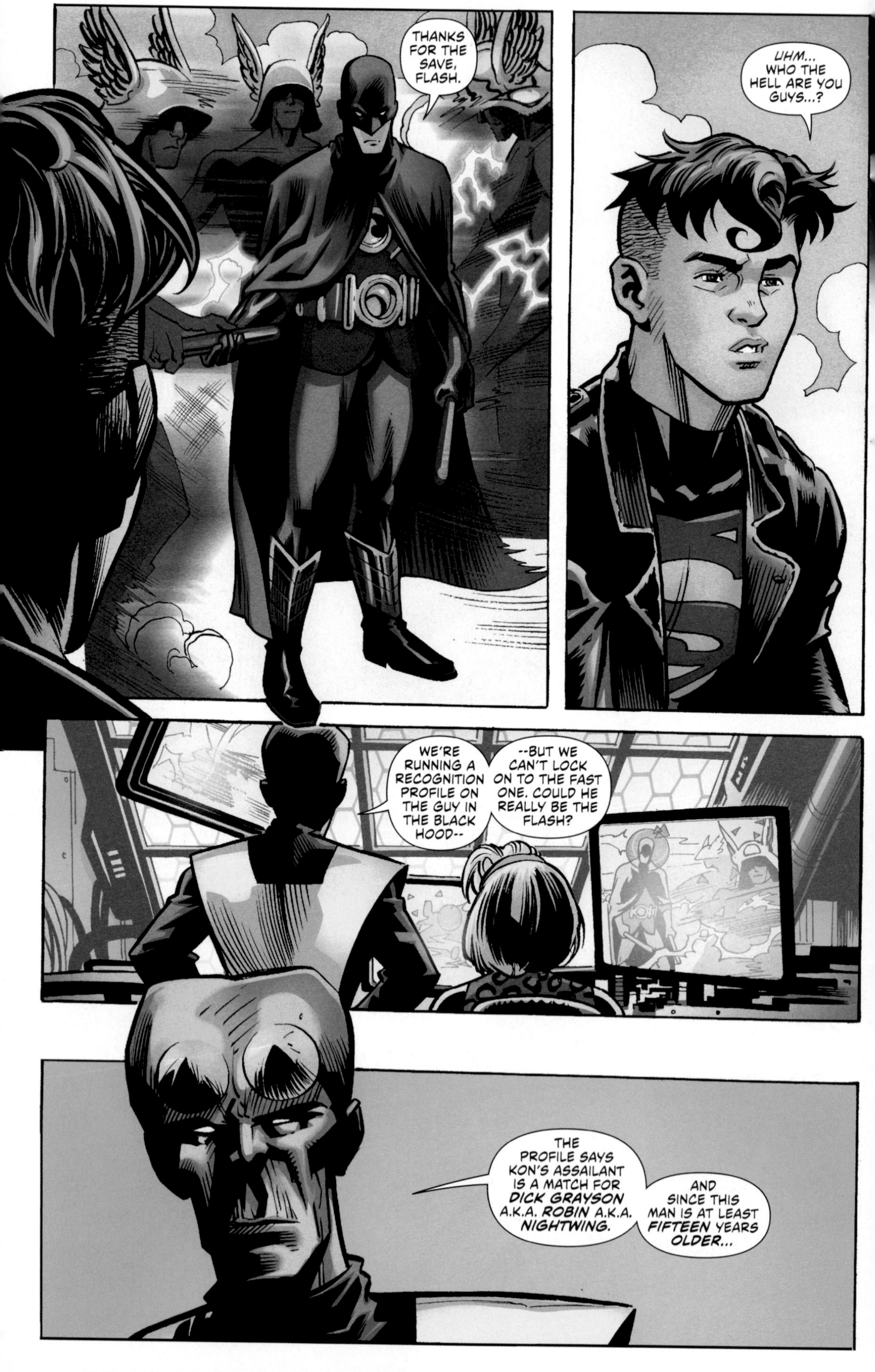
THANKS FOR THE SAVE, FLASH.
UHM... WHO THE HELL ARE YOU GUYS...?
WE'RE RUNNING A RECOGNITION PROFILE ON THE GUY IN THE BLACK HOOD--
--BUT WE CAN'T LOCK ON TO THE FAST ONE. COULD HE REALLY BE THE FLASH?
THE PROFILE SAYS KON'S ASSAILANT IS A MATCH FOR DICK GRAYSON A.K.A. ROBIN A.K.A. NIGHTWING.
AND SINCE THIS MAN IS AT LEAST FIFTEEN YEARS OLDER...

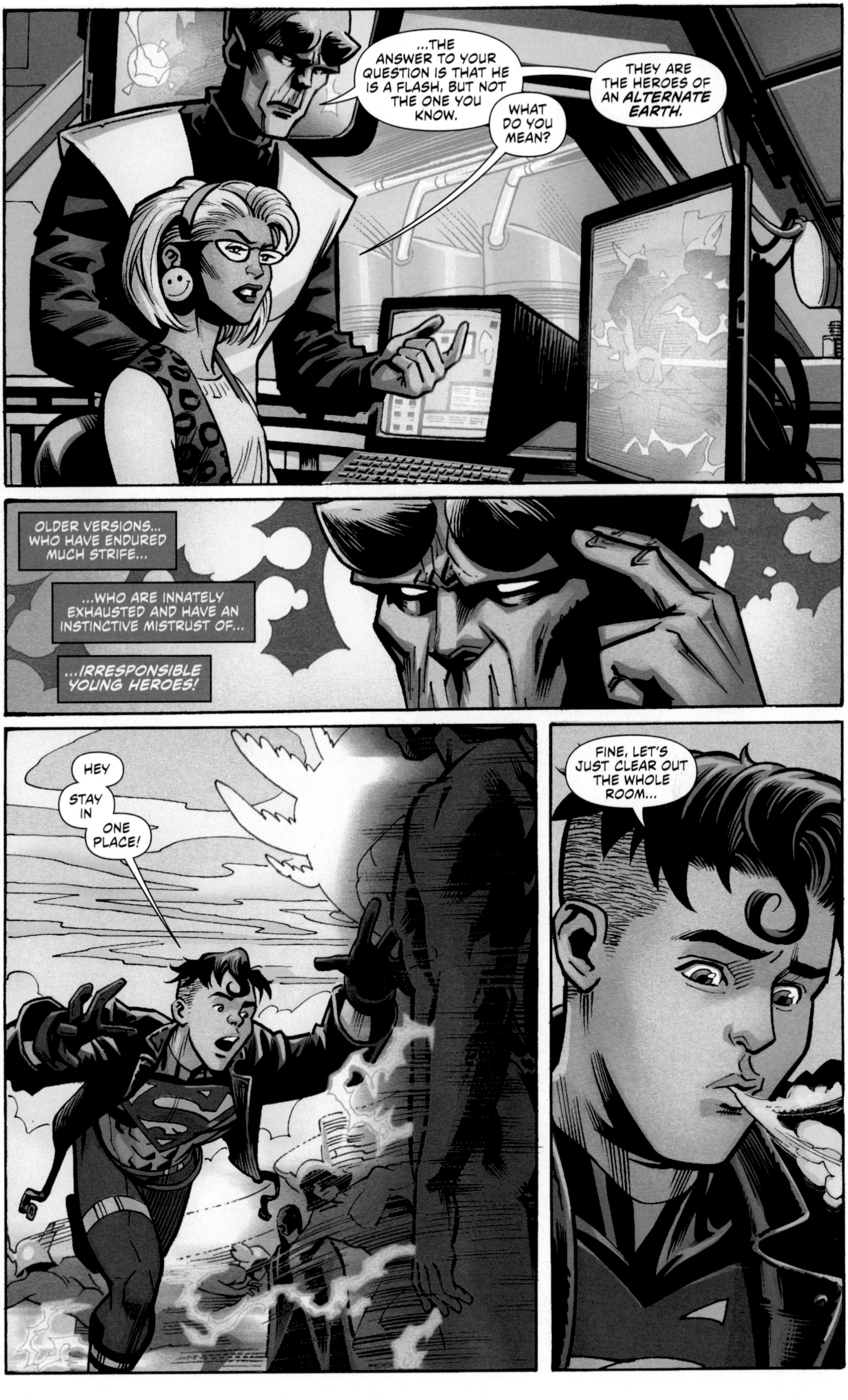
...THE ANSWER TO YOUR QUESTION IS THAT HE IS A FLASH, BUT NOT THE ONE YOU KNOW.
WHAT DO YOU MEAN?
THEY ARE THE HEROES OF AN *ALTERNATE EARTH.*
OLDER VERSIONS... WHO HAVE ENDURED MUCH STRIFE...
...WHO ARE INNATELY EXHAUSTED AND HAVE AN INSTINCTIVE MISTRUST OF...
...*IRRESPONSIBLE YOUNG HEROES!*
HEY
STAY IN
ONE PLACE!
FINE, LET'S JUST CLEAR OUT THE WHOLE ROOM...

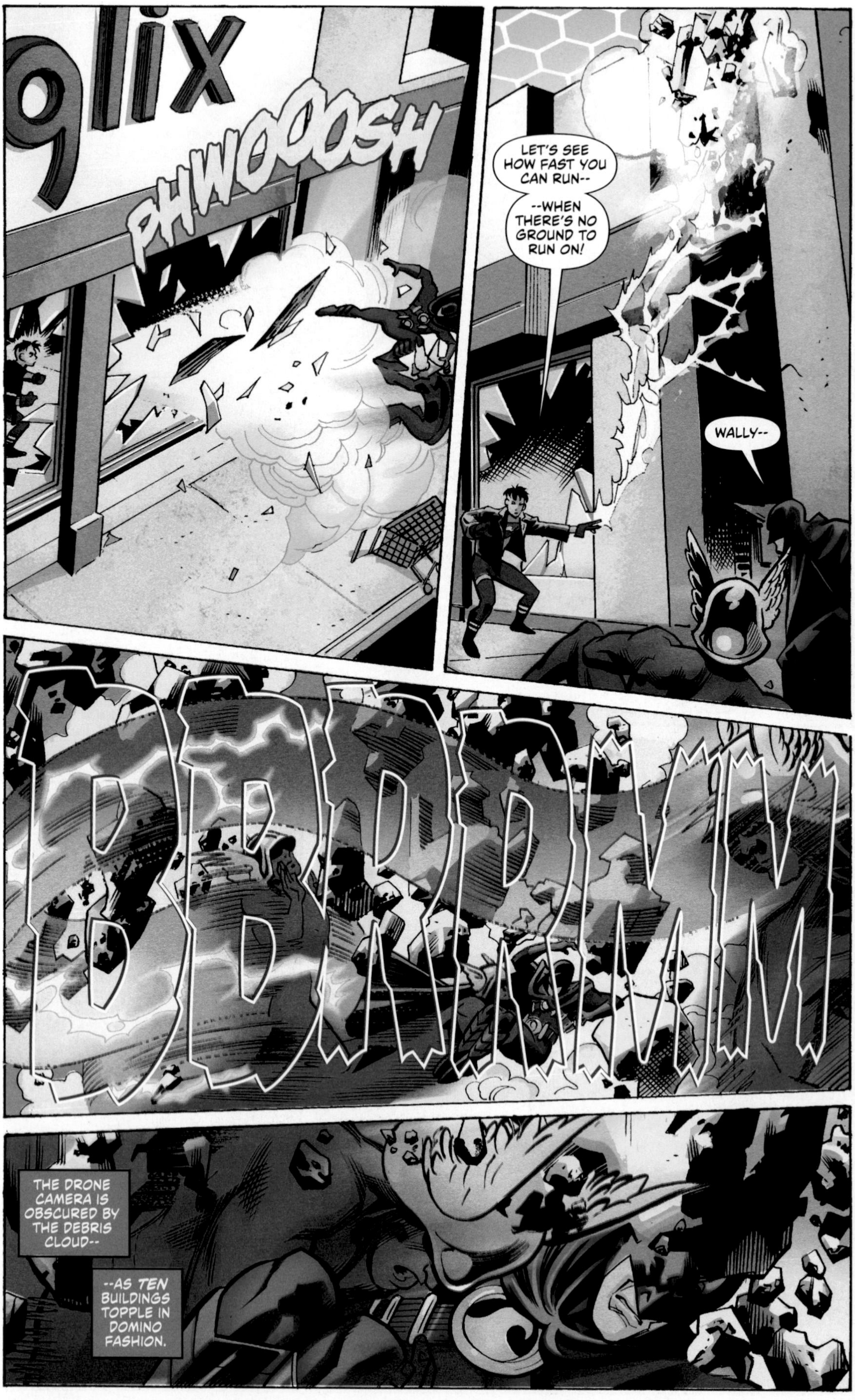
glix
PHWOOOSH
LET'S SEE HOW FAST YOU CAN RUN--
--WHEN THERE'S NO GROUND TO RUN ON!
WALLY--
DBRRMMM
THE DRONE CAMERA IS OBSCURED BY THE DEBRIS CLOUD--
--AS TEN BUILDINGS TOPPLE IN DOMINO FASHION.

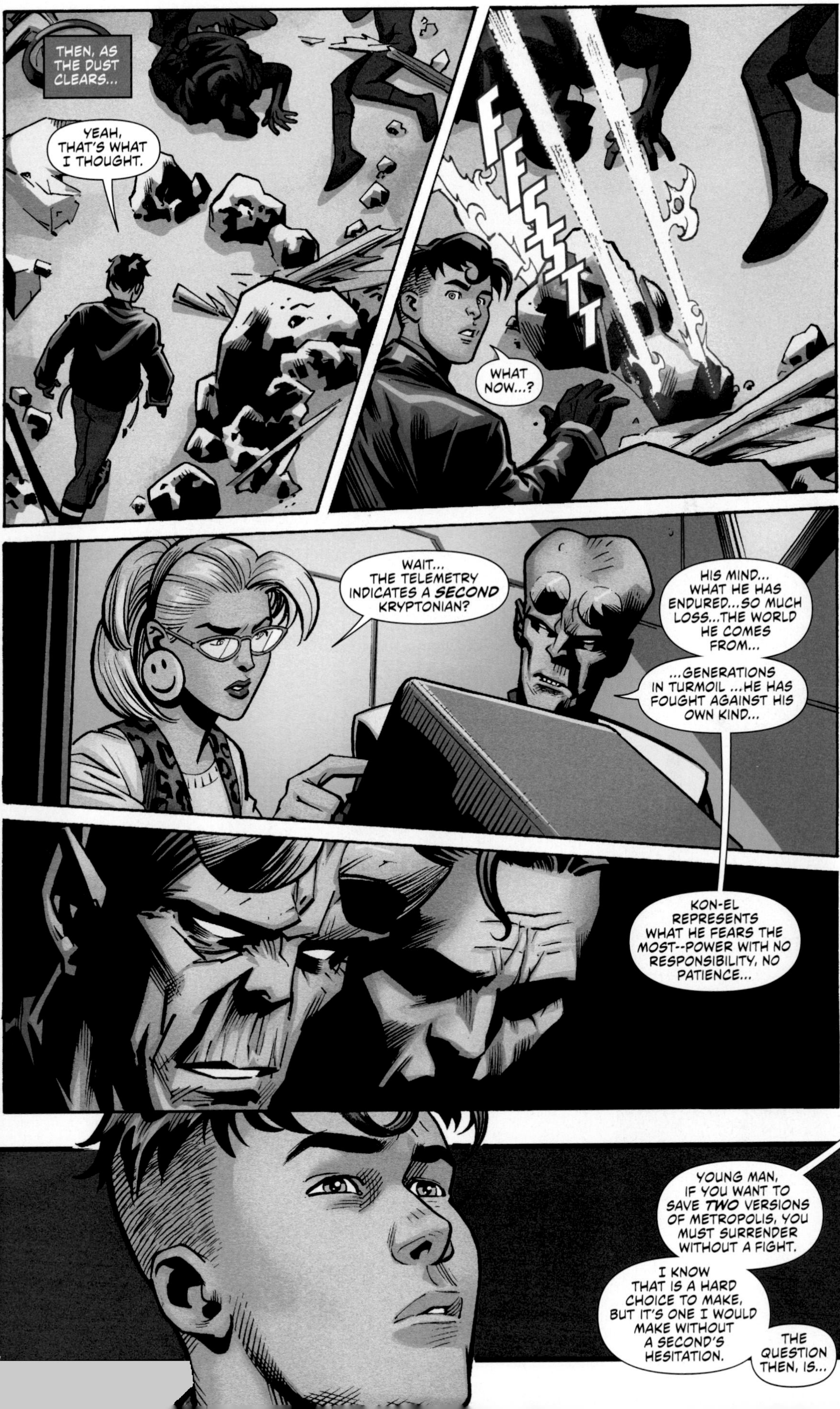
THEN, AS THE DUST CLEARS...
YEAH, THAT'S WHAT I THOUGHT.
FFSSTT
WHAT NOW...?
WAIT... THE TELEMETRY INDICATES A *SECOND* KRYPTONIAN?
HIS MIND... WHAT HE HAS ENDURED...SO MUCH LOSS...THE WORLD HE COMES FROM...
...GENERATIONS IN TURMOIL ...HE HAS FOUGHT AGAINST HIS OWN KIND...
KON-EL REPRESENTS WHAT HE FEARS THE MOST--POWER WITH NO RESPONSIBILITY, NO PATIENCE...
YOUNG MAN, IF YOU WANT TO SAVE *TWO* VERSIONS OF METROPOLIS, YOU MUST SURRENDER WITHOUT A FIGHT.
I KNOW THAT IS A HARD CHOICE TO MAKE, BUT IT'S ONE I WOULD MAKE WITHOUT A SECOND'S HESITATION.
THE QUESTION THEN, IS...

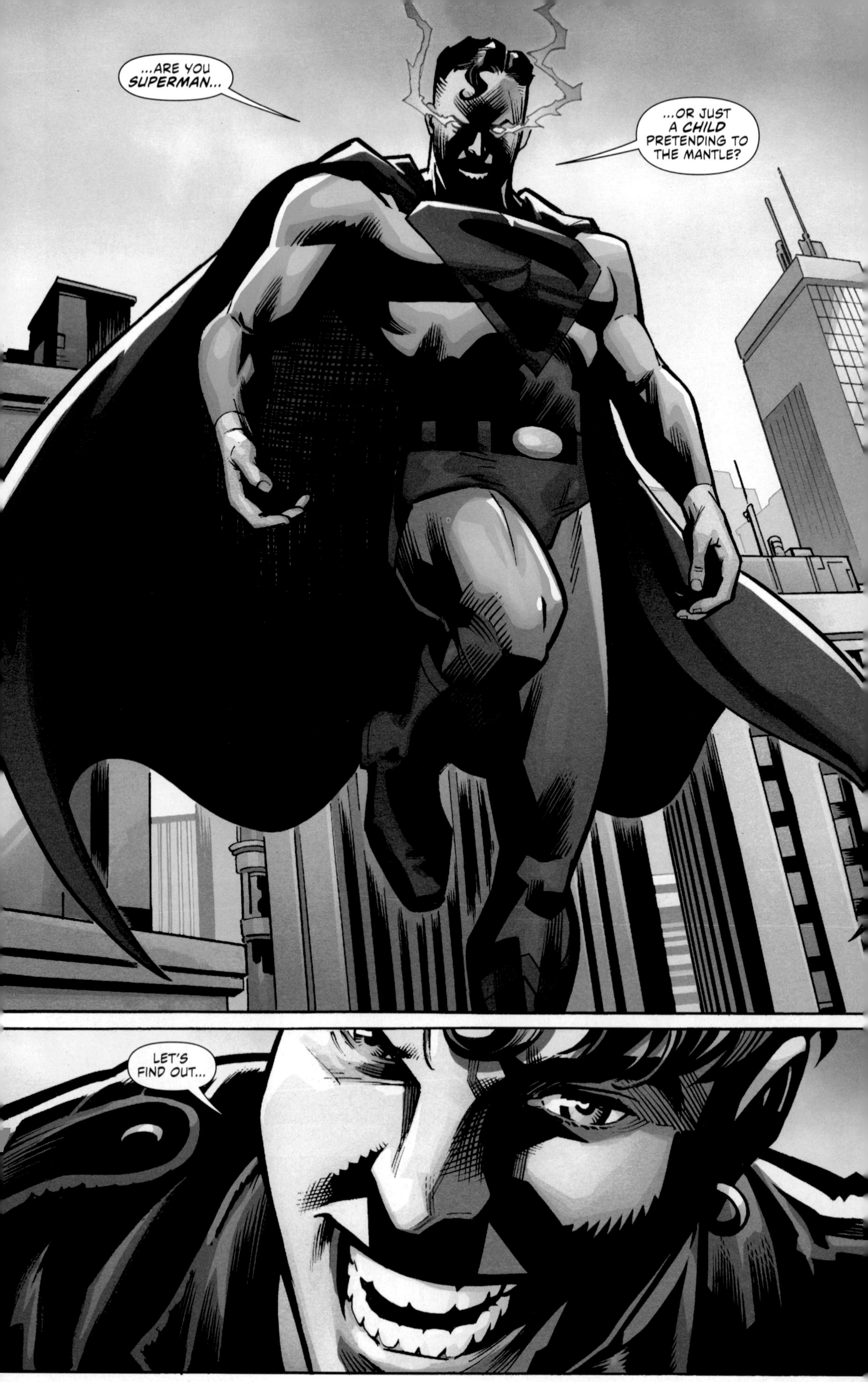
...ARE YOU SUPERMAN...
...OR JUST A CHILD PRETENDING TO THE MANTLE?
LET'S FIND OUT...

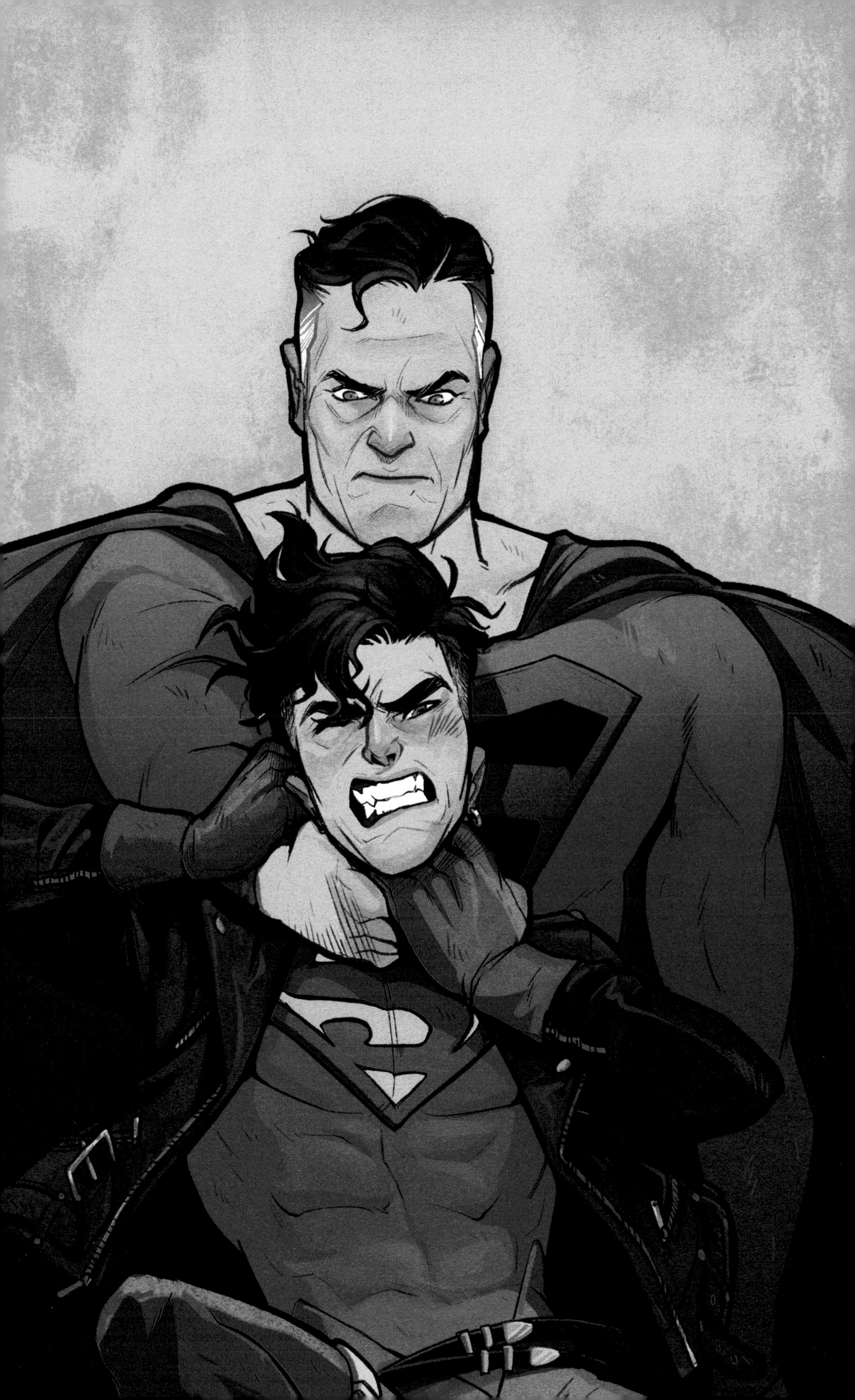

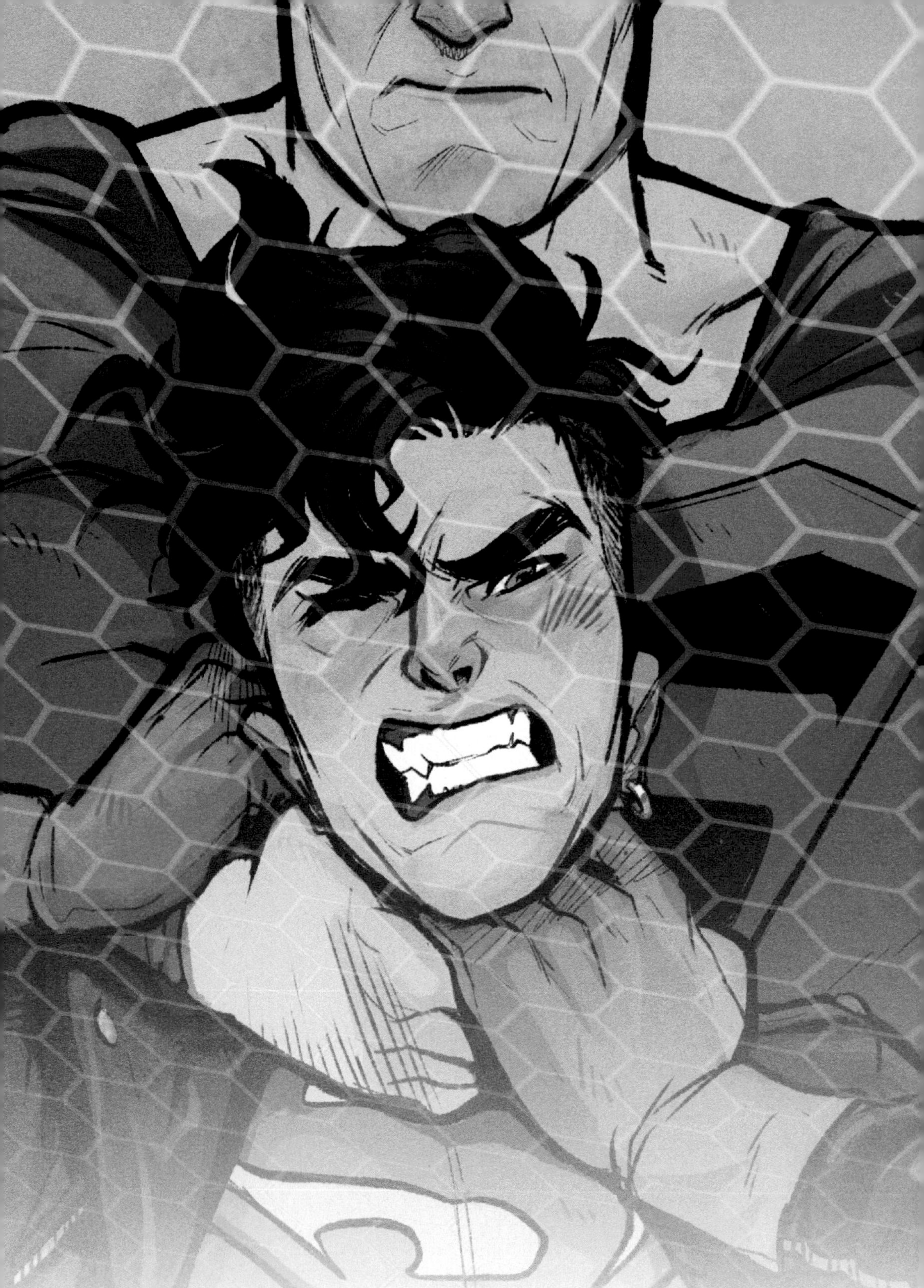

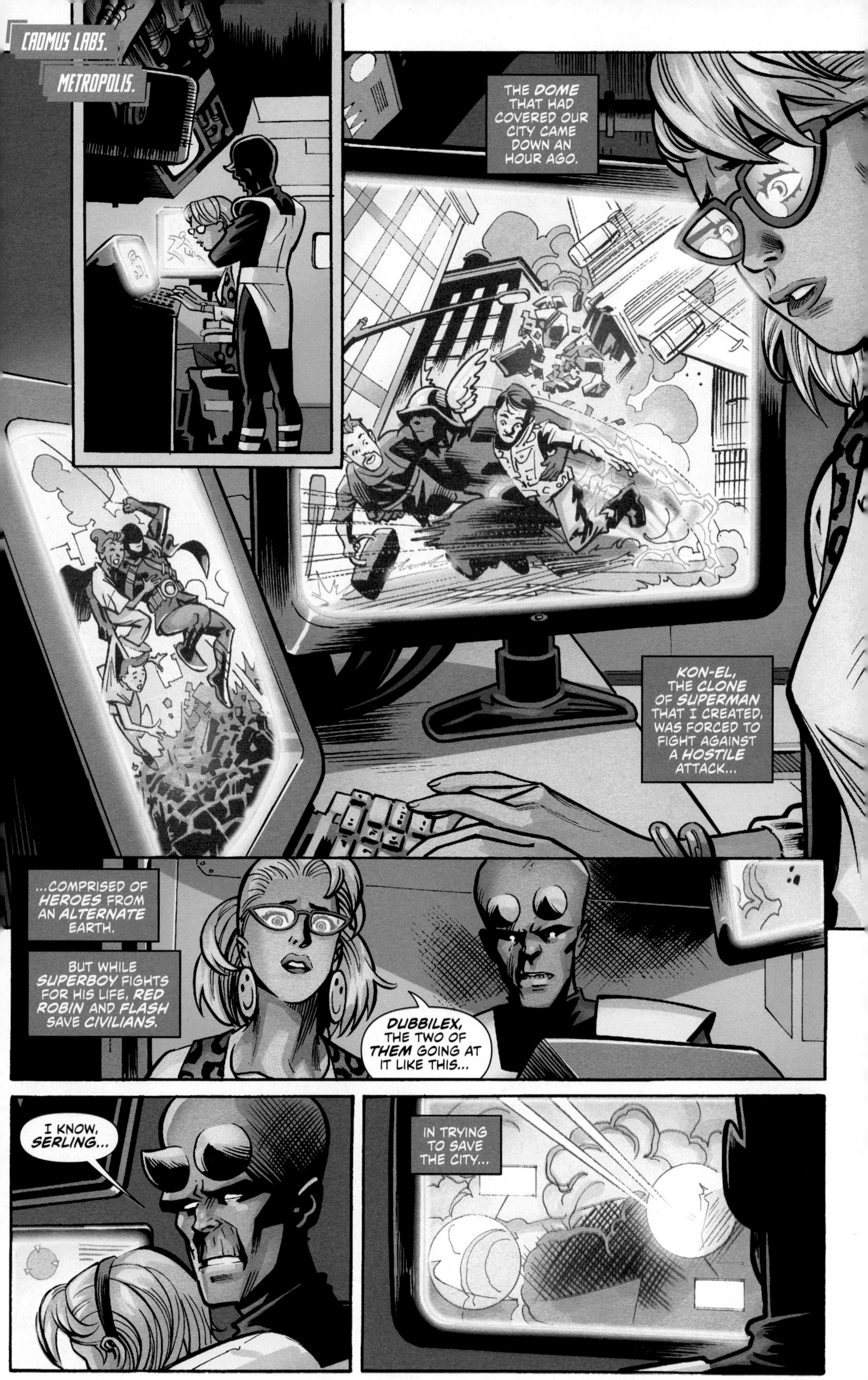
CADMUS LABS.
METROPOLIS.
THE DOME THAT HAD COVERED OUR CITY CAME DOWN AN HOUR AGO.
KON-EL, THE CLONE OF SUPERMAN THAT I CREATED, WAS FORCED TO FIGHT AGAINST A HOSTILE ATTACK...
...COMPRISED OF HEROES FROM AN ALTERNATE EARTH.
BUT WHILE SUPERBOY FIGHTS FOR HIS LIFE, RED ROBIN AND FLASH SAVE CIVILIANS.
DUBBILEX, THE TWO OF THEM GOING AT IT LIKE THIS...
I KNOW, SERLING...
IN TRYING TO SAVE THE CITY...

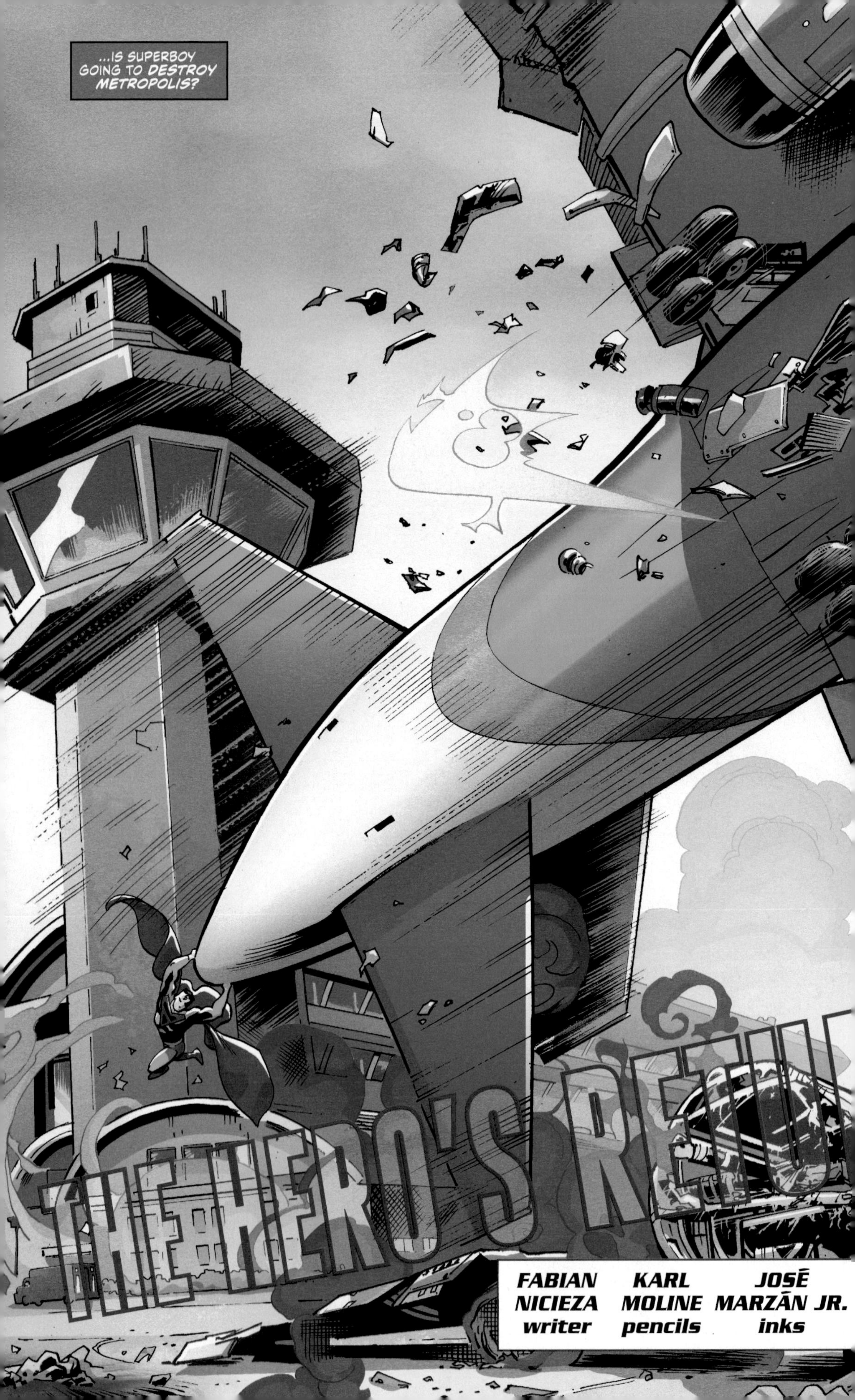
...IS SUPERBOY GOING TO DESTROY METROPOLIS?
THE HERO'S RETU
FABIAN NICIEZA writer
KARL MOLINE pencils
JOSÉ MARZÁN JR. inks

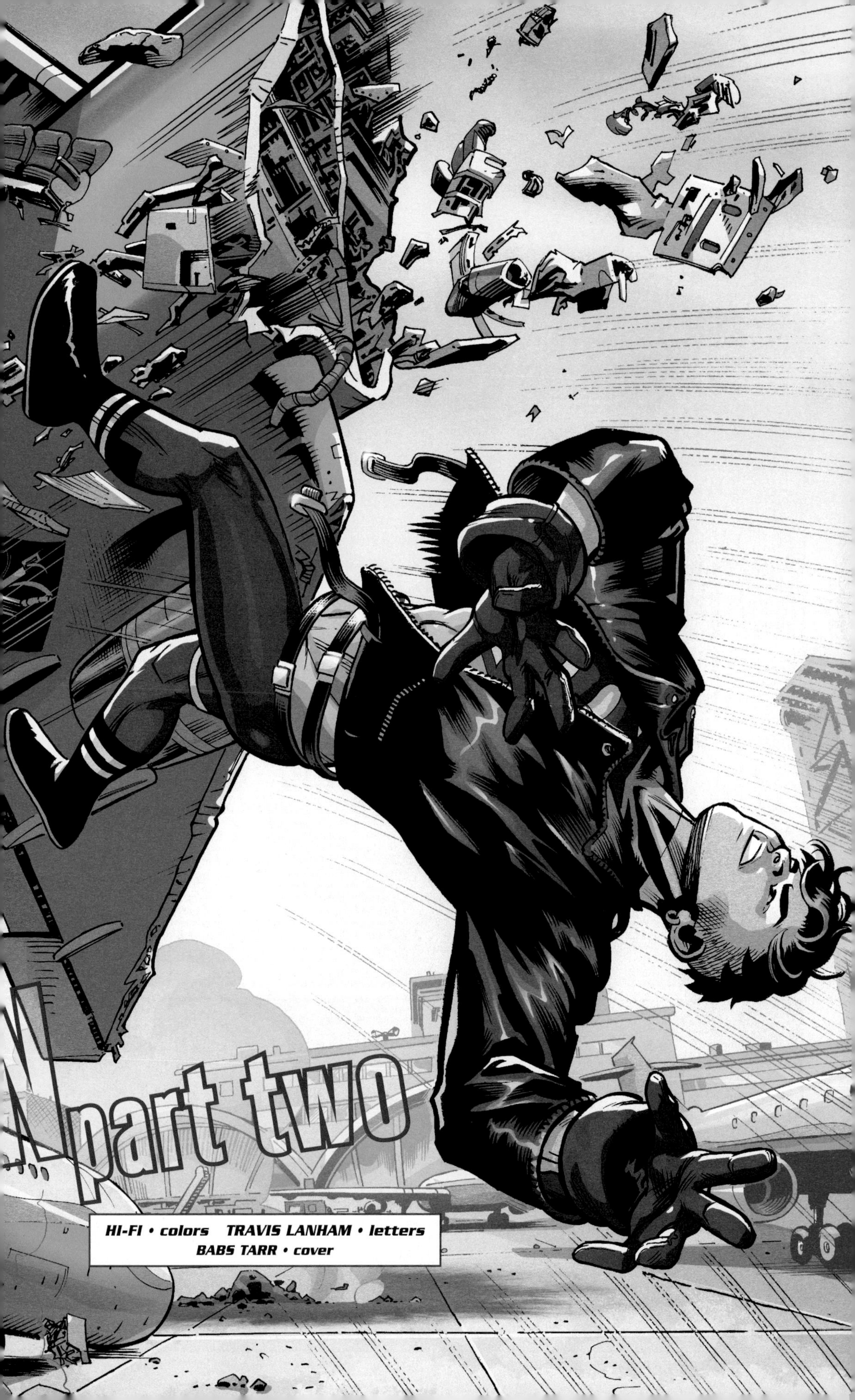
part two
HI-FI • colors TRAVIS LANHAM • letters
BABS TARR • cover

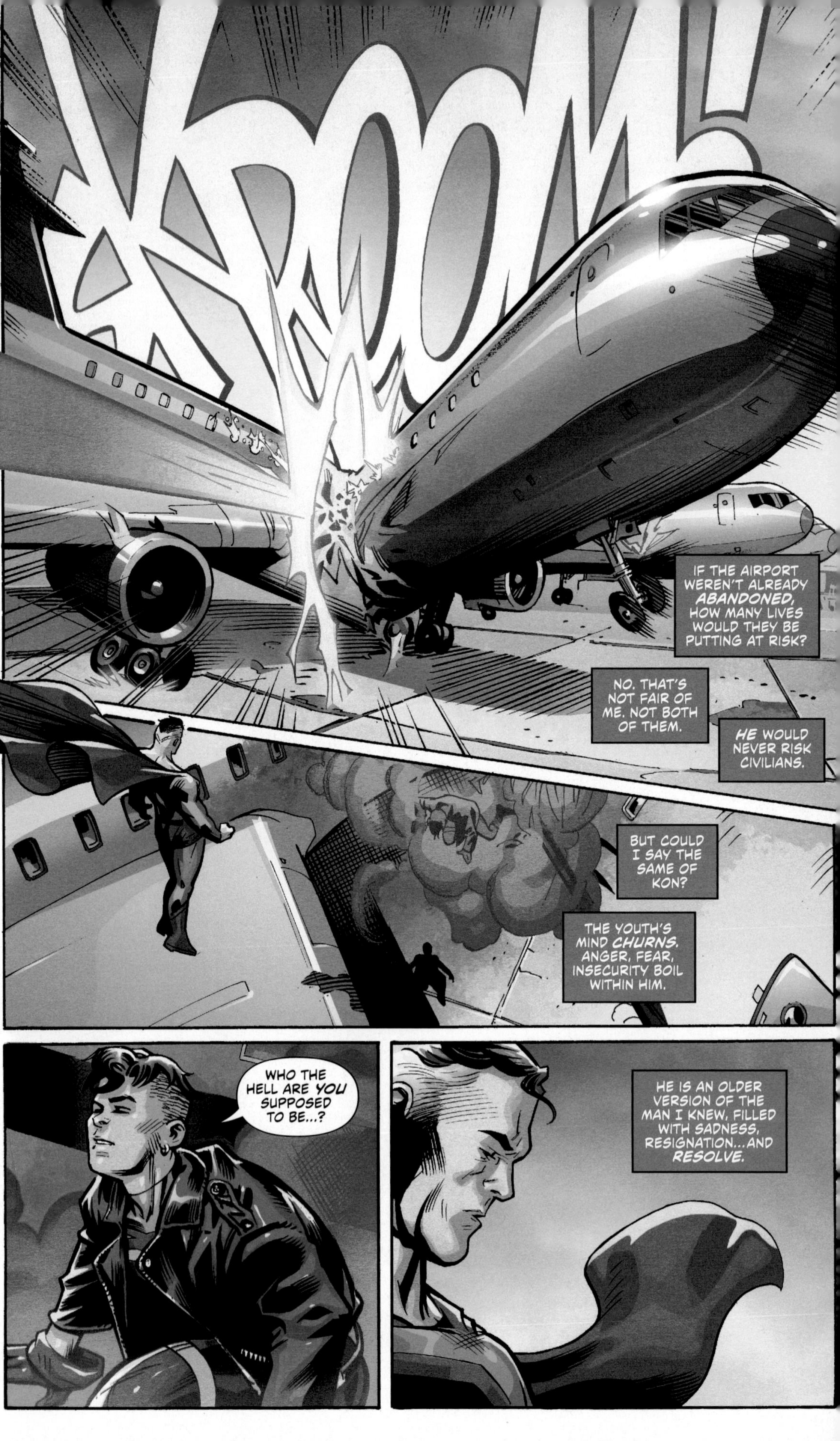
IF THE AIRPORT WEREN'T ALREADY ABANDONED, HOW MANY LIVES WOULD THEY BE PUTTING AT RISK?
NO. THAT'S NOT FAIR OF ME. NOT BOTH OF THEM.
HE WOULD NEVER RISK CIVILIANS.
BUT COULD I SAY THE SAME OF KON?
THE YOUTH'S MIND CHURNS. ANGER, FEAR, INSECURITY BOIL WITHIN HIM.
WHO THE HELL ARE YOU SUPPOSED TO BE...?
HE IS AN OLDER VERSION OF THE MAN I KNEW, FILLED WITH SADNESS, RESIGNATION...AND RESOLVE.

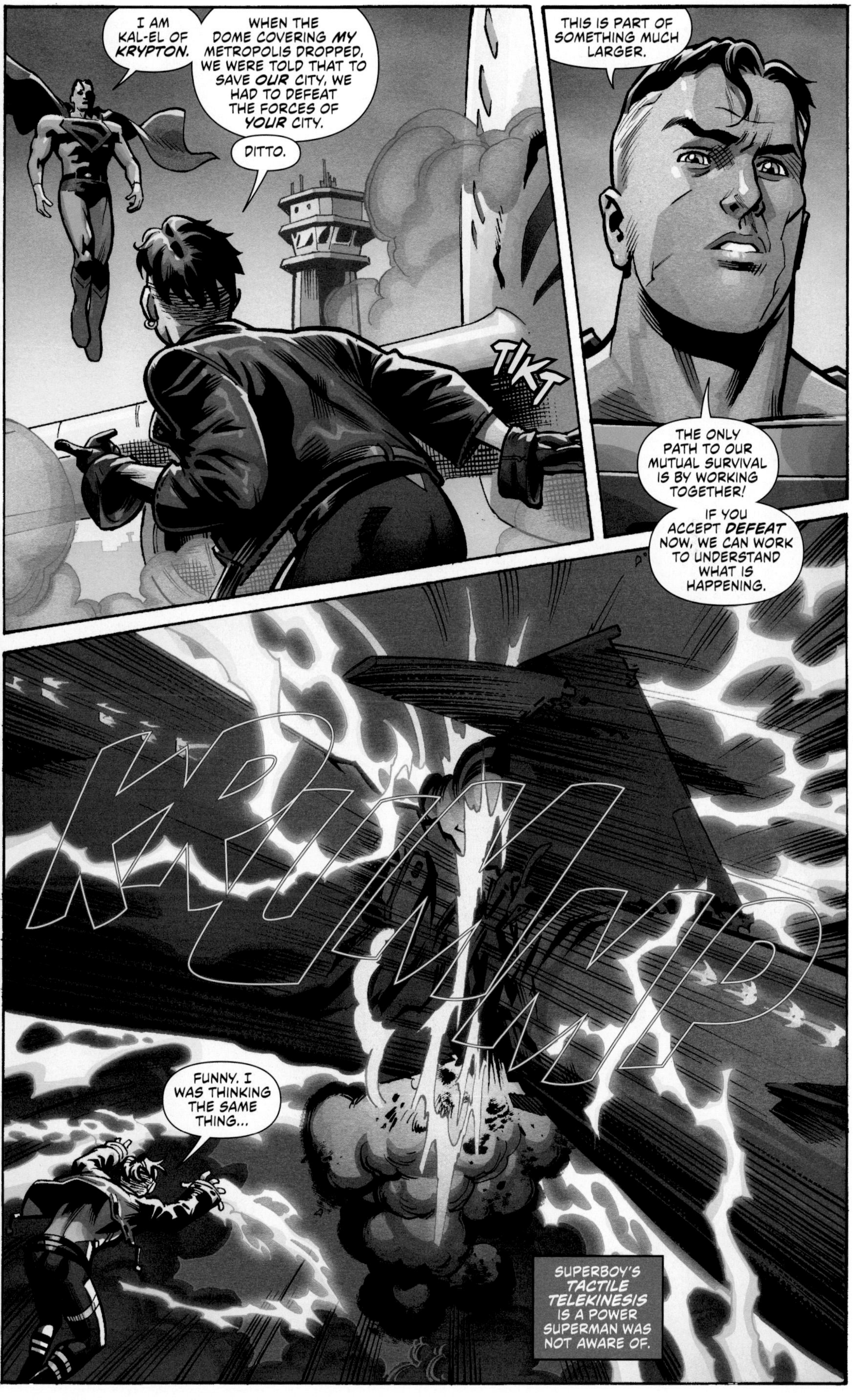
I AM KAL-EL OF KRYPTON.
WHEN THE DOME COVERING MY METROPOLIS DROPPED, WE WERE TOLD THAT TO SAVE OUR CITY, WE HAD TO DEFEAT THE FORCES OF YOUR CITY.
DITTO.
TIKT
THIS IS PART OF SOMETHING MUCH LARGER.
THE ONLY PATH TO OUR MUTUAL SURVIVAL IS BY WORKING TOGETHER!
IF YOU ACCEPT DEFEAT NOW, WE CAN WORK TO UNDERSTAND WHAT IS HAPPENING.
KROOMP
FUNNY. I WAS THINKING THE SAME THING...
SUPERBOY'S TACTILE TELEKINESIS IS A POWER SUPERMAN WAS NOT AWARE OF.

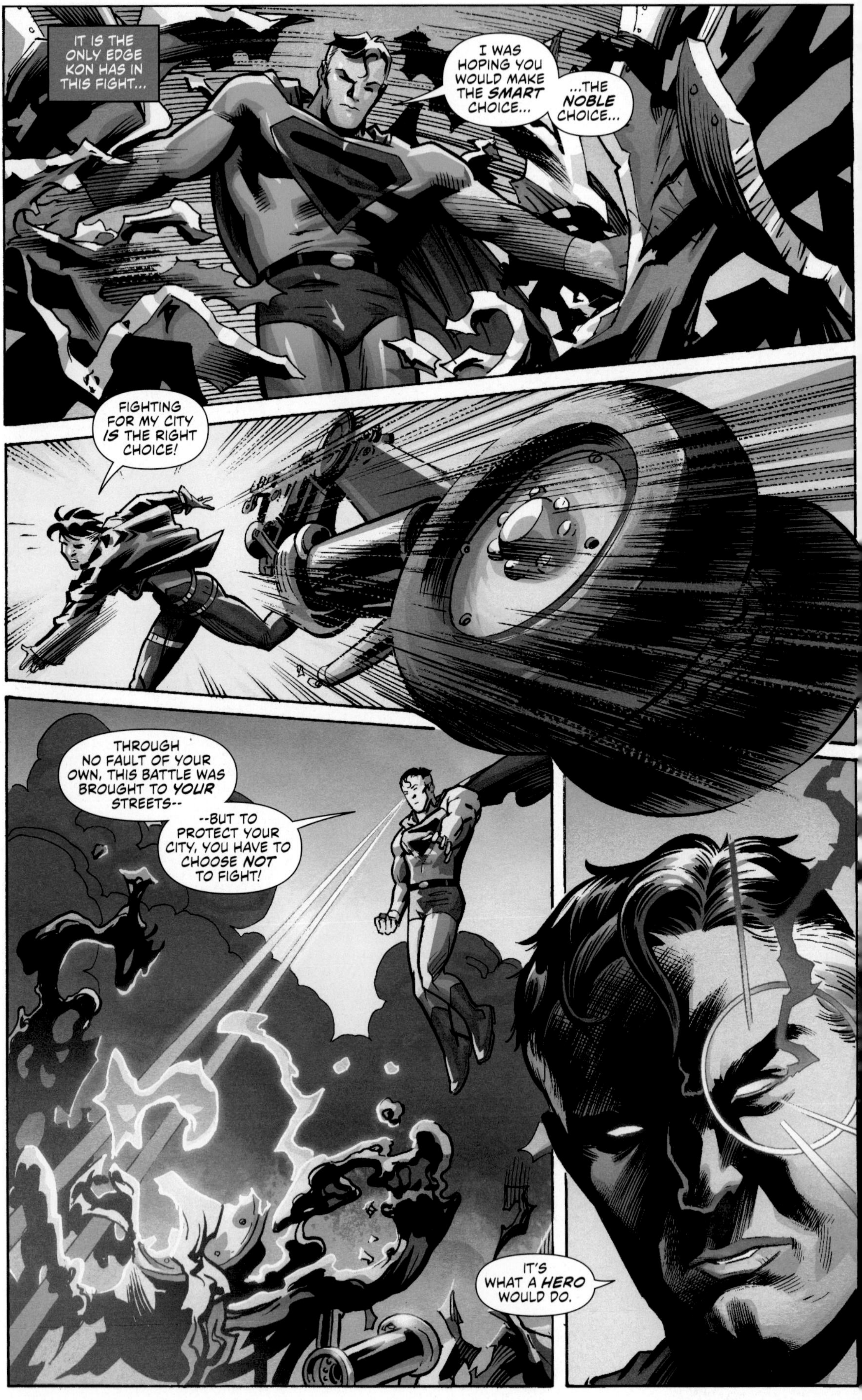
IT IS THE ONLY EDGE KON HAS IN THIS FIGHT...
I WAS HOPING YOU WOULD MAKE THE SMART CHOICE...
...THE NOBLE CHOICE...
FIGHTING FOR MY CITY IS THE RIGHT CHOICE!
THROUGH NO FAULT OF YOUR OWN, THIS BATTLE WAS BROUGHT TO YOUR STREETS--
--BUT TO PROTECT YOUR CITY, YOU HAVE TO CHOOSE NOT TO FIGHT!
IT'S WHAT A HERO WOULD DO.

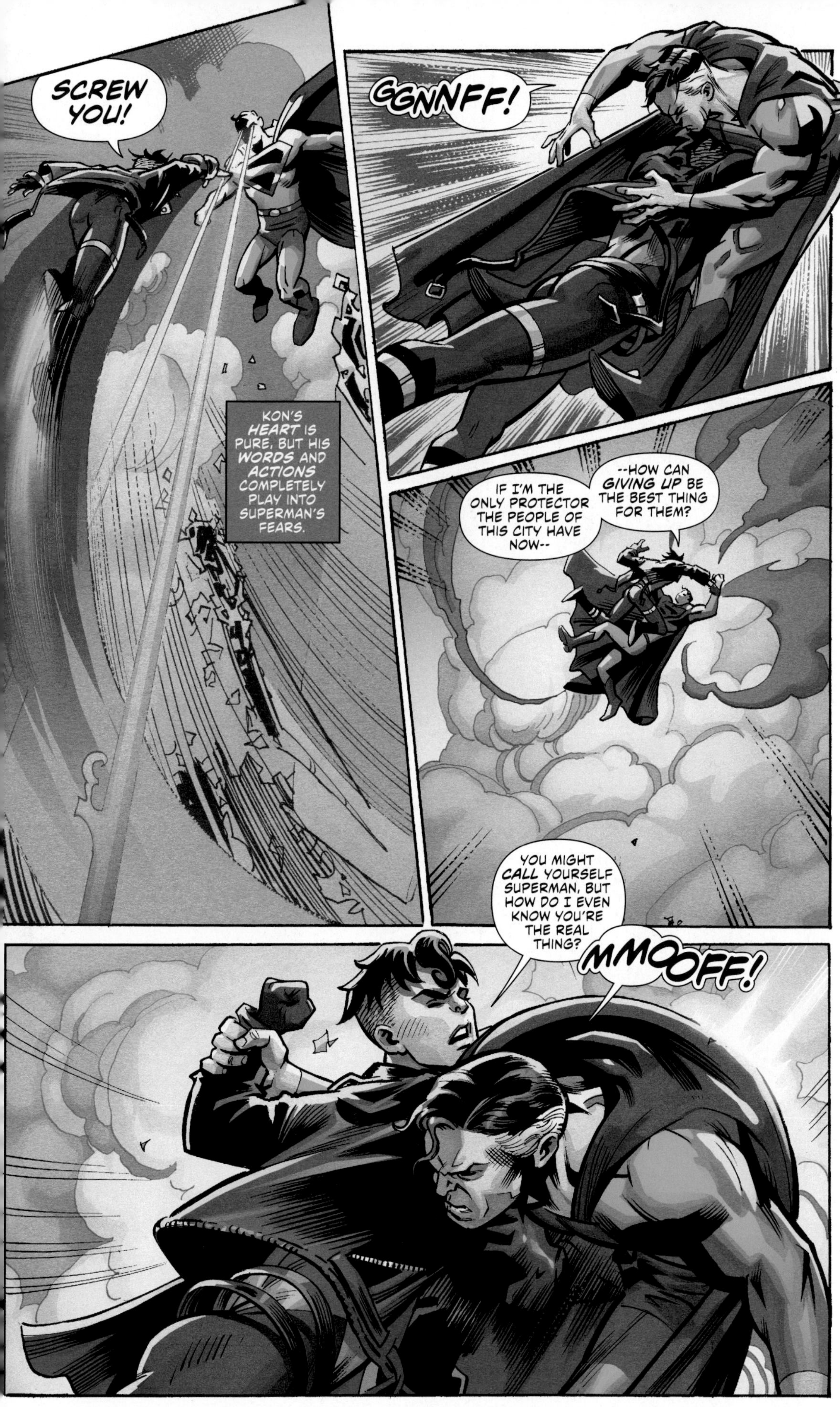
SCREW YOU!
GGNNFF!
KON'S HEART IS PURE, BUT HIS WORDS AND ACTIONS COMPLETELY PLAY INTO SUPERMAN'S FEARS.
IF I'M THE ONLY PROTECTOR THE PEOPLE OF THIS CITY HAVE NOW--
--HOW CAN GIVING UP BE THE BEST THING FOR THEM?
YOU MIGHT CALL YOURSELF SUPERMAN, BUT HOW DO I EVEN KNOW YOU'RE THE REAL THING?
MMOOFF!

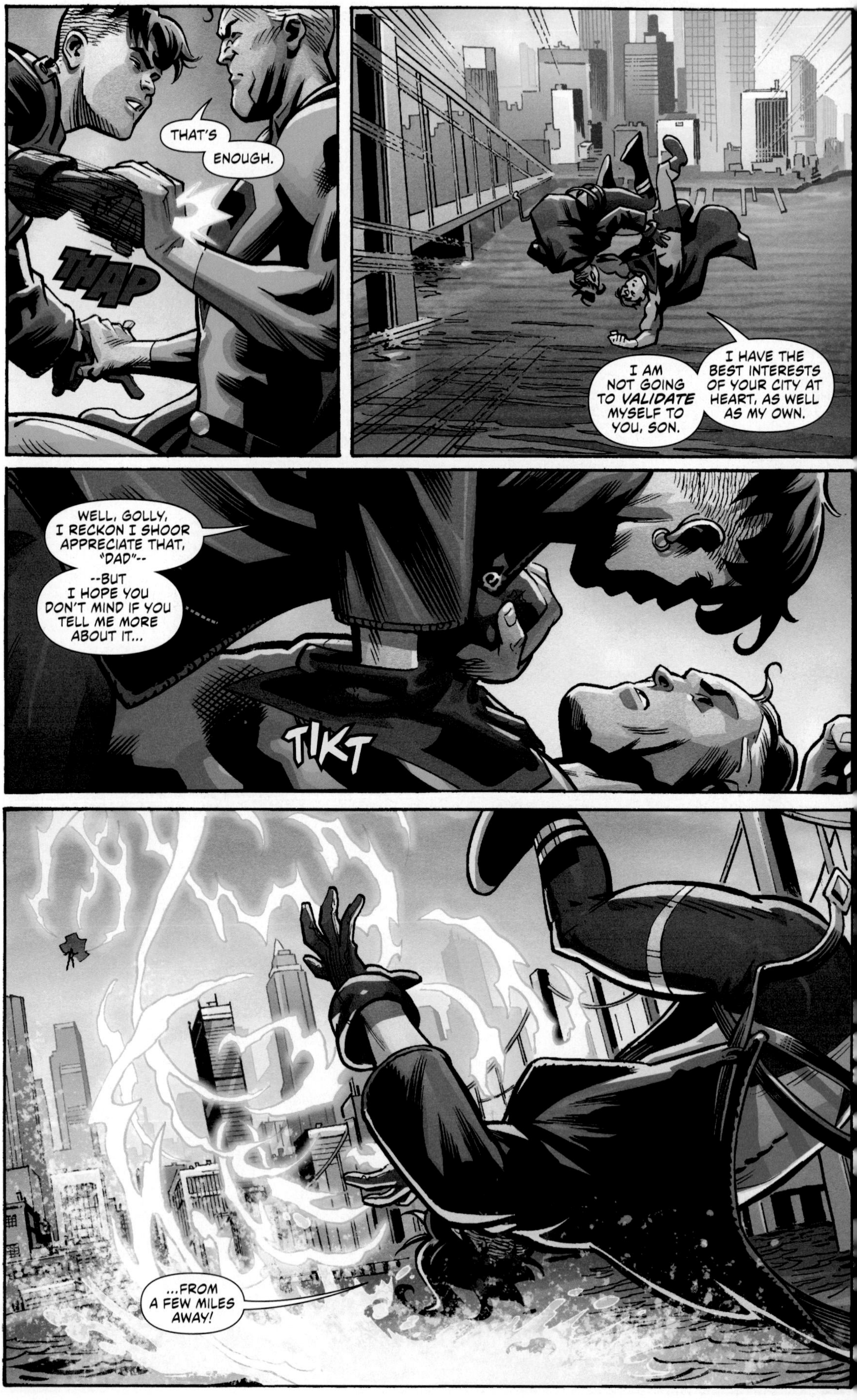
THAT'S ENOUGH.
THAP
I HAVE THE BEST INTERESTS OF YOUR CITY AT HEART, AS WELL AS MY OWN.
I AM NOT GOING TO *VALIDATE* MYSELF TO YOU, SON.
WELL, GOLLY, I RECKON I SHOOR APPRECIATE THAT, "DAD"--
--BUT I HOPE YOU DON'T MIND IF YOU TELL ME MORE ABOUT IT...
TIKT
...FROM A FEW MILES AWAY!

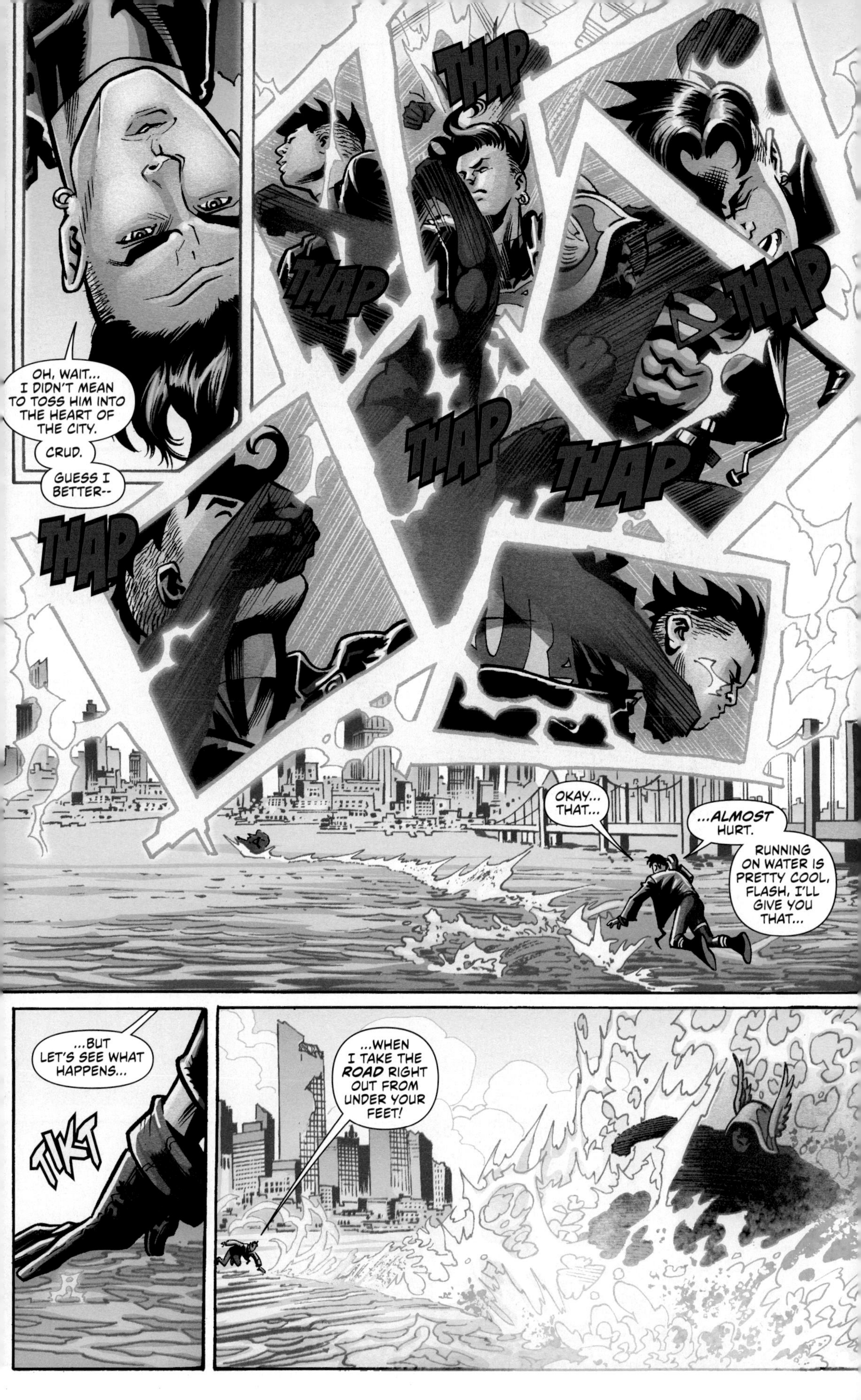
THAP
OH, WAIT... I DIDN'T MEAN TO TOSS HIM INTO THE HEART OF THE CITY.
CRUD.
GUESS I BETTER--
THAP
THAP
THAP
THAP
THAP
OKAY... THAT...
...ALMOST HURT.
RUNNING ON WATER IS PRETTY COOL, FLASH, I'LL GIVE YOU THAT...
...BUT LET'S SEE WHAT HAPPENS...
TIKT
...WHEN I TAKE THE ROAD RIGHT OUT FROM UNDER YOUR FEET!

WE CAN TRACK HIM FROM *PROJECT CADMUS*, BUT WE CAN'T PREVENT HIM FROM MAKING A MISTAKE.

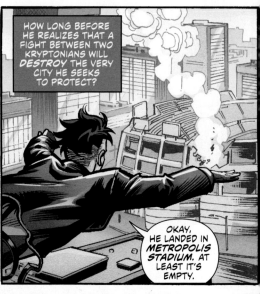

HOW LONG BEFORE HE REALIZES THAT A FIGHT BETWEEN TWO KRYPTONIANS WILL *DESTROY* THE VERY CITY HE SEEKS TO PROTECT?

OKAY, HE LANDED IN *METROPOLIS STADIUM*. AT LEAST IT'S EMPTY.

FLASH IS THERE ALREADY? DANG, HE'S *FAST*...

I ASK SERLING TO RUN AN ACCELERATED *CATACLYSM SCENARIO* THAT INCLUDES FLASH IN THE FIGHT.

BURGERS R US | Daily Planet | Sports W

I AM A *TELEPATH* OF THE HIGHEST ORDER, ONE OF THE MOST *INTELLIGENT* BEINGS ON THE PLANET.

AND YET... I CAN ONLY *WATCH*, HELPLESS...

...AS SUPERBOY PLAYS INTO ALL MY WORST FEARS...

HE WILL NOT LISTEN TO REASON.

YOU AGREE THAT KON SHOULD JUST *SURRENDER*?

HE CANNOT HOPE TO *WIN*, SERLING.

WHAT OTHER OPTION WOULD YOU PROPOSE?

I DON'T KNOW...FIGHT FOR HIS LIFE-- FOR OURS?

BREEP

THE SIMULATION IS DONE.

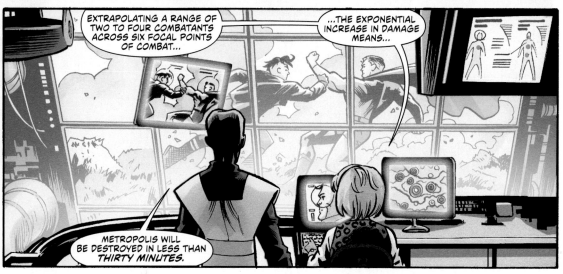

EXTRAPOLATING A RANGE OF TWO TO FOUR COMBATANTS ACROSS SIX FOCAL POINTS OF COMBAT...

...THE EXPONENTIAL INCREASE IN DAMAGE MEANS...

METROPOLIS WILL BE DESTROYED IN LESS THAN *THIRTY MINUTES.*

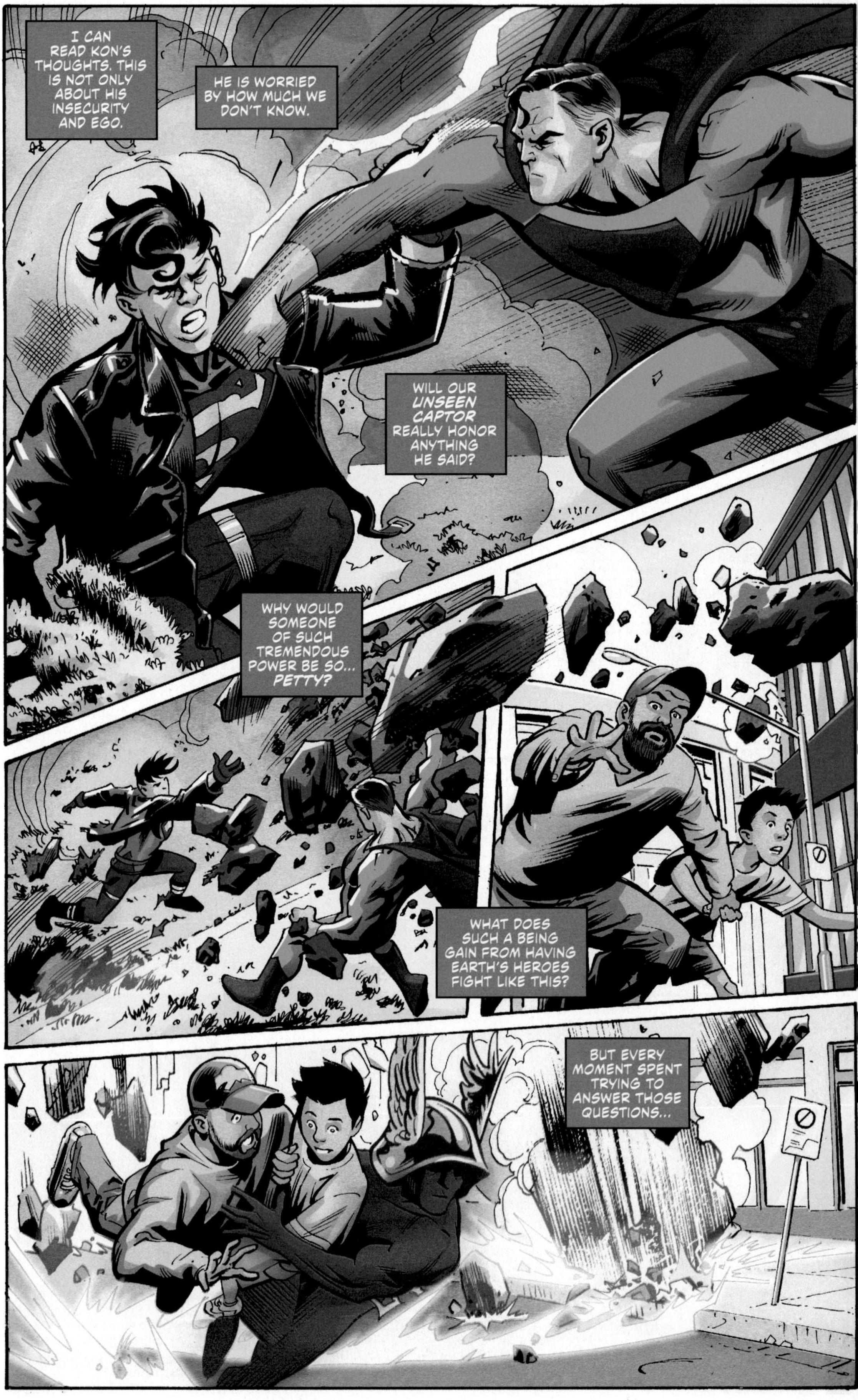
I CAN READ KON'S THOUGHTS. THIS IS NOT ONLY ABOUT HIS INSECURITY AND EGO.
HE IS WORRIED BY HOW MUCH WE DON'T KNOW.
WILL OUR *UNSEEN CAPTOR* REALLY HONOR ANYTHING HE SAID?
WHY WOULD SOMEONE OF SUCH TREMENDOUS POWER BE SO... *PETTY?*
WHAT DOES SUCH A BEING GAIN FROM HAVING EARTH'S HEROES FIGHT LIKE THIS?
BUT EVERY MOMENT SPENT TRYING TO ANSWER THOSE QUESTIONS...

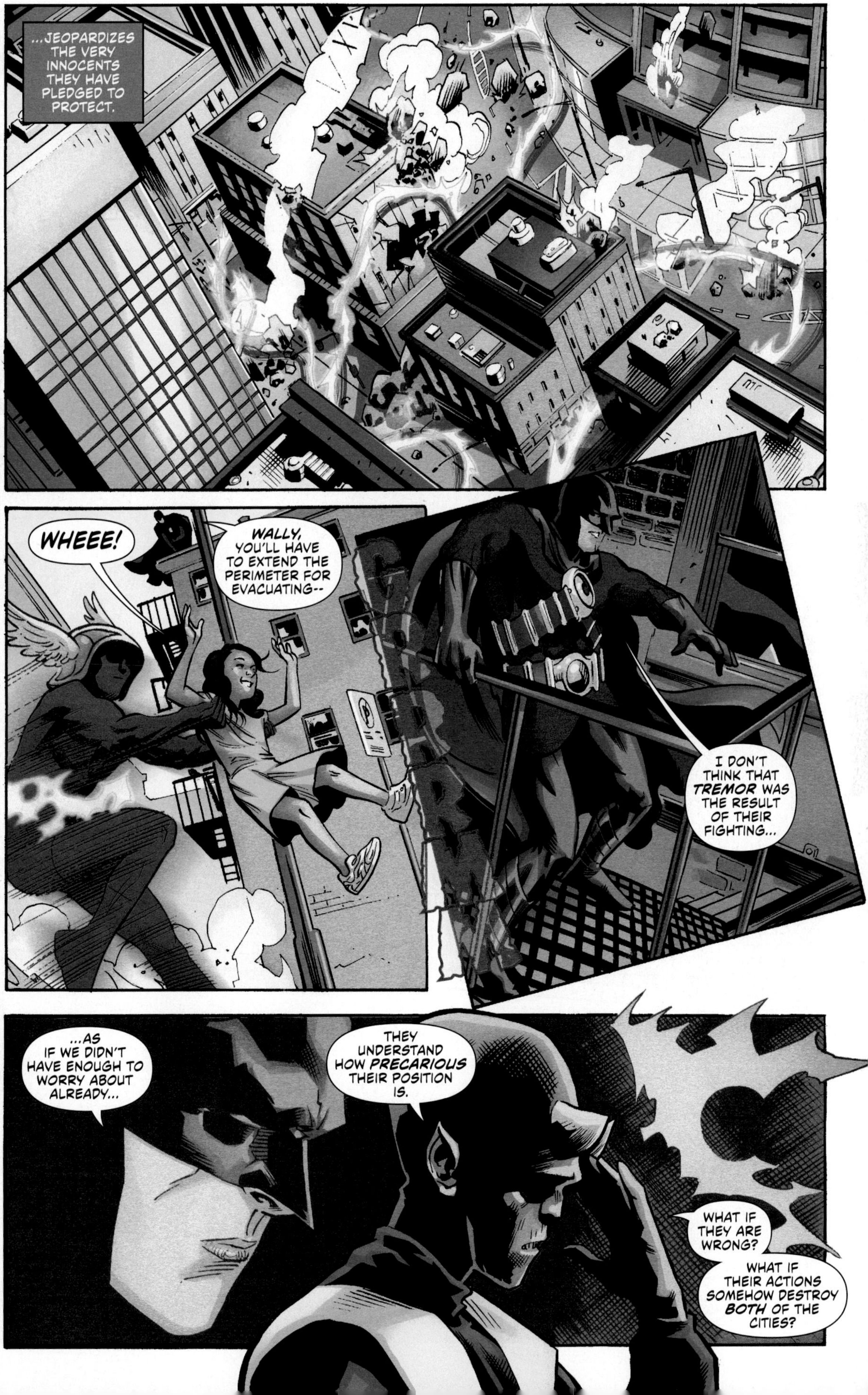
...JEOPARDIZES THE VERY INNOCENTS THEY HAVE PLEDGED TO PROTECT.
WHEEE!
WALLY, YOU'LL HAVE TO EXTEND THE PERIMETER FOR EVACUATING--
I DON'T THINK THAT TREMOR WAS THE RESULT OF THEIR FIGHTING...
...AS IF WE DIDN'T HAVE ENOUGH TO WORRY ABOUT ALREADY...
THEY UNDERSTAND HOW PRECARIOUS THEIR POSITION IS.
WHAT IF THEY ARE WRONG?
WHAT IF THEIR ACTIONS SOMEHOW DESTROY BOTH OF THE CITIES?

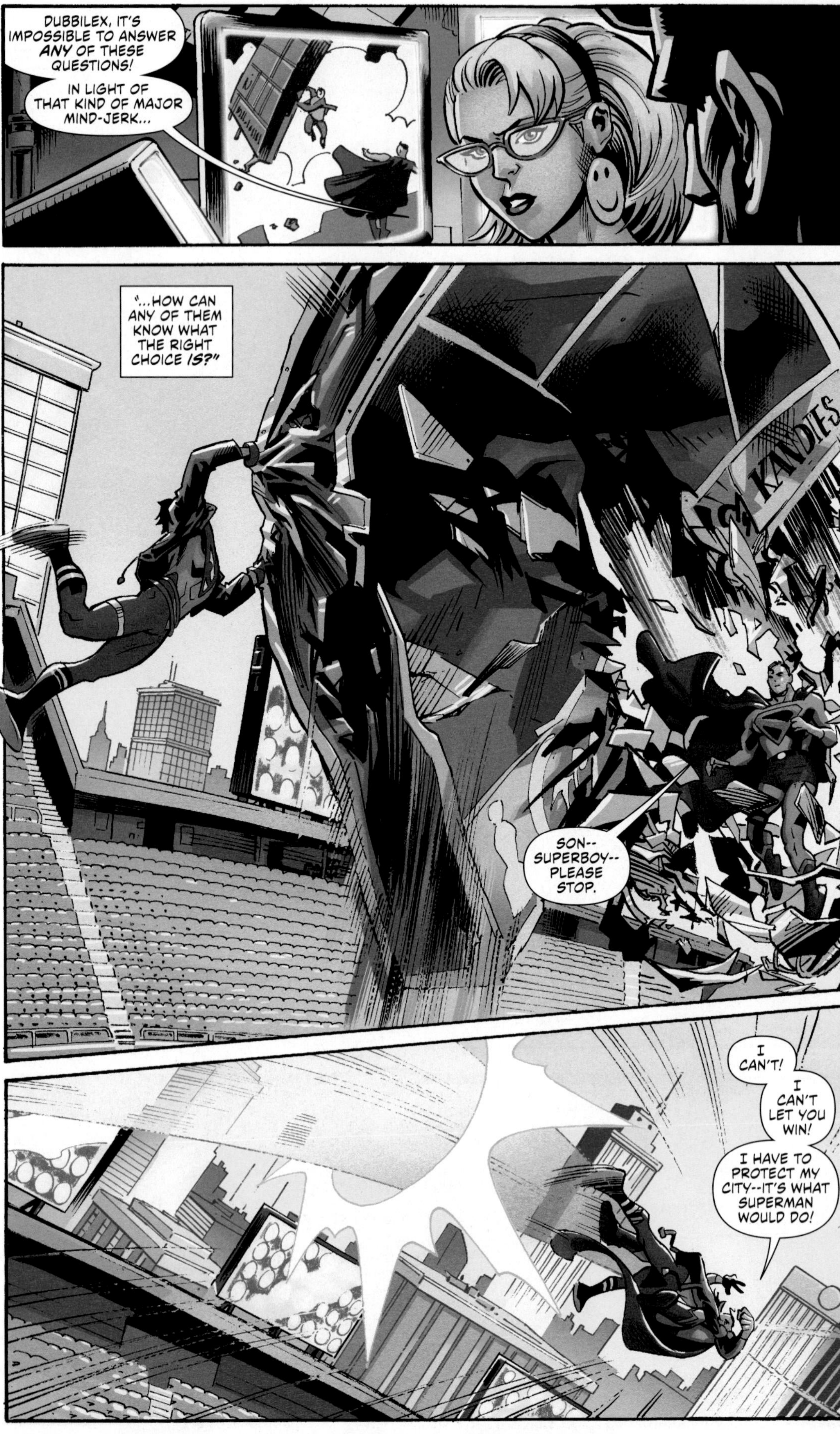
DUBBILEX, IT'S IMPOSSIBLE TO ANSWER ANY OF THESE QUESTIONS!
IN LIGHT OF THAT KIND OF MAJOR MIND-JERK...
"...HOW CAN ANY OF THEM KNOW WHAT THE RIGHT CHOICE IS?"
KANDIES
SON-- SUPERBOY-- PLEASE STOP.
I CAN'T!
I CAN'T LET YOU WIN!
I HAVE TO PROTECT MY CITY--IT'S WHAT SUPERMAN WOULD DO!

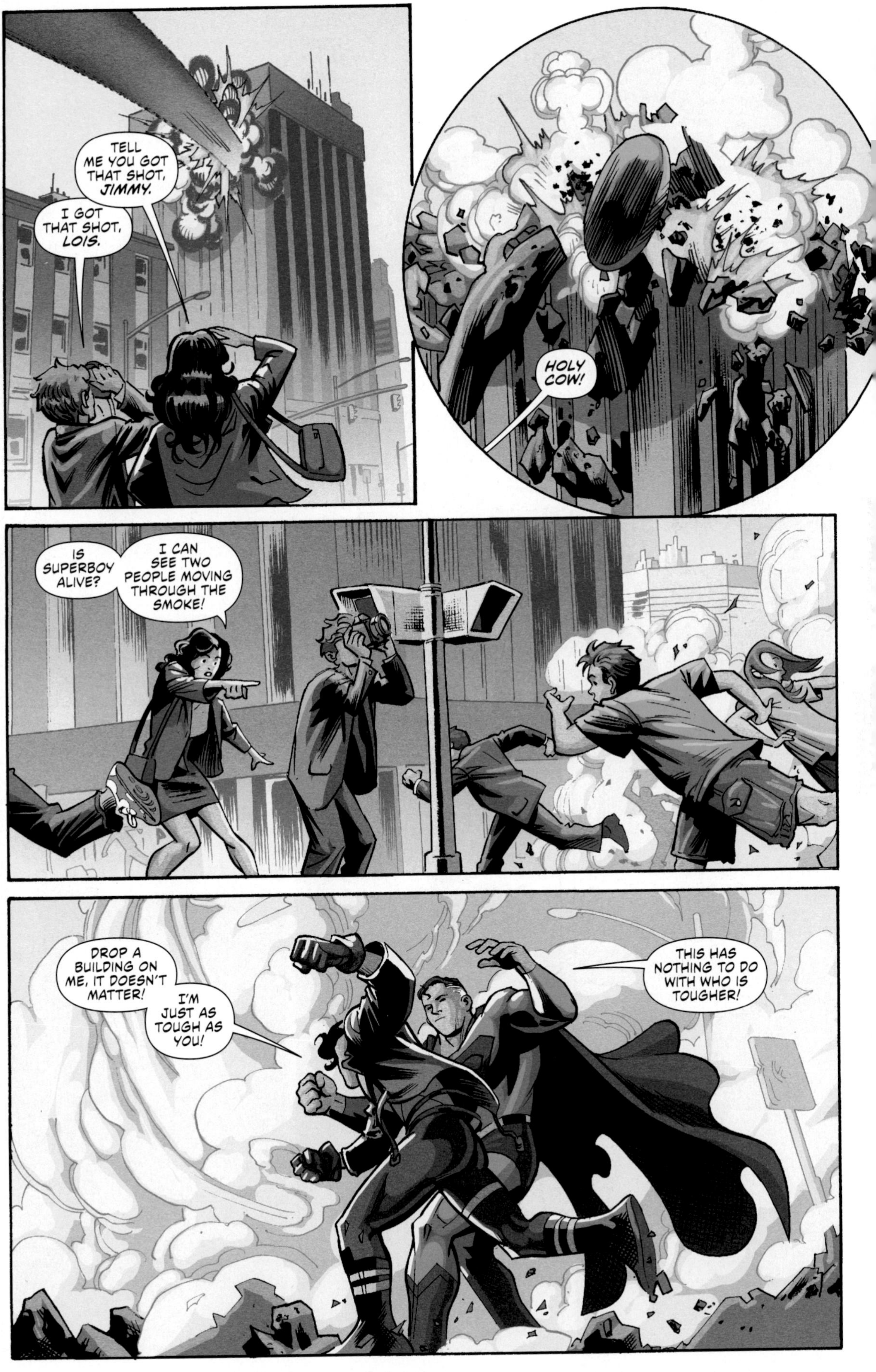
TELL ME YOU GOT THAT SHOT, JIMMY.
I GOT THAT SHOT, LOIS.
HOLY COW!
IS SUPERBOY ALIVE?
I CAN SEE TWO PEOPLE MOVING THROUGH THE SMOKE!
DROP A BUILDING ON ME, IT DOESN'T MATTER!
I'M JUST AS TOUGH AS YOU!
THIS HAS NOTHING TO DO WITH WHO IS TOUGHER!

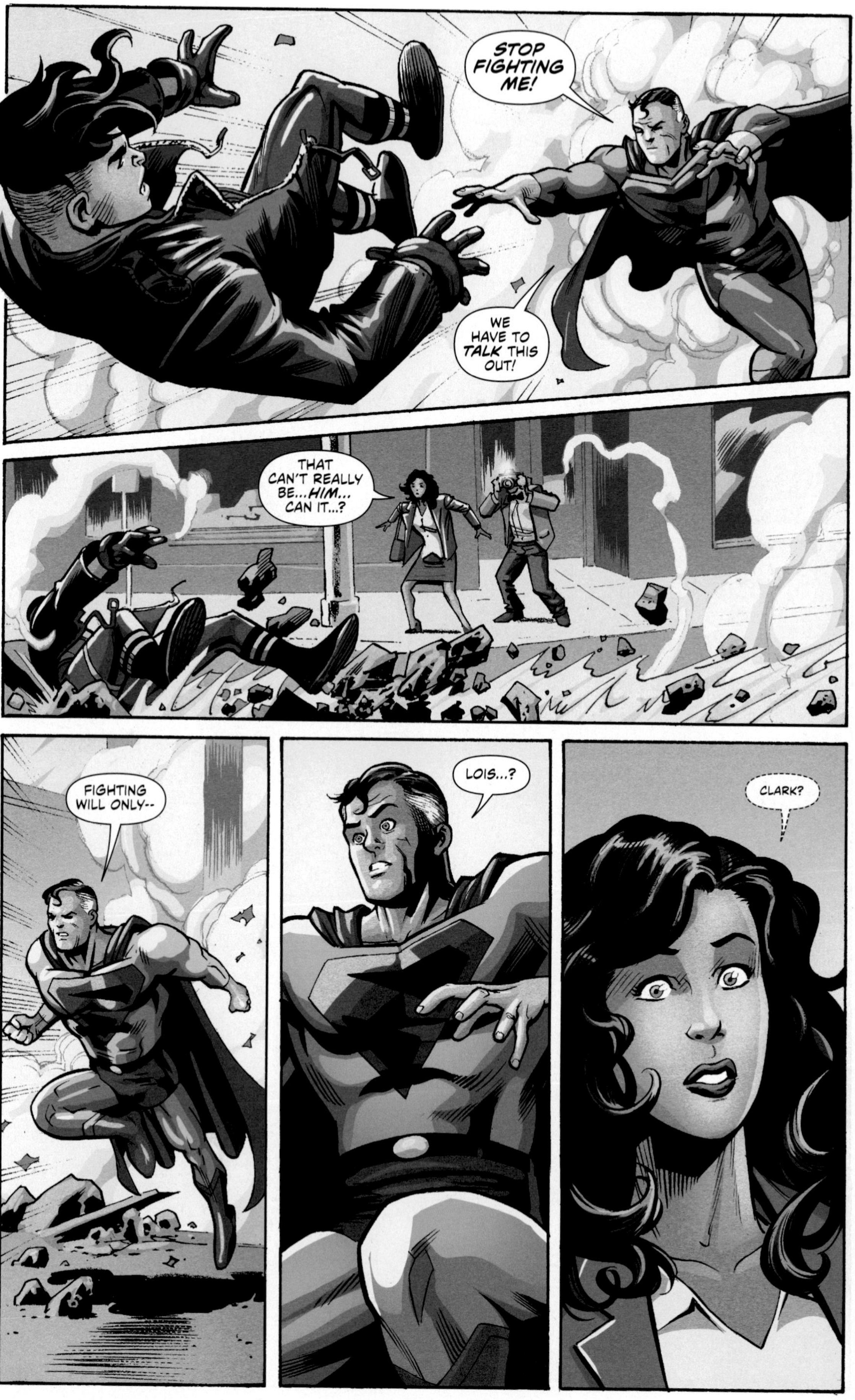
STOP FIGHTING ME!
WE HAVE TO TALK THIS OUT!
THAT CAN'T REALLY BE...HIM... CAN IT...?
FIGHTING WILL ONLY--
LOIS...?
CLARK?

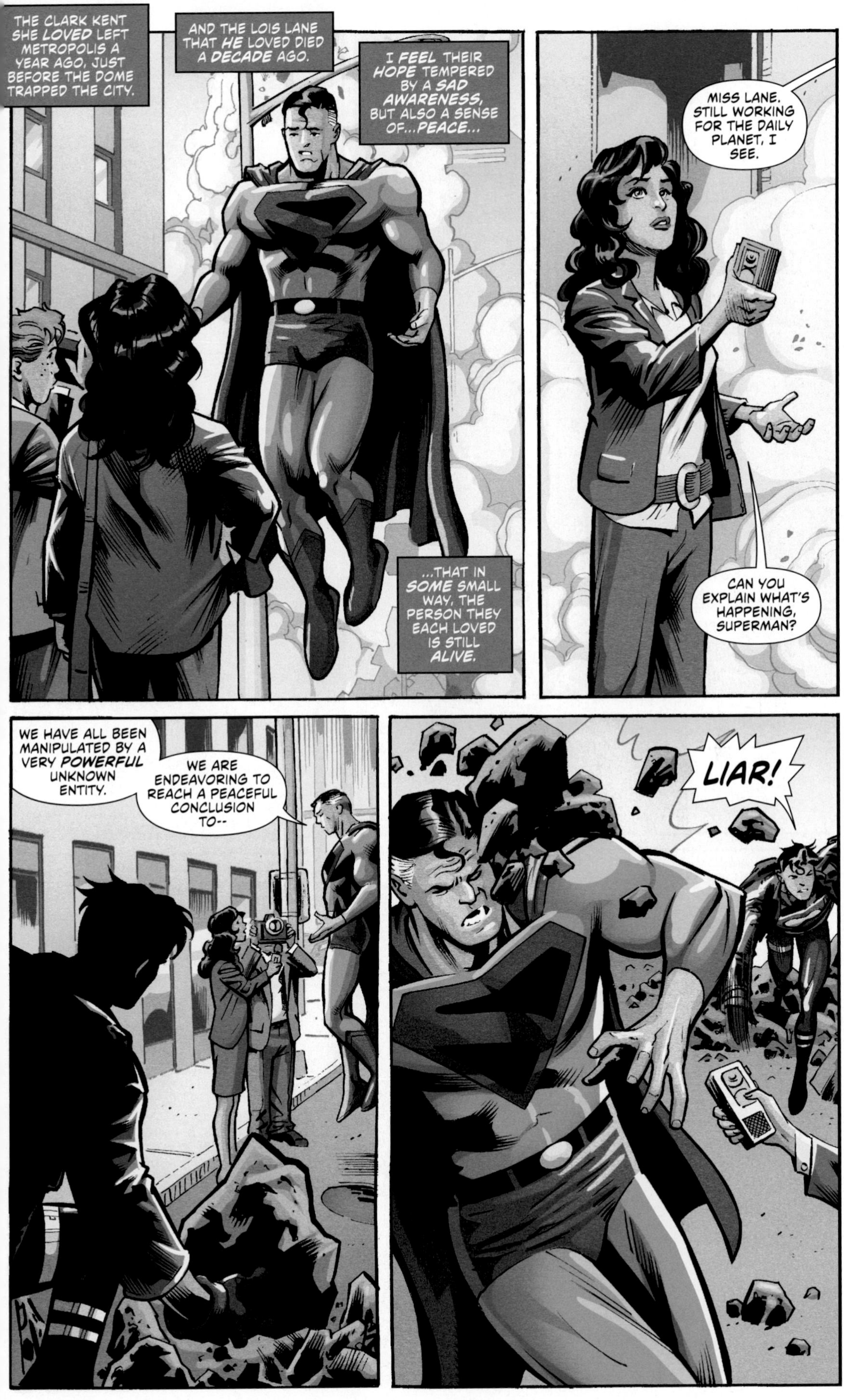
THE CLARK KENT SHE LOVED LEFT METROPOLIS A YEAR AGO, JUST BEFORE THE DOME TRAPPED THE CITY.
AND THE LOIS LANE THAT HE LOVED DIED A DECADE AGO.
I FEEL THEIR HOPE TEMPERED BY A SAD AWARENESS, BUT ALSO A SENSE OF...PEACE...
...THAT IN SOME SMALL WAY, THE PERSON THEY EACH LOVED IS STILL ALIVE.
MISS LANE. STILL WORKING FOR THE DAILY PLANET, I SEE.
CAN YOU EXPLAIN WHAT'S HAPPENING, SUPERMAN?
WE HAVE ALL BEEN MANIPULATED BY A VERY POWERFUL UNKNOWN ENTITY.
WE ARE ENDEAVORING TO REACH A PEACEFUL CONCLUSION TO--
LIAR!

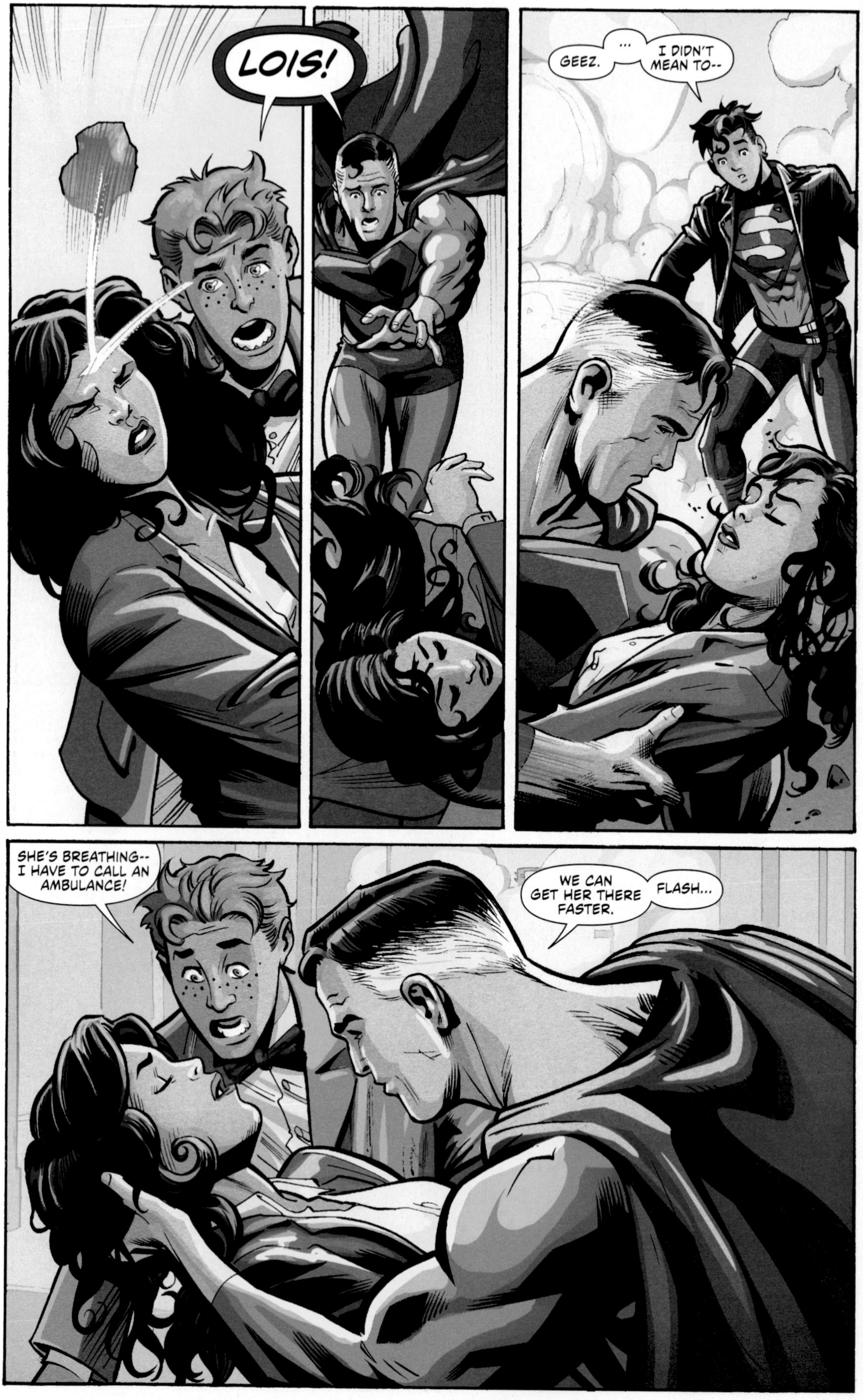
LOIS!
GEEZ.
...
I DIDN'T MEAN TO--
SHE'S BREATHING-- I HAVE TO CALL AN AMBULANCE!
FLASH...
WE CAN GET HER THERE FASTER.

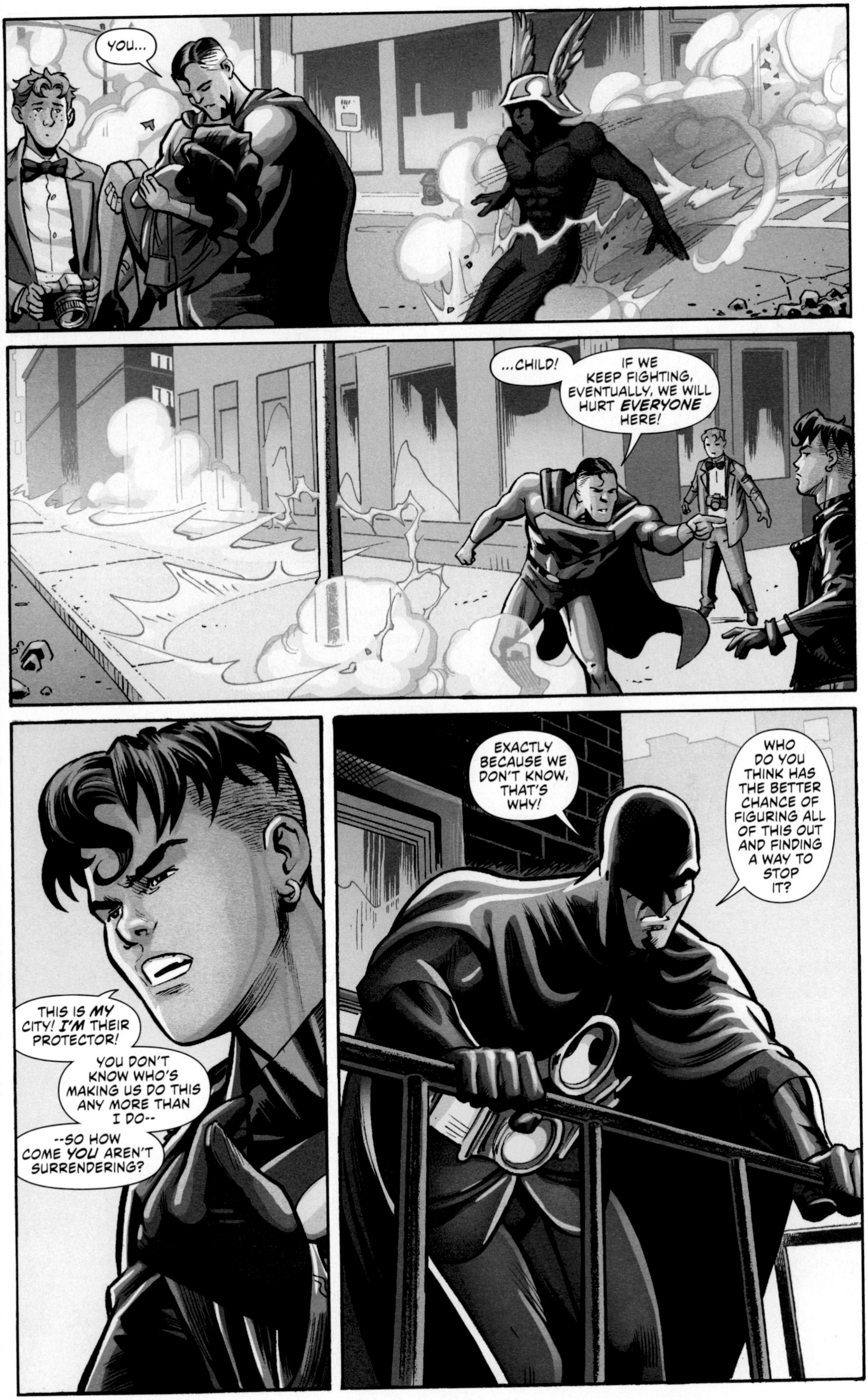
YOU...
...CHILD!
IF WE KEEP FIGHTING, EVENTUALLY, WE WILL HURT EVERYONE HERE!
THIS IS MY CITY! I'M THEIR PROTECTOR!
YOU DON'T KNOW WHO'S MAKING US DO THIS ANY MORE THAN I DO--
--SO HOW COME YOU AREN'T SURRENDERING?
EXACTLY BECAUSE WE DON'T KNOW, THAT'S WHY!
WHO DO YOU THINK HAS THE BETTER CHANCE OF FIGURING ALL OF THIS OUT AND FINDING A WAY TO STOP IT?

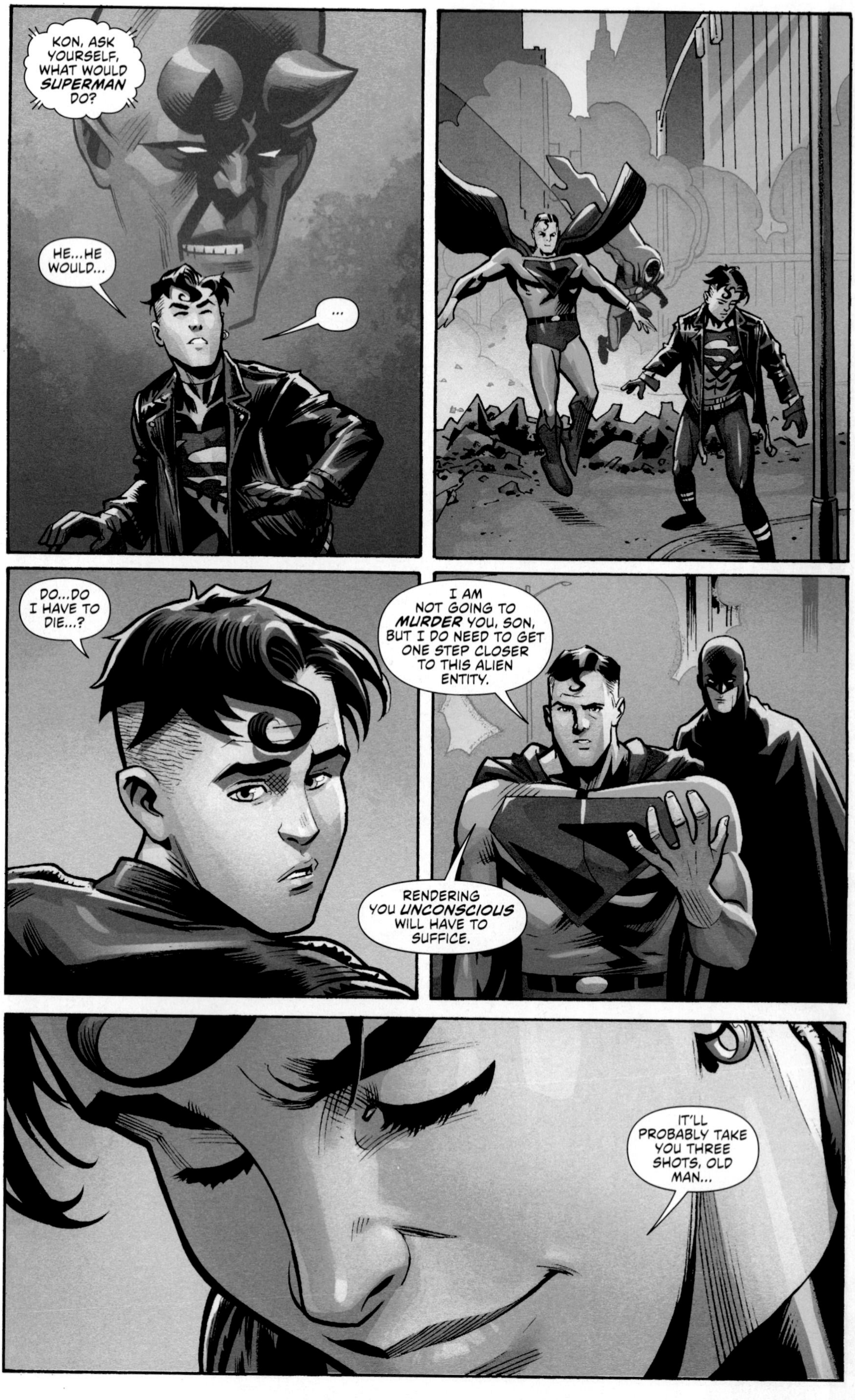
KON, ASK YOURSELF, WHAT WOULD SUPERMAN DO?
HE...HE WOULD...
...
DO...DO I HAVE TO DIE...?
I AM NOT GOING TO MURDER YOU, SON, BUT I DO NEED TO GET ONE STEP CLOSER TO THIS ALIEN ENTITY.
RENDERING YOU UNCONSCIOUS WILL HAVE TO SUFFICE.
IT'LL PROBABLY TAKE YOU THREE SHOTS, OLD MAN...

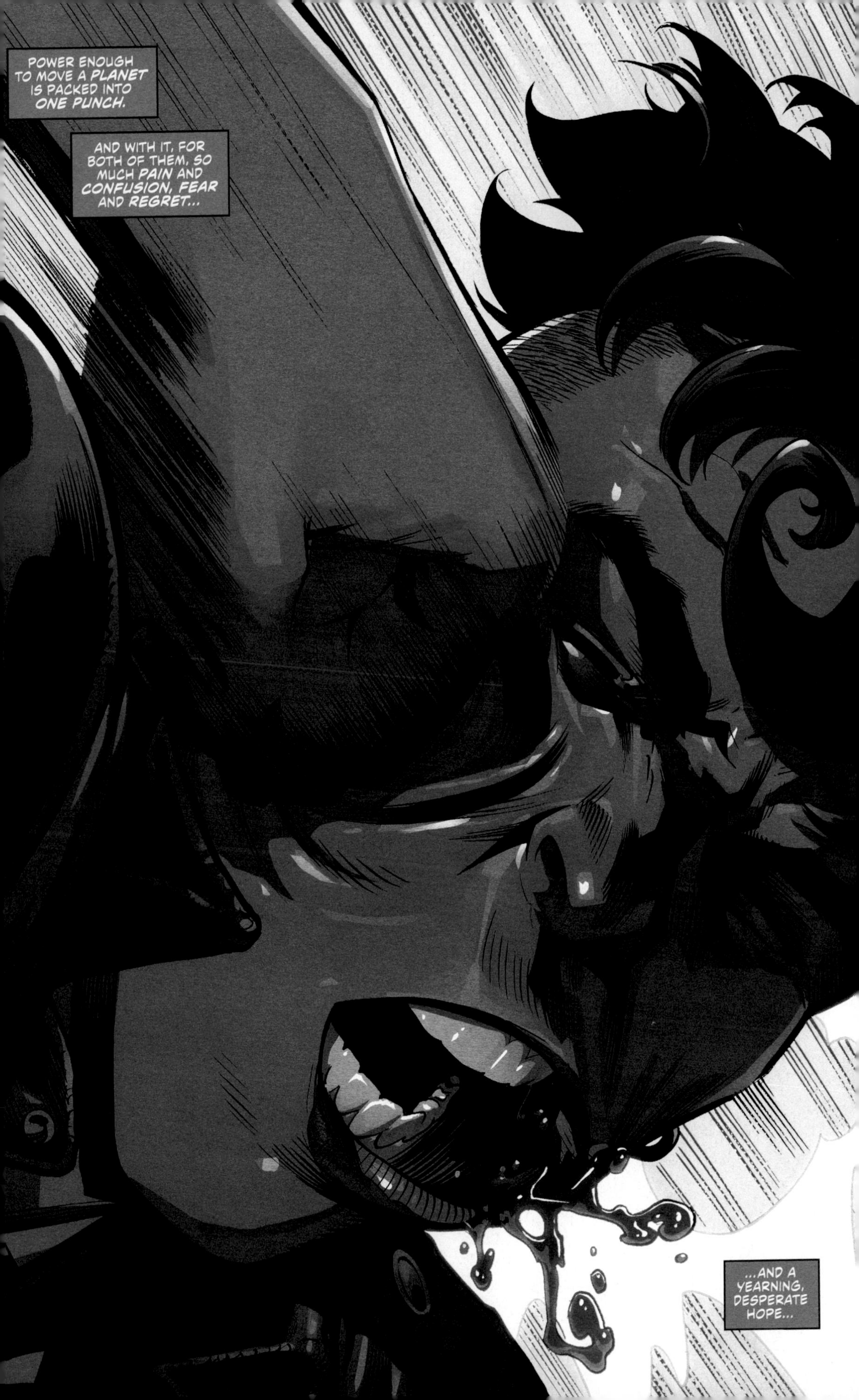
POWER ENOUGH TO MOVE A *PLANET* IS PACKED INTO *ONE PUNCH.*
AND WITH IT, FOR BOTH OF THEM, SO MUCH *PAIN* AND *CONFUSION, FEAR* AND *REGRET...*
...AND A YEARNING, DESPERATE HOPE...

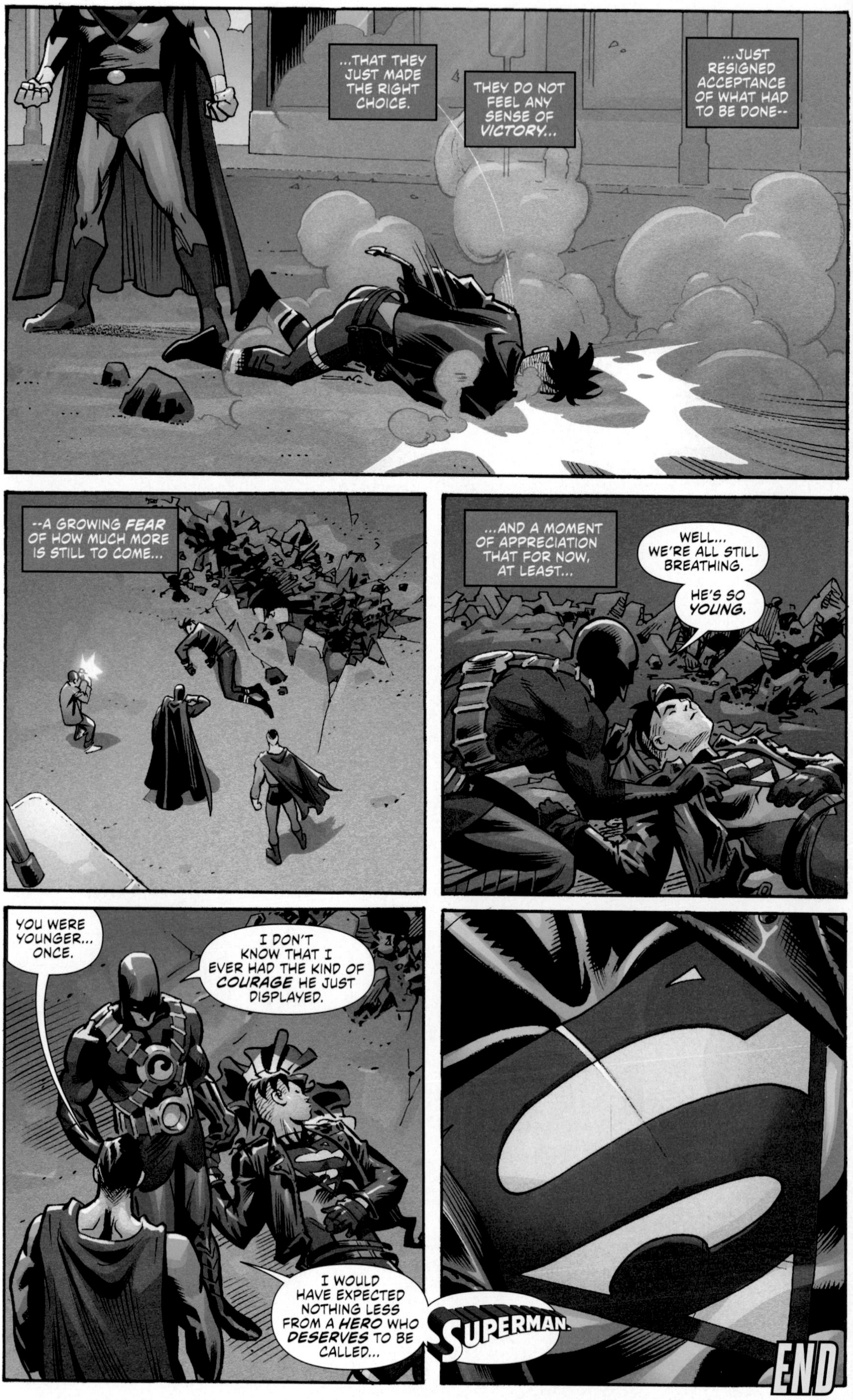
...THAT THEY JUST MADE THE RIGHT CHOICE.
THEY DO NOT FEEL ANY SENSE OF VICTORY...
...JUST RESIGNED ACCEPTANCE OF WHAT HAD TO BE DONE--
--A GROWING FEAR OF HOW MUCH MORE IS STILL TO COME...
...AND A MOMENT OF APPRECIATION THAT FOR NOW, AT LEAST...
WELL... WE'RE ALL STILL BREATHING.
HE'S SO YOUNG.
YOU WERE YOUNGER... ONCE.
I DON'T KNOW THAT I EVER HAD THE KIND OF COURAGE HE JUST DISPLAYED.
I WOULD HAVE EXPECTED NOTHING LESS FROM A HERO WHO DESERVES TO BE CALLED...
SUPERMAN.
END

FIGHT FOR YOUR CITY

WHO'S WHO IN
CONVERGENCE
ZERO HOUR

Special Thanks to Steve Korté and Joey Cavalieri

Selina Kyle was the most accomplished thief Gotham City had ever known. Blessed with natural acrobatic skills and keen wits, she became a cat who darted over the rooftops of Gotham, eluding capture by the police. But it wasn't until she slipped on a mask and costume—including gloves with built-in razor-sharp claws—that Selina became Catwoman.

CATWOMAN

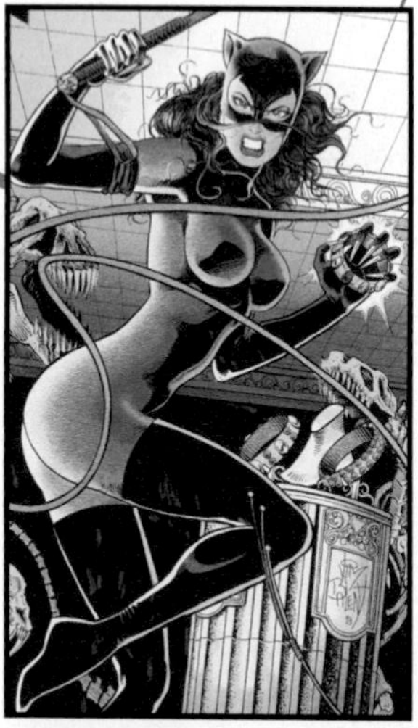

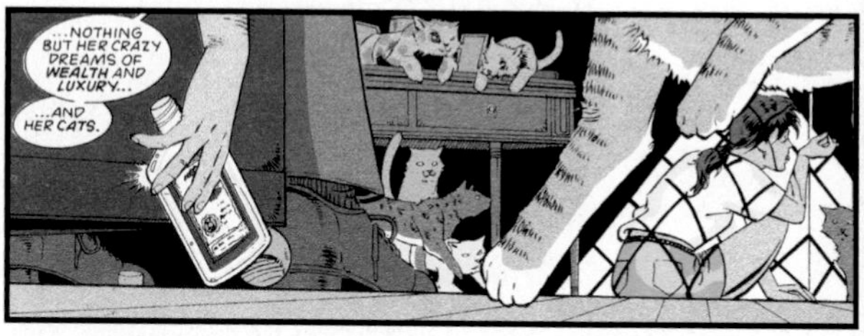

...NOTHING BUT HER CRAZY DREAMS OF WEALTH AND LUXURY...
...AND HER CATS.

Selina's childhood was filled with tragedy. Her mother committed suicide, and her father drank himself to death shortly thereafter. Selina even lost her beloved cats when she ran away and was consigned to the abusive Seagate school for delinquent girls.

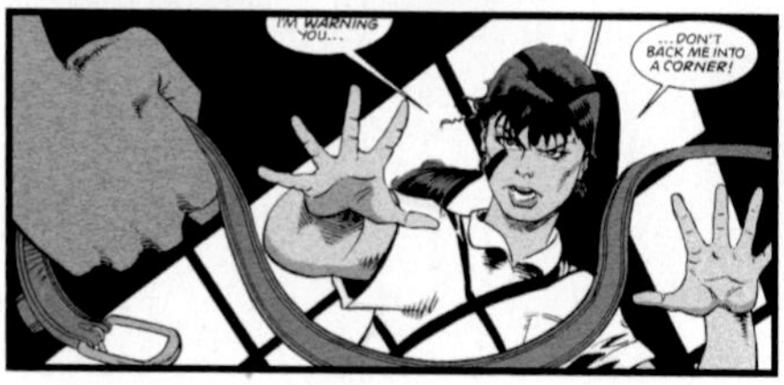

I'M WARNING YOU...
...DON'T BACK ME INTO A CORNER!

Selina dreamed of freedom, and one night she deactivated the alarm at Seagate and used her gymnastic skills to clamber to the roof. Her punishment the next day was a vicious whipping from the director of the school. But Selina would have her revenge!

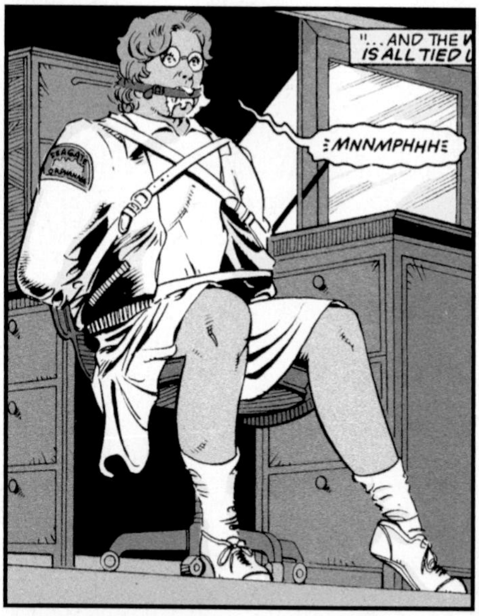

"...AND THE
IS ALL TIED
MNNMPHHH
SEAGATE

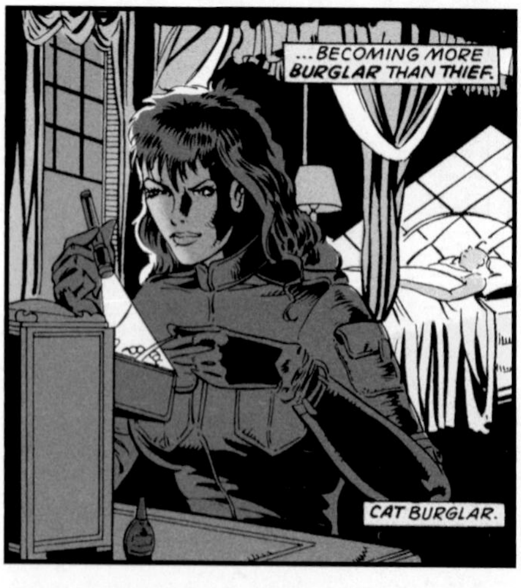

...BECOMING MORE BURGLAR THAN THIEF.
CAT BURGLAR.

After leaving Seagate, Selina decided to take her chances on the dark streets of Gotham City. She began with petty theft and eventually became a skilled cat burglar, always one step ahead of the Gotham police.

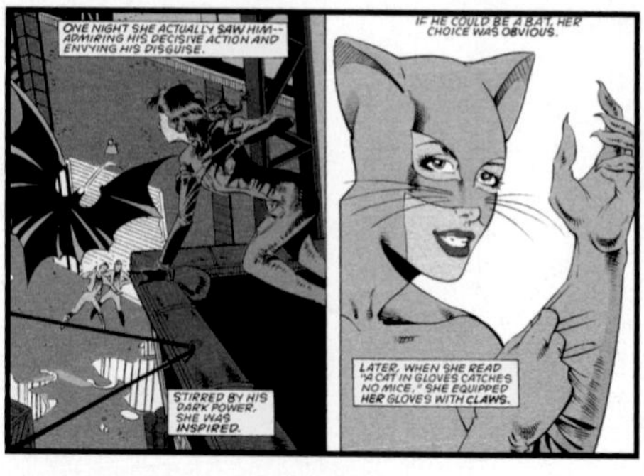

ONE NIGHT SHE ACTUALLY SAW HIM-- ADMIRING HIS DECISIVE ACTION AND ENVYING HIS DISGUISE.
STIRRED BY HIS DARK POWER, SHE WAS INSPIRED.
IF HE COULD BE A BAT, HER CHOICE WAS OBVIOUS.
LATER, WHEN SHE READ "A CAT IN GLOVES CATCHES NO MICE," SHE EQUIPPED HER GLOVES WITH CLAWS.

Selina also honed her martial arts and boxing skills. After she saw Batman in action, Selina was inspired to fashion a mask and costume for herself: The cat burglar became Catwoman!

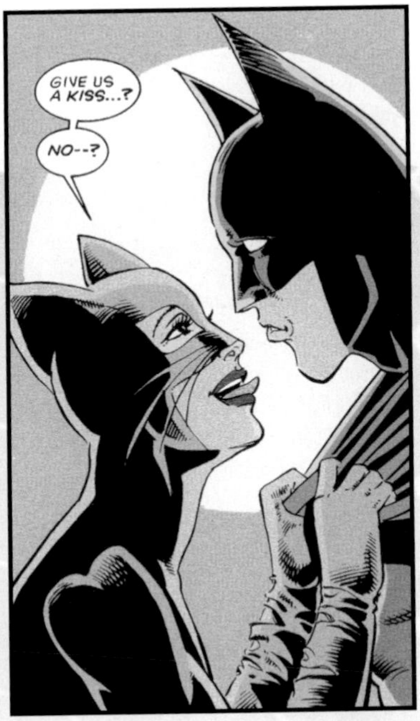
GIVE US A KISS...?
NO--?

Eventually, Catwoman's criminal activities brought her to the attention of Batman. When they finally met face-to-face, they acknowledged a powerful—and for Batman, confounding—mutual attraction.

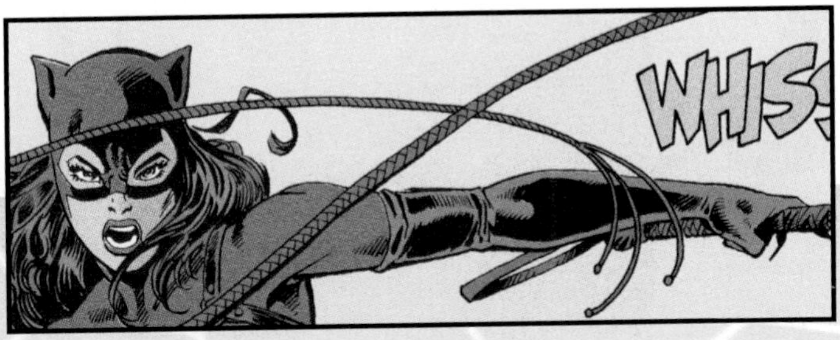
WHIS

Perhaps remembering the whipping she received at Seagate, Catwoman began wielding both a fearsome eight-foot bullwhip and a steel-bearing-tipped cat-o'-nine-tails.

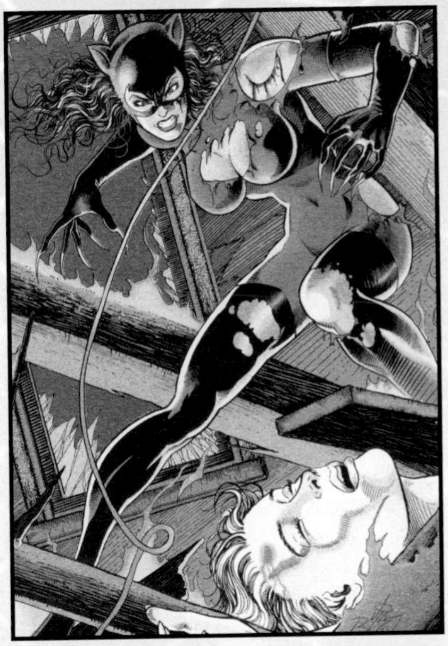

Selina took pity on a teenage runaway named Arizona and invited the girl to live with her. After their apartment was bombed and Arizona was injured, Selina discovered that the hit had been ordered by her employer, Bane, the villain who had broken Batman's back.

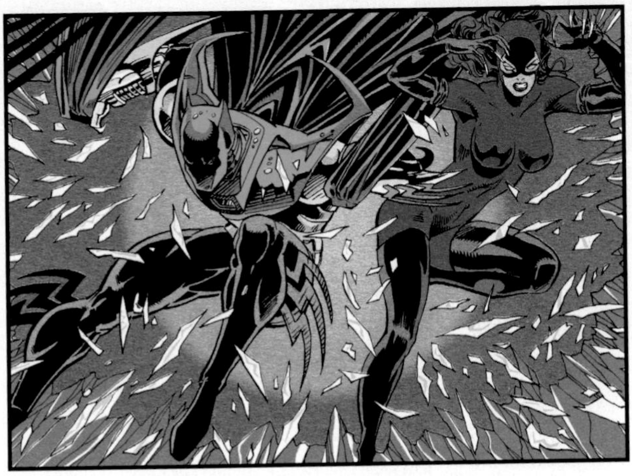

As always, Catwoman had her revenge. She betrayed Bane to Azrael, the vigilante who had temporarily become Batman. She even worked briefly alongside Azrael.

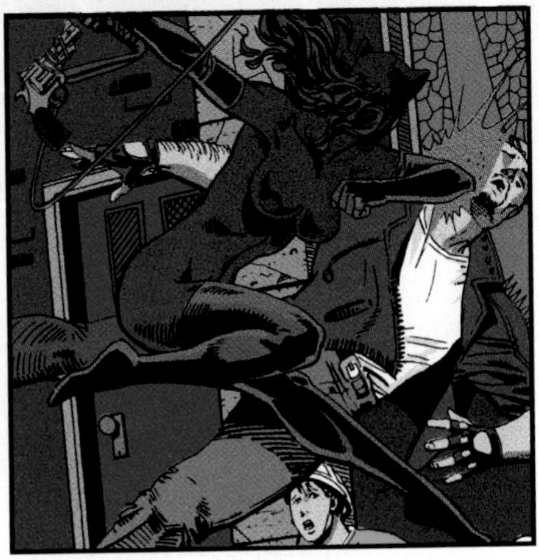

Catwoman has her own moral code. If anyone crosses her, she will retaliate swiftly and mercilessly. She also has utter—and violent—contempt for those who prey upon the helpless.

GREEN ARROW

Young Oliver Queen's lack of character and integrity was made abundantly clear to Sandra Hawke when she told him that she was pregnant following a one-night stand. He urged her to terminate the pregnancy or get a paternity test to prove it was his child.

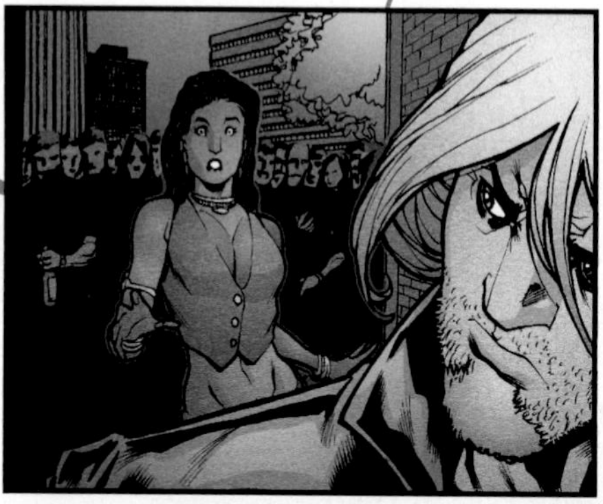

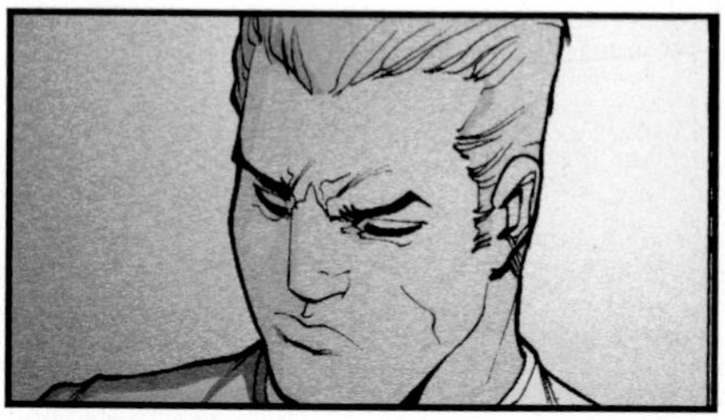

Queen's life-altering time on a deserted island might have set him on the path to becoming Green Arrow, but it failed to provide him with a sense of responsibility when it came to his newborn son, Connor. He offered Sandra financial assistance, but nothing else.

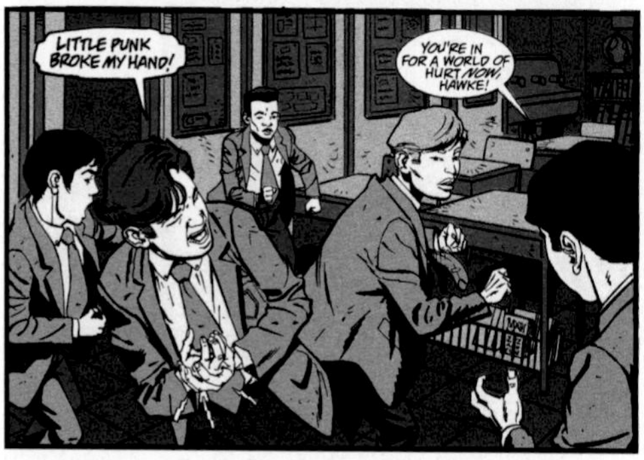
LITTLE PUNK BROKE MY HAND!
YOU'RE IN FOR A WORLD OF HURT NOW, HAWKE!

Even as a child, Connor Hawke proved to be a capable fighter, taking on four bullies who hoped to rob his ample allowance.

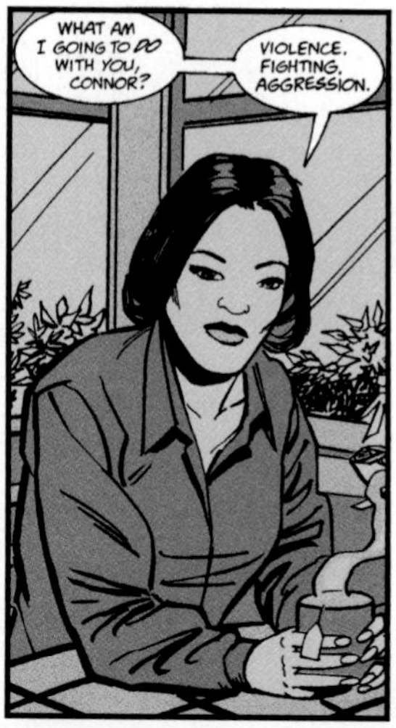
WHAT AM I GOING TO DO WITH YOU, CONNOR?
VIOLENCE. FIGHTING. AGGRESSION.

Sandra made her son promise not to get into any more fights, to which he agreed. And for a while, he honored that promise, running from future confrontations even when it meant being mocked by his peers.

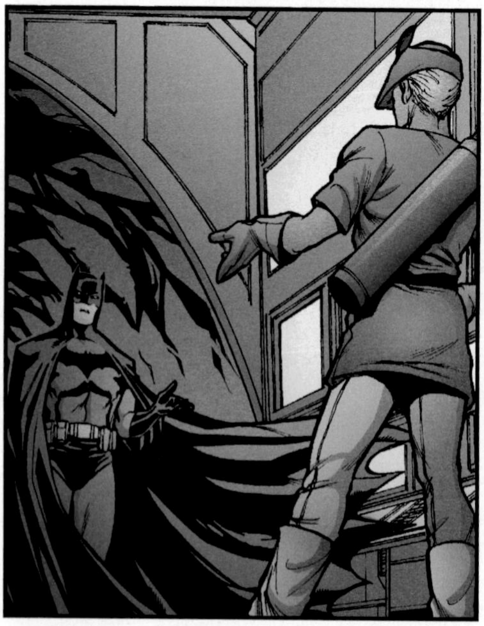

Oliver Queen never forgot about his son. And when he was unable to locate Sandra and Connor, he turned to the world's greatest detective for help.

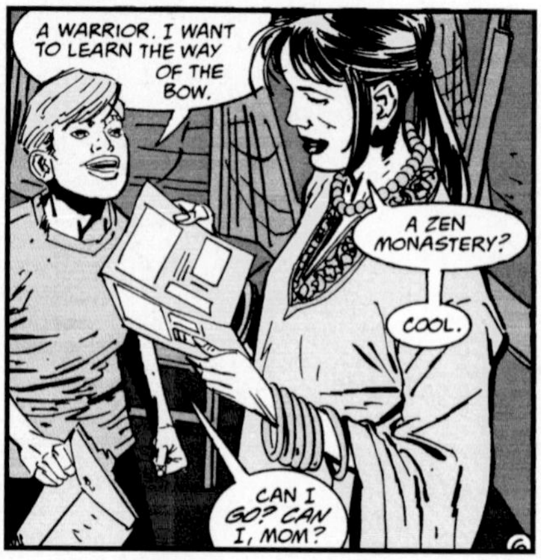
A WARRIOR. I WANT TO LEARN THE WAY OF THE BOW.
A ZEN MONASTERY?
COOL.
CAN I GO? CAN I, MOM?

That spark inside Connor couldn't be tamed. Sandra was surprised when he asked to join an ashram in Napa Valley. She agreed, hoping it would provide him with control and focus for both his talents and his demons.

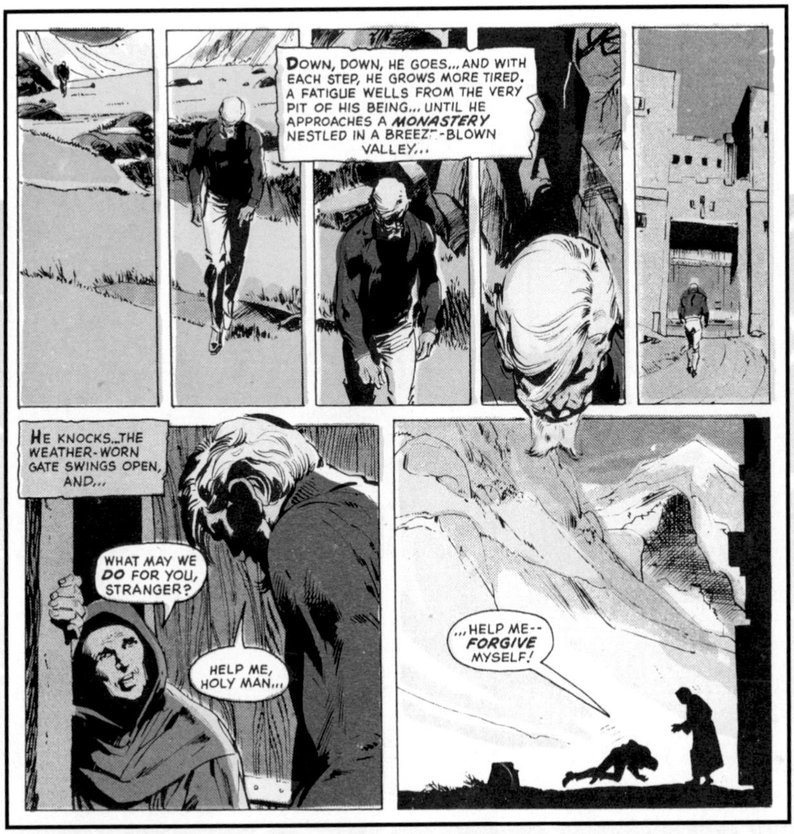
DOWN, DOWN, HE GOES... AND WITH EACH STEP, HE GROWS MORE TIRED. A FATIGUE WELLS FROM THE VERY PIT OF HIS BEING... UNTIL HE APPROACHES A MONASTERY NESTLED IN A BREEZE-BLOWN VALLEY...
HE KNOCKS... THE WEATHER-WORN GATE SWINGS OPEN, AND...
WHAT MAY WE DO FOR YOU, STRANGER?
HELP ME, HOLY MAN...
...HELP ME-- FORGIVE MYSELF!

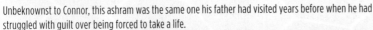

Unbeknownst to Connor, this ashram was the same one his father had visited years before when he had struggled with guilt over being forced to take a life.

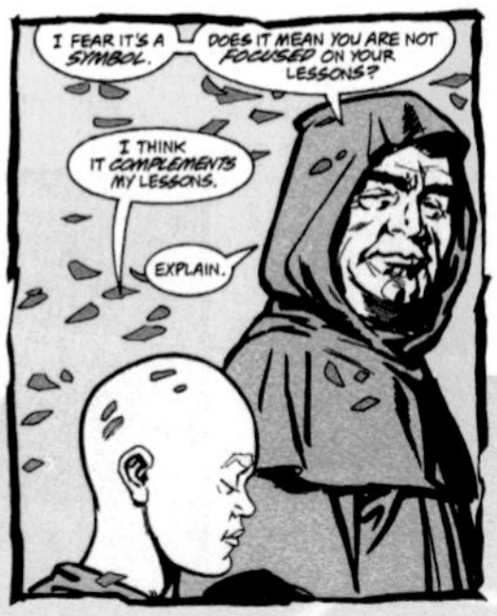
I FEAR IT'S A SYMBOL.
DOES IT MEAN YOU ARE NOT FOCUSED ON YOUR LESSONS?
I THINK IT COMPLEMENTS MY LESSONS.
EXPLAIN.

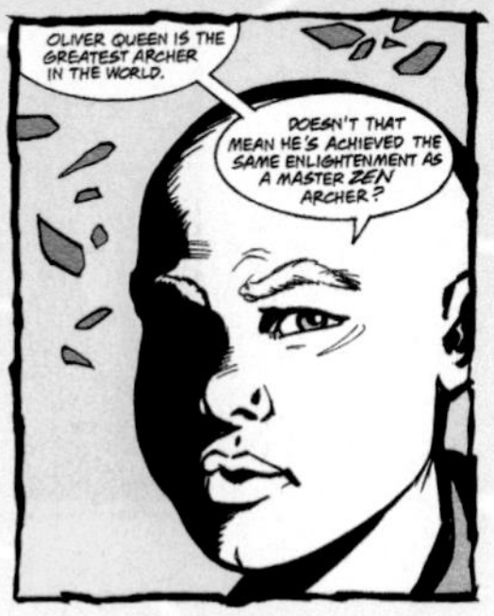
OLIVER QUEEN IS THE GREATEST ARCHER IN THE WORLD.
DOESN'T THAT MEAN HE'S ACHIEVED THE SAME ENLIGHTENMENT AS A MASTER ZEN ARCHER?

Even at the ashram, Connor found himself in trouble. Master Jansen admonished the child for hiding a magazine featuring his idol, Green Arrow. Jansen felt Oliver Queen had learned little from his time spent there and worried that Queen's exploits would only distract Connor.

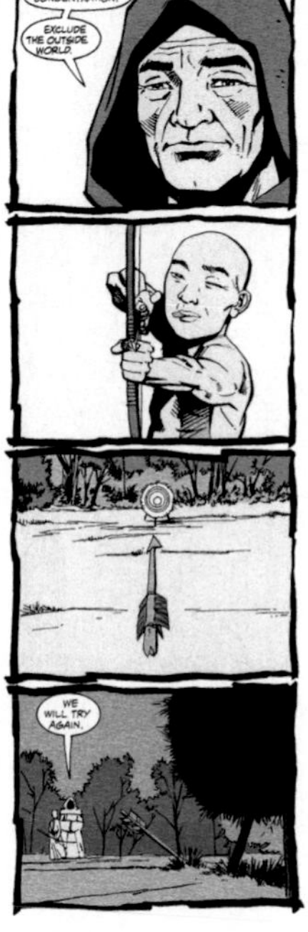
CONCENTRATION.
EXCLUDE THE OUTSIDE WORLD.
WE WILL TRY AGAIN.

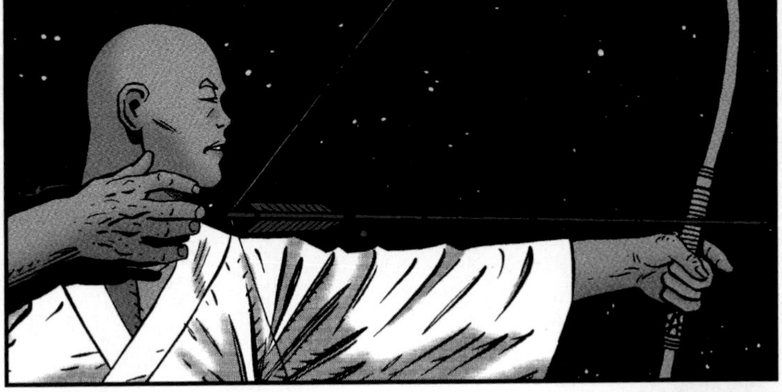

The years spent at the ashram served Connor well, affording him the inner peace and training he had hoped for.

Despite his heritage, mastering the bow didn't come easy to Connor. It took practice and the guidance of Master Jansen.

That's not to say he didn't continue to break a few rules, such as keeping a scrapbook about Green Arrow. He was his father's son, after all.

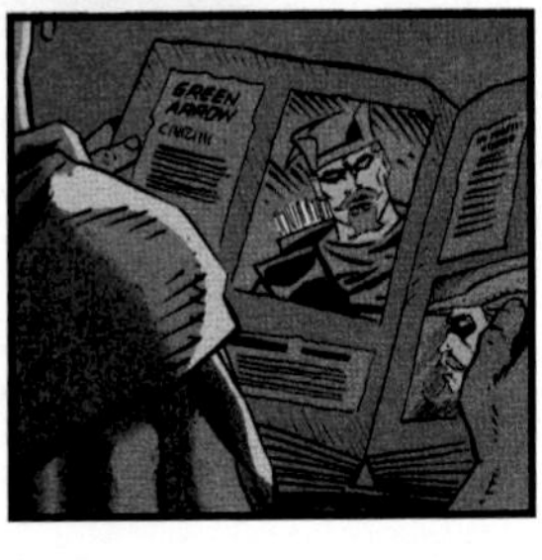
GREEN ARROW

Shrewd businessman Maxwell Lord IV had a vision of the Justice League that extended far beyond the United States of America. With his money and political connections, Lord inserted himself into the team's affairs. They would be chartered by the United Nations and have embassies on every continent. Justice League International was born.

JUSTICE LEAGUE INTERNATIONAL

BUT IN TODAY'S WORLD THERE'S NO LONGER ROOM FOR BORDERS AND BOUNDARIES. THE WALLS BETWEEN NATIONS HAVE TO FALL IF OUR PLANET IS TO SURVIVE.
SO, FOR THE NEW ERA-- A NEW LEAGUE:

BONK
I'LL SAY THIS FOR BATMAN: HE'S EFFICIENT.
ONE PUNCH! ONE PUNCH!
GOOD AFTERNOON, EVERYONE. HOPE WE HAVEN'T--
IS THAT GUY ON THE FLOOR?
WHAT HAPPENED TO HIM? IS HE DEAD?
NAH... WE COULDN'T BE THAT LUCKY!

The personalities on the team led to many conflicts, the first and most infamous occurring when Guy Gardner instigated a fight with Batman. Batman ended it with a single punch.

...WOW-- I AM WIPED OUT! I'VE NEVER TRIED ANYTHING THAT AMBITIOUS BEFORE!
WELL, YOU DID A BEAUTIFUL JOB OF IT, ICEY! I DON'T KNOW WHY EVERYONE SAYS YOUR POWERS ARE SO STUPID!
YEAH, WELL, I--
HEY! WHO SAYS MY POWERS ARE STUPID?!

PROBLEM?
NO PROBLEM HERE, MAX. NO PROBLEM AT ALL. ALL UNDER CONTROL. REALLY. EVERYTHING IS FINE.

Martian Manhunter's greatest weakness wasn't his vulnerability to fire, but a fondness for cookies. His body responded to them the same way humans responded to highly addictive drugs.

Former members of the Global Guardians, Fire and Ice waltzed into the nearest Justice League embassy one day to apply for membership. Martian Manhunter decided to give them a chance. They quickly became stalwarts of the League, even if their teammates weren't quick to praise them.

WELL, THE GOOD NEWS IS -- I FINALLY GOT THIS THING WORKING AGAIN. WE CAN CALL HOME FOR THE SHUTTLE CRAFT... GET THESE PEOPLE OUT OF HERE... GET BACK TO THE EMBASSY.
OH, GOOD. I CAN'T WAIT TO GET HOME AND HAVE MAX PUT A BULLET THROUGH MY HEAD.
OH, COME ON, BOOSTER-- MAX'D NEVER DO THAT.
HE'D AIM FOR THE SPINAL CORD... CRIPPLE YOU FOR LIFE.

Blue Beetle and Booster Gold wondered how Maxwell Lord would react to their disastrous Club Justice League, a casino and resort built on Kooey Kooey Kooey, a sentient island in the South Pacific. The island didn't react well to its new residents and uprooted itself to swim away, causing earthquakes.

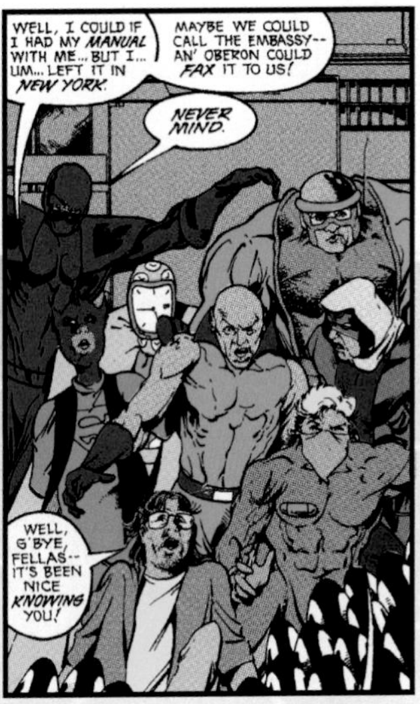
WELL, I COULD IF I HAD MY MANUAL WITH ME... BUT I... UM... LEFT IT IN NEW YORK.
MAYBE WE COULD CALL THE EMBASSY-- AN' OBERON COULD FAX IT TO US!
NEVER MIND.
WELL, G'BYE, FELLAS-- IT'S BEEN NICE KNOWING YOU!

After inadvertently foiling a terrorist attack, the largely incompetent Injustice League decided to go straight. To monitor the group and keep them out of trouble, Maxwell Lord appointed them as Justice League Antarctica. They were all fired by Lord after destroying the Antarctica embassy in a fight with crazed killer penguins.

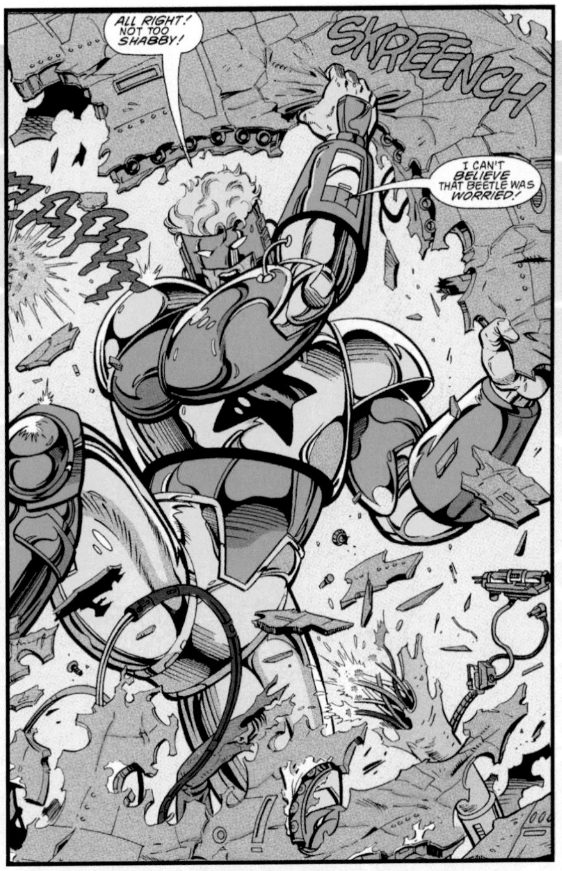
ALL RIGHT! NOT TOO SHABBY!
SKREEENCH
I CAN'T BELIEVE THAT BEETLE WAS WORRIED!

Booster Gold's original suit was damaged beyond repair in the fight against Doomsday. Blue Beetle built him a rather clunky replacement that worked most of the time, until a blast fried the suit's circuits and rendered Booster immobile.

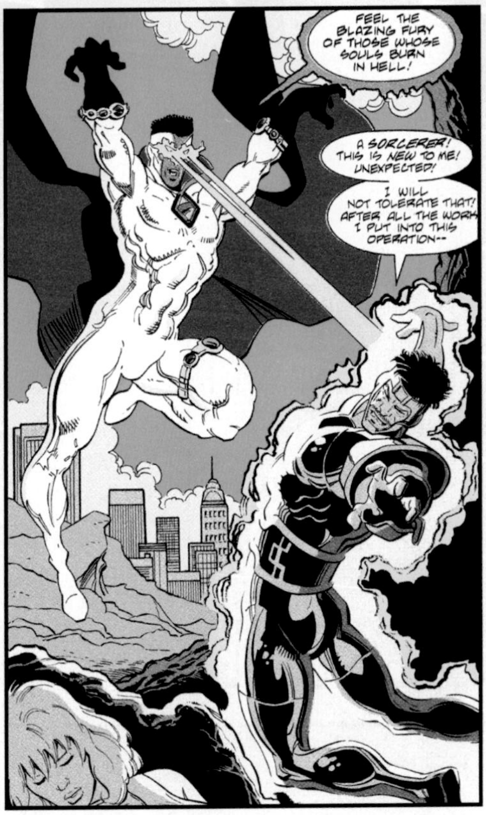
FEEL THE BLAZING FURY OF THOSE WHOSE SOULS BURN IN HELL!
A SORCERER! THIS IS NEW TO ME! UNEXPECTED!
I WILL NOT TOLERATE THAT! AFTER ALL THE WORK I PUT INTO THIS OPERATION--

The mysterious Bloodwynd joined the League after rescuing the team from the clutches of the Weapons Master. Much later, it was revealed that Bloodwynd was actually Martian Manhunter in disguise. Through the gem attached to his chest, Martian Manhunter was possessed by the monstrous Rott, who was trapped within the gem. Rott planned to manipulate Martian Manhunter into finding a power source that would help him escape.

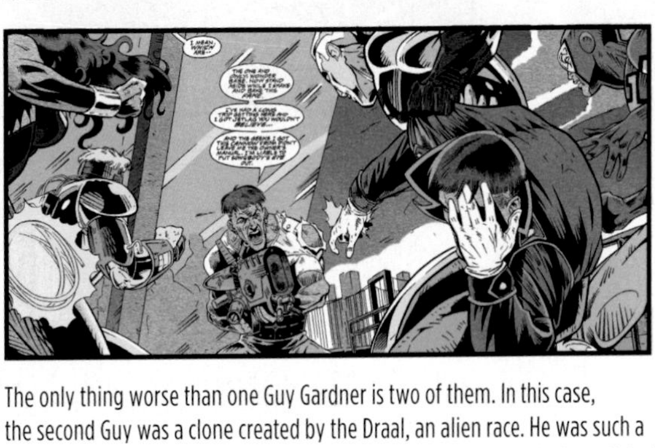

The only thing worse than one Guy Gardner is two of them. In this case, the second Guy was a clone created by the Draal, an alien race. He was such a convincing jerk that no one on the League even noticed he wasn't the real deal until Gardner showed up to stop him and get his power ring back.

Congressional aide Amanda "The Wall" Waller reactivated a covert government operation known as Task Force X with the ingenious plan of using imprisoned super-villains to carry out secret and dangerous missions. She was joined by Rick Flag, a member of the previous iteration of Task Force X. They made a very simple offer to each villain: Succeed in the mission and all criminal charges would be dropped. With such high stakes, the group was known as the Suicide Squad.

SUICIDE SQUAD

LOOK, COLONEL--WE'VE GOT A JOB TO DO HERE, AND I WAS TOLD YOU WERE THE MAN TO DO IT!
THE QUESTION ISN'T WHETHER YOU LIKE THE JOB--OR ME--OR ANY OF THE OTHERS I'VE CHOSEN!
THE ONLY THING THAT MATTERS IS --CAN YOU DO THE JOB WELL?
PERFECTLY.
IF NOT, TELL ME NOW-- SO I CAN FIND SOMEONE WHO CAN!

'EY, WHAT IS THIS?
IT'S AN EXPLOSIVE BRACELET, EXACTLY LIKE MINE!
CALL IT A LITTLE INSURANCE POLICY, AUSSIE! YOU DECIDE TO WANDER AWAY FROM COLONEL FLAG DURING THIS MISSION--
--AND FROM NOW ON YOU'LL BE APPLAUDING ONE-HANDED!

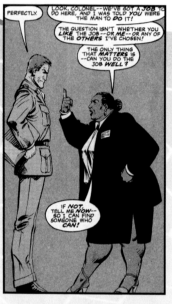

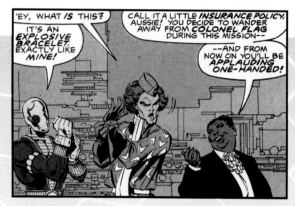

Dealing with criminals wasn't something Waller took lightly. She had them fitted with explosive bracelets that would detonate if they strayed too far from the mission or Flag. Additionally, the hero known as the Bronze Tiger joined Flag as added security on the missions.

HALF A MO'! WHAT DO I CARE? BLOODY BIKE MADE ME A LAFFING STOCK IN FRONT OF TH' OTHERS!
NOBODY DOES THAT T' ME!
BRRAAAAK

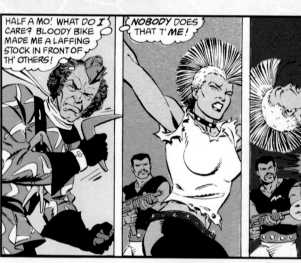

Loyalty among Squad members was rare. Captain Boomerang had the opportunity to save Mindboggler on her first mission but chose to do nothing because she had used her illusion powers to embarrass him in front of the team earlier in the day.

Batman was angered to learn of the Suicide Squad's existence, objecting to unreformed criminals being allowed back on the streets (especially criminals he had put away). He wanted to expose the group, but Waller threatened to uncover his secret identity and reveal it. Much to the surprise and amusement of the Squad, Batman backed down.

WHAT'S YOUR PROBLEM, BATMAN?
MY PROBLEM, MRS. WALLER, IS YOUR SUICIDE SQUAD.
THE GOVERNMENT IS NOW INVOLVED IN PUTTING UNREFORMED MENACES BACK OUT ON THE STREET. MENACES THAT I AND MANY OTHERS, COSTUMED AND OTHERWISE, SPENT A LOT OF TIME AND TROUBLE PUTTING AWAY.

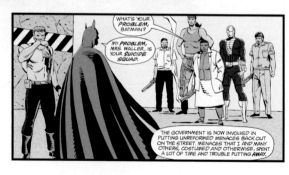

CONVERGENCE

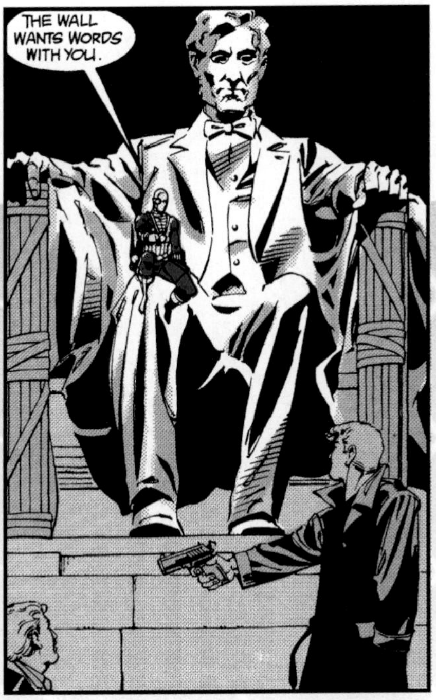
THE WALL WANTS WORDS WITH YOU.

After Senator Joseph Cray and the team's National Security Council liaison Derek Tolliver attempted to blackmail Amanda Waller, Rick Flag killed Tolliver first and then went after Cray. Waller ordered the team to stop Flag by any means necessary. In a standoff at the Lincoln Memorial, Deadshot knew the only way to stop Flag was to kill him. He then shot Senator Cray himself, arguing that the mission was completed because he prevented Flag from doing it.

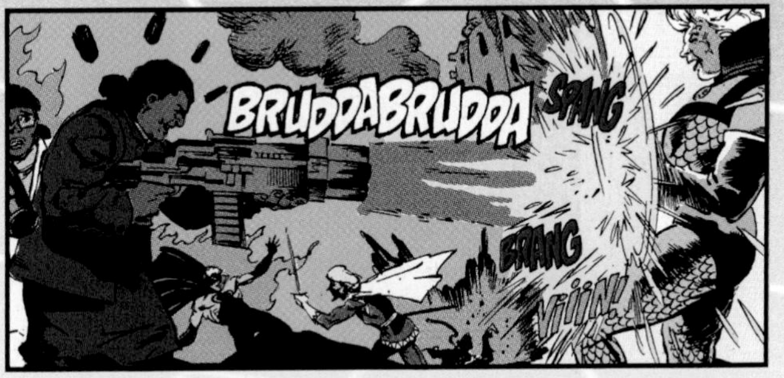
BRUDDABRUDDA
SPANG
BRANG

At first Waller didn't join the Suicide Squad on missions, but she showed her mettle when the Suicide Squad was dragged to Apokolips by Lashina, who hoped to regain her leadership of the Female Furies. Waller stood toe-to-toe with the frightening and powerful Granny Goodness, taking a savage beating but refusing to give up.

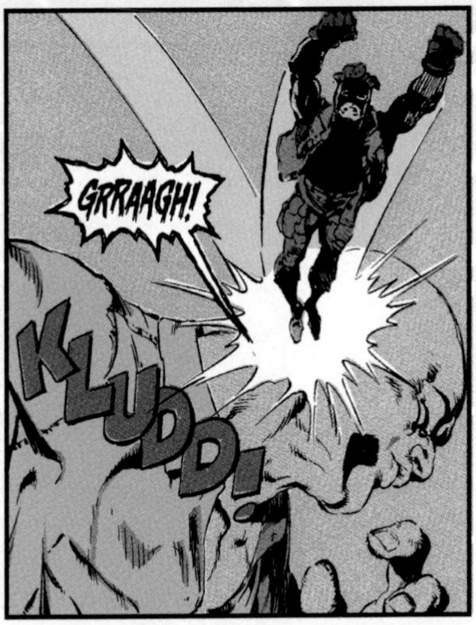
GRRAAGH!
KLUDD!

Cutting their ties with the U.S. government, the Suicide Squad became mercenaries for hire and eschewed their traditional costumes in favor of less conspicuous wardrobes. With his shrinking ability, the Atom proved to be a fine secret asset to the team. Underneath the mask was Adam Cray, son of the murdered senator, filling in for Ray Palmer.

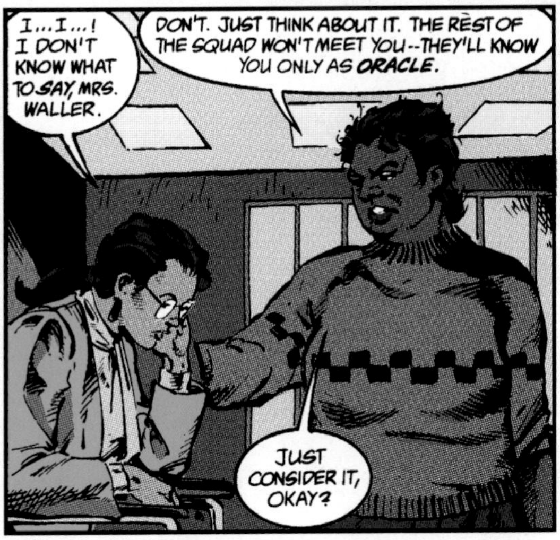
I...I...! I DON'T KNOW WHAT TO SAY, MRS. WALLER.
DON'T. JUST THINK ABOUT IT. THE REST OF THE SQUAD WON'T MEET YOU--THEY'LL KNOW YOU ONLY AS ORACLE.
JUST CONSIDER IT, OKAY?

Expert hacker Oracle began anonymously aiding Task Force X and later officially became part of the team after meeting Amanda Waller face-to-face. Waller made a bold offer to Oracle, despite not even knowing her real name (Oracle used the alias Amy Beddoes, and Waller vowed never to pry). If Waller didn't come back from a mission, she wanted Oracle to take over running the Squad.

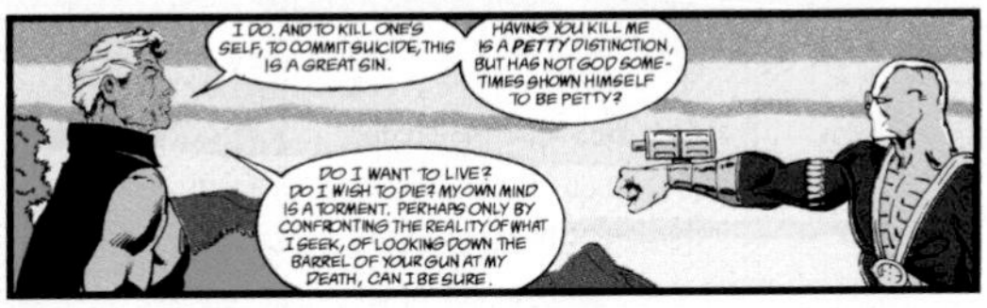
I DO. AND TO KILL ONE'S SELF, TO COMMIT SUICIDE, THIS IS A GREAT SIN.
HAVING YOU KILL ME IS A PETTY DISTINCTION, BUT HAS NOT GOD SOMETIMES SHOWN HIMSELF TO BE PETTY?
DO I WANT TO LIVE? DO I WISH TO DIE? MY OWN MIND IS A TORMENT. PERHAPS ONLY BY CONFRONTING THE REALITY OF WHAT I SEEK, OF LOOKING DOWN THE BARREL OF YOUR GUN AT MY DEATH, CAN I BE SURE.

Count Vertigo questioned if life was worth living due to his struggles with mental illness and the indignity of being mind-controlled by both Poison Ivy and Vlatavan rebels. Unable to take his own life, Count Vertigo asked Deadshot if he'd be willing to kill him. His teammate replied, "So be damned sure that's what you really want before you really ask me to do it." After the team's final mission, Count Vertigo stared down the barrel of Deadshot's gun and knew he wanted to live.

SUPERBOY

Superman had been killed at the hands of Doomsday. In the wake of the Man of Steel's death, the secretive Cadmus Project began experimenting to create a new Superman. One dark night a young man, genetically engineered to resemble Superman, escaped from the facility. This headstrong teenager in sunglasses called himself Superman, but the world would come to know him as Superboy.

DON'T EVER CALL ME SUPERBOY!

"OR CADMUS."

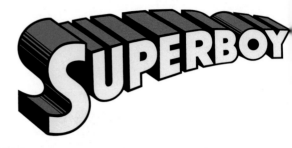

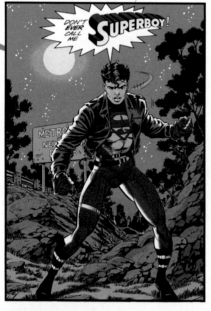

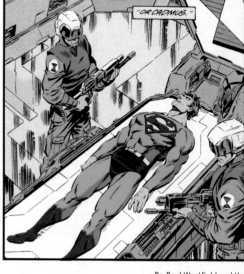

Dr. Paul Westfield and the scientists at Cadmus grafted some of Superman's Kryptonian DNA onto a human DNA strand. Using a rapid-aging process, they created a 16-year-old clone of Superman who had the power of tactile-telekinesis, giving him super-strength and the ability to fly.

LOIS, LOIS, LOIS... I THOUGHT WE HAD A DEAL.
YOU KNOW--I SAVE THE WORLD... YOU WRITE IT UP... WE BOTH END UP ON PAGE ONE...
BUT NO. I GET PAGE SIX. NO BY-LINE. RIGHT UNDER "HAMMER HOBBLES HOME."
ORDWAY TO SPONSOR BATSON EXPEDITION
Daily Planet
Y'KNOW, I WOULD'VE GOTTEN RID OF DOOMSDAY, TOO... WAS GETTIN' AROUND TO IT.

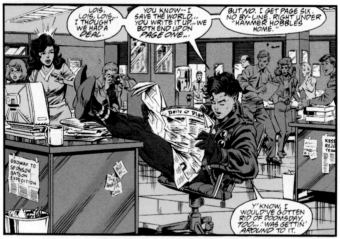

Brash, boastful, and calling himself Superman, the Kid of Steel caused a stir in the *Daily Planet* newsroom when he met Lois Lane and Jimmy Olsen.

Was Superman really dead? The world was startled by the appearance of four new Supermen, each claiming to be the Man of Steel! Superboy was badly injured during a battle with one of them, the Cyborg-Superman.

KANG
...AND I SAID THEY'D DIE IN HERE!
SUPERMAN ALWAYS KEEPS HIS WORD!
AS FOR YOU...

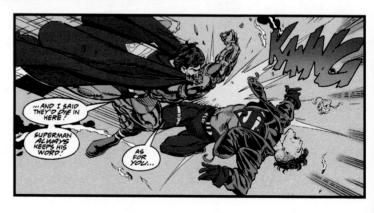

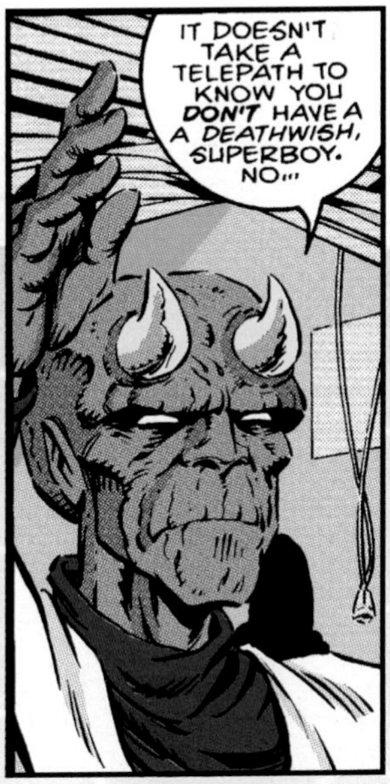
IT DOESN'T TAKE A TELEPATH TO KNOW YOU DON'T HAVE A A DEATHWISH, SUPERBOY. NO...

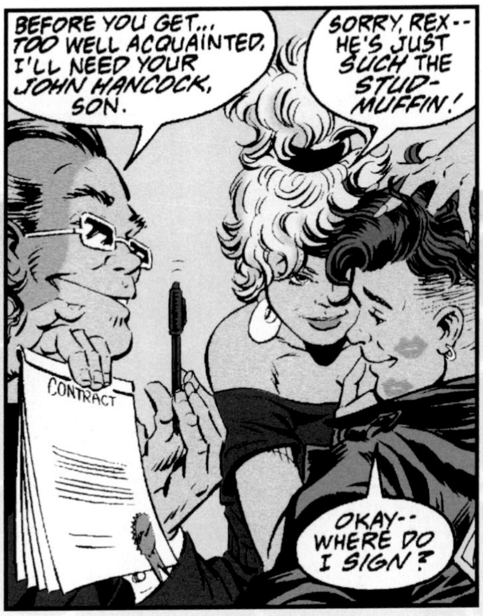
BEFORE YOU GET... TOO WELL ACQUAINTED, I'LL NEED YOUR JOHN HANCOCK, SON.
SORRY, REX-- HE'S JUST SUCH THE STUD-MUFFIN!
CONTRACT
OKAY-- WHERE DO I SIGN?

After the return of the original Man of Steel to Metropolis, Superboy relinquished his claim to the Superman name and went on a world publicity tour engineered by shady publicist Rex Leech. Eventually the Teen of Steel moved to Hawaii, where he was joined by Leech and his daughter Roxy, along with Dubbilex, a telepath assigned by Cadmus to chaperone Superboy.

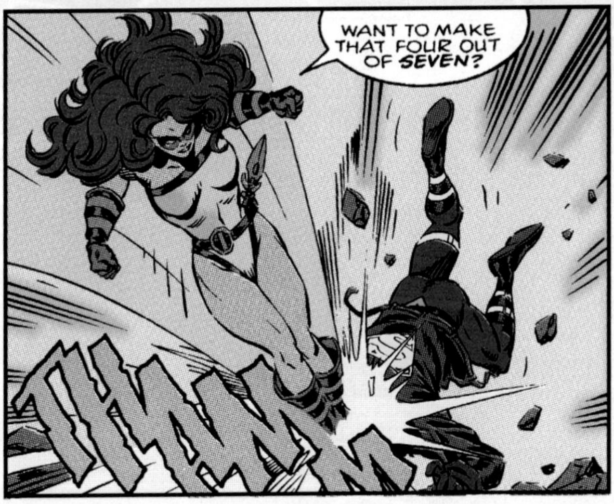
WANT TO MAKE THAT FOUR OUT OF SEVEN?

Knockout was a Female Fury from Apokolips who landed in Hawaii and both fought and flirted with Superboy: "It's your first time, isn't it, Superboy? Fighting a woman, I mean. Maybe I should start a little more gentle." Knockout was the first to call him "pup," a nickname he despised.

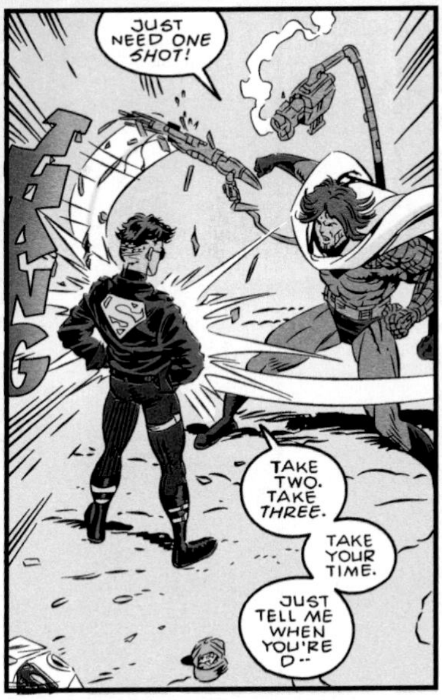
JUST NEED ONE SHOT!
TAKE TWO. TAKE THREE.
TAKE YOUR TIME.
JUST TELL ME WHEN YOU'RE D--

Superboy's first Hawaiian battle was a savage fight on Waikiki Beach with Sidearm, a criminal equipped with a cybernetic vest and deadly appendages.

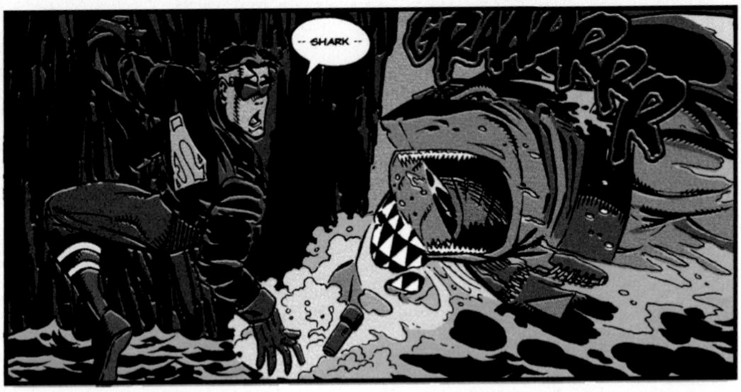
-- SHARK --

One of the perils of life in Hawaii was Superboy's ferocious enemy King Shark. Some thought the creature a savage mutation, but according to Hawaiian legend, he was the spawn of a mortal woman and a Shark god.

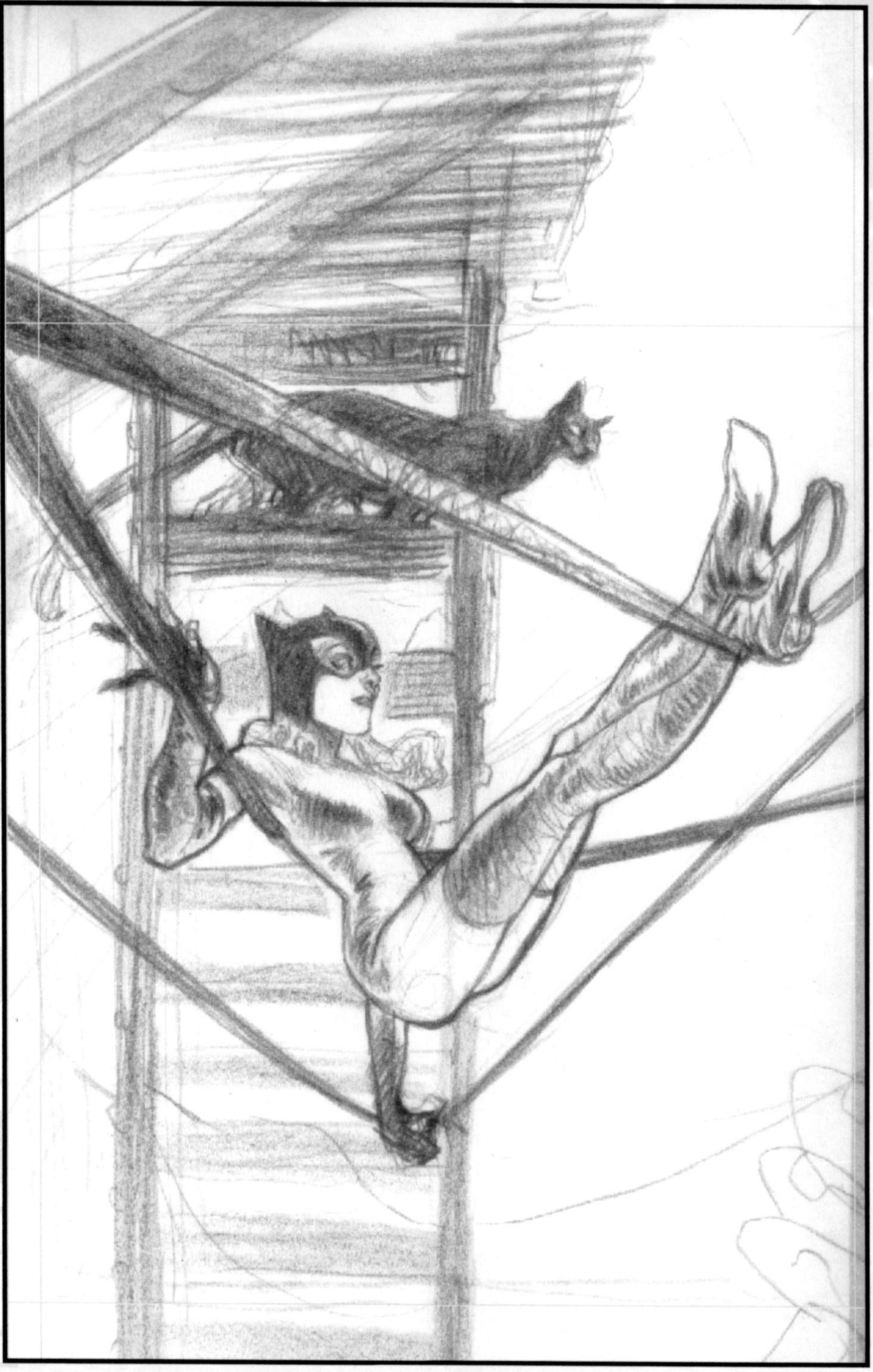

CONVERGENCE: CATWOMAN #1
COVER SKETCH BY CLAIRE WENDLING

CONVERGENCE: SUICIDE SQUAD #1
PAGES 15–16 PENCILS BY TOM MANDRAKE

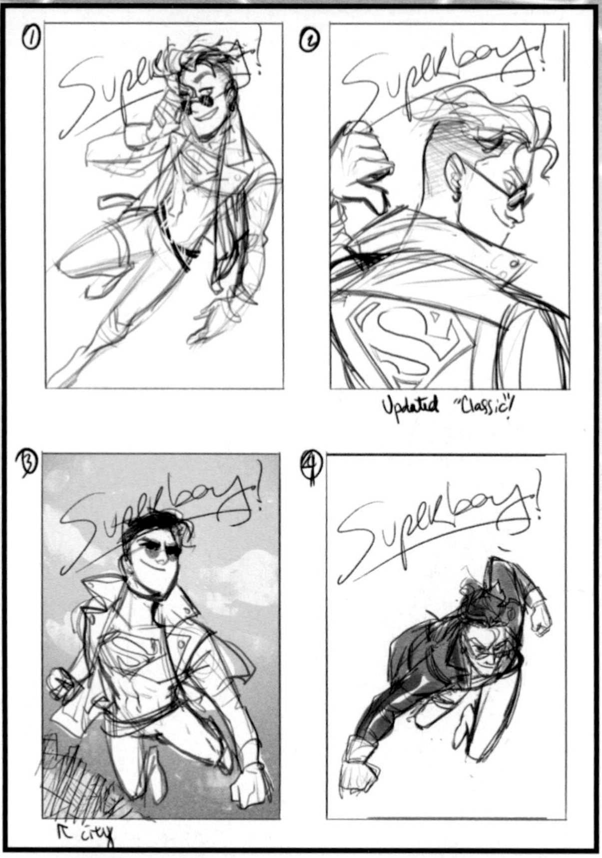
1
Superboy!
2
Superboy!
Updated "Classic"!
3
Superboy!
city
4
Superboy!

CONVERGENCE: SUPERBOY #1 COVER SKETCHES BY BABS TARR

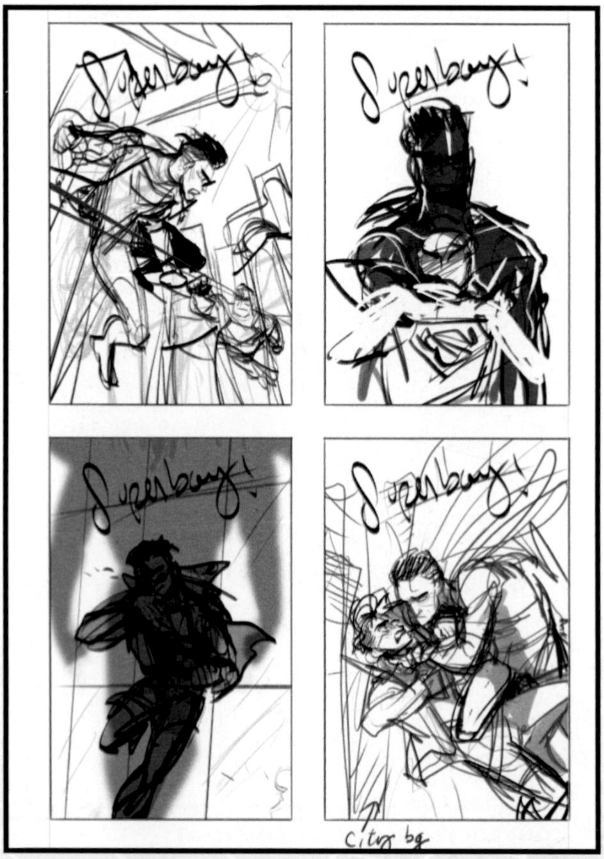
Superboy!
Superboy!
Superboy!
Superboy!
city bg

CONVERGENCE: SUPERBOY #2 COVER SKETCHES BY BABS TARR

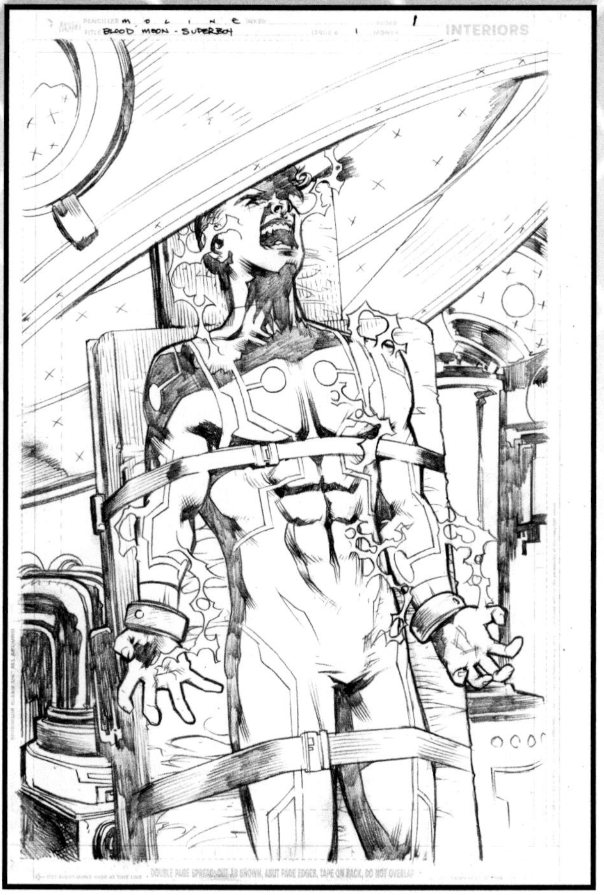
MOLINE
BLOOD MOON - SUPERBOY
INTERIORS
DOUBLE PAGE SPREAD: CUT AS SHOWN, ABUT PAGE EDGES, TAPE ON BACK, DO NOT OVERLAP

CONVERGENCE: SUPERBOY #1

PAGES 1–3 PENCILS BY KARL MOLINE

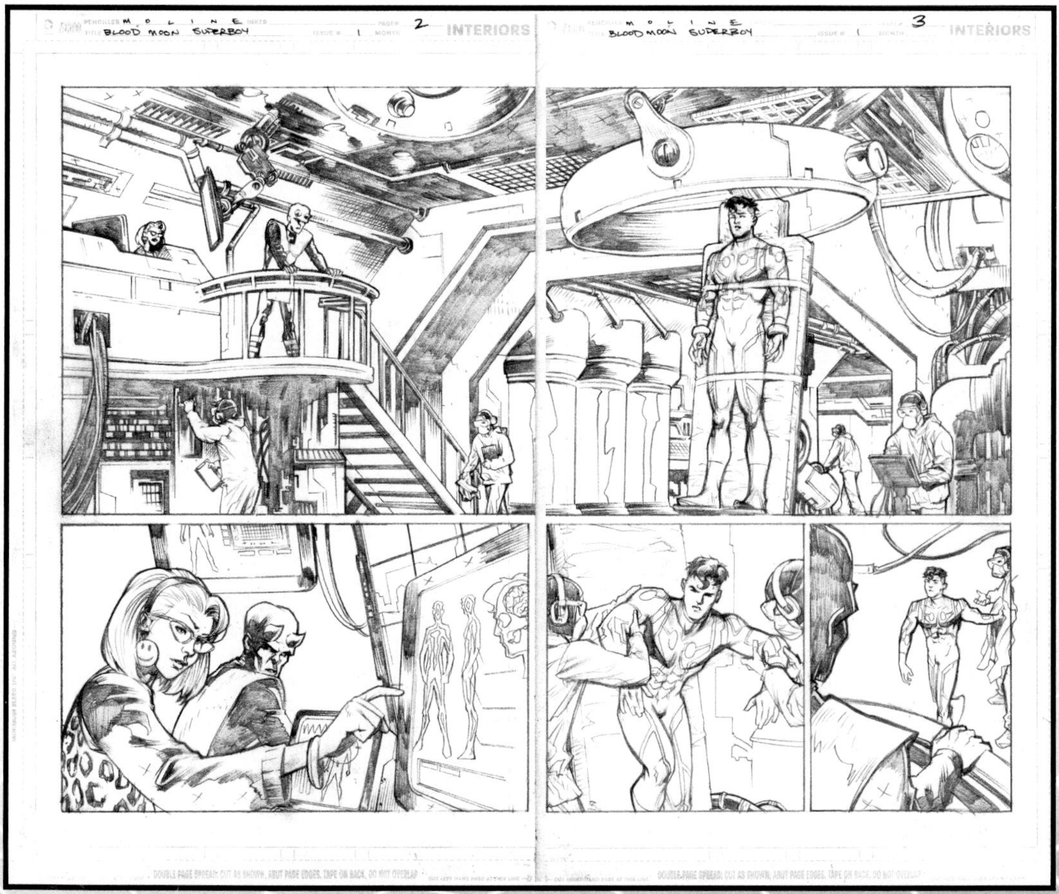
MOLINE
BLOOD MOON SUPERBOY
INTERIORS
MOLINE
BLOOD MOON SUPERBOY
INTERIORS
DOUBLE PAGE SPREAD: CUT AS SHOWN, ABUT PAGE EDGES, TAPE ON BACK, DO NOT OVERLAP
DOUBLE PAGE SPREAD: CUT AS SHOWN, ABUT PAGE EDGES, TAPE ON BACK, DO NOT OVERLAP

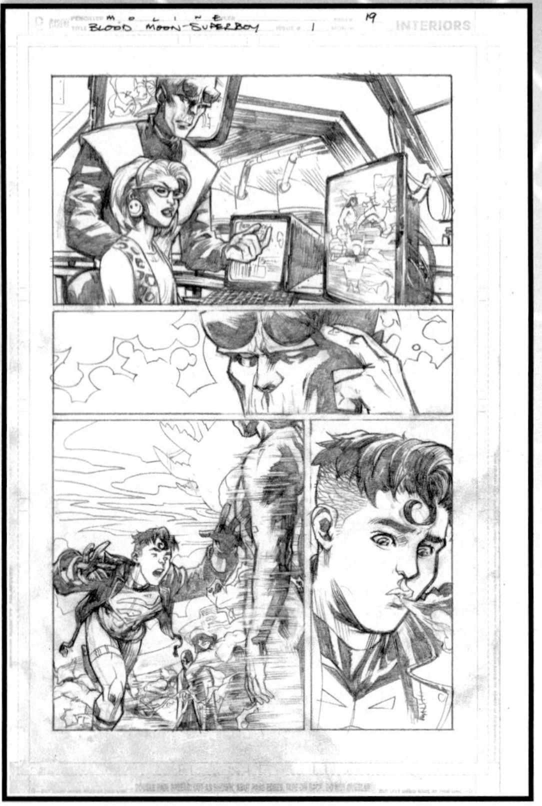
MOLINE
BLOOD MOON - SUPERBOY
1
19
INTERIORS

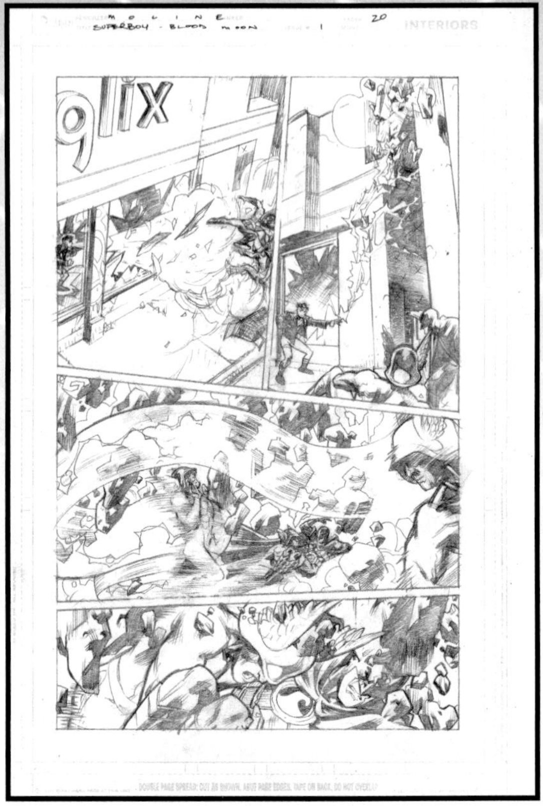
MOLINE
SUPERBOY - BLOOD MOON
1
20
INTERIORS

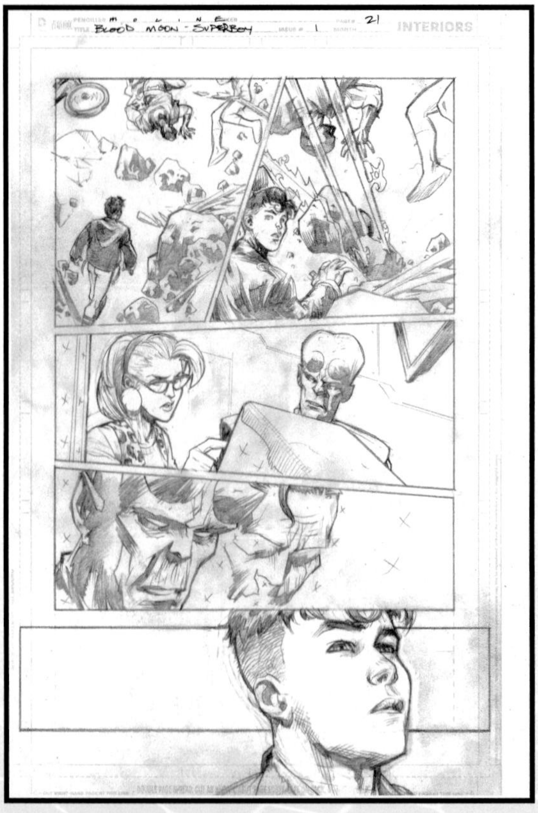
MOLINE
BLOOD MOON - SUPERBOY
1
21
INTERIORS

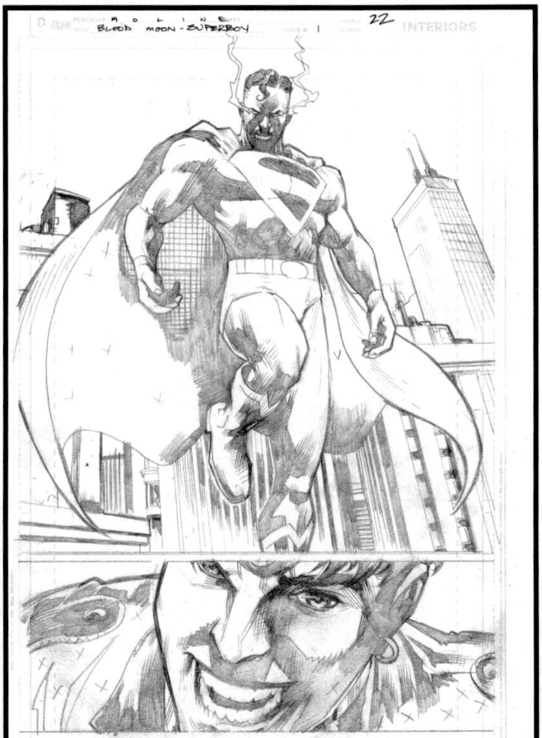
MOLINE
BLOOD MOON - SUPERBOY
1
22
INTERIORS

CONVERGENCE: SUPERBOY #1

PAGES 19–22 PENCILS BY KARL MOLINE